THE BODLEY HEAD
Bernard Shaw
VOLUME

I

THE BODLEY HEAD

Bernard Shaw

COLLECTED PLAYS WITH

THEIR PREFACES

⌈VOLUME I⌉

PLAYS UNPLEASANT

Widowers' Houses, The Philanderer
Mrs Warren's Profession

PLAYS PLEASANT

Arms and the Man
Candida, The Man of Destiny
You Never Can Tell

MAX REINHARDT
THE BODLEY HEAD
LONDON   SYDNEY
TORONTO

EDITORIAL SUPERVISOR

Dan H. Laurence

Publisher's Note

Bernard Shaw was, throughout his publishing career, an inveterate reviser. His most extensive revision of his plays was undertaken in 1930-32 for the Collected Edition. This text was subsequently reset and issued in 1931-32 as the Standard Edition: it contained corrections but no further textual revision. Shaw, however, did make further alterations in some of the plays and prefaces in the Standard Edition in later years. Accordingly, to ensure a definitive text, we have set type for the Bodley Head edition from the last printing of each volume of plays in the Standard Edition which was authorized for press by Shaw in his lifetime.

Shaw had strong personal opinions about style in printing, many of them highly idiosyncratic, and as he was his own publisher he had no difficulty implementing them. His spellings and contractions were often bizarre (*enterprize* and *wernt*), and sometimes archaic (*shew* for *show*, as in the title of his play *The Shewing-up of Blanco Posnet*). He had equally strong convictions about the superfluous use of punctuation, noting in *The Author* in April 1902:

"The apostrophes in ain't, don't, haven't, etc., look so ugly that the most careful printing cannot make a page of colloquial dialogue as handsome as a page of classical dialogue. Besides, shan't should be sha"n't, if the wretched pedantry of indicating the elision is to be carried out. I have written aint, dont, havnt, shant, shouldnt and wont for twenty years with perfect impunity, using the apostrophe only where its omission would suggest another word: for example, hell for he'll. There is not the faintest reason for persisting in the ugly and silly trick of peppering pages with these uncouth bacilli. I also write thats, whats, lets, for the colloquial forms of that is, what is, let us; and I have not yet been prosecuted."

Throughout this definitive edition we have undertaken to follow Shaw's dictates in all matters of spelling and punctuation. Except for a small number of corrections of obvious misprints, the texts are faithfully reproduced.

One additional technical matter must be noted here. Shaw's aesthetics of typography required that italics be reserved for stage directions. In all editions of Shaw's plays up to and including the Collected Edition emphasis within dialogue passages was obtained by letter-spacing. For technical reasons, however, Shaw's printer (William Maxwell, director of R. & R. Clark, Edinburgh) prevailed upon him to permit the setting of emphasised words in the Standard Edition in a slightly larger type. In the present edition the original spaced lettering has been restored. This move, we like to think, would have pleased Shaw.

CONTENTS

[*see over*

PLAYS PLEASANT

PLAYS
UNPLEASANT

Preface
Mainly about Myself

There is an old saying that if a man has not fallen in love before forty, he had better not fall in love after. I long ago perceived that this rule applied to many other matters as well: for example, to the writing of plays; and I made a rough memorandum for my own guidance that unless I could produce at least half a dozen plays before I was forty, I had better let playwriting alone. It was not so easy to comply with this provision as might be supposed. Not that I lacked the dramatist's gift. As far as that is concerned, I have encountered no limit but my own laziness to my power of conjuring up imaginary people in imaginary places, and finding pretexts for theatrical scenes between them. But to obtain a livelihood by this insane gift, I must have conjured so as to interest not only my own imagination, but that of at least some seventy or a hundred thousand contemporary London playgoers. To fulfil this condition was hopelessly out of my power. I had no taste for what is called popular art, no respect for popular morality, no belief in popular religion, no admiration for popular heroics. As an Irishman I could pretend to patriotism neither for the country I had abandoned nor the country that had ruined it. As a humane person I detested violence and slaughter, whether in war, sport, or the butcher's yard. I was a Socialist, detesting our anarchical scramble for money, and believing in equality as the only possible permanent basis of social organization, discipline, subordination, good manners, and selection of fit persons for high functions. Fashionable life, open on indulgent terms to unencumbered "brilliant" persons, I could not endure, even if I had not feared its demoralizing effect on a character which required looking after as much as my own. I was neither a sceptic nor a cynic in these matters: I simply understood life differently from the average respectable man; and as I certainly enjoyed myself more—mostly in ways which would have made him unbearably miserable—I was not splenetic over our variance.

Judge then, how impossible it was for me to write fiction that should delight the public. In my nonage I had tried to obtain a foothold in literature by writing novels, and had actually produced five long works in that form without getting further than an encouraging compliment or two from the most dignified of the London and American publishers, who unanimously declined to venture their capital upon me. Now it is clear that a novel cannot be too bad to be worth publishing, provided it is a novel at all, and not merely an ineptitude. I was not convinced that the publishers' view was commercially sound until I got a clue to my real condition from a friend of mine, a physician who had devoted himself specially to ophthalmic surgery. He tested my eyesight one evening, and informed me that it was quite uninteresting to him because it was normal. I naturally took this to mean that it was like everybody else's; but he rejected this construction as paradoxical, and hastened to explain to me that I was an exceptional and highly fortunate person optically, normal sight conferring the power of seeing things accurately, and being enjoyed by only about ten per cent of the population, the remaining ninety per cent being abnormal. I immediately perceived the explanation of my want of success in fiction. My mind's eye, like my body's, was "normal": it saw things differently from other people's eyes, and saw them better.

This revelation produced a considerable effect on me. At first it struck me that I might live by selling my works to the ten per cent who were like myself; but a moment's reflection shewed me that these must all be as penniless as I, and that we could not live by taking in oneanother's literary washing. How to earn daily bread by my pen was then the problem. Had I been a practical commonsense moneyloving Englishman, the matter would have been easy enough: I should have put on a pair of abnormal spectacles and aberred my vision to the liking of the ninety per cent of potential bookbuyers. But I was so prodigiously self-satisfied with my superiority, so flattered by my abnormal normality, that the resource of hypocrisy never occurred to me. Better see rightly on a pound a week than squint on a million. The question was, how to get the pound a week. The matter, once I gave up writing novels, was not so very difficult. Every despot must have one disloyal subject to keep him sane. Even Louis the Eleventh had to tolerate his confessor, standing for the eternal against the temporal throne. Democracy has now handed the sceptre of the despot to the sovereign people; but they, too, must have their confessor, whom they call Critic. Criticism is not only medicinally salutary: it has positive popular attractions in its cruelty, its gladiatorship, and the gratification given to envy by its attacks on the great, and to enthusiasm by its praises. It may say things which many would like to say, but dare not, and indeed for want of skill could not even if they durst. Its iconoclasms, seditions, and blasphemies, if well turned, tickle those whom they shock; so that the critic adds the privileges of the court jester to those of the confessor. Garrick, had he called Dr Johnson Punch, would have spoken profoundly and wittily; whereas Dr Johnson, in hurling that epithet at him, was but picking up the cheapest sneer an actor is subject to.

It was as Punch, then, that I emerged from obscurity. All I had to do was to open my normal eyes, and with my utmost literary skill put the case exactly as it struck me, or describe the thing exactly as I saw it, to be applauded as the most humorously extravagant paradoxer in London. The only reproach with which I became familiar was the everlasting "Why can you not be serious?" Soon my privileges were enormous and my wealth immense. I had a prominent place reserved for me on a prominent journal every week to say my say as if I were the most important person in the kingdom. My pleasing toil was to report upon all the works of fine art the capital of the world can attract to its exhibitions, its opera house, its concerts and its theatres. The classes eagerly read my essays: the masses patiently listened to my harangues. I enjoyed the immunities of impecuniosity with the opportunities of a millionaire. If ever there was a man without a grievance, I was that man.

But alas! the world grew younger as I grew older: its vision cleared as mine dimmed: it began to read with the naked eye the writing on the wall which now began to remind me that the age of spectacles was at hand. My opportunities were still there: nay, they multiplied tenfold; but the strength and youth to cope with them began to fail, and to need eking out with the shifty cunning of experience. I had to shirk the platform; to economize my health; even to take holidays. In my weekly columns, which I once filled

full from a magic well that never ran dry or lost its
sparkle provided I pumped hard enough, I began to
repeat myself; to fall into a style which, to my great
peril, was recognized as at least partly serious; to
find the pump tiring me and the water lower in the
well; and, worst symptom of all, to reflect with little
tremors on the fact that my mystic wealth could not,
like the money for which other men threw it away, be
stored up against my second childhood. The younger
generation, reared in an enlightenment unknown to
my schooldays, came knocking at the door too: I
glanced back at my old columns and realized that I
had timidly botched at thirty what newer men do now
with gay confidence in their cradles. I listened to their
vigorous knocks with exultation for the race, with
penurious alarm for my own old age. When I talked
to this generation, it called me Mister, and, with its
frank, charming humanity, respected me as one who
had done good work in my time. A famous playwright
wrote a long play to shew that people of my age were
on the shelf; and I laughed at him with the wrong side
of my mouth.

It was at this bitter moment that my fellow citizens,
who had previously repudiated all my offers of political
service, contemptuously allowed me to become a
vestryman: *me*, the author of Widowers' Houses!
Then, like any other harmless useful creature, I took
the first step rearward. Up to that fateful day I had
never penuriously spooned up the spilt drops of my
well into bottles. Time enough for that when the well
was empty. But now I listened to the voice of the
publisher for the first time since he had refused to
listen to mine. I turned over my articles again; but
to serve up the weekly paper of five years ago as a
novelty! no: I had not yet fallen so low, though I see

that degradation looming before me as an agricultural laborer sees the workhouse. So I said "I will begin with small sins: I will publish my plays."

How! you will cry: plays! What plays?

Let me explain. One of the worst privations of life in London for persons of serious intellectual and artistic interests is the want of a suitable playhouse. I am fond of the play, and am, as intelligent readers of this preface will have observed, myself a bit of an actor. Consequently, when I found myself coming across projects of all sorts for the foundation of a theatre which should be to the newly gathered intellectual harvest of the nineteenth century what Shakespear's theatre was to the harvest of the Renascence, I was warmly interested. But it soon appeared that the languid demand of a small and uppish group for a form of entertainment which it had become thoroughly accustomed to do without, could never provide the intense energy necessary for the establishment of the New Theatre (we of course called everything advanced "the New" at that time: see The Philanderer, the second play in this volume). That energy could be set free only by the genius of the actor and manager finding in the masterpieces of the New Drama its characteristic and necessary mode of expression, and revealing their fascination to the public. Clearly the way to begin was to pick up a masterpiece or two. Masterpieces, however, do not grow on the bushes. The New Theatre would never have come into existence but for the plays of Ibsen, just as the Bayreuth Festival Playhouse would never have come into existence but for Wagner's Nibelungen tetralogy. Every attempt to extend the repertory proved that it is the drama that makes the theatre and not the theatre the drama. Not that this needed fresh proof, since the whole difficulty had arisen through the drama of the day being written for the theatres instead of from its own inner necessity. Still, a thing that nobody believes cannot be proved too often.

Ibsen, then, was the hero of the new departure. It was in 1889 that the first really effective blow was struck by the production of A Doll's House by Charles Charrington and Janet Achurch. Whilst they were taking that epoch making play round the world, Mr Grein followed up the campaign in London with his Independent Theatre. It got on its feet by producing Ibsen's Ghosts; but its search for unacted native dramatic masterpieces was so complete a failure that in the autumn of 1892 it had not yet produced a single original piece of any magnitude by an English author. In this humiliating national emergency, I proposed to Mr Grein that he should boldly announce a play by me. Being an extraordinarily sanguine and enterprising man, he took this step without hesitation. I then raked out, from my dustiest pile of discarded and rejected manuscripts, two acts of a play I had begun in 1885, shortly after the close of my novel writing period, in collaboration with my friend William Archer.

Archer has himself described how I proved the most impossible of collaborators. Laying violent hands on his thoroughly planned scheme for a sympathetically romantic "well made play" of the Parisian type then in vogue, I perversely distorted it into a grotesquely realistic exposure of slum landlordism, municipal jobbery, and the pecuniary and matrimonial ties between them and the pleasant people with "independent" incomes who imagine that such sordid matters do not touch their own lives. The result was

revoltingly incongruous; for though I took my theme
seriously enough, I did not then take the theatre
quite seriously, even in taking it more seriously than
it took itself. The farcical trivialities in which I
followed the fashion of the times became silly and
irritating beyond all endurance when intruded upon
a subject of such depth, reality, and force as that into
which I had plunged my drama. Archer, perceiving
that I had played the fool both with his plan and my
own theme, promptly disowned me; and the project,
which neither of us had much at heart, was dropped,
leaving me with two abortive acts of an unfinished
and condemned play. Exhuming this as aforesaid
seven years later, I saw that the very qualities which
had made it impossible for ordinary commercial
purposes in 1885 might be exactly those needed by
the Independent Theatre in 1892. So I completed
it by a third act; gave it the farfetched Scriptural
title of Widowers' Houses; and handed it over to
Mr Grein, who launched it at the public in the Royalty
Theatre with all its original tomfooleries on its head.
It made a sensation out of all proportion to its merits
or even its demerits; and I at once became infamous
as a playwright. The first performance was sufficiently
exciting: the Socialists and Independents applauded
me furiously on principle; the ordinary playgoing
first-nighters hooted me frantically on the same
ground; I, being at that time in some practice as
what is impolitely called a mob orator, made a speech
before the curtain; the newspapers discussed the play
for a whole fortnight not only in the ordinary theatrical
notices and criticisms, but in leading articles and
letters; and finally the text of the play was published
with an introduction by Mr Grein, an amusing account
by Archer of the original collaboration, and a long

preface and several elaborate controversial appendices in my most energetically egotistic fighting style. The volume, forming number one of the Independent Theatre series of plays, now extinct, is a curious relic of that nine days wonder; and as it contains the original text of the play with all its silly pleasantries, I can recommend it to collectors of quarto Hamlets, and of all those scarce and superseded early editions which the unfortunate author would so gladly annihilate if he could.

I had not achieved a success; but I had provoked an uproar; and the sensation was so agreeable that I resolved to try again. In the following year, 1893, when the discussion about Ibsenism, "the New Woman," and the like, was at its height, I wrote for the Independent Theatre the topical comedy called The Philanderer. But even before I finished it, it was apparent that its demands on the most expert and delicate sort of high comedy acting went beyond the resources then at the disposal of Mr Grein. I had written a part which nobody but Charles Wyndham could act, in a play which was impossible at his theatre: a feat comparable to the building of Robinson Crusoe's first boat. I immediately threw it aside, and, returning to the vein I had worked in Widowers' Houses, wrote a third play, Mrs Warren's Profession, on a social subject of tremendous force. That force justified itself in spite of the inexperience of the playwright. The play was everything that the Independent Theatre could desire: rather more, if anything, than it bargained for. But at this point I came upon the obstacle that makes dramatic authorship intolerable in England to writers accustomed to the freedom of the Press. I mean, of course, the Censorship.

In 1737, Henry Fielding, the greatest practising

dramatist, with the single exception of Shakespear, produced by England between the Middle Ages and the nineteenth century, devoted his genius to the task of exposing and destroying parliamentary corruption, then at its height. Walpole, unable to govern without corruption, promptly gagged the stage by a censorship which is in full force at the present moment. Fielding, driven out of the trade of Molière and Aristophanes, took to that of Cervantes; and since then the English novel has been one of the glories of literature, whilst the English drama has been its disgrace. The extinguisher which Walpole dropped on Fielding descends on me in the form of the Lord Chamberlain's Examiner of Plays, a gentleman who robs, insults, and suppresses me as irresistibly as if he were the Tsar of Russia and I the meanest of his subjects. The robbery takes the form of making me pay him two guineas for reading every play of mine that exceeds one act in length. I do not want him to read it (at least officially: personally he is welcome): on the contrary, I strenuously resent that impertinence on his part. But I must submit in order to obtain from him an insolent and insufferable document, which I cannot read without boiling of the blood, certifiying that in his opinion—*his* opinion!—my play "does not in its general tendency contain anything immoral or otherwise improper for the stage," and that the Lord Chamberlain therefore "allows" its performance (confound his impudence!). In spite of this certificate he still retains his right, as an ordinary citizen, to prosecute me, or instigate some other citizen to prosecute me, for an outrage on public morals if he should change his mind later on. Besides, if he really protects the public against my immorality, why does not the public pay him for the service? The police-

man does not look to the thief for his wages, but to
the honest man whom he protects against the thief.
And yet, if I refuse to pay, this tyrant can practically
ruin any manager who produces my play in defiance
of him. If, having been paid, he is afraid to license
the play: that is, if he is more afraid of the clamor of
the opponents of my opinions than of their supporters,
then he can suppress it, and impose a mulct of £50
on everybody who takes part in a representation of it,
from the callboy to the principal tragedian. And there
is no getting rid of him. Since he lives, not at the
expense of the taxpayer, but by blackmailing the
author, no political party would gain ten votes by
abolishing him. Private political influence cannot touch
him; for such private influence, moving only at the
promptings of individual benevolence to individuals,
makes nice little places to job nice little people into
instead of doing away with them. Nay, I myself,
though I know that the Examiner is necessarily an
odious and mischievous official, and that if I were
appointed to his post (which I shall probably apply
for at the next vacancy) I could no more help being
odious and mischievous than a ramrod could if it were
stuck into the wheels of a steam engine, am loth to
stir up the question lest the Press, having now lost
all tradition of liberty, and being able to conceive no
alternative to the Lord Chamberlain's Examiner than
a Home Secretary's Examiner or some other seven-
headed devil to replace the oneheaded one, should
make the remedy worse than the disease. Thus I
cling to the Censorship as many Radicals cling to the
House of Lords or the Throne, or as domineering
women shun masterful men, and marry weak and
amiable ones. Until the nation is prepared for Freedom of The Stage on the same terms as it now enjoys

Freedom of The Press, by allowing the playwright and manager to perform anything they please and take the consequences before the ordinary law as authors and editors do, I shall cherish the Lord Chamberlain's Examiner as the apple of my eye. I once thought of organizing a Petition of Right from all the managers and authors to the Prime Minister; but as it was obvious that nine out of ten of these victims of oppression, far from daring to offend their despot, would promptly extol him as the most salutary of English institutions, and spread themselves with unctuous flattery on the perfectly irrelevant question of his estimable personal character, I abandoned the notion. What is more, many of them, in taking this safe course, would be pursuing a sound business policy, since the managers and authors to whom the existing system has brought success not only have no incentive to change it for another which would expose them to wider competition, but have for the most part the greatest dread of the "New" ideas which the abolition of the Censorship would let loose on the stage. And so long live the Lord Chamberlain's Examiner!

In 1893 this post was occupied by a gentleman, now deceased, whose ideas had in the course of nature become quite obsolete. He was openly hostile to the New movement; and his evidence before the Select Committee of the House of Commons on Theatres and Places of Entertainment in 1892 (Blue Book No. 240, pp. 328-335) is probably the best compendium in existence of every fallacy that can make a Censor obnoxious. In dealing with him Mr Grein was at a heavy disadvantage. Without a license, Mrs Warren's Profession could only be performed in some building not a theatre, and therefore not subject to reprisals from the Lord Chamberlain. The audience would have to be invited as guests only; so that the support of the public paying money at the doors, a support with which the Independent Theatre could not afford to dispense, was out of the question. To apply for a license was to court a practically certain refusal, entailing the £50 penalty on all concerned in any subsequent performance whatever. The deadlock was complete. The play was ready; the Independent Theatre was ready; and the cast was ready; but the mere existence of the Censorship, without any action or knowledge of the play on its part, was sufficient to paralyze all these forces. So I threw Mrs Warren's Profession aside too, and, like another Fielding, closed my career as playwright in ordinary to the Independent Theatre.

Fortunately, though the Stage is bond, the Press is free. And even if the Stage were freed, none the less would it be necessary to publish plays as well as perform them. Had the two performances of Widowers' Houses achieved by Mr Grein been multiplied by fifty, it would still have remained unknown to those who either dwell out of reach of a theatre, or, as a matter of habit, prejudice, comfort, health or age, abstain altogether from playgoing. Many people who read with delight all the classic dramatists, from Eschylus to Ibsen, only go to the theatre on the rare occasions when they are offered a play by an author whose work they have already learnt to value as literature, or a performance by an actor of the first rank. Even our habitual playgoers have no true habit of playgoing. If on any night at the busiest part of the theatrical season in London, the audiences were cordoned by the police and examined individually as to their views on the subject, there would probably not be a single house-owning native among them who would not conceive a visit to the theatre, or indeed to any public assembly, artistic or political, as an exceptional way of spending an evening, the normal English way being to sit in separate families in separate houses, each person silently occupied with a book, a paper, or a game of halma, cut off equally from the blessings of society and solitude. You may make the acquaintance of a thousand streets of middle-class English families without coming on a trace of any consciousness of citizenship, or any artistic cultivation of the senses. The condition of the men is bad enough, in spite of their daily escape into the city, because they carry the exclusive and unsocial habits of "the home" with them into the wider world of their business. Amiable and companionable enough by nature, they are, by home training, so incredibly ill-mannered, that not even their interest as men of business in welcoming a possible customer in every inquirer can correct their habit of treating everybody who has not been "introduced" as a stranger and intruder. The women, who have not even the city to educate them, are much worse: they are positively unfit for civilized intercourse: graceless, ignorant, narrow-minded to a quite appalling degree. In public places these home-bred people cannot be taught to understand that the right they are themselves exercising is a common right. Whether they are in a second-class railway carriage or in a church, they receive every additional fellow-passenger or worshipper as a Chinaman receives the "foreign devil" who has forced him to open his ports.

In proportion as this horrible domestic institution is broken up by the active social circulation of the upper classes in their own orbit, or its stagnant isolation made impossible by the conditions of working class life, manners improve enormously. In the middle

classes themselves the revolt of a single clever daughter
(nobody has yet done justice to the modern clever
Englishwoman's loathing of the very word Home),
and her insistence on qualifying herself for an independent working life, humanizes her whole family in
an astonishingly short time; and such communal
enjoyments as a visit to the suburban theatre once a
week, or to the Monday Popular Concerts, or both,
softens the worst symptoms of its unsociableness. But
none of these breaches in the English survival of the
hareem can be made without a cannonade of books
and pianoforte music. The books and music cannot
be kept out, because they alone can make the hideous
boredom of the hearth bearable. If its victims may not
live real lives, they may at least read about imaginary
ones, and perhaps learn from them to doubt whether a
class that not only submits to home life, but actually
boasts about it, is really a class worth belonging to.
For the sake of the unhappy prisoners of the home,
then, let my plays be printed as well as acted.

But the dramatic author has reasons for publishing
his plays which would hold good even if English
families went to the theatre as regularly as they take
in the newspaper. A perfectly adequate and successful
stage representation of a play requires a combination
of circumstances so extraordinarily fortunate that I
doubt whether it has ever occurred in the history of the
world. Take the case of the most successful English
dramatist of the first rank: Shakespear. Although he
wrote three centuries ago, he still holds his own so well
that it is not impossible to meet old playgoers who
have witnessed public performances of more than
thirty out of his thirty-seven reputed plays, a dozen of
them fairly often, and half a dozen over and over again.
I myself, though I have by no means availed myself

of all my opportunities, have seen twenty-three of his plays publicly acted. But if I had not read them as well, my impression of them would be not merely incomplete, but violently distorted and falsified. It is only within the last few years that some of our younger actor-managers have been struck with the idea, quite novel in their profession, of performing Shakespear's plays as he wrote them, instead of using them as a cuckoo uses a sparrow's nest. In spite of the success of these experiments, the stage is still dominated by Garrick's conviction that the manager and actor must adapt Shakespear's plays to the modern stage by a process which no doubt presents itself to the adapter's mind as one of masterly amelioration, but which must necessarily be mainly one of debasement and mutilation whenever, as occasionally happens, the adapter is inferior to the author. The living author can protect himself against this extremity of misrepresentation; but the more unquestioned his authority is on the stage, and the more friendly and willing the co-operation of the manager and the company, the more completely does he get convinced of the impossibility of achieving an authentic representation of his piece as well as an effective and successful one. It is quite possible for a piece to enjoy the most sensational success on the basis of a complete misunderstanding of its philosophy: indeed, it is not too much to say that it is only by a capacity for succeeding in spite of its philosophy that a dramatic work of serious poetic import can become popular. In the case of the first part of Goethe's Faust we have this frankly avowed by the extraction from the great original of popular entertainments like Gounod's opera or the Lyceum version, in which poetry and philosophy are replaced by romance, which is the recognized spurious substitute for both and is

destructive of them. Not even when a drama is performed without omission or alteration by actors who
are enthusiastic disciples of the author does it escape
transfiguration. We have lately seen some remarkably
sympathetic stage interpretations of poetic drama,
from the experiments of Charles Charrington with
Ibsen, and of Lugné Poë with Maeterlinck, under
comparatively inexpensive conditions, to those of
the Wagner Festival Playhouse at Bayreuth on the
costliest scale; and readers of Ibsen and Maeterlinck,
and pianoforte students of Wagner, are rightly warned
that they cannot fully appreciate the force of a dramatic masterpiece without the aid of the theatre. But
I have never found an acquaintance with a dramatist
founded on the theatre alone, or with a composer
founded on the concert room alone, a really intimate
and accurate one. The very originality and genius
of the performers conflicts with the originality and
genius of the author. Imagine Shakespear confronted
with Sir Henry Irving at a rehearsal of The Merchant
of Venice, or Sheridan with Miss Ada Rehan at one
of The School for Scandal. It is easy to imagine the
speeches that might pass on such occasions. For
example "As I look at your playing, Sir Henry, I
seem to see Israel mourning the Captivity and crying,
'How long, O Lord, how long?' It is a little startling
to see Shylock's strong feelings operating through a
romantic intellect instead of through an entirely
commercial one; but pray dont alter your conception,
which will be abundantly profitable to us both." Or
"My dear Miss Rehan: let me congratulate you on a
piece of tragic acting which has made me ashamed of
the triviality of my play, and obliterated Sir Peter
Teazle from my consciousness, though I meant him
to be the hero of the scene. I foresee an enormous

success for both of us in this fortunate misrepresentation of my intention." Even if the author had nothing to gain pecuniarily by conniving at the glorification of his play by the performer, the actor's excess of power would still carry its own authority and win the sympathy of the author's histrionic instinct, unless he were a Realist of fanatical integrity. And that would not save him either; for his attempts to make powerful actors do less than their utmost would be as futile as his attempts to make feeble ones do more.

In short, the fact that a skilfully written play is infinitely more adaptable to all sorts of acting than available acting is to all sorts of plays (the actual conditions thus exactly reversing the desirable ones) finally drives the author to the conclusion that his own view of his work can only be conveyed by himself. And since he could not act the play singlehanded even if he were a trained actor, he must fall back on his powers of literary expression, as other poets and fictionists do. So far, this has hardly been seriously attempted by dramatists. Of Shakespear's plays we have not even complete prompt copies: the folio gives us hardly anything but the bare lines. What would we not give for the copy of Hamlet used by Shakespear at rehearsal, with the original stage business scrawled by the prompter's pencil? And if we had in addition the descriptive directions which the author gave on the stage: above all, the character sketches, however brief, by which he tried to convey to the actor the sort of person he meant him to incarnate, what a light they would shed, not only on the play, but on the history of the sixteenth century! Well, we should have had all this and much more if Shakespear, instead of merely writing out his lines, had prepared the plays for publication in competition with fiction as elaborate as that of Meredith. It is for want of this elaboration that Shakespear, unsurpassed as poet, storyteller, character draughtsman, humorist, and rhetorician, has left us no intellectually coherent drama, and could not afford to pursue a genuinely scientific method in his studies of character and society, though in such unpopular plays as All's Well, Measure for Measure, and Troilus and Cressida, we find him ready and willing to start at the twentieth century if the seventeenth would only let him.

Such literary treatment is much more needed by modern plays than by Shakespear's, because in his time the acting of plays was very imperfectly differentiated from the declamation of verses; and descriptive or narrative recitation did what is now done by scenery, furniture, and stage business. Anyone reading the mere dialogue of an Elizabethan play understands all but half a dozen unimportant lines of it without difficulty; whilst many modern plays, highly successful on the stage, are not merely unreadable but positively unintelligible without visible stage business. Recitation on a platform, with the spectators seated round the reciter in the Elizabethan fashion, would reduce them to absurdity. The extreme instance is a pure pantomime, like L'Enfant Prodigue, in which the dialogue, though it exists, is not spoken. If a dramatic author were to publish a pantomime, it is clear that he could make it intelligible to a reader only by giving him the words which the pantomimist is supposed to be uttering. Now it is not a whit less impossible to make a modern practical stage play intelligible to an audience by dialogue alone, than to make a pantomime intelligible to a reader without it.

Obvious as this is, the presentation of plays through

the literary medium has not yet become an art; and the result is that it is very difficult to induce the English public to buy and read plays. Indeed, why should they, when they find nothing in them except the bare words, with a few carpenter's and costumier's directions as to the heroine's father having a grey beard and the drawing room having three doors on the right, two doors and an entrance through the conservatory on the left, and a French window in the middle? It is astonishing to me that Ibsen, devoting two years to the production of a three-act play, the extraordinary quality of which depends on a mastery of character and situation which can only be achieved by working out a good deal of the family and personal history of the individuals represented, should nevertheless give the reading public very little more than the technical memorandum required by the carpenter, the electrician, and the prompter. Who will deny that the resultant occasional mysteriousness of effect, enchanting though it may be, is produced at the cost of intellectual obscurity? Ibsen, interrogated as to his meaning, replied "What I have said, I have said." Precisely; but the point is that what he hasnt said, he hasnt said. There are perhaps people (though I doubt it, not being one of them myself) to whom Ibsen's plays, as they stand, speak sufficiently for themselves. There are certainly others who could not understand them on any terms. Granting that on both these classes further explanations would be thrown away, is nothing to be done for the vast majority to whom a word of explanation makes all the difference?

Finally, may I put in a plea for actors themselves? Born actors have a susceptibility to dramatic emotion which enables them to seize the moods of their parts intuitively. But to expect them to be intuitive as to intellectual meaning and circumstantial conditions as well, is to demand powers of divination from them: one might as well expect the Astronomer Royal to tell the time in a catacomb. And yet the actor generally finds his part full of emotional directions which he could supply as well or better than the author, whilst he is left quite in the dark as to the political or religious conditions under which the character he impersonates is supposed to be acting. Definite conceptions of these are always implicit in the best plays, and are often the key to their appropriate rendering; but most actors are so accustomed to do without them that they would object to being troubled with them, although it is only by such educative trouble that an actor's profession can place him on the level of the lawyer, the physician, the churchman, and the statesman. Even as it is, Shylock as a Jew and usurer, Othello as a Moor and a soldier, Cæsar, Cleopatra and Antony as figures in defined political circumstances, are enormously more real to the actor than the countless heroes as to whom nothing is ever known except that they wear nice clothes, love the heroine, baffle the villain, and live happily ever after.

The case, then, is overwhelming not only for printing and publishing the dialogue of plays, but for a serious effort to convey their full content to the reader. This means the institution of a new art; and I daresay that before these two volumes are ten years old, the bald attempt they make at it will be left far behind, and that the customary brief and unreadable scene specification at the head of an act will have expanded into a chapter, or even a series of chapters. No doubt one result of this will be the production, under cover of the above arguments, of works of a mixture of kinds, part narrative, part homily, part description, part dialogue, and (possibly) part drama: works that could be read, but not acted. I have no objection to such works; but my own aim has been that of the practical dramatist: if anything my eye has been too much on the stage. At all events, I have tried to put down nothing that is irrelevant to the actor's performance, and, through it, to the audience's comprehension of the play. I have of course been compelled to omit many things that a stage representation could convey, simply because the art of letters, though highly developed grammatically, is still in its infancy as a technical speech notation: for example, there are fifty ways of saying Yes, and five hundred of saying No, but only one way of writing them down. Even the use of spaced letters instead of italics for underlining, though familiar to foreign readers, will have to be learned by the English public before it becomes effective. But if my readers do their fair share of the work, I daresay they will understand nearly as much of the plays as I do myself.

Finally, a word as to why I have labelled the three plays in this first volume Unpleasant. The reason is pretty obvious: their dramatic power is used to force the spectator to face unpleasant facts. No doubt all plays which deal sincerely with humanity must wound the monstrous conceit which it is the business of romance to flatter. But here we are confronted, not only with the comedy and tragedy of individual character and destiny, but with those social horrors which arise from the fact that the average homebred Englishman, however honorable and goodnatured he may be in his private capacity, is, as a citizen, a wretched creature who, whilst clamoring for a gratuitous millennium, will shut his eyes to the most villainous abuses if the remedy threatens to add another

penny in the pound to the rates and taxes which he
has to be half cheated, half coerced into paying. In
Widowers' Houses I have shewn middle-class respectability and younger son gentility fattening on the
poverty of the slum as flies fatten on filth. That is not
a pleasant theme.

In The Philanderer I have shewn the grotesque
sexual compacts made between men and women
under marriage laws which represent to some of us a
political necessity (especially for other people), to
some a divine ordinance, to some a romantic ideal, to
some a domestic profession for women, and to some
that worst of blundering abominations, an institution
which society has outgrown but not modified, and
which "advanced" individuals are therefore forced to
evade. The scene with which The Philanderer opens,
the atmosphere in which it proceeds, and the marriage
with which it ends, are, for the intellectually and ar-
tistically conscious classes in modern society, typical;
and it will hardly be denied, I think, that they are
unpleasant.

In Mrs Warren's Profession I have gone straight at
the fact that, as Mrs Warren puts it, "the only way
for a woman to provide for herself decently is for her
to be good to some man that can afford to be good to
her." There are certain questions on which I am, like
most Socialists, an extreme Individualist. I believe
that any society which desires to found itself on a
high standard of integrity of character in its units
should organize itself in such a fashion as to make it
possible for all men and all women to maintain themselves in reasonable comfort by their industry without
selling their affections and their convictions. At
present we not only condemn women as a sex to
attach themselves to breadwinners, licitly or illicitly,

on pain of heavy privation and disadvantage; but we have great prostitute classes of men: for instance, the playwrights and journalists, to whom I myself belong, not to mention the legions of lawyers, doctors, clergymen, and platform politicians who are daily using their highest faculties to belie their real sentiments: a sin compared to which that of a women who sells the use of her person for a few hours is too venial to be worth mentioning; for rich men without conviction are more dangerous in modern society than poor women without chastity. Hardly a pleasant subject, this!

I must, however, warn my readers that my attacks are directed against themselves, not against my stage figures. They cannot too thoroughly understand that the guilt of defective social organization does not lie alone on the people who actually work the commercial makeshifts which the defects make inevitable, and who often, like Sartorius and Mrs Warren, display valuable executive capacities and even high moral virtues in their administration, but with the whole body of citizens whose public opinion, public action, and public contribution as ratepayers, alone can replace Sartorius's slums with decent dwellings, Charteris's intrigues with reasonable marriage contracts, and Mrs Warren's profession with honorable industries guarded by a humane industrial code and a "moral minimum" wage.

How I came, later on, to write plays which, dealing less with the crimes of society, and more with its romantic follies and with the struggles of individuals against those follies, may be called, by contrast, Pleasant, is a story which I shall tell on resuming this discourse for the edification of the readers of the second volume. 1898

Widowers' Houses

WITH

The Author's Preface to the 1893 Edition

The Playwright on His First Play

Composition begun 18 August 1884; completed
20 October 1892. Published 1893. Revised
text in *Plays Pleasant and Unpleasant*, 1898.
Further revision in Collected Edition, 1930

First presented by the Independent Theatre
at the Royalty Theatre, London, on 9 December 1892; repeated on 13 December (matinée).

Dr Harry Trench   *W. J. Robertson*
William de Burgh Cokane   *Arthur Whittaker*
Sartorius   *T. W. Percyval*
Lickcheese   *James Welch*
Waiter   *E. P. Donne*
Porter   *W. Alison*
Blanche Sartorius   *Florence Farr*
Annie (parlormaid)   *N. de Silva*

ACT I *In the Grounds of a Hotel-Restaurant at Remagen, on the Rhine*
ACT II *Library in Sartorius' House at Surbiton*
ACT III *The Drawing-Room—Evening*

The Author's Preface

(to 1893 edition)

The early history of the play which forms this first volume of the "Independent Theatre Series" has been given by Mr. William Archer in *The World* of the 14th December, 1892, in the following terms:—

"Partly to facilitate the labours of Mr. George Bernard Shaw's biographers, and partly by way of relieving my own conscience, I think I ought to give a short history of the genesis of *Widowers' Houses*. Far away back in the olden days [1885], while as yet the Independent Theatre slumbered in the womb of Time, together with the New Drama, the New Criticism, the New Humour, and all the other glories of our renovated world, I used to be a daily frequenter of the British Museum Reading Room. Even more assiduous in his attendance was a young man of tawny complexion and attire, beside whom I used frequently to find myself seated. My curiosity was piqued by the odd conjunction of his subjects of research. Day after day for weeks he had before him two books, which he studied alternately, if not simultaneously—Karl Marx's *Das Kapital* (in French), and an orchestral score of *Tristan und Isolde*. I did not know then how exactly this quaint juxtaposition symbolised the main interests of his life. Presently I met him at the house of a common acquaintance, and we conversed for the first time. I learned from himself that he was the author of several unpublished masterpieces of fiction. Construction, he owned with engaging modesty, was not his strong point, but his dialogue was incomparable. Now, in those days, I had still a certain hankering after the rewards, if not the

glories, of the playwright. With a modesty in no way
inferior to Mr. Shaw's, I had realised that I could not
write dialogue a bit; but I still considered myself
a born constructor. So I proposed, and Mr. Shaw
agreed to, a collaboration. I was to provide him with
one of the numerous plots I kept in stock, and he was
to write the dialogue. So said, so done. I drew out,
scene by scene, the scheme of a twaddling cup-and-
saucer comedy vaguely suggested by Augier's *Ceinture
Dorée*. The details I forget, but I know it was to be
called *Rhinegold*, was to open, as *Widowers' Houses*
actually does, in a hotel-garden on the Rhine, and was
to have two heroines, a sentimental and a comic one,
according to the accepted Robertson-Byron-Carton
formula. I fancy the hero was to propose to the sentimental heroine, believing her to be the poor niece
instead of the rich daughter of the sweater, or slum-
landlord, or whatever he may have been; and I know
he was to carry on in the most heroic fashion, and was
ultimately to succeed in throwing the tainted treasure
of his father-in-law, metaphorically speaking, into
the Rhine. All this I gravely propounded to Mr. Shaw,
who listened with no less admirable gravity. Then I
thought the matter had dropped, for I heard no more
of it for many weeks. I used to see Mr. Shaw at the
Museum, laboriously writing page after page of the
most exquisitely neat shorthand at the rate of about
three words a minute; but it did not occur to me that
this was our play. After about six weeks he said to me
'Look here, I've written half the first act of that
comedy, and I've used up all your plot. Now I want
some more to go on with.' I told him that my plot
was a rounded and perfect organic whole, and that I
could no more eke it out in this fashion than I could
provide him or myself with a set of supplementary

arms and legs. I begged him to extend his shorthand
and let me see what he had done; but this would have
taken him far too long. He tried to decipher some of it
orally, but the process was too lingering and painful
for endurance. So he simply gave me an outline in
narrative of what he had done; and I saw that, so far
from having used up my plot, he had not even touched
it. There the matter rested for months and years. Mr.
Shaw would now and then hold out vague threats of
finishing 'our play,' but I felt no serious alarm. I
thought (judging from my own experience in other
cases) that when he came to read over in cold blood
what he had written, he would see what impossible
stuff it was. Perhaps my free utterance of this view
piqued him; perhaps he felt impelled to remove from
the Independent Theatre the reproach of dealing
solely in foreign products. The fire of his genius, at
all events, was not to be quenched by my persistent
applications of the wet-blanket. He finished his play;
Mr Grein, as in duty bound, accepted it; and the
result was the performance of Friday last [9th Dec.
1892] at the Independent Theatre."

To this history I have little to add. The circumstances occurred, in the main, as Mr. Archer states
them. But I most strenuously deny that there is any
such great difference between his *Rhinegold* and
Widowers' Houses as he supposes. I appeal to the
impartial public, which has now both my play and
Mr. Archer's story before it, to judge whether I did
not deal faithfully with him. The Rhine hotel garden,
the hero proposing to the heroine in ignorance of the
source of her father's wealth, the "tainted treasure of
the father-in-law," the renunciation of it by the lover:
all these will be found as prominently in the following

pages as in Mr. Archer's description of the fable which he persists in saying I did "not even touch." As a matter of fact the dissolution of partnership between us came when I told him that I had finished up the renunciation and wanted some more story to go on with, as I was only in the middle of the second act. He said that according to his calculation the renunciation ought to have landed me at the end of the play. I could only reply that his calculation did not work out, and that he must supply further material. This he most unreasonably refused to do; and I had eventually to fish up the tainted treasure out of the Rhine, so to speak, and make it last out another act and a half, which I had to invent all by myself. Clearly, then, he was the defaulter; and I am the victim.

It will have been noted by the attentive reader that what I have called a story, Mr. Archer calls a plot; and that he mentions two heroines, introduced for the sole purpose of being mistaken for one another. Now, I must confess to discarding the second daughter. She was admittedly a mere joist in the plot; and I had then, have now, and have always had, an utter contempt for "constructed" works of art. How any man in his senses can deliberately take as his model the sterile artifice of Wilkie Collins or Scribe, and repudiate the natural artistic activity of Fielding, Goldsmith, Defoe and Dickens, not to mention Æschylus and Shakespear, is beyond argument with me: those who entertain such preferences are obviously incapable people, who prefer a "well made play" to *King Lear* exactly as they prefer acrostics to sonnets. As a fictionist, my natural way is to imagine characters and spin out a story about them, whether I am writing a novel or a play; and I please myself by reflecting that this has been the way of all great masters of fiction. At the same time I am quite aware that a writer with the necessary constructive ingenuity, and the itch for exercising it for its own sake, can entertain audiences or readers very agreeably by carefully constructing and unravelling mysteries and misunderstandings; and that this ingenuity may be associated with sufficient creative imagination to give a considerable show of humanity and some interest of character to the puppets contrived for the purpose of furthering the plot. The line between the authors who place their imagination at the service of their ingenuity and those who place their ingenuity at the service of their imagination may be hard to draw with precise justice (to Edgar Allan Poe, for instance!); but it is clear that if we draw it as an equator, Scribe and the plot constructors will be at the south pole, and Æschylus and the dramatic poets at the north. Now, Archer's *Rhinegold*, in the absence of any convincing evidence that I was an Æschylus, was designed for the southern hemisphere; and *Widowers' Houses* was built for the north. I told the story, but discarded the plot; and Archer at once perceived that this step made the enterprise entirely my own, since the resultant play, whether good or bad, must on my method be a *growth* out of the stimulated imagination of the actual writer, and not a manufactured article constructed by an artisan according to plans and specifications supplied by an inventor. The collaboration was therefore dropped; and after finishing the second act, so as to avoid leaving a loose end, and noting such beginnings of the third as had already sprouted, I left the work aside for seven years and thought no more of it. Last August, having been rather overworked by the occurrence of a General Election at the busiest part of the journalistic season in London, I could do nothing for a while but potter aimlessly over my old papers, among which I came across the manuscript of the play; and it so tickled me that I there and then sat down and finished it. But for Mr. Grein and the Independent Theatre Society it would probably have gone back to its drawer and lain there for another seven years, if not for ever.

Some idea of the discussion which followed the performance may be gathered from the appendices which will be found at the end of this volume. The entire novelty on the stage of the standpoint taken, which is impartially Socialistic, greatly confused the critics, especially those who are in the habit of accepting as Socialism that spirit of sympathy with the poor and indignant protest against suffering and injustice which, in modern literature, culminated in Victor Hugo's *Les Miserables*, and has lately been forced into the theatre by the pressure of the Socialist propaganda outside. This "stage Socialism" is represented in my play by the good-natured compunction of my hero, who conceives the horrors of the slums as merely the result of atrocious individual delinquency on the part of the slum landlord. In spite of the unanswerable way in which the shallowness and impracticability of this view are exposed at once by a single speech from a practical business man, many of my critics were unable to rid themselves of it. They dismissed the man of business as a sophistical villain, and so got hopelessly astray as to the characterization in the piece. My portraiture of Lickcheese, the slum rent collector, an effective but quite common piece of work, pleased better than any of the rest. My technical skill as a playwright sustained many attacks, all based on the assumption that the only admissible stage technique is the technique of plot construction, an assumption which excludes Shakespear and Goethe from the ranks of competent stage workmen, and which therefore appears to me to reduce itself to absurdity, although I am well aware that many of our critics look on Shakespear and Goethe as literary men who were unfortunately disabled from producing good acting plays by their deficiency in the stage craft of the ordinary farcical comedy writer and melodramatist. It was further objected that my play, being didactic, was therefore not a work of art—a proposition which, if examined, will be found to mean either that the world's acknowledged masterpieces are not works of art, or else exactly nothing at all. Now, I submit that I could not reasonably be expected to defer to the authority of canons of art which no artist acknowledges, and in subjection to which no art would be possible, even if I had not, by my practice in the profession of music critic during the remarkable development effected both in that art and in its criticism by Richard Wagner, been sufficiently trained in critical processes to recognize the objections I have cited as nothing more than the common fallacies and ineptitudes into which all critics fall when first confronted with a progressive movement. I have also practised picture criticism, and have had to make up my mind as to the pre-Raphaelite movement and the Impressionist movement, with the result that I have come to suspect dramatic critics of never having had to make up their minds about anything, owing to the fact that until the advent of Ibsen the other day there had not for many years been anything worth calling a movement in dramatic art. I by no means undervalued their like or dislike of my work, which was written as much to please them as any one else; but, as an expert, I found their critical analysis anything but skilful, and their power of imposing on themselves by phrase-making, boundless. Even the best of the younger school will occasionally be satisfied that he has quite accounted for an unexpected speech by dismissing it as a wanton paradox (without any consciousness of having insulted the author); or he will dispose of an incident by pointing out that it is "inconsistent"; or, if he wishes to be specially ingenious, he will say of a character—a red-haired one, for instance—that it is not a human being at all, but a type of the red-haired variety of mankind. I make free to criticize my critics thus because some of them are my personal friends; others have dealt so handsomely by me that I cannot very well except them without a ridiculous appearance of returning the compliment; and the rest will be all the better for being brought to book. Besides, I may offer my *Quintessence of Ibsenism*, written and published before there was any question of finishing or producing *Widowers' Houses*, as a substantial proof that my interest in the art of criticism is not at bottom merely the protest of my own sensitiveness against the very disrespectful way in which my work has been handled in various quarters. There must, however, be no mistake as to the ground upon which I challenge criticism for the play, now that I submit it in print to the public. It is a propagandist play—a didactic play—a play with a purpose; but I do not therefore claim any special indulgence for it from people who go to the theatre to be entertained. I offer it as a technically good practicable stage play, one which will, if adequately acted, hold its proper audience and drive its story home to the last word.

But in claiming place for my play among works of art, I must make a melancholy reservation. One or two friendly readers may find it interesting, amusing, even admirable, as far as a mere topical farce can excite admiration; but nobody will find it a beautiful or lovable work. It is saturated with the vulgarity of the life it represents: the people do not speak nobly, live gracefully, or sincerely face their own position: the author is not giving expression in pleasant fancies to the underlying beauty and romance of happy life, but dragging up to the smooth surface of "respectability" a handful of the slime and foulness of its polluted bed, and playing off your laughter at the scandal of the exposure against your shudder at its blackness. I offer it as my own criticism of the author of *Widowers' Houses* that the disillusion which makes all great dramatic poets tragic has here made him only derisive; and derision is by common consent a baser atmosphere than that of tragedy. I had better have written a beautiful play, like *Twelfth Night*, or a grand play, like the tragic masterpieces; but, frankly, I was not able to: modern commercialism is a bad art school, and cannot, with all its robberies, murders and prostitutions, move us in the grand manner to pity and terror: it is squalid, futile, blundering, mean, ridiculous, for ever uneasily pretending to be the wide-minded, humane, enterprising thing it is not. It is not my fault, reader, that my art is the expression of my sense of moral and intellectual perversity rather than of my sense of beauty. My life has been passed mostly in big modern towns, where my sense of beauty has been starved whilst my intellect has been gorged with problems like that of the slums in this play, until at last I have come, in a horrible sort of way, to relish them enough to make them the subjects of my essays as an artist. Such art as can come out of these conditions for a man of my endowment I claim to have put into my work; and therefore you will please judge it, not as a pamphlet in dialogue, but as in intention a work of art as much as any comedy of Molière's is a work of art, and as pretending to be a better made play for actual use and long wear on the boards than anything that has yet been turned out by the patent constructive machinery. And I claim that its value in both respects is enhanced by the fact that it deals with a burning social question, and is deliberately intended to induce people to vote on the Progressive side at the next County Council election in London. So, as the clown says in *All's Well*, "Spare not me." I am no novice in the current critical theories of dramatic art; and what I have done I have done on purpose.

LONDON, *March* 1893

[ACT I]

In the garden restaurant of a hotel at Remagen on the Rhine, on a fine afternoon in August in the eighteen-eighties. Looking down the Rhine towards Bonn, the gate leading from the garden to the riverside is seen on the right. The hotel is on the left. It has a wooden annexe with an entrance marked Table d'Hôte. A waiter is in attendance.

A couple of English tourists come out of the hotel. The younger, Dr Harry Trench, is about 24, stoutly built, thick in the neck, close-cropped and black in the hair, with undignified medical-student manners, frank, hasty, rather boyish. The other, Mr William de Burgh Cokane, is probably over 40, possibly 50: an ill-nourished, scanty-haired gentleman, with affected manners: fidgety, touchy, and constitutionally ridiculous in uncompassionate eyes.

COKANE [*on the threshold of the hotel, calling peremptorily to the waiter*] Two beers for us out here. [*The waiter goes for the beer. Cokane comes into the garden*]. We have secured the room with the best view in the hotel, Harry, thanks to my tact. We'll leave in the morning, and do Mainz and Frankfurt. There is a very graceful female statue in the private house of a nobleman in Frankfurt. Also a zoo. Next day, Nuremberg! finest collection of instruments of torture in the world.

TRENCH. All right. You look out the trains, will you?

[*He takes a Continental Bradshaw from his pocket, and tosses it on one of the tables*].

COKANE [*baulking himself in the act of sitting down*] Pah! the seat is all dusty. These foreigners are deplorably unclean in their habits.

TRENCH [*buoyantly*] Never mind: it dont matter, old chappie. Buck up, Billy, buck up. Enjoy yourself. [*He throws Cokane into the chair, and sits down opposite him, taking out his pipe, and singing noisily*]

> Pour out the Rhine wine: let it flow
> Like a free and bounding river—

COKANE [*scandalized*] In the name of common decency, Harry, will you remember that you are a Gentleman, and not a coster on Hampstead Heath on Bank Holiday? Would you dream of behaving like this in London?

TRENCH. Oh, rot! Ive come abroad to enjoy myself. So would you if youd just passed an examination after four years in the medical school and walking the hospital. [*He again bursts into song*].

COKANE [*rising*] Trench: either you travel as a gentleman, or you travel alone. This is what makes Englishmen unpopular on the Continent. It may not matter before the natives; but the people who came on board the steamer at Bonn are English. I have been uneasy all the afternoon about what they must think of us. Look at our appearance.

TRENCH. Whats wrong with our appearance?

COKANE. Négligé, my dear fellow, négligé. On the steamboat a little négligé was quite en règle; but here, in this hotel, some of them are sure to dress for dinner; and you have nothing but that Norfolk jacket. How are they to know that you are well connected if you do not shew it by your costume?

[48]

TRENCH. Pooh! the steamboat people were the scum of the earth: Americans and all sorts. They may go hang themselves, Billy. I shall not bother about them. [*He strikes a match, and proceeds to light his pipe*].

COKANE. Do drop calling me Billy in public, Trench. My name is Cokane. I am sure they were persons of consequence: you were struck with the distinguished appearance of the father yourself.

TRENCH [*sobered at once*] What! those people? [*He blows out the match and puts up his pipe*].

COKANE [*following up his advantage triumphantly*] Here, Harry, here: at this hotel. I recognized the father's umbrella in the hall.

TRENCH [*with a touch of genuine shame*] I suppose I ought to have brought a change. But a lot of luggage is such a nuisance; and [*rising abruptly*] at all events we can go and have a wash. [*He turns to go into the hotel, but stops in consternation, seeing some people coming up to the riverside gate*]. Oh, I say! Here they are.

A lady and gentleman, followed by a porter with some light parcels, not luggage, but shop purchases, come into the garden. They are apparently father and daughter. The gentleman is 50, tall, well preserved, and of upright carriage. His incisive, domineering utterance and imposing style, with his strong aquiline nose and resolute clean-shaven mouth, give him an air of importance. He wears a light frock-coat with silk linings, a white hat, and a field-glass slung in a new leather case. A self-made man, formidable to servants, not easily accessible to anyone. His daughter is a well-dressed, well-fed, good-looking, strongminded young woman, presentably lady-like, but still her father's daughter. Nevertheless fresh and attractive, and none the worse for being vital and energetic rather than delicate and refined.

COKANE [*quickly taking the arm of Trench, who is*

staring as if transfixed] Recollect yourself, Harry:
presence of mind, presence of mind! [*He strolls with
him towards the hotel. The waiter comes out with the
beer*]. Kellner: ceci-là est notre table. Est-ce que
vous comprenez Français?

WAITER. Yes zare. Oll right, zare.

THE GENTLEMAN [*to his porter*] Place those things
on that table. [*The porter does not understand*].

WAITER [*interposing*] Zese zhentellmen are using zis
table, zare. Vould you mind—

THE GENTLEMAN [*severely*] You should have told
me so before. [*To Cokane, with fierce condescension*]
I regret the mistake, sir.

COKANE. Dont mention it, my dear sir: dont mention
it. Retain the place, I beg.

THE GENTLEMAN [*coldly turning his back on him*]
Thank you. [*To the porter*] Place them on that table.
[*The porter makes no movement until the gentleman
points to the parcels and peremptorily raps on another
table, nearer the gate*].

PORTER. Ja wohl, gnäd'g' Herr. [*He puts down the
parcels*].

THE GENTLEMAN [*taking out a handful of money*]
Waiter.

WAITER [*awestruck*] Yes, zare.

THE GENTLEMAN. Tea. For two. Out here.

WAITER. Yes, zare. [*He goes into the hotel*].

*The gentleman selects a small coin from his handful of
money, and gives it to the porter, who receives it with a
submissive touch to his cap, and goes out, not daring to
speak. His daughter sits down and opens a parcel of
photographs. The gentleman takes out a Baedeker;
places a chair for himself; and then, before sitting down,
looks truculently at Cokane, as if waiting for him to
take himself off. Cokane, not at all abashed, resumes his*

place at the other table with an air of modest good breeding, and calls to Trench, who is prowling irresolutely in the background.

COKANE. Trench, my dear fellow: your beer is waiting for you. [*He drinks*].

TRENCH [*glad of the excuse to come back to his chair*] Thank you, Cokane. [*He also drinks*].

COKANE. By the way, Harry, I have often meant to ask you: is Lady Roxdale your mother's sister or your father's?

This shot tells immediately. The gentleman is perceptibly interested.

TRENCH. My mother's, of course. What put that into your head?

COKANE. Nothing. I was just thinking—hm! She will expect you to marry, Harry: a doctor ought to marry.

TRENCH. What has she got to do with it?

COKANE. A great deal, dear boy. She looks forward to floating your wife in society in London.

TRENCH. What rot!

COKANE. Ah, you are young, dear boy: you dont know the importance of these things; apparently idle ceremonial trifles, really the springs and wheels of a great aristocratic system. [*The waiter comes back with the tea things, which he brings to the gentleman's table. Cokane rises and addresses the gentleman*]. My dear sir, excuse my addressing you; but I cannot help feeling that you prefer this table, and that we are in your way.

THE GENTLEMAN [*graciously*] Thank you. Blanche: this gentleman very kindly offers us his table, if you would prefer it.

BLANCHE. Oh, thanks: it makes no difference.

THE GENTLEMAN [*to Cokane*] We are fellow travellers, I believe, sir.

COKANE. Fellow travellers and fellow countrymen.

[51]

Ah, we rarely feel the charm of our own tongue until it reaches our ears under a foreign sky. You have no doubt noticed that?

THE GENTLEMAN [*a little puzzled*] Hm! From a romantic point of view, possibly, very possibly. As a matter of fact, the sound of English makes me feel at home; and I dislike feeling at home when I am abroad. It is not precisely what one goes to the expense for. [*He looks at Trench*]. I think this gentleman travelled with us also.

COKANE [*acting as master of the ceremonies*] My valued friend, Dr Trench. [*The gentleman and Trench rise*]. Trench, my dear fellow, allow me to introduce you to—er—? [*He looks inquiringly at the gentleman, waiting for the name*].

THE GENTLEMAN. Permit me to shake your hand, Dr Trench. My name is Sartorius; and I have the honor of being known to Lady Roxdale, who is, I believe, a near relative of yours. Blanche. [*She looks up.*] Dr Trench. [*They bow*].

TRENCH. Perhaps I should introduce my friend Cokane to you, Mr Sartorius: Mr William de Burgh Cokane. [*Cokane makes an elaborate bow. Sartorius accepts it with dignity. The waiter meanwhile returns with the tea things.*]

SARTORIUS [*to the waiter*] Two more cups.

WAITER. Yes, zare. [*He goes into the hotel*].

BLANCHE. Do you take sugar, Mr Cokane?

COKANE. Thank you. [*To Sartorius*] This is really too kind. Harry: bring your chair round.

SARTORIUS. You are very welcome. [*Trench brings his chair to the tea table; and they all sit round it. The waiter returns with two more cups*].

WAITER. Table d'hôte at alf pass zeex, zhentellmenn. Somesing else now, zare?

SARTORIUS. No. You can go. [*The waiter goes*].

COKANE [*very agreeably*] Do you contemplate a long stay here, Miss Sartorius?

BLANCHE. We were thinking of going on to Rolandseck. Is it as nice as this place?

COKANE. Harry: the Baedeker. [*Trench produces it from the other pocket*]. Thank you. [*He consults the index for Rolandseck*].

BLANCHE. Sugar, Dr Trench?

TRENCH. Thanks. [*She hands him the cup, and looks meaningly at him for an instant. He looks down hastily, and glances apprehensively at Sartorius, who is preoccupied with the bread and butter*].

COKANE. Rolandseck appears to be an extremely interesting place. [*He reads*] "It is one of the most beautiful and frequented spots on the river, and is surrounded with numerous villas and pleasant gardens, chiefly belonging to wealthy merchants from the Lower Rhine, and extending along the wooded slopes at the back of the village."

BLANCHE. That sounds civilized and comfortable. I vote we go there.

SARTORIUS. Quite like our place at Surbiton, my dear.

BLANCHE. Quite.

COKANE. You have a place down the river? Ah, I envy you.

SARTORIUS. No: I have merely taken a furnished villa at Surbiton for the summer. I live in Bedford Square. I am a vestryman, and must reside in the parish.

BLANCHE. Another cup, Mr Cokane?

COKANE. Thank you, no. [*To Sartorius*] I presume you have been round this little place. Not much to see here, except the Apollinaris Church.

SARTORIUS [*scandalized*] The what!

COKANE. The Apollinaris Church.

[53]

SARTORIUS. A strange name to give a church. Very continental, I must say.

COKANE. Ah, yes, yes, yes. That is where our neighbors fall short sometimes, Mr Sartorius. Taste! taste is what they occasionally fail in. But in this instance they are not to blame. The water is called after the church, not the church after the water.

SARTORIUS [*as if this were an extenuating circumstance, but not a complete excuse*] I am glad to hear it. Is the church a celebrated one?

COKANE. Baedeker stars it.

SARTORIUS [*respectfully*] Oh, in that case I should like to see it.

COKANE [*reading*] "—erected in 1839 by Zwirner, the late eminent architect of the cathedral of Cologne, at the expense of Count Fürstenberg-Stammheim."

SARTORIUS [*much impressed*] We must certainly see that, Mr Cokane. I had no idea that the architect of Cologne cathedral lived so recently.

BLANCHE. Dont let us bother about any more churches, papa: theyre all the same. I'm tired to death of them.

SARTORIUS. Well, my dear, if you think it sensible to take a long and expensive journey to see what there is to be seen, and then go away without seeing it—

BLANCHE. Not this afternoon, papa, please.

SARTORIUS. My dear: I should like you to see everything. It is part of your education—

BLANCHE [*rising, with a petulant sigh*] Oh, my education! Very well, very well: I suppose I must go through with it. Are you coming, Dr Trench? [*With a grimace*] I'm sure the Johannis Church will be a treat for you.

COKANE [*laughing softly and archly*] Ah, excellent, excellent: very good indeed. [*Seriously*] But do you know, Miss Sartorius, there actually are Johannis churches here—several of them—as well as Apollinaris ones?

SARTORIUS [*sententiously, taking out his field-glass and leading the way to the gate*] There is many a true word spoken in jest, Mr Cokane.

COKANE [*accompanying him*] How true! How true!

They go out together, ruminating profoundly. Blanche makes no movement to follow them. She watches until they are safely out of sight, and then posts herself before Trench, looking at him with an enigmatic smile, which he returns with a half sheepish, half conceited grin.

BLANCHE. Well! So you have done it at last.

TRENCH. Yes. At least Cokane's done it. I told you he'd manage it. He's rather an ass in some ways; but he has tremendous tact.

BLANCHE [*contemptuously*] Tact! Thats not tact; thats inquisitiveness. Inquisitive people always have a lot of practice in getting into conversation with strangers. Why didnt you speak to my father yourself on the boat? You were ready enough to speak to me without any introduction.

TRENCH. I didnt particularly want to talk to him.

BLANCHE. It didnt occur to you, I suppose, that you put me in a false position by that.

TRENCH. Oh, I dont see that, exactly. Besides, your father isnt an easy man to tackle. Of course, now that I know him, I see that he's pleasant enough; but then youve got to know him first, havnt you?

BLANCHE [*impatiently*] Everybody is afraid of papa: I'm sure I dont know why. [*She sits down again, pouting a little*].

TRENCH [*tenderly*] However, it's all right now: isnt it? [*He sits near her*].

BLANCHE [*sharply*] I dont know. How should I?

You had no right to speak to me that day on board the steamer. You thought I was alone, because [*with false pathos*] I had no mother with me.

TRENCH [*protesting*] Oh, I say! Come! It was you who spoke to me. Of course I was only too glad of the chance; but on my word I shouldnt have moved an eyelid if you hadnt given me a lead.

BLANCHE. I only asked you the name of a castle. There was nothing unladylike in that.

TRENCH. Of course not. Why shouldnt you? [*With renewed tenderness*] But it's all right now: isnt it?

BLANCHE [*softly, looking subtly at him*] Is it?

TRENCH [*suddenly becoming shy*] I—I suppose so. By the way, what about the Apollinaris Church? Your father expects us to follow him, doesnt he?

BLANCHE [*with suppressed resentment*] Dont let me detain you if you wish to see it.

TRENCH. Wont you come?

BLANCHE. No [*She turns her face away moodily*].

TRENCH [*alarmed*] I say: youre not offended, are you? [*She looks round at him for a moment with a reproachful film on her eyes*]. Blanche. [*She bristles instantly; overdoes it; and frightens him*]. I beg your pardon for calling you by your name; but I—er—[*She corrects her mistake by softening her expression eloquently. He responds with a gush*] You dont mind, do you? I felt sure you wouldnt, somehow. Well, look here. I have no idea how you will receive this: it must seem horribly abrupt; but the circumstances do not admit of—the fact is, my utter want of tact—[*he flounders more and more, unable to see that she can hardly contain her eagerness*]. Now, if it were Cokane—

BLANCHE [*impatiently*] Cokane!

TRENCH [*terrified*] No, not Cokane. Though I assure you I was only going to say about him that—

BLANCHE. That he will be back presently with papa.

TRENCH [*stupidly*] Yes: they cant be very long now. I hope I'm not detaining you.

BLANCHE. I thought you were detaining me because you had something to say.

TRENCH [*totally unnerved*] Not at all. At least, nothing very particular. That is, I'm afraid you wouldnt think it very particular. Another time, perhaps—

BLANCHE. What other time? How do you know that we shall ever meet again? [*Desperately*] Tell me now. I want you to tell me now.

TRENCH. Well, I was thinking that if we could make up our minds to—or not to—at least—er—[*His nervousness deprives him of the power of speech*].

BLANCHE [*giving him up as hopeless*] I dont think theres much danger of your making up your mind, Dr Trench.

TRENCH [*stammering*] I only thought—[*He stops and looks at her piteously. She hesitates a moment, and then puts her hands into his with calculated impulsiveness. He snatches her into his arms with a cry of relief*]. Dear Blanche! I thought I should never have said it. I believe I should have stood stuttering here all day if you hadnt helped me out with it.

BLANCHE [*indignantly trying to break loose from him*] I didnt help you out with it.

TRENCH [*holding her*] I dont mean that you did it on purpose, of course. Only instinctively.

BLANCHE [*still a little anxious*] But you havnt said anything.

TRENCH. What more can I say than this? [*He kisses her again*].

BLANCHE [*overcome by the kiss, but holding on to her point*] But Harry—

TRENCH [*delighted at the name*] Yes.

BLANCHE. When shall we be married?

TRENCH. At the first church we meet: the Apollinaris Church, if you like.

BLANCHE. No, but seriously. This is serious, Harry: you mustnt joke about it.

TRENCH [*looking suddenly round to the riverside gate and quickly releasing her*] Sh! Here they are back again.

BLANCHE. Oh, d— [*The word is drowned by the clangor of a bell from within the hotel. The waiter appears on the steps, ringing it. Cokane and Sartorious are seen returning by the river gate*].

WAITER. Table d'hôte in dwendy minutes, ladies and zhentellmenn. [*He goes into the hotel*].

SARTORIUS [*gravely*] I intended you to accompany us, Blanche.

BLANCHE. Yes, papa. We were just about to start.

SARTORIUS. We are rather dusty: we must make ourselves presentable at the table d'hôte. I think you had better come in with me, my child, Come.

He offers Blanche his arm. The gravity of his manner overawes them all. Blanche silently takes his arm and goes into the hotel with him. Cokane, hardly less momentous than Sartorius himself, contemplates Trench with the severity of a judge.

COKANE [*with reprobation*] No, my dear boy. No, no. Never. I blush for you. I was never so ashamed in my life. You have been taking advantage of that unprotected girl.

TRENCH [*hotly*] Cokane!

COKANE [*inexorable*] Her father seems to be a perfect gentleman. I obtained the privilege of his acquaintance: I introduced you: I allowed him to believe that he might leave his daughter in your charge with absolute confidence. And what did I see on our return?

what did her father see? Oh, Trench, Trench!
No, my dear fellow, no, no. Bad taste, Harry, bad
form!

TRENCH. Stuff! There was nothing to see.

COKANE. Nothing to see! She, a perfect lady, a person
of highest breeding, actually in your arms; and you
say there was nothing to see! with a waiter there
actually ringing a heavy bell to call attention to his
presence! [*Lecturing him with redoubled severity*] Have
you no principles, Trench? Have you no religious
convictions? Have you no acquaintance with the
usages of society? You actually kissed—

TRENCH. You didnt see me kiss her.

COKANE. We not only saw but heard it: the report
positively reverberated down the Rhine. Dont condescend to subterfuge, Trench.

TRENCH. Nonsense, my dear Billy. You—

COKANE. There you go again. Dont use that low
abbreviation. How am I to preserve the respect of
fellow travellers of position and wealth, if I am to be
Billied at every turn? My name is William: William
de Burgh Cokane.

TRENCH. Oh, bother! There: dont be offended, old
chap. Whats the use of putting your back up at every
trifle? It comes natural to me to call you Billy: it
suits you, somehow.

COKANE [*mortified*] You have no delicacy of feeling,
Trench: no tact. I never mention it to any one; but
nothing, I am afraid, will ever make a true gentleman
of you. [*Sartorius appears on the threshold of the hotel*].
Here is my friend Sartorius, coming, no doubt, to
ask you for an explanation of your conduct. I really
should not have been surprised to see him bring a
horsewhip with him. I shall not intrude on the painful
scene.

TRENCH. Dont go, confound it. I dont want to meet him alone just now.

COKANE [*shaking his head*] Delicacy, Harry, delicacy! Good taste! Savoir faire! [*He walks away. Trench tries to escape in the opposite direction by strolling off towards the garden entrance*].

SARTORIUS [*mesmerically*] Dr Trench.

TRENCH [*stopping and turning*] Oh, is that you, Mr Sartorius? How did you find the church?

Sartorius, without a word, points to a seat. Trench, half hypnotized by his own nervousness and the impressiveness of Sartorius, sits down helplessly.

SARTORIUS [*also seating himself*] You have been speaking to my daughter, Dr Trench.

TRENCH [*with an attempt at ease of manner*] Yes: we had a conversation—quite a chat, in fact—while you were at the church with Cokane. How did you get on with Cokane, Mr Sartorius? I always think he has such wonderful tact.

SARTORIUS [*ignoring the digression*] I have just had a word with my daughter, Dr Trench; and I find her under the impression that something has passed between you which it is my duty as a father—the father of a motherless girl—to inquire into at once. My daughter, perhaps foolishly, has taken you quite seriously; and—

TRENCH. But—

SARTORIUS. One moment, if you will be so good. I have been a young man myself: younger, perhaps, than you would suppose from my present appearance. I mean, of course, in character. If you were not serious—

TRENCH [*ingenuously*] But I was perfectly serious. I want to marry your daughter, Mr Sartorius. I hope you dont object.

[60]

SARTORIUS [*condescending to Trench's humility from the mere instinct to seize an advantage, and yet deferring to Lady Roxdale's relative*] So far, no. I may say that your proposal seems to be an honorable and straightforward one, and that it is very gratifying to me personally.

TRENCH [*agreeably surprised*] Then I suppose we may consider the affair as settled. It's really very good of you.

SARTORIUS. Gently, Dr Trench, gently. Such a transaction as this cannot be settled off-hand.

TRENCH. Not off-hand, no. There are settlements and things, of course. But it may be regarded as settled between ourselves, maynt it?

SARTORIUS. Hm! Have you nothing further to mention?

TRENCH. Only that—that—No: I dont know that I have, except that I love—

SARTORIUS [*interrupting*] Anything about your family, for example? You do not anticipate any objection on their part, do you?

TRENCH. Oh, they have nothing to do with it.

SARTORIUS [*warmly*] Excuse me, sir: they have a great deal to do with it. [*Trench is abashed*]. I am resolved that my daughter shall approach no circle in which she will not be received with the full consideration to which her education and her breeding [*here his self-control slips a little; and he repeats, as if Trench had contradicted him*]—I say, her breeding—entitle her.

TRENCH [*bewildered*] Of course not. But what makes you think my family wont like Blanche? Of course my father was a younger son; and Ive had to take to a profession and all that; so my people wont expect us to entertain them: theyll know we cant afford it. But theyll entertain us: they always ask me.

[61]

SARTORIUS. That wont do for me, sir. Families often think it due to themselves to turn their backs on new-comers whom they may not think quite good enough for them.

TRENCH. But I assure you my people arnt a bit snobbish. Blanche is a lady: thatll be good enough for them.

SARTORIUS [*moved*] I am glad you think so. [*He offers his hand. Trench, astonished, takes it*]. I think so myself. [*He presses Trench's hand gratefully and releases it*]. And now, Dr Trench, since you have acted handsomely, you shall have no cause to complain of me. There shall be no difficulty about money: you shall entertain as much as you please: I will guarantee all that. But I must have a guarantee on my side that she will be received on equal terms by your family.

TRENCH. Guarantee!

SARTORIUS. Yes, a reasonable guarantee. I shall expect you to write to your relatives explaining your intention, and adding what you think proper as to my daughter's fitness for the best society. When you can shew me a few letters from the principal members of your family, congratulating you in a fairly cordial way, I shall be satisfied. Can I say more?

TRENCH [*much puzzled, but grateful*] No indeed. You are really very good. Many thanks. Since you wish it, I'll write to my people. But I assure you youll find them as jolly as possible over it. I'll make them write by return.

SARTORIUS. Thank you. In the meantime, I must ask you not to regard the matter as settled.

TRENCH. Oh! Not to regard the—I see. You mean between Blanche and—

SARTORIUS. I mean between you and Miss Sartorius.

When I interrupted your conversation here some time ago, you and she were evidently regarding it as settled. In case difficulties arise, and the match—you see I call it a match—is broken off, I should not wish Blanche to think that she had allowed a gentleman to—to—[*Trench nods sympathetically*] Quite so. May I depend on you to keep a fair distance, and so spare me the necessity of having to restrain an intercourse which promises to be very pleasant to us all?

TRENCH. Certainly; since you prefer it. [*They shake hands on it*].

SARTORIUS [*rising*] You will write today, I think you said?

TRENCH [*eagerly*] I'll write now, before I leave here: straight off.

SARTORIUS. I will leave you to yourself then. [*He hesitates, the conversation having made him self-conscious and embarrassed; then recovers himself with an effort, and adds with dignity, as he turns to go*] I am pleased to have come to an understanding with you. [*He goes into the hotel; and Cokane, who has been hanging about inquisitively, emerges from the shrubbery*].

TRENCH [*excitedly*] Billy, old chap: youre just in time to do me a favor. I want you to draft a letter for me to copy out.

COKANE. I came with you on this tour as a friend, Trench: not as a secretary.

TRENCH. Well, youll write as a friend. It's to my Aunt Maria, about Blanche and me. To tell her, you know.

COKANE. Tell her about Blanche and you! Tell her about your conduct! Betray you, my friend; and forget that I am writing to a lady? Never!

TRENCH. Bosh, Billy: dont pretend you dont understand. We're engaged: engaged, my boy! what do you think of that? I must write by tonight's post. You are the man to tell me what to say. Come, old chap [*coaxing him to sit down at one of the tables*]: heres a pencil. Have you a bit of—oh, here: thisll do: write it on the back of the map. [*He tears the map out of his Baedeker and spreads it face downwards on the table. Cokane takes the pencil and prepares to write*]. Thats right. Thanks awfully, old chap. Now fire away. [*Anxiously*] Be careful how you word it though, Cokane.

COKANE [*putting down the pencil*] If you doubt my ability to express myself becomingly to Lady Roxdale—

TRENCH [*propitiating him*] All right, old fellow, all right: theres not a man alive who could do it half so well as you. I only wanted to explain. You see, Sartorius has got it into his head, somehow, that my people will snub Blanche; and he wont consent unless they send letters and invitations and congratulations and the deuce knows what not. So just put it in such a way that Aunt Maria will write by return saying she is delighted, and asking us—Blanche and me, you know —to stay with her, and so forth. You know what I mean. Just tell her all about it in a chatty way; and—

COKANE [*crushingly*] If you will tell me all about it in a chatty way, I daresay I can communicate it to Lady Roxdale with becoming delicacy. What is Sartorius?

TRENCH [*taken aback*] I dont know: I didnt ask. It's a sort of question you cant very well put to a man— at least a man like him. Do you think you could word the letter so as to pass all that over? I really dont like to ask him.

COKANE. I can pass it over if you wish. Nothing easier. But if you think Lady Roxdale will pass it over, I differ from you. I may be wrong: no doubt I am. I generally am wrong, I believe; but that is my opinion.

TRENCH [*much perplexed*] Oh, confound it! What the deuce am I to do? Cant you say he's a gentleman: that wont commit us to anything. If you dwell on his being well off, and Blanche an only child, Aunt Maria will be satisfied.

COKANE. Henry Trench: when will you begin to get a little sense? This is a serious business. Act responsibly, Harry: act responsibly.

TRENCH. Bosh! Dont be moral!

COKANE. I am not moral, Trench. At least I am not a moralist: that is the expression I should have used. Moral, but not a moralist. If you are going to get money with your wife, doesnt it concern your family to know how that money was made? Doesnt it concern you—you, Harry? [*Trench looks at him helplessly, twisting his fingers nervously. Cokane throws down the pencil and leans back with ostentatious indifference*]. Of course it is no business of mine: I only throw out the suggestion. Sartorius may be a retired burglar for all I know. [*Sartorius and Blanche, ready for dinner, come from the hotel*].

TRENCH. Sh! Here they come. Get the letter finished before dinner, like a good old chappie: I shall be awfully obliged to you.

COKANE [*impatiently*] Leave me, leave me: you disturb me. [*He waves him off, and begins to write*].

TRENCH [*humbly and gratefully*] Yes, old chap. Thanks awfully. [*By this time Blanche has left her father, and is strolling off towards the riverside. Sartorius comes down the garden, Baedeker in hand, and sits near Cokane, reading. Trench addresses him*]. You wont mind my taking Blanche in to dinner, I hope, sir?

SARTORIUS. By all means, Dr Trench. Pray do so.

[*He graciously waves him off to join Blanche. Trench hurries after her through the gate. The light reddens as the Rhenish sunset begins. Cokane, making wry faces in the agonies of composition, is disconcerted to find Sartorius's eye upon him*].

SARTORIUS. I do not disturb you, I hope, Mr Cokane.

COKANE. By no means. Our friend Trench has entrusted me with a difficult and delicate task. He has requested me, as a friend of the family, to write to them on a subject that concerns you.

SARTORIUS. Indeed, Mr Cokane! Well, the communication could not be in better hands.

COKANE [*with an air of modesty*] Ah, that is going too far, my dear sir, too far. Still, you see what Trench is. A capital fellow in his way, Mr Sartorius, an excellent young fellow. But family communications like these require good manners. They require tact; and tact is Trench's weak point. He has an excellent heart, but no tact: none whatever. Everything depends on the way the matter is put to Lady Roxdale. But as to that, you may rely on me. I understand the sex.

SARTORIUS. Well, however she may receive it—and I care as little as any man, Mr Cokane, how people may choose to receive me—I trust I may at least have the pleasure of seeing you sometimes at my house when we return to England.

COKANE [*overwhelmed*] My dear sir! You express yourself in the true spirit of an English gentleman.

SARTORIUS. Not at all. You will always be most welcome. But I fear I have disturbed you in the composition of your letter. Pray resume it. I shall leave you to yourself. [*He pretends to rise, but checks himself to add*] Unless indeed I can assist you in any way? by clearing up any point on which you are not informed, for instance? or even, if I may so far presume on my years, giving you the benefit of my experience as to the best way of wording the matter? [*Cokane looks a little surprised at this. Sartorius looks hard at him, and continues deliberately and meaningly*] I shall always be happy to help any friend of Dr Trench's, in any way, to the best of my ability and of my means.

COKANE. My dear sir: you are really very good. Trench and I were putting our heads together over the letter just now; and there certainly were one or two points on which we were a little in the dark. [*Scrupulously*] But I would not permit Harry to question you. No. I pointed out to him that, as a matter of taste, it would be more delicate to wait until you volunteered the necessary information.

SARTORIUS. Hm! May I ask what you have said, so far?

COKANE. "My dear Aunt Maria." That is, Trench's dear Aunt Maria, my friend Lady Roxdale. You understand that I am only drafting a letter for Trench to copy.

SARTORIUS. Quite so. Will you proceed; or would it help you if I were to suggest a word or two?

COKANE [*effusively*] Your suggestions will be most valuable, my dear sir, most welcome.

SARTORIUS. I think I should begin in some such way as this. "In travelling with my friend Mr Cokane up the Rhine—"

COKANE [*murmuring as he writes*] Invaluable, invaluable. The very thing. "—my friend Mr Cokane up the Rhine—"

SARTORIUS. "I have made the acquaintance of"— or you may say "picked up," or "come across," if

you think that would suit your friend's style better.
We must not be too formal.

COKANE. "Picked up"! oh no: too dégagé, Mr
Sartorius, too dégagé. I should say "had the privilege
of becoming acquainted with."

SARTORIUS [*quickly*] By no means: Lady Roxdale
must judge of that for herself. Let it stand as I have
said. "I have made the acquaintance of a young lady,
the daughter of—" [*He hesitates*].

COKANE [*writing*] "acquaintance of a young lady,
the daughter of"—yes?

SARTORIUS. "of"—you had better say "a gentleman."

COKANE [*surprised*] Of course.

SARTORIUS [*with sudden passion*] It is not of course,
sir. [*Cokane, startled, looks at him with dawning
suspicion. Sartorius recovers himself somewhat shamefacedly*]. Hm! "—of a gentleman of considerable
wealth and position—"

COKANE [*echoing with a new note of coldness in his
voice as he writes the last words*] "—and position"

SARTORIUS. "which, however, he has made entirely
for himself." [*Cokane, now fully enlightened, stares at
him instead of writing*]. Have you written that?

COKANE [*expanding into an attitude of patronage and
encouragement*] Ah, indeed. Quite so, quite so. [*He
writes*] "—entirely for himself." Just so. Proceed,
Sartorius, proceed. Very clearly expressed.

SARTORIUS. "The young lady will inherit the bulk
of her father's fortune, and will be liberally treated on
her marriage. Her education has been of the most
expensive and complete kind obtainable; and her
surroundings have been characterized by the strictest
refinement. She is in every essential particular—"

COKANE [*interrupting*] Excuse the remark; but dont

[68]

you think this is rather too much in the style of a
prospectus of the young lady ? I throw out the suggestion as a matter of taste.

SARTORIUS [*troubled*] Perhaps you are right. I am of
course not dictating the exact words;—

COKANE. Of course not: of course not.

SARTORIUS. —but I desire that there may be no
wrong impression as to my daughter's—er—breeding.
As to myself—

COKANE. Oh, it will be sufficient to mention your
profession, or pursuits, or— [*He pauses; and they
look pretty hard at one another*].

SARTORIUS [*very deliberately*] My income, sir, is
derived from the rental of a very extensive real estate
in London. Lady Roxdale is one of the head landlords; and Dr Trench holds a mortgage from which,
if I mistake not, his entire income is derived. The truth
is, Mr Cokane, I am quite well acquainted with Dr
Trench's position and affairs; and I have long desired
to know him personally.

COKANE [*again obsequious, but still inquisitive*] What
a remarkable coincidence! In what quarter is the
estate situated, did you say ?

SARTORIUS. In London, sir. Its management occu-
pies as much of my time as is not devoted to the
ordinary pursuits of a gentleman. [*He rises and takes out
his card case*]. The rest I leave to your discretion.
[*He leaves a card on the table*]. That is my address at
Surbiton. If it should unfortunately happen, Mr
Cokane, that this leads to nothing but a disappointment for Blanche, probably she would rather not see
you afterwards. But if all turns out as we hope, Dr
Trench's best friends will then be our best friends.

COKANE [*rising and confronting Sartorius confidently,
pencil and paper in hand*] Rely on me, Mr Sartorius.

The letter is already finished here [*pointing to his brain*]. In five minutes it will be finished there [*He points to the paper; nods to emphasize the assertion; and begins to pace up and down the garden, writing, and tapping his forehead from time to time as he goes, with every appearance of severe intellectual exertion*].

SARTORIUS [*calling through the gate after a glance at his watch*] Blanche.

BLANCHE [*replying in the distance*] Yes?

SARTORIUS. Time, my dear. [*He goes into the table d'hôte*].

BLANCHE [*nearer*] Coming. [*She comes back through the gate, followed by Trench*].

TRENCH [*in a half whisper, as Blanche goes towards the table d'hôte*] Blanche: stop. One moment. [*She stops*]. We must be careful when your father is by. I had to promise him not to regard anything as settled until I hear from my people at home.

BLANCHE [*chilled*] Oh, I see. Your family may object to me; and then it will be all over between us. They are almost sure to.

TRENCH [*anxiously*] Dont say that, Blanche: it sounds as if you didnt care. I hope you regard it as settled. You havnt made any promise, you know.

BLANCHE [*earnestly*] Yes, I have: *I* promised papa too. But I have broken my promise for your sake. I suppose I am not so conscientious as you. And if the matter is not to be regarded as settled, family or no family, promise or no promise, let us break it off here and now.

TRENCH [*intoxicated with affection*] Blanche: on my most sacred honor, family or no family, promise or no promise—[*The waiter reappears at the table d'hôte entrance, ringing his bell*]. Damn that noise!

COKANE [*as he comes to them, flourishing the letter*] Finished, dear boy, finished. Done to a turn, punctually to the second, C'est fini, mon cher garçon, c'est fini. [*Sartorius returns*].

SARTORIUS. Will you take Blanche in, Dr Trench? [*Trench takes Blanche in to the table d'hôte*]. Is the letter finished, Mr Cokane?

COKANE [*with an author's pride, handing his draft to Sartorius*] There! [*Sartorius reads it, nodding gravely over it with complete approval*].

SARTORIUS [*returning the draft*] Thank you, Mr Cokane. You have the pen of a ready writer.

COKANE [*as they go in together*] Not at all, not at all. A little tact, Mr Sartorius, a little knowledge of the world, a little experience of women—[*They disappear into the annexe*].

[ACT II]

In the library of a handsomely appointed villa at Surbiton on a sunny forenoon in September. Sartorius is busy at a writing table littered with business letters. The fireplace, decorated for summer, is close behind him: the window is in the opposite wall. Between the table and the window Blanche, in her prettiest frock, sits reading The Queen. The door is in the middle. All the walls are lined with shelves of smartly tooled books, fitting into their places like bricks.

SARTORIUS. Blanche.

BLANCHE. Yes, papa.

SARTORIUS. I have some news here.

BLANCHE. What is it?

SARTORIUS. I mean news for you—from Trench.

BLANCHE [*with affected indifference*] Indeed?

SARTORIUS. "Indeed?"! Is that all you have to say to me? Oh, very well.

He resumes his work. Silence.

BLANCHE. What do his people say, papa?

SARTORIUS. His people? I dont know. [*Still busy*].

Another pause.

BLANCHE. What does he say?

SARTORIUS. He! He says nothing. [*He folds a letter leisurely, and looks for the envelope*]. He prefers to communicate the result of his—where did I put?—oh, here. Yes: he prefers to communicate the result in person.

BLANCHE [*springing up*] Oh, papa! When is he coming?

SARTORIUS. If he walks from the station, he may arrive in the course of the next half-hour. If he drives, he may be here at any moment.

BLANCHE [*making hastily for the door*] Oh!

SARTORIUS. Blanche.

BLANCHE. Yes, papa.

SARTORIUS. You will of course not meet him until he has spoken to me.

BLANCHE [*hypocritically*] Of course not, papa. I shouldnt have thought of such a thing.

SARTORIUS. That is all. [*She is going, when he puts out his hand, and says with fatherly emotion*] My dear child. [*She responds by going over to kiss him. A tap at the door*]. Come in.

Lickcheese enters, carrying a black handbag. He is a shabby, needy man, with dirty face and linen, scrubby beard and whiskers, going bald. A nervous, wiry, pertinacious human terrier, judged by his mouth and eyes, but miserably apprehensive and servile before Sartorius. He bids Blanche "Good morning, miss"; and she passes out with a slight and contemptuous recognition of him.

LICKCHEESE. Good morning, sir.

SARTORIUS [*harsh and peremptory*] Good morning.

LICKCHEESE [*taking a little sack of money from his bag*] Not much this morning, sir. I have just had the honor of making Dr Trench's acquaintance, sir.

SARTORIUS [*looking up from his writing, displeased*] Indeed?

LICKCHEESE. Yes, sir. Dr Trench asked his way of me, and was kind enough to drive me from the station.

SARTORIUS. Where is he, then?

LICKCHEESE. I left him in the hall, with his friend, sir. I should think he is speaking to Miss Sartorius.

[73]

SARTORIUS. Hm! What do you mean by his friend?

LICKCHEESE. There is a Mr Cokane with him, sir.

SARTORIUS. I see you have been talking to him, eh?

LICKCHEESE. As we drove along: yes, sir.

SARTORIUS [*sharply*] Why did you not come by the nine o'clock train?

LICKCHEESE. I thought—

SARTORIUS. It cannot be helped now; so never mind what you thought. But do not put off my business again to the last moment. Has there been any further trouble about the St Giles property?

LICKCHEESE. The Sanitary Inspector has been complaining again about No. 13 Robbins's Row. He says he'll bring it before the vestry.

SARTORIUS. Did you tell him that I am on the vestry?

LICKCHEESE. Yes, sir.

SARTORIUS. What did he say to that?

LICKCHEESE. Said he supposed so, or you wouldnt dare to break the law so scand'lous. I only tell you what he said.

SARTORIUS. Hm! Did you know his name?

LICKCHEESE. Yes, sir. Speakman.

SARTORIUS. Write it down in the diary for the day of the next meeting of the Health Committee. I will teach Mr Speakman his duty to members of the vestry.

LICKCHEESE [*doubtfully*] The vestry cant hurt him, sir. He's under the Local Government Board.

SARTORIUS. I did not ask you that. Let me see the books. [*Lickcheese produces the rent book, and hands it to Sartorius; then makes the desired entry in the diary on the table, watching Sartorius with misgivings as the rent book is examined. Sartorius rises, frowning*]. One pound four for repairs to number thirteen! What does this mean?

LICKCHEESE. Well, sir, it was the staircase on the

third floor. It was downright dangerous: there werent but three whole steps in it, and no handrail. I thought it best to have a few boards put in.

SARTORIUS. Boards! Firewood, sir, firewood! They will burn every stick of it. You have spent twenty-four shillings of my money on firewood for them.

LICKCHEESE. There ought to be stone stairs, sir: it would be a saving in the long run. The clergyman says—

SARTORIUS. What! Who says?

LICKCHEESE. The clergyman, sir, only the clergyman. Not that I make much account of him; but if you knew how he has worried me over that staircase—

SARTORIUS. I am an Englishman; and I will suffer no priest to interfere in my business. [*He turns suddenly on Lickcheese*]. Now look here, Mr Lick-cheese! This is the third time this year that you have brought me a bill of over a pound for repairs. I have warned you repeatedly against dealing with these tenement houses as if they were mansions in a West-End square. I have had occasion to warn you too against discussing my affairs with strangers. You have chosen to disregard my wishes. You are discharged.

LICKCHEESE [*dismayed*] Oh, sir, dont say that.

SARTORIUS [*fiercely*] You are discharged.

LICKCHEESE. Well, Mr Sartorius, it is hard, so it is. No man alive could have screwed more out of them poor destitute devils for you than I have, or spent less in doing it. I have dirtied my hands at it until theyre not fit for clean work hardly; and now you turn me—

SARTORIUS [*interrupting him menacingly*] What do you mean by dirtying your hands? If I find that you have stepped an inch outside the letter of the law, Mr Lickcheese, I will prosecute you myself. The way to keep your hands clean is to gain the confidence of your

[75]

employers. You will do well to bear that in mind in your next situation.

THE PARLORMAID [*opening the door*] Mr Trench and Mr Cokane.

Cokane and Trench come in: Trench festively dressed and in buoyant spirits: Cokane highly self-satisfied.

SARTORIUS. How do you do, Dr Trench? Good morning, Mr Cokane. I am pleased to see you here. Mr Lickcheese: you will place your accounts and money on the table: I will examine them and settle with you presently.

Lickcheese retires to the table, and begins to arrange his accounts, greatly depressed. The parlormaid withdraws.

TRENCH [*glancing at Lickcheese*] I hope we're not in the way.

SARTORIUS. By no means. Sit down, pray. I fear you have been kept waiting.

TRENCH [*taking Blanche's chair*] Not at all. Weve only just come in. [*He takes out a packet of letters, and begins untying them*].

COKANE [*going to a chair nearer the window, but stopping to look admiringly round before sitting down*] You must be happy here with all these books, Mr Sartorius. A literary atmosphere.

SARTORIUS [*resuming his seat*] I have not looked into them. They are pleasant for Blanche occasionally when she wishes to read. I chose the house because it is on gravel. The death-rate is very low.

TRENCH [*triumphantly*] I have any amount of letters for you. All my people are delighted that I am going to settle. Aunt Maria wants Blanche to be married from her house. [*He hands Sartorius a letter*].

SARTORIUS. Aunt Maria?

COKANE. Lady Roxdale, my dear sir: he means Lady

Roxdale. Do express yourself with a little more tact, my dear fellow.

TRENCH. Lady Roxdale, of course. Uncle Harry—

COKANE. Sir Harry Trench. His godfather, my dear sir, his godfather.

TRENCH. Just so. The pleasantest fellow for his age you ever met. He offers us his house at St Andrews for a couple of months, if we care to pass our honeymoon there. [*He hands Sartorius another letter*]. It's the sort of house nobody can live in, you know; but it's a nice thing for him to offer. Dont you think so?

SARTORIUS [*dissembling a thrill at the titles*] No doubt. These seem very gratifying, Dr Trench.

TRENCH. Yes, arnt they? Aunt Maria has really behaved like a brick. If you read the postscript youll see she spotted Cokane's hand in my letter. [*Chuckling*] He wrote it for me.

SARTORIUS [*glancing at Cokane*] Indeed! Mr Cokane evidently did it with great tact.

COKANE [*returning the glance*] Dont mention it.

TRENCH [*gleefully*] Well, what do you say now, Mr Sartorius? May we regard the matter as settled at last?

SARTORIUS. Quite settled. [*He rises and offers his hand. Trench, glowing with gratitude, rises and shakes it vehemently, unable to find words for his feelings*].

COKANE [*coming between them*]. Allow me to congratulate you both. [*He shakes hands with the two at the same time*].

SARTORIUS. And now, gentlemen, I have a word to say to my daughter. Dr Trench: you will not, I hope, grudge me the pleasure of breaking this news to her: I have had to disappoint her more than once since I last saw you. Will you excuse me for ten minutes?

COKANE [*in a flush of friendly protest*] My dear sir: can you ask?

TRENCH. Certainly.

SARTORIUS. Thank you. [*He goes out*].

TRENCH [*chuckling again*] He wont have any news to break, poor old boy: she's seen all the letters already.

COKANE. I must say your behaviour has been far from straightforward, Harry. You have been carrying on a clandestine correspondence.

LICKCHEESE [*stealthily*] Gentlemen—

TRENCH ⎱ [*turning: they had forgotten his presence*]
COKANE ⎰ Hallo!

LICKCHEESE [*coming between them very humbly, but in mortal anxiety and haste*] Look here, gentlemen. [*To Trench*] You, sir, I address myself to more particlar. Will you say a word in my favor to the guvnor? He's just given me the sack; and I have four children looking to me for their bread. A word from you, sir, on this happy day, might get him to take me on again.

TRENCH [*embarrassed*] Well, you see, Mr Lickcheese, I dont see how I can interfere. I'm very sorry, of course.

COKANE. Certainly you cannot interfere. It would be in the most execrable taste.

LICKCHEESE. Oh, gentlemen, youre young; and you dont know what loss of employment means to the like of me. What harm would it do you to help a poor man? Just listen to the circumstances, sir. I only—

TRENCH [*moved, but snatching at an excuse for taking a high tone in avoiding the unpleasantness of helping him*] No: I had rather not. Excuse my saying plainly that I think Mr Sartorius is a not a man to act hastily or harshly. I have always found him very fair and generous; and I believe he is a better judge of the circumstances than I am.

COKANE [*inquisitive*] I think you ought to hear the

[78]

circumstances, Harry. It can do no harm. Hear the circumstances by all means.

LICKCHEESE. Never mind, sir: it aint any use. When I hear that man called generous and fair!—well, never mind.

TRENCH [*severely*] If you wish me to do anything for you, Mr Lickcheese, let me tell you that you are not going the right way about it in speaking ill of Mr Sartorius.

LICKCHEESE. Have I said one word against him, sir? I leave it to your friend: have I said a word?

COKANE. True: true. Quite true. Harry: be just.

LICKCHEESE. Mark my words, gentlemen: he'll find what a man he's lost the very first week's rents the new man'll bring him. Youll find the difference yourself, Dr Trench, if you or your children come into the property. Ive took money there when no other collector alive would have wrung it out. And this is the thanks I get for it! Why, see here, gentlemen! Look at that bag of money on the table. Hardly a penny of that but there was a hungry child crying for the bread it would have bought. But I got it for him—screwed and worried and bullied it out of them. I—look here, gentlemen: I'm pretty seasoned to the work; but theres money there that I couldnt have taken if it hadnt been for the thought of my own children depending on me for giving him satisfaction. And because I charged him four-and-twenty shillin to mend a staircase that three women have been hurt on, and that would have got him prosecuted for manslaughter if it had been let go much longer, he gives me the sack. Wouldnt listen to a word, though I would have offered to make up the money out of my own pocket: aye, and am willing to do it still if you will only put in a word for me.

TRENCH [*aghast*] You took money that ought to have fed starving children! Serve you right! If I had been the father of one of those children, I'd have given you something worse than the sack. I wouldnt say a word to save your soul, if you have such a thing. Mr Sartorius was quite right.

LICKCHEESE [*staring at him, surprised into contemptuous amusement in the midst of his anxiety*] Just listen to this! Well, you are an innocent young gentleman. Do you suppose he sacked me because I was too hard? Not a bit on it: it was because I wasnt hard enough. I never heard him say he was satisfied yet: no, nor he wouldnt, not if I skinned em alive. I dont say he's the worst landlord in London: he couldnt be worse than some; but he's no better than the worst I ever had to do with. And, though I say it, I'm better than the best collector he ever done business with. Ive screwed more and spent less on his properties than anyone would believe that knows what such properties are. I know my merits, Dr Trench, and will speak for myself if no one else will.

COKANE. What description of properties? Houses?

LICKCHEESE. Tenement houses, let from week to week by the room or half room: aye, or quarter room. It pays when you know how to work it, sir. Nothing like it. It's been calculated on the cubic foot of space, sir, that you can get higher rents letting by the room than you can for a mansion in Park Lane.

TRENCH. I hope Mr Sartorius hasnt much of that sort of property, however it may pay.

LICKCHEESE. He has nothing else, sir; and he shews his sense in it, too. Every few hundred pounds he could scrape together he bought old houses with: houses that you wouldnt hardly look at without holding your nose. He has em in St Giles's: he has em in Marylebone: he has em in Bethnal Green. Just look how he lives himself, and youll see the good of it to him. He likes a low deathrate and a gravel soil for himself, he does. You come down with me to Robbins's Row; and I'll shew you a soil and a death-rate, I will! And, mind you, it's me that makes it pay him so well. Catch him going down to collect his own rents! Not likely!

TRENCH. Do you mean to say that all his property—all his means—come from this sort of thing?

LICKCHEESE. Every penny of it, sir.

Trench, overwhelmed, has to sit down.

COKANE [*looking compassionately at him*] Ah, my dear fellow, the love of money is the root of all evil.

LICKCHEESE. Yes, sir; and we'd all like to have the tree growing in our garden.

COKANE [*revolted*] Mr Lickcheese: I did not address myself to you. I do not wish to be severe with you; but there is something peculiarly repugnant to my feelings in the calling of a rent collector.

LICKCHEESE. It's no worse than many another. I have my children looking to me.

COKANE. True: I admit it. So has our friend Sartorius. His affection for his daughter is a redeeming point—a redeeming point, certainly.

LICKCHEESE. She's a lucky daughter, sir. Many another daughter has been turned out upon the streets to gratify his affection for her. Thats what business is, sir, you see. Come, sir: I think your friend will say a word for me now he knows I'm not in fault.

TRENCH [*rising angrily*] I will not. It's a damnable business from beginning to end; and you deserve no better luck for helping in it. Ive seen it all among the out-patients at the hospital; and it used to make my blood boil to think that such things couldnt be prevented.

LICKCHEESE [*his suppressed spleen breaking out*] Oh indeed, sir. But I suppose youll take your share when you marry Miss Blanche, all the same. [*Furiously*] Which of us is the worse. I should like to know? me that wrings the money out to keep a home over my children, or you that spend it and try to shove the blame on to me?

COKANE. A most improper observation to address to a gentleman, Mr Lickcheese! A most revolutionary sentiment!

LICKCHEESE. Perhaps so. But then Robbins's Row aint a school for manners. You collect a week or two there—youre welcome to my place if I cant keep it for myself—and youll hear a little plain speaking, you will.

COKANE [*with dignity*] Do you know to whom you are speaking, my good man?

LICKCHEESE [*recklessly*] I know well enough who I'm speaking to. What do I care for you, or a thousand such? I'm poor: thats enough to make a rascal of me. No consideration for me! nothing to be got by saying a word for me! [*Suddenly cringing to Trench*] Just a word, sir. It would cost you nothing. [*Sartorius appears at the door, unobserved*]. Have some feeling for the poor.

TRENCH. I'm afraid you have shewn very little, by your own confession.

LICKCHEESE [*breaking out again*] More than your precious father-in-law, anyhow. I— [*Sartorius's voice, striking in with deadly coldness, paralyzes him*].

SARTORIUS. You will come here tomorrow not later than ten, Mr Lickcheese, to conclude our business. I shall trouble you no further today. [*Lickcheese, cowed, goes out amid dead silence. Sartorius continues, after an awkward pause*] He is one of my agents, or rather was; for I have unfortunately had to dismiss him for repeatedly disregarding my instructions. [*Trench says nothing. Sartorius throws off his embarrassment, and assumes a jocose, rallying air, unbecoming to him under any circumstances, and just now almost unbearably jarring*]. Blanche will be down presently, Harry [*Trench recoils*]—I suppose I must call you Harry now. What do you say to a stroll through the garden, Mr Cokane? We are celebrated here for our flowers.

COKANE. Charmed, my dear sir, charmed. Life here is an idyll—a perfect idyll. We were just dwelling on it.

SARTORIUS [*slyly*] Harry can follow with Blanche. She will be down directly.

TRENCH [*hastily*] No. I cant face her just now.

SARTORIUS [*rallying him*] Indeed! Ha, ha!

The laugh, the first they have heard from him, sets Trench's teeth on edge. Cokane is taken aback, but instantly recovers himself.

COKANE. Ha! ha! ha! Ho! ho!

TRENCH. But you dont understand.

SARTORIUS. Oh, I think we do, I think we do. Eh, Mr Cokane? Ha! ha!

COKANE. I should think we do. Ha! ha! ha!

They go out together, laughing at him. He collapses into a chair, shuddering in every nerve. Blanche appears at the door. Her face lights up when she sees that he is alone. She trips noiselessly to the back of his chair and clasps her hands over his eyes. With a convulsive start and exclamation he springs up and breaks away from her.

BLANCHE [*astonished*] Harry!

TRENCH [*with distracted politeness*] I beg your pardon. I was thinking—wont you sit down?

BLANCHE [*looking suspiciously at him*] Is anything

the matter? [*She sits down slowly near the writing table. He takes Cokane's chair*].

TRENCH. No. Oh no.

BLANCHE. Papa has not been disagreeable, I hope.

TRENCH. No: I have hardly spoken to him since I was with you. [*He rises; takes up his chair; and plants it beside hers. This pleases her better. She looks at him with her most winning smile. A sort of sob breaks from him; and he catches her hands and kisses them passionately. Then, looking into her eyes with intense earnestness, he says*] Blanche: are you fond of money?

BLANCHE [*gaily*] Very. Are you going to give me any?

TRENCH [*wincing*] Dont make a joke of it: I'm serious. Do you know that we shall be very poor?

BLANCHE. Is that what made you look as if you had neuralgia?

TRENCH [*pleadingly*] My dear: it's no laughing matter. Do you know that I have a bare seven hundred a year to live on?

BLANCHE. How dreadful!

TRENCH. Blanche: it's very serious indeed: I assure you it is.

BLANCHE. It would keep me rather short in my housekeeping, dearest boy, if I had nothing of my own. But papa has promised me that I shall be richer than ever when we are married.

TRENCH. We must do the best we can with seven hundred. I think we ought to be self-supporting.

BLANCHE. Thats just what I mean to be, Harry. If I were to eat up half your seven hundred, I should be making you twice as poor; but I'm going to make you twice as rich instead. [*He shakes his head*]. Has papa made any difficulty?

TRENCH [*rising with a sigh and taking his chair back to its former place*] No. None at all. [*He sits down *dejectedly. When Blanche speaks again her face and voice betray the beginning of a struggle with her temper*].

BLANCHE. Harry are you too proud to take money from my father?

TRENCH. Yes, Blanche: I am too proud.

BLANCHE [*after a pause*] That is not nice to me, Harry.

TRENCH. You must bear with me, Blanche. I—I cant explain. After all, it's very natural.

BLANCHE. Has it occurred to you that I may be proud, too?

TRENCH. Oh, thats nonsense. No one will accuse you of marrying for money.

BLANCHE. No one would think the worse of me if I did, or of you either. [*She rises and begins to walk restlessly about*]. We really cannot live on seven hundred a year, Harry; and I dont think it quite fair of you to ask me merely because you are afraid of people talking.

TRENCH. It's not that alone, Blanche.

BLANCHE. What else is it, then?

TRENCH. Nothing. I—

BLANCHE [*getting behind him, and speaking with forced playfulness as she bends over him, her hands on his shoulders*] Of course it's nothing. Now dont be absurd, Harry: be good; and listen to me: I know how to settle it. You are too proud to owe anything to me; and I am too proud to owe anything to you. You have seven hundred a year. Well, I will take just seven hundred a year from papa at first; and then we shall be quits. Now, now, Harry, you know youve not a word to say against that.

TRENCH. It's impossible.

BLANCHE. Impossible!

TRENCH. Yes, impossible. I have resolved not to take any money from your father.

BLANCHE. But he'll give the money to me, not to you.

TRENCH. It's the same thing. [*With an effort to be sentimental*] I love you too well to see any distinction. [*He puts up his hand halfheartedly: she takes it over his shoulder with equal indecision. They are both trying hard to conciliate one another*].

BLANCHE. Thats a very nice way of putting it, Harry; but I'm sure theres something I ought to know. Has papa been disagreeable?

TRENCH. No: he has been very kind—to me, at least. It's not that. It's nothing you can guess, Blanche. It would only pain you—perhaps offend you. I dont mean, of course, that we shall live always on seven hundred a year. I intend to go at my profession in earnest, and work my fingers to the bone.

BLANCHE [*playing with his fingers, still over his shoulder*] But I shouldnt like you with your fingers worked to the bone, Harry: I must be told what the matter is. [*He takes his hand quickly away: she flushes angrily; and her voice is no longer even an imitation of the voice of a lady as she exclaims*] I hate secrets; and I dont like to be treated as if I were a child.

TRENCH [*annoyed by her tone*] Theres nothing to tell. I dont choose to trespass on your father's generosity: thats all.

BLANCHE. You had no objection half an hour ago, when you met me in the hall, and shewed me all the letters. Your family doesnt object. Do you object?

TRENCH [*earnestly*] I do not indeed. It's only a question of money.

BLANCHE [*imploringly, the voice softening and refining for the last time*] Harry: theres no use in our fencing in this way. Papa will never consent to my being absolutely dependent on you; and I dont like the idea of it

[86]

myself. If you even mention such a thing to him you
will break off the match: you will indeed.

TRENCH [*obstinately*] I cant help that.

BLANCHE [*white with rage*] You cant help—! Oh,
I'm beginning to understand. I will save you the
trouble. You can tell papa that *I* have broken off the
match; and then there will be no further difficulty.

TRENCH [*taken aback*] What do you mean, Blanche?
Are you offended?

BLANCHE. Offended! How dare you ask me?

TRENCH. Dare!

BLANCHE. How much more manly it would have
been to confess that you were trifling with me that
time on the Rhine! Why did you come here today?
Why did you write to your people?

TRENCH. Well, Blanche, if you are going to lose your
temper—

BLANCHE. Thats no answer. You depended on your
family to get you out of your engagement; and they
did not object: they were only too glad to be rid of you.
You were not mean enough to stay away, and not
manly enough to tell the truth. You thought you could
provoke me to break the engagement: thats so like
a man—to try to put the woman in the wrong. Well,
you have your way: I release you. I wish youd opened
my eyes by downright brutality; by striking me; by
anything rather than shuffling as you have done.

TRENCH [*hotly*] Shuffling! If I'd thought you capable
of turning on me like this, I'd never have spoken to
you. Ive a good mind never to speak to you again.

BLANCHE. You shall not—not ever. I will take care of
that [*going to the door*].

TRENCH [*alarmed*] What are you going to do?

BLANCHE. To get your letters: your false letters, and
your presents: your hateful presents, to return them

to you. I'm very glad it's all broken off; and if— [*as she puts her hand to the door it is opened from without by Sartorius, who enters and shuts it behind him*].

SARTORIUS [*interrupting her severely*] Hush, pray, Blanche: you are forgetting yourself: you can be heard all over the house. What is the matter?

BLANCHE [*too angry to care whether she is overheard or not*] You had better ask him. He has some excuse about money.

SARTORIUS. Excuse! Excuse for what?

BLANCHE. For throwing me over.

TRENCH [*vehemently*] I declare I never—

BLANCHE [*interrupting him still more vehemently*] You did. You did. You are doing nothing else—

TRENCH ⎱ *together: each trying to* ⎰ I am doing nothing
BLANCHE ⎰ *shout down the other* ⎱ What else is it but
⎰ of the sort. You know very well that what you are
⎱ throwing me over? But I dont care for you. I hate
⎰ saying is disgracefully untrue. It's a damned lie.
⎱ you. I always hated you. Beastly—dirty—vile—
⎰ I wont stand—
⎱

SARTORIUS [*in desperation at the noise*] Silence! [*Still more formidably*] Silence!! [*They obey. He proceeds firmly*] Blanche: you must control your temper: I will not have these repeated scenes within hearing of the servants. Dr Trench will answer for himself to me. You had better leave us. [*He opens the door, and calls*] Mr Cokane: will you kindly join us here.

COKANE [*in the conservatory*] Coming, my dear sir, coming. [*He appears at the door*].

BLANCHE. I'm sure I have no wish to stay. I hope I shall find you alone when I come back. [*An inarticulate exclamation bursts from Trench. She goes out, passing*

Cokane resentfully. He looks after her in surprise;
then looks questioningly at the two men. Sartorius shuts
the door with an angry stroke, and turns to Trench].

SARTORIUS [*aggressively*] Sir—

TRENCH [*interrupting him more aggressively*] Well, sir?

COKANE [*getting between them*] Gently, dear boy,
gently. Suavity, Harry, suavity.

SARTORIUS [*mastering himself*] If you have anything
to say to me, Dr Trench, I will listen to you patiently.
You will then allow me to say what I have to say on
my part.

TRENCH [*ashamed*] I beg your pardon. Of course, yes.
Fire away.

SARTORIUS. May I take it that you have refused to
fulfil your engagement with my daughter?

TRENCH. Certainly not: your daughter has refused
to fulfil her engagement with me. But the match is
broken off, if thats what you mean.

SARTORIUS. Dr Trench: I will be plain with you. I
know that Blanche has a quick temper. It is part of
her strong character and her physical courage, which
is greater than that of most men, I can assure you. You
must be prepared for that. If this quarrel is only
Blanche's temper, you may take my word for it that
it will be over before tomorrow. But I understood
from what she said just now that you have made some
difficulty on the score of money.

TRENCH [*with renewed excitement*] It was Miss Sartorius who made the difficulty. I shouldnt have
minded that so much, if it hadnt been for the things
she said. She shewed that she doesnt care that [*snapping his fingers*] for me.

COKANE [*soothingly*] Dear boy—

TRENCH. Hold your tongue, Billy: it's enough to
make a man wish he'd never seen a woman. Look

here, Mr Sartorius: I put the matter to her as delicately and considerately as possible, never mentioning
a word of my reasons, but just asking her to be content to live on my own little income; and yet she
turned on me as if I'd behaved like a savage.

SARTORIUS. Live on your income! Impossible:
my daughter is accustomed to a proper establishment.
Did I not expressly undertake to provide for that?
Did she not tell you I promised her to do so?

TRENCH. Yes, I know all about that, Mr Sartorius; and
I'm greatly obliged to you; but I'd rather not take
anything from you except Blanche herself.

SARTORIUS. And why did you not say so before?

TRENCH. No matter why. Let us drop the subject.

SARTORIUS. No matter! But it does matter, sir. I
insist on an answer. Why did you not say so before?

TRENCH. I didnt know before.

SARTORIUS [*provoked*] Then you ought to have
known your own mind on a point of such vital importance.

TRENCH [*much injured*] I ought to have known!
Cokane: is this reasonable? [*Cokane's features are
contorted by an air of judicial consideration; but he
says nothing; and Trench again addresses Sartorius,
this time with a marked diminution of respect*]. How
the deuce could I have known? You didn't tell me.

SARTORIUS. You are trifling with me, sir. You said
that you did not know your own mind before.

TRENCH. I said nothing of the sort. I say that I did
not know where your money came from before.

SARTORIUS. That is not true, sir. I—

COKANE. Gently, my dear sir. Gently, Harry, dear
boy. Suaviter in modo: fort—

TRENCH. Let him begin, then. What does he mean by
attacking me in this fashion?

[90]

SARTORIUS. Mr Cokane: you will bear me out. I was explicit on the point. I said I was a self-made man; and I am not ashamed of it.

TRENCH. You are nothing of the sort. I found out this morning from your man—Lickcheese, or whatever his confounded name is—that your fortune has been made out of a parcel of unfortunate creatures that have hardly enough to keep body and soul together—made by screwing, and bullying, and threatening, and all sorts of pettifogging tyranny.

SARTORIUS [*outraged*] Sir! [*They confront one another threateningly*].

COKANE [*softly*] Rent must be paid, dear boy. It is inevitable, Harry, inevitable. [*Trench turns away petulantly. Sartorius looks after him reflectively for a moment; then resumes his former deliberate and dignified manner, and addresses Trench with studied consideration, but with a perceptible condescension to his youth and folly*].

SARTORIUS. I am afraid, Dr Trench, that you are a very young hand at business; and I am sorry I forgot that for a moment or so. May I ask you to suspend your judgment until we have had a little quiet discussion of this sentimental notion of yours? if you will excuse me for calling it so. [*He takes a chair, and motions Trench to another on his right*].

COKANE. Very nicely put, my dear sir. Come, Harry: sit down and listen; and consider the matter calmly and judicially. Dont be headstrong.

TRENCH. I have no objection to sit down and listen; but I dont see how that can make black white; and I am tired of being turned on as if I were in the wrong. [*He sits down*].

Cokane sits at Trench's elbow, on his right. They compose themselves for a conference.

SARTORIUS. I assume, to begin with, Dr Trench, that you are not a Socialist, or anything of that sort.

TRENCH. Certainly not. I'm a Conservative. At least, if I ever took the trouble to vote, I should vote for the Conservative and against the other fellow.

COKANE. True blue, Harry, true blue!

SARTORIUS. I am glad to find that so far we are in perfect sympathy. I am, of course, a Conservative. Not a narrow or prejudiced one, I hope, nor at all opposed to true progress. Still, a sound Conservative. As to Lickcheese, I need say no more about him than that I have dismissed him from my service this morning for a breach of trust; and you will hardly accept his testimony as friendly or disinterested. As to my business, it is simply to provide homes suited to the small means of very poor people, who require roofs to shelter them just like other people. Do you suppose I can keep up those roofs for nothing?

TRENCH. Yes: thats all very fine; but the point is, what sort of homes do you give them for their money? People must live somewhere, or else go to jail. Advantage is taken of that to make them pay for houses that are not fit for dogs. Why dont you build proper dwellings, and give fair value for the money you take?

SARTORIUS [*pitying his innocence*] My young friend: these poor people do not know how to live in proper dwellings: they would wreck them in a week. You doubt me: try it for yourself. You are welcome to replace all the missing banisters, handrails, cistern lids and dusthole tops at your own expense; and you will find them missing again in less than three days: burnt, sir, every stick of them. I do not blame the poor creatures: they need fires, and often have no other way of getting them. But I really cannot spend pound after pound in repairs for them to pull down, when I can barely get them to pay me four and sixpence a week for a room, which is the recognized fair London rent. No, gentlemen: when people are very poor, you cannot help them, no matter how much you may sympathize with them. It does them more harm than good in the long run. I prefer to save my money in order to provide additional houses for the homeless, and to lay by a little for Blanche. [*He looks at them. They are silent: Trench unconvinced, but talked down; Cokane humanely perplexed. Sartorius bends his brows; comes forward in his chair as if gathering himself for a spring; and addresses himself, with impressive significance, to Trench*]. And now, Dr Trench, may I ask what your income is derived from?

TRENCH [*defiantly*] From interest: not from houses. My hands are clean as far as that goes. Interest on a mortgage.

SARTORIUS [*forcibly*] Yes: a mortgage on my property. When I, to use your own words, screw, and bully, and drive these people to pay what they have freely undertaken to pay me, I cannot touch one penny of the money they give me until I have first paid you your seven hundred a year out of it. What Lickcheese did for me, I do for you. He and I are alike intermediaries: you are the principal. It is because of the risks I run through the poverty of my tenants that you exact interest from me at the monstrous and exorbitant rate of seven per cent, forcing me to exact the uttermost farthing in my turn from the tenants. And yet, Dr Trench, you, who have never done a hand's turn of work in connection with the place, you have not hesitated to speak contemptuously of me because I have applied my industry and forethought to the management of our property, and am maintaining it by the same honorable means.

COKANE [*greatly relieved*] Admirable, my dear sir, excellent! I felt instinctively that Trench was talking unpractical nonsense. Let us drop the subject, my dear boy: you only make an ass of yourself when you meddle in business matters. I told you it was inevitable.

TRENCH [*dazed*] Do you mean to say that I am just as bad as you are?

COKANE. Shame, Harry, shame! Grossly bad taste! Be a gentleman. Apologize.

SARTORIUS. Allow me, Mr Cokane. [*To Trench*] If, when you say you are just as bad as I am, you mean that you are just as powerless to alter the state of society, then you are unfortunately quite right.

Trench does not at once reply. He stares at Sartorius, and then hangs his head and gazes stupidly at the floor, morally beggared, with his clasped knuckles between his knees, a living picture of disillusion. Cokane comes sympathetically to him and puts an encouraging hand on his shoulder.

COKANE [*gently*] Come, Harry, come! Pull yourself together. You owe a word to Mr Sartorius.

TRENCH [*still stupefied, slowly unlaces his fingers; puts his hands on his knees, and lifts himself upright; pulls his waistcoat straight with a tug; and tries to take his disenchantment philosophically as he says, turning to Sartorius*] Well, people who live in glass houses have no right to throw stones. But, on my honor, I never knew that my house was a glass one until you pointed it out. I beg your pardon. [*He offers his hand*].

SARTORIUS. Say no more, Harry: your feelings do you credit: I assure you I feel exactly as you do, myself. Every man who has a heart must wish that a better state of things was practicable. But unhappily it is not.

TRENCH [*a little consoled*] I suppose not.

COKANE. Not a doubt of it, my dear sir: not a doubt of it. The increase of the population is at the bottom of it all.

SARTORIUS [*to Trench*] I trust I have convinced you that you need no more object to Blanche sharing my fortune, than I need object to her sharing yours.

TRENCH [*with dull wistfulness*] It seems so. We're all in the same swim, it appears. I hope youll excuse my making such a fuss.

SARTORIUS. Not another word. In fact, I thank you for refraining from explaining the nature of your scruples to Blanche: I admire that in you, Harry. Perhaps it will be as well to leave her in ignorance.

TRENCH [*anxiously*] But I must explain now. You saw how angry she was.

SARTORIUS. You had better leave that to me. [*He looks at his watch, and rings the bell*]. Lunch is nearly due: while you are getting ready for it I can see Blanche; and I hope the result will be quite satisfactory to us all. [*The parlormaid answers the bell: he addresses her with his habitual peremptoriness*]. Tell Miss Blanche I want her.

THE PARLORMAID [*her face falling expressively*] Yes, sir. [*She turns reluctantly to go*].

SARTORIUS [*on second thoughts*] Stop. [*She stops*]. My love to Miss Blanche; and I am alone here and would like to see her for a moment if she is not busy.

THE PARLORMAID [*relieved*] Yes sir. [*She goes out*].

SARTORIUS. I will shew you your room, Harry. I hope you will soon be perfectly at home in it. You also, Mr Cokane, must learn your way about here. Let us go before Blanche comes. [*He leads the way to the door*].

COKANE [*cheerily, following him*] Our little discussion
has given me quite an appetite.

TRENCH [*moodily*] It's taken mine away.

*The two friends go out, Sartorius holding the door
for them. He is following when the parlormaid reappears.
She is a snivelling sympathetic creature, and is on the
verge of tears.*

SARTORIUS. Well: is Miss Blanche coming?

THE PARLORMAID. Yes, sir. I think so, sir.

SARTORIUS. Wait here until she comes; and tell her
that I will be back in a moment. I have to shew Dr
Trench his room.

THE PARLORMAID. Yes, sir. [*She comes into the
room. A sound between a sob and a sniff escapes her*].

*Sartorius looks suspiciously at her. He half closes
the door.*

SARTORIUS [*lowering his voice*] Whats the matter
with you?

THE PARLORMAID [*whimpering*] Nothing, sir.

SARTORIUS [*at the same pitch, more menacingly*] Take
care how you behave yourself when there are visitors
present. Do you hear?

THE PARLORMAID. Yes, sir. [*Sartorius goes out*].

SARTORIUS [*outside*] Excuse me: I had a word to say
to the servant.

Trench is heard replying "Not at all," *and Cokane*
"Dont mention it, my dear sir."

*Their voices pass out of hearing. The parlormaid sniffs;
dries her eyes; and takes some brown paper and a ball
of string from a cupboard under the bookcase. She puts
them on the table, and wrestles with another sob.
Blanche comes in, with a jewel box in her hands. Her
expression is that of a strong and determined woman in
an intense passion. The maid looks at her with abject
wounded affection and bodily terror.*

BLANCHE [*looking round*] Wheres my father?

THE PARLORMAID [*tremulously propitiatory*] He left word he'd be back directly, miss. I'm sure he wont be long. Heres the paper and string all ready, miss. [*She spreads the paper on the table*]. Can I do the parcel for you, miss?

BLANCHE. No. Mind your own business. [*She empties the box in the sheet of brown paper. It contains a packet of letters and some jewellery. She plucks a ring from her finger and throws it down on the heap so angrily that it rolls away and falls on the carpet. The maid submissively picks it up and puts it on the table, again sniffing and drying her eyes.*] What are you crying for?

THE PARLORMAID [*plaintively*] You speak so brutal to me, Miss Blanche; and I do love you so. I'm sure no one else would stay and put up with what I have to put up with.

BLANCHE. Then go. I dont want you. Do you hear. Go.

THE PARLORMAID [*piteously, falling on her knees*] Oh no, Miss Blanche. Dont send me away from you: dont—

BLANCHE [*with fierce disgust*] Agh! I hate the sight of you. [*The maid, wounded to the heart, cries bitterly*]. Hold your tongue. Are those two gentlemen gone?

THE PARLORMAID [*weeping*] Oh, how could you say such a thing to me, Miss Blanche: me that—

BLANCHE [*seizing her by the hair and throat*] Stop that noise, I tell you, unless you want me to kill you.

THE PARLORMAID [*protesting and imploring, but in a carefully subdued voice*] Let me go, Miss Blanche: you know youll be sorry: you always are. Remember how dreadfully my head was cut last time.

BLANCHE [*raging*] Answer me, will you. Have they gone?

THE PARLORMAID. Lickcheese has gone, looking dreadf—[*she breaks off with a stifled cry as Blanche's fingers tighten furiously on her*].

BLANCHE. Did I ask you about Lickcheese? You beast: you know who I mean: youre doing it on purpose.

THE PARLORMAID [*in a gasp*] Theyre staying to lunch.

BLANCHE [*looking intently into her face*] He?

THE PARLORMAID [*whispering with a sympathetic nod*] Yes, miss. [*Blanche lets her drop, and stands forlorn, with despair in her face. The parlormaid, recognizing the passing of the crisis of passion, and fearing no further violence, sits discomfitedly on her heels, and tries to arrange her hair and cap, whimpering a little with exhaustion and soreness*]. Now youve set my hands all trembling; and I shall jingle the things on the tray at lunch so that everybody will notice me. It's too bad of you, Miss Bl— [*Sartorius coughs outside*].

BLANCHE [*quickly*] Sh! Get up. *The parlormaid hastily rises, and goes out as demurely as she can. Sartorius glances sternly at her and comes to Blanche.*

SARTORIUS [*mournfully*] My dear: can you not make a little better fight with your temper?

BLANCHE [*panting with the subsidence of her fit*] No I cant. I wont. I do my best. Nobody who really cares for me gives me up because of my temper. I never shew my temper to any of the servants but that girl; and she is the only one that will stay with us.

SARTORIUS. But, my dear, remember that we have to meet our visitors at luncheon presently. I have run down before them to say that I have arranged that little difficulty with Trench. It was only a piece of mischief made by Lickcheese. Trench is a young fool; but it is all right now.

BLANCHE. I dont want to marry a fool.

SARTORIUS. Then you will have to take a husband over thirty, Blanche. You must not expect too much, my child. You will be richer than your husband, and, I think, cleverer too. I am better pleased that it should be so.

BLANCHE [*seizing his arm*] Papa.

SARTORIUS. Yes, my dear.

BLANCHE. May I do as I like about this marriage; or must I do as you like?

SARTORIUS [*uneasily*] Blanche—

BLANCHE. No, papa: you must answer me.

SARTORIUS [*abandoning his self-control, and giving way recklessly to his affection for her*] You shall do as you like now and always, my beloved child. I only wish to do as my own darling pleases.

BLANCHE. Then I will not marry him. He has played fast and loose with me. He thinks us beneath him: he is ashamed of us: he dared to object to being benefited by you—as if it were not natural for him to owe you everything; and yet the money tempted him after all. [*She throws her arms hysterically about his neck*] Papa: I dont want to marry: I only want to stay with you and be happy as we have always been. I hate the thought of being married: I dont care for him: I dont want to leave you. [*Trench and Cokane come in; but she can hear nothing but her own voice and does not notice them*]. Only send him away: promise me that you will send him away and keep me here with you as we have always—[*seeing Trench*] Oh! [*She hides her face on her father's breast*].

TRENCH [*nervously*] I hope we are not intruding.

[99]

SARTORIUS [*formidably*] Dr Trench: my daughter has changed her mind.

TRENCH [*disconcerted*] Am I to understand—

COKANE [*striking in in his most vinegary manner*] I think, Harry, under the circumstances, we have no alternative but to seek luncheon elsewhere.

TRENCH. But, Mr Sartorius, have you explained?

SARTORIUS [*straight in Trench's face*] I have explained, sir. Good morning. [*Trench, outraged, advances a step. Blanche sinks away from her father into a chair. Sartorius stands his ground rigidly*].

TRENCH [*turning away indignantly*] Come on, Cokane.

COKANE. Certainly, Harry, Certainly. [*Trench goes out, very angry. The parlormaid, with a tray jingling in her hands, passes outside*]. You have disappointed me, sir, very acutely. Good morning. [*He follows Trench*].

[ACT III]

The drawing-room in Sartorius's house in Bedford Square, London. Winter evening: fire burning, curtains drawn, and lamps lighted. Sartorius and Blanche are sitting glumly near the fire. The parlormaid, who has just brought in coffee, is placing it on a small table between them. There is a large table in the middle of the room. Looking from it towards the two windows, the pianoforte, a grand, is on the right, with a photographic portrait of Blanche on a miniature easel on a sort of bedspread which covers the top, shewing that the instrument is seldom, if ever, opened. There are two doors: one on the left, further forward than the fireplace leading to the study; the other by the corner nearest the right hand window, leading to the lobby. Blanche has her workbasket at hand, and is knitting. Sartorius, closer to the fire, has a newspaper. The parlormaid goes out.

SARTORIUS. Blanche, my love.

BLANCHE. Yes.

SARTORIUS. I had a long talk to the doctor today about our going abroad.

BLANCHE [*impatiently*] I am quite well; and I will not go abroad. I loathe the very thought of the Continent. Why will you bother me so about my health?

SARTORIUS. It was not about your health, Blanche, but about my own.

BLANCHE [*rising*] Yours! [*She goes anxiously to him*].

[101]

Oh, papa, theres nothing the matter with you, I hope?

SARTORIUS. There will be: there must be, Blanche, long before you begin to consider yourself an old woman.

BLANCHE. But theres nothing the matter now?

SARTORIUS. Well, my dear, the doctor says I need change, travel, excitement—

BLANCHE. Excitement! You need excitement! [*She laughs joylessly, and sits down on the rug at his feet*]. How is it, papa, that you, who are so clever with everybody else, are not a bit clever with me? Do you think I cant see through your little plan to take me abroad? Since I will not be the invalid and allow you to be the nurse, you are to be the invalid and I am to be the nurse.

SARTORIUS. Well, Blanche, if you will have it that you are well and have nothing preying on your spirits, I must insist on being ill and have something preying on mine. And indeed, my girl, there is no use in our going on as we have for the last four months. You have not been happy; and I have been very far from comfortable. [*Blanche's face clouds; she turns away from him, and sits dumb and brooding. He waits in vain for some reply; then adds in a lower tone*] Need you be so inflexible, Blanche?

BLANCHE. I thought you admired inflexibility: you have always prided yourself on it.

SARTORIUS. Nonsense, my dear, nonsense! I have had to give in often enough. And I could shew you plenty of soft fellows who have done as well as I, and enjoyed themselves more, perhaps. If it is only for the sake of inflexibility that you are standing out—

BLANCHE. I am not standing out. I dont know what you mean. [*She tries to rise and go away*].

SARTORIUS [*catching her arm and arresting her on her knees*] Come, my child! you must not trifle with me as if I were a stranger. You are fretting because—

BLANCHE [*violently twisting herself free and speaking as she rises*] If you say it, papa, I will kill myself. It is not true. If he were here on his knees tonight, I would walk out of the house sooner than endure it. [*She goes out excitedly*].

Sartorius, greatly troubled, turns again to the fire with a heavy sigh.

SARTORIUS [*gazing gloomily into the glow*] Now if I fight it out with her, no more comfort for months! I might as well live with my clerk or my servant. And if I give in now, I shall have to give in always. Well! I cant help it. I have stuck to having my own way all my life; but there must be an end to that drudgery some day. She is young: let her have her turn at it.

The parlormaid comes in, evidently excited.

THE PARLORMAID. Please, sir, Mr Lickcheese wants to see you very particlar. On important business. Your business, he told me to say.

SARTORIUS. Mr Lickcheese! Do you mean Lickcheese who used to come here on my business?

THE PARLORMAID. Yes, sir. But indeed, sir, youd scarcely know him.

SARTORIUS [*frowning*] Hm! Starving, I suppose. Come to beg?

THE PARLORMAID [*intensely repudiating the idea*] O-o-o-o-h NO, sir. Quite the gentleman, sir! Sealskin overcoat, sir! Come in a hansom, all shaved and clean! I'm sure he's come into a fortune, sir.

SARTORIUS. Hm! Shew him up.

Lickcheese, who has been waiting at the door, instantly comes in. The change in his appearance is dazzling. He is in evening dress, with an overcoat lined throughout with furs presenting all the hues of the tiger. His shirt is fastened at the breast with a single diamond stud. His silk hat is of the glossiest black; a handsome gold watch-chain hangs like a garland on his filled-out waistcoat; he has shaved his whiskers and grown a moustache, the ends of which are waxed and pointed. As Sartorius stares speechless at him, he stands, smiling, to be admired, intensely enjoying the effect he is producing. The parlormaid, hardly less pleased with her own share in this coup-de-théâtre, goes out beaming, full of the news for the kitchen. Lickcheese clinches the situation by a triumphant nod at Sartorius.

SARTORIUS [*bracing himself: hostile*] Well?

LICKCHEESE. Quite well, Sartorius, thankee.

SARTORIUS. I was not asking after your health, sir, as you know, I think, as well as I do. What is your business?

LICKCHEESE. Business that I can take elsewhere if I meet with less civility than I please to put up with, Sartorius. You and me is man and man now. It was money that used to be my master, and not you: dont think it. Now that I'm independent in respect of money—

SARTORIUS [*crossing determinedly to the door, and holding it open*] You can take your independence out of my house, then. I wont have it here.

LICKCHEESE [*indulgently*] Come, Sartorius: dont be stiffnecked. I come here as a friend to put money in your pocket. No use your lettin on to me that youre above money. Eh?

SARTORIUS [*hesitates, and at last shuts the door, saying guardedly*] How much money?

LICKCHEESE [*victorious, going to Blanche's chair and taking off his overcoat*] Ah! there you speak like yourself, Sartorius. Now suppose you ask me to sit down and make myself comfortable?

SARTORIUS [*coming from the door*] I have a mind to put you downstairs by the back of your neck, you infernal blackguard.

LICKCHEESE [*not a bit ruffled, hangs his overcoat on the back of Blanche's chair, pulling a cigar case out of one of the pockets as he does so*] You and me is too much of a pair for me to take anything you say in bad part, Sartorius. Ave a cigar?

SARTORIUS. No smoking here: this is my daughter's room. However, sit down, sit down. [*They sit*].

LICKCHEESE. I' bin gittin on a little since I saw you last.

SARTORIUS. So I see.

LICKCHEESE. I owe it partly to you, you know. Does that surprise you?

SARTORIUS. It doesnt concern me.

LICKCHEESE. So you think, Sartorius; because it never did concern you how *I* got on, so long as I got you on by bringin in the rents. But I picked up something for myself down at Robbins's Row.

SARTORIUS. I always thought so. Have you come to make restitution?

LICKCHEESE. You wouldnt take it if I offered it to you, Sartorius. It wasnt money: it was knowledge: knowledge of the great public question of the Ousing of the Working Classes. You know theres a Royal Commission on it, dont you?

SARTORIUS. Oh, I see. Youve been giving evidence.

LICKCHEESE. Giving evidence! Not me. What good would that do me? Only my expenses; and that not on the professional scale, neither. No: I gev no evidence. But I'll tell you what I did. I kep it back, jast to oblige one or two people whose feelins would 'a bin urt by seeing their names in a bluebook as keepin a fever den. Their Agent got so friendly with me over it that he put his name on a bill of mine to the tune of— well, no matter: it gev me a start; and a start was all I ever wanted to get on my feet. Ive got a copy of the first report of the Commission in the pocket of my overcoat. [*He rises and gets at his overcoat, from a pocket of which he takes a bluebook*]. I turned down the page to shew you: I thought youd like to see it. [*He doubles the book back at the place indicated, and hands it to Sartorius*].

SARTORIUS. So blackmail is the game, eh? [*He puts the book on the table without looking at it, and strikes it emphatically with his fist*]. I dont care that for my name being in bluebooks. My friends dont read them; and I'm neither a Cabinet Minister nor a candidate for Parliament. Theres nothing to be got out of me on that lay.

LICKCHEESE [*shocked*] Blackmail! Oh, Mr Sartorius, do you think I would let out a word about your premises? Round on an old pal! no: that aint Lickcheese's way. Besides, they know all about you already. Them stairs that you and me quarrelled about, they was a whole arternoon examinin the clergyman that made such a fuss—you remember?—about the women that was urt on it. He made the worst he could of it, in an ungentlemanly, unchristian spirit. I wouldnt have that clergyman's disposition for worlds. Oh no: thats not what was in my thoughts.

SARTORIUS. Come, come, man! what was in your thoughts? Out with it.

LICKCHEESE [*with provoking deliberation, smiling and looking mysteriously at him*] You aint spent a few hundreds in repairs since we parted, ave you? [*Sartorius, losing patience, makes a threatening move-*

ment]. Now dont fly out at me. I know a landlord that owned as beastly a slum as you could find in London, down there by the Tower. By my advice that man put half the houses into first-class repair, and let the other half to a new Company: the North Thames Iced Mutton Depot Company, of which I hold a few shares: promoters' shares. And what was the end of it, do you think?

SARTORIUS. Smash, I suppose.

LICKCHEESE. Smash! not a bit of it. Compensation, Mr Sartorius, compensation. Do you understand that?

SARTORIUS. Compensation for what?

LICKCHEESE. Why, the land was wanted for an extension of the Mint; and the Company had to be bought out, and the buildings compensated for. Somebody has to know these things beforehand, you know, no matter how dark theyre kept.

SARTORIUS [*interested, but cautious*] Well?

LICKCHEESE. Is that all you have to say to me, Mr Sartorius? "Well"! as if I was next door's dog! Suppose I'd got wind of a new street that would knock down Robbins's Row and turn Burke's Walk into a frontage worth thirty pound a foot! would you say no more to me than [*mimicking*] "Well"? [*Sartorius hesitates, looking at him in great doubt. Lickcheese rises and exhibits himself*]. Come! look at my get-up, Mr Sartorius. Look at this watch-chain! Look at the corporation Ive got on me! Do you think all that came from keeping my mouth shut? No: it came from keeping my ears and eyes open.

Blanche comes in, followed by the parlormaid, who has a silver tray on which she collects the coffee cups. Sartorius, impatient at the interruption, rises and motions Lickcheese to the door of the study.

SARTORIUS. Sh! We must talk this over in the study. There is a good fire there; and you can smoke. Blanche: an old friend of ours.

LICKCHEESE. And a kind one to me. I hope I see you well, Miss Blanche.

BLANCHE. Why, it's Mr Lickcheese! I hardly knew you.

LICKCHEESE. I find you a little changed yourself, miss.

BLANCHE [*hastily*] Oh, I am the same as ever. How are Mrs Lickcheese and the chil—

SARTORIUS [*impatiently*] We have business to transact, Blanche. You can talk to Mr Lickcheese afterwards. Come on.

Sartorius and Lickcheese go into the study. Blanche, surprised at her father's abruptness, looks after them for a moment. Then, seeing Lickcheese's overcoat on her chair, she takes it up, amused, and looks at the fur.

THE PARLORMAID. Oh, we are fine, aint we, Miss Blanche? I think Mr Lickcheese must have come into a legacy. [*Confidentially*] I wonder what he can want with the master, Miss Blanche! He brought him this big book. [*She shews the bluebook to Blanche*].

BLANCHE [*her curiosity roused*] Let me see. [*She takes the book down and looks at it*]. Theres something about papa in it. [*She sits down and begins to read*].

THE PARLORMAID [*folding the tea-table and putting it out of the way*] He looks ever s'much younger, Miss Blanche, dont he? I couldnt help laughing when I saw him with his whiskers shaved off: it do look so silly when youre not accustomed to it. [*No answer from Blanche*]. You havnt finished your coffee, miss: I suppose I may take it away? [*No answer*]. Oh, you are interested in Mr Lickcheese's book, miss.

Blanche springs up. The parlormaid looks at her

face, and instantly hurries out of the room on tiptoe with her tray.

BLANCHE. So that was why he would not touch the money. [*She tries to tear the book across. Finding this impossible she throws it violently into the fireplace. It falls into the fender*]. Oh, if only a girl could have no father, no family, just as I have no mother! Clergyman! beast! "The worst slum landlord in London." "Slum landlord." Oh! [*She covers her face with her hands, and sinks shuddering into the chair on which the overcoat lies. The study door opens*].

LICKCHEESE [*in the study*] You just wait five minutes: I'll fetch him. [*Blanche snatches a piece of work from her basket, and sits erect and quiet, stitching at it. Lickcheese comes back, speaking to Sartorius, who follows him*]. He lodges round the corner in Gower Street; and my private ansom's at the door. By your leave, Miss Blanche [*pulling gently at his overcoat*].

BLANCHE [*rising*] I beg your pardon. I hope I havnt crushed it.

LICKCHEESE [*gallantly, as he gets into the coat*] Youre welcome to crush it again now, Miss Blanche. Dont say good evenin to me, miss: I'm comin back presently: me and a friend or two. Ta ta, Sartorius: I shant be long. [*He goes out*].

Sartorius looks about for the bluebook.

BLANCHE. I thought we were done with Lickcheese.

SARTORIUS. Not quite yet, I think. He left a book here for me to look over: a large book in a blue paper cover. Has the girl put it away? [*He sees it in the fender; looks at Blanche; and adds*] Have you seen it?

BLANCHE. No. Yes. [*Angrily*] No: I have not seen it. What have I to do with it?

Sartorius picks the book up and dusts it; then sits down quietly to read. After a glance up and down the columns, he nods assentingly, as if he found there exactly what he expected.

SARTORIUS. It's a curious thing, Blanche, that the Parliamentary gentlemen who write such books as these should be so ignorant of practical business. One would suppose, to read this, that we are the most grasping, grinding, heartless pair in the world, you and I.

BLANCHE. Is it not true? About the state of the houses, I mean?

SARTORIUS [*calmly*] Oh, quite true.

BLANCHE. Then it is not our fault?

SARTORIUS. My dear: if we made the houses any better, the rents would have to be raised so much that the poor people would be unable to pay, and would be thrown homeless on the streets.

BLANCHE. Well, turn them out and get in a respectable class of people. Why should we have the disgrace of harboring such wretches?

SARTORIUS [*opening his eyes*] That sounds a little hard on them, doesnt it, my child?

BLANCHE. Oh, I hate the poor. At least, I hate those dirty, drunken, disreputable people who live like pigs. If they must be provided for, let other people look after them. How can you expect any one to think well of us when such things are written about us in that infamous book?

SARTORIUS [*coldly and a little wistfully*] I see I have made a real lady of you, Blanche.

BLANCHE [*defiantly*] Well? Are you sorry for that?

SARTORIUS. No, my dear: of course not. But do you know, Blanche, that my mother was a very poor woman, and that her poverty was not her fault?

BLANCHE. I suppose not; but the people we want to mix with now dont know that. And it was not my fault; so I dont see why *I* should be made to suffer for it.

SARTORIUS [*enraged*] Who makes you suffer for it, miss? What would you be now but for what your grandmother did for me when she stood at her washtub for thirteen hours a day and thought herself rich when she made fifteen shillings a week?

BLANCHE [*angrily*] I suppose I should have been down on her level instead of being raised above it, as I am now. Would you like us to go and live in that place in the book for the sake of grandmamma? I hate the idea of such things. I dont want to know about them. I love you because you brought me up to something better. [*Half aside, as she turns away from him*] I should hate you if you had not.

SARTORIUS [*giving in*] Well, my child, I suppose it is natural for you to feel that way, after your bringing up. It is the ladylike view of the matter. So dont let us quarrel, my girl. You shall not be made to suffer any more. I have made up my mind to improve the property, and get in quite a new class of tenants. There! does that satisfy you? I am only waiting for the consent of the ground landlord, Lady Roxdale.

BLANCHE. Lady Roxdale!

SARTORIUS. Yes. But I shall expect the mortgagee to take his share of the risk.

BLANCHE. The mortgagee! Do you mean—[*She cannot finish the sentence: Sartorius does it for her*].

SARTORIUS. Harry Trench. Yes. And remember, Blanche: if he consents to join me in the scheme, I shall have to be friends with him.

BLANCHE. And to ask him to the house?

SARTORIUS. Only on business. You need not meet him unless you like.

BLANCHE [*overwhelmed*] When is he coming?

SARTORIUS. There is no time to be lost. Lickcheese
has gone to ask him to come round.

BLANCHE [in dismay] Then he will be here in a few
minutes! What shall I do?

SARTORIUS. I advise you to receive him as if nothing
had happened, and then go out and leave us to our
business. You are not afraid to meet him?

BLANCHE. Afraid! No: most certainly not. But—

LICKCHEESE'S VOICE [without] Straight in front of
you, doctor. You never bin here before; but I know
the house better than my own.

BLANCHE. Here they are. Dont say I'm here, papa.
[She rushes away into the study].

   Lickcheese comes in with Trench and Cokane. Both
are in evening dress. Cokane shakes hands effusively with
Sartorius. Trench, who is coarsened and sullen, and has
evidently not been making the best of his disappointment,
bows shortly and resentfully. Lickcheese covers the
general embarrassment by talking cheerfully until they
are all seated round the large table: Trench nearest the
fireplace; Cokane nearest the piano; and the other two
between them, with Lickcheese next Cokane].

LICKCHEESE. Here we are, all friends round St
Paul's. You remember Mr Cokane? he does a little
business for me now as a friend, and gives me a help
with my correspondence: sekketerry we call it. Ive no
litery style, and thats the truth; so Mr Cokane kindly
puts it into my letters and draft prospectuses and advertisements and the like. Dont you, Cokane? Of
course you do: why shouldnt you? He's been helping
me to persuade his old friend, Dr Trench, about the
matter we were speaking of.

COKANE [austerely] No, Mr Lickcheese, not trying
to persuade him. No: this is a matter of principle
with me. I say it is your duty, Henry—your duty—to

put those abominable buildings into proper and habitable repair. As a man of science you owe it to the community to perfect the sanitary arrangements. In questions of duty there is no room for persuasion, even from the oldest friend.

SARTORIUS [to Trench] I certainly feel, as Mr Cokane puts it, that it is our duty: one which I have perhaps too long neglected out of regard for the poorest class of tenants.

LICKCHEESE. Not a doubt of it, gents: a dooty. I can be as sharp as any man when it's a question of business; but dooty's another pair o' shoes.

TRENCH. Well, I dont see that it's any more my duty now than it was four months ago. I look at it simply as a question of so much money.

COKANE. Shame, Harry, shame! Shame!

TRENCH. Oh, shut up, you fool. [Cokane springs up].

LICKCHEESE [catching his coat and holding him] Steady! steady! Mr Sekketerry. Dr Trench is only joking.

COKANE. I insist on the withdrawal of that expression. I have been called a fool.

TRENCH [morosely] So you are a fool.

COKANE. Then you are a damned fool. Now, sir!

TRENCH. All right. Now weve settled that. [Cokane, with a snort, sits down]. What I mean is this. Dont lets have any nonsense about this job. As I understand it, Robbins's Row is to be pulled down to make way for the new street into the Strand; and the straight tip now is to go for compensation.

LICKCHEESE [chuckling] That'so, Dr Trench. Thats it.

TRENCH [continuing] Well, it appears that the dirtier a place is the more rent you get; and the decenter it is, the more compensation you get. So we're to give up dirt and go in for decency.

SARTORIUS. I should not put it exactly in that way; but—

COKANE. Quite right, Mr Sartorius, quite right. The case could not have been stated in worse taste or with less tact.

LICKCHEESE. Sh-sh-sh-sh!

SARTORIUS. I do not quite go with you there, Mr Cokane. Dr Trench puts the case frankly as a man of business. I take the wider view of a public man. We live in a progressive age; and humanitarian ideas are advancing and must be taken into account. But my practical conclusion is the same as his. I should hardly feel justified in making a large claim for compensation under existing circumstances.

LICKCHEESE. Of course not; and you wouldnt get it if you did. You see, it's like this, Dr Trench. Theres no doubt that the Vestries has legal powers to play old Harry with slum properties, and spoil the house-knacking game if they please. That didn't matter in the good old times, because the Vestries used to be us ourselves. Nobody ever knew a word about the election; and we used to get ten of us into a room and elect one another, and do what we liked. Well, that cock wont fight any longer; and, to put it short, the game is up for men in the position of you and Mr Sartorius. My advice to you is, take the present chance of getting out of it. Spend a little money on the block at the Cribbs Market end: enough to make it look like a model dwelling, you know; and let the other block to me on fair terms for a depot of the North Thames Iced Mutton Company. Theyll be knocked down inside of two year to make room for the new north and south main thoroughfare; and youll be compensated to the tune of double the present valuation, with the cost of improvements thrown in. Leave things as they are; and you stand a good chance of being fined, or condemned, or pulled down before long. Now's your time.

COKANE. Hear, hear! Hear, hear! Hear, hear! Admirably put from the business point of view! I recognize the uselessness of putting the moral point of view to you, Trench; but even you must feel the cogency of Mr Lickcheese's business statement.

TRENCH. But why cant you act without me? What have I got to do with it? I'm only a mortgagee.

SARTORIUS. There is a certain risk in this compensation investment, Dr Trench. The County Council may alter the line of the new street. If that happens, the money spent in improving the houses will be thrown away: simply thrown away. Worse than thrown away, in fact; for the new buildings may stand unlet or half let for years. But you will expect your seven per cent as usual.

TRENCH. A man must live.

COKANE. Je n'en vois pas la nécessité.

TRENCH. Shut up, Billy; or else speak some language you understand. No, Mr Sartorius: I should be very glad to stand in with you if I could afford it; but I cant; so you may leave me out of it.

LICKCHEESE. Well, all I can say is that youre a very foolish young man.

COKANE. What did I tell you, Harry?

TRENCH. I dont see that it's any business of yours, Mr Lickcheese.

LICKCHEESE. It's a free country: every man has a right to his opinion.

COKANE. Hear, hear!

LICKCHEESE. Come! wheres your feelins for them poor people, Dr Trench? Remember how it went to your heart when I first told you about them. What! are you going to turn hard?

TRENCH. No: it wont do: you cant get over me that way. You proved to me before that there was no use in being sentimental over that slum shop of ours; and it's no good your turning round on the philanthropic tack now that you want me to put my capital into your speculation. Ive had my lesson; and I'm going to stick to my present income. It's little enough for me as it is.

SARTORIUS. It really matters nothing to me, Dr Trench, how you decide. I can easily raise the money elsewhere and pay you off. Then, since you are resolved to run no risks, you can invest your ten thousand pounds in Consols and get two hundred and fifty pounds a year for it instead of seven hundred.

Trench, completely outwitted, stares at them in consternation. Cokane breaks the silence.

COKANE. This is what comes of being avaricious, Harry. Two thirds of your income gone at one blow. And I must say it serves you right.

TRENCH. Thats all very fine; but I dont understand it. If you can do this to me, why didnt you do it long ago?

SARTORIUS. Because, as I should probably have had to borrow at the same rate, I should have saved nothing; whereas you would have lost over four hundred a year: a very serious matter for you. I had no desire to be unfriendly; and even now I should be glad to let the mortgage stand, were it not that the circumstances mentioned by Mr Lickcheese force my hand. Besides, Dr Trench, I hoped for some time that our interests might be joined by closer ties even than those of friendship.

LICKCHEESE [*jumping up, relieved*] There! Now the

[116]

murder's out. Excuse me, Dr Trench. Ex-cuse me,
Mr Sartorius: excuse my freedom. Why not Dr
Trench marry Miss Blanche, and settle the whole
affair that way?

Sensation. Lickcheese sits down triumphant.

COKANE. You forget, Mr Lickcheese, that the young
lady, whose taste has to be considered, decisively
objected to him.

TRENCH. Oh! Perhaps you think she was struck with
you.

COKANE. I do not say so, Trench. No man of any
delicacy would suggest such a thing. You have an
untutored mind, Trench, an untutored mind.

TRENCH. Well, Cokane: Ive told you my opinion of
you already.

COKANE [*rising wildly*] And I have told you my
opinion of you. I will repeat it if you wish. I am
ready to repeat it.

LICKCHEESE. Come, Mr Sekketerry: you and me, as
married men, is out of the unt as far as young ladies
is concerned. I know Miss Blanche: she has her
father's eye for business. Explain this job to her; and
she'll make it up with Dr Trench. Why not have a bit
of romance in business when it costs nothing? We all
have our feelins: we aint mere calculatin machines.

SARTORIUS [*revolted*] Do you think, Lickcheese, that
my daughter is to be made part of a money bargain
between you and these gentlemen?

LICKCHEESE. Oh come, Sartorius! dont talk as if you
was the only father in the world. I have a daughter too;
and my feelins in that matter is just as fine as yours.
I propose nothing but what is for Miss Blanche's
advantage and Dr Trench's.

COKANE. Lickcheese expresses himself roughly, Mr
Sartorius; but his is a sterling nature; and what he

says is to the point. If Miss Sartorius can really bring herself to care for Harry, I am far from desiring to stand in the way of such an arrangement.

TRENCH. Why, what have you got to do with it?

LICKCHEESE. Easy, Dr Trench, easy. We want your opinion. Are you still on for marrying Miss Blanche if she's agreeable?

TRENCH [*shortly*] I dont know that I am. [*Sartorius rises indignantly*].

LICKCHEESE. Easy one moment, Mr Sartorius. [*To Trench*] Come now, Dr Trench! you say you dont know that you are. But do you know that you aint? thats what we want to know.

TRENCH [*sulkily*] I wont have the relations between Miss Sartorius and myself made part of a bargain. [*He rises to leave the table*].

LICKCHEESE [*rising*] Thats enough: a gentleman could say no less. [*Insinuatingly*] Now, would you mind me and Cokane and the guvnor steppin into the study to arrange about the lease to the North Thames Iced Mutton Company?

TRENCH. Oh, *I* don't mind. I'm going home. Theres nothing more to say.

LICKCHEESE. No: dont go. Only just a minute: me and Cokane will be back in no time to see you home. Youll wait for us, wont you?

TRENCH. Oh, well, if you wish, yes.

LICKCHEESE [*cheerily*] Didnt I know you would!

SARTORIUS [*at the study door, to Cokane*] After you, sir.

Cokane bows formally and goes into the study.

LICKCHEESE [*at the door, aside to Sartorius*] You never ad such a managin man as me, Sartorius. [*He goes into the study chuckling, followed by Sartorius*].

Trench, left alone, looks round carefully and listens

[118]

*a moment. Then he goes on tiptoe to the piano and leans
upon it with folded arms, gazing at Blanche's portrait.
Blanche herself appears presently at the study door.
When she sees how he is occupied, she closes it softly
and steals over to him, watching him intently. He rises
from his leaning attitude, and takes the portrait from
the easel, and is about to kiss it when, taking a second
look round to reassure himself that nobody is watching
him, he finds Blanche close upon him. He drops the
portrait, and stares at her without the least presence of
mind.*

BLANCHE [*shrewishly*] Well? So you have come back
here. You have had the meanness to come into this
house again. [*He flushes and retreats a step. She follows
him up remorselessly*]. What a poor spirited creature
you must be! Why dont you go? [*Red and wincing,
he starts huffily to get his hat from the table; but when
he turns to the door with it she deliberately stands in his
way; so that he has to stop*]. I dont want you to stay.
[*For a moment they stand face to face, quite close to
one another, she is provocative, taunting, half defying,
half inviting him to advance, in a flush of undisguised
animal excitement. It suddenly flashes on him that all
this ferocity is erotic: that she is making love to him. His
eye lights up: a cunning expression comes into the corners
of his mouth: with a heavy assumption of indifference
he walks straight back to his chair, and plants himself in it
with his arms folded. She comes down the room after
him*]. But I forgot: you have found that there is some
money to be made here. Lickcheese told you. You,
who were so disinterested, so independent, that you
could not accept anything from my father! [*At the end
of every sentence she waits to see what execution she
has done*]. I suppose you will try to persuade me that
you have come down here on a great philanthropic

enterprise—to befriend the poor by having those houses rebuilt, eh? [*Trench maintains his attitude and makes no sign*]. Yes: when my father makes you do it. And when Lickcheese has discovered some way of making it profitable. Oh, I know papa; and I know you. And for the sake of that, you come back here—into the house where you were refused—ordered out. [*Trench's face darkens: her eyes gleam as she sees it*]. Aha! you remember that. You know it's true: you cant deny it. [*She sits down, and softens her tone a little as she affects to pity him*]. Well, let me tell you that you cut a poor figure, a very, very poor figure, Harry. [*At the word Harry he relaxes the fold of his arms; and a faint grin of anticipated victory appears on his face*]. And you, too, a gentleman! so highly connected! with such distinguished relations! so particular as to where your money comes from! I wonder at you. I really wonder at you. I should have thought that if your fine family gave you nothing else, it might at least have given you some sense of personal dignity. Perhaps you think you look dignified at present: eh? [*No reply*]. Well, I can assure you that you dont: you look most ridiculous—as foolish as a man could look—you dont know what to say; and you dont know what to do. But after all, I really dont see what any one could say in defence of such conduct. [*He looks straight in front of him, and purses up his lips as if whistling. This annoys her; and she becomes affectedly polite*]. I am afraid I am in your way, Dr Trench. [*She rises*]. I shall not intrude on you any longer. You seem so perfectly at home that I need make no apology for leaving you to yourself. [*She makes a feint of going to the door; but he does not budge; and she returns and comes behind his chair*]. Harry. [*He does not turn. She comes a step nearer*]. Harry: I want you to answer me a question. [*Earnestly, stooping over him*] Look me in the face. [*No reply*]. Do you hear? [*Seizing his cheeks and twisting his head round*] Look—me—in—the—face. [*He shuts his eyes tight and grins. She suddenly kneels down beside him with her breast against his shoulder*]. Harry: what were you doing with my photograph just now, when you thought you were alone? [*He opens his eyes: they are full of delight. She flings her arms round him, and crushes him in an ecstatic embrace as she adds, with furious tenderness*] How dare you touch anything belonging to me?

The study door opens and voices are heard.

TRENCH. I hear some one coming.

She regains her chair with a bound, and pushes it back as far as possible. Cokane, Lickcheese, and Sartorius come from the study. Sartorius and Lickcheese come to Trench. Cokane crosses to Blanche in his most killing manner.

COKANE. How do you do, Miss Sartorius? Nice weather for the return of l'enfant prodigue, eh?

BLANCHE. Capital, Mr Cokane. So glad to see you. [*She gives him her hand, which he kisses with gallantry*].

LICKCHEESE [*on Trench's left, in a low voice*] Any noos for us, Dr Trench?

TRENCH [*to Sartorius, on his right*] I'll stand in, compensation or no compensation. [*He shakes Sartorius's hand*].

The parlormaid has just appeared at the door.

THE PARLORMAID. Supper is ready, miss.

COKANE. Allow me.

Exeunt omnes: Blanche on Cokane's arm; Lickcheese jocosely taking Sartorius on one arm, and Trench on the other.

The Playwright on
His First Play

(An interview,
drafted by Shaw, on *Widowers' Houses*.
The Star, 29 November 1892)

I am an experienced interviewer; but I confess that
when *The Star* editor directed me to tackle Bernard
Shaw on the subject of the play he has written for the
Independent Theatre, I felt nervous. "Keep him to
the point," said the editor. "Be firm, or he will talk
your head off without once alluding to the play."
Though quaking inwardly, I looked bold as I assured
my chief he might rely on me. Then I went off to
the well-known number in Fitzroy-sq., and arrived
there about half-past eleven in the morning. The door
was furnished with several bells, one of them bearing
the name SHAW. I performed on this instrument for
some 12 minutes in vain, concluding with a five
minutes' fantasia on all the other bells. Then I was
joined by a rather attractive young woman in an ulster,
come, as I gathered, to help the eminent Socialist
by looking after the household work. She informed me
that it was extremely improbable that Mr. Shaw would
be up at that early hour, and, on my criticising the
bells, remarked apologetically that there was one of
them that rang sometimes. However, she let me in,
which was, after all, the main thing; and brought me
up some desolate stone steps to the second floor,

WHERE I FOUND MR. SHAW

in a very small room, completely blocking up the
narrow passage between the wide-open window and
the door as he sat between the fire and the table in a

substantial chair fortified by a strong wooden rail, with a typewriter on its stand before him. The table was untidy beyond belief: dusty heaps of letters and papers in utter disorder were mixed up with stationery, inkstands, *Stars*, *Chronicles*, butter, sugar, stray apples, knives and spoons, a full breakfast cup of cocoa, and a plate upon which Mr. Shaw, as I entered, was dumping down a helping of porridge which he had just extracted from a saucepan on the hob. I confess I felt embarrassed. Not so my host. He received me affably, with entire confidence in the propriety of his surroundings, and piloted me between the Scylla of the typewriter and the Charybdis of the blazing fire to a chair by the window. Before I was fairly seated he began a most brilliant account of the entire history of *The Star* newspaper from its inception to the present time. This gave me 15 minutes to make a note of two photographs—one of Mr. Toft's bust of Cunninghame Graham over the mantelshelf, and the other, over the table, of the well-known horse's head from the Naples museum. Also to study Mr. Shaw's costume, and to observe that he wore

A GRAY COLLAR AND SANDALS.

"And now, Mr. Shaw," I said, "what about 'Wendover's Horses'?"

"What do you mean?"

"Your play, Mr. Shaw. That is the title given by one of the evening papers."

"Nonsense. 'Widowers' Houses' is the title."

"Why 'Widowers' Houses,' if I may ask?"

"I thought you would have recognised the allusion. I have been assured that in one of the sections of the Bible dealing with the land question there is a clause against the destruction of widows' houses. There is

[123]

no widow in my play; but there is a widower who owns slum property. Hence the title. Perhaps you are not familiar with the Bible."

I apologised for not catching the reference. My next question was,

"To what genre does the play belong? Comedy, tragedy, farce, or melodrama?"

"To none of them. To Humanity solely. That is the only genre I recognize."

"Is it true, Mr. Shaw, that Sir Augustus Harris has consented to play one of the leading parts?"

"Unhappily, no. It's only an idle rumor. I wish it were true. It would give me a practical opportunity of imparting my views on stage management to Sir Augustus, who recognises my merits as an operatic critic."

"Have you heard that Mr. Clement Scott is returning from the East to be present at the performance?"

"I have not heard it; but it is, of course, quite possible."

"I see that your play is announced by the Independent Theatre as 'a didactic, realistic drama.' May I venture to hope that it will

NOT BE TOO DIDACTIC?"

"Sir," said Mr. Shaw sternly, "it will be nothing else than didactic. Do you suppose I have gone to all this trouble to *amuse* the public? No, if they want that, there is the Criterion for them, the Comedy, the Garrick, and so on. My object is to instruct them."

"Quite so. Do you find that the stage manager takes that view?"

"I am sorry to say that he does not. I cannot understand it in so clever a man. You know him—Hermann de Lange, who did that perfect bit of acting in

'Thérèse Raquin'—an artist to the tip of his fingers, a master of nuances that not one actor in ten can distinguish, one from whom even I have learnt something—a man with such a confounded vivacity of imagination that he conceives every character in my play six times over at each rehearsal, and conceives it differently every time. Well, I cannot make de Lange see the importance of appealing to the audience on the solid ground of political economy. There is a situation in the second act—the climax of the play—which really requires to be explained by one of the leading characters on a blackboard by means of a diagram. They actually want to cut out the blackboard. De Lange keeps saying, 'My dear boy you can't get a blackboard over the footlights.' I explain to him that I don't want to get it over the footlights—that I want it to stand on the stage, not to have it handed round the stalls. But he only laughs at me and says I don't understand the theatre. All I can say is that I will not be responsible for the success of the scene IF THE BLACKBOARD IS OMITTED.

The public cannot possibly understand the economic point without the diagram." (Here Mr. Shaw drew the diagram for me, and explained at great length the bearing on the play of the value theory of the late Professor Stanley Jevons. It was most interesting.)

"You must not suppose, however, that this is my only difficulty with the Independent Theatre. They have the most limited ideas as to the proper length for a play. They say two hours and a half. I say that this may be all very well for the idle pleasure-seekers, but that an audience of genuine enthusiasts, attending the theatre with serious aims, would not grudge five hours. That is clear, is it not?"

"Unquestionably, Mr. Shaw. And is the play to last five hours, if I may ask?"

"No. There is only time to learn three acts of it, which will occupy no more than the usual time."

"How many acts, then, are there in the whole play?"

"Seventeen. 'Widowers' Houses' is a mere episode in a historic drama." (Here Mr. Shaw held me spellbound for nearly an hour with a brilliant aperçu of the social and industrial development of England from the Reformation up to the twenty-second century, of which he has the clearest prevision.)

"May I ask for a sketch of the plot of your play, Mr. Shaw? As you do not wish to amuse the public, you need not, I presume, hesitate to disclose it."

"There is no plot. The hero, who has no conventionally heroic qualities, loves the heroine, who has no conventionally amiable ones. She has, in fact,
AN ABOMINABLE TEMPER.
Her father, a widower, offers to provide handsomely for the young couple. But the hero discovers that the widower's money comes from the rents of a slum property—a horrible example of house knacking. Like a true son of the middle-class, he recoils with horror from the idea of profiting by such an iniquity until he discovers that his own little income is equally compromised. He then sorrowfully admits that 'such things must be.' This is the point which I wanted to have demonstrated on the blackboard."

"May we anticipate some of your unrivalled touches of humor, Mr. Shaw?"

"Certainly not. I have removed with the greatest care every line that could possibly provoke a smile. I have been greatly misunderstood in this matter. Being an Irishman, I do not always see things exactly as an Englishman would: consequently my most serious and blunt statements sometimes raise a laugh and create an impression that I am intentionally jesting. I admit that some Irishmen do take advantage of the public in this way. Wilde, unquestionably the ablest of our dramatists, has done so in 'Lady Windermere's Fan.' There are lines in that play which were put in for no other purpose than to make the audience laugh."

"'Widowers' Houses' will be quite free from that sort of thing, then?"

"Absolutely. However, I do not blame Wilde. He wrote for the stage as an artist. I am simply a propagandist."

"Has the play been refused by many London managers?"

'It has never been offered to one. Why should it? They are not interested in propaganda. Since I wrote it in 1885, I have been too busy to concern myself about its production. The entire credit of its appearance is due to Mr. Grein, the founder of the Independent Theatre."

"And the cast, Mr. Shaw?"

"Nothing can exceed the devotion of the cast. They are presenting their services to the Independent Theatre at considerable expense to themselves, and without the least prospect of making the sort of personal success which an ambitious actor might score in the work of a practised dramatist bent on a popular success. As the whole play is carried on by five persons, the parts are not only thankless but

VERY LONG AND TROUBLESOME.

The part of the widower is as difficult as that of Digby Grand in 'The Two Roses,' which first brought Mr. Irving to the front. It has been undertaken by Mr.

T. W. Percyval, whom you may remember as Count Evitoff in 'Gloriana.' He finds the part the most difficult he has ever studied; and he is by no means a novice. I remember his telling me that he began his career by playing eight different parts in 'Hamlet.'"

"Do you mean on the same evening?"

"I am not sufficiently familiar with the play to know whether that is possible. Let us say on the same tour, not on the same evening. Then there is the hero. His part, strangely enough, revolted the moral sense of several actors who were asked to play it. They complained of his being 'a feeder'—I cannot think why, as I have made no allusion to his appetite, nor does he eat anything on the stage. Fortunately Mr. W. J. Robertson stepped in to save the performance from being postponed, and will do his best to sustain his reputation in this ungrateful part. But my great trouble is with Mr. Arthur Whittaker, the representative of the hero's confidant. Mr. Whittaker is, unfortunately a practised and versatile comedian, who is accustomed to play the most popular parts of Mr. Penley, Mr. Hawtrey, and Mr. Hare. He has made me laugh several times at rehearsal; and I foresee great danger of his

UPSETTING THE GRAVITY OF THE AUDIENCE

He seems only imperfectly sensible of the force of my remonstrances. By the bye, I am forgetting to mention the part that appeals most to the actor. It is that of the slum rent collector; and I shall be glad to have your opinion of it when it has been played by Mr. James Welch, whom you have seen as the Artful Dodger at the Olympic."

"I think you said something about a heroine, Mr. Shaw?"

"To be sure. There is a heroine and a housemaid.

The housemaid was the great difficulty; for the part is small and yet so important that the end of the second act depends entirely on it. Mr. Grein said that nobody but a first-rate actress could be trusted with it. I said, 'Very good, let us have a first-rate actress: there is more hope for us in the modesty of a finished artist than in the vanity of a beginner.' And we boldly asked Miss Kate Phillips, who consented with the utmost goodnature. For the heroine I had long before set my heart on Miss Florence Farr, if only she could be persuaded to undertake so odious a task as the impersonation of a rich upstart's wilful, violent daughter, who hates the class from which her father sprang. Miss Farr is an actress trained only in farcical comedy, with obvious gifts for such stage work as demands a lively sense of humor and personal grace and address, but without the formidable physical equipment for tragedy which distinguishes Miss Robins and Miss Achurch, for instance. I first met Miss Farr in the days of the Ibsen controversy. The only Ibsen part which seemed at all within her means was 'The Lady from the Sea,' which she was about to attempt when I directed her attention to the most difficult tragic part in the whole Ibsen repertory—that of Rebecca West in 'Rosmersholm.' You remember how she actually produced that extraordinary play, and what an impression she made as Rebecca, and how, later on, in spite of appalling difficulties created by our corrupt censorship, she saved us from having to let the Shelley centenary pass without at least a glimpse of Beatrice Cenci. And all this, remember,

NOT AS PART OF HER ORDINARY BUSINESS; for she is not a tragédienne, but a quite unassuming member of Mr. Hawtrey's company at the Comedy Theatre. This sort of thing can only be done by a highly intelligent woman. No mere genius—everybody on the stage is a genius—could achieve it. I appealed to Miss Farr on the ground that the play was impossible without her; and she, too, consented, though her part is a specially hazardous and disagreeable one."

"Do you really think the censorship is corrupt, Mr. Shaw?"

"Of course. All irresponsible authorities are corrupt. It is a law of nature—a commonplace of political philosophy. Besides, look at the second act of 'Incognita,' licensed for a rich financier who was supposed at the time to have bought up the *Pall Mall Gazette;* and compare it with Brandes' 'Visit,' for which a license was refused to the comparatively poor and socially uninfluential Independent Theatre. Look at Mr. Pigott's evidence before the Royal Commission —how he assumed as a matter of course that Mr. William Archer was simply booming Ibsen to make money out of him. Corrupt!—the Lord Chamberlain's office is a sink of corruption. I do not mean that they take £50 notes there for licenses, though I have no guarantee whatever that they don't; but that they are respecters of persons and their pretence of keeping the theatre pure is an impudent sham are facts too flagrant to be overlooked. The only comfort is that as the censorship is

A DESPOTIC STATE DEPARTMENT,

the right to denounce them is part of the public right of free speech against the Government."

"As a playwright, Mr. Shaw, you are of course a follower of Ibsen?"

"What! *I* a follower of Ibsen! My good sir, as far as England is concerned, Ibsen is a follower of mine. In 1880, when I was only 24, I wrote a book called

'The Irrational Knot,' which reads nowadays like an Ibsenite novel. When I wrote the first two acts of 'Widowers' Houses' I had never heard of Ibsen. My 'Quintessence of Ibsenism' proved that I understood Ibsen's drift better than he understood it himself."

"Shakespeare is your model, perhaps?"

"Shakespeare! stuff! Shakespeare—a disillusioned idealist! a pessimist! a rationalist! a capitalist! If the fellow had not been a great poet, his rubbish would have been forgotten long ago. Molière, as a thinker, was worth a thousand Shakespeares. If my play is not better than Shakespeare, let it be damned promptly."

"I suppose there is no doubt that you are an exceptionally clever man, Mr. Shaw?"

"Not the slightest. Ah, if I had only realised that years ago!—if I had only had courage and faith in myself

AS WELL AS BRAINS!

Be warned by me—you are a young man still—beware of timidity and diffidence. They have done me a world of harm and very little good."

"I will bear it in mind, Mr. Shaw. Many thanks. I am afraid I have detained you unconscionably."

"Not at all. May I offer you some refreshment—a glass of water and few carrots?"

"Thanks, I never take anything at this hour. Have I your full permission to publish what has passed?"

"Verbatim, if you please. Tell the exact truth Remember me to all at Stonecutter-st. Good day."

"Good day, Mr. Shaw. Again many thanks. Never mind coming down. By the bye, where and when is the performance to take place?"

"On the 9th, I believe. I don't know where—

perhaps at the Avenue, or the Royalty. Ask Grein: he knows. Good-bye."

And I left him beaming flatteringly after me from the stairhead. He was the most copious talker I ever interviewed.

The Philanderer

WITH

Prefatory Note, 1930

Composition begun 14 March 1893; completed 27 June 1893. Published in *Plays Pleasant and Unpleasant*, 1898. Revised text in Collected Edition, 1930. Copyright reading at the Victoria Hall (Bijou Theatre), London, on 30 March 1898. First presented by the New Stage Club (amateurs) at the Cripplegate Institute, London, on 20 February 1905. First professional performance presented by J. E. Vedrenne and H. Granville Barker at the Royal Court Theatre, London, on 5 February 1907 (for a series of eight matinées).

Leonard Charteris   *Ben Webster*
Mrs Grace Tranfield   *Wynne Matthison*
Julia Craven   *Mary Barton*
Colonel Daniel Craven, V.C.   *Eric Lewis*
Joseph Cuthbertson   *Luigi Lablache*
Sylvia Craven   *Dorothy Minto*
Dr Percy Paramore   *Hubert Harben*
The Club Page   *Cyril Bruce*

Period—During the first vogue of Ibsen in London after 1889

ACT I *Mr Joseph Cuthbertson's Flat in Ashley Gardens*

ACTS II AND III *The Library of the Ibsen Club in Cork Street*

ACT IV *Dr Paramore's Rooms in Savile Row*

Prefatory Note

There is a disease to which plays as well as men become liable with advancing years. In men it is called doting, in plays dating. The more topical the play the more it dates. The Philanderer suffers from this complaint. In the eighteen-nineties, when it was written, not only dramatic literature but life itself was staggering from the impact of Ibsen's plays, which reached us in 1889. The state of mind represented by the Ibsen Club in this play was familiar then to our Intelligentsia. That far more numerous body which may be called the Unintelligentsia was as unconscious of Ibsen as of any other political influence: quarter of a century elapsed before an impatient heaven rained German bombs down on them to wake them from their apathy. That accustomed them to much more startling departures from Victorian routine than those that shock the elderly colonel and the sentimental theatre critic in The Philanderer; but they do not associate their advance in liberal morals with the great Norwegian. Even the Intelligentsia have forgotten that the lesson that might have saved the lives of ten million persons hideously slaughtered was offered to them by Ibsen.

I make no attempt to bring the play up to date. I should as soon think of bringing Ben Jonson's Bartholomew Fair up to date by changing the fair into a Woolworth store. The human nature in it is still in the latest fashion: indeed I am far from sure that its ideas, instead of being 36 years behind the times, are not for a considerable section of the community 36 years ahead of them. My picture of the past may be for many people a picture of the future. At all events I

shall leave the play as it is; for all the attempts within
my experience to modernize ancient plays have only
produced worse anachronisms than those they aimed
at remedying.

1930

[ACT I]

---

*A lady and gentleman are making love to one another
in the drawing room of a flat in Ashley Gardens in the
Victoria district of London. It is past ten at night. The
walls are hung with theatrical engravings and photographs: Kemble as Hamlet, Mrs Siddons as Queen
Katherine pleading in court, Macready as Werner (after
Maclise), Sir Henry Irving as Richard III (after Long),
Ellen Terry, Mrs Kendal, Ada Rehan, Sarah Bernhardt,
Henry Arthur Jones, Sir Arthur Pinero, Sydney Grundy,
and so on, but not Eleonora Duse nor any one connected
with Ibsen. The room is not rectangular, one corner being
cut off diagonally by the doorway, and the opposite one
rounded by a turret window filled up with a stand of
flowers surrounding a statuet of Shakespear. The fireplace is on the doorway side, with an armchair near it.
A small round table, further from the door on the same
side, with a chair beside it, has a yellow backed French
novel lying open on it. The piano, a grand, is on the
Shakespear side, open, with the keyboard at right angles
to the wall. The piece of music on the desk is When
Other Lips. Incandescent lights, well shaded, are on the
piano and mantelpiece. Near the piano is a sofa, on
which the lady and gentleman are seated affectionately
side by side, in one another's arms.*

*The lady, Grace Tranfield, is about 32, slight of
build, delicate of feature, and sensitive in expression.
She is just now given up to the emotion of the moment;
but her well closed mouth, proudly set brows, firm chin,*

[137]

and elegant carriage shew plenty of determination and self-respect. She is in evening dress.

The gentleman, Leonard Charteris, a few years older, is unconventionally but smartly dressed in a velvet jacket and cashmere trousers. His collar, dyed Wotan blue, is part of his shirt, and turns over a garnet colored scarf of Indian silk, secured by a turquoise ring. He wears blue socks and leather sandals. The arrangement of his tawny hair, and of his moustache and short beard, is apparently left to Nature; but he has taken care that Nature shall do him the fullest justice. His amative enthusiasm, at which he is himself laughing, and his clever, imaginative, humorous ways, contrast strongly with the sincere tenderness and dignified quietness of the woman.

CHARTERIS [*impulsively clasping Grace*] My dearest love.

GRACE [*responding affectionately*] My darling. Are you happy?

CHARTERIS. In Heaven.

GRACE. My own.

CHARTERIS. My heart's love. [*He sighs happily, and takes her hands in his, looking quaintly at her*]. That must positively be my last kiss, Grace; or I shall become downright silly. Let us talk. [*He releases her and sits a little apart*]. Grace: is this your first love affair?

GRACE. Have you forgotten that I am a widow? Do you think I married Tranfield for money?

CHARTERIS. How do I know? Besides, you might have married him not because you loved him, but because you didnt love anybody else. When one is young, one marries out of mere curiosity, just to see what it's like.

GRACE. Well, since you ask me, I never was in love with Tranfield, though I only found that out when I fell in love with you. But I used to like him for being in love with me. It brought out all the good in him so much that I have wanted to be in love with someone ever since. I hope, now that I am in love with you, you will like me for it just as I liked Tranfield.

CHARTERIS. My dear: it is because I like you that I want to marry you. I could love anybody—any pretty woman, that is.

GRACE. Do you really mean that, Leonard?

CHARTERIS. Of course. Why not?

GRACE [*reflecting*] Never mind. Now tell me, is this your first love affair?

CHARTERIS [*amazed at the simplicity of the question*] No, bless my soul, no; nor my second, nor my third.

GRACE. But I mean your first serious one?

CHARTERIS [*with a certain hesitation*] Yes. [*There is a pause. She is not convinced. He adds, with a very perceptible load on his conscience*] It is the first in which *I* have been serious.

GRACE [*searchingly*] I see. The other parties were always serious.

CHARTERIS. Not always. Heaven forbid!

GRACE. How often?

CHARTERIS. Well, once.

GRACE. Julia Craven?

CHARTERIS [*recoiling*] Who told you that? [*She shakes her head mysteriously. He turns away from her moodily and adds*] You had much better not have asked.

GRACE [*gently*] I'm sorry, dear. [*She puts out her hand and pulls softly at him to bring him near her again*].

CHARTERIS [*yielding mechanically to the pull, and allowing her hand to rest on his arm, but sitting squarely without the least attempt to return the caress*] Do I feel harder to the touch than I did five minutes ago?

GRACE. What nonsense!

CHARTERIS. I feel as if my body had turned into the toughest hickory. That is what comes of reminding me of Julia Craven. [*Brooding, with his chin on his right hand and his elbow on his knee*] I have sat alone with her just as I am sitting with you—

GRACE [*shrinking from him*] Just!

CHARTERIS [*sitting upright and facing her steadily*] Just exactly. She has put her hands in mine, and laid her cheek against mine, and listened to me saying all sorts of silly things. [*Grace, chilled to the soul, rises from the sofa and sits down on the piano stool, with her back to the keyboard*]. Ah, you dont want to hear any more of the story. So much the better.

GRACE [*deeply hurt, but controlling herself*] When did you break it off?

CHARTERIS [*guiltily*] Break it off?

GRACE [*firmly*] Yes: break it off.

CHARTERIS. Well: let me see. When did I fall in love with you?

GRACE. Did you break it off then?

CHARTERIS [*making it plainer and plainer that it has not been broken off*] It was clear then, of course, that it must be broken off.

GRACE. And did you break it off?

CHARTERIS. Oh, yes: *I* broke it off.

GRACE. But did she break it off?

CHARTERIS [*rising*] As a favor to me, dearest, change the subject. Come away from the piano: I want you to sit here with me. [*He takes a step towards her*].

GRACE. No. I also have grown hard to the touch: much harder than hickory for the present. Did she break it off?

CHARTERIS. My dear, be reasonable. It was fully explained to her that it was to be broken off.

GRACE. Did she accept the explanation?

CHARTERIS. She did what a woman like Julia always does. When I explained personally, she said it was not my better self that was speaking, and that she knew I still really loved her. When I wrote it to her with brutal explicitness, she read the letter carefully and then sent it back to me with a note to say that she had not had the courage to open it, and that I ought to be ashamed of having written it. [*He comes beside Grace, and puts his left hand caressingly round her neck*]. You see, dearie, she wont look the situation in the face.

GRACE [*shaking off his hand and turning a little away on the stool*] I am afraid, from the light way you speak of it, you did not sound the right chord.

CHARTERIS. My dear: when you are doing what a woman calls breaking her heart, you may sound the very prettiest chords you can find on the piano; but to her ears it is just like this. [*He sits down on the bass end of the keyboard. Grace puts her fingers in her ears. He rises and moves away from the piano, saying*] No, my dear: Ive been kind; Ive been frank; Ive been everything that a good-natured man can be; but she only takes it as the making up of a lovers' quarrel. [*Grace winces*]. Frankness and kindness: one is as base as the other. Especially frankness. Ive tried both. [*He crosses to the fireplace, and stands facing the fire, looking at the ornaments on the mantelpiece, and warming his hands*].

GRACE [*her voice a little strained*] What are you going to try now?

CHARTERIS [*on the hearthrug, turning to face her*] Action, my dear. Marriage. In that she must believe.

She wont be convinced by anything short of it; because, you see, Ive had some tremendous philanderings before, and have gone back to her after them.

GRACE. And so that is why you want to marry me?

CHARTERIS. I cannot deny it, my love. Yes: it is your mission to rescue me from Julia.

GRACE [*rising*] Then, if you please, I decline to be made use of for any such purpose. I will not steal you from another woman. [*She walks up and down the room with ominous disquiet*].

CHARTERIS. Steal me! [*He comes towards her*]. Grace: I have a question to put to you as an advanced woman. Mind! as an advanced woman. Does Julia belong to me? Am I her owner—her master?

GRACE. Certainly not. No woman is the property of a man. A woman belongs to herself and to nobody else.

CHARTERIS. Quite right. Ibsen for ever! Thats exactly my opinion. Now tell me, do I belong to Julia; or have I a right to belong to myself?

GRACE [*puzzled*] Of course you have; but—

CHARTERIS [*interrupting her triumphantly*] Then how can you steal me from Julia if I dont belong to her? [*He catches her by the shoulders and holds her out at arms length in front of him*]. Eh, little philosopher? No, my dear: if Ibsen sauce is good for the goose, it's good for the gander as well. Besides [*coaxing her*] it was nothing but a philander with Julia. Nothing else in the world, I assure you.

GRACE [*breaking away from him*] So much the worse! I hate your philanderings: they make me ashamed of you and of myself. [*She goes to the sofa and sits in the corner furthest from the piano, leaning gloomily on her elbow with her face averted*].

CHARTERIS. Grace: you utterly misunderstand the

[142]

origin of my philanderings. [*He sits down beside her*].
Listen to me. Am I a particularly handsome man?

GRACE [*astonished at his conceit*] No.

CHARTERIS [*triumphantly*] You admit it. Am I a
well dressed man?

GRACE. Not particularly.

CHARTERIS. Of course not. Have I a romantic mysterious charm about me? do I look as if a secret sorrow
preyed on me? am I gallant to women?

GRACE. Not in the least.

CHARTERIS. Certainly not. No one can accuse me of it.
Then whose fault is it that half the women I speak to
fall in love with me? Not mine: I hate it: it bores me
to distraction. At first it flattered me—delighted me—
that was how Julia got me, because she was the first
woman who had the pluck to make me a declaration.
But I soon had enough of it; and at no time have I
taken the initiative and persecuted women with my
advances as women have persecuted me. Never,
Except, of course, in your case.

GRACE. Oh, you need not make any exception. I had
a good deal of trouble to induce you to come and see
us. You were very coy.

CHARTERIS [*fondly, taking her hand*] With you,
dearest, the coyness was sheet coquetry. I loved you
from the first, and fled only that you might pursue.
But come! let us talk about something really interesting. [*He takes her in his arms*]. Do you love me
better than anyone else in the world?

GRACE. I dont think you like to be loved too much.

CHARTERIS. That depends on who the person is.
You [*pressing her to his heart*] cannot love me too
much: you cannot love me half enough. I reproach
you every day for your coldness, your—[*A violent
double knock without. They start and listen, still in one*

another's arms, hardly daring to breathe]. Who the
deuce is calling at this hour?

GRACE. I cant imagine. [*They listen guiltily. The door
of the flat is opened without. They hastily get away
from one another*].

A WOMAN'S VOICE OUTSIDE. Is Mr Charteris
here?

CHARTERIS [*springing up*] Julia! The devil! [*He
stands at the end of the sofa with his eyes fixed on the
door and his heart beating very unpleasantly*].

GRACE [*rising also*] What can she want?

THE VOICE. Never mind: I will announce myself.
[*A beautiful, dark, tragic looking woman, in mantle
and toque, appears at the door, raging*]. Oh, this is
charming. I have interrupted a pretty tete-à-tete.
Oh, you villain! [*She comes straight at Grace. Charteris
runs across behind the sofa, and stops her. She struggles
furiously with him. Grace preserves her self-possession,
but retreats quietly to the piano. Julia, finding Charteris
too strong for her, gives up her attempt to get at Grace,
but strikes him in the face as she frees herself*].

CHARTERIS [*shocked*] Oh, Julia, Julia! This is too bad.

JULIA. Is it, indeed, too bad? What are you doing
up here with that woman? You scoundrel! But now
listen to me, Leonard: you have driven me to desperation; and I dont care what I do, or who hears
me. I'll not bear it. She shall not have my place with
you—

CHARTERIS. Sh-sh!

JULIA. No, no: I dont care: I will expose her true
character before everybody. You belong to me: you
have no right to be here; and she knows it.

CHARTERIS. I think you had better let me take you
home, Julia.

JULIA. I will not. I am not going home: I am going

[144]

to stay here—here—until I have made you give her up.

CHARTERIS. My dear: you must be reasonable. You really cannot stay in Mrs Tranfield's house if she objects. She can ring the bell and have us both put out.

JULIA. Let her do it then. Let her ring the bell if she dares. Let us see how this pure virtuous creature will face the scandal of what I will declare about her. Let us see how you will face it. I have nothing to lose. Everybody knows how you have treated me: you have boasted of your conquests, you poor pitiful vain creature: I am the common talk of your acquaintances and hers. Oh, I have calculated my advantage [*she tears off her mantle*]: I am a most unhappy and injured woman; but I am not the fool you take me to be. I am going to stay: see? [*She flings the mantle on the round table; puts her toque on it; and sits down*]. Now, Mrs Tranfield: theres the bell [*pointing to the button beside the fireplace*]: why dont you ring? [*Grace, looking attentively at Charteris, does not move*]. Ha! ha! I thought so.

CHARTERIS [*quietly, without relaxing his watch on Julia*] Mrs Tranfield: I think you had better go into another room. [*Grace makes a movement towards the door, but stops and looks inquiringly at Charteris as Julia springs up to intercept her. He advances a step to guard the way to the door*].

JULIA. She shall not. She shall stay here. She shall know what you are, and how you have been in love with me: how it is not two days since you kissed me and told me that the future would be as happy as the past. [*Screaming at him*] You did: deny it if you dare.

CHARTERIS [*to Grace in a low voice*] Go.

GRACE [*with nonchalant disgust, going*] Get her away as soon as you can, Leonard.

Julia, with a stifled cry of rage, rushes at Grace, who is crossing behind the sofa towards the door. Charteris seizes Julia, and prevents her from getting past the sofa. Grace goes out. Charteris, holding Julia fast, looks round to the door to see whether Grace is safely out of the room.

JULIA [*suddenly ceasing to struggle, and speaking with the most pathetic dignity*] Oh, there is no need to be violent. [*He passes her across to the sofa, and leans against the end of it, panting and mopping his forehead*]. That is worthy of you! to use brute force! to humiliate me before her! [*She bursts into tears*].

CHARTERIS [*to himself, with melancholy conviction*] This is going to be a cheerful evening. Now patience! patience! patience! [*He sits down on a chair near the round table*].

JULIA [*in anguish*] Leonard: have you no feeling for me?

CHARTERIS. Only an intense desire to get you safely out of this.

JULIA [*fiercely*] I am not going to stir.

CHARTERIS [*wearily*] Well, well. [*He heaves a long sigh*].

They sit silent for a while: Julia striving, not to regain her self-control, but to maintain her rage at boiling point.

JULIA [*rising suddenly*] I am going to speak to that woman.

CHARTERIS [*jumping up*] No, no. Hang it, Julia, dont lets have another wrestling match. Remember: I'm getting on for forty: youre too young for me. Sit down; or else let me take you home. Suppose her father comes in!

JULIA. I dont care. It rests with you. I am ready to go if she will give you up: until then I stay. Those are

[146]

my terms: you owe me that. [*She sits down deter-minedly*].

Charteris looks at her for a moment, then, making up his mind, goes resolutely to the sofa; sits down near the end of it, she being at the opposite end; and speaks with biting emphasis.

CHARTERIS. I owe you just exactly nothing.

JULIA [*reproachfully*] Nothing! You can look me in the face and say that? Oh, Leonard!

CHARTERIS. Let me remind you, Julia, that when first we became acquainted, the position you took up was that of a woman of advanced views.

JULIA. That should have made you respect me the more.

CHARTERIS [*placably*] So it did, my dear. But that is not the point. As a woman of advanced views, you were determined to be free. You regarded marriage as a degrading bargain, by which a woman sells herself to a man for the social status of a wife and the right to be supported and pensioned in old age out of his income. Thats the advanced view: our view. Besides, if you had married me, I might have turned out a drunkard, a criminal, an imbecile, a horror to you; and you couldnt have released yourself. Too big a risk, you see. Thats the rational view: our view. Accordingly, you reserved the right to leave me at any time if you found our companionship incompatible with—what was the expression you used?—with your full development as a human being. I think that was how you put the Ibsenist view: our view. So I had to be content with a charming philander, which taught me a great deal, and brought me some hours of exquisite happiness.

JULIA. Leonard: you confess then, that you owe me something?

CHARTERIS [*haughtily*] No: what I received, I paid. Did you learn nothing from me? was there no delight for you in our friendship?

JULIA [*vehemently and movingly; for she is now sincere*] No. You made me pay dearly for every moment of happiness. You revenged yourself on me for the humiliation of being the slave of your passion for me. I was never sure of you for a moment. I trembled whenever a letter came from you, lest it should contain some stab for me. I dreaded your visits almost as much as I longed for them. I was your plaything, not your companion. [*She rises, exclaiming*] Oh, there was such suffering in my happiness that I hardly knew joy from pain. [*She sinks on the piano stool, and adds, as she buries her face in her hands and turns away from him*] Better for me if I had never met you!

CHARTERIS [*rising indignantly*] You ungenerous wretch! Is this your gratitude for the way I have just been flattering you? What have I not endured from you? endured with angelic patience? Did I not find out, before our friendship was a fortnight old, that all your advanced views were merely a fashion picked up and followed like any other fashion, without understanding or meaning a word of them? Did you not, in spite of your care for your own liberty, set up claims on me compared to which the claims of the most jealous wife would have been trifles? Have I a single woman friend whom you have not abused as old, ugly, vicious—

JULIA [*quickly looking up*] So they are.

CHARTERIS. Well, then, I'll come to grievances that even you can understand. I accuse you of habitual and intolerable jealousy and ill temper; of insulting me on imaginary provocation; of positively beating me; of stealing letters of mine—

JULIA. Yes, nice letters!

CHARTERIS. —of breaking your solemn promises not to do it again; of spending hours—aye, days! piecing together the contents of my waste paper basket in your search for more letters; and then representing yourself as an ill used saint and martyr wantonly betrayed and deserted by a selfish monster of a man.

JULIA [*rising*] I was justified in reading your letters. Our perfect confidence in one another gave me the right to do it.

CHARTERIS. Thank you. Then I hasten to break off a confidence which gives such rights. [*He sits down sulkily on the sofa*].

JULIA [*bending over him threateningly*] You have no right to break it off.

CHARTERIS. I have. You refused to marry me because—

JULIA. I did not. You never asked me. If we were married, you would never dare treat me as you are doing now.

CHARTERIS [*laboriously going back to his argument*] It was understood between us as people of advanced views that we were not to marry; because, as the law stands, I might have become a drunkard, a—

JULIA. —a criminal, an imbecile or a horror. You said that before. [*She sits down beside him with a fling*].

CHARTERIS [*politely*] I beg your pardon, my dear. I know I have a habit of repeating myself. The point is that you reserved your freedom to give me up when you pleased.

JULIA. Well, what of that? I do not please to give you up; and I will not. You have not become a drunkard or a criminal.

CHARTERIS. You dont see the point yet, Julia. You

[149]

seem to forget that in reserving your freedom to leave me in case I should turn out badly, you also reserved my freedom to leave you in case you should turn out badly.

JULIA. Very ingenious. And pray, have *I* become a drunkard, or a criminal, or an imbecile?

CHARTERIS. You have become what is infinitely worse than all three together: a jealous termagant.

JULIA [*shaking her head bitterly*] Yes: abuse me: call me names.

CHARTERIS. I now assert the right I reserved: the right of breaking with you when I please. Advanced views, Julia, involve advanced duties: you cannot be an advanced woman when you want to bring a man to your feet, and a conventional woman when you want to hold him there against his will. Advanced people form charming friendships: conventional people marry. Marriage suits a good many people; and its first duty is fidelity. Friendship suits some people; and its first duty is unhesitating uncomplaining acceptance of a notice of change of feeling from either side. You chose friendship instead of marriage. Now do your duty, and accept your notice.

JULIA. Never. We are engaged in the eye of—the eye of—

CHARTERIS. Yes, Julia? Cant you get it out? In the eye of something that advanced women dont believe in, eh?

JULIA [*throwing herself at his feet*] Oh, Leonard, dont be cruel. I'm too miserable to argue—to think. I only know I love you. You reproach me with not wanting to marry you. I would have married you at any time after I came to love you, if you had asked me. I will marry you now if you will.

CHARTERIS. I wont, my dear. Thats flat. We're intellectually incompatible.

JULIA. But why? We could be so happy. You love me: I know you love me. I feel it. You say "My dear" to me: you have said it several times this evening. I know I have been wicked, odious, bad: I say nothing in defence of myself. But dont be hard on me. I was distracted by the thought of losing you. I cant face life without you, Leonard. I was happy when I met you: I had never loved any one; and if you had only let me alone, I could have gone on contentedly by myself. But I cant now. I must have you with me. Dont cast me off without a thought of all I have at stake. I could be a friend to you if you would only let me; if you would only tell me your plans; give me a share in your work; treat me as something more than the amusement of an idle hour. Oh, Leonard, Leonard, youve never given me a chance: indeed you havnt. I'll take pains; I'll read; I'll try to think; I'll conquer my jealousy I'll—[*she breaks down, rocking her head desperately on his knees and writhing*]. Oh, I'm mad: I'm mad: youll kill me if you desert me.

CHARTERIS [*petting her*] My dear love, dont cry: dont go on in this way. You know I cant help it.

JULIA [*sobbing as he rises and tenderly lifts her with him*] Oh, you can, you can. One word from you will make us happy for ever.

CHARTERIS [*diplomatically*] Come, my dear: we really must go. We cant stay until Cuthbertson comes. [*He releases her gently, and takes her mantle from the table*]. Here is your mantle: put it on and be good. You have given me a terrible evening: you must have some consideration for me.

JULIA [*dangerous again*] Then I am to be cast off?

CHARTERIS [*coaxingly*] You are to put on your bonnet, dearest. [*He puts the mantle on her shoulders*].

JULIA [*with a bitter half laugh, half sob*] Well, I suppose I must do what I am told. [*She goes to the table, and looks for her toque. She sees the yellow backed French novel*]. Ah, look at that [*holding it out to him*]! Look at what the creature reads! filthy, vile French stuff that no decent woman would touch. And you—you have been reading it with her.

CHARTERIS. You recommended that book to me yourself.

JULIA. Faugh! [*She dashes it on the floor*].

CHARTERIS [*running anxiously to the book*] Dont damage property, Julia. [*He picks it up and dusts it*]. Making scenes is an affair of sentiment: damaging property is serious. [*He replaces it on the table*]. And now do pray come along.

JULIA [*implacably*] You can go: there is nothing to prevent you. I will not stir. [*She sits down stubbornly on the sofa*].

CHARTERIS [*losing patience*] Oh come! I am not going to begin all this over again. There are limits even to my forbearance. Come on.

JULIA. I will not, I tell you.

CHARTERIS. Then goodnight. [*He makes resolutely for the door. With a rush, she gets there before him and bars his way*]. I thought you wanted me to go.

JULIA [*at the door*] You shall not leave me here alone.

CHARTERIS. Then come with me.

JULIA. Not until you have sworn to me to give up that woman.

CHARTERIS. My dear: I will swear anything if youll only come away and put an end to this.

JULIA [*perplexed, doubting him*] You will swear?

CHARTERIS. Solemnly. Propose the oath. I have been on the point of swearing for the last half hour.

JULIA [*despairingly*] You are only making fun of me. I want no oaths. I want your promise: your sacred word of honor.

CHARTERIS. Certainly: anything you demand, on condition that you come away immediately. On my sacred word of honor as a gentleman—as an Englishman—as anything you like—I will never see her again, never speak to her, never think of her. Now come.

JULIA. But are you in earnest? Will you keep your word?

CHARTERIS [*smiling subtly*] Now you are getting unreasonable. Do come along without any more nonsense. At any rate, I am going. I am not strong enough to carry you home; but I am strong enough to make my way through that door in spite of you. You will then have a new grievance against me for my brutal violence. [*He takes a step towards the door*].

JULIA [*solemnly*] If you do, I swear I will throw myself from that window, Leonard, as you pass out.

CHARTERIS [*unimpressed*] That window is at the back of the building. I shall pass out at the front; so you will not hurt me. Goodnight. [*He approaches the door*].

JULIA. Leonard: have you no pity?

CHARTERIS. Not the least. When you condescend to these antics you force me to despise you. How can a woman who behaves like a spoiled child and talks like a sentimental novel have the audacity to dream of being a companion for a man of any sort of sense or character? [*She gives an inarticulate cry, and throws herself sobbing on his breast*]. Come! dont cry, my dear Julia: you dont look half so beautiful as when youre happy; and it makes me all damp. Come along.

JULIA [*affectionately*] I'll come, dear, if you wish it. Give me one kiss.

CHARTERIS [*exasperated*] This is too much. No: I'm dashed if I will. Here: let me go, Julia. [*She clings to him*]. Will you come without another word if I give you a kiss?

JULIA. I will do anything you wish, darling.

CHARTERIS. Well, here. [*He takes her in his arms and gives her an unceremonious kiss*]. Now remember your promise. Come along.

JULIA. That was not a nice kiss, dearest. I want one of our old real kisses.

CHARTERIS [*furious*] Oh, go to the deuce. [*He disengages himself impulsively; and she, as if he had flung her down, falls pathetically with a stifled moan. With an angry look at her, he strides out and slams the door. She raises herself on one hand, listening to his retreating footsteps. They stop. Her face lights with eager triumphant cunning. The steps return hastily. She throws herself down again as before. Charteris reappears, in the utmost dismay, exclaiming*] Julia: we're done. Cuthbertson's coming upstairs with your father [*she sits up quickly*] Do you hear? the two fathers!

JULIA [*sitting on the floor*] Impossible. They dont know one another.

CHARTERIS [*desperately*] I tell you theyre coming up together like twins. What on earth are we to do?

JULIA [*scrambling up with the help of his hand*] Quick: the lift: we can go down in that. [*She rushes to the table for her toque*].

CHARTERIS. No: the man's gone home; and the lift's locked.

JULIA [*putting on her toque at express speed*] Lets go up to the next floor.

CHARTERIS. Theres no next floor. We're at the top

of the house. No, no: you must invent some thumping lie. I cant think of one: you can, Julia. Exercise all your genius. I'll back you up.

JULIA. But—

CHARTERIS. Sh-sh! Here they are. Sit down and look at home. [*Julia tears off her toque and mantle; throws them on the table; and darts to the piano, at which she seats herself*].

JULIA. Come and sing.

She plays the symphony to When Other Lips. *Charteris stands at the piano, as if about to sing. Two elderly gentlemen enter. Julia stops playing.*

The elder of the two newcomers, Colonel Daniel Craven, affects the bluff simple veteran, and carries it off pleasantly and well, having a fine upright figure, and being, in fact, a goodnaturedly impulsive credulous person who, after an entirely thoughtless career as an officer and a gentleman, is now being startled into some sort of self-education by the surprising proceedings of his children.

His companion, Mr Joseph Cuthbertson, Grace's father, has none of the Colonel's boyishness. He is a man of fervent idealistic sentiment, so frequently outraged by the facts of life that he has acquired an habitually indignant manner, which unexpectedly becomes enthusiastic or affectionate when he speaks.

The two men differ greatly in expression. The Colonel's face is lined with weather, with age, with eating and drinking, and with the cumulative effect of many petty vexations, but not with thought: he is still fresh, still full of expectations of pleasure and novelty. Cuthbertson has the lines of sedentary London brain work, with its chronic fatigue and longing for rest and recreative emotion, and its disillusioned indifference to adventure and enjoyment, except as a means of recuperation. His

*vigilant, irascible, eye, piled-up hair, and the honorable
seriousness with which he takes himself, give him an air
of considerable consequence.*

*They are both in evening dress. Cuthberton has not
taken off his fur-collared overcoat.*

CUTHBERTSON [*with a hospitable show of delight at
finding visitors*] Dont stop, Miss Craven. Go on,
Charteris.

*He comes behind the sofa, and hangs his overcoat on it,
after taking an opera glass and a theatre program from
the pockets, and putting them down on the piano.
Craven meanwhile goes to the fireplace, and plants
himself on the hearthrug.*

CHARTERIS. No, thank you. Miss Craven has just
been taking me through an old song; and Ive had
enough of it. [*He takes the song off the piano desk
and lays it aside; then closes the lid over the keyboard.*]

JULIA [*passing between the sofa and piano to shake
hands with Cuthbertson*] Why, youve brought Daddy!
What a surprise! [*Looking across to Craven*] So glad
youve come, Dad. [*She takes a chair near the window,
and sits there*].

CUTHBERTSON. Craven: let me introduce you to
Mr Leonard Charteris, the famous Ibsenist philosopher.

CRAVEN. Oh, we know one another already. Charteris
is quite at home in our house, Jo.

CUTHBERTSON. I beg both your pardons. He's quite
at home here too. [*Charteris sits down on the piano
stool*]. By the bye, wheres Grace?

JULIA AND CHARTERIS. Er—[*They stop and look
at one another*].

JULIA [*politely*] I beg your pardon, Mr Charteris:
I interrupted you.

CHARTERIS. Not at all, Miss Craven. [*An awkward pause*].

CUTHBERTSON [*to help them out*] You were going to tell us about Grace, Charteris.

CHARTERIS. I was only going to say that I didnt know that you and Craven were acquainted.

CRAVEN. Why, *I* didnt know it until tonight. It's a most extraordinary thing. We met by chance at the theatre; and he turns out to be my oldest friend.

CUTHBERTSON [*energetically*] Yes, Craven; and do you see how this proves what I was saying to you about the break-up of family life? Here are all our young people bosom friends, inseparables; and yet they never said a word of it to us. We two, who knew each other before they were born, might never have met again if you hadnt popped into the stall next mine tonight by pure chance. Come: sit down [*bustling over to him affectionately, and pushing him into the armchair above the fire*]: theres your place, by my fireside, whenever you choose to fill it. [*He posts himself at the end of the sofa, leaning against it and admiring Craven*]. Just imagine you being Dan Craven!

CRAVEN. Just imagine you being Jo Cuthbertson, though! Thats a far more extraordinary coincidence; because I'd got it into my head that your name was Tranfield.

CUTHBERTSON. Oh, thats my daughter's name. She's a widow, you know. How uncommonly well you look, Dan! The years havnt hurt you much.

CRAVEN [*suddenly becoming unnaturally gloomy*] I look well. I even feel well. But my days are numbered.

CUTHBERTSON [*alarmed*] Oh, dont say that, my dear fellow. I hope not.

JULIA [*with anguish in her voice*] Daddy! [*Cuthbertson looks inquiringly round at her*].

CRAVEN. There, there, my dear: I was wrong to talk of it. It's a sad subject. But it's better that Cuthbertson should know. We used to be very close friends, and are so still, I hope. [*Cuthbertson goes to Craven and presses his hand silently; then returns to the sofa and sits down, pulling out his handkerchief, and displaying some emotion*].

CHARTERIS [*a little impatiently*] The fact is, Cuthbertson, Craven's a devout believer in the department of witchcraft called medical science. He's celebrated in all the medical schools as an example of the newest sort of liver complaint. The doctors say he cant last another year; and he has fully made up his mind not to survive next Easter, just to oblige them.

CRAVEN [*with military affectation*] It's very kind of you to try to keep up my spirits by making light of it, Charteris. But I shall be ready when my time comes. I'm a soldier. [*A sob from Julia*]. Dont cry, Julia.

CUTHBERTSON [*huskily*] I hope you may long be spared, Dan.

CRAVEN. To oblige me, Jo, change the subject. [*He gets up, and again posts himself on the hearthrug with his back to the fire*].

CHARTERIS. Persuade him to join our club, Cuthbertson. He mopes.

JULIA. It's no use. Sylvia and I are always at him to join; but he wont.

CRAVEN. My child: I have my own club.

CHARTERIS [*contemptuously*] Yes: the Junior Army and Navy! Do you call that a club? Why, they darent let a woman cross the doorstep!

CRAVEN [*a little ruffled*] Clubs are a matter of taste, Charteris. You like a cock-and-hen club: I dont. It's bad enough to have Julia and her sister—a girl under twenty!—spending half their time at such a place. Besides, now really, such a name for a club! The Ibsen club! I should be laughed out of London. The Ibsen club! Come, Cuthbertson! back me up. I'm sure you agree with me.

CHARTERIS. Cuthbertson's a member.

CRAVEN [*amazed*] No! Why he's been talking to me all the evening about the way in which everything is going to the dogs through advanced ideas in the younger generation.

CHARTERIS. Of course. He's been studying it in the club. He's always there.

CUTHBERTSON [*warmly*] Not always. Dont exaggerate, Charteris. You know very well that though I joined the club on Grace's account, thinking that her father's presence there would be a protection and a—a sort of sanction, as it were, I never approved of it.

CRAVEN [*tactlessly harping on Cuthbertson's inconsistency*] Well, you know, this is unexpected: now it's really very unexpected. I should never have thought it from hearing you talk, Jo. Why, you said the whole modern movement was abhorrent to you because your life had been passed in witnessing scenes of suffering nobly endured and sacrifice willingly rendered by womanly women and manly men and deuce knows what else. Is it at the Ibsen club that you see all this manliness and womanliness?

CHARTERIS. Certainly not: the rules of the club forbid anything of the sort. Every candidate for membership must be nominated by a man and a woman, who both guarantee that the candidate, if female, is not womanly, and if male, not manly.

CRAVEN [*chuckling cunningly as he stoops to press his heated trousers against his legs, which are chilly*] Wont do, Charteris. Cant take me in with so thin a story as that.

CUTHBERTSON [*vehemently*] It's true. It's monstrous; but it's true.

CRAVEN [*with rising indignation, as he begins to draw the inevitable inferences*] Do you mean to say that somebody had the audacity to guarantee that my Julia is not a womanly woman?

CHARTERIS [*darkly*] It sounds incredible; but a man was found ready to take that inconceivable lie on his conscience.

JULIA [*firing up*] If he has nothing worse than that on his conscience, he may sleep pretty well. In what way am I more womanly than any of the rest of them, I should like to know? They are always saying things like that behind my back: I hear of them from Sylvia. Only the other day a member of the committee said I ought never to have been elected—that you [*to Charteris*] had smuggled me in. I should like to see her say it to my face: thats all.

CRAVEN. But, my precious, I most sincerely hope she was right. She paid you the highest compliment. Why, the place must be a den of infamy.

CUTHBERTSON [*emphatically*] So it is, Craven: so it is.

CHARTERIS. Exactly. Thats what keeps it so select: nobody but people whose reputations are above suspicion dare belong to it. If we once got a good name, we should become a mere whitewashing shop for all the shady characters in London. Better join us, Craven. Let me put you up.

CRAVEN. What! Join a club where theres some scoundrel who guaranteed my daughter to be an unwomanly woman! If I werent an invalid, I'd kick him.

CHARTERIS. Oh dont say that. It was I.

CRAVEN [*reproachfully*] You! Now upon my soul, Charteris, this is very vexing. Now how could you bring yourself to do such a thing?

CHARTERIS. She made me. Why, I had to guarantee Cuthbertson as unmanly; and he's the leading representative of manly sentiment in London.

CRAVEN. That didnt do Jo any harm; but it took away my Julia's character.

JULIA [*outraged*] Daddy!

CHARTERIS. Not at the Ibsen club: quite the contrary. After all, what can we do? You know what breaks up most clubs for men and women. Theres a quarrel—a scandal—cherchez la femme—always a woman at the bottom of it. Well, we knew this when we founded the club; but we noticed that the woman at the bottom of it was always a womanly woman. The unwomanly women who work for their living, and know how to take care of themselves, never give any trouble. So we simply said we wouldnt have any womanly women; and when one gets smuggled in she has to take care not to behave in a womanly way. We get on all right. [*He rises*]. Come to lunch with me there tomorrow and see the place.

CUTHBERTSON [*rising*] No: he's engaged to me. But you can join us.

CHARTERIS. What hour?

CUTHBERTSON. Any time after twelve. [*To Craven*] It's at 90 Cork Street, at the other end of the Burlington Arcade.

CRAVEN [*making a note on his cuff*] 90, you say. After twelve. [*Suddenly relapsing into gloom*] By the bye, dont order anything special for me. I'm not allowed wine: only Apollinaris. No meat either: only a scrap of fish occasionally. I'm to have a short life, but not a merry one. [*Sighing*] Well, well! [*Bracing himself up*] Now, Julia: it's time for us to be off. [*Julia rises*].

CUTHBERTSON. But where on earth is Grace? I must go and look for her. [*He turns to the door*].

JULIA [*stopping him*] Oh pray dont disturb her, Mr Cuthbertson. She's so tired.

CUTHBERTSON. But just for a moment, to say goodnight. [*Julia and Charteris look at one another in dismay. Cuthbertson looks quickly at them, perceiving that something is wrong*].

CHARTERIS. We must make a clean breast of it, I see.

CUTHBERTSON. Of what?

CHARTERIS. The truth is, Cuthbertson, Mrs Tranfield, who is, as you know, the most thoughtful of women, took it into her head that I—well, that I particularly wanted to speak to Miss Craven alone. So she said she was tired, and went to bed.

CRAVEN [*scandalized*] Tut! tut!

CUTHBERTSON. Oho! is that it? Then it's all right: she never goes to bed as early as this. I'll fetch her in a moment. [*He goes out confidently, leaving Charteris aghast*].

JULIA. Now youve done it. [*She rushes to the round table, and snatches up her mantle and toque*]. I'm off. [*She makes for the door*].

CRAVEN [*horrified*] What are you doing, Julia? You cant go until youve said goodnight to Mrs Tranfield. It'd be horribly rude.

JULIA. You can stay if you like, Daddy: I cant. I'll wait for you in the hall. [*She hurries out*].

CRAVEN [*following her*] But what on earth am I to say? [*She disappears, shutting the door behind her in his face. He turns to Charteris, grumbling*]. Now really you know, Charteris, this is devilish awkward: upon my life it is. That was a most indelicate thing of you to say plump out before us all: that about you and Julia.

CHARTERIS. I'll explain it all tomorrow. Just at present we'd really better follow Julia's example and bolt. [*He starts for the door*].

CRAVEN [*intercepting him*] Stop! dont leave me like this: I shall look like a fool. Now I shall really take it in bad part if you run away, Charteris.

CHARTERIS. All right. I'll stay. [*He lifts himself on to the shoulder of the grand piano and sits there swinging his legs and contemplating Craven resignedly*].

CRAVEN [*pacing up and down*] I'm excessively vexed about Julia's conduct: I am indeed. She cant bear to be crossed in the slightest thing, poor child. I'll have to apologize for her, you know: her going away is a downright slap in the face for these people here. Cuthbertson may be offended already for all I know.

CHARTERIS. Oh, never mind about him. Mrs Tranfield bosses this establishment.

CRAVEN [*cunningly*] Ah, thats it, is it? He's just the sort of fellow that would have no control over his daughter. [*He goes back to his former place on the hearthrug with his back to the fire*]. By the bye, what the dickens did he mean by all that about passing his life amid—what was it?—"scenes of suffering nobly endured and sacrifice willingly rendered by womanly women and manly men" and a lot more of the same sort? I suppose he's something in a hospital.

CHARTERIS. Hospital! Nonsense! he's a dramatic critic. Didnt you hear me say he was the leading representative of manly sentiment in London?

CRAVEN. You dont say so! Now really, who'd have thought it! How jolly it must be to be able to go to the theatre for nothing! I must ask him to get me a few tickets occasionally. But isnt it ridiculous for a man to talk like that ? I'm hanged if he dont take what he sees on the stage quite seriously.

CHARTERIS. Of course: thats why he's a good critic. Besides, if you take people seriously off the stage, why shouldnt you take them seriously on it, where theyre under some sort of decent restraint ? [*He jumps down from the piano, and goes to the window*].

Cuthbertson comes back.

CUTHBERTSON [*to Craven, rather sheepishly*] The fact is, Grace has gone to bed. I must apologize to you and Miss— [*He turns to Julia's seat, and stops on seeing it vacant*].

CRAVEN [*embarrassed*] It is I who have to apologize for Julia, Jo. She—

CHARTERIS [*interrupting*] She said she was quite sure that if we didnt go, youd persuade Mrs Tranfield to get up to say goodnight for the sake of politeness; so she went straight off.

CUTHBERTSON. Very kind of her indeed. I'm really ashamed—

CRAVEN. Dont mention it, Jo: dont mention it. She's waiting for me below. [*Going*] Goodnight. Goodnight, Charteris.

CHARTERIS. Goodnight.

CUTHBERTSON [*seeing Craven out*] Goodnight. Say goodnight and thanks to Miss Craven for me. Tomorrow any time after twelve, remember. [*They go out*].

Charteris, with a long sigh, crosses to the fireplace, thoroughly tired out.

CRAVEN [*outside*] All right.

CUTHBERTSON [*outside*] Take care of the stairs: theyre rather steep. Goodnight. [*The outside door shuts*].

Cuthbertson returns. Instead of entering, he stands

[164]

impressively in the doorway with one hand in the breast of his waistcoat, eyeing Charteris sternly.

CHARTERIS. Whats the matter?

CUTHBERTSON [*sternly*] Charteris: what has been going on here? I insist on knowing. Grace has not gone to bed: I have seen and spoken with her. What is it all about?

CHARTERIS. Ask your theatrical experience, Cuthbertson. A man, of course.

CUTHBERTSON [*coming forward and confronting him*] Dont play the fool with me, Charteris: I'm too old a hand to be amused by it. I ask you, seriously, what is the matter?

CHARTERIS. I tell you, seriously, I'm the matter. Julia wants to marry me: I want to marry Grace. I came here tonight to sweetheart Grace. Enter Julia. Alarums and excursions. Exit Grace. Enter you and Craven. Subterfuges and excuses. Exeunt Craven and Julia. And here we are. Thats the whole story. Sleep over it. Goodnight. [*He leaves*].

CUTHBERTSON [*staring after him*] Well I'll be—

$\lceil$ ACT II $\rceil$

*Next day at noon, in the library of the Ibsen club. A
long room, with glass doors half-way down on both sides,
leading respectively to the dining room corridor and the
main staircase. At the end, in the middle, is the fireplace,
surmounted by a handsome mantelpiece, with a bust of
Ibsen, and decorative inscriptions of the titles of his
plays. There are circular recesses at each side of the
fireplace, with divan seats running round them, the space
above the divans lined with books. A long settee faces
the fire. Along the back of the settee, and touching it,
is a green table, littered with journals. Ibsen, looking
down the room, has the dining room door on his left,
and further on, nearly in the middle of the library, a
revolving bookcase, with an easy chair close to it. On
his right, between the door and the recess, is a light
library step-ladder. Further on, past the door an easy
chair, and a smaller one between it and the middle of the
room. Placards inscribed* SILENCE *are conspicuously
exhibited here and there.*

*Cuthbertson is seated in the easy chair at the revolving
bookstand, reading* The Daily Graphic. *Dr Paramore
is on the divan in the recess on Ibsen's right, reading* The
British Medical Journal. *He is young as age is counted
in the professions: barely forty. His hair is wearing bald
on his forehead; and his dark arched eyebrows, coming
rather close together, give him a conscientiously sinister
appearance. He wears the frock coat of the fashionable
physician, and cultivates the professional bedside manner
with scrupulous conventionality. Not at all a happy or*

frank man, but not consciously unhappy nor intentionally insincere, and highly self-satisfied intellectually.

Sylvia Craven is sitting in the middle of the settee before the fire, reading a volume of Ibsen, only the back of her head being visible from the middle of the room. She is a pretty girl of eighteen, small and trim, wearing a mountaineering suit of Norfolk jacket and breeches with neat town stockings and shoes. A detachable cloth skirt lies ready to her hand across the end of the settee.

A page boy's voice, monotonously calling for Dr Paramore, is heard approaching outside on the right.

THE PAGE [*outside*] Dr Paramore, Dr Paramore, Dr Paramore [*he enters, carrying a salver with a card on it*] Dr Par—

PARAMORE [*sharply, sitting up*] Here, boy. [*The boy presents the salver. Paramore takes the card and looks at it*]. All right: I'll come down to him. [*The boy goes. Paramore rises, and comes from the recess, throwing his paper on the table*]. Good morning, Mr Cuthbertson [*stopping to pull out his cuffs, and shake his coat straight*]. Mrs Tranfield quite well, I hope?

SYLVIA [*turning her head indignantly*] Sh—sh—sh!

Paramore turns, surprised. Cuthbertson rises energetically and looks across the bookstand to see who is the author of this impertinence.

PARAMORE [*to Sylvia, stiffly*] I beg your pardon, Miss Craven: I did not mean to disturb you.

SYLVIA [*flustered and self-assertive*] You may talk as much as you like if you will have the common consideration to ask first whether the other people object. What I protest against is your assumption that my presence doesnt matter because I'm only a female member. Thats all. Now go on, pray: you dont disturb me in the least. [*She turns to the fire, and again buries herself in Ibsen*].

CUTHBERTSON [*with emphatic dignity*] No gentleman would have dreamt of objecting to our exchanging a few words, madam. [*She takes no notice. He resumes angrily*] As a matter of fact I was about to say to Dr Paramore that if he would care to bring his visitor up here, *I* should not object. The impudence! [*He dashes his paper down on the chair*].

PARAMORE. Oh, many thanks; but it's only an instrument maker.

CUTHBERTSON. Any new medical discoveries doctor?

PARAMORE. Well, since you ask me, yes: perhaps a most important one. I have discovered something that has hitherto been overlooked: a minute duct in the liver of the guinea pig. Miss Craven will forgive my mentioning it when I say that it may throw an important light on her father's case. The first thing, of course, is to find out what the duct is there for.

CUTHBERTSON [*reverently, feeling that he is in the presence of Science*] Indeed? How will you do that?

PARAMORE. Oh, easily enough, by simply cutting the duct, and seeing what will happen to the guinea pig. [*Sylvia rises, horrified*]. I shall require a knife specially made to get at it. The man who is waiting for me downstairs has brought me a few handles to try before fitting it and sending it to the laboratory. I am afraid it would not do to bring such weapons up here.

SYLVIA. If you attempt such a thing, Dr Paramore, I will complain to the committee. A majority of the members are anti-vivisectionists. You ought to be ashamed of yourself. [*She snatches up the detachable skirt, and begins buttoning it on as she flounces out at the staircase door*].

PARAMORE [*with patient contempt*] Thats the sort of

thing we scientific men have to put up with nowadays, Mr Cuthbertson. Ignorance, superstition, sentimentality: they are all one. A guinea pig's convenience is set above the health and lives of the entire human race.

CUTHBERTSON [*vehemently*] It's not ignorance nor superstition, Paramore: it's sheer downright Ibsenism: thats what it is. Ive been wanting to sit comfortably at that fire the whole morning; but Ive never had a chance with that girl there. I couldnt go and plump myself down on a seat beside her: goodness knows what she'd think I wanted! Thats one of the delights of having women in the club: when they come in here they all want to sit at the fire and adore that bust. I sometimes feel that I should like to take the poker, and fetch it a wipe across the nose. Ugh!

PARAMORE. I must say I prefer the elder Miss Craven to her sister.

CUTHBERTSON [*his eyes lighting up*] Ah, Julia! I believe you. A splendid fine creature: every inch a woman. No Ibsenism about her!

PARAMORE. I quite agree with you there, Mr Cuthbertson. Er—by the way, do you think is Miss Craven attached to Charteris at all?

CUTHBERTSON. What! that fellow! Not he. He hangs about after her; but he's not man enough for her. A woman of that sort likes a strong, manly, deep throated, broad chested man.

PARAMORE [*anxiously*] Hm! a sort of sporting character, you think?

CUTHBERTSON. Oh, no, no. A scientific man, perhaps, like yourself. But you know what I mean: a MAN. [*He strikes himself a sounding blow on the chest*].

PARAMORE. Of course; but Charteris is a man.

CUTHBERTSON. Pah! you dont see what I mean.

[169]

The page boy returns with his salver.

THE PAGE [*calling monotonously as before*] Mr Cuthbertson, Mr Cuthbertson, Mr Cuth—

CUTHBERTSON. Here, boy. [*He takes the card from the salver*]. Bring the gentleman up here. [*The boy goes out*]. It's Craven. He's coming to lunch with me and Charteris. You might join us if youve nothing better to do, when youve finished with the instrument man. If Julia turns up I'll ask her too.

PARAMORE [*flushing with pleasure*] I shall be very pleased. Thank you. [*He is going out at the staircase door when Craven enters*]. Good morning, Colonel Craven.

CRAVEN [*at the door*] Good morning: glad to see you. I'm looking for Cuthbertson.

PARAMORE [*smiling*] There he is. [*He goes out*].

CUTHBERTSON [*greeting Craven effusively*] Delighted to see you. Now will you come to the smoking room; or will you sit down here, and have a chat while we're waiting for Charteris? If you like company, the smoking room's always full of women. Here in the library we shall have it pretty well all to ourselves until about three o'clock.

CRAVEN. I dont like to see women smoking. I'll make myself comfortable here. [*He sits in the easy chair on the staircase side*].

CUTHBERTSON [*taking the smaller chair on his left*] Neither do I. Theres not a room in this club where I can enjoy a pipe quietly without a woman coming in and beginning to roll a cigaret. It's a disgusting habit in a woman: it's not natural to her sex.

CRAVEN [*sighing*] Ah, Jo, times have changed since we both courted Molly Ebden all those years ago. I took my defeat well, old chap, didnt I?

CUTHBERTSON [*with earnest approval*] You did,

Dan. The thought of it has often helped me to behave well myself: it has, on my honor.

CRAVEN. Yes: you always believed in hearth and home, Jo: in a true English wife, and a happy wholesome fireside. How did Molly turn out?

CUTHBERTSON [*trying to be fair to Molly*] Well, not bad. She might have been worse. You see, I couldnt stand her relations: all the men were roaring cads; and she couldnt get on with my mother. And then she hated being in town; and of course I couldnt live in the country on account of my work. But we hit it off as well as most people until we separated.

CRAVEN [*taken aback*] Separated! [*He is irresistibly amused*]. Oh! that was the end of the hearth and home, Jo, was it?

CUTHBERTSON [*warmly*] It was not my fault, Dan. [*Sentimentally*] Some day the world will know how I loved that woman. But she was incapable of valuing a true man's affection. Do you know, she often said she wished she'd married you instead.

CRAVEN [*sobered by the suggestion*] Dear me! dear me! Well, perhaps it was better as it was. You heard about my marriage, I suppose.

CUTHBERTSON. Oh yes: we all heard of it.

CRAVEN. Well, Jo, I may as well make a clean breast of it: everybody knew it. *I* married for money.

CUTHBERTSON [*encouragingly*] And why not, Dan? Why not? We cant get on without it, you know.

CRAVEN [*with sincere feeling*] I got to be very fond of her, Jo. I had a home until she died. Now everything's changed. Julia's always here. Sylvia's of a different nature; but she's always here too.

CUTHBERTSON [*sympathetically*] I know. It's the same with Grace. She's always here.

CRAVEN. And now they want me to be always here.

Theyre at me every day to join the club. To stop my grumbling, I suppose. Thats what I want to consult you about. Do you think I ought to join?

CUTHBERTSON. Well, if you have no conscientious objection—

CRAVEN [*testily interrupting him*] I object to the existence of the place on principle; but whats the use of that? Here it is in spite of my objection; and I may as well have the benefit of any good that may be in it.

CUTHBERTSON [*soothing him*] Of course: thats the only reasonable view of the matter. Well, the fact is, it's not so inconvenient as you might think. When youre at home, you have the house more to yourself; and when you want to have your family about you, you can dine with them at the club.

CRAVEN [*not much attracted by this*] True.

CUTHBERTSON. Besides, if you dont want to dine with them, you neednt.

CRAVEN [*convinced*] True, very true. But dont they carry on here, rather?

CUTHBERTSON. Oh no: they dont exactly carry on. Of course the usual tone of the club is low, because the women smoke, and earn their own living, and all that; but still theres nothing actually to complain of. And it's convenient, certainly.

Charteris comes in, looking round for them.

CRAVEN [*rising*] Do you know, Ive a great mind to join, just to see what it's like.

CHARTERIS [*coming between them*] Do so by all means. I hope I havnt disturbed your chat by coming too soon.

CRAVEN. Not at all. [*He shakes his hand cordially*].

CHARTERIS. Thats right. I'm earlier than I intended. The fact is, I have something rather pressing to say to Cuthbertson.

CRAVEN. Private?

CHARTERIS. Not particularly. [*To Cuthbertson*] Only what we were speaking of last night.

CUTHBERTSON. Well, Charteris, I think that is private, or ought to be.

CRAVEN [*retiring discreetly towards the table*] I'll just take a look at The Times—

CHARTERIS [*stopping him*] Oh, it's no secret: everybody in the club guesses it. [*To Cuthbertson*] Has Grace never mentioned to you that she wants to marry me?

CUTHBERTSON [*indignantly*] She has mentioned that you want to marry her.

CHARTERIS. Ah; but then it's not what I want, but what Grace wants, that will weigh with you.

CRAVEN [*a little shocked*] Excuse me, Charteris: this is private. I'll leave you to yourselves [*again moving towards the table*].

CHARTERIS. Wait a bit, Craven: youre concerned in this. Julia wants to marry me too.

CRAVEN [*in a tone of the strongest remonstrance*] Now really! Now upon my life and soul!

CHARTERIS. It's a fact, I assure you. Didnt it strike you as rather odd, our being up there last night, and Mrs Tranfield not with us?

CRAVEN. Well, yes it did. But you explained it. And now really, Charteris, I must say your explanation was in shocking bad taste before Julia.

CHARTERIS. Never mind. It was a good, fat, healthy, bouncing lie.

CRAVEN AND CUTHBERTSON. Lie!

CHARTERIS. Didnt you suspect that?

CRAVEN. Certainly not. Did you, Jo?

CUTHBERTSON. Not at the moment.

CRAVEN. Whats more, I dont believe you. I'm sorry

to have to say such a thing; but you forget that Julia
was present, and didnt contradict you.

CHARTERIS. She didnt want to.

CRAVEN. Do you mean to say that my daughter
deceived me?

CHARTERIS. Delicacy towards me compelled her to,
Craven.

CRAVEN [*taking a very serious tone*] Now look here,
Charteris: have you any proper sense of the fact
that youre standing between two fathers?

CUTHBERTSON. Quite right, Dan, quite right. I
repeat the question on my own account.

CHARTERIS. Well, I'm a little dazed still by standing
for so long between two daughters; but I think I
grasp the situation. [*Cuthbertson flings away with an
exclamation of disgust*].

CRAVEN. Then I'm sorry for your manners, Charteris:
thats all. [*He turns away sulkily; then suddenly flares
up and comes back at Charteris*]. How dare you tell me
my daughter wants to marry you? Who are you,
pray, that she should have any such ambition?

CHARTERIS. Just so: you're quite right: she couldnt
have made a worse choice. But she wont listen to
reason. I assure you, my dear Craven, Ive said everything that fifty fathers could have said; but it's no
use: she wont give me up. And if she wont listen to
me, what likelihood is there of her listening to you?

CRAVEN [*in angry bewilderment*] Cuthbertson: did
you ever hear anything like this?

CUTHBERTSON. Never! Never!

CHARTERIS. Oh, bother! Come! dont behave like a
couple of conventional old fathers: this is a serious
affair. Look at these letters [*producing a letter and a
letter-card*]! This [*shewing the card*] is from Grace—
by the way, Cuthbertson, I wish youd ask her not

to write on letter-cards: the blue color makes it so easy for Julia to pick the bits out of my waste paper basket and piece them together. Now listen. "My dear Leonard: Nothing could make it worth my while to be exposed to such scenes as last night's. You had much better go back to Julia, and forget me. Yours sincerely, Grace Tranfield."

CUTHBERTSON. I approve of every word of that letter.

CHARTERIS [*turning to Craven and preparing to read the letter*] Now for Julia. [*The Colonel turns away to hide his face from Charteris, anticipating a shock, and puts his hand on a chair to steady himself*]. "My dearest boy: Nothing will make me believe that this odious woman can take my place in your heart. I send some of the letters you wrote me when we first met; and I ask you to read them. They will recall what you felt when you wrote them. You cannot have changed so much as to be indifferent to me: whoever may have struck your fancy for the moment, your heart is still mine"—and so on: you know the sort of thing— "Ever and always your loving Julia." [*The Colonel sinks on the chair, and covers his face with his hand*]. You dont suppose she's serious, do you? thats the sort of thing she writes me three times a day. [*To Cuthbertson*] Grace is in earnest though, confound it. [*He holds out Grace's letter*]. A blue card as usual! This time I shall not trust the waste paper basket. [*He goes to the fire, and throws the letters into it*].

CUTHBERTSON [*facing him with folded arms as he comes back to them*] May I ask, Mr Charteris, is this the New Humor?

CHARTERIS [*still too preoccupied with his own affairs to have any sense of the effect he is producing on the others*] Oh, stuff! Do you suppose it's a joke to be situated as I am? Youve got your head so stuffed with the New Humor and the New Woman and the New This, That, and The Other, all mixed up with your own old Adam, that youve lost your senses.

CUTHBERTSON [*strenuously*] Do you see that old man, grown grey in the honored service of his country, whose last days you have blighted?

CHARTERIS [*surprised, looking at Craven and realizing his distress with genuine concern*] I'm very sorry. Come, Craven: dont take it to heart. [*Craven shakes his head*]. I assure you it means nothing: it happens to me constantly.

CUTHBERTSON. There is only one excuse for you. You are not fully responsible for your actions. Like all advanced people, you have got neurasthenia.

CHARTERIS [*appalled*] Great Heavens! whats that?

CUTHBERTSON. I decline to explain. You know as well as I do. I'm going downstairs now to order lunch. I shall order it for three; but the third place is for Paramore, whom I have invited, not for you. [*He goes out through the dining room door*].

CHARTERIS [*putting his hand on Craven's shoulder*] Come, Craven: advise me. Youve been in this sort of fix yourself probably.

CRAVEN. Charteris: no woman writes such a letter to a man unless he has made advances to her.

CHARTERIS [*mournfully*] How little you know the world, Colonel! The New Woman is not like that.

CRAVEN. I can only give you very oldfashioned advice, my boy; and that is that it's well to be off with the Old Woman before youre on with the New. I'm sorry you told me. You might have waited for my death: it's not far off now. [*His head droops again*].

Julia and Paramore come in from the staircase. Julia stops as she catches sight of Charteris, her face clouding, and her breast heaving. Paramore, seeing the Colonel apparently ill, hurries down to him with his bedside manner in full play.

CHARTERIS [*seeing Julia*] Oh, Lord! [*He retreats under the lee of the revolving bookstand.*]

PARAMORE [*sympathetically to the Colonel, taking his wrist, and beginning to count his pulse*] Allow me.

CRAVEN [*looking up*] Eh? [*He withdraws his hand and rises rather crossly*]. No, Paramore: it's not my liver now: it's private business.

A chase begins between Julia and Charteris, all the more exciting to them because the huntress and her prey alike must conceal the real object of their movements from the others. Charteris first makes for the staircase door. Julia immediately retreats to it, barring his path. He doubles back round the bookstand, setting it whirling as he makes for the other door, Julia crossing in pursuit of him. He is about to escape when he is cut off by the return of Cuthbertson. Turning back, he sees Julia close upon him. There being nothing else for it, he bolts into the recess on Ibsen's left.

CUTHBERTSON. Good morning, Miss Craven. [*They shake hands*]. Wont you join us at lunch? Paramore's coming too.

JULIA. Thanks: I shall be very pleased. [*She strolls with affected purposelessness towards the recess, Charteris, almost trapped in it, crosses to the opposite recess by way of the fender, knocking down the fireirons with a crash as he does so*].

CRAVEN [*who has crossed to the whirling bookcase and stopped it*] What the dickens are you doing there, Charteris?

CHARTERIS. Nothing. It's such a confounded room to get about in.

JULIA [*maliciously*] Yes: isnt it? [*She is about to*

[177]

*move to guard the staircase door when Cuthbertson offers
her his arm*].

CUTHBERTSON. May I take you down?

JULIA. No, really: you know it's against the rules of
the club to coddle women in any way. Whoever is
nearest the door goes first.

CUTHBERTSON. Oh, well, if you insist. Come, gentlemen: let us go to lunch in the Ibsen fashion: the
unsexed fashion. [*He turns and goes out, followed by
Paramore, who raises his politest consulting-room laugh.
Craven goes last.*]

CRAVEN [*at the door, gravely*] Come, Julia.

JULIA [*with patronizing affection*] Yes, Daddy dear,
presently. Dont wait for me: I'll come in a moment.
[*The Colonel hesitates*]. It's all right, Daddy.

CRAVEN [*very gravely*] Dont be long, my dear. [*He
goes out*].

CHARTERIS. I'm off. [*He makes a dash for the staircase door*].

JULIA [*darting at him and seizing his wrists*] Arnt you
coming?

CHARTERIS. No. Unhand me, Julia. [*He tries to get
away: she holds him*]. If you dont let me go, I'll scream
for help.

JULIA [*reproachfully*] Leonard! [*He breaks away from
her*]. Oh, how can you be so rough with me, dear! Did
you get my letter?

CHARTERIS. Burnt it—

  *Julia turns away, struck to the heart, and buries her
face in her hands.*

CHARTERIS [*continuing*]—along with hers.

JULIA [*quickly turning again*] Hers! Has she written
to you?

CHARTERIS. Yes: to break off with me on your account!

JULIA [*her eyes gleaming*] Ah!

CHARTERIS. You are pleased. Wretch! Now you have lost the last scrap of my regard. [*He turns to go, but is stopped by the return of Sylvia. Julia turns away and stands pretending to read a paper which she picks up from the table*].

SYLVIA [*offhandedly*] Hallo Charteris! how are you getting on? [*She takes his arm familiarly, and walks down the room with him*]. Have you seen Grace Tranfield this morning? [*Julia drops the paper, and comes a step nearer to listen*]. You generally know where she's to be found.

CHARTERIS. I shall never know any more, Sylvia. She's quarrelled with me.

SYLVIA. Sylvia! How often am I to tell you that I am not Sylvia at the club?

CHARTERIS. I forgot. I beg your pardon, Craven, old chap [*slapping her on the shoulder*].

SYLVIA. Thats better. A little overdone, but better.

JULIA. Dont be a fool, Silly.

SYLVIA. Remember, Julia, if you please, that here we are members of the club, not sisters. I dont take liberties with you here on family grounds: dont you take any with me. [*She goes to the settee, and resumes her former place*].

CHARTERIS. Quite right, Craven. Down with the tyranny of the elder sister!

JULIA. You ought to know better than to encourage a child to make herself ridiculous, Leonard, even at my expense.

CHARTERIS [*seating himself on the edge of the table*] Your lunch will be cold, Julia.

Julia is about to retort furiously when she is checked by the reappearance of Cuthbertson at the dining room door.

CUTHBERTSON. What has become of you, Miss Craven? Your father is getting quite uneasy. We're all waiting for you.

JULIA. So I have just been reminded, thank you. [*She goes out angrily past him, Sylvia looking round to see*].

CUTHBERTSON [*looking first after her, then at Charteris*] More neurasthenia! [*He follows her*].

SYLVIA [*jumping up on her knees on the settee, and speaking over the back of it*] Whats up, Charteris? Julia been making love to you?

CHARTERIS [*speaking to her over his shoulder*] No. Jealous of Grace.

SYLVIA. Serve you right. You are an awful devil for philandering.

CHARTERIS [*calmly*] Do you consider it good club form to talk that way to a man who might nearly be your father?

SYLVIA [*knowingly*] Oh, I know you, my lad.

CHARTERIS. Then you know that I never pay any special attention to any woman.

SYLVIA [*thoughtfully*] Do you know, Leonard, I really believe you. I dont think you care a bit more for one woman than for another.

CHARTERIS. You mean I dont care a bit less for one woman than another.

SYLVIA. That makes it worse. But what I mean is that you never bother about their being only women: you talk to them just as you do to me or any other fellow. Thats the secret of your success. You cant think how sick they get of being treated with the respect due to their sex.

CHARTERIS. Ah, if Julia only had your wisdom, Craven! [*He gets off the table with a sigh, and perches himself reflectively on the step ladder*].

[180]

SYLVIA. She cant take things easy: can she, old man?
But dont you be afraid of breaking her heart: she gets
over her little tragedies. We found that out at home
when our great sorrow came.

CHARTERIS. What was that?

SYLVIA. I mean when we learned that poor papa had
Paramore's disease.

CHARTERIS. Paramore's disease! Why, whats the
matter with Paramore?

SYLVIA. Oh, not a disease that he suffers from, but
one that he discovered.

CHARTERIS. The liver business?

SYLVIA. Yes: thats what made Paramore's reputation,
you know. Papa used to get bad occasionally; but we
always thought that it was partly his Indian service,
and partly his eating and drinking too much. He
used to wolf down a lot in those days, did Dad. The
doctor never knew what was wrong with him until
Paramore discovered a dreadful little microbe in his
liver. There are forty millions of them to every square
inch of liver. Paramore discovered them first; and
now he declares that everybody should be inoculated
against them as well as vaccinated. But it was too late
to inoculate poor papa. All they could do was to pro-
long his life for two years more by putting him on a
strict diet. Poor old boy! they cut off his liquor; and
he's not allowed to eat meat.

CHARTERIS. Your father appears to me to be uncommonly well.

SYLVIA. Yes: you would think he was a great deal
better. But the microbe is at work, slowly but surely.
In another year it will be all over. Poor old Dad!
it's unfeeling to talk about him in this attitude: I
must sit down properly. [*She comes down from the
settee, and takes the chair near the bookstand*]. I should

like papa to live for ever just to take the conceit out of Paramore. I believe he's in love with Julia.

CHARTERIS [*starting up excitedly*] In love with Julia! A ray of hope on the horizon! Do you really mean it?

SYLVIA. I should think I do. Why do you suppose he's hanging about the club today in a beautiful new coat and tie instead of attending to his patients? That lunch with Julia will finish him. He'll ask Daddy's consent before they come back: I'll bet you three to one he will, in anything you please.

CHARTERIS. Gloves?

SYLVIA. No: cigarets.

CHARTERIS. Done! But what does she think about it? Does she give him any encouragement?

SYLVIA. Oh, the usual thing. Enough to keep any other woman from getting him.

CHARTERIS. Just so. I understand. Now listen to me: I am going to speak as a philosopher. Julia is jealous of everybody: everybody. If she saw you flirting with Paramore she'd begin to value him directly. You might play up a little, Craven, for my sake: eh?

SYLVIA [*rising*] Youre too awful, Leonard. For shame! However, anything to oblige a fellow Ibsenite. I'll bear your affair in mind. But I think it would be more effective if you got Grace to do it.

CHARTERIS. Think so? Hm! perhaps youre right.

THE PAGE [*outside as before*] Dr Paramore, Dr Paramore, Dr Paramore—

SYLVIA. They ought to get that boy's voice properly cultivated: it's a disgrace to the club. [*She goes into the recess on Ibsen's left*].

The page enters, carrying the British Medical Journal.

CHARTERIS [*calling to the page*] Dr Paramore is in the dining room.

THE PAGE. Thank you, sir. [*He is about to go into the dining room when Sylvia swoops on him*].

SYLVIA. Here: where are you taking that paper? It belongs to this room.

THE PAGE. It's Dr Paramore's particular orders, miss. The British Medical Journal has always to be brought to him dreckly it comes.

SYLVIA. What cheek! Charteris: oughtnt we to stop this on principle?

CHARTERIS. Certainly not. Principle's the poorest reason I know for making yourself nasty.

SYLVIA. Bosh! Ibsen!

CHARTERIS [*to the page*] Off with you, my boy: Dr Paramore's waiting breathless with expectation.

THE PAGE [*seriously*] Indeed, sir? [*He hurries off*].

CHARTERIS. That boy will make his way in this country. He has no sense of humor.

Grace comes in. Her dress, very convenient and businesslike, is made to please herself and serve her own purposes without the slightest regard to fashion, though by no means without a careful concern for her personal elegance. She enters briskly, like an habitually busy woman.

SYLVIA [*running to her*] Here you are at last, Tranfield, old girl. Ive been waiting for you this last hour. I'm starving.

GRACE. All right, dear. [*To Charteris*] Did you get my letter?

CHARTERIS. Yes. I wish you wouldnt write on those confounded blue letter-cards.

SYLVIA [*to Grace*] Shall I go down first, and secure a table?

CHARTERIS [*taking the reply out of Grace's mouth*] Do, old boy.

SYLVIA. Dont be too long. [*She goes into the dining room*].

GRACE. Well?

CHARTERIS. I'm afraid to face you after last night. Can you imagine a more horrible scene? Dont you hate the very sight of me after it?

GRACE. Oh no.

CHARTERIS. Then you ought to. Ugh! it was hideous: an insult: an outrage. A nice end to all my plans for making you happy: for making you an exception to all the women who swear I have made made them miserable!

GRACE [*sitting down placidly*] I am not at all miserable. I'm sorry; but I shant break my heart.

CHARTERIS. No: yours is a thoroughbred heart: you dont scream and cry every time it's pinched. Thats why you are the only possible woman for me.

GRACE [*shaking her head*] Not now. Never any more.

CHARTERIS. Never! What do you mean?

GRACE. What I say, Leonard.

CHARTERIS. Jilted again! The fickleness of the women I love is only equalled by the infernal constancy of the women who love me. Well, well! I see how it is, Grace: you cant forget that horrible scene last night. Imagine her saying I had kissed her within the last two days!

GRACE [*rising eagerly*] Was that not true?

CHARTERIS. True! No: a thumping lie.

GRACE. Oh, I'm so glad. That was the only thing that really hurt me.

CHARTERIS. Just why she said it. How adorable of you to care! My darling. [*He seizes her hands, and presses them to his breast*].

GRACE. Remember! it's all broken off.

CHARTERIS. Ah yes: you have my heart in your

hands. Break it. Throw my happiness out of the window.

GRACE. Oh, Leonard, does your happiness really depend on me?

CHARTERIS [*tenderly*] Absolutely. [*She beams with delight. A sudden revulsion comes to him at the sight: he recoils, dropping her hands and crying*] Ah no: why should I lie to you? [*He folds his arms and adds firmly*] My happiness depends on nobody but myself. I can do without you.

GRACE [*nerving herself*] So you shall. Thank you for the truth. Now *I* will tell you the truth.

CHARTERIS [*unfolding his arms in terror*] No, please. Dont. As a philosopher, it's my business to tell other people the truth; but it's not their business to tell it to me. I dont like it: it hurts.

GRACE [*quietly*] It's only that I love you.

CHARTERIS. Ah! thats not a philosophic truth. You may tell me that as often as you like. [*He takes her in his arms*].

GRACE. Yes, Leonard; but I'm an advanced woman. [*He checks himself, and looks at her in some consternation*]. I'm what my father calls the New Woman. [*He lets her go, and stares at her*]. I quite agree with all your ideas.

CHARTERIS [*scandalized*] Thats a nice thing for a respectable woman to say! You ought to be ashamed of yourself.

GRACE. I am quite in earnest about them too, though you are not. That is why I will never marry a man I love too much. It would give him a terrible advantage over me: I should be utterly in his power. Thats what the New Woman is like. Isnt she right, Mr Philosopher?

CHARTERIS. The struggle between the Philosopher

and the Man is fearful, Grace. But the Philosopher says you are right.

GRACE. I know I am right. And so we must part.

CHARTERIS. Not at all. You must marry some one else; and then I'll come and philander with you.

Sylvia comes back.

SYLVIA [*holding the door open*] Oh, I say: come along. I'm starving.

CHARTERIS. So am I. I'll lunch with you if I may.

SYLVIA. I thought you would. Ive ordered soup for three. [*Grace passes out. Sylvia continues, to Charteris*] You can watch Paramore from our table: he's pretending to read the British Medical Journal; but he must be making up his mind for the plunge: he looks green with nervousness. [*She goes out*].

CHARTERIS. Good luck to him! [*He follows her*].

The library remains unoccupied for ten minutes.

Then Julia, angry and miserable, comes in from the dining room, followed by Craven. She crosses the room tormentedly, and throws herself into a chair.

CRAVEN [*impatiently*] What is the matter? Has every one gone mad today? What do you mean by suddenly getting up from the table and tearing away like that? What does Paramore mean by reading his paper, and not answering when he's spoken to? [*Julia writhes impatiently*]. Come, come [*tenderly*]: wont my pet tell her own Daddy what—[*irritably*] what the devil is wrong with everybody. Do pull yourself together, Julia, before Cuthbertson comes. He's only paying the bill: he'll be here in a moment.

JULIA. I couldnt bear it any longer. Oh, to see them sitting there at lunch together, laughing, chatting, making game of me! I should have screamed out in another moment. I should have taken a knife and killed her. I should have—

Cuthbertson appears, stuffing the luncheon bill into his waistcoat pocket as he comes to them. He begins speaking the moment he enters.

CUTHBERTSON. I'm afraid youve had a very poor lunch, Dan. It's disheartening to see you picking at a few beans, and drinking soda water. I wonder how you live!

JULIA. Thats all he ever takes, Mr Cuthbertson, I assure you. He hates to be bothered about it.

CRAVEN. Wheres Paramore?

CUTHBERTSON. Reading his paper. I asked him wasnt he coming; but he didnt hear me. It's amazing how anything scientific absorbs him. Clever man! Monstrously clever man!

CRAVEN [*pettishly*] Oh yes, thats all very well, Jo; but it's not good manners at table: he should shut up the shop sometimes. Heaven knows I am only too anxious to forget his science, since it has pronounced my doom. [*He sits down with a melancholy air*].

CUTHBERTSON [*compassionately*] You mustnt think about that, Craven: perhaps he was mistaken. [*He sighs deeply and sits down*]. But he certainly is a very clever fellow. He thinks twice before he commits himself.

They sit in silence, full of gloom. Suddenly Paramore enters, pale and in the utmost disorder, with The British Medical Journal in his clenched hand. They rise in alarm. He tries to speak, but chokes, clutches at his throat, and staggers. Cuthbertson quickly takes his chair and places it behind Paramore, who sinks into it as they crowd about him, Craven at his right shoulder, Cuthbertson on his left, and Julia behind.

CRAVEN. Whats the matter, Paramore?

JULIA. Are you ill?

CUTHBERTSON. No bad news, I hope?

PARAMORE [*despairingly*] The worst of news! Terrible news! Fatal news! My disease—

CRAVEN [*quickly*] Do you mean my disease?

PARAMORE [*fiercely*] I mean my disease: Paramore's disease: the disease I discovered: the work of my life! Look here [*he points to the journal with a ghastly expression of horror*]! If this is true, it was all a mistake: there is no such disease.

Cuthbertson and Julia look at one another, hardly daring to believe the good news.

CRAVEN [*in strong remonstrance*] And you call this bad news! Now really, Paramore—

PARAMORE [*cutting him short hoarsely*] It's natural for you to think only of yourself. I dont blame you: all invalids are selfish. Only a scientific man can feel what I feel now. [*Writhing under a sense of intolerable injustice*] It's the fault of the wickedly sentimental laws of this country. I was not able to make experiments enough: only three dogs and a monkey. Think of that, with all Europe full of my professional rivals! men burning to prove me wrong! There is freedom in France: enlightened republican France! One Frenchman experiments on two hundred monkeys to disprove my theory. Another sacrifices £36— three hundred dogs at three francs apiece—to upset the monkey experiments. A third proves them both wrong by a single experiment in which he gets the temperature of a camel's liver sixty degrees below zero. And now comes this cursed Italian who has ruined me. He has a government grant to buy animals with, besides having the run of the largest hospital in Italy. [*With desperate resolution*] But I wont be beaten by any Italian. I'll go to Italy myself. I'll rediscover my disease: I know it exists; I feel it; and I'll prove it if I have to experiment on every mortal animal thats got a liver at all. [*He folds his arms and breathes hard at them*].

CRAVEN [*his sense of injury growing on him*] Am I to understand, Paramore, that you took it on yourself to pass sentence of death on me: yes, of Death! on the strength of three dogs and an infernal monkey?

PARAMORE [*utterly contemptuous of Craven's narrow personal view of the matter*] Yes. That was all I could get a license for.

CRAVEN. Now upon my soul, Paramore, I'm vexed at this. I dont wish to be unfriendly; but I'm extremely vexed, really. Why, confound it, do you realize what youve done? Youve cut off my meat and drink for a year! made me an object of public scorn! a miserable vegetarian and teetotaller.

PARAMORE [*rising*] Well, you can make up for lost time now. [*Bitterly, shewing Craven the Journal*] There! you can read for yourself. The camel was fed on beef dissolved in alcohol; and he gained half a ton on it. Eat and drink as much as you please. [*Still unable to stand without support, he makes his way past Cuthbertson, to the revolving bookcase, and stands there with his back to them, leaning on it with his head on his hands*].

CRAVEN [*grumbling*] Oh yes: it's very easy for you to talk, Paramore. But what am I to say to the Humanitarian societies and the Vegetarian societies that have made me Vice President?

CUTHBERTSON [*chuckling*] Aha! You made a virtue of it, did you, Dan?

CRAVEN [*warmly*] I made a virtue of necessity, Jo. No one can blame me.

JULIA [*soothing him*] Well, never mind, Daddy. Come back to the dining room, and have a good beefsteak.

CRAVEN [*shuddering*] Ugh! [*Plaintively*] No: Ive lost

my old manly taste for it. My very nature's been corrupted by living on pap. [*To Paramore*] Thats what comes of all this vivisection. You go experimenting on horses; and of course the result is that you try to get me into condition by feeding me on beans.

PARAMORE [*curtly, without changing his position*] Well, if theyve done you good, so much the better for you.

CRAVEN [*querulously*] Thats all very well; but it's very vexing. You dont half see how serious it is to make a man believe that he has only another year to live: you really dont, Paramore: I cant help saying it. Ive made my will, which was altogether unnecessary; and Ive been reconciled to a lot of people I'd quarrelled with: people I cant stand under ordinary circumstances. Then Ive let the girls get round me at home to an extent I should never have done if I'd had my life before me. Ive done a lot of serious thinking and reading and extra church going. And now it turns out simple waste of time. On my soul, it's too disgusting: I'd far rather die like a man when I said I would.

PARAMORE [*as before*] Perhaps you may. Your heart's shaky, if thats any satisfaction to you.

CRAVEN [*offended*] You must excuse me, Paramore, if I say that I no longer feel any confidence in your opinion as a medical man. [*Paramore's eye flashes: he straightens himself and listens*]. I paid you a pretty stiff fee for that consultation when you condemned me; and I cant say I think you gave me value for it.

PARAMORE [*turning and facing Craven with dignity*] Thats unanswerable, Colonel Craven. I shall return the fee.

CRAVEN. Oh, it's not the money; but I think you

[190]

ought to realize your position. [*Paramore turns stiffly away. Craven follows him impulsively, exclaiming remorsefully*] Well, perhaps it was a nasty thing of me to allude to it. [*He offers Paramore his hand*].

PARAMORE [*conscientiously taking it*] Not at all. You are quite in the right, Colonel Craven: my diagnosis was wrong; and I must take the consequences.

CRAVEN [*holding his hand*] No, dont say that. It was natural enough: my liver is enough to set any man's diagnosis wrong. [*A long handshake, very trying to Paramore's nerves. Paramore then retires to the recess on Ibsen's left, and throws himself on the divan with a half suppressed sob, bending over The British Medical Journal with his head on his hands and his elbows on his knees*].

CUTHBERTSON [*who has been rejoicing with Julia at the other side of the room*] Well, lets say no more about it. I congratulate you, Craven, and hope you may long be spared. [*Craven offers his hand*]. No, Dan: your daughter first. [*He takes Julia's hand gently and hands her across to Craven, into whose arms she flies with a gush of feeling*].

JULIA. Dear old Daddy!

CRAVEN. Ah, is Julia glad that the old Dad is let off for a few years more?

JULIA [*almost crying*] Oh, so glad! so glad!

Cuthbertson sobs audibly. The Colonel is affected. Sylvia, entering from the dining room, stops abruptly at the door on seeing the three. Paramore, in the recess, escapes her notice.

SYLVIA. Hallo!

CRAVEN. Tell her the news, Julia: it would sound ridiculous from me. [*He goes to the weeping Cuthbertson, and pats him consolingly on the shoulder*].

JULIA. Silly: only think! Dad's not ill at all. It was only

a mistake of Dr Paramore's. Oh, dear! [*She catches Craven's left hand and stoops to kiss it, his right hand being still on Cuthbertson's shoulder*].

SYLVIA [*contemptuously*] I knew it. Of course it was nothing but eating too much. I always said Paramore was an ass. [*Sensation. The group of Cuthbertson, Craven, and Julia breaks up as they turn in dismay*].

PARAMORE [*without malice*] Never mind, Miss Craven. That is what is being said all over Europe now. Never mind.

SYLVIA [*a little abashed*] I'm so sorry, Dr Paramore. You must excuse a daughter's feelings.

CRAVEN [*huffed*] It evidently doesnt make much difference to you, Sylvia.

SYLVIA. I'm not going to be sentimental over it, Dad, you may bet. [*Coming to Craven*] Besides, I knew it was nonsense all along. [*Petting him*] Poor dear old Dad! why should your days be numbered any more than any one's else's? [*He pats her cheek, mollified. Julia impatiently turns away from them*]. Come to the smoking room; and lets see what you can do after teetotalling for a year.

CRAVEN [*playfully*] Vulgar little girl! [*He pinches her ear*]. Shall we come, Jo! Youll be the better for a pick-me-up after all this emotion.

CUTHBERTSON. I'm not ashamed of it, Dan. It has done me good. [*He goes up to the table and shakes his fist at the bust over the mantelpiece*]. It would do you good too, if you had eyes and ears to take it in.

CRAVEN [*astonished*] Who?

SYLVIA. Why, good old Henrik, of course.

CRAVEN [*puzzled*] Henrik?

CUTHBERTSON [*impatiently*] Ibsen, man: Ibsen. [*He goes out by the staircase door, followed by Sylvia, who kisses her hand to the bust as she passes. Craven*

*stares blankly after her, and then at the bust. Giving
the problem up as insoluble, he shakes his head and
follows them. Near the door, he checks himself, and
comes back*].

CRAVEN [*softly*] By the way, Paramore?

PARAMORE [*rousing himself with an effort*] Yes?

CRAVEN. You werent in earnest that time about my
heart, were you?

PARAMORE. Oh, nothing, nothing. Theres a slight
murmur: mitral valves a little worn perhaps; but
theyll last your time if youre careful. Dont smoke
too much.

CRAVEN. What! More privations! Now really, Paramore, really—

PARAMORE [*rising distractedly*] Excuse me: I cant
pursue the subject. I—I—

JULIA. Dont worry him now, Daddy.

CRAVEN. Well, well: I wont. [*He comes to Paramore,
who is pacing restlessly up and down the middle of the
room*] Come, Paramore! I'm not selfish, believe me:
I can feel for your disappointment. But you must face
it like a man. And after all, now really, doesnt this
shew that theres a lot of rot about modern science?
Between ourselves, you know, it's horribly cruel: you
must admit that it's a deuced nasty thing to go
ripping up and crucifying camels and monkeys. It
must blunt all the finer feelings sooner or later.

PARAMORE [*turning on him*] How many camels and
horses and men were ripped up in that Soudan campaign where you won your Victoria Cross, Colonel
Craven?

CRAVEN [*firing up*] That was fair fighting: a very
different thing, Paramore.

PARAMORE. Yes: Martinis and machine guns against
naked spearmen.

CRAVEN [*hotly*] Naked spearmen can kill, Paramore. I risked my life: dont forget that.

PARAMORE [*with equal spirit*] And I have risked mine, as all doctors do, oftener than any soldier.

CRAVEN [*handsomely*] Thats true. I didnt think of that. I beg your pardon, Paramore: I'll never say another word against your profession. But I hope youll let me stick to the good oldfashioned shaking-up treatment for my liver: a clinking run across country with the hounds.

PARAMORE [*with bitter irony*] Isnt that rather cruel? a pack of dogs ripping up a fox?

JULIA [*coming coaxingly between them*] Oh please dont begin arguing again. Do go to the smoking room, Daddy: Mr Cuthbertson will wonder what has become of you.

CRAVEN. Very well, very well: I'll go. But youre really not reasonable today, Paramore, to talk that way of fair sport—

JULIA. Sh—sh [*coaxing him towards the door*].

CRAVEN. Well, well, I'm off. [*He goes goodhumoredly, pushed out by Julia*].

JULIA [*turning at the door with her utmost witchery of manner*] Dont look so disappointed, Dr Paramore. Cheer up. Youve been most kind to us; and youve done papa a lot of good.

PARAMORE [*delighted, rushing over to her*] How beautiful it is of you to say that to me, Miss Craven!

JULIA. I hate to see any one unhappy. I cant bear unhappiness. [*She runs out, casting a Parthian glance at him as she flies*].

Paramore stands enraptured, gazing after her through the glass door. Whilst he is thus absorbed, Charteris comes in from the dining room and touches him on the arm.

PARAMORE [*starting*] Eh? Whats the matter?

CHARTERIS [*significantly*] Charming woman, isnt she, Paramore? [*Looking admiringly at him*] How have you managed to fascinate her?

PARAMORE. I! Do you really mean—[*He looks at him; then recovers himself, and adds coldly*] Excuse me: this is a subject I do not care to jest about. [*He walks away from Charteris, and sits down in the nearest easy chair, reading his journal to intimate that he does not wish to pursue the conversation*].

CHARTERIS [*ignoring the hint, and coolly sitting down beside him*] Why dont you get married, Paramore? You know it's a scandalous thing for a man in your profession to be single.

PARAMORE [*shortly, still pretending to read*] Thats my own business: not yours.

CHARTERIS. Not at all: it's pre-eminently a social question. Youre going to get married, arnt you?

PARAMORE. Not that I am aware of.

CHARTERIS [*alarmed*] No! Dont say that. Why?

PARAMORE [*rising angrily and rapping one of the SILENCE placards*] Allow me to call your attention to that. [*He crosses the room to the easy chair near the revolving bookstand, and flings himself into it with determined hostility*].

CHARTERIS [*following him, too deeply concerned to mind the rebuff*] Paramore: you alarm me more than I can say. Youve muffed this business somehow. I fully expected to find you a joyful accepted suitor.

PARAMORE [*angrily*] Yes, you have been watching me because you admire Miss Craven yourself. Well, you may go in and win now. You will be pleased to hear that I am a ruined man.

CHARTERIS. You! Ruined! How? The turf?

PARAMORE [*contemptuously*] The turf!! Certainly not.

CHARTERIS. Paramore: if the loan of all I possess will help you over this difficulty, you have only to ask.

PARAMORE [*rising in surprise*] Charteris! I— [*Suspiciously*] Are you joking?

CHARTERIS. Why on earth do you always suspect me of joking? I never was more serious in my life.

PARAMORE [*shamed by Charteris's generosity*] Then I beg your pardon. I thought the news would please you.

CHARTERIS [*deprecating this injustice to his good feeling*] My dear fellow!

PARAMORE. I see I was wrong. I am really very sorry. [*They shake hands*]. And now you may as well learn the truth. I had rather you heard it from me than from the gossip of the club. My liver discovery has been—er—er—[*he cannot bring himself to say it*].

CHARTERIS [*helping him out*] Confirmed? [*Sadly*] I see: the poor Colonel's doomed.

PARAMORE. No: on the contrary, it has been—er—called in question. The Colonel now believes himself to be in perfectly good health; and my friendly relations with the Cravens are entirely spoilt.

CHARTERIS. Who told him about it?

PARAMORE. I did, of course, the moment I read the news in this. [*He shews the journal, and puts it down on the bookstand*].

CHARTERIS. Why, man, youve been a messenger of glad tidings! Didnt you congratulate him?

PARAMORE [*scandalized*] Congratulate him! Congratulate a man on the worst blow pathological science has received for the last three hundred years!

CHARTERIS. No, no, no. Congratulate him on having his life saved. Congratulate Julia on having her father spared. Swear that your discovery and your reputation are as nothing to you compared with the pleasure of restoring happiness to the household in which the best hopes of your life are centred. Confound it, man, youll never get married if you cant turn things to account with a woman in these little ways.

PARAMORE [*gravely*] Excuse me; but my self-respect is dearer to me even than Miss Craven. I cannot trifle with scientific questions for the sake of a personal advantage. [*He turns away coldly, and goes towards the table*].

CHARTERIS. Well, this beats me! The Nonconformist conscience is bad enough; but the scientific conscience is the very devil. [*He follows Paramore, and puts his arm familiarly round his shoulder, bringing him back again whilst he speaks*]. Now look here, Paramore: I have no conscience in that sense at all: I loathe it as I loathe all the snares of idealism; but I have some common humanity and common sense. [*He replaces him in the easy chair, and sits down opposite him*]. Come! what is a really scientific theory? A true theory, isnt it?

PARAMORE. No doubt.

CHARTERIS. For instance, you have a theory about Craven's liver, eh?

PARAMORE. I still believe that to be a true theory, though it has been upset for the moment.

CHARTERIS. And you have a theory that it would be pleasant to be married to Julia?

PARAMORE. I suppose so. In a sense.

CHARTERIS. That theory also will be upset, probably, before youre a year older.

PARAMORE. Always cynical, Charteris.

CHARTERIS. Never mind that. Now it's a perfectly damnable thing for you to hope that your liver theory is true, because it amounts to hoping that Craven will die an agonizing death.

PARAMORE. And always paradoxical, Charteris.

CHARTERIS. Well, at least youll admit that it's amiable and human to hope that your theory about Julia is right, because it amounts to hoping that she may live happily ever after.

PARAMORE. I do hope that with all my soul—[*correcting himself*] I mean with all my function of hoping.

CHARTERIS. Then, since both theories are equally scientific, why not devote yourself, as a humane man, to proving the amiable theory rather than the damnable one?

PARAMORE. But how?

CHARTERIS. I'll tell you. You think I'm fond of Julia myself. So I am; but then I'm fond of everybody; so I dont count. Besides, if you try the scientific experiment of asking her whether she loves me, she'll tell you that she hates and despises me. So I'm out of the running. Nevertheless, like you, I hope that she may be happy with all my—what did you call your soul?

PARAMORE [*impatiently*] Oh, go on, go on: finish what you were going to say.

CHARTERIS [*suddenly affecting complete indifference, and rising carelessly*] I dont know that I was going to say anything more. If I were you I should invite the Cravens to tea in honor of the Colonel's escape from a horrible doom. By the way, if youve done with that British Medical Journal, I should like to see how theyve smashed your theory up.

PARAMORE [*wincing as he also rises*] Oh, certainly, if you wish it. I have no objection. [*He takes the journal from the bookstand*] I admit that the Italian experiments apparently upset my theory. But please remember that it is doubtful—extremely doubtful—

whether anything can be proved by experiments on animals. [*He hands Charteris the journal*].

CHARTERIS [*taking it*] It doesnt matter: I dont intend to make any. [*He retires to the recess on Ibsen's right, picking up the step-ladder as he passes and placing it so that he is able to use it for a leg rest as he settles himself to read on the divan with his back to the corner of the mantelpiece*].

Paramore goes to the dining room door, and is about to leave the library when he meets Grace entering.

GRACE. How do you do, Dr Paramore? So glad to see you. [*They shake hands*].

PARAMORE. Thanks. Quite well, I hope?

GRACE. Quite, thank you. Youre looking overworked. We must take more care of you, Doctor.

PARAMORE. You are too kind.

GRACE. It is you who are too kind—to your patients. You sacrifice yourself. Have a little rest. Come and talk to me. Tell me all about the latest scientific discoveries, and what I ought to read to keep myself up to date. But perhaps youre busy.

PARAMORE. No, not at all. Only too delighted. [*They go into the recess on Ibsen's left, and sit there chatting in whispers, very confidentially*].

CHARTERIS. How they all love a doctor! They can say what they like to him. [*Julia returns, but does not look his way. He takes his feet from the ladder and sits up*] Whew! [*Julia wanders along his side of the room, apparently looking for some one. Charteris steals after her*].

CHARTERIS [*in a low voice*] Looking for me, Julia?

JULIA [*starting violently*] Oh! How you startled me!

CHARTERIS. Sh! I want to shew you something. Look! [*He points to the pair in the recess*].

JULIA [*jealously*] That woman!

CHARTERIS. My young woman, carrying off your young man.

JULIA. What do you mean? Do you dare insinuate—

CHARTERIS. Sh—sh—sh! Dont disturb them.

Paramore rises; takes down a book; and sits on a footstool at Grace's feet.

JULIA. Why are they whispering like that?

CHARTERIS. Because they dont want any one to hear what they are saying to one another.

Paramore shews Grace a picture in the book. They both laugh heartily over it.

JULIA. What is he shewing her?

CHARTERIS. Probably a diagram of the liver. [*Julia, with an exclamation of disgust, makes for the recess. Charteris catches her sleeve*]. Stop: be careful, Julia. [*She frees herself by giving him a push which upsets him into the easy chair; then crosses to the recess, and stands looking down at Grace and Paramore from the corner next the fireplace*].

JULIA [*with suppressed fury*] You seem to have found a very interesting book, Dr Paramore. [*They look up, astonished*]. May I ask what it is? [*She stoops swiftly; snatches the book from Paramore; and comes down to the table quickly to look at it whilst they rise in amazement*]. Good Words! [*She flings it on the table, and sweeps back past Charteris, exclaiming contemptuously*] You fool! [*Paramore and Grace, meanwhile, come from the recess: Paramore bewildered: Grace very determined*].

CHARTERIS [*aside to Julia as he gets out of the easy chair*] Idiot! She'll have you turned out of the club for this.

JULIA [*terrified*] She cant: can she?

PARAMORE. What is the matter, Miss Craven?

CHARTERIS [*hastily*] Nothing. My fault: a stupid practical joke. I beg your pardon and Mrs Tranfield's.

GRACE [*firmly*] It is not your fault in the least, Mr Charteris. Dr Paramore: will you oblige me by finding Sylvia Craven for me, if you can?

PARAMORE [*hesitating*] But—

GRACE. I want you to go now, if you please.

PARAMORE [*succumbing*] Certainly. [*He bows and goes out by the staircase door*].

GRACE. You are going with him, Charteris.

JULIA. You will not leave me here to be insulted by this woman, Mr Charteris. [*She takes his arm as if to go with him*].

GRACE. When two ladies quarrel in this club, it is against the rules to settle it when there are gentlemen present: especially the gentleman they are quarrelling about. I presume you do not wish to break that rule, Miss Craven. [*Julia sullenly drops Charteris's arm. Grace turns to Charteris, and adds*] Now! Trot off.

CHARTERIS. Certainly. Certainly. [*He follows Paramore ignominiously*].

GRACE [*to Julia, with quiet peremptoriness*] Now: what have you to say to me?

JULIA [*suddenly throwing herself tragically on her knees at Grace's feet*] Dont take him from me. Oh dont—dont be so cruel. Give him back to me. You dont know what youre doing—what our past has been —how I love him. You dont know—

GRACE. Get up; and dont be a fool. Suppose any one comes in and sees you in that ridiculous attitude!

JULIA. I hardly know what I'm doing. I dont care what I'm doing: I'm too miserable. Oh, wont you listen to me?

GRACE. Do you suppose I am a man, to be imposed on by this sort of rubbish?

JULIA [*getting up and looking darkly at her*] You intend to take him from me, then?

GRACE. Do you expect me to help you to keep him after the way you have behaved?

JULIA [*trying her theatrical method in a milder form: reasonable and impulsively goodnatured instead of tragic*] I know I was wrong to act as I did last night. I beg your pardon. I am sorry. I was mad.

GRACE. Not a bit mad. You calculated to an inch how far you could go. When he is present to stand between us and play out the scene with you, I count for nothing. When we are alone, you fall back on your natural way of getting anything you want: crying for it like a baby until it is given to you.

JULIA [*with unconcealed hatred*] You learnt this from him.

GRACE. I learnt it from yourself, last night and now. How I hate to be a woman when I see, by you, what wretched childish creatures we are! Those two men would cut you dead and have you turned out of the club if you were a man, and had behaved in such a way before them. But because you are only a woman, they are forbearing! sympathetic! gallant! Oh, if you had a scrap of self-respect, their indulgence would make you creep all over. I understand now why Charteris has no respect for women.

JULIA. How dare you say that?

GRACE. Dare! I love him. And I have refused his offer to marry me.

JULIA [*incredulous, but hopeful*] You have refused!

GRACE. Yes; because I will not give myself to any man who has learnt how to treat women from you and your like. I can do without his love, but not without his respect; and it is your fault that I cannot have both. Take his love then; and much good may it do you! Run to him, and beg him to take you back.

JULIA. Oh, what a liar you are! He loved me before he ever saw you—before he ever dreamt of you, you pitiful thing. Do you think *I* need go down on my knees to men to make them come to me? That may be your experience, you creature with no figure: it is not mine. There are dozens of men who would give their souls for a look from me. I have only to lift my finger.

GRACE. Lift it then; and see whether he will come.

JULIA. How I should like to kill you! I dont know why I dont.

GRACE. Yes: you like to get out of your difficulties at other people's expense. It is something to boast of, isnt it, that dozens of men would make love to you if you invited them?

JULIA [*sullenly*] I suppose it's better to be like you, with a cold heart and a serpent's tongue. Thank Heaven, I have a heart: that is why you can hurt me as I cannot hurt you. And you are a coward. You are giving him up to me without a struggle.

GRACE. Yes: it is for you to struggle. I wish you success. [*She turns away contemptuously, and is going to the dining room door when Sylvia enters on the opposite side, followed by Cuthbertson and Craven, who come to Julia, whilst Sylvia crosses to Grace*].

SYLVIA. Here I am, sent by the faithful Paramore. He hinted that I'd better bring the elder members of the family too: here they are. Whats the row?

GRACE [*quietly*] Nothing, dear. Theres no row.

JULIA [*hysterically, tottering and stretching out her arms to Craven*] Daddy!

CRAVEN [*taking her in his arms*] My precious! Whats the matter?

JULIA [*through her tears*] She's going to have me

[203]

expelled from the club; and we shall all be disgraced. Can she do it, Daddy?

CRAVEN. Well, really, the rules of this club are so extraordinary that I dont know. [*To Grace*] May I ask, madam, whether you have any complaint to make of my daughter's conduct?

GRACE. Yes, sir. I am going to complain to the committee.

SYLVIA. I knew youd overdo it some day, Julia.

CRAVEN. Do you know this lady, Jo?

CUTHBERTSON. This is my daughter, Mrs Tranfield, Dan. Grace: this is my old friend Colonel Craven.

Grace and Craven bow to one another constrainedly.

CRAVEN. May I ask the ground of complaint, Mrs Tranfield?

GRACE. Simply that Miss Craven is essentially a womanly woman, and, as such, not eligible for membership.

JULIA. It's false. I'm not a womanly woman. I was guaranteed when I joined just as you were.

GRACE. By Mr Charteris, I think, at your own request. I shall call him as a witness to your thoroughly womanly conduct just now in his presence and Dr Paramore's.

CRAVEN. Cuthbertson: are they joking? or am I dreaming?

CUTHBERTSON [*grimly*] It's real, Dan: youre awake.

SYLVIA [*taking Craven's left arm, and hugging it affectionately*] Dear old Rip Van Winkle!

CRAVEN. Well, Mrs Tranfield, all I can say is that I hope you will succeed in establishing your complaint, and that Julia may soon see the last of this most outrageous institution.

Charteris returns.

CHARTERIS [*at the door*] May I come in?

SYLVIA. Yes: youre wanted here as a witness. [*Charteris comes in, and places himself with evident misgiving between Julia and Grace*]. It's a bad case of womanliness.

GRACE [*half aside to him, significantly*] You understand? [*Julia, watching them jealously, leaves her father and gets close to Charteris. Grace adds aloud*] I shall expect your support before the committee.

JULIA. If you have a scrap of manhood in you you will take my part.

CHARTERIS. But then I shall be expelled for being a manly man. Besides, I'm on the committee myself: I cant act as judge and witness too. You must apply to Paramore: he saw it all.

GRACE. Where is Dr Paramore?

CHARTERIS. Just gone home.

JULIA [*with sudden resolution*] What is Dr Paramore's number in Savile Row?

CHARTERIS. Seventy-nine.

Julia goes out quickly by the staircase door, to their astonishment. Charteris follows her to the door, which swings back in his face, leaving him staring after her through the glass.

SYLVIA [*running to Grace*] Grace: go after her. Dont let her get beforehand with Paramore. She'll tell him the most heartbreaking stories about how she's been treated, and get round him completely.

CRAVEN [*thundering*] Sylvia! is that the way to speak of your sister, miss? [*Grace squeezes Sylvia's hand to console her; takes a magazine from the table; and sits down calmly. Sylvia posts herself behind Grace's chair, leaning over the back to watch the ensuing colloquy between the three men*]. I assure you, Mrs Tranfield, Dr Paramore has just invited us all to take afternoon tea with him; and if my daughter has gone to his house, she is simply taking advantage of his invitation to extricate herself from a very embarrassing scene here. We're all going there. Come, Sylvia. [*He turns to go, followed by Cuthbertson*].

CHARTERIS [*in consternation*] Stop! [*He gets between Craven and Cuthbertson*]. What hurry is there? Cant you give the man time?

CRAVEN. Time! What for?

CHARTERIS [*talking foolishly in his agitation*] Well, to get a little rest, you know: a busy professional man like that! He's not had a moment to himself all day.

CRAVEN. But Julia's with him.

CHARTERIS. Well, no matter: she's only one person. And she ought to have an opportunity of laying her case before him. As a member of the committee, I think thats only just. Be reasonable, Craven: give him half an hour.

CUTHBERTSON [*sternly*] What do you mean by this, Charteris?

CHARTERIS. Nothing, I assure you. Only common consideration for poor Paramore.

CUTHBERTSON. Youve some motive. Craven: I strongly advise that we go at once. [*He grasps the door handle*].

CHARTERIS [*coaxingly*] No, no. [*He puts his hand persuasively on Craven's arm, adding*] It's not good for your liver, Craven, to rush about immediately after lunch.

CUTHBERTSON. His liver's cured. Come on, Craven. [*He opens the door*].

CHARTERIS [*catching Cuthbertson by the sleeve*] Cuthbertson: youre mad. Paramore's going to propose to Julia. We must give him time: he's not the man to come to the point in three seconds as you or I would. [*Turning to Craven*] Dont you see? that will get me out of the difficulty we were speaking of this morning: you and I and Cuthbertson. You remember?

CRAVEN. Now is this a thing to say plump out before everybody, Charteris? Confound it, have you no decency?

CUTHBERTSON [*severely*] None whatever.

CHARTERIS [*turning to Cuthbertson*] No: dont be unkind, Cuthbertson. Back me up. My future, her future, Mrs Tranfield's future, Craven's future, everybody's future depends on Julia being Paramore's affianced bride when we arrive. He's certain to propose if youll only give him time. You know youre a kindly and sensible man as well as a deucedly clever one, Cuthbertson, in spite of all the nonsense you pick up in the theatre. Say a word for me.

CRAVEN. I'm quite willing to leave the decision to Cuthbertson; and I have no doubt whatever as to what that decision will be.

Cuthbertson carefully shuts the door, and comes back into the room with an air of weighty reflection.

CUTHBERTSON. I am now going to speak as a man of the world: that is, without moral responsibility.

CRAVEN. Quite so, Jo. Of course.

CUTHBERTSON. Therefore, though I have no sympathy whatever with Charteris's views, I think we can do no harm by waiting—say ten minutes or so. [*He sits down*].

CHARTERIS [*delighted*] Ah, theres nobody like you after all, Cuthbertson, when theres a difficult situation to be judged. [*He sits down on the settee back*].

CRAVEN [*deeply disappointed*] Oh well, Jo, if that is your decision, I must keep my word and abide by it. Better sit down and make ourselves comfortable, I suppose. [*He sits also, under protest*].

A pause, very trying for the three men.

GRACE [*looking up from her magazine*] Dont fidget, Leonard.

CHARTERIS [*slipping off the settee back*] I cant help it: I'm too restless. The fact is, Julia has made me so nervous that I cant answer for myself until I know her decision. Mrs Tranfield will tell you what a time Ive had lately. Julia's really a most determined woman, you know.

CRAVEN [*starting up*] Well, upon my life! Upon my honour and conscience!! Now really!!! I shall go this instant. Come on, Sylvia. Cuthbertson: I hope youll mark your sense of this sort of thing by coming on to Paramore's with us at once. [*He marches to the door*].

CHARTERIS [*desperately*] Craven: youre trifling with your daughter's happiness. I ask only five minutes more.

CRAVEN. Not five seconds, sir. Fie for shame, Charteris! [*He goes out*].

CUTHBERTSON [*to Charteris, as he passes him on his way to the door*] Bungler! [*He follows Craven*].

SYLVIA. Serve you right, you duffer! [*She follows Cuthbertson*].

CHARTERIS. Oh, these headstrong old men! [*To Grace*] Nothing to be done now but go with them, and delay the Colonel as much as possible. So I'm afraid I must leave you.

GRACE [*rising*] Not at all. Paramore invited me, too.

CHARTERIS [*aghast*] You dont mean to say youre coming!

GRACE. Most certainly. Do you suppose I will let that woman think I am afraid to meet her? [*Charteris sinks on a chair with a prolonged groan*]. Come: dont be silly: youll not overtake the Colonel if you delay any longer.

CHARTERIS. Why was I ever born, child of misfortune that I am! [*He rises despairingly*]. Well, if you must come, you must. [*He offers his arm, which she takes*]. By the way, what happened after I left you?

GRACE. I gave her a lecture on her behavior which she will remember to the last day of her life.

CHARTERIS [*approvingly*] That was right, darling. [*He slips his arm round her waist*] Just one kiss. To soothe me.

GRACE [*complacently offering her cheek*] Foolish boy! [*He kisses her*]. Now come along. [*They go out together*].

[ACT III]

Paramore's reception room in Savile Row. Viewing the room from the front windows, the door is seen in the opposite wall near the left hand corner. Another door, a light noiseless one covered with green baize, leading to the consulting room, is in the right hand wall towards the back. The fireplace is on the left. At the nearest corner of it a couch is placed at right angles to the wall, settlewise. At the other corner, an easy chair. On the right the wall is occupied by a bookcase, further forward than the green baize door. Beyond the door is a cabinet of anatomical preparations, with a framed photograph of Rembrandt's School of Anatomy hanging on the wall above it. In front, a little to the right, a teatable.

Paramore is seated in a round-backed chair, on castors, pouring out tea. Julia sits opposite him, with her back to the fire. He is in high spirits: she very downcast.

PARAMORE [*handing her the cup he has just filled*] There! Making tea is one of the few things I consider myself able to do thoroughly well. Cake?

JULIA. No, thank you. I dont like sweet things. [*She sets down the cup untasted*].

PARAMORE. Anything wrong with the tea?

JULIA. No. It's very nice.

PARAMORE. I'm afraid I'm a bad entertainer. The fact is, I am too professional. I shine only in consultation. I almost wish you had something serious the

matter with you; so that you might call out my knowledge and sympathy. As it is, I can only admire you,
and feel how pleasant it is to have you here.

JULIA [*bitterly*] And pet me, and say pretty things to
me. I wonder you dont offer me a saucer of milk at
once.

PARAMORE [*astonished*] Why?

JULIA. Because you seem to regard me very much as
if I were a Persian cat.

PARAMORE [*in strong remonstrance*] Miss Cra—

JULIA [*cutting him short*] Oh, you neednt protest. I'm
used to it: it's the sort of attachment I seem always to
inspire. [*Ironically*] You cant think how flattering it is.

PARAMORE. My dear Miss Craven, what a cynical
thing to say! You! who are loved at first sight by the
people in the street as you pass. Why, in the club I can
tell by the faces of the men whether you have been
lately in the room or not.

JULIA [*shrinking fiercely*] Oh, I hate that look in their
faces. Do you know that I have never had one human
being care for me since I was born?

PARAMORE. Thats not true, Miss Craven. Even if it
were true of your father, and of Charteris, who loves
you madly in spite of your dislike for him, it is not
true of me.

JULIA [*startled*] Who told you that about Charteris?

PARAMORE. Why, he himself.

JULIA [*with deep, poignant conviction*] He cares for only
one person in the world; and that is himself. There is
not in his whole nature one unselfish spot. He would
not spend one hour of his real life with— [*a sob
chokes her: she rises passionately, crying*] You are all
alike, every one of you. Even my father only makes a
pet of me. [*She goes away to the fireplace, and stands
with her back to him to hide her face*].

PARAMORE [*following her humbly*] I dont deserve this from you: indeed I do not.

JULIA [*rating him*] Then why do you gossip about me behind my back with Charteris?

PARAMORE. We said nothing disparaging of you. Nobody shall ever do that in my presence. We spoke of the subject nearest our hearts.

JULIA. His heart! Oh God, his heart! [*She sits down on the couch, and covers her face*].

PARAMORE [*sadly*] I am afraid you love him, for all that, Miss Craven.

JULIA [*raising her head instantly*] If he says that, he lies. If ever you hear it said that I cared for him, contradict it: it is false.

PARAMORE [*quickly advancing to her*] Miss Craven: is the way clear for me then?

JULIA [*losing interest in the conversation, and looking crossly away from him*] What do you mean?

PARAMORE [*impetuously*] You must see what I mean. Contradict the rumor of your attachment to Charteris, not by words—it has gone too far for that—but by becoming my wife. [*Earnestly*] Believe me: it is not merely your beauty that attracts me [*Julia, interested, looks up at him quickly*]: I know other beautiful women. It is your heart, your sincerity, your sterling reality, [*Julia rises and gazes at him, breathless with a new hope*] your great gifts of character that are only half developed because you have never been understood by those about you.

JULIA [*looking intently at him, and yet beginning to be derisively sceptical in spite of herself*] Have you really seen all that in me?

PARAMORE. I have felt it. I have been alone in the world; and I need you, Julia. That is how I have divined that you, also, are alone in the world.

JULIA [*with theatrical pathos*] You are right there. I am indeed alone in the world.

PARAMORE [*timidly approaching her*] With you I should not be alone. And you? with me?

JULIA. You [*She gets quickly out of his reach, taking refuge at the teatable*]. No, no. I cant bring myself— [*She breaks off, perplexed, and looks uneasily about her*]. Oh, I dont know what to do. You will expect too much from me. [*She sits down*].

PARAMORE. I have more faith in you than you have in yourself. Your nature is richer than you think.

JULIA [*doubtfully*] Do you really believe that I am not the shallow, jealous, devilish tempered creature they all pretend I am?

PARAMORE. I am ready to place my happiness in your hands. Does that prove what I think of you?

JULIA. Yes: I believe you really care for me. [*He approaches her eagerly: she has a violent revulsion, and rises with her hands up as if to beat him off, crying*] No, no, no, no. I cannot. It's impossible. [*She goes towards the door*].

PARAMORE [*looking wistfully after her*] Is it Charteris?

JULIA [*stopping and turning*] Ah, you think that! [*She comes back*]. Listen to me. If I say yes, will you promise not to touch me? Will you give me time to accustom myself to our new relations?

PARAMORE. I promise most faithfully. I would not press you for the world.

JULIA. Then—then— Yes: I promise.

PARAMORE. Oh, how unspeakably hap—

JULIA [*stopping his raptures*] No: not another word. Let us forget it. [*She resumes her seat at the table*]. I havnt touched my tea. [*He hastens to his former seat. As he passes, she puts her left hand on his arm and says*] Be good to me, Percy: I need it sorely.

PARAMORE [*transported*] You have called me Percy! Hurrah!

Charteris and Craven come in. Paramore hastens to meet them, beaming.

PARAMORE. Delighted to see you here with me, Colonel Craven. And you too, Charteris. Sit down. [*The Colonel sits down on the end of the couch*]. Where are the others?

CHARTERIS. Sylvia has dragged Cuthbertson off into the Burlington Arcade to buy some caramels. He likes to encourage her in eating caramels: he thinks it's a womanly taste. Besides, he likes them himself. Theyll be here presently. [*He strolls across to the cabinet, and pretends to study the Rembrandt photograph, so as to be as far out of Julia's reach as possible*].

CRAVEN. Yes; and Charteris has been trying to persuade me that theres a short cut between Cork Street and Savile Row somewhere in Conduit Street. Now did you ever hear such nonsense? Then he said my coat was getting shabby, and wanted me to go into Poole's and order a new one. Paramore: is my coat shabby?

PARAMORE. Not that I can see.

CRAVEN. I should think not. Then he wanted to draw me into an argument about the Egyptian war. We should have been here quarter of an hour ago only for his nonsense.

CHARTERIS [*still contemplating Rembrandt*] I did my best to keep him from disturbing you, Paramore.

PARAMORE [*gratefully*] You kept him exactly the right time, to a second. [*Formally*] Colonel Craven: I have something very particular to say to you.

CRAVEN [*springing up in alarm*] In private, Paramore: now really it must be in private.

PARAMORE [*surprised*] Of course. I was about to

[214]

suggest my consulting room: theres nobody there.
Miss Craven: will you excuse me: Charteris will entertain you until I return. [*He leads the way to the
green baize door*].

CHARTERIS [*aghast*] Oh, I say, hadnt you better wait
until the others come?

PARAMORE [*exultant*] No need for further delay now,
my best friend. [*He wrings Charteris's hand*]. Will you
come, Colonel?

CRAVEN. At your service, Paramore: at your service.

*Craven and Paramore go into the consulting room.
Julia turns her head, and stares insolently at Charteris.
His nerves play him false: he is completely out of
countenance in a moment. She rises suddenly. He starts,
and comes hastily forward between the table and the
bookcase. She crosses to that side behind the table; and
he immediately crosses to the opposite side in front of it,
dodging her.*

CHARTERIS [*nervously*] Dont, Julia. Now dont abuse
your advantage. Youve got me here at your mercy. Be
good for once; and dont make a scene.

JULIA [*contemptuously*] Do you suppose I am going
to touch you?

CHARTERIS. No. Of course not.

*She comes forward on her side of the table. He retreats
on his side of it. She looks at him with utter scorn;
sweeps across to the couch; and sits down imperially.
With a great sigh of relief he drops into Paramore's
chair.*

JULIA. Come here. I have something to say to you.

CHARTERIS. Yes? [*He rolls the chair a few inches
towards her*].

JULIA. Come here, I say. I am not going to shout
across the room at you. Are you afraid of me?

CHARTERIS. Horribly. [*He moves the chair slowly, with great misgiving, to the end of the couch*].

JULIA [*with studied insolence*] Has that woman told you that she has given you up to me without an attempt to defend her conquest?

CHARTERIS [*whispering persuasively*] Shew that you are capable of the same sacrifice. Give me up too.

JULIA. Sacrifice! And so you think I'm dying to marry you, do you?

CHARTERIS. I am afraid your intentions have been honorable, Julia.

JULIA. You cad!

CHARTERIS [*with a sigh*] I confess I am something either more or less than a gentleman, Julia. You once gave me the benefit of the doubt.

JULIA. Indeed! I never told you so. If you cannot behave like a gentleman, you had better go back to the society of the woman who has given you up: if such a coldblooded, cowardly creature can be called a woman. [*She rises majestically: he makes his chair fly back to the table*]. I know you now, Leonard Charteris, through and through, in all your falseness, your petty spite, your cruelty and your vanity. The place you coveted has been won by a man more worthy of it.

CHARTERIS [*springing up, and coming close to her, gasping with eagerness*] What do you mean? Out with it. Have you accep—

JULIA. I am engaged to Dr Paramore.

CHARTERIS [*enraptured*] My own Julia! [*He attempts to embrace her*].

JULIA [*recoiling: he catching her hands and holding them*] How dare you! Are you mad? Do you wish me to call Dr Paramore?

CHARTERIS. Call everybody, my darling—everybody in London. Now I shall no longer have to be brutal; to defend myself; to go in fear of you. How I have looked forward to this day! You know now that I dont want you to marry me or to love me: Paramore can have all that. I only want to look on and rejoice disinterestedly in the happiness of [*kissing her hand*] my dear Julia, [*kissing the other*] my beautiful Julia. [*She tears her hands away and raises them as if to strike him, as she did the night before at Cuthbertson's: he faces them with joyous recklessness*]. No use to threaten me now: I am not afraid of those hands: the loveliest hands in the world.

JULIA. How have you the face to turn round like this after insulting and torturing me?

CHARTERIS. Never mind, dearest: you never did understand me; and you never will. Our vivisecting friend has made a successful experiment at last.

JULIA [*earnestly*] It is you who are the vivisector: a far crueller, more wanton vivisector than he.

CHARTERIS. Yes; but then I learn so much more from my experiments than he does! And the victims learn as much as I do. Thats where my moral superiority comes in.

JULIA [*sitting down again on the couch with rueful humor*] Well, you shall not experiment on me any more. Go to your Grace if you want a victim. She'll be a tough one.

CHARTERIS [*reproachfully, sitting down beside her*] And you drove me to propose to her to escape from you! Suppose she had accepted me, where should I be now?

JULIA. Where *I* am, I suppose, now that I have accepted Paramore.

CHARTERIS. But I should have made Grace unhappy. [*Julia sneers*]. However, now I come to think

[217]

of it, youll make Paramore unhappy. And yet if you refused him he would be in despair. Poor devil!

JULIA [*her temper flashing up for a moment again*] He is a better man than you.

CHARTERIS [*humbly*] I grant you that, my dear.

JULIA [*impetuously*] Dont call me your dear. And what do you mean by saying that I shall make him unhappy? Am I not good enough for him?

CHARTERIS [*dubiously*] Well, that depends on what you mean by good enough.

JULIA [*earnestly*] You might have made me good if you had chosen to. You had a great power over me. I was like a child in your hands; and you knew it.

CHARTERIS. Yes, my dear. That means that whenever you got jealous and flew into a tearing rage, I could always depend on its ending happily if I only waited long enough, and petted you very hard all the time. When you had had your fling, and called the object of your jealousy every name you could lay your tongue to, and abused me to your heart's content for a couple of hours, then the reaction would come; and you would at last subside into a soothing rapture of affection which gave you a sensation of being angelically good and forgiving. Oh, I know that sort of goodness! You may have thought on these occasions that I was bringing out your latent amiability; but I thought you were bringing out mine, and using up rather more than your fair share of it.

JULIA. According to you, then, I have no good in me. I am an utterly vile worthless woman. Is that it?

CHARTERIS. Yes, if you are to be judged as you judge others. From the conventional point of view, theres nothing to be said for you, Julia: nothing. Thats why I have to find some other point of view to save my self-respect when I remember how I have loved you.

Oh, what I have learnt from you! from you! who
could learn nothing from me! I made a fool of you;
and you brought me wisdom: I broke your heart; and
you brought me joy: I made you curse your womanhood; and you revealed my manhood to me. Blessings
for ever and ever on my Julia's name! [*With genuine
emotion, he takes her hand to kiss it again*].

JULIA [*snatching her hand away in disgust*] Oh, stop
talking that nasty sneering stuff.

CHARTERIS [*laughingly appealing to the heavens*] She
calls it nasty sneering stuff! Well, well: I'll never talk
like that to you again, dearest. It only means that you
are a beautiful woman, and that we all love you.

JULIA. Dont say that: I hate it. It sounds as if I were
a mere animal.

CHARTERIS. Hm! A fine animal is a very wonderful
thing. Dont let us disparage animals, Julia.

JULIA. That is what you really think me.

CHARTERIS. Come, Julia! you dont expect me to
admire you for your moral qualities, do you?

*Julia turns and looks hard at him. He starts up
apprehensively, and backs away from her. She rises and
follows him up slowly and intently.*

JULIA [*deliberately*] I have seen you very much infatuated with this depraved creature who has no
moral qualities.

CHARTERIS [*retreating*] Keep off, Julia. Remember
your new obligations to Paramore.

JULIA [*overtaking him in the middle of the room*] Never
mind Paramore: that is my business. [*She grasps the
lappels of his coat in her hands, and looks fixedly at him*].
Oh, if the people you talk so cleverly to could only
know you as I know you! Sometimes I wonder at
myself for ever caring for you.

CHARTERIS [*beaming at her*] Only sometimes?

JULIA. You fraud! You humbug! You miserable little plaster saint! [*He looks delighted*]. Oh! [*In a paroxysm half of rage, half of tenderness, she shakes him, growling over him like a tigress over her cub*].

Paramore and Craven return from the consulting room, and are thunderstruck at the spectacle.

CRAVEN [*shouting, utterly scandalized*] Julia!!

Julia releases Charteris, but stands her ground disdainfully as they come forward, Craven on her left, Paramore on her right.

PARAMORE. Whats the matter?

CHARTERIS. Nothing, nothing. Youll soon get used to this, Paramore.

CRAVEN. Now really, Julia, this is a very extraordinary way to behave. It's not fair to Paramore.

JULIA [*coldly*] If Dr Paramore objects, he can break off our engagement. [*To Paramore*] Pray dont hesitate.

PARAMORE [*looking doubtfully and anxiously at her*] Do you wish me to break it off?

CHARTERIS [*alarmed*] Nonsense! dont act so hastily. It was my fault. I annoyed Miss Craven—insulted her. Hang it all, dont go and spoil everything like this.

CRAVEN. This is most infernally perplexing. I cant believe that you insulted Julia, Charteris. Ive no doubt you annoyed her: youd annoy anybody: upon my soul you would; but insult! now what do you mean by that?

PARAMORE [*very earnestly*] Miss Craven: in all delicacy and sincerity I ask you to be frank with me. What are the relations between you and Charteris?

JULIA [*enigmatically*] Ask him. [*She goes to the fireplace, turning her back on them*].

CHARTERIS. Certainly: I'll confess. I'm in love with Miss Craven. Ive persecuted her with my addresses ever since I knew her. It's been no use: she utterly despises me. A moment ago the spectacle of a rival's happiness stung me to make a nasty sneering speech; and she—well, she just shook me a little, as you saw.

PARAMORE [*chivalrously*] I shall never forget that you helped me to win her, Charteris. [*Julia turns quickly, a spasm of fury in her face*].

CHARTERIS. Sh! For Heaven's sake dont mention it.

CRAVEN. This is a very different story to the one you told Cuthbertson and myself this morning. Youll excuse my saying that it sounds much more like the truth. Come! you were humbugging us, werent you?

CHARTERIS [*enigmatically*] Ask Julia.

Paramore and Craven turn to Julia. Charteris remains doggedly looking straight before him.

JULIA. It's quite true. He has been in love with me; he has persecuted me; and I utterly despise him.

CRAVEN. Dont rub it in, Julia: it's not kind. No man is quite himself when he's crossed in love. [*To Charteris*] Now listen to me, Charteris. When I was a young fellow, Cuthbertson and I fell in love with the same woman. She preferred Cuthbertson. I was taken aback: I wont deny it. But I knew my duty; and I did it. I gave her up, and wished Cuthbertson joy. He told me this morning, when we met after many years, that he has respected and liked me ever since for it. And I believe him, and feel the better for it. [*Impressibly*] Now, Charteris: Paramore and you stand today where Cuthbertson and I stood on a certain July evening thirty-five years ago. How are you going to take it?

JULIA [*indignantly*] How is he going to take it, indeed! Really, papa, this is too much. If Mrs Cuthbertson wouldnt have you, it may have been very noble of you to make a virtue of giving her up, just as you made a virtue of being a teetotaller when Percy cut off your wine. But he shant be virtuous over me. I have refused him; and if he doesnt like it he can— he can—

CHARTERIS. I can lump it. Precisely. Craven: you can depend on me. I'll lump it. [*He moves off nonchalantly, and leans against the bookcase with his hands in his pockets*].

CRAVEN [*hurt*] Julia: you dont treat me respectfully. I dont wish to complain; but that was not a becoming speech.

JULIA [*bursting into tears, and throwing herself into the easy chair*] Is there any one in the world who has any feeling for me? who does not think me utterly vile?

Craven and Paramore hurry to her in the greatest consternation.

CRAVEN [*remorsefully*] My pet: I didnt for a moment mean—

JULIA. Must I stand to be bargained for by two men— passed from one to the other like a slave in the market, and not say a word in my own defence?

CRAVEN. But, my love—

JULIA. Oh, go away, all of you. Leave me. I—oh— [*she gives way to a passion of tears*].

PARAMORE [*reproachfully to Craven*] Youve wounded her cruelly, Colonel Craven. Cruelly.

CRAVEN. But I didn't mean to: I said nothing. Charteris: was I harsh?

CHARTERIS. You forget the revolt of the daughters, Craven. And you certainly wouldnt have gone on like that to any grown-up woman who was not your daughter.

CRAVEN. Do you mean to say that I am expected to treat my daughter the same as I would any other girl?

PARAMORE. I should say certainly, Colonel Craven.

CRAVEN. Well, dash me if I will. There!

PARAMORE. If you take that tone, I have nothing more to say. [*He crosses the room with offended dignity, and posts himself with his back to the bookcase beside Charteris*].

JULIA [*with a sob*] Daddy.

CRAVEN [*turning solicitously to her*] Yes, my love.

JULIA [*looking up at him tearfully, and kissing his hand*] Dont mind them. You didnt mean it, Daddy, did you?

CRAVEN. No, no, my precious. Come: dont cry.

PARAMORE [*to Charteris, looking at Julia with delight*] How beautiful she is!

CHARTERIS [*throwing up his hands*] Oh, Lord help you, Paramore! [*He leaves the bookcase, and sits at the end of the couch farthest from the fire*].

Sylvia arrives.

SYLVIA [*contemplating Julia*] Crying again! Well, you are a womanly one!

CRAVEN. Dont worry your sister, Sylvia. You know she cant bear it.

SYLVIA. I speak for her good, Dad. All the world cant be expected to know that she's the family baby.

JULIA. You will get your ears boxed presently, Silly.

CRAVEN. Now! now! my dear children, really now! Come, Julia: put up your handkerchief before Mrs Tranfield sees you. She's coming along with Jo.

JULIA [*rising*] That woman again!

SYLVIA. Another row! Go it, Julia!

CRAVEN. Hold your tongue, Sylvia. [*He turns commandingly to Julia*]. Now look here, Julia.

CHARTERIS. Hallo! A revolt of the fathers!

CRAVEN. Silence, Charteris. [*To Julia, unanswerably*] The test of a man's or woman's breeding is how they behave in a quarrel. Anybody can behave well when things are going smoothly. Now you said today, at that iniquitous club, that you were not a womanly woman. Very well: I dont mind. But if you are not going to behave like a lady when Mrs Tranfield comes into this room, youve got to behave like a gentleman; or fond as I am of you, I'll cut you dead exactly as I would if you were my son.

PARAMORE [*remonstrating*] Colonel Craven—

CRAVEN [*cutting him short*] Dont be a fool, Paramore.

JULIA [*tearfully excusing herself*] I'm sure, Daddy—

CRAVEN. Stop snivelling. I'm not speaking as your Daddy now: I'm speaking as your commanding officer.

SYLVIA. Good old Victoria Cross! [*Craven turns sharply on her; and she darts away behind Charteris, and presently seats herself on the couch, so that she and Charteris are shoulder to shoulder, facing opposite ways*].

Cuthbertson arrives with Grace, who remains near the door whilst her father joins the others.

CRAVEN. Ah, Jo, here you are. Now, Paramore: tell em the news.

PARAMORE. Mrs Tranfield: Cuthbertson: allow me to introduce you to my future wife.

CUTHBERTSON [*coming forward to shake hands with Paramore*] My heartiest congratulations! Miss Craven: you will accept Grace's congratulations as well as mine, I hope.

CRAVEN. She will, Jo. [*Peremptorily*] Now, Julia.

Julia slowly rises.

CUTHBERTSON. Now, Grace. [*He conducts her to Julia's right; then posts himself on the hearthrug, with his back to the fire, watching them, whilst the Colonel keeps guard on the other side*].

GRACE [*speaking in a low voice to Julia alone*] So you

have shewn him that you can do without him! Now I take back everything I said. Will you shake hands with me? [*Julia gives her hand painfully, with her face averted*]. They think this a happy ending, Julia, these men: our lords and masters!

The two stand silent hand in hand.

SYLVIA [*leaning back across the couch, aside to Charteris*] Has she really chucked you? [*He nods assent. She looks at him dubiously, and adds*] I expect you chucked her.

CUTHBERTSON. And now, Paramore, mind you dont stand any chaff from Charteris about this. He's in the same predicament himself. He's engaged to Grace.

JULIA [*dropping Grace's hand, and speaking with breathless anguish, but not violently*] Again!

CHARTERIS [*rising hastily*] Dont be alarmed. It's all off.

SYLVIA [*rising indignantly*] What! Youve chucked Grace too! What a shame! [*She goes to the other side of the room, fuming*].

CHARTERIS [*following her, and putting his hand soothingly on her shoulder*] She wont have me, old chap. That is [*turning to the others*], unless Mrs Tranfield has changed her mind again.

GRACE. No: we shall remain very good friends, I hope; but nothing would induce me to marry you. [*She takes the easy chair at the fireplace, and sits down with perfect composure*].

JULIA. Ah! [*She sits down on the couch with a great sigh of relief*].

SYLVIA [*consoling Charteris*] Poor old Leonard!

CHARTERIS. Yes: this is the doom of the philanderer. I shall have to go on philandering now all my life. No domesticity, no fireside, no little ones, nothing at all in Cuthbertson's line! Nobody will marry me—unless you, Sylvia: eh?

SYLVIA. Not if I know it, Charteris.

CHARTERIS [*to them all*] You see!

CRAVEN [*coming between Charteris and Sylvia*] Now you really shouldnt make a jest of these things: upon my life and soul you shouldnt, Charteris.

CUTHBERTSON [*on the hearthrug*] The only use he can find for sacred things is to make a jest of them. Thats the New Order. Thank Heaven, we belong to the Old Order, Dan!

CHARTERIS. Cuthbertson: dont be symbolic.

CUTHBERTSON [*outraged*] Symbolic! That is an accusation of Ibsenism. What do you mean?

CHARTERIS. Symbolic of the Old Order. Dont persuade yourself that you represent the Old Order. There never was any Old Order.

CRAVEN. There I flatly contradict you, and stand up for Jo. I'd no more have behaved as you do when I was a young man than I'd have cheated at cards. *I* belong to the Old Order.

CHARTERIS. Youre getting old, Craven; and you want to make a merit of it, as usual.

CRAVEN. Come now, Charteris: youre not offended, I hope. [*With a conciliatory outburst*] Well, perhaps I shouldnt have said that about cheating at cards. I withdraw it [*offering his hand*].

CHARTERIS [*taking Craven's hand*] No offence, my dear Craven: none in the world. I didnt mean to shew any temper. But [*aside, after looking round to see whether the others are listening*] only just consider! the spectacle of a rival's happiness! the—

CRAVEN [*aloud, decisively*] Charteris: now youve got to behave like a man. Your duty's plain before you. [*To Cuthbertson*] Am I right, Jo?

CUTHBERTSON [*firmly*] You are, Dan.

CRAVEN [*to Charteris*] Go straight up and congratulate Julia. And do it like a gentleman, smiling.

CHARTERIS. Colonel: I will. Not a quiver shall betray the conflict within.

CRAVEN. Julia: Charteris has not congratulated you yet. He's coming to do it.

Julia rises, and fixes a dangerous look on Charteris.

SYLVIA [*whispering quickly behind Charteris as he is about to advance*] Take care. She's going to hit you. I know her.

Charteris stops and looks cautiously at Julia, measuring the situation. They regard one another steadfastly for a moment. Grace softly rises and gets close to Julia.

CHARTERIS [*whispering over his shoulder to Sylvia*] I'll chance it. [*He walks confidently up to Julia*]. Julia? [*He proffers his hand*].

JULIA [*exhausted, allowing herself to take it*] You are right. I am a worthless woman.

CHARTERIS [*triumphant, and gaily remonstrating*] Oh, Why?

JULIA. Because I am not brave enough to kill you.

GRACE [*taking her in her arms as she sinks, almost fainting, away from him*] Oh no. Never make a hero of a philanderer.

Charteris, amused and untouched, shakes his head laughingly. The rest look at Julia with concern, and even a little awe, feeling for the first time the presence of a keen sorrow.

Mrs Warren's Profession

WITH

Preface
Mr Shaw's Method and Secret
Shaw Proud of His Play
Shaw Replies to His Critics
Mr Shaw Hits Back
Author's Note to 1926 Production

Composition begun 27 June 1893; completed 2 November 1893. Published in *Plays Pleasant and Unpleasant*, 1898. Separate edition, 1902 (containing a new preface "The Author's Apology"). Revised text in Collected Edition, 1930.

Copyright reading at the Victoria Hall (Bijou Theatre), London, on 30 March 1898. First presented by the Stage Society at the New Lyric Club on 5 January 1902; repeated on 6 January.

Praed   *Julius Knight*
Sir George Crofts   *Charles Goodhart*
The Reverend Samuel Gardner   *Cosmo Stuart*
Frank Gardner   *H. Granville Barker*
Vivie Warren   *Madge McIntosh*
Mrs Kitty Warren   *Fanny Brough*

ACT I *The Garden of Vivie Warren's Holiday Cottage at Haslemere*

ACT II *Inside the Cottage*

ACT III *The Vicarage Garden*

ACT IV *Honoria Fraser's Chambers in Chancery Lane*

Preface

Mrs Warren's Profession was written in 1894 to draw attention to the truth that prostitution is caused, not by female depravity and male licentiousness, but simply by underpaying, undervaluing, and overworking women so shamefully that the poorest of them are forced to resort to prostitution to keep body and soul together. Indeed all attractive unpropertied women lose money by being infallibly virtuous or contracting marriages that are not more or less venal. If on the large social scale we get what we call vice instead of what we call virtue it is simply because we are paying more for it. No normal woman would be a professional prostitute if she could better herself by being respectable, nor marry for money if she could afford to marry for love.

Also I desired to expose the fact that prostitution is not only carried on without organization by individual enterprise in the lodgings of solitary women, each her own mistress as well as every customer's mistress, but organized and exploited as a big international commerce for the profit of capitalists like any other commerce, and very lucrative to great city estates, including Church estates, through the rents of the houses in which it is practised.

I could not have done anything more injurious to my prospects at the outset of my career. My play was immediately stigmatized by the Lord Chamberlain, who by Act of Parliament has despotic and even supermonarchical power over our theatres, as "immoral and otherwise improper for the stage." Its performance was prohibited, I myself being branded by implication, to my great damage, as an unscrupulous and blackguardly author. True, I have lived this defamation down, and am apparently none the worse. True too that the stage under the censorship became so licentious after the war that the ban on a comparatively prudish play like mine became ridiculous and had to be lifted. Also I admit that my career as a revolutionary critic of our most respected social institutions kept me so continually in hot water that the addition of another jugful of boiling fluid by the Lord Chamberlain troubled me too little to entitle me to personal commiseration, especially as the play greatly strengthened my repute among serious readers. Besides, in 1894 the ordinary commercial theatres would have nothing to say to me, Lord Chamberlain or no Lord Chamberlain. None the less the injury done me, now admittedly indefensible, was real and considerable, and the injury to society much greater; for when the White Slave Traffic, as Mrs Warren's profession came to be called, was dealt with legislatively, all that Parliament did was to enact that prostitutes' male bullies and parasites should be flogged, leaving Mrs Warren in complete command of the situation, and its true nature more effectually masked than ever. It was the fault of the Censorship that our legislators and journalists were not better instructed.

In 1902 the Stage Society, technically a club giving private performances for the entertainment of its own members, and therefore exempt from the Lord Chamberlain's jurisdiction, resolved to perform the play. None of the public theatres dared brave his displeasure (he has absolute power to close them if they offend him) by harboring the performance; but another club which had a little stage, and which rather courted a pleasantly scandalous reputation, opened its doors for one night and one afternoon. Some idea of the resultant sensation may be gathered from the following polemic, which appeared as a preface to a special edition of the play, and was headed

THE AUTHOR'S APOLOGY

Mrs Warren's Profession has been performed at last, after a delay of only eight years; and I have once more shared with Ibsen the triumphant amusement of startling all but the strongest-headed of the London theatre critics clean out of the practice of their profession. No author who has ever known the exultation of sending the Press into an hysterical tumult of protest, of moral panic, of involuntary and frantic confession of sin, of a horror of conscience in which the power of distinguishing between the work of art on the stage and the real life of the spectator is confused and overwhelmed, will ever care for the stereotyped compliments which every successful farce or melodrama elicits from the newspapers. Give me that critic who rushed from my play to declare furiously that Sir George Crofts ought to be kicked. What a triumph for the actor, thus to reduce a jaded London journalist to the condition of the simple sailor in the Wapping gallery, who shouts execrations at Iago and warnings to Othello not to believe him! But dearer still than such simplicity is that sense of the sudden earthquake shock to the foundations of morality which sends a pallid crowd of critics into the street shrieking that the pillars of society are cracking and the ruin of the State at hand. Even the Ibsen champions of ten years ago remonstrate with me just as the veterans of those brave days remonstrated with them. Mr Grein, the hardy iconoclast who first launched my plays on the stage alongside Ghosts and The Wild Duck,

[233]

exclaims that I have shattered his ideals. Actually his ideals! What would Dr Relling say? And Mr William Archer himself disowns me because I "cannot touch pity without wallowing in it." Truly my play must be more needed than I knew; and yet I thought I knew how little the others know.

Do not suppose, however, that the consternation of the Press reflects any consternation among the general public. Anybody can upset the theatre critics, in a turn of the wrist, by substituting for the romantic commonplaces of the stage the moral commonplaces of the pulpit, the platform, or the library. Play Mrs Warren's Profession to an audience of clerical members of the Christian Social Union and of women well experienced in Rescue, Temperance, and Girls' Club work, and no moral panic will arise: every man and woman present will know that as long as poverty makes virtue hideous and the spare pocket-money of rich bachelordom makes vice dazzling, their daily hand-to-hand fight against prostitution with prayer and persuasion, shelters and scanty alms, will be a losing one. There was a time when they were able to urge that though "the white-lead factory where Anne Jane was poisoned" may be a far more terrible place than Mrs Warren's house, yet hell is still more dreadful. Nowadays they no longer believe in hell; and the girls among whom they are working know that they do not believe in it, and would laugh at them if they did. So well have the rescuers learnt that Mrs Warren's defence of herself and indictment of society is the thing that most needs saying, that those who know me personally reproach me, not for writing this play, but for wasting my energies on "pleasant plays" for the amusement of frivolous people, when I can build up such excellent stage sermons on their own work.

Mrs Warren's Profession is the one play of mine which I could submit to a censorship without doubt of the result; only, it must not be the censorship of the minor theatre critic, nor of an innocent court official like the Lord Chamberlain's Examiner, much less of people who consciously profit by Mrs Warren's profession, or who personally make use of it, or who hold the widely whispered view that it is an indispensable safety-valve for the protection of domestic virtue, or, above all, who are smitten with a sentimental affection for our fallen sister, and would "take her up tenderly, lift her with care, fashioned so slenderly, young, and *so* fair." Nor am I prepared to accept the verdict of the medical gentlemen who would compulsorily examine and register Mrs Warren, whilst leaving Mrs Warren's patrons, especially her military patrons, free to destroy her health and anybody else's without fear of reprisals. But I should be quite content to have my play judged by, say, a joint committee of the Central Vigilance Society and the Salvation Army. And the sterner moralists the members of the committee were, the better.

Some of the journalists I have shocked reason so unripely that they will gather nothing from this but a confused notion that I am accusing the National Vigilance Association and the Salvation Army of complicity in my own scandalous immorality. It will seem to them that people who would stand this play would stand anything. They are quite mistaken. Such an audience as I have described would be revolted by many of our fashionable plays. They would leave the theatre convinced that the Plymouth Brother who still regards the playhouse as one of the gates of hell is perhaps the safest adviser on the subject of which he knows so little. If I do not draw the same conclusion, it is not because I am one of those who claim that art is exempt from moral obligations, and deny that the writing or performance of a play is a moral act, to be treated on exactly the same footing as theft or murder if it produces equally mischievous consequences. I am convinced that fine art is the subtlest, the most seductive, the most effective instrument of moral propaganda in the world, excepting only the example of personal conduct; and I waive even this exception in favor of the art of the stage, because it works by exhibiting examples of personal conduct made intelligible and moving to crowds of unobservant unreflecting people to whom real life means nothing. I have pointed out again and again that the influence of the theatre in England is growing so great that private conduct, religion, law, science, politics, and morals are becoming more and more theatrical, whilst the theatre itself remains impervious to common sense, religion, science, politics, and morals. That is why I fight the theatre, not with pamphlets and sermons and treatises, but with plays; and so effective do I find the dramatic method that I have no doubt I shall at last persuade even London to take its conscience and its brains with it when it goes to the theatre, instead of leaving them at home with its prayer-book as it does at present. Consequently, I am the last man to deny that if the net effect of performing Mrs Warren's Profession were an increase in the number of persons entering that profession or employing it, its performance might well be made an indictable offence.

Now let us consider how such recruiting can be encouraged by the theatre. Nothing is easier. Let the Lord Chamberlain's Examiner of Plays, backed by the Press, make an unwritten but perfectly well understood regulation that members of Mrs Warren's profession shall be tolerated on the stage only when they are beautiful, exquisitely dressed, and sumptuously lodged and fed; also that they shall, at the end of the play, die of consumption to the sympathetic tears of the whole audience, or step into the next room to commit suicide, or at least be turned out by their protectors and passed on to be "redeemed" by old and faithful lovers who have adored them in spite of all their levities. Naturally the poorer girls in the gallery will believe in the beauty, in the exquisite dresses, and the luxurious living, and will see that there is no real necessity for the consumption, the suicide, or the ejectment: mere pious forms, all of them, to save the Censor's face. Even if these purely official catastrophes carried any conviction, the majority of English girls remain so poor, so dependent, so well aware that the drudgeries of such honest work as is within their reach are likely enough to lead them eventually to lung disease, premature death, and domestic desertion or brutality, that they would still see reason to prefer the primrose path to the stony way of virtue, since both, vice at worst and virtue at best, lead to the same end in poverty and overwork. It is true that the Elementary School mistress will tell you that only girls of a certain kind will reason in this way. But alas! that certain kind turns out on inquiry to be simply the pretty, dainty kind: that is, the only kind that gets the chance of acting on such reasoning. Read the first report of the Commission on the Housing of the Working Classes [Bluebook C 4402, 1889]; read the Report on Home Industries (sacred word, Home!) issued by the Women's Industrial Council [Home Industries of Women in London, 1897, 1s.]; and ask yourself whether, if the lot in life therein described were your lot in life, you would not rather be a jewelled Vamp. If you can go deep enough into things to be able to say no, how many ignorant half-starved girls will believe you are speaking sincerely? To them the lot of the stage courtesan is heavenly in comparison with their own. Yet the Lord Chamberlain's Examiner, being an officer of the Royal Household, places the King in the position of saying to the dramatist "Thus, and thus only, shall you present Mrs Warren's profession on the stage, or you shall starve. Witness Shaw, who told the untempting truth about it, and whom We, by the Grace of God, accordingly disallow and suppress, and do what in Us lies to silence." Fortunately, Shaw cannot be silenced. "The harlot's cry from street to street" is louder than the voices of all the kings. I am not dependent on the theatre, and cannot be starved into making my play a standing advertisement of the attractive side of Mrs Warren's business.

Here I must guard myself against a misunderstanding. It is not the fault of their authors that the long string of wanton's tragedies, from Antony and Cleopatra to Iris, are snares to poor girls, and are objected to on that account by many earnest men and women who consider Mrs Warren's Profession an excellent sermon. Pinero is in no way bound to suppress the fact that his Iris is a person to be envied by millions of better women. If he made his play false to life by inventing fictitious disadvantages for her, he would be acting as unscrupulously as any tract-writer. If society chooses to provide for its Irises better than for its working women, it must not expect honest playwrights to manufacture spurious evidence to save its credit. The mischief lies in the deliberate suppression of the other side of the case: the refusal to allow Mrs Warren to expose the drudgery and repulsiveness of plying for hire among coarse tedious drunkards. All that, says the Examiner in effect, is horrifying, loathsome. Precisely: what does he expect it to be? would he have us represent it as beautiful and gratifying? His answer to this question amounts, I fear, to a blunt Yes; for it seems impossible to root out of an Englishman's mind the notion that vice is delightful, and that abstention from it is privation. At all events, as long as the tempting side of it is kept towards the public, and softened by plenty of sentiment and sympathy, it is welcomed by our Censor, whereas the slightest attempt to place it in the light of the policeman's lantern or the Salvation Army shelter is checkmated at once as not merely disgusting, but, if you please, unnecessary.

Everybody will, I hope, admit that this state of things is intolerable; that the subject of Mrs Warren's profession must be either tapu altogether, or else exhibited with the warning side as freely displayed as the tempting side. But many persons will vote for a complete tapu, and an impartial clean sweep from the boards of Mrs Warren and Gretchen and the rest: in short, for banishing the sexual instincts from the stage altogether. Those who think this impossible can hardly have considered the number and importance of the subjects which are actually banished from the stage. Many plays, among them Lear, Hamlet, Macbeth, Coriolanus, Julius Cæsar, have no sex complications: the thread of their action can be followed by children who could not understand a single scene of Mrs Warren's Profession or Iris. None of our plays rouse the sympathy of the audience by an exhibition of the pains of maternity, as Chinese plays constantly do. Each nation has its particular set of tapus in addition to the common human stock; and though each of these tapus limits the scope of the dramatist, it does not make drama impossible. If the Examiner were to refuse to license plays with female characters in them, he would only be doing to the stage what our tribal customs already do to the pulpit and the bar. I have myself written a rather entertaining play with only one woman in it, and she quite heartwhole; and I could just as easily write a play without a woman in it at all. I will even go as far as to promise the Examiner my support if he will introduce this limitation for part of the year, say during Lent, so as to make a close season for that dullest of stock dramatic subjects, adultery, and force our managers and authors to find out what all great dramatists find out spontaneously: to wit, that people who sacrifice every other consideration to love are as hopelessly unheroic on the stage as lunatics or dipsomaniacs. Hector and Hamlet are the world's heroes; not Paris and Antony.

But though I do not question the possibility of a drama in which love should be as effectively ignored as cholera is at present, there is not the slightest chance of that way out of the difficulty being taken by the Examiner. If he attempted it there would be a revolt in which he would be swept away, in spite of my singlehanded efforts to defend him. A complete tapu is politically impossible. A complete toleration is equally impossible to the Examiner, because his occupation would be gone if there were no tapu to enforce. He is therefore compelled to maintain the present compromise of a partial tapu, applied, to the best of his judgment, with a careful respect to persons and to public opinion. And a very sensible English solution of the difficulty, too, most readers will say. I should not dispute it if dramatic poets really were what English public opinion generally assumes them to be during their lifetime: that is, a licentiously irregular group to be kept in order in a rough and ready way by a magistrate who will stand no nonsense from them. But I cannot admit that the class represented by Eschylus, Sophocles, Aristophanes, Euripides, Shakespear, Goethe, Ibsen, and Tolstoy, not to mention our own contemporary playwrights, is as much in place in the Examiner's office as a pickpocket is in Bow Street. Further, it is not true that the Censorship, though it certainly suppresses Ibsen and Tolstoy, and would suppress Shakespear but for the absurd rule that a play once licensed is always licensed (so that Wycherly is permitted and Shelley prohibited), also suppresses unscrupulous playrights. I challenge the Examiner to mention any extremity of sexual misconduct which any manager in his senses would risk presenting on the London stage that has not been presented under his license and that of his predecessor. The compromise, in fact, works out in practice in favor of loose plays as against earnest ones.

To carry conviction on this point, I will take the extreme course of narrating the plots of two plays witnessed within the last ten years by myself at London West End theatres, one licensed under Queen Victoria, the other under her successor. Both plots conform to the strictest rules of the period when La Dame aux Camellias was still a forbidden play, and when The Second Mrs Tanqueray would have been tolerated only on condition that she carefully explained to the audience that when she met Captain Ardale she sinned "but in intention."

Play number one. A prince is compelled by his parents to marry the daughter of a neighboring king, but loves another maiden. The scene represents a hall in the king's palace at night. The wedding has taken place that day; and the closed door of the nuptial chamber is in view of the audience. Inside, the princess awaits her bridegroom. A duenna is in attendance. The bridegroom enters. His sole desire is to escape from a marriage which is hateful to him. A means occurs to him. He will assault the duenna, and be ignominiously expelled from the palace by his indignant father-in-law. To his horror, when he proceeds to carry out this stratagem, the duenna, far from raising an alarm, is flattered, delighted, and compliant. The assaulter becomes the assaulted. He flings her angrily to the ground, where she remains placidly. He flies. The father enters; dismisses the duenna; and listens at the keyhole of his daughter's nuptial chamber, uttering various pleasantries, and declaring, with a shiver, that a sound of kissing, which he supposes to proceed from within, makes him feel young again.

Story number two. A German officer finds himself in an inn with a French lady who has wounded his national vanity. He resolves to humble her by committing a rape upon her. He announces his purpose. She remonstrates, implores, flies to the doors and finds them locked, calls for help and finds none at hand, runs screaming from side to side, and, after a harrowing scene, is overpowered and faints. Nothing further being possible on the stage without actual felony, the officer then relents and leaves her. When she recovers, she believes that he has carried out his threat; and during the rest of the play she is represented as vainly vowing vengeance upon him, whilst she is really falling in love with him under the influence of his imaginary crime against her. Finally she consents to marry him; and the curtain falls on their happiness.

The story was certified by the Examiner, acting for the Lord Chamberlain, as void in its general tendency of "anything immoral or otherwise improper for the stage." But let nobody conclude therefore that the Examiner is a monster, whose policy it is to deprave the theatre. As a matter of fact, both the above stories are strictly in order from the official point of view. The incidents of sex which they contain, though carried in both to the extreme point at which another step would be dealt with, not by the Examiner, but by the police, do not involve adultery, nor any allusion to Mrs Warren's profession, nor to the fact that the children of any polyandrous group will, when they grow up, inevitably be confronted, as those of Mrs Warren's group are in my play, with the insoluble problem of their own possible consanguinity. In short, by depending wholly on the coarse humors and the physical fascination of sex, they comply with all the formulable requirements of the Censorship, whereas plays in which these humors and fascinations are discarded, and the social problems created by sex seriously faced and dealt with, inevitably ignore the official formula and are suppressed. If the old rule against the exhibition of illicit sex relations on the stage were revived, and the subject absolutely barred, the only result would be that Antony and Cleopatra, Othello (because of the Bianca episode), Troilus and Cressida, Henry IV, Measure for Measure, Timon of Athens, La Dame aux Camellias, the Profligate, The Second Mrs Tanqueray, The Notorious Mrs Ebbsmith, The Gay Lord Quex, Mrs Dane's Defence, and Iris would be swept from the stage, and placed under the same ban as Tolstoy's Dominion of Darkness and Mrs Warren's Profession, whilst such plays as the two described above would have a monopoly of the theatre as far as sexual interest is concerned.

What is more, the repulsiveness of the worst of the certified plays would protect Censorship against effective exposure and criticism. Not long ago an American Review of high standing asked me for an article on the Censorship of the English Stage. I replied that such an article would involve passages too disagreeable for publication in a magazine for general family reading. The editor persisted nevertheless; but not until he had declared his readiness to face this, and had pledged himself to insert the article unaltered (the particularity of the pledge extending even to a specification of the exact number of words in the article) did I consent to the proposal. What was the result? The editor, confronted with the two stories, given above, threw his pledge to the winds, and instead of returning the article, printed it with the illustrative examples omitted, and nothing left but the argument from political principle against the Censorship. In doing this he fired my broadside after withdrawing the cannon balls; for neither the Censor nor any other Englishman, except perhaps a few veterans of the dwindling old guard of Benthamism, cares a dump about political principle. The ordinary Briton thinks that if every other Briton is not under some form of tutelage, the more childish the better, he will abuse his freedom viciously. As far as its principle is concerned, the Censorship is the most popular institution in England; and the playwright who criticizes it is slighted as a blackguard agitating for impunity. Consequently nothing can really shake the confidence of the public in the Lord Chamberlain's department except a remorseless and unbowdlerized narration of the licentious fictions which slip through its net, and are hallmarked by it with the approval of the royal household. But as such stories cannot be made public without great difficulty, owing to the obligation an editor is under not to deal unexpectedly with matters that are not *virginibus puerisque*, the chances are heavily in favor of the Censor escaping all remonstrance. With the exception of such comments as I was able to make in my own critical articles in The World and The Saturday Review when the pieces I have described were first produced, and a few ignorant protests by churchmen against much better plays which they confessed they had not seen nor read, nothing has been said in the press that could seriously disturb the easygoing notion that the stage would be much worse than it admittedly is but for the vigilance of the Examiner. The truth is, that no manager would dare produce on his own responsibility the pieces he can now get royal certificates for at two guineas per piece.

I hasten to add that I believe these evils to be inherent in the nature of all censorship, and not merely a consequence of the form the institution takes in London. No doubt there is a staggering absurdity in appointing an ordinary clerk to see that the leaders of European literature do not corrupt the morals of the nation, and to restrain Sir Henry Irving from presuming to impersonate Samson or David on the stage, though any other sort of artist may daub these scriptural figures on a signboard or carve them on a tombstone without hindrance. If the General Medical Council, the Royal College of Physicians, the Royal Academy of Arts, the Incorporated Law Society, and Convocation were abolished, and their functions handed over to the Examiner, the Concert of Europe would presumably certify England as mad. Yet, though neither medicine nor painting nor law nor the Church moulds the character of the nation as potently as the theatre does, nothing can come on the stage unless its dimensions admit of its first passing through the Examiner's mind! Pray do not think that I question his honesty. I am quite sure that he sincerely thinks me a blackguard, and my play a grossly improper one, because, like Tolstoy's Dominion of Darkness, it produces, as they are both meant to produce, a very strong and very painful impression of evil. I do not doubt for a moment that the rapine play which I have described, and which he licensed, was quite incapable in manuscript of producing any particular effect on his mind at all, and that when he was once satisfied that the ill-conducted hero was a German and not an English officer, he passed the play without studying its moral tendencies. Even if he had undertaken that study, there is no more reason to suppose that he is a competent moralist than there is to suppose that I am a competent mathematician. But truly it does not matter whether he is a moralist or not. Let nobody dream for a moment that what is wrong with the Censorship is the shortcoming of the gentleman who happens at any moment to be acting as Censor. Replace him tomorrow by an Academy of Letters and an Academy of Dramatic Poetry, and the new filter will still exclude original and epoch-making work, whilst passing conventional, old-fashioned, and vulgar work. The conclave which compiles the expurgatory index of the Roman Catholic Church is the most august, ancient, learned, famous, and authoritative censorship in Europe. Is it more enlightened more liberal, more tolerant than the comparatively un-qualified office of the Lord Chamberlain? On the contrary, it has reduced itself to a degree of absurdity which makes a Catholic university a contradiction in terms. All censorships exist to prevent anyone from challenging current conceptions and existing institutions. All progress is initiated by challenging current conceptions, and executed by supplanting existing institutions. Consequently the first condition of progress is the removal of censorships. There is the whole case against censorships in a nutshell.

It will be asked whether theatrical managers are to be allowed to produce what they like, without regard to the public interest. But that is not the alternative. The managers of our London music-halls are not subject to any censorship. They produce their entertainments on their own responsibility, and have no two-guinea certificates to plead if their houses are conducted viciously. They know that if they lose their character, the County Council will simply refuse to renew their license at the end of the year; and nothing in the history of popular art is more amazing than the improvement in music-halls that this simple arrangement has produced within a few years. Place the theatres on the same footing, and we shall promptly have a similar revolution: a whole class of frankly blackguardly plays, in which unscrupulous low comedians attract crowds to gaze at bevies of girls who have nothing to exhibit but their prettiness, will vanish like the obscene songs which were supposed to enliven the squalid dullness, incredible to the younger generation, of the music-halls fifteen years ago. On the other hand, plays which treat sex questions as problems for thought instead of as aphrodisiacs will be freely performed. Gentlemen of the Examiner's way of thinking will have plenty of opportunity of protesting against them in Council;

but the result will be that the Examiner will find his natural level; Ibsen and Tolstoy theirs; so no harm will be done.

This question of the Censorship reminds me that I have to apologize to those who went to the recent performance of Mrs Warren's Profession expecting to find it what I have just called an aphrodisiac. That was not my fault: it was the Examiner's. After the specimens I have given of the tolerance of his department, it was natural enough for thoughtless people to infer that a play which overstepped his indulgence must be a very exciting play indeed. Accordingly, I find one critic so explicit as to the nature of his disappointment as to say candidly that "such airy talk as there is upon the matter is utterly unworthy of acceptance as being a representation of what people with blood in them think or do on such occasions." Thus am I crushed between the upper millstone of the Examiner, who thinks me a libertine, and the nether popular critic, who thinks me a prude. Critics of all grades and ages, middle-aged fathers of families no less than ardent young enthusiasts, are equally indignant with me. They revile me as lacking in passion, in feeling, in manhood. Some of them even sum the matter up by denying me any dramatic power: a melancholy betrayal of what dramatic power has come to mean on our stage under the Censorship! Can I be expected to refrain from laughing at the spectacle of a number of respectable gentlemen lamenting because a playwright lures them to the theatre by a promise to excite their senses in a very special and sensational manner, and then, having successfully trapped them in exceptional numbers, proceeds to ignore their senses and ruthlessly improve their minds? But I protest again that lure was not mine. The play had been in print for four years; and I have spared no pains to make known that my plays are built to induce, not voluptuous reverie but intellectual interest, not romantic rhapsody but humane concern. Accordingly, I do not find those critics who are gifted with intellectual appetite and political conscience complaining of want of dramatic power. Rather do they protest, not altogether unjustly, against a few relapses into staginess and caricature which betray the young playwright and the old playgoer in this early work of mine. As to the voluptuaries, I can assure them that the playwright, whether he be myself or another, will always disappoint them. The drama can do little to delight the senses: all the apparent instances to the contrary are instances of the personal fascination of the performers. The drama of pure feeling is no longer in the hands of the playwright: it has been conquered by the musician, after whose enchantments all the verbal arts seem cold and tame. Romeo and Juliet with the loveliest Juliet is dry, tedious, and rhetorical in comparison with Wagner's Tristan, even though Isolde be both fourteen stone and forty, as she often is in Germany. Indeed, it needed no Wagner to convince the public of this. The voluptuous sentimentality of Gounod's Faust and Bizet's Carmen has captured the common playgoer; and there is, flatly, no future now for any drama without music except the drama of thought. The attempt to produce a genus of opera without music (and this absurdity is what our fashionable theatres have been driving at for a long time past without knowing it) is far less hopeful than my own determination to accept problem as the normal material of the drama.

That this determination will throw me into a long conflict with our theatre critics, and with the few

playgoers who go to the theatre as often as the critics,
I well know; but I am too well equipped for the strife
to be deterred by it, or to bear malice towards the
losing side. In trying to produce the sensuous effects
of opera, the fashionable drama has become so flaccid
in its sentimentality, and the intellect of its frequenters
so atrophied by disuse, that the reintroduction of
problem, with its remorseless logic and iron frame-
work of fact, inevitably produces at first an overwhelming impression of coldness and inhuman
rationalism. But this will soon pass away. When the
intellectual muscle and moral nerve of the critics has
been developed in the struggle with modern problem
plays, the pettish luxuriousness of the clever ones,
and the sulky sense of disadvantaged weakness in the
sentimental ones, will clear away; and it will be seen
that only in the problem play is there any real drama,
because drama is no mere setting up of the camera
to nature: it is the presentation in parable of the conflict between Man's will and his environment: in a
word, of problem. The vapidness of such drama as
the pseudo-operatic plays contain lies in the fact that
in them animal passion, sentimentally diluted, is
shewn in conflict, not with real circumstances, but
with a set of conventions and assumptions half of
which do not exist off the stage, whilst the other half
can either be evaded by a pretence of compliance or
defied with complete impunity by any reasonably
strong-minded person. Nobody can feel that such
conventions are really compulsory; and consequently
nobody can believe in the stage pathos that accepts
them as an inexorable fate, or in the reality of the
figures who indulge in such pathos. Sitting at such
plays we do not believe: we make-believe. And the
habit of make-believe becomes at last so rooted, that

criticism of the theatre insensibly ceases to be criticism at all, and becomes more and more a chronicle of the fashionable enterprises of the only realities left on the stage: that is, the performers in their own persons. In this phase the playwright who attempts to revive genuine drama produces the disagreeable impression of the pedant who attempts to start a serious discussion at a fashionable at-home. Later on, when he has driven the tea services out and made the people who had come to use the theatre as a drawing-room understand that it is they and not the dramatists who are the intruders, he has to face the accusation that his plays ignore human feeling, an illusion produced by that very resistance of fact and law to human feeling which creates drama. It is the *deus ex machina* who, by suspending that resistance, makes the fall of the curtain an immediate necessity, since drama ends exactly where resistance ends. Yet the introduction of this resistance produces so strong an impression of heartlessness nowadays that a distinguished critic has summed up the impression made on him by Mrs Warren's Profession, by declaring that "the difference between the spirit of Tolstoy and the spirit of Mr Shaw is the difference between the spirit of Christ and the spirit of Euclid." But the epigram would be as good if Tolstoy's name were put in place of mine and D'Annunzio's in place of Tolstoy's. At the same time I accept the enormous compliment to my reasoning powers with sincere complacency; and I promise my flatterer that when he is sufficiently accustomed to and therefore undazzled by problem on the stage to be able to attend to the familiar factor of humanity in it as well as to the unfamiliar one of a real environment, he will both see and feel that Mrs Warren's Profession is no mere theorem, but a play of instincts and temperaments in conflict with each other and with a flinty social problem that never yields an inch to mere sentiment.

I go further than this. I declare that the real secret of the cynicism and inhumanity of which shallower critics accuse me is the unexpectedness with which my characters behave like human beings, instead of conforming to the romantic logic of the stage. The axioms and postulates of that dreary mimanthropometry are so well known that it is almost impossible for its slaves to write tolerable last acts to their plays, so conventionally do their conclusions follow from their premises. Because I have thrown this logic ruthlessly overboard, I am accused of ignoring, not stage logic, but, of all things, human feeling. People with completely theatrified imaginations tell me that no girl would treat her mother as Vivie Warren does, meaning that no stage heroine would in a popular sentimental play. They say this just as they might say that no two straight lines would enclose a space. They do not see how completely inverted their vision has become even when I throw its preposterousness in their faces, as I repeatedly do in this very play. Praed, the sentimental artist (fool that I was not to make him a theatre critic instead of an architect!) burlesques them by expecting all through the piece that the feelings of the others will be logically deducible from their family relationships and from his "conventionally unconventional" social code. The sarcasm is lost on the critics: they, saturated with the same logic, only think him the sole sensible person on the stage. Thus it comes about that the more completely the dramatist is emancipated from the illusion that men and women are primarily reasonable beings, and the more powerfully he insists on the ruthless indifference of their great dramatic antagonist, the external world, to their whims and emotions, the surer he is to be denounced as blind to the very distinction on which his whole work is built. Far from ignoring idiosyncrasy, will, passion, impulse, whim, as factors in human action, I have placed them so nakedly on the stage that the elderly citizen, accustomed to see them clothed with the veil of manufactured logic about duty, and to disguise even his own impulses from himself in this way, finds the picture as unnatural as Carlyle's suggested painting of parliament sitting without its clothes.

I now come to those critics who, intellectually baffled by the problem in Mrs Warren's Profession, have made a virtue of running away from it on the gentlemanly ground that the theatre is frequented by women as well as by men, and that such problems should not be discussed or even mentioned in the presence of women. With that sort of chivalry I cannot argue: I simply affirm that Mrs Warren's Profession is a play for women; that it was written for women; that it has been performed and produced mainly through the determination of women that it should be performed and produced; that the enthusiasm of women made its first performance excitingly successful; and that not one of these women had any inducement to support it except their belief in the timeliness and the power of the lesson the play teaches. Those who were "surprised to see ladies present" were men; and when they proceeded to explain that the journals they represented could not possibly demoralize the public by describing such a play, their editors cruelly devoted the space saved by their delicacy to reporting at unusual length an exceptionally abominable police case.

My old Independent Theatre manager, Mr Grein, besides that reproach to me for shattering his ideals, complains that Mrs Warren is not wicked enough, and names several romancers who would have clothed her black soul with all the terrors of tragedy. I have no doubt they would; but that is just what I did not want to do. Nothing would please our sanctimonious British public more than to throw the whole guilt of Mrs Warren's profession on Mrs Warren herself. Now the whole aim of my play is to throw that guilt on the British public itself. Mr Grein may remember that when he produced my first play, Widowers' Houses, exactly the same misunderstanding arose. When the virtuous young gentleman rose up in wrath against the slum landlord, the slum landlord very effectually shewed him that slums are the product, not of individual Harpagons, but of the indifference of virtuous young gentlemen to the condition of the city they live in, provided they live at the west end of it on money earned by somebody else's labor. The notion that prostitution is created by the wickedness of Mrs Warren is as silly as the notion—prevalent, nevertheless, to some extent in Temperance circles—that drunkenness is created by the wickedness of the publican. Mrs Warren is not a whit a worse woman than the reputable daughter who cannot endure her. Her indifference to the ultimate social consequences of her means of making money, and her discovery of that means by the ordinary method of taking the line of least resistance to getting it, are too common in English society to call for any special remark. Her vitality, her thrift, her energy, her outspokenness, her wise care of her daughter, and the managing capacity which has enabled her and her sister to climb from the fried fish shop down by the Mint to the establishments of which she boasts, are all high English social virtues. Her defence of herself is so overwhelming that it provokes the St James's Gazette to declare that "the tendency of the play is wholly evil" because "it contains one of the boldest and most specious defences of an immoral life for poor women that has ever been penned." Happily the St James's Gazette here speaks in haste. Mrs Warren's defence of herself is not only bold and specious, but valid and unanswerable. But it is no defence at all of the vice which she organizes. It is no defence of an immoral life to say that the alternative offered by society collectively to poor women is a miserable life, starved, overworked, fetid, ailing, ugly. Though it is quite natural and *right* for Mrs Warren to choose what is, according to her lights, the least immoral alternative, it is none the less infamous of society to offer such alternatives. For the alternatives offered are not morality and immorality, but two sorts of immorality. The man who cannot see that starvation, overwork, dirt, and disease are as anti-social as prostitution—that they are the vices and crimes of a nation, and not merely its misfortunes—is (to put it as politely as possible) a hopelessly Private Person.

The notion that Mrs Warren must be a fiend is only an example of the violence and passion which the slightest reference to sex rouses in undisciplined minds, and which makes it seem natural to our law-givers to punish silly and negligible indecencies with a ferocity unknown in dealing with, for example, ruinous financial swindling. Had my play been entitled Mr Warren's Profession, and Mr Warren been a bookmaker, nobody would have expected me to make him a villain as well. Yet gambling is a vice, and book-making an institution, for which there is absolutely nothing to be said. The moral and economic evil done by trying to get other people's money without working for it (and this is the essence of gambling) is not only enormous but uncompensated. There are no two sides to the question of gambling, no circumstances which force us to tolerate it lest its suppression lead to worse things, no consensus of opinion among responsible classes, such as magistrates and military commanders, that it is a necessity, no Athenian records of gambling made splendid by the talents of its professors, no contention that instead of violating morals it only violates a legal institution which is in many respects oppressive and unnatural, no possible plea that the instinct on which it is founded is a vital one. Prostitution can confuse the issue with all these excuses: gambling has none of them. Consequently, if Mrs Warren must needs be a demon, a bookmaker must be a cacodemon. Well, does anybody who knows the sporting world really believe that bookmakers are worse than their neighbors? On the contrary, they have to be a good deal better; for in that world nearly everybody whose social rank does not exclude such an occupation would be a bookmaker if he could; but the strength of character required for handling large sums of money and for strict settlements and unflinching payment of losses is so rare that successful bookmakers are rare too. It may seem that at least public spirit cannot be one of a bookmaker's virtues; but I can testify from personal experience that excellent public work is done with money subscribed by bookmakers. It is true that there are abysses in bookmaking: for example, welshing. Mr Grein hints that there are abysses in Mrs Warren's profession also. So there are in every profession: the error lies in supposing that every member of them sounds these depths. I sit on a public body which prosecutes Mrs Warren zealously; and I can assure Mr Grein that she is often leniently dealt with because she has conducted her business "respectably" and held herself above its vilest branches. The degrees in infamy are as numerous and as scrupulously observed as the degrees in the peerage: the moralist's notion that there are depths at which the moral atmosphere ceases is as delusive as the rich man's notion that there are no social jealousies or snobberies among the very poor. No: had I drawn Mrs Warren as a fiend in human form, the very people who now rebuke me for flattering her would probably be the first to deride me for deducing character logically from occupation instead of observing it accurately in society.

One critic is so enslaved by this sort of logic that he calls my portraiture of the Reverend Samuel Gardner an attack on religion. According to this view Subaltern Iago is an attack on the army, Sir John Falstaff an attack on knighthood, and King Claudius an attack on royalty. Here again the clamor for naturalness and human feeling, raised by so many critics when they are confronted by the real thing on the stage, is really a clamor for the most mechanical and superficial sort of logic. The dramatic reason for making the clergyman what Mrs Warren calls "an old stick-in-the-mud," whose son, in spite of much capacity and charm, is a cynically worthless member of society, is to set up a mordant contrast between him and the woman of infamous profession, with her well brought-up, straightforward, hardworking daughter. The critics who have missed the contrast have doubtless observed often enough that many clergymen are in the Church through no genuine calling, but simply because, in circles which can command preferment, it is the refuge of the fool of the family; and that clergymen's sons are often conspicuous reactionists against the restraints imposed on them in childhood by their father's profession. These critics must know, too, from history if not from experience, that women as unscrupulous as Mrs Warren have distinguished themselves as administrators and rulers, both commercially and politically. But both observation and knowledge are left behind when journalists go to the theatre. Once in their stalls, they assume that it is "natural" for clergymen to be saintly, for soldiers to be heroic, for lawyers to be hard-hearted, for sailors to be simple and generous, for doctors to perform miracles with little bottles, and for Mrs Warren to be a beast and a demon. All this is not only not natural, but not dramatic. A man's profession only enters into the drama of his life when it comes into conflict with his nature. The result of this conflict is tragic in Mrs Warren's case, and comic in the clergyman's case (at least we are savage enough to laugh at it); but in both cases it is illogical, and in both cases natural. I repeat, the critics who accuse me of sacrificing nature to logic are so sophisticated by their profession that to them logic is nature, and nature absurdity.

Many friendly critics are too little skilled in social questions and moral discussions to be able to conceive that respectable gentlemen like themselves, who would instantly call the police to remove Mrs Warren if she ventured to canvass them personally, could possibly be in any way responsible for her proceedings. They remonstrate sincerely, asking me what good such painful exposures can possibly do. They might as well ask what good Lord Shaftesbury did by devoting his life to the exposure of evils (by no means yet remedied) compared to which the worst things brought into view or even into surmise in this play are trifles. The good of mentioning them is that you make people so extremely uncomfortable about them that they finally stop blaming "human nature" for them, and begin to support measures for their reform. Can anything be more absurd than the copy of The Echo which contains a notice of the performance of my play? It is edited by a gentleman who, having devoted his life to work of the Shaftesbury type, exposes social evils and clamors for their reform in every column except one; and that one is occupied by the declaration of the paper's kindly theatre critic, that the performance left him "wondering what useful purpose the play was intended to serve." The balance has to be redressed by the more fashionable papers, which usually combine capable art criticism with West-End solecism on politics and sociology. It is very noteworthy, however, on comparing the press explosion produced by Mrs Warren's Profession in 1902 with that produced by Widowers' Houses about ten years earlier, that whereas in 1892 the facts were frantically denied and the persons of the drama flouted as monsters of wickedness, in 1902 the facts are admitted, and the characters recognized, though it is suggested that this is exactly why no gentleman should mention them in public. Only one writer has ventured to imply this time that the poverty mentioned by Mrs Warren has since been quietly relieved, and need not have been dragged back to the footlights. I compliment him on his splendid mendacity, in which he is unsupported, save by a little plea in a theatrical paper which is innocent enough to think that ten guineas a year with board and lodging is an impossibly low wage for a barmaid. It goes on to cite Mr Charles Booth as having testified that there are many laborers' wives who are happy and contented on eighteen shillings a week. But I can go further than that myself. I have seen an Oxford agricultural laborer's wife looking cheerful on eight shillings a week; but that does not console me for the fact that agriculture in England is a ruined industry. If poverty does not matter as long as it is contented, then crime does not matter as long as it is unscrupulous. The truth is that it is only then that it does matter most desperately. Many persons are more comfortable when they are dirty than when they are clean; but that does not recommend dirt as a national policy.

In 1905 Arnold Daly produced Mrs Warren's Profession in New York. The press of that city instantly raised a cry that such persons as Mrs Warren are "ordure" and should not be mentioned in the presence of decent people. This hideous repudiation of humanity and social conscience so took possession of the New York journalists that the few among them who kept their feet morally and intellectually could do nothing to check the epidemic of foul language, gross suggestion, and raving obscenity of word and thought that broke out. The writers abandoned all self-restraint under the impression that they were upholding virtue instead of outraging it. They infected each other with their hysteria until they were for all practical purposes indecently mad. They finally forced the police to arrest Daly and his company, and led the magistrate to express his loathing of the duty thus forced upon him of reading an unmentionable and abominable play. Of course the convulsion soon exhausted itself. The magistrate, naturally somewhat impatient when he found that what he had to read was a strenuously ethical play forming part of a book which had been in circulation unchallenged for eight years, and had been received without protest by the whole London and New York Press, gave the journalists a piece of his mind as to their moral taste in plays. By consent, he passed the case on to a higher court, which declared that the play was not immoral; acquitted Daly; and made an end of the attempt to use the law to declare living women to be "ordure," and thus enforce silence as to the far-reaching fact that you cannot cheapen women in the market for industrial purposes without cheapening them for other purposes as well. I hope Mrs Warren's Profession will be played everywhere, in season and out of season, until Mrs Warren has bitten that fact into the public conscience, and shamed the newspapers which support a tariff to keep up the price of every American commodity except American manhood and womanhood.

Unfortunately, Daly had already suffered the usual fate of those who direct public attention to the profits of the sweater or the pleasures of the voluptuary. He was morally lynched side by side with me. Months elapsed before the decision of the courts vindicated him; and even then, since his vindication implied the condemnation of the Press, which was by that time sober again, and ashamed of its orgie, his triumph received a rather sulky and grudging publicity. In the meantime he had hardly been able to approach an American city, including even those cities which had heaped applause on him as the defender of hearth and home when he produced Candida, without having to face articles discussing whether mothers could allow their daughters to attend such plays as You Never Can Tell, written by the infamous author of Mrs Warren's Profession, and acted by the monster who produced it. What made this harder to bear was that though no fact is better established in theatrical business than the financial disastrousness of moral discredit, the journalists who had done all the mischief kept paying vice the homage of assuming that it is enormously popular and lucrative, and that Daly and I, being exploiters of vice, must therefore be making colossal fortunes out of the abuse heaped on us, and had in fact provoked it and welcomed it with that express object. Ignorance of real life could hardly go further.

I was deeply disgusted by this unsavory mobbing. And I have certain sensitive places in my soul: I do not like that word "ordure." Apply it to my work, and I can afford to smile, since the world, on the whole, will smile with me. But to apply it to the woman in the street, whose spirit is of one substance with your own and her body no less holy: to look your women folk in the face afterwards and not go out and hang yourself: that is not on the list of pardonable sins.

Shortly after these events a leading New York newspaper, which was among the most abusively clamorous for the suppression of Mrs Warren's Profession, was fined heavily for deriving part of its revenue from advertisements of Mrs Warren's houses.

Many people have been puzzled by the fact that whilst stage entertainments which are frankly meant to act on the spectators as aphrodisiacs are everywhere tolerated, plays which have an almost horrifying contrary effect are fiercely attacked by persons and papers notoriously indifferent to public morals on all other occasions. The explanation is very simple. The profits of Mrs Warren's profession are shared not only by Mrs Warren and Sir George Crofts, but by the landlords of their houses, the newspapers which advertize them, the restaurants which cater for them, and, in short, all the trades to which they are good customers, not to mention the public officials and representatives whom they silence by complicity, corruption, or blackmail. Add to these the employers who profit by cheap female labor, and the shareholders whose dividends depend on it (you find such people everywhere, even on the judicial bench and in the highest places in Church and State) and you get a large and powerful class with a strong pecuniary incentive to protect Mrs Warren's profession, and a correspondingly strong incentive to conceal, from their own consciences no less than from the world, the real sources of their gain. These are the people who declare that it is feminine vice and not poverty that drives women to the streets, as if vicious women with independent incomes ever went there. These are the people who, indulgent or indifferent to aphrodisiac plays, raise the moral hue and cry against performances of Mrs Warren's Profession, and drag actresses to the police court to be insulted, bullied, and threatened for fulfilling their engagements. For please observe that the judicial decision in New York State in favor of the play did not end the matter. In Kansas City, for instance, the municipality, finding itself restrained by the courts from preventing the performance, fell back on a local bye-law against indecency. It summoned the actress who impersonated Mrs Warren to the police court, and offered her and her colleagues the alternative of leaving the city or being prosecuted under this bye-law.

Now nothing is more possible than that the city councillors who suddenly displayed such concern for the morals of the theatre were either Mrs Warren's landlords, or employers of women at starvation wages, or restaurant keepers, or newspaper proprietors, or in some other more or less direct way sharers of the profits of her trade. No doubt it is equally possible that they were simply stupid men who thought that indecency consists, not in evil, but in mentioning it. I have, however, been myself a member of a municipal council, and have not found municipal councillors quite so simple and inexperienced as this. At all events I do not propose to give the Kansas councillors the benefit of the doubt. I therefore advise the public at large, which will finally decide the matter, to keep a vigilant eye on gentlemen who will stand anything at the theatre except a performance of Mrs Warren's Profession, and who assert in the same breath that (*a*) the play is too loathsome to be bearable by civilized people, and (*b*) that unless its performance is prohibited the whole town will throng to see it. They may be merely excited and foolish; but I am bound to warn the public that it is equally likely that they may be collected and knavish.

At all events, to prohibit the play is to protect the evil which the play exposes; and in view of that fact, I see no reason for assuming that the prohibitionists are disinterested moralists, and that the author, the managers, and the performers, who depend for their livelihood on their personal reputations and not on rents, advertisements, or dividends, are grossly inferior to them in moral sense and public responsibility.

It is true that in Mrs Warren's Profession, Society, and not any individual, is the villain of the piece; but it does not follow that the people who take offence at it are all champions of society. Their credentials cannot be too carefully examined.

PICCARD'S COTTAGE, *January* 1902

P.S. (1930) On reading the above after a lapse of 28 years, with the ban on Mrs Warren withdrawn and forgotten, I should have discarded it as an overdone fuss about nothing that now matters were it not for a recent incident. Before describing this I must explain that with the invention of the cinematograph a new censorship has come into existence, created, not this time by Act of Parliament, but by the film manufacturers to provide themselves with the certificates of propriety which have proved so useful to the theatre managers. This private censorship has acquired public power through its acceptance by the local authorities, without whose licence the films cannot be exhibited in place of public entertainment.

A lady who has devoted herself to the charitable work of relieving the homeless and penniless people who are to be found every night in London on the Thames Embankment had to deal largely with working men who had come to London from the country under the mistaken impression that there is always employment there for everybody, and with young women, also from the provinces, who had been lured to London by offers of situations which were really traps set for them by the agents of the White Slave traffic. The lady rightly concluded that much the best instrument for warning the men, and making known to the women the addresses of the organization for befriending unprotected girl travellers, is the cinema. She caused a film to be made for this purpose. The Film Censor immediately banned the part of the film which gave the addresses to the girls and shewed them the risks they ran. The lady appealed to me to help her to protest. After convincing myself by witnessing a private exhibition of the film that it was quite innocent I wrote to the Censor, begging him to examine the film personally, and remedy what seemed to be a rule-of-thumb mistake by his examiners. He not only confirmed their veto, but left uncontradicted a report in all the papers that he had given as his reason that the lady had paraded the allurements of vice, and that such parades could not be tolerated by him. The sole allurements were the smart motor car in which the heroine of the film was kidnapped, and the fashionable clothes of the two very repulsive agents who drugged her in it. In every other respect her experiences were as disagreeable as the sternest moralist could desire.

I then made a tour of the picture houses to see what the Film Censor considers allowable. Of the films duly licensed by him two were so nakedly pornographic that their exhibition could hardly have been risked without the Censor's certificate of purity. One of them presented the allurements of a supposedly French brothel so shamelessly that I rose and fled in disgust long before the end, though I am as hardened to vulgar salacity in the theatre as a surgeon is to a dissecting room.

The only logical conclusion apparent is that the White Slave traffickers are in complete control of our picture theatres, and can close them to our Rescue workers as effectively as they can reserve them for advertisements of their own trade. I spare the Film Censor that conclusion. The conclusion I press upon him and on the public is my old one of twentyeight years ago: that all the evil effects of such corrupt control are inevitably produced gratuitously by Censors with the best intentions.

Mr Shaw's Method and Secret

(A letter to the Editor of *The Daily Chronicle*,
London, 30 April 1898)

28th April 1898

Sir,—

I notice that your columns are agitated at present
by the question whether my dramatic works are due
to the influence of Ibsen or De Maupassant.

Allow me to give you a few instances of the real
living influences under which I work. I live in the
parish of St. Pancras, and am a vestryman thereof.
St. Pancras contains quarter of a million inhabitants.
An appalling number of them live in single-room
tenements. The districts in which these tenements are
most plentiful have been frankly given up by our
most energetic sanitary inspectors, who have no time
to do anything more than attend to complaints which,
I need hardly say, are only made by the people who
are enlightened enough to be least in need of attention.
A recent very careful inquiry by a sub-committee in
the Health Department pointed out the means of
dealing with this evil. The vestry positively declined
to take them. It gave no reasons. It freely accused its
Health Committee of incompetence and its Sanitary
Staff of negligence; but it took no steps to reconstitute
the committee, nor to set on foot an inquiry into the
alleged negligence. It knew perfectly well that more
sanitary inspectors were required; and it was resolved
not to pay for them even at the risk of being ignominiously compelled by the County Council to do
its duty.

There is in St. Pancras the usual public sanitary
accommodation, including a single underground

[267]

convenience for women. The accommodation is perfectly free to men, and is used by thousands daily without payment. It is only when the lavatory or a closet is used that a charge is made. Free accommodation is refused altogether to women. Six months ago the one woman on the vestry, supported by a few humane and decent men, succeeded in shaming the vestry into making the accommodation in the women's convenience partly free. Since then, 1,725 women, or thirteen per cent., of the total number using the convenience, have availed themselves of the free accommodation. Yesterday the vestry deliberately abolished it. I remonstrated, and was seconded by our lady member. An eminent member of the vestry immediately rose and expressed his horror at my venturing to speak in public on so disgusting a subject. He then accused my seconder of indecency. At this point the vestrymen, to their credit, revolted, and squashed the unhappy apostle of gentlemanly delicacy; but they voted on his side in a majority of about seven to one, and the poor women of St. Pancras will in future have to pay a penny for the privilege, enjoyed for nothing by the men, of observing the common decencies of traffic in a city.

Later on we came to a subject which has lately been well in evidence in the "Chronicle"—I mean the Bill now before Parliament for interfering very mildly with shop slavery. The vestry was warned by its Parliamentary Committee that this Bill would compel the provision of sitting accommodation for women employed in shops; would save them from being kept more than a certain number of hours without rest or refreshment; and would secure proper sanitary accommodation and ventilation for them. We were told that the vestry of St. Anne, Limehouse, has re-

[268]

solved to oppose the Bill, "for the reason that it would injuriously affect the interests of retail traders." The vestry of St. Pancras, a ghastly centre of shop slavery, promptly assured St. Anne of its approval and cordial agreement.

It must not be inferred that vestrymen are an inhuman and merciless class. On the contrary, they are stuffed, every man of them, with good intentions, intense respectability, piety, theoretical humanity and the most exalted ideas of womanly purity. All their finest instincts are jarred unendurably when their minds are dragged down from the contemplation of photographs of princesses to sanitary conveniences for charwomen. Every drop of their blood is so sweetened by charity that they pay starvation wages to their scavengers lest they should be compelled to discharge the worn-out men whom they have employed out of benevolence. At most of their meetings they commit crimes against society for which they would get twenty years' penal servitude if they committed them as individuals against private property instead of as public representatives against the common weal. But they do it from the loftiest, kindliest, most self-sacrificing reasons; and all remonstrance strikes them as being half ludicrous, half cynical, and altogether a breach of good sense and good manners—much as "The Philanderer" strikes my friend Mr. Archer, in fact.

Looking away from local politics to the broader world-horizon, I see two nations busily engaged in shiplifting, arson and murder, and all the newspapers gravely calling it war, patriotism, "Feeling in America," "Feeling in Spain," and so forth. And if I were to propose that the European Concert should promptly take steps to capture the shiplifters and restrain them by force, I daresay I should discover that the European Press is precisely like the St. Pancras Vestry; and your literary columns would proceed to discuss whether my proposals were borrowed from Ibsen or Maupassant.

If a dramatist living in a world like this has to go to books for his ideas and his inspiration, he must be both blind and deaf. Most dramatists are.

For the satisfaction of my friend Cunninghame Graham, I may say that if I have fallen into the ways of De Maupassant, the fault is Mr. Archer's. He once lent me, and insisted on my reading, a book by that author entitled "Une Vie." It took me two years to get through it; but it was a very honest and able bit of photography. I believe I also once read a short Maupassant story about a man who shot himself because he was afraid to fight a duel. As to "Mrs. Warren's Profession," it came about in this way. Miss Janet Achurch mentioned to me a novel by some French writer [De Maupassant's *Yvette*] as having a dramatisable story in it. It being hopeless to get me to read anything, she told me the story, which was ultra-romantic. I said, "Oh, I will work out the real truth about that mother some day." In the following autumn I was the guest of a lady [Beatrice Webb] of very distinguished ability—one whose knowledge of English social types is as remarkable as her command of industrial and political questions. She suggested that I should put on the stage a real modern lady of the governing class—not the sort of thing that theatrical and critical authorities imagine such a lady to be. I did so; and the result was Miss Vivie Warren, who has laid the intellect of Mr. William Archer in ruins. The fact is the modern lady expresses so freely the ideas that were first introduced to Mr. Archer by me in the course of the fruitless pains I have bestowed for years on his neglected sociological education, that he sees nothing in her but a Shaw in petticoats— a dreadful phenomenon. Mrs. Warren herself was my version of the heroine of the romance narrated by Miss Achurch. The tremendously effective scene— which a baby could write if its sight were normal— in which she justifies herself, is only a paraphrase of a scene in a novel of my own, "Cashel Byron's Profession" (hence the title, "Mrs. Warren's Profession"), in which a prize-fighter shows how he was driven into the ring exactly as Mrs. Warren was driven on the streets. Never was there a more grossly obvious derivation. I finally persuaded Miss Achurch, who is clever with her pen, to dramatise her story herself on its original romantic lines. Her version is called "Mrs. Daintry's Daughter." That is the history of "Mrs. Warren's Profession." I never dreamt of Ibsen or De Maupassant, any more than a blacksmith shoeing a horse thinks of the blacksmith in the next county.

Yours truly,
G. Bernard Shaw

⌈ACT I⌉

Summer afternoon in a cottage garden on the eastern slope of a hill a little south of Haslemere in Surrey. Looking up the hill, the cottage is seen in the left hand corner of the garden, with its thatched roof and porch, and a large latticed window to the left of the porch. A paling completely shuts in the garden, except for a gate on the right. The common rises uphill beyond the paling to the sky line. Some folded canvas garden chairs are leaning against the side bench in the porch. A lady's bicycle is propped against the wall, under the window. A little to the right of the porch a hammock is slung from two posts. A big canvas umbrella, stuck in the ground, keeps the sun off the hammock, in which a young lady lies reading and making notes, her head towards the cottage and her feet towards the gate. In front of the hammock, and within reach of her hand, is a common kitchen chair, with a pile of serious-looking books and a supply of writing paper on it.

A gentleman walking on the common comes into sight from behind the cottage. He is hardly past middle age, with something of the artist about him, unconventionally but carefully dressed, and clean-shaven except for a moustache, with an eager susceptible face and very amiable and considerate manners. He has silky black hair, with waves of grey and white in it. His eyebrows are white, his moustache black. He seems not certain of his way. He looks over the paling; takes stock of the place; and sees the young lady.

THE GENTLEMAN [*taking off his hat*] I beg your pardon. Can you direct me to Hindhead View—Mrs Alison's?

THE YOUNG LADY [*glancing up from her book*] This is Mrs Alison's. [*She resumes her work*].

THE GENTLEMAN. Indeed! Perhaps—may I ask are you Miss Vivie Warren?

THE YOUNG LADY [*sharply, as she turns on her elbow to get a good look at him*] Yes.

THE GENTLEMAN [*daunted and conciliatory*] I'm afraid I appear intrusive. My name is Praed. [*Vivie at once throws her books upon the chair, and gets out of the hammock*]. Oh, pray dont let me disturb you.

VIVIE [*striding to the gate and opening it for him*] Come in, Mr Praed. [*He comes in*]. Glad to see you. [*She proffers her hand and takes his with a resolute and hearty grip. She is an attractive specimen of the sensible, able, highly-educated young middle-class Englishwoman. Age 22. Prompt, strong, confident, self-possessed. Plain business-like dress, but not dowdy. She wears a chatelaine at her belt, with a fountain pen and a paper knife among its pendants*].

PRAED. Very kind of you indeed, Miss Warren. [*She shuts the gate with a vigorous slam. He passes in to the middle of the garden, exercising his fingers, which are slightly numbed by her greeting*]. Has your mother arrived?

VIVIE [*quickly, evidently scenting aggression*] Is she coming?

PRAED [*surprised*] Didnt you expect us?

VIVIE. No.

PRAED. Now, goodness me, I hope Ive not mistaken the day. That would be just like me, you know. Your mother arranged that she was to come down from

London and that I was to come over from Horsham to be introduced to you.

VIVIE [*not at all pleased*] Did she? Hm! My mother has rather a trick of taking me by surprise—to see how I behave myself when she's away, I suppose. I fancy I shall take my mother very much by surprise one of these days, if she makes arrangements that concern me without consulting me beforehand. She hasnt come.

PRAED [*embarrassed*] I'm really very sorry.

VIVIE [*throwing off her displeasure*] It's not your fault, Mr Praed, is it? And I'm very glad youve come. You are the only one of my mother's friends I have ever asked her to bring to see me.

PRAED [*relieved and delighted*] Oh, now this is really very good of you, Miss Warren!

VIVIE. Will you come indoors; or would you rather sit out here and talk?

PRAED. It will be nicer out here, dont you think?

VIVIE. Then I'll go and get you a chair. [*She goes to the porch for a garden chair*].

PRAED [*following her*] Oh, pray, pray! Allow me. [*He lays hands on the chair*].

VIVIE [*letting him take it*] Take care of your fingers: theyre rather dodgy things, those chairs. [*She goes across to the chair with the books on it; pitches them into the hammock; and brings the chair forward with one swing*].

PRAED [*who has just unfolded his chair*] Oh, now do let me take that hard chair. I like hard chairs.

VIVIE. So do I. Sit down, Mr Praed. [*This invitation she gives with genial peremptoriness, his anxiety to please her clearly striking her as a sign of weakness of character on his part. But he does not immediately obey*].

PRAED. By the way, though, hadnt we better go to the station to meet your mother?

VIVIE [*coolly*] Why? She knows the way.

PRAED [*disconcerted*] Er—I suppose she does [*he sits down*].

VIVIE. Do you know, you are just like what I expected. I hope you are disposed to be friends with me.

PRAED [*again beaming*] Thank you, my dear Miss Warren: thank you. Dear me! I'm so glad your mother hasnt spoilt you!

VIVIE. How?

PRAED. Well, in making you too conventional. You know, my dear Miss Warren, I am a born anarchist. I hate authority. It spoils the relations between parent and child: even between mother and daughter. Now I was always afraid that your mother would strain her authority to make you very conventional. It's such a relief to find that she hasnt.

VIVIE. Oh! have I been behaving unconventionally?

PRAED. Oh no: oh dear no. At least not conventionally unconventionally, you understand. [*She nods and sits down. He goes on, with a cordial outburst*] But it was so charming of you to say that you were disposed to be friends with me! You modern young ladies are splendid: perfectly splendid!

VIVIE [*dubiously*] Eh? [*watching him with dawning disappointment as to the quality of his brains and character*].

PRAED. When I was your age, young men and women were afraid of each other: there was no good fellowship. Nothing real. Only gallantry copied out of novels, and as vulgar and affected as it could be. Maidenly reserve! gentlemanly chivalry! always saying no when you meant yes! simple purgatory for shy and sincere souls.

[275]

VIVIE. Yes, I imagine there must have been a frightful waste of time. Especially women's time.

PRAED. Oh, waste of life, waste of everything. But things are improving. Do you know, I have been in a positive state of excitement about meeting you ever since your magnificent achievements at Cambridge: a thing unheard of in my day. It was perfectly splendid, you tieing with the third wrangler. Just the right place, you know. The first wrangler is always a dreamy, morbid fellow, in whom the thing is pushed to the length of a disease.

VIVIE. It doesnt pay. I wouldnt do it again for the same money.

PRAED [*aghast*] The same money!

VIVIE. I did it for £50.

PRAED. Fifty pounds!

VIVIE. Yes. Fifty pounds. Perhaps you dont know how it was. Mrs Latham, my tutor at Newnham, told my mother that I could distinguish myself in the mathematical tripos if I went in for it in earnest. The papers were full just then of Phillipa Summers beating the senior wrangler. You remember about it, of course.

PRAED [*shakes his head energetically*]!!!

VIVIE. Well anyhow she did; and nothing would please my mother but that I should do the same thing. I said flatly it was not worth my while to face the grind since I was not going in for teaching; but I offered to try for fourth wrangler or thereabouts for £50. She closed with me at that, after a little grumbling; and I was better than my bargain. But I wouldnt do it again for that. £200 would have been nearer the mark.

PRAED [*much damped*] Lord bless me! Thats a very practical way of looking at it.

VIVIE. Did you expect to find me an unpractical person?

PRAED. But surely it's practical to consider not only the work these honors cost, but also the culture they bring.

VIVIE. Culture! My dear Mr Praed: do you know what the mathematical tripos means? It means grind, grind, grind for six to eight hours a day at mathematics, and nothing but mathematics. I'm supposed to know something about science; but I know nothing except the mathematics it involves. I can make calculations for engineers, electricians, insurance companies, and so on; but I know next to nothing about engineering or electricity or insurance. I dont even know arithmetic well. Outside mathematics, lawn-tennis, eating, sleeping, cycling, and walking, I'm a more ignorant barbarian than any woman could possibly be who hadnt gone in for the tripos.

PRAED [*revolted*] What a monstrous, wicked, rascally system! I knew it! I felt at once that it meant destroying all that makes womanhood beautiful.

VIVIE. I dont object to it on that score in the least. I shall turn it to very good account, I assure you.

PRAED. Pooh! In what way?

VIVIE. I shall set up in chambers in the City, and work at actuarial calculations and conveyancing. Under cover of that I shall do some law, with one eye on the Stock Exchange all the time. Ive come down here by myself to read law: not for a holiday, as my mother imagines. I hate holidays.

PRAED. You make my blood run cold. Are you to have no romance, no beauty in your life?

VIVIE. I dont care for either, I assure you.

PRAED. You cant mean that.

VIVIE. Oh yes I do. I like working and getting paid

[277]

for it. When I'm tired of working, I like a comfortable chair, a cigar, a little whisky, and a novel with a good detective story in it.

PRAED [*rising in a frenzy of repudiation*] I dont believe it. I am an artist; and I cant believe it: I refuse to believe it. It's only that you havnt discovered yet what a wonderful world art can open up to you.

VIVIE. Yes I have. Last May I spent six weeks in London with Honoria Fraser. Mamma thought we were doing a round of sightseeing together; but I was really at Honoria's chambers in Chancery Lane every day, working away at actuarial calculations for her, and helping her as well as a greenhorn could. In the evenings we smoked and talked, and never dreamt of going out except for exercise. And I never enjoyed myself more in my life. I cleared all my expenses, and got initiated into the business without a fee into the bargain.

PRAED. But bless my heart and soul, Miss Warren, do you call that discovering art?

VIVIE. Wait a bit. That wasnt the beginning. I went up to town on an invitation from some artistic people in Fitzjohn's Avenue: one of the girls was a Newnham chum. They took me to the National Gallery—

PRAED [*approving*] Ah!! [*He sits down, much relieved*].

VIVIE [*continuing*]—to the Opera—

PRAED [*still more pleased*] Good!

VIVIE. —and to a concert where the band played all the evening: Beethoven and Wagner and so on. I wouldnt go through that experience again for anything you could offer me. I held out for civility's sake until the third day; and then I said, plump out, that I couldnt stand any more of it, and went off to Chancery Lane. Now you know the sort of perfectly splendid modern young lady I am. How do you think I shall get on with my mother?

PRAED [*startled*] Well, I hope—er—

VIVIE. It's not so much what you hope as what you believe, that I want to know.

PRAED. Well, frankly, I am afraid your mother will be a little disappointed. Not from any shortcoming on your part, you know: I dont mean that. But you are so different from her ideal.

VIVIE. Her what?!

PRAED. Her ideal.

VIVIE. Do you mean her ideal of ME?

PRAED. Yes.

VIVIE. What on earth is it like?

PRAED. Well, you must have observed, Miss Warren, that people who are dissatisfied with their own bringing-up generally think that the world would be all right if everybody were to be brought up quite differently. Now your mother's life has been—er—I suppose you know—

VIVIE. Dont suppose anything, Mr Praed. I hardly know my mother. Since I was a child I have lived in England, at school or college, or with people paid to take charge of me. I have been boarded out all my life. My mother has lived in Brussels or Vienna and never let me go to her. I only see her when she visits England for a few days. I dont complain: it's been very pleasant; for people have been very good to me; and there has always been plenty of money to make things smooth. But dont imagine I know anything about my mother. I know far less than you do.

PRAED [*very ill at ease*] In that case—[*He stops, quite at a loss. Then, with a forced attempt at gaiety*] But what nonsense we are talking! Of course you and your mother will get on capitally. [*He rises, and looks abroad at the view*]. What a charming little place you have here!

VIVIE [*unmoved*] Rather a violent change of subject, Mr Praed. Why wont my mother's life bear being talked about?

PRAED. Oh, you really mustnt say that. Isnt it natural that I should have a certain delicacy in talking to my old friend's daughter about her behind her back? You and she will have plenty of opportunity of talking about it when she comes.

VIVIE. No: she wont talk about it either. [*Rising*] However, I daresay you have good reasons for telling me nothing. Only, mind this, Mr Praed. I expect there will be a battle royal when my mother hears of my Chancery Lane project.

PRAED [*ruefully*] I'm afraid there will.

VIVIE. Well, I shall win, because I want nothing but my fare to London to start there to-morrow earning my own living by devilling for Honoria. Besides, I have no mysteries to keep up; and it seems she has. I shall use that advantage over her if necessary.

PRAED [*greatly shocked*] Oh no! No, pray. Youd not do such a thing.

VIVIE. Then tell me why not.

PRAED. I really cannot. I appeal to your good feeling. [*She smiles at his sentimentality*]. Besides you may be too bold. Your mother is not to be trifled with when she's angry.

VIVIE. You cant frighten me, Mr Praed. In that month at Chancery Lane I had opportunities of taking the measure of one or two women very like my mother. You may back me to win. But if I hit harder in my ignorance than I need, remember that it is you who refuse to enlighten me. Now, let us drop the subject.

[*She takes her chair and replaces it near the hammock with the same vigorous swing as before*].

PRAED [*taking a desperate resolution*] One word, Miss Warren. I had better tell you. It's very difficult; but—

Mrs Warren and Sir George Crofts arrive at the gate. Mrs Warren is between 40 and 50, formerly pretty, showily dressed in a brilliant hat and a gay blouse fitting tightly over her bust and flanked by fashionable sleeves. Rather spoilt and domineering, and decidedly vulgar, but, on the whole, a genial and fairly presentable old blackguard of a woman.

Crofts is a tall powerfully-built man of about 50, fashionably dressed in the style of a young man. Nasal voice, reedier than might be expected from his strong frame. Clean-shaven bulldog jaws, large flat ears, and thick neck: gentlemanly combination of the most brutal types of city man, sporting man, and man about town.

VIVIE. Here they are. [*Coming to them as they enter the garden*] How do, mater? Mr Praed's been here this half hour waiting for you.

MRS WARREN. Well, if youve been waiting, Praddy, it's your own fault: I thought youd have the gumption to know I was coming by the 3.10 train. Vivie: put your hat on, dear: youll get sunburnt. Oh, I forgot to introduce you. Sir George Crofts: my little Vivie.

Crofts advances to Vivie with his most courtly manner. She nods, but makes no motion to shake hands.

CROFTS. May I shake hands with a young lady whom I have known by reputation very long as the daughter of one of my oldest friends?

VIVIE [*who has been looking him up and down sharply*] If you like. [*She takes his tenderly proffered hand and gives it a squeeze that makes him open his eyes; then turns away, and says to her mother*] Will you come in,

[281]

or shall I get a couple more chairs ? [*She goes into the porch for the chairs*].

MRS WARREN. Well George, what do you think of her ?

CROFTS [*ruefully*] She has a powerful fist. Did you shake hands with her, Praed ?

PRAED. Yes: it will pass off presently.

CROFTS. I hope so. [*Vivie reappears with two more chairs. He hurries to her assistance*]. Allow me.

MRS WARREN [*patronizingly*] Let Sir George help you with the chairs, dear.

VIVIE [*pitching them into his arms*] Here you are. [*She dusts her hands and turns to Mrs Warren*]. Youd like some tea, wouldnt you ?

MRS WARREN [*sitting in Praed's chair and fanning herself*] I'm dying for a drop to drink.

VIVIE. I'll see about it. [*She goes into the cottage*].

Sir George has by this time managed to unfold a chair and plant it beside Mrs Warren, on her left. He throws the other on the grass and sits down, looking dejected and rather foolish, with the handle of his stick in his mouth. Praed, still very uneasy, fidgets about the garden on their right.

MRS WARREN [*to Praed, looking at Crofts*] Just look at him, Praddy: he looks cheerful, dont he ? He's been worrying my life out these three years to have that little girl of mine shewn to him; and now that Ive done it, he's quite out of countenance. [*Briskly*] Come! sit up, George; and take your stick out of your mouth. [*Crofts sulkily obeys*].

PRAED. I think, you know—if you dont mind my saying so—that we had better get out of the habit of thinking of her as a little girl. You see she has really distinguished herself; and I'm not sure, from what I have seen of her, that she is not older than any of us.

[282]

MRS WARREN [*greatly amused*] Only listen to him, George! Older than any of us! Well, she has been stuffing you nicely with her importance.

PRAED. But young people are particularly sensitive about being treated in that way.

MRS WARREN. Yes; and young people have to get all that nonsense taken out of them, and a good deal more besides. Dont you interfere, Praddy: I know how to treat my own child as well as you do. [*Praed, with a grave shake of his head, walks up the garden with his hands behind his back. Mrs Warren pretends to laugh, but looks after him with perceptible concern. Then she whispers to Crofts*] Whats the matter with him? What does he take it like that for?

CROFTS [*morosely*] Youre afraid of Praed.

MRS WARREN. What! Me! Afraid of dear old Praddy! Why, a fly wouldnt be afraid of him.

CROFTS. Youre afraid of him.

MRS WARREN [*angry*] I'll trouble you to mind your own business, and not try any of your sulks on me. I'm not afraid of you, anyhow. If you cant make yourself agreeable, youd better go home. [*She gets up, and, turning her back on him, finds herself face to face with Praed*]. Come, Praddy, I know it was only your tender-heartedness. Youre afraid I'll bully her.

PRAED. My dear Kitty: you think I'm offended. Dont imagine that: pray dont. But you know I often notice things that escape you; and though you never take my advice, you sometimes admit afterwards that you ought to have taken it.

MRS WARREN. Well, what do you notice now?

PRAED. Only that Vivie is a grown woman. Pray, Kitty, treat her with every respect.

MRS WARREN [*with genuine amazement*] Respect!

[283]

Treat my own daughter with respect! What next, pray!

VIVIE [*appearing at the cottage door and calling to Mrs Warren*] Mother: will you come to my room before tea?

MRS WARREN. Yes, dearie. [*She laughs indulgently at Praed's gravity, and pats him on the cheek as she passes him on her way to the porch*]. Dont be cross, Praddy. [*She follows Vivie into the cottage*].

CROFTS [*furtively*] I say, Praed.

PRAED. Yes.

CROFTS. I want to ask you a rather particular question.

PRAED. Certainly. [*He takes Mrs Warren's chair and sits close to Crofts*].

CROFTS. Thats right: they might hear us from the window. Look here: did Kitty ever tell you who that girl's father is?

PRAED. Never.

CROFTS. Have you any suspicion of who it might be?

PRAED. None.

CROFTS [*not believing him*] I know, of course, that you perhaps might feel bound not to tell if she had said anything to you. But it's very awkward to be uncertain about it now that we shall be meeting the girl every day. We dont exactly know how we ought to feel towards her.

PRAED. What difference can that make? We take her on her own merits. What does it matter who her father was?

CROFTS [*suspiciously*] Then you know who he was?

PRAED [*with a touch of temper*] I said no just now. Did you not hear me?

CROFTS. Look here, Praed. I ask you as a particular favor. If you do know [*movement of protest from*

[284]

Praed]—I only say, if you know, you might at least set my mind at rest about her. The fact is, I feel attracted.

PRAED [*sternly*] What do you mean?

CROFTS. Oh, dont be alarmed: it's quite an innocent feeling. Thats what puzzles me about it. Why, for all I know, *I* might be her father.

PRAED. You! Impossible!

CROFTS [*catching him up cunningly*] You know for certain that I'm not?

PRAED. I know nothing about it, I tell you, any more than you. But really, Crofts—oh no, it's out of the question. Theres not the least resemblance.

CROFTS. As to that, theres no resemblance between her and her mother that I can see. I suppose she's not your daughter, is she?

PRAED [*rising indignantly*] Really, Crofts—!

CROFTS. No offence, Praed. Quite allowable as between two men of the world.

PRAED [*recovering himself with an effort and speaking gently and gravely*] Now listen to me, my dear Crofts. [*He sits down again*]. I have nothing to do with that side of Mrs Warren's life, and never had. She has never spoken to me about it; and of course I have never spoken to her about it. Your delicacy will tell you that a handsome woman needs some friends who are not—well, not on that footing with her. The effect of her own beauty would become a torment to her if she could not escape from it occasionally. You are probably on much more confidential terms with Kitty than I am. Surely you can ask her the question yourself.

CROFTS. I have asked her, often enough. But she's so determined to keep the child all to herself that she would deny that it ever had a father if she could.

[*Rising*] I'm thoroughly uncomfortable about it, Praed.

PRAED [*rising also*] Well, as you are, at all events, old enough to be her father, I dont mind agreeing that we both regard Miss Vivie in a parental way, as a young girl whom we are bound to protect and help. What do you say?

CROFTS [*aggressively*] I'm no older than you, if you come to that.

PRAED. Yes you are, my dear fellow: you were born old. I was born a boy: Ive never been able to feel the assurance of a grown-up man in my life. [*He folds his chair and carries it to the porch*].

MRS WARREN [*calling from within the cottage*] Prad-dee! George! Tea-ea-ea-ea!

CROFTS [*hastily*] She's calling us. [*He hurries in*].

Praed shakes his head bodingly, and is following Crofts when he is hailed by a young gentleman who has just appeared on the common, and is making for the gate. He is pleasant, pretty, smartly dressed, cleverly good-for-nothing, not long turned 20, with a charming voice and agreeably disrespectful manners. He carries a light sporting magazine rifle.

THE YOUNG GENTLEMAN. Hallo! Praed!

PRAED. Why, Frank Gardner! [*Frank comes in and shakes hands cordially*]. What on earth are you doing here?

FRANK. Staying with my father.

PRAED. The Roman father?

FRANK. He's rector here. I'm living with my people this autumn for the sake of economy. Things came to a crisis in July: the Roman father had to pay my debts. He's stony broke in consequence; and so am I. What are you up to in these parts? Do you know the people here?

PRAED. Yes: I'm spending the day with a Miss Warren.

FRANK [*enthusiastically*] What! Do you know Vivie?
Isnt she a jolly girl? I'm teaching her to shoot with
this (*putting down the rifle*). I'm so glad she knows
you: youre just the sort of fellow she ought to know.
[*He smiles, and raises the charming voice almost to a
singing tone as he exclaims*] It's ever so jolly to find
you here, Praed.

PRAED. I'm an old friend of her mother. Mrs Warren
brought me over to make her daughter's acquaintance.

FRANK. The mother! Is she here?

PRAED. Yes: inside, at tea.

MRS WARREN [*calling from within*] Prad-dee-ee-ee-
eee! The tea-cake'll be cold.

PRAED [*calling*] Yes, Mrs Warren. In a moment. Ive
just met a friend here.

MRS WARREN. A what?

PRAED [*louder*] A friend

MRS WARREN. Bring him in.

PRAED. All right. [*To Frank*] Will you accept the
invitation?

FRANK [*incredulous, but immensely amused*] Is that
Vivie's mother?

PRAED. Yes.

FRANK. By Jove! What a lark! Do you think she'll like
me?

PRAED. Ive no doubt youll make yourself popular, as
usual. Come in and try [*moving towards the house*].

FRANK. Stop a bit. [*Seriously*] I want to take you into
my confidence.

PRAED. Pray dont. It's only some fresh folly, like the
barmaid at Redhill.

FRANK. It's ever so much more serious than that.
You say youve only just met Vivie for the first time?

PRAED. Yes.

FRANK [*rhapsodically*] Then you can have no idea what a girl she is. Such character! Such sense! And her cleverness! Oh, my eye, Praed, but I can tell you she is clever! And—need I add?—she loves me.

CROFTS [*putting his head out of the window*] I say, Praed: what are you about? Do come along. [*He disappears*].

FRANK. Hallo! Sort of chap that would take a prize at a dog show, aint he? Who's he?

PRAED. Sir George Crofts, an old friend of Mrs Warren's. I think we had better come in.

On their way to the porch they are interrupted by a call from the gate. Turning, they see an elderly clergyman looking over it.

THE CLERGYMAN [*calling*] Frank!

FRANK. Hallo! [*To Praed*] The Roman father. [*To the clergyman*] Yes, gov'nor: all right: presently. [*To Praed*] Look here, Praed: youd better go in to tea. I'll join you directly.

PRAED. Very good. [*He goes into the cottage*].

The clergyman remains outside the gate, with his hands on the top of it. The Rev. Samuel Gardner, a beneficed clergyman of the Established Church, is over 50. Externally he is pretentious, booming, noisy, important. Really he is that obsolescent social phenomenon the fool of the family dumped on the Church by his father, the patron, clamorously asserting himself as father and clergyman without being able to command respect in either capacity.

REV. S. Well, sir. Who are your friends here, if I may ask?

FRANK. Oh, it's all right, gov'nor! Come in.

REV. S. No sir; not until I know whose garden I am entering.

FRANK. It's all right. It's Miss Warren's.

REV. S. I have not seen her at church since she came.

FRANK. Of course not: she's a third wrangler. Ever so intellectual. Took a higher degree than you did; so why should she go to hear you preach?

REV. S. Dont be disrespectful, sir.

FRANK. Oh, it dont matter: nobody hears us. Come in. [*He opens the gate, unceremoniously pulling his father with it into the garden*]. I want to introduce you to her. Do you remember the advice you gave me last July, gov'nor?

REV. S. [*severely*] Yes. I advised you to conquer your idleness and flippancy, and to work your way into an honorable profession and live on it and not upon me.

FRANK. No: thats what you thought of afterwards. What you actually said was that since I had neither brains nor money, I'd better turn my good looks to account by marrying somebody with both. Well, look here. Miss Warren has brains: you cant deny that.

REV. S. Brains are not everything.

FRANK. No, of course not: theres the money—

REV. S. [*interrupting him austerely*] I was not thinking of money, sir. I was speaking of higher things. Social position, for instance.

FRANK. I dont care a rap about that.

REV. S. But I do, sir.

FRANK. Well, nobody wants you to marry her. Anyhow, she has what amounts to a high Cambridge degree; and she seems to have as much money as she wants.

REV. S. [*sinking into a feeble vein of humor*] I greatly doubt whether she has as much money as you will want.

FRANK. Oh, come: I havnt been so very extravagant. I live ever so quietly; I dont drink; I dont bet much;

and I never go regularly on the razzle-dazzle as you did when you were my age.

REV. S. [*booming hollowly*] Silence, sir.

FRANK. Well, you told me yourself, when I was making ever such an ass of myself about the barmaid at Redhill, that you once offered a woman £50 for the letters you wrote to her when—

REV. S. [*terrified*] Sh-sh-sh, Frank, for Heaven's sake! [*He looks round apprehensively. Seeing no one within earshot he plucks up courage to boom again, but more subduedly*]. You are taking an ungentlemanly advantage of what I confided to you for your own good, to save you from an error you would have repented all your life long. Take warning by your father's follies, sir; and dont make them an excuse for your own.

FRANK. Did you ever hear the story of the Duke of Wellington and his letters?

REV. S. No, sir; and I dont want to hear it.

FRANK. The old Iron Duke didnt throw away £50: not he. He just wrote: "Dear Jenny: publish and be damned! Yours affectionately, Wellington." Thats what you should have done.

REV. S. [*piteously*] Frank, my boy: when I wrote those letters I put myself into that woman's power. When I told you about them I put myself, to some extent, I am sorry to say, in your power. She refused my money with these words, which I shall never forget. "Knowledge is power" she said; "and I never sell power." Thats more than twenty years ago; and she has never made use of her power or caused me a moment's uneasiness. You are behaving worse to me than she did, Frank.

FRANK. Oh yes I dare say! Did you ever preach at her the way you preach at me every day?

[290]

REV. S. [*wounded almost to tears*] I leave you sir. You are incorrigible. [*He turns towards the gate*].

FRANK [*utterly unmoved*] Tell them I shant be home to tea, will you, gov'nor, like a good fellow? [*He moves towards the cottage door and is met by Praed and Vivie coming out*].

VIVIE [*to Frank*] Is that your father, Frank? I do so want to meet him.

FRANK. Certainly. [*Calling after his father*] Gov'nor. Youre wanted. [*The parson turns at the gate, fumbling nervously at his hat. Praed crosses the garden to the opposite side, beaming in anticipation of civilities*]. My father: Miss Warren.

VIVIE [*going to the clergyman and shaking his hand*] Very glad to see you here, Mr Gardner. [*Calling to the cottage*] Mother: come along: youre wanted.

Mrs Warren appears on the threshold, and is immediately transfixed recognizing the clergyman.

VIVIE [*continuing*] Let me introduce—

MRS WARREN [*swooping on the Reverend Samuel*] Why, it's Sam Gardner, gone into the Church! Well, I never! Dont you know us, Sam? This is George Crofts, as large as life and twice as natural. Dont you remember me?

REV. S. [*very red*] I really—er—

MRS WARREN. Of course you do. Why, I have a whole album of your letters still: I came across them only the other day.

REV. S. [*miserably confused*] Miss Vavasour, I believe.

MRS WARREN [*correcting him quickly in a loud whisper*] Tch! Nonsense! Mrs Warren: dont you see my daughter there?

[ACT II]

Inside the cottage after nightfall. Looking eastward from within instead of westward from without, the latticed window, with its curtains drawn, is now seen in the middle of the front wall of the cottage, with the porch door to the left of it. In the left-hand side wall is the door leading to the kitchen. Farther back against the same wall is a dresser with a candle and matches on it, and Frank's rifle standing beside them, with the barrel resting in the plate-rack. In the centre a table stands with a lighted lamp on it. Vivie's books and writing materials are on a table to the right of the window, against the wall. The fireplace is on the right, with a settle: there is no fire. Two of the chairs are set right and left of the table.

The cottage door opens, shewing a fine starlit night without; and Mrs Warren, her shoulders wrapped in a shawl borrowed from Vivie, enters, followed by Frank, who throws his cap on the window seat. She has had enough of walking, and gives a gasp of relief as she unpins her hat; takes it off; sticks the pin through the crown; and puts it on the table.

MRS WARREN. O Lord! I dont know which is the worst of the country, the walking or the sitting at home with nothing to do. I could do with a whisky and soda now very well, if only they had such a thing in this place.

FRANK. Perhaps Vivie's got some.

MRS WARREN. Nonsense! What would a young girl

like her be doing with such things! Never mind: it
dont matter. I wonder how she passes her time here!
I'd a good deal rather be in Vienna.

FRANK. Let me take you there. [*He helps her to take
off her shawl, gallantly giving her shoulders a very perceptible squeeze as he does so*].

MRS WARREN. Ah! would you? I'm beginning to
think youre a chip of the old block.

FRANK. Like the gov'nor, eh? [*He hangs the shawl
on the nearest chair, and sits down*].

MRS WARREN. Never you mind. What do you know
about such things? Youre only a boy. [*She goes to the
hearth, to be farther from temptation*].

FRANK. Do come to Vienna with me? It'd be ever
such larks.

MRS WARREN. No, thank you. Vienna is no place for
you—at least not until youre a little older. [*She nods
at him to emphasize this piece of advice. He makes a
mock-piteous face, belied by his laughing eyes. She looks
at him; then comes back to him*]. Now, look here, little
boy [*taking his face in her hands and turning it up to
her*]: I know you through and through by your like-
ness to your father, better than you know yourself.
Dont you go taking any silly ideas into your head
about me. Do you hear?

FRANK [*gallantly wooing her with his voice*] Cant help
it, my dear Mrs Warren: it runs in the family.

*She pretends to box his ears; then looks at the pretty
laughing upturned face for a moment, tempted. At last
she kisses him, and immediately turns away, out of
patience with herself.*

MRS WARREN. There! I shouldnt have done that. I
am wicked. Never you mind, my dear: it's only a
motherly kiss. Go and make love to Vivie.

FRANK. So I have.

MRS WARREN [*turning on him with a sharp note of alarm in her voice*] What!

FRANK. Vivie and I are ever such chums.

MRS WARREN. What do you mean? Now see here: I wont have any young scamp tampering with my little girl. Do you hear? I wont have it.

FRANK [*quite unabashed*] My dear Mrs Warren: dont you be alarmed. My intentions are honorable: ever so honorable; and your little girl is jolly well able to take care of herself. She dont need looking after half so much as her mother. She aint so handsome, you know.

MRS WARREN [*taken aback by his assurance*] Well, you have got a nice healthy two inches thick of cheek all over you. I dont know where you got it. Not from your father, anyhow.

CROFTS [*in the garden*] The gipsies, I suppose?

REV. S. [*replying*] The broomsquires are far worse.

MRS WARREN [*to Frank*] S-sh! Remember! youve had your warning.

Crofts and the Reverend Samuel come in from the garden, the clergyman continuing his conversation as he enters.

REV. S. The perjury at the Winchester assizes is deplorable.

MRS WARREN. Well? What became of you two? And wheres Praddy and Vivie?

CROFTS [*putting his hat on the settle and his stick in the chimney corner*] They went up the hill. We went to the village. I wanted a drink. [*He sits down on the settle, putting his legs up along the seat*].

MRS WARREN. Well, she oughtnt to go off like that without telling me. [*To Frank*] Get your father a chair, Frank: where are your manners? [*Frank springs up and gracefully offers his father his chair; and then takes another from the wall and sits down at the table, in the middle, with his father on his right and Mrs Warren on his left].* George: where are you going to stay tonight? You cant stay here. And whats Praddy going to do?

CROFTS. Gardner'll put me up.

MRS WARREN. Oh, no doubt youve taken care of yourself! But what about Praddy?

CROFTS. Dont know. I suppose he can sleep at the inn.

MRS WARREN. Havnt you room for him, Sam?

REV. S. Well—er—you see, as rector here, I am not free to do as I like. Er—what is Mr Praed's social position?

MRS WARREN. Oh, he's all right: he's an architect. What an old stick-in-the-mud you are, Sam!

FRANK. Yes, it's all right, gov'nor. He built that place down in Wales for the Duke. Caernarvon Castle they call it. You must have heard of it. *[He winks with lightning smartness at Mrs Warren, and regards his father blandly].*

REV. S. Oh, in that case, of course we shall only be too happy. I suppose he knows the Duke personally.

FRANK. Oh, ever so intimately! We can stick him in Georgina's old room.

MRS WARREN. Well, thats settled. Now if those two would only come in and let us have supper. Theyve no right to stay out after dark like this.

CROFTS *[aggressively]* What harm are they doing you?

MRS WARREN. Well, harm or not, I dont like it.

FRANK. Better not wait for them, Mrs Warren. Praed will stay out as long as possible. He has never known before what it is to stray over the heath on a summer night with my Vivie.

CROFTS *[sitting up in some consternation]* I say, you know! Come!

REV. S. [*rising, startled out of his professional manner into real force and sincerity*] Frank, once for all, it's out of the question. Mrs Warren will tell you that it's not to be thought of.

CROFTS. Of course not.

FRANK [*with enchanting placidity*] Is that so, Mrs Warren?

MRS WARREN [*reflectively*] Well, Sam, I dont know. If the girl wants to get married, no good can come of keeping her unmarried.

REV. S. [*astounded*] But married to him!—your daughter to my son! Only think: it's impossible.

CROFTS. Of course it's impossible. Dont be a fool, Kitty.

MRS WARREN [*nettled*] Why not? Isnt my daughter good enough for your son?

REV. S. But surely, my dear Mrs Warren, you know the reasons—

MRS WARREN [*defiantly*] I know no reasons. If you know any, you can tell them to the lad, or to the girl, or to your congregation, if you like.

REV. S. [*collapsing helplessly into his chair*] You know very well that I couldnt tell anyone the reasons. But my boy will believe me when I tell him there are reasons.

FRANK. Quite right, Dad: he will. But has your boy's conduct ever been influenced by your reasons?

CROFTS. You cant marry her; and thats all about it. [*He gets up and stands on the hearth, with his back to the fireplace, frowning determinedly*].

MRS WARREN [*turning on him sharply*] What have you got to do with it, pray?

FRANK [*with his prettiest lyrical cadence*] Precisely what I was going to ask, myself, in my own graceful fashion.

[296]

CROFTS [*to Mrs Warren*] I suppose you dont want to marry the girl to a man younger than herself and without either a profession or twopence to keep her on. Ask Sam, if you dont believe me. [*To the parson*] How much more money are you going to give him?

REV. S. Not another penny. He has had his patrimony; and he spent the last of it in July. [*Mrs Warren's face falls*].

CROFTS [*watching her*] There! I told you. [*He resumes his place on the settle and puts up his legs on the seat again, as if the matter were finally disposed of*].

FRANK [*plaintively*] This is ever so mercenary. Do you suppose Miss Warren's going to marry for money? If we love one another—

MRS WARREN. Thank you. Your love's a pretty cheap commodity, my lad. If you have no means of keeping a wife, that settles it: you cant have Vivie.

FRANK [*much amused*] What do you say, gov'nor, eh?

REV S. I agree with Mrs Warren.

FRANK. And good old Crofts has already expressed his opinion.

CROFTS [*turning angrily on his elbow*] Look here: I want none of your cheek.

FRANK [*pointedly*] I'm ever so sorry to surprise you, Crofts, but you allowed yourself the liberty of speaking to me like a father a moment ago. One father is enough, thank you.

CROFTS [*contemptuously*] Yah! [*He turns away again*].

FRANK [*rising*] Mrs Warren: I cannot give my Vivie up, even for your sake.

MRS WARREN [*muttering*] Young scamp!

FRANK [*continuing*] And as you no doubt intend to hold out other prospects to her, I shall lose no time in placing my case before her. [*They stare at him; and he begins to declaim gracefully*]

He either fears his fate too much,
Or his deserts are small,
That dares not put it to the touch
To gain or lose it all.

The cottage door opens whilst he is reciting; and Vivie and Praed come in. He breaks off. Praed puts his hat on the dresser. There is an immediate improvement in the company's behavior. Crofts takes down his legs from the settle and pulls himself together as Praed joins him at the fireplace. Mrs Warren loses her ease of manner and takes refuge in querulousness.

MRS WARREN. Wherever have you been, Vivie?

VIVIE [*taking off her hat and throwing it carelessly on the table*] On the hill.

MRS WARREN. Well, you shouldnt go off like that without letting me know. How could I tell what had become of you? And night coming on too!

VIVIE [*going to the door of the kitchen and opening it, ignoring her mother*] Now, about supper? [*All rise except Mrs Warren*]. We shall be rather crowded in here, I'm afraid.

MRS WARREN. Did you hear what I said, Vivie?

VIVIE [*quietly*] Yes, mother. [*Reverting to the supper difficulty*] How many are we? [*Counting*] One, two, three, four, five, six. Well, two will have to wait until the rest are done: Mrs Alison has only plates and knives for four.

PRAED. Oh, it doesnt matter about me. I—

VIVIE. You have had a long walk and are hungry, Mr Praed: you shall have your supper at once. I can wait myself. I want one person to wait with me. Frank: are you hungry?

FRANK. Not the least in the world. Completely off my peck, in fact.

MRS WARREN [*to Crofts*] Neither are you, George. You can wait.

CROFTS. Oh, hang it, Ive eaten nothing since tea-time. Cant Sam do it?

FRANK. Would you starve my poor father?

REV. S. [*testily*] Allow me to speak for myself, sir. I am perfectly willing to wait.

VIVIE [*decisively*] Theres no need. Only two are wanted. [*She opens the door of the kitchen*]. Will you take my mother in, Mr Gardner. [*The parson takes Mrs Warren; and they pass into the kitchen. Praed and Crofts follow. All except Praed clearly disapprove of the arrangement, but do not know how to resist it. Vivie stands at the door looking in at them*]. Can you squeeze past to that corner, Mr Praed: it's rather a tight fit. Take care of your coat against the white-wash: thats right. Now, are you all comfortable?

PRAED [*within*] Quite, thank you.

MRS WARREN [*within*] Leave the door open, dearie. [*Vivie frowns; but Frank checks her with a gesture, and steals to the cottage door, which he softly sets wide open*]. Oh Lor, what a draught! Youd better shut it, dear.

Vivie shuts it with a slam, and then, noting with disgust that her mother's hat and shawl are lying about, takes them tidily to the window seat, whilst Frank noiselessly shuts the cottage door.

FRANK [*exulting*] Aha! Got rid of em. Well, Vivvums: what do you think of my guvernor?

VIVIE [*preoccupied and serious*] Ive hardly spoken to him. He doesnt strike me as being a particularly able person.

FRANK. Well, you know, the old man is not altogether such a fool as he looks. You see, he was shoved into the Church rather; and in trying to live up to it he makes a much bigger ass of himself than he really is.

I dont dislike him as much as you might expect. He means well. How do you think youll get on with him?

VIVIE [*rather grimly*] I dont think my future life will be much concerned with him, or with any of that old circle of my mother's, except perhaps Praed. [*She sits down on the settle*]. What do you think of my mother?

FRANK. Really and truly?

VIVIE. Yes, really and truly.

FRANK. Well, she's ever so jolly. But she's rather a caution, isn't she? And Crofts! Oh, my eye, Crofts! [*He sits beside her*].

VIVIE. What a lot, Frank!

FRANK. What a crew!

VIVIE [*with intense contempt for them*] If I thought that *I* was like that—that I was going to be a waster, shifting along from one meal to another with no purpose, and no character, and no grit in me, I'd open an artery and bleed to death without one moment's hesitation.

FRANK. Oh no, you wouldnt. Why should they take any grind when they can afford not to? I wish I had their luck. No: what I object to is their form. It isnt the thing: it's slovenly, ever so slovenly.

VIVIE. Do you think your form will be any better when youre as old as Crofts, if you dont work?

FRANK. Of course I do. Ever so much better. Vivvums mustnt lecture: her little boy's incorrigible. [*He attempts to take her face caressingly in his hands*].

VIVIE [*striking his hands down sharply*] Off with you: Vivvums is not in a humor for petting her little boy this evening. [*She rises and comes forward to the other side of the room*].

FRANK [*following her*] How unkind!

VIVIE [*stamping at him*] Be serious. I'm serious.

FRANK. Good. Let us talk learnedly. Miss Warren: do you know that all the most advanced thinkers are agreed that half the diseases of modern civilization are due to starvation of the affections in the young. Now, I—

VIVIE [*cutting him short*] You are very tiresome. [*She opens the inner door*]. Have you room for Frank there? He's complaining of starvation.

MRS WARREN [*within*] Of course there is [*clatter of knives and glasses as she moves the things on the table*]. Here! theres room now beside me. Come along, Mr Frank.

FRANK. Her little boy will be ever so even with his Vivvums for this. [*He passes into the kitchen*].

MRS WARREN [*within*] Here, Vivie: come on you too, child. You must be famished. [*She enters, followed by Crofts, who holds the door open for Vivie with marked deference. She goes out without looking at him; and he shuts the door after her*]. Why, George, you cant be done: youve eaten nothing. Is there anything wrong with you?

CROFTS. Oh, all I wanted was a drink. [*He thrusts his hands in his pockets, and begins prowling about the room, restless and sulky*].

MRS WARREN. Well, I like enough to eat. But a little of that cold beef and cheese and lettuce goes a long way. [*With a sigh of only half repletion she sits down lazily on the settle*].

CROFTS. What do you go encouraging that young pup for?

MRS WARREN [*on the alert at once*] Now see here, George: what are you up to about that girl? Ive been watching your way of looking at her. Remember: I know you and what your looks mean.

CROFTS. Theres no harm in looking at her, is there?

MRS WARREN. I'd put you out and pack you back to London pretty soon if I saw any of your nonsense. My girl's little finger is more to me than your whole body and soul. [*Crofts receives this with a sneering grin. Mrs Warren, flushing a little at her failure to impose on him in the character of a theatrically devoted mother, adds in a lower key*] Make your mind easy: the young pup has no more chance than you have.

CROFTS. Maynt a man take an interest in a girl?

MRS WARREN. Not a man like you.

CROFTS. How old is she?

MRS WARREN. Never you mind how old she is.

CROFTS. Why do you make such a secret of it?

MRS WARREN. Because I choose.

CROFTS. Well, I'm not fifty yet; and my property is as good as ever it was—

MRS WARREN [*interrupting him*] Yes; because youre as stingy as youre vicious.

CROFTS [*continuing*] And a baronet isnt to be picked up every day. No other man in my position would put up with you for a mother-in-law. Why shouldnt she marry me?

MRS WARREN. You!

CROFTS. We three could live together quite comfortably. I'd die before her and leave her a bouncing widow with plenty of money. Why not? It's been growing in my mind all the time Ive been walking with that fool inside there.

MRS WARREN [*revolted*] Yes: it's the sort of thing that would grow in your mind.

He halts in his prowling; and the two look at one another, she steadfastly, with a sort of awe behind her contemptuous disgust: he stealthily, with a carnal gleam in his eye and a loose grin.

CROFTS [*suddenly becoming anxious and urgent as he*

sees no sign of sympathy in her] Look here, Kitty: youre a sensible woman: you neednt put on any moral airs. I'll ask no more questions; and you need answer none. I'll settle the whole property on her; and if you want a cheque for yourself on the wedding day, you can name any figure you like—in reason.

MRS WARREN. So it's come to that with you, George, like all the other worn-out old creatures!

CROFTS [*savagely*] Damn you!

Before she can retort the door of the kitchen is opened; and the voices of the others are heard returning. Crofts, unable to recover his presence of mind, hurries out of the cottage. The clergyman appears at the kitchen door.

REV. S. [*looking round*] Where is Sir George?

MRS WARREN. Gone out to have a pipe. [*The clergyman takes his hat from the table, and joins Mrs Warren at the fireside. Meanwhile Vivie comes in, followed by Frank, who collapses into the nearest chair with an air of extreme exhaustion. Mrs Warren looks round at Vivie and says, with her affectation of maternal patronage even more forced than usual*] Well, dearie: have you had a good supper?

VIVIE. You know what Mrs Alison's suppers are. [*She turns to Frank and pets him*]. Poor Frank! was all the beef gone? did it get nothing but bread and cheese and ginger beer? [*Seriously, as if she had done quite enough trifling for one evening*] Her butter is really awful. I must get some down from the stores.

FRANK. Do, in Heaven's name!

Vivie goes to the writing-table and makes a memorandum to order the butter. Praed comes in from the kitchen, putting up his handkerchief, which he has been using as a napkin.

REV. S. Frank, my boy: it is time for us to be thinking

of home. Your mother does not know yet that we have visitors.

PRAED. I'm afraid we're giving trouble.

FRANK [*rising*] Not the least in the world: my mother will be delighted to see you. She's a genuinely intellectual artistic woman; and she sees nobody here from one year's end to another except the gov'nor; so you can imagine how jolly dull it pans out for her. [*To his father*] Youre not intellectual or artistic are you, pater? So take Praed home at once; and I'll stay here and entertain Mrs Warren. Youll pick up Crofts in the garden. He'll be excellent company for the bull-pup.

PRAED [*taking his hat from the dresser, and coming close to Frank*] Come with us, Frank. Mrs Warren has not seen Miss Vivie for a long time; and we have prevented them from having a moment together yet.

FRANK [*quite softened, and looking at Praed with romantic admiration*] Of course. I forgot. Ever so thanks for reminding me. Perfect gentleman, Praddy. Always were. My ideal through life. [*He rises to go, but pauses a moment between the two older men, and puts his hand on Praed's shoulder*]. Ah, if you had only been my father instead of this unworthy old man! [*He puts his other hand on his father's shoulder*].

REV. S. [*blustering*] Silence, sir, silence: you are profane.

MRS WARREN [*laughing heartily*] You should keep him in better order, Sam. Goodnight. Here: take George his hat and stick with my compliments.

REV. S. [*taking them*] Goodnight. [*They shake hands. As he passes Vivie he shakes hands with her also and bids her goodnight. Then, in booming command, to Frank*] Come along, sir, at once. [*He goes out*].

MRS WARREN. Byebye, Praddy.

PRAED. Byebye, Kitty.

They shake hands affectionately and go out together, she accompanying him to the garden gate.

FRANK [*to Vivie*] Kissums?

VIVIE [*fiercely*] No. I hate you. [*She takes a couple of books and some paper from the writing-table, and sits down with them at the middle table, at the end next the fireplace*].

FRANK [*grimacing*] Sorry. [*He goes for his cap and rifle. Mrs Warren returns. He takes her hand*] Goodnight, dear Mrs Warren. [*He kisses her hand. She snatches it away, her lips tightening, and looks more than half disposed to box his ears. He laughs mischievously and runs off, clapping-to the door behind him*].

MRS WARREN [*resigning herself to an evening of boredom now that the men are gone*] Did you ever in your life hear anyone rattle on so? Isnt he a tease? [*She sits at the table*]. Now that I think of it, dearie, dont you go on encouraging him. I'm sure he's a regular good-for-nothing.

VIVIE [*rising to fetch more books*] I'm afraid so. Poor Frank! I shall have to get rid of him; but I shall feel sorry for him, though he's not worth it. That man Crofts does not seem to me to be good for much either: is he? [*She throws the books on the table rather roughly*].

MRS WARREN [*galled by Vivie's indifference*] What do you know of men, child, to talk that way about them? Youll have to make up your mind to see a good deal of Sir George Crofts, as he's a friend of mine.

VIVIE [*quite unmoved*] Why? [*She sits down and opens a book*]. Do you expect that we shall be much together? You and I, I mean?

MRS WARREN [*staring at her*] Of course: until youre married. Youre not going back to college again.

VIVIE. Do you think my way of life would suit you?
I doubt it.

MRS WARREN. Your way of life! What do you mean?

VIVIE [*cutting a page of her book with the paper knife on her chatelaine*] Has it really never occurred to you, mother, that I have a way of life like other people?

MRS WARREN. What nonsense is this youre trying to talk? Do you want to shew your independence, now that youre a great little person at school? Dont be a fool, child.

VIVIE [*indulgently*] Thats all you have to say on the subject, is it, mother?

MRS WARREN [*puzzled, then angry*] Dont you keep on asking me questions like that. [*Violently*] Hold your tongue. [*Vivie works on, losing no time, and saying nothing*]. You and your way of life, indeed! What next? [*She looks at Vivie again. No reply*]. Your way of life will be what I please, so it will. [*Another pause*]. Ive been noticing these airs in you ever since you got that tripos or whatever you call it. If you think I'm going to put up with them youre mistaken; and the sooner you find it out, the better. [*Muttering*] All I have to say on the subject, indeed! [*Again raising her voice angrily*] Do you know who youre speaking to, Miss?

VIVIE [*looking across at her without raising her head from her book*] No. Who are you? What are you?

MRS WARREN [*rising breathless*] You young imp!

VIVIE. Everybody knows my reputation, my social standing, and the profession I intend to pursue. I know nothing about you. What is that way of life which you invite me to share with you and Sir George Crofts, pray?

MRS WARREN. Take care. I shall do something I'll be sorry for after, and you too.

VIVIE [*putting aside her books with cool decision*] Well, let us drop the subject until you are better able to face it. [*Looking critically at her mother*] You want some good walks and a little lawn tennis to set you up. You are shockingly out of condition: you were not able to manage twenty yards uphill today without stopping to pant; and your wrists are mere rolls of fat. Look at mine. [*She holds out her wrists*].

MRS WARREN [*after looking at her helplessly, begins to whimper*] Vivie—

VIVIE [*springing up sharply*] Now pray dont begin to cry. Anything but that. I really cannot stand whimpering. I will go out of the room if you do.

MRS WARREN [*piteously*] Oh, my darling, how can you be so hard on me? Have I no rights over you as your mother?

VIVIE. Are you my mother?

MRS WARREN [*appalled*] Am I your mother! Oh, Vivie!

VIVIE. Then where are our relatives? my father? our family friends? You claim the rights of a mother: the right to call me fool and child; to speak to me as no woman in authority over me at college dare speak to me; to dictate my way of life; and to force on me the acquaintance of a brute whom anyone can see to be the most vicious sort of London man about town. Before I give myself the trouble to resist such claims, I may as well find out whether they have any real existence.

MRS WARREN [*distracted, throwing herself on her knees*] Oh no, no. Stop, stop. I am your mother: I swear it. Oh, you cant mean to turn on me—my own child! it's not natural. You believe me, dont you? Say you believe me.

VIVIE. Who was my father?

MRS WARREN. You dont know what youre asking. I cant tell you.

VIVIE [*determinedly*] Oh yes you can, if you like. I have a right to know; and you know very well that I have that right. You can refuse to tell me, if you please; but if you do, you will see the last of me tomorrow morning.

MRS WARREN. Oh, it's too horrible to hear you talk like that. You wouldnt—you couldnt leave me.

VIVIE [*ruthlessly*] Yes, without a moment's hesitation, if you trifle with me about this. [*Shivering with disgust*] How can I feel sure that I may not have the contaminated blood of that brutal waster in my veins?

MRS WARREN. No, no. On my oath it's not he, nor any of the rest that you have ever met. I'm certain of that, at least.

Vivie's eyes fasten sternly on her mother as the significance of this flashes on her.

VIVIE [*slowly*] You are certain of that, at least. Ah! You mean that that is all you are certain of. [*Thoughtfully*] I see. [*Mrs Warren buries her face in her hands*]. Dont do that, mother: you know you dont feel it a bit. [*Mrs Warren takes down her hands and looks up deplorably at Vivie, who takes out her watch and says*] Well, that is enough for tonight. At what hour would you like breakfast? Is half-past eight too early for you?

MRS WARREN [*wildly*] My God, what sort of woman are you?

VIVIE [*coolly*] The sort the world is mostly made of, I should hope. Otherwise I dont understand how it gets its business done. Come [*taking her mother by the wrist, and pulling her up pretty resolutely*]: pull yourself together. Thats right.

MRS WARREN [*querulously*] Youre very rough with me, Vivie.

VIVIE. Nonsense. What about bed? It's past ten.

MRS WARREN [*passionately*] Whats the use of my going to bed? Do you think I could sleep?

VIVIE. Why not? I shall.

MRS WARREN. You! youve no heart. [*She suddenly breaks out vehemently in her natural tongue—the dialect of a woman of the people—with all her affectations of maternal authority and conventional manners gone, and an overwhelming inspiration of true conviction and scorn in her*] Oh, I wont bear it: I wont put up with the injustice of it. What right have you to set yourself up above me like this? You boast of what you are to me— to me, who gave you the chance of being what you are. What chance had I! Shame on you for a bad daughter and a stuck-up prude!

VIVIE [*sitting down with a shrug, no longer confident; for her replies, which have sounded sensible and strong to her so far, now begin to ring rather woodenly and even priggishly against the new tone of her mother*] Dont think for a moment I set myself above you in any way. You attacked me with the conventional authority of a mother: I defended myself with the conventional superiority of a respectable woman. Frankly, I am not going to stand any of your nonsense; and when you drop it I shall not expect you to stand any of mine. I shall always respect your right to your own opinions and your own way of life.

MRS WARREN. My own opinions and my own way of life! Listen to her talking! Do you think I was brought up like you? able to pick and choose my own way of life? Do you think I did what I did because I liked it, or thought it right, or wouldnt rather have gone to college and been a lady if I'd had the chance? VIVIE. Everybody has some choice, mother. The poorest girl alive may not be able to choose between being Queen of England or Principal of Newnham; but she can choose between ragpicking and flower-selling, according to her taste. People are always blaming their circumstances for what they are. I dont believe in circumstances. The people who get on in this world are the people who get up and look for the circumstances they want, and, if they cant find them, make them.

MRS WARREN. Oh, it's easy to talk, very easy, isnt it? Here! would you like to know what my circumstances were?

VIVIE. Yes: you had better tell me. Wont you sit down?

MRS WARREN. Oh, I'll sit down: dont you be afraid. [*She plants her chair farther forward with brazen energy, and sits down. Vivie is impressed in spite of herself*]. D'you know what your gran'mother was?

VIVIE. No.

MRS WARREN. No you dont. I do. She called herself a widow and had a fried-fish shop down by the Mint, and kept herself and four daughters out of it. Two of us were sisters: that was me and Liz; and we were both good-looking and well made. I suppose our father was a well-fed man: mother pretended he was a gentleman; but I dont know. The other two were only half sisters: undersized, ugly, starved looking, hard working, honest poor creatures: Liz and I would have half-murdered them if mother hadnt half-murdered us to keep our hands off them. They were the respectable ones. Well, what did they get by their respectability? I'll tell you. One of them worked in a whitelead factory twelve hours a day for nine shillings a week until she died of lead poisoning. She only expected to get her hands a little paralyzed; but she died. The other was always held up to us as a model because she married a Government laborer in the Deptford victualling yard, and kept his room and the three children neat and tidy on eighteen shillings a week—until he took to drink. That was worth being respectable for, wasnt it?

VIVIE [*now thoughtfully attentive*] Did you and your sister think so?

MRS WARREN. Liz didnt, I can tell you: she had more spirit. We both went to a church school— that was part of the ladylike airs we gave ourselves to be superior to the children that knew nothing and went nowhere—and we stayed there until Liz went out one night and never came back. I know the schoolmistress thought I'd soon follow her example; for the clergyman was always warning me that Lizzie'd end by jumping off Waterloo Bridge. Poor fool: that was all he knew about it! But I was more afraid of the whitelead factory than I was of the river; and so would you have been in my place. That clergyman got me a situation as a scullery maid in a temperance restaurant where they sent out for anything you liked. Then I was waitress; and then I went to the bar at Waterloo station: fourteen hours a day serving drinks and washing glasses for four shillings a week and my board. That was considered a great promotion for me. Well, one cold, wretched night, when I was so tired I could hardly keep myself awake, who should come up for a half of Scotch but Lizzie, in a long fur cloak, elegant and comfortable, with a lot of sovereigns in her purse.

VIVIE [*grimly*] My aunt Lizzie!

MRS WARREN. Yes; and a very good aunt to have, too. She's living down at Winchester now, close to the cathedral, one of the most respectable ladies there. Chaperones girls at the county ball, if you

please. No river for Liz, thank you! You remind me
of Liz a little: she was a first-rate business woman—
saved money from the beginning—never let herself
look too like what she was—never lost her head or
threw away a chance. When she saw I'd grown up
good-looking she said to me across the bar "What are
you doing there, you little fool? wearing out your
health and your appearance for other people's profit!"
Liz was saving money then to take a house for herself in Brussels; and she thought we two could
save faster than one. So she lent me some money and
gave me a start; and I saved steadily and first paid
her back, and then went into business with her as her
partner. Why shouldnt I have done it? The house in
Brussels was real high class: a much better place for
a woman to be in than the factory where Anne Jane
got poisoned. None of our girls were ever treated as
I was treated in the scullery of that temperance place,
or at the Waterloo bar, or at home. Would you have
had me stay in them and become a worn out old
drudge before I was forty?

VIVIE [*intensely interested by this time*] No; but why
did you choose that business? Saving money and
good management will succeed in any business.

MRS WARREN. Yes, saving money. But where can a
woman get the money to save in any other business?
Could you save out of four shillings a week and keep
yourself dressed as well? Not you. Of course, if youre
a plain woman and cant earn anything more; or if you
have a turn for music, or the stage, or newspaper-
writing: thats different. But neither Liz nor I had
any turn for such things: all we had was our appearance
and our turn for pleasing men. Do you think we were
such fools as to let other people trade in our good looks
by employing us as shopgirls, or barmaids, or wait-

resses, when we could trade in them ourselves and get all the profits instead of starvation wages? Not likely.

VIVIE. You were certainly quite justified—from the business point of view.

MRS WARREN. Yes; or any other point of view. What is any respectable girl brought up to do but to catch some rich man's fancy and get the benefit of his money by marrying him?—as if a marriage ceremony could make any difference in the right or wrong of the thing! Oh! the hypocrisy of the world makes me sick! Liz and I had to work and save and calculate just like other people; elseways we should be as poor as any good-for-nothing drunken waster of a woman that thinks her luck will last for ever. [*With great energy*] I despise such people: theyve no character; and if theres a thing I hate in a woman, it's want of character.

VIVIE. Come now, mother: frankly! Isnt it part of what you call character in a woman that she should greatly dislike such a way of making money?

MRS WARREN. Why, of course. Everybody dislikes having to work and make money; but they have to do it all the same. I'm sure Ive often pitied a poor girl, tired out and in low spirits, having to try to please some man that she doesnt care two straws for—some half-drunken fool that thinks he's making himself agreeable when he's teasing and worrying and disgusting a woman so that hardly any money could pay her for putting up with it. But she has to bear with disagreeables and take the rough with the smooth, just like a nurse in a hospital or anyone else. It's not work that any woman would do for pleasure, goodness knows; though to hear the pious people talk you would suppose it was a bed of roses.

VIVIE. Still, you consider it worth while. It pays.

MRS WARREN. Of course it's worth while to a poor girl, if she can resist temptation and is good-looking and well conducted and sensible. It's far better than any other employment open to her. I always thought that oughtnt to be. It cant be right, Vivie, that there shouldnt be better opportunities for women. I stick to that: it's wrong. But it's so, right or wrong; and a girl must make the best of it. But of course it's not worth while for a lady. If you took to it youd be a fool; but I should have been a fool if I'd taken to anything else.

VIVIE [*more and more deeply moved*] Mother: suppose we were both as poor as you were in those wretched old days, are you quite sure that you wouldnt advise me to try the Waterloo bar, or marry a laborer, or even go into the factory?

MRS WARREN [*indignantly*] Of course not. What sort of mother do you take me for! How could you keep your self-respect in such starvation and slavery? And whats a woman worth? whats life worth? without self-respect! Why am I independent and able to give my daughter a first-rate education, when other women that had just as good opportunities are in the gutter? Because I always knew how to respect myself and control myself. Why is Liz looked up to in a cathedral town? The same reason. Where would we be now if we'd minded the clergyman's foolishness? Scrubbing floors for one and sixpence a day and nothing to look forward to but the workhouse infirmary. Dont you be led astray by people who dont know the world, my girl. The only way for a woman to provide for herself decently is for her to be good to some man that can afford to be good to her. If she's in his own station of life, let her make him marry her; but if she's far beneath him she cant expect it:

why should she? it wouldnt be for her own happiness. Ask any lady in London society that has daughters; and she'll tell you the same, except that I tell you straight and she'll tell you crooked. Thats all the difference.

VIVIE [*fascinated, gazing at her*] My dear mother: you are a wonderful woman: you are stronger than all England. And are you really and truly not one wee bit doubtful—or—or—ashamed?

MRS WARREN. Well, of course, dearie, it's only good manners to be ashamed of it: it's expected from a woman. Women have to pretend to feel a great deal that they dont feel. Liz used to be angry with me for plumping out the truth about it. She used to say that when every woman could learn enough from what was going on in the world before her eyes, there was no need to talk about it to her. But then Liz was such a perfect lady! She had the true instinct of it; while I was always a bit of a vulgarian. I used to be so pleased when you sent me your photos to see that you were growing up like Liz: youve just her ladylike, determined way. But I cant stand saying one thing when everyone knows I mean another. Whats the use in such hypocrisy? If people arrange the world that way for women, theres no good pretending it's arranged the other way. No: I never was a bit ashamed really. I consider I had a right to be proud of how we managed everything so respectably, and never had a word against us, and how the girls were so well taken care of. Some of them did very well: one of them married an ambassador. But of course now I darent talk about such things: whatever would they think of us! [*She yawns*]. Oh dear! I do believe I'm getting sleepy after all. [*She stretches herself lazily, thoroughly relieved by her explosion, and placidly ready for her night's rest*].

VIVIE. I believe it is I who will not be able to sleep now. [*She goes to the dresser and lights the candle. Then she extinguishes the lamp, darkening the room a good deal*]. Better let in some fresh air before locking up. [*She opens the cottage door, and finds that it is broad moonlight*]. What a beautiful night! Look! [*She draws aside the curtains of the window. The landscape is seen bathed in the radiance of the harvest moon rising over Blackdown*].

MRS WARREN [*with a perfunctory glance at the scene*] Yes, dear; but take care you dont catch your death of cold from the night air.

VIVIE [*contemptuously*] Nonsense.

MRS WARREN [*querulously*] Oh yes: everything I say is nonsense, according to you.

VIVIE [*turning to her quickly*] No: really that is not so, mother. You have got completely the better of me tonight, though I intended it to be the other way. Let us be good friends now.

MRS WARREN [*shaking her head a little ruefully*] So it has been the other way. But I suppose I must give in to it. I always got the worst of it from Liz; and now I suppose it'll be the same with you.

VIVIE. Well, never mind. Come: goodnight, dear old mother. [*She takes her mother in her arms*].

MRS WARREN [*fondly*] I brought you up well, didnt I, dearie?

VIVIE. You did.

MRS WARREN. And youll be good to your poor old mother for it, wont you?

VIVIE. I will, dear. [*Kissing her*] Goodnight.

MRS WARREN [*with unction*] Blessings on my own dearie darling! a mother's blessing!

She embraces her daughter protectingly, instinctively looking upward for divine sanction.

[ACT III]

In the Rectory garden next morning, with the sun shining from a cloudless sky. The garden wall has a five-barred wooden gate, wide enough to admit a carriage, in the middle. Beside the gate hangs a bell on a coiled spring, communicating with a pull outside. The carriage drive comes down the middle of the garden and then swerves to its left, where it ends in a little gravelled circus opposite the Rectory porch. Beyond the gate is seen the dusty high road, parallel with the wall, bounded on the farther side by a strip of turf and an unfenced pine wood. On the lawn, between the house and the drive, is a clipped yew tree, with a garden bench in its shade. On the opposite side the garden is shut in by a box hedge; and there is a sundial on the turf, with an iron chair near it. A little path leads off through the box hedge, behind the sundial.

Frank, seated on the chair near the sundial, on which he has placed the morning papers, is reading The Standard. His father comes from the house, red-eyed and shivery, and meets Frank's eye with misgiving.

FRANK [*looking at his watch*] Half-past eleven. Nice hour for a rector to come down to breakfast!

REV. S. Dont mock, Frank: dont mock. I am a little— er— [*Shivering*]—

FRANK. Off color?

REV. S. [*repudiating the expression*] No, sir: unwell this morning. Wheres your mother?

FRANK. Dont be alarmed: she's not here. Gone to town by the 11.13 with Bessie. She left several messages for you. Do you feel equal to receiving them now, or shall I wait til youve breakfasted?

REV. S. I have breakfasted, sir. I am surprised at your mother going to town when we have people staying with us. Theyll think it very strange.

FRANK. Possibly she has considered that. At all events, if Crofts is going to stay here, and you are going to sit up every night with him until four, recalling the incidents of your fiery youth, it is clearly my mother's duty, as a prudent housekeeper, to go up to the stores and order a barrel of whisky and a few hundred siphons.

REV. S. I did not observe that Sir George drank excessively.

FRANK. You were not in a condition to, gov'nor.

REV. S. Do you mean to say that I—?

FRANK [calmly] I never saw a beneficed clergyman less sober. The anecdotes you told about your past career were so awful that I really dont think Praed would have passed the night under your roof if it hadnt been for the way my mother and he took to one another.

REV. S. Nonsense, sir. I am Sir George Croft's host. I must talk to him about something; and he has only one subject. Where is Mr Praed now?

FRANK. He is driving my mother and Bessie to the station.

REV. S. Is Crofts up yet?

FRANK. Oh, long ago. He hasnt turned a hair: he's in much better practice than you. Has kept it up ever since, probably. He's taken himself off somewhere to smoke.

Frank resumes his paper. The parson turns disconsolately towards the gate; then comes back irresolutely.

[318]

REV. S. Er—Frank.

FRANK. Yes.

REV. S. Do you think the Warrens will expect to be asked here after yesterday afternoon?

FRANK. Theyve been asked already.

REV. S. [*appalled*] What!!!

FRANK. Crofts informed us at breakfast that you told him to bring Mrs Warren and Vivie over here today, and to invite them to make this house their home. My mother then found she must go to town by the 11.13 train.

REV. S. [*with despairing vehemence*] I never gave any such invitation. I never thought of such a thing.

FRANK [*compassionately*] How do you know, gov'nor, what you said and thought last night?

PRAED [*coming in through the hedge*] Good morning.

REV. S. Good morning. I must apologize for not having met you at breakfast. I have a touch of—of—

FRANK. Clergyman's sore throat, Praed. Fortunately not chronic.

PRAED [*changing the subject*] Well, I must say your house is in a charming spot here. Really most charming.

REV. S. Yes: it is indeed. Frank will take you for a walk, Mr Praed, if you like. I'll ask you to excuse me: I must take the opportunity to write my sermon while Mrs Gardner is away and you are all amusing yourselves. You wont mind, will you?

PRAED. Certainly not. Dont stand on the slightest ceremony with me.

REV. S. Thank you. I'll—er—er—[*He stammers his way to the porch and vanishes into the house*].

PRAED. Curious thing it must be writing a sermon every week.

[319]

FRANK. Ever so curious, if he did it. He buys em. He's gone for some soda water.

PRAED. My dear boy: I wish you would be more respectful to your father. You know you can be so nice when you like.

FRANK. My dear Praddy: you forget that I have to live with the governor. When two people live together—it doesnt matter whether theyre father and son or husband and wife or brother and sister—they cant keep up the polite humbug thats so easy for ten minutes on an afternoon call. Now the governor, who unites to many admirable domestic qualities the irresoluteness of a sheep and the pompousness and aggressiveness of a jackass—

PRAED. No, pray, pray, my dear Frank, remember! He is your father.

FRANK. I give him due credit for that. [*Rising and flinging down his paper*] But just imagine his telling Crofts to bring the Warrens over here! He must have been ever so drunk. You know, my dear Praddy, my mother wouldnt stand Mrs Warren for a moment. Vivie mustnt come here until she's gone back to town.

PRAED. But your mother doesnt know anything about Mrs Warren, does she? [*He picks up the paper and sits down to read it*].

FRANK. I dont know. Her journey to town looks as if she did. Not that my mother would mind in the ordinary way: she has stuck like a brick to lots of women who had got into trouble. But they were all nice women. Thats what makes the real difference. Mrs Warren, no doubt, has her merits; but she's ever so rowdy; and my mother simply wouldnt put up with her. So—hallo! [*This exclamation is provoked by the reappearance of the clergyman, who comes out of the house in haste and dismay*].

[320]

REV. S. Frank: Mrs Warren and her daughter are coming across the heath with Crofts: I saw them from the study windows. What am I to say about your mother?

FRANK. Stick on your hat and go out and say how delighted you are to see them; and that Frank's in the garden; and that mother and Bessie have been called to the bedside of a sick relative, and were ever so sorry they couldnt stop; and that you hope Mrs Warren slept well; and—and—say any blessed thing except the truth, and leave the rest to Providence.

REV. S. But how are we to get rid of them afterwards?

FRANK. Theres no time to think of that now. Here! [*He bounds into the house*].

REV. S. He's so impetuous. I dont know what to do with him, Mr Praed.

FRANK [*returning with clerical felt hat, which he claps on his father's head*] Now: off with you. [*Rushing him through the gate*]. Praed and I'll wait here, to give the thing an unpremeditated air. [*The clergyman, dazed but obedient, hurries off*].

FRANK. We must get the old girl back to town somehow, Praed. Come! Honestly, dear Praddy, do you like seeing them together?

PRAED. Oh, why not?

FRANK [*his teeth on edge*] Dont it make your flesh creep ever so little? that wicked old devil, up to every villainy under the sun, I'll swear, and Vivie—ugh!

PRAED. Hush, pray. Theyre coming.

The clergyman and Crofts are seen coming along the road, followed by Mrs Warren and Vivie walking affectionately together.

FRANK. Look: she actually has her arm round the old woman's waist. It's her right arm: she began it. She's gone sentimental, by God! Ugh! ugh! Now do you feel the creeps? [*The clergyman opens the gate; and Mrs Warren and Vivie pass him and stand in the middle of the garden looking at the house. Frank, in an ecstasy of dissimulation, turns gaily to Mrs Warren, exclaiming*] Ever so delighted to see you, Mrs Warren. This quiet old rectory garden becomes you perfectly.

MRS WARREN. Well, I never! Did you hear that, George? He says I look well in a quiet old rectory garden.

REV. S. [*still holding the gate for Crofts, who loafs through it, heavily bored*] You look well everywhere, Mrs Warren.

FRANK. Bravo, gov'nor! Now look here: lets have a treat before lunch. First lets see the church. Everyone has to do that. It's a regular old thirteenth century church, you know: the gov'nor's ever so fond of it, because he got up a restoration fund and had it completely rebuilt six years ago. Praed will be able to shew its points.

PRAED [*rising*] Certainly, if the restoration has left any to shew.

REV. S. [*mooning hospitably at them*] I shall be pleased, I'm sure, if Sir George and Mrs Warren really care about it.

MRS WARREN. Oh, come along and get it over.

CROFTS [*turning back towards the gate*] Ive no objection.

REV. S. Not that way. We go through the fields, if you dont mind. Round here. [*He leads the way by the little path through the box hedge*].

CROFTS. Oh, all right. [*He goes with the parson*].

Praed follows with Mrs Warren. Vivie does not stir: she watches them until they have gone, with all the lines of purpose in her face marking it strongly.

FRANK. Aint you coming?

VIVIE. No. I want to give you a warning, Frank. You were making fun of my mother just now when you said that about the rectory garden. That is barred in future. Please treat my mother with as much respect as you treat your own.

FRANK. My dear Viv: she wouldnt appreciate it: the two cases require different treatment. But what on earth has happened to you? Last night we were perfectly agreed as to your mother and her set. This morning I find you attitudinizing sentimentally with your arm round your parent's waist.

VIVIE [*flushing*] Attitudinizing!

FRANK. That was how it struck me. First time I ever saw you do a second-rate thing.

VIVIE [*controlling herself*] Yes, Frank: there has been a change; but I dont think it a change for the worse. Yesterday I was a little prig.

FRANK. And today?

VIVIE [*wincing; then looking at him steadily*] Today I know my mother better than you do.

FRANK. Heaven forbid!

VIVIE. What do you mean?

FRANK. Viv: theres a freemasonry among thoroughly immoral people that you know nothing of. Youve too much character. Thats the bond between your mother and me: thats why I know her better than youll ever know her.

VIVIE. You are wrong: you know nothing about her. If you knew the circumstances against which my mother had to struggle—

FRANK [*adroitly finishing the sentence for her*] I should know why she is what she is, shouldnt I? What difference would that make? Circumstances or no circumstances, Viv, you wont be able to stand your mother.

VIVIE [*very angrily*] Why not?

FRANK. Because she's an old wretch, Viv. If you ever put your arm round her waist in my presence again, I'll shoot myself there and then as a protest against an exhibition which revolts me.

VIVIE. Must I choose between dropping your acquaintance and dropping my mother's?

FRANK [*gracefully*] That would put the old lady at ever such a disadvantage. No, Viv: your infatuated little boy will have to stick to you in any case. But he's all the more anxious that you shouldnt make mistakes. It's no use, Viv: your mother's impossible. She may be a good sort; but she's a bad lot, a very bad lot.

VIVIE [*hotly*] Frank—! [*He stands his ground. She turns away and sits down on the bench under the yew tree, struggling to recover her self-command. Then she says*] Is she to be deserted by all the world because she's what you call a bad lot? Has she no right to live?

FRANK. No fear of that, Viv: she wont ever be deserted. [*He sits on the bench beside her*].

VIVIE. But I am to desert her, I suppose.

FRANK [*babyishly, lulling her and making love to her with his voice*] Mustnt go live with her. Little family group of mother and daughter wouldnt be a success. Spoil our little group.

VIVIE [*falling under the spell*] What little group?

FRANK. The babes in the wood: Vivie and little Frank. [*He nestles against her like a weary child*]. Lets go and get covered up with leaves.

VIVIE [*rhythmically, rocking him like a nurse*] Fast asleep, hand in hand, under the trees.

FRANK. The wise little girl with her silly little boy.

VIVIE. The dear little boy with his dowdy little girl.

FRANK. Ever so peaceful, and relieved from the im-

becility of the little boy's father and the questionable-
ness of the little girl's—

VIVIE [*smothering the word against her breast*] Sh-sh-
sh-sh! little girl wants to forget all about her mother.
[*They are silent for some moments, rocking one another.
Then Vivie wakes up with a shock, exclaiming*] What a
pair of fools we are! Come: sit up. Gracious! your
hair. [*She smoothes it*]. I wonder do all grown up
people play in that childish way when nobody is looking. I never did it when I was a child.

FRANK. Neither did I. You are my first playmate.
[*He catches her hand to kiss it, but checks himself to
look round first. Very unexpectedly, he sees Crofts
emerging from the box hedge*]. Oh damn!

VIVIE. Why damn, dear?

FRANK [*whispering*] Sh! Here's this brute Crofts. [*He
sits farther away from her with an unconcerned air*].

CROFTS. Could I have a few words with you, Miss
Vivie?

VIVIE. Certainly.

CROFTS [*to Frank*] Youll excuse me, Gardner. Theyre
waiting for you in the church, if you don't mind.

FRANK [*rising*] Anything to oblige you, Crofts—except
church. If you should happen to want me, Vivvums,
ring the gate bell. [*He goes into the house with unruffled suavity*].

CROFTS [*watching him with a crafty air as he disappears,
and speaking to Vivie with an assumption of being on
privileged terms with her*] Pleasant young fellow that,
Miss Vivie. Pity he has no money, isnt it?

VIVIE. Do you think so?

CROFTS. Well, whats he to do? No profession. No
property. Whats he good for?

VIVIE. I realize his disadvantages, Sir George.

CROFTS [*a little taken aback at being so precisely*

interpreted] Oh, it's not that. But while we're in this world we're in it; and money's money. [*Vivie does not answer*]. Nice day, isnt it?

VIVIE [*with scarcely veiled contempt for this effort at conversation*] Very.

CROFTS [*with brutal good humor, as if he liked her pluck*] Well, thats not what I came to say. [*Sitting down beside her*] Now listen, Miss Vivie. I'm quite aware that I'm not a young lady's man.

VIVIE. Indeed, Sir George?

CROFTS. No; and to tell you the honest truth I dont want to be either. But when I say a thing I mean it; when I feel a sentiment I feel it in earnest; and what I value I pay hard money for. Thats the sort of man I am.

VIVIE. It does you great credit, I'm sure.

CROFTS. Oh, I dont mean to praise myself. I have my faults, Heaven knows: no man is more sensible of that than I am. I know I'm not perfect: thats one of the disadvantages of being a middle-aged man; for I'm not a young man, and I know it. But my code is a simple one, and, I think, a good one. Honor between man and man; fidelity between man and woman; and no cant about this religion or that religion, but an honest belief that things are making for good on the whole.

VIVIE [*with biting irony*] "A power, not ourselves, that makes for righteousness," eh?

CROFTS [*taking her seriously*] Oh certainly. Not ourselves, of course. You understand what I mean. Well, now as to practical matters. You may have an idea that Ive flung my money about; but I havnt: I'm richer today than when I first came into the property. Ive used my knowledge of the world to invest my money in ways that other men have overlooked; and whatever else I may be, I'm a safe man from the money point of view.

VIVIE. It's very kind of you to tell me all this.

CROFTS. Oh well, come, Miss Vivie: you neednt pretend you dont see what I'm driving at. I want to settle down with a Lady Crofts. I suppose you think me very blunt, eh?

VIVIE. Not at all: I am much obliged to you for being so definite and business-like. I quite appreciate the offer: the money, the position, Lady Crofts, and so on. But I think I will say no, if you dont mind. I'd rather not. [*She rises, and strolls across to the sundial to get out of his immediate neighborhood*].

CROFTS [*not at all discouraged, and taking advantage of the additional room left him on the seat to spread himself comfortably, as if a few preliminary refusals were part of the inevitable routine of courtship*] I'm in no hurry. It was only just to let you know in case young Gardner should try to trap you. Leave the question open.

VIVIE [*sharply*] My no is final. I wont go back from it.

Crofts is not impressed. He grins; leans forward with his elbows on his knees to prod with his stick at some unfortunate insect in the grass; and looks cunningly at her. She turns away impatiently.

CROFTS. I'm a good deal older than you. Twenty-five years: quarter of a century. I shant live for ever; and I'll take care that you shall be well off when I'm gone.

VIVIE. I am proof against even that inducement, Sir George. Dont you think youd better take your answer? There is not the slightest chance of my altering it.

CROFTS [*rising, after a final slash at a daisy, and coming nearer to her*] Well, no matter. I could tell you some things that would change your mind fast enough; but I wont, because I'd rather win you by honest affection. I was a good friend to your mother: ask her whether I wasnt. She'd never have made the money that paid for your education if it hadnt been for my advice and help, not to mention the money I advanced her. There are not many men would have stood by her as I have. I put not less than £40,000 into it, from first to last.

VIVIE [*staring at him*] Do you mean to say you were my mother's business partner?

CROFTS. Yes. Now just think of all the trouble and the explanations it would save if we were to keep the whole thing in the family, so to speak. Ask your mother whether she'd like to have to explain all her affairs to a perfect stranger.

VIVIE. I see no difficulty, since I understand that the business is wound up, and the money invested.

CROFTS [*stopping short, amazed*] Wound up! Wind up a business thats paying 35 per cent in the worst years! Not likely. Who told you that?

VIVIE [*her color quite gone*] Do you mean that it is still—? [*She stops abruptly, and puts her hand on the sundial to support herself. Then she gets quickly to the iron chair and sits down*]. What business are you talking about?

CROFTS. Well, the fact is it's not what would be considered exactly a high-class business in my set— the county set, you know—our set it will be if you think better of my offer. Not that theres any mystery about it: dont think that. Of course you know by your mother's being in it that it's perfectly straight and honest. Ive known her for many years; and I can say of her that she'd cut off her hands sooner than touch anything that was not what it ought to be. I'll tell you all about it if you like. I dont know whether youve found in travelling how hard it is to find a really comfortable private hotel.

VIVIE [*sickened, averting her face*] Yes: go on.

CROFTS. Well, thats all it is. Your mother has a genius for managing such things. We've got two in Brussels, one in Ostend, one in Vienna, and two in Budapest. Of course there are others besides ourselves in it; but we hold most of the capital; and your mother's indispensable as managing director. Youve noticed, I daresay, that she travels a good deal. But you see you cant mention such things in society. Once let out the word hotel and everybody says you keep a public-house. You wouldnt like people to say that of your mother, would you? Thats why we're so reserved about it. By the way, youll keep it to yourself, wont you? Since it's been a secret so long, it had better remain so.

VIVIE. And this is the business you invite me to join you in?

CROFTS. Oh no. My wife shant be troubled with business. Youll not be in it more than youve always been.

VIVIE. *I* always been! What do you mean?

CROFTS. Only that youve always lived on it. It paid for your education and the dress you have on your back. Dont turn up your nose at business, Miss Vivie: where would your Newnhams and Girtons be without it?

VIVIE [*rising, almost beside herself*] Take care. I know what this business is.

CROFTS [*starting, with a suppressed oath*] Who told you?

VIVIE. Your partner. My mother.

CROFTS [*black with rage*] The old—

VIVIE. Just so.

He swallows the epithet and stands for a moment swearing and raging foully to himself. But he knows that his cue is to be sympathetic. He takes refuge in generous indignation.

CROFTS. She ought to have had more consideration for you. *I'd* never have told you.

VIVIE. I think you would probably have told me when we were married: it would have been a convenient weapon to break me in with.

CROFTS [*quite sincerely*] I never intended that. On my word as a gentleman I didnt.

Vivie wonders at him. Her sense of the irony of his protest cools and braces her. She replies with contemptuous self-possession.

VIVIE. It does not matter. I suppose you understand that when we leave here today our acquaintance ceases.

CROFTS. Why? Is it for helping your mother?

VIVIE. My mother was a very poor woman who had no reasonable choice but to do as she did. You were a rich gentleman; and you did the same for the sake of 35 per cent. You are a pretty common sort of scoundrel, I think. That is my opinion of you.

CROFTS [*after a stare: not at all displeased, and much more at ease on these frank terms than on their former ceremonious ones*] Ha! ha! ha! ha! Go it, little missie, go it: it doesnt hurt me and it amuses you. Why the devil shouldnt I invest my money that way? I take the interest on my capital like other people: I hope you dont think I dirty my own hands with the work. Come! you wouldnt refuse the acquaintance of my mother's cousin the Duke of Belgravia because some of the rents he gets are earned in queer ways. You wouldnt cut the Archbishop of Canterbury, I suppose, because the Ecclesiastical Commissioners have a few publicans and sinners among their tenants. Do you

[330]

remember your Crofts scholarship at Newnham? Well, that was founded by my brother the M.P. He gets his 22 per cent out of a factory with 600 girls in it, and not one of them getting wages enough to live on. How d'ye suppose they manage when they have no family to fall back on? Ask your mother. And do you expect me to turn my back on 35 per cent when all the rest are pocketing what they can, like sensible men? No such fool! If youre going to pick and choose your acquaintances on moral principles, youd better clear out of this country, unless you want to cut yourself out of all decent society.

VIVIE [*conscience stricken*] You might go on to point out that I myself never asked where the money I spent came from. I believe I am just as bad as you.

CROFTS [*greatly reassured*] Of course you are; and a very good thing too! What harm does it do after all? [*Rallying her jocularly*] So you dont think me such a scoundrel now you come to think it over. Eh?

VIVIE. I have shared profits with you; and I admitted you just now to the familiarity of knowing what I think of you.

CROFTS [*with serious friendliness*] To be sure you did. You wont find me a bad sort: I dont go in for being superfine intellectually; but Ive plenty of honest human feeling; and the old Crofts breed comes out in a sort of instinctive hatred of anything low, in which I'm sure youll sympathize with me. Believe me, Miss Vivie, the world isnt such a bad place as the croakers make out. As long as you dont fly openly in the face of society, society doesnt ask any inconvenient questions; and it makes precious short work of the cads who do. There are no secrets better kept than the secrets everybody guesses. In the class of people I can introduce you to, no lady or gentleman would so far forget themselves as to discuss my business affairs or your mother's. No man can offer you a safer position.

VIVIE [*studying him curiously*] I suppose you really think youre getting on famously with me.

CROFTS. Well, I hope I may flatter myself that you think better of me than you did at first.

VIVIE [*quietly*] I hardly find you worth thinking about at all now. When I think of the society that tolerates you, and the laws that protect you! when I think of how helpless nine out of ten young girls would be in the hands of you and my mother! the unmentionable woman and her capitalist bully—

CROFTS [*livid*] Damn you!

VIVIE. You need not. I feel among the damned already.

She raises the latch of the gate to open it and go out. He follows her and puts his hand heavily on the top bar to prevent its opening.

CROFTS [*panting with fury*] Do you think I'll put up with this from you, you young devil?

VIVIE [*unmoved*] Be quiet. Some one will answer the bell. [*Without flinching a step she strikes the bell with the back of her hand. It clangs harshly; and he starts back involuntarily. Almost immediately Frank appears at the porch with his rifle*].

FRANK [*with cheerful politeness*] Will you have the rifle, Viv; or shall I operate?

VIVIE. Frank: have you been listening?

FRANK [*coming down into the garden*] Only for the bell, I assure you; so that you shouldn't have to wait. I think I shewed great insight into your character, Crofts.

CROFTS. For two pins I'd take that gun from you and break it across your head.

FRANK [*stalking him cautiously*] Pray dont. I'm ever

[332]

so careless in handling firearms. Sure to be a fatal accident, with a reprimand from the coroner's jury for my negligence.

VIVIE. Put the rifle away, Frank: it's quite unnecessary.

FRANK. Quite right, Viv. Much more sportsmanlike to catch him in a trap. [*Crofts, understanding the insult, makes a threatening movement*]. Crofts: there are fifteen cartridges in the magazine here; and I am a dead shot at the present distance and at an object of your size.

CROFTS. Oh, you neednt be afraid. I'm not going to touch you.

FRANK. Ever so magnanimous of you under the circumstances! Thank you!

CROFTS. I'll tell you this before I go. It may interest you, since youre so fond of one another. Allow me, Mister Frank, to introduce you to your half-sister, the eldest daughter of the Reverend Samuel Gardner. Miss Vivie: your half-brother. Good morning. [*He goes out through the gate and along the road*].

FRANK [*after a pause of stupefaction, raising the rifle*] Youll testify before the coroner that it's an accident, Viv. [*He takes aim at the retreating figure of Crofts. Vivie seizes the muzzle and pulls it round against her breast*].

VIVIE. Fire now. You may.

FRANK [*dropping his end of the rifle hastily*] Stop! take care. [*She lets it go. It falls on the turf*] Oh, youve given your little boy such a turn. Suppose it had gone off! ugh! [*He sinks on the garden seat, overcome*].

VIVIE. Suppose it had: do you think it would not have been a relief to have some sharp physical pain tearing through me?

FRANK [*coaxingly*] Take it ever so easy, dear Viv.

Remember: even if the rifle scared that fellow into telling the truth for the first time in his life, that only makes us the babes in the wood in earnest. [*He holds out his arms to her*]. Come and be covered up with leaves again.

VIVIE [*with a cry of disgust*] Ah, not that, not that. You make all my flesh creep.

FRANK. Why, whats the matter?

VIVIE. Goodbye. [*She makes for the gate*].

FRANK [*jumping up*] Hallo! Stop! Viv! Viv! [*She turns in the gateway*] Where are you going to? Where shall we find you?

VIVIE. At Honoria Fraser's chambers, 67 Chancery Lane, for the rest of my life. [*She goes off quickly in the opposite direction to that taken by Crofts*].

FRANK. But I say—wait—dash it! [*He runs after her*].

[ACT IV]

Honoria Fraser's chambers in Chancery Lane. An office at the top of New Stone Buildings, with a plate-glass window, distempered walls, electric light, and a patent stove. Saturday afternoon. The chimneys of Lincoln's Inn and the western sky beyond are seen through the window. There is a double writing table in the middle of the room, with a cigar box, ash pans, and a portable electric reading lamp almost snowed up in heaps of papers and books. This table has knee holes and chairs right and left and is very untidy. The clerk's desk, closed and tidy, with its high stool, is against the wall, near a door communicating with the inner rooms. In the opposite wall is the door leading to the public corridor. Its upper panel is of opaque glass, lettered in black on the outside, FRASER AND WARREN. A baize screen hides the corner between this door and the window.

Frank, in a fashionable light-colored coaching suit, with his stick, gloves, and white hat in his hands, is pacing up and down the office. Somebody tries the door with a key.

FRANK [*calling*] Come in. It's not locked.

Vivie comes in, in her hat and jacket. She stops and stares at him.

VIVIE [*sternly*] What are you doing here?

FRANK. Waiting to see you. Ive been here for hours. Is this the way you attend to your business? [*He puts his hat and stick on the table, and perches himself with a vault on the clerk's stool, looking at her with every appearance of being in a specially restless, teasing flippant mood*].

VIVIE. Ive been away exactly twenty minutes for a cup of tea. [*She takes off her hat and jacket and hangs them up behind the screen*]. How did you get in?

FRANK. The staff had not left when I arrived. He's gone to play cricket on Primrose Hill. Why dont you employ a woman, and give your sex a chance?

VIVIE. What have you come for?

FRANK [*springing off the stool and coming close to her*] Viv: lets go and enjoy the Saturday half-holiday somewhere, like the staff. What do you say to Richmond, and then a music hall, and a jolly supper?

VIVIE. Cant afford it. I shall put in another six hours work before I go to bed.

FRANK. Cant afford it, cant we? Aha! Look here. [*He takes out a handful of sovereigns and makes them chink*]. Gold, Viv: gold!

VIVIE. Where did you get it?

FRANK. Gambling, Viv: gambling. Poker.

VIVIE. Pah! It's meaner than stealing it. No: I'm not coming. [*She sits down to work at the table, with her back to the glass door, and begins turning over the papers*].

FRANK [*remonstrating piteously*] But, my dear Viv, I want to talk to you ever so seriously.

VIVIE. Very well: sit down in Honoria's chair and talk here. I like ten minutes chat after tea. [*He murmurs*]. No use groaning: I'm inexorable. [*He takes the opposite seat disconsolately*]. Pass that cigar box, will you?

FRANK [*pushing the cigar box across*] Nasty womanly habit. Nice men dont do it any longer.

VIVIE. Yes: they object to the smell in the office; and weve had to take to cigarets. See! [*She opens the box*

*and takes out a cigaret, which she lights. She offers him
one; but he shakes his head with a wry face. She settles
herself comfortably in her chair, smoking*]. Go ahead.

FRANK. Well, I want to know what youve done—
what arrangements youve made.

VIVIE. Everything was settled twenty minutes after
I arrived here. Honoria has found the business too
much for her this year; and she was on the point of
sending for me and proposing a partnership when I
walked in and told her I hadnt a farthing in the world.
So I installed myself and packed her off for a fortnight's holiday. What happened at Haslemere when
I left?

FRANK. Nothing at all. I said youd gone to town on
particular business.

VIVIE. Well?

FRANK. Well, either they were too flabbergasted to
say anything, or else Crofts had prepared your
mother. Anyhow, she didnt say anything; and Crofts
didnt say anything; and Praddy only stared. After tea
they got up and went; and Ive not seen them since.

VIVIE [*nodding placidly with one eye on a wreath of
smoke*] Thats all right.

FRANK [*looking round disparagingly*] Do you intend
to stick in this confounded place?

VIVIE [*blowing the wreath decisively away, and sitting
straight up*] Yes. These two days have given me back
all my strength and self-possession. I will never take
a holiday again as long as I live.

FRANK [*with a very wry face*] Mps! You look quite
happy. And as hard as nails.

VIVIE [*grimly*] Well for me that I am!

FRANK [*rising*] Look here, Viv: we must have an
explanation. We parted the other day under a complete
misunderstanding. [*He sits on the table, close to her*].

VIVIE [*putting away the cigaret*] Well: clear it up.

FRANK. You remember what Crofts said?

VIVIE. Yes.

FRANK. That revelation was supposed to bring about a complete change in the nature of our feeling for one another. It placed us on the footing of brother and sister.

VIVIE. Yes.

FRANK. Have you ever had a brother?

VIVIE. No.

FRANK. Then you dont know what being brother and sister feels like? Now I have lots of sisters; and the fraternal feeling is quite familiar to me. I assure you my feeling for you is not the least in the world like it. The girls will go their way; I will go mine; and we shant care if we never see one another again. Thats brother and sister. But as to you, I cant be easy if I have to pass a week without seeing you. Thats not brother and sister. It's exactly what I felt an hour before Crofts made his revelation. In short, dear Viv, it's love's young dream.

VIVIE [*bitingly*] The same feeling, Frank, that brought your father to my mother's feet. Is that it?

FRANK [*so revolted that he slips off the table for a moment*] I very strongly object, Viv, to have my feelings compared to any which the Reverend Samuel is capable of harboring; and I object still more to a comparison of you to your mother. [*Resuming his perch*]. Besides, I dont believe the story. I have taxed my father with it, and obtained from him what I consider tantamount to a denial.

VIVIE. What did he say?

FRANK. He said he was sure there must be some mistake.

VIVIE. Do you believe him?

FRANK. I am prepared to take his word as against Crofts'.

VIVIE. Does it make any difference? I mean in your imagination or conscience; for of course it makes no real difference.

FRANK [shaking his head] None whatever to me.

VIVIE. Nor to me.

FRANK [staring] But this is ever so surprising! [He goes back to his chair]. I thought our whole relations were altered in your imagination and conscience, as you put it, the moment those words were out of that brute's muzzle.

VIVIE. No: it was not that. I didnt believe him. I only wish I could.

FRANK. Eh?

VIVIE. I think brother and sister would be a very suitable relation for us.

FRANK. You really mean that?

VIVIE. Yes. It's the only relation I care for, even if we could afford any other. I mean that.

FRANK [raising his eyebrows like one on whom a new light has dawned, and rising with quite an effusion of chivalrous sentiment] My dear Viv: why didnt you say so before? I am ever so sorry for persecuting you. I understand, of course.

VIVIE [puzzled] Understand what?

FRANK. Oh, I'm not a fool in the ordinary sense: only in the Scriptural sense of doing all the things the wise men declared to be folly, after trying them himself on the most extensive scale. I see I am no longer Vivvums's little boy. Dont be alarmed: I shall never call you Vivvums again—at least unless you get tired of your new little boy, whoever he may be.

VIVIE. My new little boy!

FRANK [*with conviction*] Must be a new little boy. Always happens that way. No other way, in fact.

VIVIE. None that you know of, fortunately for you.

Someone knocks at the door.

FRANK. My curse upon yon caller, whoe'er he be!

VIVIE. It's Praed. He's going to Italy and wants to say goodbye. I asked him to call this afternoon. Go and let him in.

FRANK. We can continue our conversation after his departure for Italy. I'll stay him out. [*He goes to the door and opens it*]. How are you, Praddy? Delighted to see you. Come in.

Praed, dressed for travelling, comes in, in high spirits.

PRAED. How do you do, Miss Warren? [*She presses his hand cordially, though a certain sentimentality in his high spirits jars on her*]. I start in an hour from Holborn Viaduct. I wish I could persuade you to try Italy.

VIVIE. What for?

PRAED. Why, to saturate yourself with beauty and romance, of course.

Vivie, with a shudder, turns her chair to the table, as if the work waiting for her were a support to her. Praed sits opposite to her. Frank places a chair near Vivie, and drops lazily and carelessly into it, talking at her over his shoulder.

FRANK. No use, Praddy. Viv is a little Philistine. She is indifferent to my romance, and insensible to my beauty.

VIVIE. Mr Praed: once for all, there is no beauty and no romance in life for me. Life is what it is; and I am prepared to take it as it is.

PRAED [*enthusiastically*] You will not say that if you come with me to Verona and on to Venice. You will cry with delight at living in such a beautiful world.

FRANK. This is most eloquent, Praddy. Keep it up.

PRAED. Oh, I assure you *I* have cried—I shall cry again, I hope—at fifty! At your age, Miss Warren, you would not need to go so far as Verona. Your spirits would absolutely fly up at the mere sight of Ostend. You would be charmed with the gaiety, the vivacity, the happy air of Brussels.

VIVIE [*springing up with an exclamation of loathing*] Agh!

PRAED [*rising*] Whats the matter?

FRANK [*rising*] Hallo, Viv!

VIVIE [*to Praed, with deep reproach*] Can you find no better example of your beauty and romance than Brussels to talk to me about?

PRAED [*puzzled*] Of course it's very different from Verona. I dont suggest for a moment that—

VIVIE [*bitterly*] Probably the beauty and romance come to much the same in both places.

PRAED [*completely sobered and much concerned*] My dear Miss Warren: I—[*looking inquiringly at Frank*] Is anything the matter?

FRANK. She thinks your enthusiasm frivolous, Praddy. She's had ever such a serious call.

VIVIE [*sharply*] Hold your tongue, Frank. Dont be silly.

FRANK [*sitting down*] Do you call this good manners, Praed?

PRAED [*anxious and considerate*] Shall I take him away, Miss Warren? I feel sure we have disturbed you at your work.

VIVIE. Sit down: I'm not ready to go back to work yet. [*Praed sits*]. You both think I have an attack of nerves. Not a bit of it. But there are two subjects I want dropped, if you dont mind. One of them [*to Frank*] is love's young dream in any shape or form: the other [*to Praed*] is the romance and beauty of life, especially Ostend and the gaiety of Brussels. You are welcome to any illusions you may have left on these subjects: I have none. If we three are to remain friends, I must be treated as a woman of business, permanently single [*to Frank*] and permanently unromantic [*to Praed*].

FRANK. I also shall remain permanently single until you change your mind. Praddy: change the subject. Be eloquent about something else.

PRAED [*diffidently*] I'm afraid theres nothing else in the world that I can talk about. The Gospel of Art is the only one I can preach. I know Miss Warren is a great devotee of the Gospel of Getting On; but we cant discuss that without hurting your feelings, Frank, since you are determined not to get on.

FRANK. Oh, dont mind my feelings. Give me some improving advice by all means: it does me ever so much good. Have another try to make a successful man of me, Viv. Come: lets have it all: energy, thrift, foresight, self-respect, character. Dont you hate people who have no character, Viv?

VIVIE [*wincing*] Oh, stop, stop: let us have no more of that horrible cant. Mr Praed: if there are really only those two gospels in the world, we had better all kill ourselves; for the same taint is in both, through and through.

FRANK [*looking critically at her*] There is a touch of poetry about you today, Viv, which has hitherto been lacking.

PRAED [*remonstrating*] My dear Frank: arnt you a little unsympathetic?

VIVIE [*merciless to herself*] No: it's good for me. It keeps me from being sentimental.

FRANK [*bantering her*] Checks your strong natural propensity that way, dont it?

VIVIE [*almost hysterically*] Oh yes: go on: dont spare me. I was sentimental for one moment in my life—beautifully sentimental—by moonlight; and now—

FRANK [*quickly*] I say, Viv: take care. Dont give yourself away.

VIVIE. Oh, do you think Mr Praed does not know all about my mother? [*Turning on Praed*] You had better have told me that morning, Mr Praed. You are very old fashioned in your delicacies, after all.

PRAED. Surely it is you who are a little old fashioned in your prejudices, Miss Warren. I feel bound to tell you, speaking as an artist, and believing that the most intimate human relationships are far beyond and above the scope of the law, that though I know that your mother is an unmarried woman, I do not respect her the less on that account. I respect her more.

FRANK [*airily*] Hear! Hear!

VIVIE [*staring at him*] Is that all you know?

PRAED. Certainly that is all.

VIVIE. Then you neither of you know anything. Your guesses are innocence itself compared to the truth.

PRAED [*rising, startled and indignant, and preserving his politeness with an effort*] I hope not. [*More emphatically*] I hope not, Miss Warren.

FRANK [*whistles*] Whew!

VIVIE. You are not making it easy for me to tell you, Mr Praed.

PRAED [*his chivalry drooping before their conviction*] If there is anything worse—that is, anything else—are you sure you are right to tell us, Miss Warren?

VIVIE. I am sure that if I had the courage I should spend the rest of my life in telling everybody—stamping and branding it into them until they all felt their part in its abomination as I feel mine. There is nothing

[343]

I despise more than the wicked convention that protects these things by forbidding a woman to mention them. And yet I cant tell you. The two infamous words that describe what my mother is are ringing in my ears and struggling on my tongue; but I cant utter them: the shame of them is too horrible for me. [*She buries her face in her hands. The two men, astonished, stare at one another and then at her. She raises her head again desperately and snatches a sheet of paper and a pen*]. Here: let me draft you a prospectus.

FRANK. Oh, she's mad. Do you hear, Viv? mad. Come! pull yourself together.

VIVIE. You shall see. [*She writes*]. "Paid up capital: not less than £40,000 standing in the name of Sir George Crofts, Baronet, the chief shareholder. Premises at Brussels, Ostend, Vienna and Budapest. Managing director: Mrs Warren"; and now dont let us forget her qualifications: the two words. [*She writes the words and pushes the paper to them*]. There! Oh no: dont read it: dont! [*She snatches it back and tears it to pieces; then seizes her head in her hands and hides her face on the table*].

Frank, who has watched the writing over his shoulder, and opened his eyes very widely at it, takes a card from his pocket; scribbles the two words on it; and silently hands it to Praed, who reads it with amazement, and hides it hastily in his pocket.

FRANK [*whispering tenderly*] Viv, dear: thats all right. I read what you wrote: so did Praddy. We understand. And we remain, as this leaves us at present, yours ever so devotedly.

PRAED. We do indeed, Miss Warren. I declare you are the most splendidly courageous woman I ever met.

This sentimental compliment braces Vivie. She throws it away from her with an impatient shake, and forces

*herself to stand up, though not without some support from
the table.*

FRANK. Dont stir, Viv, if you dont want to. Take it
easy.

VIVIE. Thank you. You can always depend on me for
two things: not to cry and not to faint. [*She moves a
few steps towards the door of the inner room, and stops
close to Praed to say*] I shall need much more courage
than that when I tell my mother that we have come
to the parting of the ways. Now I must go into the
next room for a moment to make myself neat again,
if you dont mind.

PRAED. Shall we go away?

VIVIE. No: I'll be back presently. Only for a moment.
[*She goes into the other room, Praed opening the door
for her*].

PRAED. What an amazing revelation! I'm extremely
disappointed in Crofts: I am indeed.

FRANK. I'm not in the least. I feel he's perfectly
accounted for at last. But what a facer for me, Praddy!
I cant marry her now.

PRAED [*sternly*] Frank! [*The two look at one another,
Frank unruffled, Praed deeply indignant*]. Let me tell
you, Gardner, that if you desert her now you will
behave very despicably.

FRANK. Good old Praddy! Ever chivalrous! But you
mistake: it's not the moral aspect of the case: it's the
money aspect. I really cant bring myself to touch
the old woman's money now?

PRAED. And was that what you were going to marry
on?

FRANK. What else? *I* havnt any money, nor the smallest turn for making it. If I married Viv now she would
have to support me; and I should cost her more than
I am worth.

PRAED. But surely a clever bright fellow like you can make something by your own brains.

FRANK. Oh yes, a little [*He takes out his money again*]. I made all that yesterday in an hour and a half. But I made it in a highly speculative business. No, dear Praddy: even if Bessie and Georgina marry millionaires and the governor dies after cutting them off with a shilling, I shall have only four hundred a year. And he wont die until he's three score and ten: he hasnt originality enough. I shall be on short allowance for the next twenty years. No short allowance for Viv, if I can help it. I withdraw gracefully and leave the field to the gilded youth of England. So thats settled. I shant worry her about it: I'll just send her a little note after we're gone. She'll understand.

PRAED [*grasping his hand*] Good fellow, Frank! I heartily beg your pardon. But must you never see her again?

FRANK. Never see her again! Hang it all, be reasonable. I shall come along as often as possible, and be her brother. I can not understand the absurd consequences you romantic people expect from the most ordinary transactions. [*A knock at the door*]. I wonder who this is. Would you mind opening the door? If it's a client it will look more respectable than if I appeared.

PRAED. Certainly. [*He goes to the door and opens it. Frank sits down in Vivie's chair to scribble a note*]. My dear Kitty: come in: come in.

Mrs Warren comes in, looking apprehensively round for Vivie. She has done her best to make herself matronly and dignified. The brilliant hat is replaced by a sober bonnet, and the gay blouse covered by a costly black silk mantle. She is pitiably anxious and ill at ease: evidently panic-stricken.

MRS WARREN [*to Frank*] What! Youre here, are you?

FRANK [*turning in his chair from his writing, but not rising*] Here, and charmed to see you. You come like a breath of spring.

MRS WARREN. Oh, get out with your nonsense. [*In a low voice*] Wheres Vivie?

Frank points expressively to the door of the inner room, but says nothing.

MRS WARREN [*sitting down suddenly and almost beginning to cry*] Praddy: wont she see me, dont you think?

PRAED. My dear Kitty: dont distress yourself. Why should she not?

MRS WARREN. Oh, you never can see why not: youre too innocent. Mr Frank: did she say anything to you?

FRANK [*folding his note*] She must see you, if [*very expressively*] you wait til she comes in.

MRS WARREN [*frightened*] Why shouldnt I wait?

Frank looks quizzically at her; puts his note carefully on the inkbottle, so that Vivie cannot fail to find it when next she dips her pen; then rises and devotes his attention entirely to her.

FRANK. My dear Mrs Warren: suppose you were a sparrow—every so tiny and pretty a sparrow hopping in the roadway—and you saw a steam roller coming in your direction, would you wait for it?

MRS WARREN. Oh, dont bother me with your sparrows. What did she run away from Haslemere like that for?

FRANK. I'm afraid she'll tell you if you rashly await her return.

MRS WARREN. Do you want me to go away?

FRANK. No: I always want you to stay. But I advise you to go away.

MRS WARREN. What! And never see her again!

FRANK. Precisely.

MRS WARREN [*crying again*] Praddy: dont let him be cruel to me. [*She hastily checks her tears and wipes her eyes*]. She'll be so angry if she sees Ive been crying.

FRANK [*with a touch of real compassion in his airy tenderness*] You know that Praddy is the soul of kindness, Mrs Warren. Praddy: what do you say? Go or stay?

PRAED [*to Mrs Warren*] I really should be very sorry to cause you unnecessary pain; but I think perhaps you had better not wait. The fact is—[*Vivie is heard at the inner door*].

FRANK. Sh! Too late. She's coming.

MRS WARREN. Dont tell her I was crying. [*Vivie comes in. She stops gravely on seeing Mrs Warren, who greets her with hysterical cheerfulness*]. Well, dearie. So here you are at last.

VIVIE. I am glad you have come: I want to speak to you. You said you were going, Frank, I think.

FRANK. Yes. Will you come with me, Mrs Warren? What do you say to a trip to Richmond, and the theatre in the evening? There is safety in Richmond. No steam roller there.

VIVIE. Nonsense, Frank. My mother will stay here.

MRS WARREN [*scared*] I dont know: perhaps I'd better go. We're disturbing you at your work.

VIVIE [*with quiet decision*] Mr Praed: please take Frank away. Sit down, mother. [*Mrs Warren obeys helplessly*].

PRAED. Come, Frank. Goodbye, Miss Vivie.

VIVIE [*shaking hands*] Goodbye. A pleasant trip.

PRAED. Thank you: thank you. I hope so.

FRANK [*to Mrs Warren*] Goodbye: youd ever so much better have taken my advice. [*He shakes hands with her. Then airily to Vivie*] Byebye, Viv.

VIVIE. Goodbye. [*He goes out gaily without shaking hands with her*].

PRAED [*sadly*] Goodbye, Kitty.

MRS WARREN [*snivelling*] —oobye!

Praed goes. Vivie, composed and extremely grave, sits down in Honoria's chair, and waits for her mother to speak. Mrs Warren, dreading a pause, loses no time in beginning.

MRS WARREN. Well, Vivie, what did you go away like that for without saying a word to me? How could you do such a thing! And what have you done to poor George? I wanted him to come with me; but he shuffled out of it. I could see that he was quite afraid of you. Only fancy: he wanted me not to come. As if [*trembling*] I should be afraid of you, dearie. [*Vivie's gravity deepens*]. But of course I told him it was all settled and comfortable between us, and that we were on the best of terms. [*She breaks down*]. Vivie: whats the meaning of this? [*She produces a commercial envelope, and fumbles at the enclosure with trembling fingers*]. I got it from the bank this morning.

VIVIE. It is my month's allowance. They sent it to me as usual the other day. I simply sent it back to be placed to your credit, and asked them to send you the lodgment receipt. In future I shall support myself.

MRS WARREN [*not daring to understand*] Wasnt it enough? Why didnt you tell me? [*With a cunning gleam in her eye*] I'll double it: I was intending to double it. Only let me know how much you want.

VIVIE. You know very well that that has nothing to do with it. From this time I go my own way in my own business and among my own friends. And you will go yours. [*She rises*]. Goodbye.

MRS WARREN [*rising, appalled*] Goodbye?

VIVIE. Yes: Goodbye. Come: dont let us make a useless scene: you understand perfectly well. Sir George Crofts has told me the whole business.

MRS WARREN [*angrily*] Silly old— [*She swallows an*

*epithet, and turns white at the narrowness of her escape
from uttering it*].

VIVIE. Just so.

MRS WARREN. He ought to have his tongue cut out.
But I thought it was ended: you said you didnt mind.

VIVIE [*steadfastly*] Excuse me: I do mind.

MRS WARREN. But I explained—

VIVIE. You explained how it came about. You did
not tell me that it is still going on [*She sits*].

*Mrs Warren, silenced for a moment, looks forlornly at
Vivie, who waits, secretly hoping that the combat is over.
But the cunning expression comes back into Mrs Warren's
face; and she bends across the table, sly and urgent, half
whispering.*

MRS WARREN. Vivie: do you know how rich I am?

VIVIE. I have no doubt you are very rich.

MRS WARREN. But you dont know all that that means:
youre too young. It means a new dress every day; it
means theatres and balls every night; it means having
the pick of all the gentlemen in Europe at your feet; it
means a lovely house and plenty of servants; it means
the choicest of eating and drinking; it means everything you like, everything you want, everything you
can think of. And what are you here? A mere drudge,
toiling and moiling early and late for your bare living
and two cheap dresses a year. Think over it. [*Soothingly*] Youre shocked, I know. I can enter into your
feelings; and I think they do you credit; but trust me,
nobody will blame you: you may take my word for
that. I know what young girls are; and I know youll
think better of it when youve turned it over in your
mind.

VIVIE. So thats how it's done, is it? You must have
said all that to many a woman, mother, to have it so
pat.

MRS WARREN [*passionately*] What harm am I asking you to do? [*Vivie turns away contemptuously. Mrs Warren continues desperately*] Vivie: listen to me: you dont understand: youve been taught wrong on purpose: you dont know what the world is really like.

VIVIE [*arrested*] Taught wrong on purpose! What do you mean?

MRS WARREN. I mean that youre throwing away all your chances for nothing. You think that people are what they pretend to be: that the way you were taught at school and college to think right and proper is the way things really are. But it's not: it's all only a pretence, to keep the cowardly slavish common run of people quiet. Do you want to find that out, like other women, at forty, when youve thrown yourself away and lost your chances; or wont you take it in good time now from your own mother, that loves you and swears to you that it's truth: gospel truth? [*Urgently*] Vivie: the big people, the clever people, the managing people, all know it. They do as I do, and think what I think. I know plenty of them. I know them to speak to, to introduce you to, to make friends of for you. I dont mean anything wrong: thats what you dont understand: your head is full of ignorant ideas about me. What do the people that taught you know about life or about people like me? When did they ever meet me, or speak to me, or let anyone tell them about me? the fools! Would they ever have done anything for you if I hadnt paid them? Havnt I told you that I want you to be respectable? Havnt I brought you up to be respectable? And how can you keep it up without my money and my influence and Lizzie's friends? Cant you see that youre cutting your own throat as well as breaking my heart in turning your back on me?

VIVIE. I recognize the Crofts philosophy of life, mother. I heard it all from him that day at the Gardners'.

MRS WARREN. You think I want to force that played-out old sot on you! I dont, Vivie: on my oath I dont.

VIVIE. It would not matter if you did: you would not succeed. [*Mrs Warren winces, deeply hurt by the implied indifference towards her affectionate intention. Vivie, neither understanding this nor concerning herself about it, goes on calmly*] Mother: you dont at all know the sort of person I am. I dont object to Crofts more than to any other coarsely built man of his class. To tell you the truth, I rather admire him for being strong-minded enough to enjoy himself in his own way and make plenty of money instead of living the usual shooting, hunting, dining-out, tailoring, loafing life of his set merely because all the rest do it. And I'm perfectly aware that if I'd been in the same circumstances as my aunt Liz, I'd have done exactly what she did. I dont think I'm more prejudiced or straitlaced than you: I think I'm less. I'm certain I'm less sentimental. I know very well that fashionable morality is all a pretence, and that if I took your money and devoted the rest of my life to spending it fashionably, I might be as worthless and vicious as the silliest woman could possibly want to be without having a word said to me about it. But I dont want to be worthless. I shouldnt enjoy trotting about the park to advertize my dressmaker and carriage builder, or being bored at the opera to shew off a shopwindowful of diamonds.

MRS WARREN [*bewildered*] But—

VIVIE. Wait a moment: Ive not done. Tell me why you continue your business now that you are inde-

pendent of it. Your sister, you told me, has left all
that behind her. Why dont you do the same?

MRS WARREN. Oh, it's all very easy for Liz: she
likes good society, and has the air of being a lady.
Imagine me in a cathedral town! Why, the very rooks
in the trees would find me out even if I could stand
the dulness of it. I must have work and excitement, or
I should go melancholy mad. And what else is there
for me to do? The life suits me: I'm fit for it and
not for anything else. If I didnt do it somebody else
would; so I dont do any real harm by it. And then it
brings in money; and I like making money. No: it's
no use: I cant give it up—not for anybody. But what
need you know about it? I'll never mention it. I'll
keep Crofts away. I'll not trouble you much: you see
I have to be constantly running about from one place
to another. Youll be quit of me altogether when I
die.

VIVIE. No: I am my mother's daughter. I am like
you: I must have work, and must make more money
than I spend. But my work is not your work, and my
way not your way. We must part. It will not make
much difference to us: instead of meeting one another
for perhaps a few months in twenty years, we shall
never meet: thats all.

MRS WARREN [*her voice stifled in tears*] Vivie: I
meant to have been more with you: I did indeed.

VIVIE. It's no use, mother: I am not to be changed by
a few cheap tears and entreaties any more than you
are, I daresay.

MRS WARREN [*wildly*] Oh, you call a mother's tears
cheap.

VIVIE. They cost you nothing; and you ask me to give
you the peace and quietness of my whole life in exchange for them. What use would my company be to

you if you could get it? What have we two in common
that could make either of us happy together?

MRS WARREN [*lapsing recklessly into her dialect*]
We're mother and daughter. I want my daughter. Ive
a right to you. Who is to care for me when I'm old?
Plenty of girls have taken to me like daughters and
cried at leaving me; but I let them all go because I
had you to look forward to. I kept myself lonely for
you. Youve no right to turn on me now and refuse
to do your duty as a daughter.

VIVIE [*jarred and antagonized by the echo of the slums
in her mother's voice*] My duty as a daughter! I
thought we should come to that presently. Now once
for all, mother, you want a daughter and Frank wants
a wife. I dont want a mother; and I dont want a husband. I have spared neither Frank nor myself in
sending him about his business. Do you think I will
spare you?

MRS WARREN [*violently*] Oh, I know the sort you are:
no mercy for yourself or anyone else. *I* know. My
experience has done that for me anyhow: I can tell
the pious, canting, hard, selfish woman when I meet
her. Well, keep yourself to yourself: *I* dont want you.
But listen to this. Do you know what I would do with
you if you were a baby again? aye, as sure as there's
a Heaven above us.

VIVIE. Strangle me, perhaps.

MRS WARREN. No: I'd bring you up to be a real
daughter to me, and not what you are now, with your
pride and your prejudices and the college education
you stole from me: yes, stole: deny it if you can: what
was it but stealing? I'd bring you up in my own house,
I would.

VIVIE [*quietly*] In one of your own houses.

MRS WARREN [*screaming*] Listen to her! listen to how

she spits on her mother's grey hairs! Oh, may you live to have your own daughter tear and trample on you as you have trampled on me. And you will: you will. No woman ever had luck with a mother's curse on her.

VIVIE. I wish you wouldnt rant, mother. It only hardens me. Come: I suppose I am the only young woman you ever had in your power that you did good to. Dont spoil it all now.

MRS WARREN. Yes, Heaven forgive me, it's true; and you are the only one that ever turned on me. Oh, the injustice of it! the injustice! the injustice! I always wanted to be a good woman. I tried honest work; and I was slave-driven until I cursed the day I ever heard of honest work. I was a good mother; and because I made my daughter a good woman she turns me out as if I was a leper. Oh, if I only had my life to live over again! I'd talk to that lying clergyman in the school. From this time forth, so help me Heaven in my last hour, I'll do wrong and nothing but wrong. And I'll prosper on it.

VIVIE. Yes: it's better to choose your line and go through with it. If I had been you, mother, I might have done as you did; but I should not have lived one life and believed in another. You are a conventional woman at heart. That is why I am bidding you goodbye now. I am right, am I not?

MRS WARREN [*taken aback*] Right to throw away all my money?

VIVIE. No: right to get rid of you? I should be a fool not to! Isnt that so?

MRS WARREN [*sulkily*] Oh well, yes, if you come to that, I suppose you are. But Lord help the world if everybody took to doing the right thing! And now I'd better go than stay where I'm not wanted. [*She turns to the door*].

VIVIE [*kindly*] Wont you shake hands?

MRS WARREN [*after looking at her fiercely for a moment with a savage impulse to strike her*] No, thank you. Goodbye.

VIVIE [*matter-of-factly*] Goodbye. [*Mrs Warren goes out, slamming the door behind her. The strain on Vivie's face relaxes; her grave expression breaks up into one of joyous content; her breath goes out in a half sob, half laugh of intense relief. She goes buoyantly to her place at the writing-table; pushes the electric lamp out of the way; pulls over a great sheaf of papers; and is in the act of dipping her pen in the ink when she finds Frank's note. She opens it unconcernedly and reads it quickly, giving a little laugh at some quaint turn of expression in it*]. And goodbye, Frank. [*She tears the note up and tosses the pieces into the wastepaper basket without a second thought. Then she goes at her work with a plunge, and soon becomes absorbed in its figures*].

Shaw Proud of His Play

(*The Sun*, New York, 1 Nov., 1905)

Police Not Protecting Public Morality in Suppressing "Mrs Warren," He Says.

Special Cable Despatch to THE SUN.

LONDON, Oct. 31.—The correspondent of THE SUN to-day interviewed George Bernard Shaw in reference to the suppression by the New York police of his play "Mrs. Warren's Profession," Mr. Shaw said:

"If Police Commissioner McAdoo has earned by his public services the confidence of the American people as a man of higher character and deeper insight into social needs, moral problems and greater concern for the good of the community than I, it is not for me to question his qualifications or to incite Mr. Daly to resist his authority. I have a certain reputation in the world; which will not be altered by Mr. McAdoo's conviction that I am a blackguard. The New York police have a certain reputation in the world, and that also will not be altered by my conviction. I know my own business better than they do.

"In the opinion of the police prostitution is a permissible subject on the stage only when it is made agreeable. In my opinion the numerous plays in which it is made agreeable should be counterbalanced by plays in which its sordid cause is exposed.

"I am extremely proud of having written the play. It has made me more friends than any other work of mine, especially among serious women. It will make me friends of the same stamp in America, and these friends will keep steadily pressing the two questions:

[357]

Are the facts exposed in 'Mrs. Warren's Profession' denied? If not, in whose interests are they suppressed?

"It will be seen more and more clearly that the police, doubtless with the best intentions, are protecting not public morality but the interests of the most dangerous class, namely, the employers who pay women less than subsistence wages and overwork them mercilessly to grind profits for themselves out of the pith of the nation. Naturally they raise the clamor of immorality and disgusting dialogue, but in the end the public conscience of America, at present a hasty, unintelligent and easily duped force, will get educated and go over them like a steam roller, with an effective factory code stated by the way.

"Mr. Daly offered to abide by the verdict of the New York press. If this is true he must have forgotten that the New York press does not go to the theatre. It only sends critics. Let the editors come and the verdict proposed by Mr. Daly will be possible, but if social and moral questions are left to the critics they will not improve on Mr. McAdoo, who probably knows the real world much better than they. For my own part I would prefer a jury of public spirited women with experience in rescue work and slum life to any other jury whatever. They know how society makes vice by refusing to pay virtue decently."

Shaw Replies to His Critics

(*The Sun*, New York, 12 Nov., 1905)

*NEW YORK REVIEWS WORSE THAN THE
SUPPRESSED PLAY*

Police Commissioner McAdoo's Reports on "Mrs
Warren's Profession" Denounced—Mr Shaw Says His
Business is to Interpret Life. Not to Teach Moral
Lessons.

Special Cable Despatch to THE SUN.

LONDON, Nov. 11—G. Bernard Shaw, after seeing
Police Commissioner McAdoo's letter in THE SUN
of November 3, and the full comments of the American newspapers writes:

"I would really rather not talk about the 'Mrs.
Warren's Profession' incident. It is extremely serious
and I feel very seriously about it. Unfortunately in
London it has got studded over with little gems of fun
that make it very difficult to maintain perfect and
becoming gravity.

"The news got on the wrong lines, because the
first announcement in the *Times* said that what would
really crush and humiliate me was New York's discovery that my play was dull. That unlucky touch of
incredibility, for in England my dullnesses, which are
frequent enough, are roared at as prime jokes, reduced the whole piece of news to an absurdity for
every reader except myself. The next notice quoted
a critic as saying, after seeing my play, that he should
not allow any of his relatives to speak to any of mine,
which, of course, simply doubled up every reader with
hysterical cachination.

"Then your Police Commissioner rushed into print

He said the only parts of the play which did not bore him were the indecent parts. Of course, the unfortunate gentleman did not mean this, but it amuses the public to laugh as if he did. Now comes his letter to a lady, a brave and honorable lady, who paid him the high compliment of letting him know what she thought of the affair, in which, having reviled my play for teaching the public too much, he recommends the Sermon on the Mount and the Ten Commandments because they teach a great deal more.

"There is a sort of fate entangling the enemies of 'Mrs. Warren's Profession.' The Commissioner was in a sufficiently difficult position in any case. He did not attempt to deny that the play was true to nature, but he had to contend that knowledge of the things mentioned in it must deprave and brutalize. Now, it is a policeman's profession to know all these things and to be in contact with them, so if the Commissioner's contention is valid he himself would be depraved and a person entirely unfit to act as the moral censor of New York.

"As a matter of fact it is the people who know about these things who are humane and understand that the victims of them are humans, often quite amiable ones. It is the people who call their ignorance purity that also call their fellow creatures filthy and outrage every literary and social decency by a torrent of bad language and an orgy of bad manners when an attempt is made to enlighten them. Look at the things said about poor *Mrs. Warren*.

"What is *Mrs. Warren* to a Christian, if such a thing exists in America? She is to the last 'the temple of the Holy Ghost.' To a policeman she is a criminal who can either be arrested or blackmailed, according to his sense of duty or his needs. To a man of honor she is at least a fellow creature, with inalienable human rights, but to the New York theatrical journalist she is a piece of mere foulness in the gutter, ordure and gangrene unmentionable, disgusting and loathsome.

"I really do not wish to be offensive, especially as I have been so severely provoked, but where do you get your journalists? Some of our own are bad enough in all conscience, but—well, I put it to you whether you would not read 'Mrs. Warren's Profession' aloud in any company ten times rather than the New York notices once. You can hardly imagine how incredible it is to Londoners that a Commissioner of Police should write sensational articles about a play and get them published in the papers as 'reports.' That he should force a manager to withdraw the play by threatening to drag the actresses in it into a police court on a charge of indecency under a statute which makes it a criminal offence for any American woman to wear a new hat or wash her face is a thing beyond all belief here. As to the climax, the publication of letters from ladies to the Commissioner, with replies at full length, one can only gasp and wonder whether it really happened.

"Pray do not misunderstand me. I am not alluding to the quality of Mr. McAdoo's letters, their contradictions, confusions and reckless inaccuracy, in regard to what he writes he has seen and the repetitions and idle rumors in regard to what he has not seen. What I mean is the public scandal of a responsible official using his reports and correspondence as copy for the newspapers and writing them accordingly in the style of the yellowest of yellow journalism. Such a thing in England would ruin a Prime Minister, much less a chief inspector of police.

"My own concern is naturally more for my own profession. I make my acknowledgement to THE SUN of the way in which it has stood almost alone in New York for the dignity of our common profession and for its liberty of speech and thought.

"Your Mr. Corbin is, I think, wrong in reproaching me for not having given that romantic charm to the play which would have adulterated it unbearably to those who know that the charm of the subject is its curse.

"Mr. Norman Hapgood, too, has shown there is still some public spirit and esprit de corps left in American literature, but the rest, hallooing for Comstock and McAdoo to arrest Miss Herne and Miss Shaw, really deserve worse than Comstock will probably some day do to them.

"As regards the play, we have no further explanations to offer except that it is a mistake to suppose my business is to teach moral lessons. My business is to interpret life by taking events occurring at haphazard in daily experiences and sorting them out so as to show their real significance and interrelation. Nothing in ordinary life tells a man when buying a box of matches he is driving some woman at the other end of New York, whom he never saw and never will see, on to the streets. My play teaches him that. Having learned it he can draw what moral lesson he is capable of from it.

"Anybody who believes he would draw better ones or be a better man from believing that the sole relation between him and the woman at the other end of New York is merely the relation between two wholly disconnected social facts, one a highly moral respectable one, and the other a vicious, disgusting one, is—excuse the phrase I am going to use, and which I am using in a scriptural sense, not expletively —a hopelessly damned fool."

Mr Shaw Hits Back

(*Evening Standard, 15 Sept. 1924*)

[*A criticism by Mr. Sisley Huddleston of Mr. George Bernard Shaw's play "Mrs. Warren's Profession," produced in Paris at the Théâtre Michel on 8 September 1924, appeared in these columns last week. To-day we have received the following reply from Mr. Shaw.*]

To the Editor of the "*Evening Standard.*"

Sir,—In the notice of "Mrs. Warren's Profession," by Mr. Sisley Huddleston, in your issue of the 10th it is said repeatedly and emphatically that the play is unreal because "it has nothing to do with our own day." It states: "Some of the conditions of labour for girls which it describes have long since been swept away. The indictment is no longer true, as doubtless it was 30 years ago. One could therefore regard some of the most important parts of the play as a picture of the past, and not of the present."

Only the other day, when my play "Getting Married" was revived at the Everyman Theatre, a leading critic calmly remarked that its discussions had lost their interest because all the objections to our marriage laws had been removed by recent legislation.

These two statements will be parroted until the public comes to believe them unless they are loudly contradicted.

May I therefore declare, in stentorian tones, that the conditions of women's labour are now worse than they were in Mrs. Warren's time, and that not one of the defects in our marriage law pointed out in the Bishop of Chelsea's kitchen has been remedied, nor do we seem any nearer to the Bishop's general remedy of sensible and humane divorce. The only change we have achieved is to make the divorce laws the same for men and women, a matter not mentioned in my play.

At the beginning of the war, when everybody was more or less mad except the rogues who reaped a huge harvest from the suspension of all the laws that protected labour from merciless exploitation, the late Mary McArthur and Miss Bondfield (who happily lives to testify to what happened) found women working twelve hours a day for 2½d. an hour under the impression that they were saving their country instead of making huge profits for their employers. These two great public-spirited ladies, with the countenance of the Queen, put a stop to that; but the monstrosity of the abuse shows what women still endure when they are outside the scope of the factory code, as many of them necessarily are.

A terrible impoverishment of the middle classes with moderate fixed incomes has been produced by the debasement of the currency and the consequent rise of prices. Women who in Mrs. Warren's time were provided for by insurances and annuities left them—often at great sacrifice—by their parents, cannot now live on their incomes except in the most abject penury. The interest on the National Debt alone is a million a day; and a famine revolution is being bought off by doles. And yet Mr. Sisley Huddleston thinks that the poverty which drives women to prostitution is now a mere tale of old unhappy far-off things and battles long ago!

During the war we had an agitation about the morals of our soldiers in the field; and we had descriptions of the endless queues that stood waiting for admission to Mrs. Warren's houses. We were anxious about the soldiers. Nobody seemed anxious about the women, or about the extremity to which they must have been driven before resorting to such an intolerable means of livelihood. Some people even seemed to regard it as a form of self-indulgence!

All that Mr. Huddleston can claim is that some attempts have been made to prevent lead poisoning and phosphorus poisoning in the factories in which Mrs. Warren's "respectable" sisters worked. If that consoles him, it does not console me, nor make the lesson of my play obsolete. It still remains as true as it was in 1894 that we praise female virtue highly and pay it poorly, and pay female vice highly whilst we deplore it verbally. We flog foreign white slave traffickers of the male sex (thus protecting Mrs. Warren against male competition); but we do not raise the wages of women to the point at which they would be independent of prostitution. That is the root of the matter.

It would be interesting if some critic had enough knowledge and public spirit to show where my play is really behind the times. There are some valuable hints in Sir Arthur Pinero's "Mind the Paint Girl."

Faithfully,

G. BERNARD SHAW

Gleneagles, Sept. 13, 1924

Author's Note

(From the programme of the production at the Strand Theatre, London, 3 March 1926)

This play, after being witheld from public performance in England by the Censorship for thirty years, has at last been released (Heaven knows why!) too late, I am sorry to say, to save Parliament from the folly of passing an Act which has only secured a monopoly of Mrs. Warren's trade to her sex by flogging all her male competitors.

On the recent experimental performance by The Macdona Players. the Press assured us all that we might now enjoy the play as a striking early specimen of my well-known artistic virtuosity, as of course the state of things it dramatizes has long since passed away. I was irresistibly reminded of the cheerful village boy who, when they told him the tragedy of the Gospels, said "Oh well, since it happened so long ago and it's all so dreadful, let's hope it ain't true."

If this play no longer had any relation to life I should not trouble the public with it now that I have so many riper and more delicate specimens of my workmanship to offer instead. But the truth is that the economic situation so forcibly demonstrated by Mrs. Warren remains as true as ever in essentials to-day. The fact that we now call Mrs. Warren's sister's eighteen shillings thirty-six, does not increase its purchasing power by one crumb. When the war came the late Mary Macarthur found women "doing their bit" for twelve hours a day at twopence-half-penny an hour. Strongly countenanced by a much more highly placed lady, whose name must not be dragged into this discussion, she put a stop to that particular atrocity; but it convicted us, twenty years after the date of my play, of making the wages of virtue lower than the wages of sin at a moment when the nation needed all its virtue very urgently. To be precise, the twopence-halfpenny is now sixpence-halfpenny, shewing that we still do everything for the virtue of British womanhood except pay for it.

In short, Mrs. Warren's profession is a vested interest; and when a woman of bold character and commercial ability applies to herself the commercial principles that are ruthlessly applied to her in the labour market, the result is Kitty Warren, whom I accordingly present to you. You will hear her justify herself completely on those principles. Whether you and I, as citizens and voters, will be able to justify ourselves, on higher principles than those of commerce, for having made her justification not only possible but unanswerable, is another matter.

I cannot pretend to feel easy about it. Can you?

G. BERNARD SHAW
2nd March, 1926

PLAYS
PLEASANT

Preface
(1898)

Readers of the discourse with which the preceding volume commences will remember that I turned my hand to play-writing when a great deal of talk about "the New Drama," followed by the actual establishment of a "New Theatre" (the Independent), threatened to end in the humiliating discovery that the New Drama, in England at least, was a figment of the revolutionary imagination. This was not to be endured. I had rashly taken up the case; and rather than let it collapse I manufactured the evidence.

Man is a creature of habit. You cannot write three plays and then stop. Besides, the New movement did not stop. In 1894, Florence Farr, who had already produced Ibsen's Rosmersholm, was placed in command of the Avenue Theatre in London for a season on the new lines by Miss A. E. F. Horniman, who had family reasons for not yet appearing openly as a pioneer-manageress. There were, as available New Dramatists, myself, discovered by the Independent Theatre (at my own suggestion); Dr John Todhunter, who had been discovered before (his play The Black Cat had been one of the Independent's successes); and Mr W. B. Yeats, a genuine discovery. Dr Todhunter supplied A Comedy of Sighs: Mr Yeats, The Land of Heart's Desire. I, having nothing but unpleasant plays in my desk, hastily completed a first attempt at a pleasant one, and called it Arms and The Man, taking the title from the first line of Dryden's Virgil. It passed for a success, the applause on the first night being as promising as could be wished; and it ran from the 21st of April to the 7th of July.

[371]

To witness it the public paid £1777:5:6, an average of £23:2:5 per representation (including nine matinées). A publisher receiving £1700 for a book would have made a satisfactory profit: experts in West End theatrical management will contemplate that figure with a grim smile.

In the autumn of 1894 I spent a few weeks in Florence, where I occupied myself with the religious art of the Middle Ages and its destruction by the Renascence. From a former visit to Italy on the same business I had hurried back to Birmingham to discharge my duties as musical critic at the Festival there. On that occasion a very remarkable collection of the works of our British "pre-Raphaelite" painters was on view. I looked at these, and then went into the Birmingham churches to see the windows of William Morris and Burne-Jones. On the whole, Birmingham was more hopeful than the Italian cities; for the art it had to shew me was the work of living men, whereas modern Italy had, as far as I could see, no more connection with Giotto than Port Said has with Ptolemy. Now I am no believer in the worth of any mere taste for art that cannot produce what it professes to appreciate. When my subsequent visit to Italy found me practising the playwright's craft, the time was ripe for a modern pre-Raphaelite play. Religion was alive again, coming back upon men, even upon clergymen, with such power that not the Church of England itself could keep it out. Here my activity as a Socialist had placed me on sure and familiar ground. To me the members of the Guild of St Matthew were no more "High Church clergymen," Dr Clifford no more "an eminent Nonconformist divine," than I was to them "an infidel." There is only one religion, though there are a hundred versions of it. We all had the same thing to say; and though some of us cleared our throats to say it by singing revolutionary lyrics and republican hymns, we thought nothing of singing them to the music of Sullivan's Onward Christian Soldiers or Haydn's God Preserve the Emperor.

Now unity, however desirable in political agitations, is fatal to drama; for every drama must present a conflict. The end may be reconciliation or destruction; or, as in life itself, there may be no end; but the conflict is indispensable: no conflict, no drama. Certainly it is easy to dramatize the prosaic conflict of Christian Socialism with vulgar Unsocialism: for instance, in Widowers' Houses, the clergyman, who does not appear on the stage at all, is the real antagonist of the slum landlord. But the obvious conflicts of unmistakeable good with unmistakeable evil can only supply the crude drama of villain and hero, in which some absolute point of view is taken, and the dissentients are treated by the dramatist as enemies to be piously glorified or indignantly vilified. In such cheap wares I do not deal. Even in my unpleasant propagandist plays I have allowed every person his or her own point of view, and have, I hope, to the full extent of my understanding of him, been as sympathetic with Sir George Crofts as with any of the more genial and popular characters in the present volume. To distil the quintessential drama from pre-Raphaelitism, medieval or modern, it must be shewn at its best in conflict with the first broken, nervous, stumbling attempts to formulate its own revolt against itself as it develops into something higher. A coherent explanation of any such revolt, addressed intelligibly and prosaically to the intellect, can only come when the work is done, and indeed *done with*: that is to say, when the development, accomplished, admitted, and assimilated, is a story of yesterday. Long before any such understanding can be reached, the eyes of men begin to turn towards the distant light of the new age. Discernible at first only by the eyes of the man of genius, it must be focussed by him on the speculum of a work of art, and flashed back from that into the eyes of the common man. Nay, the artist himself has no other way of making himself conscious of the ray: it is by a blind instinct that he keeps on building up his masterpieces until their pinnacles catch the glint of the unrisen sun. Ask him to explain himself prosaically, and you find that he "writes like an angel and talks like poor Poll," and is himself the first to make that epigram at his own expense. John Ruskin has told us clearly enough what is in the pictures of Carpaccio and Bellini: let him explain, if he can, where we shall be when the sun that is caught by the summits of the work of his favorite Tintoretto, of his aversion Rembrandt, of Mozart, of Beethoven and Wagner, of Blake and of Shelley, shall have reached the valleys. Let Ibsen explain, if he can, why the building of churches and happy homes is not the ultimate destiny of Man, and why, to thrill the unsatisfied younger generations, he must mount beyond it to heights that now seem unspeakably giddy and dreadful to him, and from which the first climbers must fall and dash themselves to pieces. He cannot explain it: he can only shew it to you as a vision in the magic glass of his artwork; so that you may catch his presentiment and make what you can of it. And this is the function that raises dramatic art above imposture and pleasure hunting, and enables the playwright to be something more than a skilled liar and pandar.

Here, then, was the higher but vaguer and timider

vision, the incoherent, mischievous, and even ridiculous unpracticalness, which offered me a dramatic antagonist for the clear, bold, sure, sensible, benevolent, salutarily shortsighted Christian Socialist idealism. I availed myself of it in Candida, the drunken scene in which has been much appreciated, I am told, in Aberdeen. I purposely contrived the play in such a way as to make the expenses of representation insignificant; so that, without pretending that I could appeal to a very wide circle of playgoers, I could reasonably sound a few of our more enlightened managers as to an experiment with half a dozen afternoon performances. They admired the play generously: indeed I think that if any of them had been young enough to play the poet, my proposal might have been acceded to, in spite of many incidental difficulties. Nay, if only I had made the poet a cripple, or at least blind, so as to combine an easier disguise with a larger claim for sympathy, something might have been done. Richard Mansfield, who had, with apparent ease, made me quite famous in America by his productions of my plays, went so far as to put the play actually into rehearsal before he would confess himself beaten by the physical difficulties of the part. But they did beat him; and Candida did not see the footlights until my old ally the Independent Theatre, making a propagandist tour through the provinces with A Doll's House, added Candida to its repertory, to the great astonishment of its audiences.

In an idle moment in 1895 I began the little scene called The Man of Destiny, which is hardly more than a bravura piece to display the virtuosity of the two principal performers.

In the meantime I had devoted the spare moments of 1896 to the composition of two more plays, only the first of which appears in this volume. You Never Can Tell was an attempt to comply with many requests for a play in which the much paragraphed "brilliancy" of Arms and The Man should be tempered by some consideration for the requirements of managers in search of fashionable comedies for West End theatres. I had no difficulty in complying, as I have always cast my plays in the ordinary practical comedy form in use at all the theatres; and far from taking an unsympathetic view of the popular preference for fun, fashionable dresses, a little music, and even an exhibition of eating and drinking by people with an expensive air, attended by an if-possible-comic waiter, I was more than willing to shew that the drama can humanize these things as easily as they, in the wrong hands, can dehumanize the drama. But as often happens it was easier to do this than to persuade those who had asked for it that they had indeed got it. A chapter in Cyril Maude's history of the Haymarket Theatre records how the play was rehearsed there, and why I withdrew it. And so I reached the point at which, as narrated in the preface to the Unpleasant volume, I resolved to avail myself of my literary expertness to put my plays before the public in my own way.

It will be noticed that I have not been driven to this expedient by any hostility on the part of our managers. I will not pretend that the modern actor-manager's talent as player can in the nature of things be often associated with exceptional critical insight. As a rule, by the time a manager has experience enough to make him as safe a judge of plays as a Bond Street dealer is of pictures he begins to be thrown out in his calculations by the slow but constant change of public taste, and by his own growing conservatism. But his need for new plays is so great, and the few accredited authors are so little able to keep pace with their commissions, that he is always apt to overrate rather than to underrate his discoveries in the way of new pieces by new authors. An original work by a man of genius like Ibsen may, of course, baffle him as it baffles many professed critics; but in the beaten path of drama no unacted works of merit, suitable to his purposes, have been discovered; whereas the production, at great expense, of very faulty plays written by novices (not "backers") is by no means an unknown event. Indeed, to anyone who can estimate, even vaguely, the complicated trouble, the risk of heavy loss, and the initial expense and thought, involved by the production of a play, the ease with which dramatic authors, known and unknown, get their works performed must needs seem a wonder.

Only, authors must not expect managers to invest many thousands of pounds in plays, however fine (or the reverse), which will clearly not attract perfectly commonplace people. Playwriting and theatrical management, on the present commercial basis, are businesses like other businesses, depending on the patronage of great numbers of very ordinary customers. When the managers and authors study the wants of these customers, they succeed: when they do not, they fail. A public-spirited manager, or an author with a keen artistic conscience, may choose to pursue his business with the minimum of profit and the maximum of social usefulness by keeping as close as he can to the highest marketable limit of quality, and constantly feeling for an extension of that limit through the advance of popular culture. An unscrupulous manager or author may aim simply at the maximum of profit with the minimum of risk. These are the opposite poles of our system, represented in practice by our first rate managements at the one end, and the syndicates which exploit pornographic farces at the other. Between them there is plenty of room for most talents to breathe freely: at all events there is a career, no harder of access than any cognate career, for all qualified playwrights who bring the manager what his customers want and understand, or even enough of it to induce them to swallow at the same time a great deal that they neither want nor understand; for the public is touchingly humble in such matters.

For all that, the commercial limits are too narrow for our social welfare. The theatre is growing in importance as a social organ. Bad theatres are as mischievous as bad schools or bad churches; for modern civilization is rapidly multiplying the class to which the theatre is both school and church. Public and private life become daily more theatrical: the modern Kaiser, Dictator, President or Prime Minister is nothing if not an effective actor; all newspapers are now edited histrionically; and the records of our law courts shew that the stage is affecting personal conduct to an unprecedented extent, and affecting it by no means for the worse, except in so far as the theatrical education of the persons concerned has been romantic: that is, spurious, cheap, and vulgar. The truth is that dramatic invention is the first effort of man to become intellectually conscious. No frontier can be marked between drama and history or religion, or between acting and conduct, nor any distinction made between them that is not also the distinction between the masterpieces of the great dramatic poets and the commonplaces of our theatrical seasons. When this chapter of science is convincingly written, the national importance of the theatre will be as unquestioned as that of the army, the fleet, the Church, the law, and the schools.

For my part, I have no doubt that the commercial limits should be overstepped, and that the highest prestige, with a financial position of reasonable security and comfort, should be attainable in theatrical management by keeping the public in constant touch with the highest achievements of dramatic art. Our managers will not dissent to this: the best of them are so willing to get as near that position as they can without ruining themselves, that they can all point to honorable losses incurred through aiming "over the heads of the public," and will no doubt risk such loss again, for the sake of their reputation as artists, as soon as a few popular successes enable them to afford it. But even if it were possible for them to educate the nation at their own private cost, why should they be expected to do it? There are much stronger objections to the pauperization of the public by private doles than were ever entertained, even by the Poor Law Commissioners of 1834, to the pauperization of private individuals by public doles. If we want a theatre which shall be to the drama what the National Gallery and British Museum are to painting and literature, we can get it by endowing it in the same way. In the meantime there are many possibilities of local activity. Groups of amateurs can form permanent societies and persevere until they develop into professional companies in established repertory theatres. In big cities it should be feasible to form influential committees, preferably without any actors, critics, or playwrights on them, and with as many persons of title as possible, for the purpose of approaching one of the leading local managers with a proposal that they shall, under a guarantee against loss, undertake a certain number of afternoon performances of the class required by the committee, in addition to their ordinary business. If the committee is influential enough, the offer will be accepted. In that case, the first performance will be the beginning of a classic repertory for the manager and his company which every subsequent performance will extend. The formation of the repertory will go hand in hand with the discovery and habituation of a regular audience for it; and it will eventually become profitable for the manager to multiply the number of performances at his own risk. It might even become worth his while to take a second theatre and establish the repertory permanently in it. In the event of any of his classic productions proving a fashionable success, he could transfer it to his fashionable house and make the most of it there. Such managership would carry a knighthood with it; and such a theatre would be the needed nucleus for municipal or national endowment. I make the suggestion quite disinterestedly; for as I am not an academic person, I should not be welcomed as an unacted classic by such a committee; and cases like mine would still leave forlorn hopes like The Independent Theatre its reason for existing. The committee plan, I may remind its critics, has been in operation in London for two hundred years in support of Italian opera.

Returning now to the actual state of things, it is clear that I have no grievance against our theatres. Knowing quite well what I was doing, I have heaped difficulties in the way of the performance of my plays by ignoring the majority of the manager's customers: nay, by positively making war on them. To the actor I have been more considerate, using all my cunning to enable him to make the most of his technical methods; but I have not hesitated on occasion to tax his intelligence very severely, making the stage effect depend not only on *nuances* of execution quite beyond the average skill produced by the routine of the English stage in its present condition, but on a perfectly sincere and straightforward conception of states of mind which still seem cynically perverse to most people, and on a goodhumoredly contemptuous or profoundly pitiful attitude towards ethical conventions which seem to them validly heroic or venerable. It is inevitable that actors should suffer more than most of us from the sophistication of their consciousness by romance; and my view of romance as the great heresy to be swept off from art and life—as the food of modern pessimism and the bane of modern self-respect, is far more puzzling to the performers than it is to the pit. It is hard for an actor whose point of honor it is to be a perfect gentleman, to sympathize with an author who regards gentility as a dishonest folly, and gallantry and chivalry as treasonable to women and stultifying to men.

The misunderstanding is complicated by the fact that actors, in their demonstrations of emotion, have made a second nature of stage custom, which is often very much out of date as a representtion of contemporary life. Sometimes the stage custom is not only obsolete, but fundamentally wrong: for instance, in the simple case of laughter and tears, in which it deals too liberally, it is certainly not based on the fact, easily enough discoverable in real life, that we only cry now in the effort to bear happiness, whilst we laugh and exult in destruction, confusion, and ruin. When a comedy is performed, it is nothing to me that the spectators laugh: any fool can make an audience laugh. I want to see how many of them, laughing or grave, are in the melting mood. And this result cannot be achieved, even by actors who thoroughly understand my purpose, except through an artistic beauty of execution unattainable without long and arduous practice, and an intellectual effort which my plays probably do not seem serious enough to call forth.

Beyond the difficulties thus raised by the nature and quality of my work, I have none to complain of. I have come upon no ill will, no inaccessibility, on the part of the very few managers with whom I have discussed it. As a rule I find that the actor-manager is over-sanguine, because he has the artist's habit of underrating the force of circumstances and exaggerating the power of the talented individual to prevail against them; whilst I have acquired the politician's habit of regarding the individual, however talented, as having no choice but to make the most of his circumstances. I half suspect that those managers who have had most to do with me, if asked to name the main obstacle to the performance of my plays, would unhesitatingly and unanimously reply "The author." And I confess that though as a matter of business I wish my plays to be performed, as a matter of instinct I fight against the inevitable misrepresentation of them with all the subtlety needed to conceal my ill will from myself as well as from the manager.

The main difficulty, of course, is the incapacity for serious drama of thousands of playgoers of all classes whose shillings and half guineas will buy as much in the market as if they delighted in the highest art. But with them I must frankly take the superior position. I know that many managers are wholly dependent on them, and that no manager is wholly independent of them; but I can no more write what they want than Joachim can put aside his fiddle and oblige a happy company of beanfeasters with a marching tune on the

German concertina. They must keep away from my plays: that is all.

There is no reason, however, why I should take this haughty attitude towards those representative critics whose complaint is that my talent, though not unentertaining, lacks elevation of sentiment and seriousness of purpose. They can find, under the surface-brilliancy for which they give me credit, no coherent thought or sympathy, and accuse me, in various terms and degrees, of an inhuman and freakish wantonness; of preoccupation with "the seamy side of life"; of paradox, cyncism, and eccentricity, reducible, as some contend, to a trite formula of treating bad as good and good as bad, important as trivial and trivial as important, serious as laughable and laughable as serious, and so forth. As to this formula I can only say that if any gentleman is simple enough to think that even a good comic opera can be produced by it, I invite him to try his hand, and see whether anything resembling one of my plays will reward him.

I could explain the matter easily enough if I chose; but the result would be that the people who misunderstand the plays would misunderstand the explanation ten times more. The particular exceptions taken are seldom more than symptoms of the underlying fundamental disagreement between the romantic morality of the critics and the natural morality of the plays. For example, I am quite aware that the much criticized Swiss officer in Arms and The Man is not a conventional stage soldier. He suffers from want of food and sleep; his nerves go to pieces after three days under fire, ending in the horrors of a rout and pursuit; he has found by experience that it is more important to have a few bits of chocolate to eat in the field than cartridges for his revolver. When many of

my critics rejected these circumstances as fantastically
improbable and cynically unnatural, it was not necessary to argue them into common sense: all I had to
do was to brain them, so to speak, with the first half
dozen military authorities at hand, beginning with the
present Commander in Chief. But when it proved that
such unromantic (but all the more dramatic) facts
implied to them a denial of the existence of courage,
patriotism, faith, hope, and charity, I saw that it was
not really mere matter of fact that was at issue between
us. One strongly Liberal critic, the late Moy Thomas,
who had, in the teeth of a chorus of dissent, received
my first play with the most generous encouragement,
declared, when Arms and The Man was produced,
that I had struck a wanton blow at the cause of
liberty in the Balkan Peninsula by mentioning that
it was not a matter of course for a Bulgarian in 1885
to wash his hands every day. He no doubt saw soon
afterwards the squabble, reported all through Europe,
between Stambouloff and an eminent lady of the
Bulgarian court who took exception to his neglect of
his fingernails. After that came the news of his ferocious assassination, with a description of the room
prepared for the reception of visitors by his widow,
who draped it with black, and decorated it with photographs of the mutilated body of her husband. Here
was a sufficiently sensational confirmation of the
accuracy of my sketch of the theatrical nature of the
first apings of western civilization by spirited races
just emerging from slavery. But it had no bearing on
the real issue between my critic and myself, which
was, whether the political and religious idealism
which had inspired Gladstone to call for the rescue
of these Balkan principalities from the despotism of
the Turk, and converted miserably enslaved pro-

vinces into hopeful and gallant little States, will survive the general onslaught on idealism which is implicit, and indeed explicit, in Arms and The Man and the naturalist plays of the modern school. For my part I hope not; for idealism, which is only a flattering name for romance in politics and morals, is as obnoxious to me as romance in ethics or religion. In spite of a Liberal Revolution or two, I can no longer be satisfied with fictitious morals and fictitious good conduct, shedding fictitious glory on robbery, starvation, disease, crime, drink, war, cruelty, cupidity, and all the other commonplaces of civilization which drive men to the theatre to make foolish pretences that such things are progress, science, morals, religion, patriotism, imperial supremacy, national greatness and all the other names the newspapers call them. On the other hand, I see plenty of good in the world working itself out as fast as the idealists will allow it; and if they would only let it alone and learn to respect reality, which would include the beneficial exercise of respecting themselves, and incidentally respecting me, we should all get along much better and faster. At all events, I do not see moral chaos and anarchy as the alternative to romantic convention; and I am not going to pretend I do merely to please the people who are convinced that the world is held together only by the force of unanimous, strenuous, eloquent, trumpet-tongued lying. To me the tragedy and comedy of life lie in the consequences, sometimes terrible, sometimes ludicrous, of our persistent attempts to found our institutions on the ideals suggested to our imaginations by our half-satisfied passions, instead of on a genuinely scientific natural history. And with that hint as to what I am driving at, I withdraw and ring up the curtain.

Arms and the Man

WITH

An Interview drafted by Shaw for
The Star, *14 April, 1894*

Ten Minutes with Mr Bernard Shaw

A Dramatic Realist to his Critics

Composition begun 26 November 1893; completed 30 March 1894. Published in *Plays Pleasant and Unpleasant*, 1898. Revised text in Collected Edition, 1930.

First presented by Florence Farr at the Avenue Theatre, London, on 21 April 1894 (50 performances).

Major Paul Petkoff *James Welch*
Major Sergius Saranoff *Bernard Gould*
Captain Bluntschli *Yorke Stephens*
Major Plechanoff *A. E. W. Mason*
Nicola *Orlando Barnett*
Catherine Petkoff *Mrs Charles Calvert*
Raïna Petkoff *Alma Murray*
Louka *Florence Farr*

The action occurs at Major Petkoff's House in a small Bulgarian town, near the Dragoman Pass. 1885-86.

ACT I *Raina's Chamber*

ACT II *The Garden*

ACT III *The Library*

Night: A lady's bedchamber in Bulgaria, in a small town near the Dragoman Pass, late in November in the year 1885. Through an open window with a little balcony a peak of the Balkans, wonderfully white and beautiful in the starlit snow, seems quite close at hand, though it is really miles away. The interior of the room is not like anything to be seen in the west of Europe. It is half rich Bulgarian, half cheap Viennese. Above the head of the bed, which stands against a little wall cutting off the left hand corner of the room, is a painted wooden shrine, blue and gold, with an ivory image of Christ, and a light hanging before it in a pierced metal ball suspended by three chains. The principal seat, placed towards the other side of the room and opposite the window, is a Turkish ottoman. The counterpane and hangings of the bed, the window curtains, the little carpet, and all the ornamental textile fabrics in the room are oriental and gorgeous: the paper on the walls is occidental and paltry. The washstand, against the wall on the side nearest the ottoman and window, consists of an enamelled iron basin with a pail beneath it in a painted metal frame, and a single towel on the rail at the side. The dressing table, between the bed and the window, is a common pine table, covered with a cloth of many colors, with an expensive toilet mirror on it. The door is on the side nearest the bed; and there is a chest of drawers between. This chest of drawers is also covered by a variegated native cloth; and on it there is a pile of paper backed novels, a box of chocolate creams, and a miniature easel with a large photograph of an extremely handsome officer, whose lofty bearing and magnetic glance can be felt even from the portrait. The room is lighted by a candle on the chest of drawers, and another on the dressing table with a box of matches beside it.

The window is hinged doorwise and stands wide open. Outside, a pair of wooden shutters, opening outwards, also stand open. On the balcony a young lady, intensely conscious of the romantic beauty of the night, and of the fact that her own youth and beauty are part of it, is gazing at the snowy Balkans. She is in her nightgown, well covered by a long mantle of furs, worth, on a moderate estimate, about three times the furniture of her room.

Her reverie is interrupted by her mother, Catherine Petkoff, a woman over forty, imperiously energetic, with magnificent black hair and eyes, who might be a very splendid specimen of the wife of a mountain farmer, but is determined to be a Viennese lady, and to that end wears a fashionable tea gown on all occasions.

CATHERINE [*entering hastily, full of good news*] Raina! [*She pronounces it Rah-eena, with the stress on the ee*]. Raina! [*She goes to the bed, expecting to find Raina there*]. Why, where—? [*Raina looks into the room*]. Heavens, child! are you out in the night air instead of in your bed? You'll catch your death. Louka told me you were asleep.

RAINA [*dreamily*] I sent her away. I wanted to be alone. The stars are so beautiful! What is the matter?

CATHERINE. Such news! There has been a battle.

RAINA [*her eyes dilating*] Ah! [*She comes eagerly to Catherine*].

CATHERINE. A great battle at Slivnitza! A victory! And it was won by Sergius.

RAINA [*with a cry of delight*] Ah! [*They embrace rapturously*] Oh, mother! [*Then, with sudden anxiety*] Is father safe?

CATHERINE. Of course: he sends me the news. Sergius is the hero of the hour, the idol of the regiment.

RAINA. Tell me, tell me. How was it? [*Ecstatically*] Oh, mother! mother! mother! [*She pulls her mother down on the ottoman; and they kiss one another frantically*].

CATHERINE [*with surging enthusiasm*] You cant guess how splendid it is. A cavalry charge! think of that! He defied our Russian commanders—acted without orders—led a charge on his own responsibility—headed it himself—was the first man to sweep through their guns. Cant you see it, Raina: our gallant splendid Bulgarians with their swords and eyes flashing, thundering down like an avalanche and scattering the wretched Serbs and their dandified Austrian officers like chaff. And you! you kept Sergius waiting a year before you would be betrothed to him. Oh, if you have a drop of Bulgarian blood in your veins, you will worship him when he comes back.

RAINA. What will he care for my poor little worship after the acclamations of a whole army of heroes? But no matter: I am so happy! so proud! [*She rises and walks about excitedly*]. It proves that all our ideas were real after all.

CATHERINE [*indignantly*] Our ideas real! What do you mean?

RAINA. Our ideas of what Sergius would do. Our patriotism. Our heroic ideals. I sometimes used to doubt whether they were anything but dreams. Oh, what faithless little creatures girls are! When I buckled on Sergius's sword he looked so noble: it was treason to think of disillusion or humiliation or failure. And yet—and yet— [*She sits down again suddenly*] Promise me youll never tell him.

CATHERINE. Dont ask me for promises until I know what I'm promising.

RAINA. Well, it came into my head just as he was holding me in his arms and looking into my eyes, that perhaps we only had our heroic ideas because we are so fond of reading Byron and Pushkin, and because we were so delighted with the opera that season at Bucharest. Real life is so seldom like that! indeed never, as far as I knew it then. [*Remorsefully*] Only think, mother: I doubted him: I wondered whether all his heroic qualities and his soldiership might not prove mere imagination when he went into a real battle. I had an uneasy fear that he might cut a poor figure there beside all those clever officers from the Tsar's court.

CATHERINE. A poor figure! Shame on you! The Serbs have Austrian officers who are just as clever as the Russians; but we have beaten them in every battle for all that.

RAINA [*laughing and snuggling against her mother*] Yes: I was only a prosaic little coward. Oh, to think that it was all true! that Sergius is just as splendid and noble as he looks! that the world is really a glorious world for women who can see its glory and men who can act its romance! What happiness! what unspeakable fulfilment!

They are interrupted by the entry of Louka, a handsome proud girl in a pretty Bulgarian peasant's dress with double apron, so defiant that her servility to Raina is almost insolent. She is afraid of Catherine, but even with her goes as far as she dares.

LOUKA. If you please, madam, all the windows are to be closed and the shutters made fast. They say there may be shooting in the streets. [*Raina and Catherine rise together, alarmed*]. The Serbs are being chased right back through the pass; and they say they may run into the town. Our cavalry will be after them; and our people will be ready for them, you may be sure, now theyre running away. [*She goes out on the balcony, and pulls the outside shutters to; then steps back into the room*].

CATHERINE [*businesslike, her housekeeping instincts aroused*] I must see that everything is made safe downstairs.

RAINA. I wish our people were not so cruel. What glory is there in killing wretched fugitives?

CATHERINE. Cruel! Do you suppose they would hesitate to kill you—or worse?

RAINA [*to Louka*] Leave the shutters so that I can just close them if I hear any noise.

CATHERINE [*authoritatively, turning on her way to the door*] Oh no, dear: you must keep them fastened. You would be sure to drop off to sleep and leave them open. Make them fast, Louka.

LOUKA. Yes, madam. [*She fastens them*].

RAINA. Dont be anxious about me. The moment I hear a shot, I shall blow out the candles and roll myself up in bed with my ears well covered.

CATHERINE. Quite the wisest thing you can do, my love. Goodnight.

RAINA. Goodnight. [*Her emotion comes back for a moment*]. Wish me joy [*They kiss*]. This is the happiest night of my life—if only there are no fugitives.

CATHERINE. Go to bed, dear; and dont think of them. [*She goes out*].

LOUKA [*secretly, to Raina*] If you would like the

shutters open, just give them a push like this [*she pushes them: they open: she pulls them to again*]. One of them ought to be bolted at the bottom; but the bolt's gone.

RAINA [*with dignity, reproving her*] Thanks, Louka; but we must do what we are told. [*Louka makes a grimace*]. Goodnight.

LOUKA [*carelessly*] Goodnight. [*She goes out, swaggering*].

Raina, left alone, takes off her fur cloak and throws it on the ottoman. Then she goes to the chest of drawers, and adores the portrait there with feelings that are beyond all expression. She does not kiss it or press it to her breast, or shew it any mark of bodily affection; but she takes it in her hands and elevates it, like a priestess.

RAINA [*looking up at the picture*] Oh, I shall never be unworthy of you any more, my soul's hero: never, never, never. [*She replaces it reverently. Then she selects a novel from the little pile of books. She turns over the leaves dreamily; finds her page; turns the book inside out at it; and, with a happy sigh, gets into bed and prepares to read herself to sleep. But before abandoning herself to fiction, she raises her eyes once more, thinking of the blessed reality, and murmurs*] My hero! my hero!

A distant shot breaks the quiet of the night. She starts, listening; and two more shots, much nearer, follow, startling her so that she scrambles out of bed, and hastily blows out the candle on the chest of drawers. Then, putting her fingers in her ears, she runs to the dressing table, blows out the light there, and hurries back to bed in the dark, nothing being visible but the glimmer of the light in the pierced ball before the image, and starlight seen through the slits at the top of the shutters. The firing breaks out again: there is a startling fusillade quite close at hand. Whilst it is still echoing, the shutters disappear, pulled open from without; and for an instant the rectangle of snowy starlight flashes out with the figure of a man silhouetted in black upon it. The shutters close immediately; and the room is dark again. But the silence is now broken by the sound of panting. Then there is a scratch and the flame of a match is seen in the middle of the room.

RAINA [*crouching on the bed*] Who's there? [*The match is out instantly*]. Who's there? Who is that?

A MAN'S VOICE [*in the darkness, subduedly, but threateningly*] Sh—sh! Dont call out; or youll be shot. Be good; and no harm will happen to you. [*She is heard leaving her bed, and making for the door*]. Take care: it's no use trying to run away.

RAINA. But who—

THE VOICE [*warning*] Remember: if you raise your voice my revolver will go off. [*Commandingly*]. Strike a light and let me see you. Do you hear. [*Another moment of silence and darkness as she retreats to the chest of drawers. Then she lights a candle; and the mystery is at an end. He is a man of about 35, in a deplorable plight, bespattered with mud and blood and snow, his belt and the strap of his revolver-case keeping together the torn ruins of the blue tunic of a Serbian artillery officer. All that the candlelight and his unwashed unkempt condition make it possible to discern is that he is of middling stature and undistinguished appearance, with strong neck and shoulders, roundish obstinate looking head covered with short crisp bronze curls, clear quick eyes and good brows and mouth, hopelessly prosaic nose like that of a strong minded baby, trim soldierlike carriage and energetic manner, and with all his wits about him in spite of his desperate predicament: even with a sense of the humor of it, without, however, the least intention of trifling with it or throwing away a chance. Reckoning up what he can guess about Raina: her age, her social position, her character, and the extent to which she is frightened, he continues, more politely but still most determinedly]* Excuse my disturbing you; but you recognize my uniform? Serb! If I'm caught I shall be killed. *[Menacingly]* Do you understand that?

RAINA. Yes.

THE MAN. Well I dont intend to get killed if I can help it. *[Still more formidably]* Do you understand that? *[He locks the door quickly but quietly]*.

RAINA *[disdainfully]* I suppose not. *[She draws herself up superbly, and looks him straight in the face, adding with cutting emphasis]* Some soldiers, I know, are afraid to die.

THE MAN *[with grim goodhumor]* All of them, dear lady, all of them, believe me. It is our duty to live as long as we can. Now, if you raise an alarm—

RAINA *[cutting him short]* You will shoot me. How do you know that *I* am afraid to die?

THE MAN *[cunningly]* Ah; but suppose I dont shoot you, what will happen then? A lot of your cavalry will burst into this pretty room of yours and slaughter me here like a pig; for I'll fight like a demon: they shant get me into the street to amuse themselves with: I know what they are. Are you prepared to receive that sort of company in your present undress? *[Raina, suddenly conscious of her nightgown, instinctively shrinks, and gathers it more closely about her neck. He watches her, and adds, pitilessly]* Hardly presentable, eh? *[She turns to the ottoman. He raises his pistol instantly, and cries]* Stop! *[She stops]*. Where are you going?

RAINA *[with dignified patience]* Only to get my cloak.

THE MAN [*passing swiftly to the ottoman and snatching the cloak*] A good idea! I'll keep the cloak; and youll take care that nobody comes in and sees you without it. This is a better weapon than the revolver: eh? [*He throws the pistol down on the ottoman*].

RAINA [*revolted*] It is not the weapon of a gentleman!

THE MAN. It's good enough for a man with only you to stand between him and death. [*As they look at one another for a moment, Raina hardly able to believe that even a Serbian officer can be so cynically and selfishly unchivalrous, they are startled by a sharp fusillade in the street. The chill of imminent death hushes the man's voice as he adds*] Do you hear? If you are going to bring those blackguards in on me you shall receive them as you are.

Clamor and disturbance. The pursuers in the street batter at the house door, shouting Open the door! Open the door! Wake up, will you! *A man servant's voice calls to them angrily from within.* This is Major Petkoff's house: you cant come in here; *but a renewal of the clamor, and a torrent of blows on the door, end with his letting a chain down with a clank, followed by a rush of heavy footsteps and a din of triumphant yells, dominated at last by the voice of Catherine, indignantly addressing an officer with* What does this mean, sir? Do you know where you are? *The noise subsides suddenly.*

LOUKA [*outside, knocking at the bedroom door*] My lady! my lady! get up quick and open the door. If you dont they will break it down.

The fugitive throws up his head with the gesture of a man who sees that it is all over with him, and drops the manner he has been assuming to intimidate Raina.

THE MAN [*sincerely and kindly*] No use, dear: I'm

[397]

done for. [*Flinging the cloak to her*] Quick! wrap yourself up: theyre coming.

RAINA. Oh, thank you. [*She wraps herself up with intense relief*].

THE MAN [*between his teeth*] Dont mention it.

RAINA [*anxiously*] What will you do?

THE MAN [*grimly*] The first man in will find out. Keep out of the way; and dont look. It wont last long; but it will not be nice. [*He draws his sabre and faces the door, waiting*].

RAINA [*impulsively*] I'll help you. I'll save you.

THE MAN. You cant.

RAINA. I can. I'll hide you. [*She drags him towards the window*]. Here! behind the curtains.

THE MAN [*yielding to her*] Theres just half a chance, if you keep your head.

RAINA [*drawing the curtain before him*] S-sh! [*She makes for the ottoman*].

THE MAN [*putting out his head*] Remember—

RAINA [*running back to him*] Yes?

THE MAN. —nine soldiers out of ten are born fools.

RAINA. Oh! [*She draws the curtain angrily before him*].

THE MAN [*looking out at the other side*] If they find me, I promise you a fight: a devil of a fight.

She stamps at him. He disappears hastily, She takes off her cloak, and throws it across the foot of the bed. Then, with a sleepy, disturbed air, she opens the door. Louka enters excitedly.

LOUKA. One of those beasts of Serbs has been seen climbing up the waterpipe to your balcony. Our men want to search for him; and they are so wild and drunk and furious. [*She makes for the other side of the room to get as far from the door as possible*]. My lady says you are to dress at once, and to—[*She sees the revolver lying on the ottoman, and stops, petrified*].

RAINA [*as if annoyed at being disturbed*] They shall not search here. Why have they been let in?

CATHERINE [*coming in hastily*] Raina, darling: are you safe? Have you seen anyone or heard anything?

RAINA. I heard the shooting. Surely the soldiers will not dare come in here?

CATHERINE. I have found a Russian officer, thank Heaven: he knows Sergius. [*Speaking through the door to someone outside*] Sir: will you come in now. My daughter will receive you.

A young Russian officer, in Bulgarian uniform, enters, sword in hand.

OFFICER [*with soft feline politeness and stiff military carriage*] Good evening, gracious lady. I am sorry to intrude; but there is a Serb hiding on the balcony. Will you and the gracious lady your mother please to withdraw whilst we search?

RAINA [*petulantly*] Nonsense, sir: you can see that there is no one on the balcony. [*She throws the shutters wide open and stands with her back to the curtain where the man is hidden, pointing to the moonlit balcony. A couple of shots are fired right under the window; and a bullet shatters the glass opposite Raina, who winks and gasps, but stands her ground; whilst Catherine screams, and the officer, with a cry of* Take care! *rushes to the balcony*].

THE OFFICER [*on the balcony, shouting savagely down to the street*] Cease firing there, you fools: do you hear? Cease firing, damn you! [*He glares down for a moment; then turns to Raina, trying to resume his polite manner*]. Could anyone have got in without your knowledge? Were you asleep?

RAINA. No: I have not been to bed.

THE OFFICER [*impatiently, coming back into the room*] Your neighbors have their heads so full of runaway

Serbs that they see them everywhere. [*Politely*] Gracious lady: a thousand pardons. Goodnight. [*Military bow, which Raina returns coldly. Another to Catherine, who follows him out*].

Raina closes the shutters, She turns and sees Louka, who has been watching the scene curiously.

RAINA. Dont leave my mother, Louka, until the soldiers go away.

Louka glances at Raina, at the ottoman, at the curtain; then purses her lips secretively, laughs insolently, and goes out. Raina, highly offended by this demonstration, follows her to the door, and shuts it behind her with a slam, locking it violently. The man immediately steps out from behind the curtain, sheathing his sabre. Then, dismissing the danger from his mind in a businesslike way, he comes affably to Raina.

THE MAN. A narrow shave; but a miss is as good as a mile. Dear young lady: your servant to the death. I wish for your sake I had joined the Bulgarian army instead of the other one. I am not a native Serb.

RAINA [*haughtily*] No: you are one of the Austrians who set the Serbs on to rob us of our national liberty, and who officer their army for them. We hate them! THE MAN. Austrian! not I. Dont hate me, dear young lady. I am a Swiss, fighting merely as a professional soldier. I joined the Serbs because they came first on the road from Switzerland. Be generous: youve beaten us hollow.

RAINA. Have I not been generous?

THE MAN. Noble! Heroic! But I'm not saved yet. This particular rush will soon pass through; but the pursuit will go on all night by fits and starts. I must take my chance to get off in a quiet interval. [*Pleasantly*] You dont mind my waiting just a minute or two, do you?

RAINA [*putting on her most genteel society manner*] Oh, not at all. Wont you sit down?

THE MAN. Thanks. [*He sits on the foot of the bed*].

Raina walks with studied elegance to the ottoman and sits down. Unfortunately she sits on the pistol, and jumps up with a shriek. The man, all nerves, shies like a frightened horse to the other side of the room.

THE MAN [*irritably*] Dont frighten me like that. What is it?

RAINA. Your revolver! It was staring that officer in the face all the time. What an escape!

THE MAN [*vexed at being unnecessarily terrified*] Oh, is that all?

RAINA [*staring at him rather superciliously as she conceives a poorer and poorer opinion of him, and feels proportionately more and more at her ease*] I am sorry I frightened you. [*She takes up the pistol and hands it to him*]. Pray take it to protect yourself against me.

THE MAN [*grinning wearily at the sarcasm as he takes the pistol*] No use, dear young lady: theres nothing in it. It's not loaded. [*He makes a grimace at it, and drops it disparagingly into his revolver case*].

RAINA. Load it by all means.

THE MAN. Ive no ammunition. What use are cartridges in battle? I always carry chocolate instead; and I finished the last cake of that hours ago.

RAINA [*outraged in her most cherished ideals of manhood*] Chocolate! Do you stuff your pockets with sweets—like a schoolboy—even in the field?

THE MAN [*grinning*] Yes: isnt it contemptible? [*Hungrily*] I wish I had some now.

RAINA. Allow me. [*She sails away scornfully to the chest of drawers, and returns with the box of confectionery in her hand*]. I am sorry I have eaten all except these. [*She offers him the box*].

THE MAN [*ravenously*] Youre an angel! [*He gobbles the contents*]. Creams! Delicious! [*He looks anxiously to see whether there are any more. There are none: he can only scrape the box with his fingers and suck them. When that nourishment is exhausted he accepts the inevitable with pathetic goodhumor, and says, with grateful emotion*] Bless you, dear lady! You can always tell an old soldier by the inside of his holsters and cartridge boxes. The young ones carry pistols and cartridges: the old ones, grub. Thank you. [*He hands back the box. She snatches it contemptuously from him and throws it away. He shies again, as if she had meant to strike him*]. Ugh! Dont do things so suddenly, gracious lady. It's mean to revenge yourself because I frightened you just now.

RAINA [*loftily*] Frighten me! Do you know, sir, that though I am only a woman, I think I am at heart as brave as you.

THE MAN. I should think so. You havnt been under fire for three days as I have. I can stand two days without shewing it much; but no man can stand three days: I'm as nervous as a mouse. [*He sits down on the ottoman, and takes his head in his hands*]. Would you like to see me cry?

RAINA [*alarmed*] No.

THE MAN. If you would, all you have to do is to scold me just as if I were a little boy and you my nurse. If I were in camp now, theyd play all sorts of tricks on me.

RAINA [*a little moved*] I'm sorry. I wont scold you. [*Touched by the sympathy in her tone, he raises his head and looks gratefully at her: immediately draws back and says stiffly*] You must excuse me: our soldiers are not like that. [*She moves away from the ottoman*].

THE MAN. Oh yes they are. There are only two sorts

of soldiers: old ones and young ones. Ive served
fourteen years: half of your fellows never smelt
powder before. Why, how is it that youve just beaten
us? Sheer ignorance of the art of war, nothing else.
[*Indignantly*] I never saw anything so unprofessional.

RAINA [*ironically*] Oh! was it unprofessional to beat
you?

THE MAN. Well, come! is it professional to throw a
regiment of cavalry on a battery of machine guns, with
the dead certainty that if the guns go off not a horse
or man will ever get within fifty yards of the fire? I
couldnt believe my eyes when I saw it.

RAINA [*eagerly turning to him, as all her enthusiasm
and her dreams of glory rush back on her*] Did you see
the great cavalry charge? Oh, tell me about it. Describe
it to me.

THE MAN. You never saw a cavalry charge, did you?

RAINA. How could I?

THE MAN. Ah, perhaps not. No: of course not! Well,
it's a funny sight. It's like slinging a handful of peas
against a window pane: first one comes; then two or
three close behind him; and then all the rest in a
lump.

RAINA [*her eyes dilating as she raises her clasped
hands ecstatically*] Yes, first One! the bravest of the
brave!

THE MAN [*prosaically*] Hm! you should see the poor
devil pulling at his horse.

RAINA. Why should he pull at his horse?

THE MAN [*impatient of so stupid a question*] It's running away with him, of course: do you suppose the
fellow wants to get there before the others and be
killed? Then they all come. You can tell the young
ones by their wildness and their slashing. The old ones
come bunched up under the number one guard: they

know that theyre mere projectiles, and that it's no use trying to fight. The wounds are mostly broken knees, from the horses cannoning together.

RAINA Ugh! But I dont believe the first man is a coward. I know he is a hero!

THE MAN [*goodhumoredly*] Thats what youd have said if youd seen the first man in the charge today.

RAINA [*breathless, forgiving him everything*] Ah, I knew it! Tell me. Tell me about him.

THE MAN. He did it like an operatic tenor. A regular handsome fellow, with flashing eyes and lovely moustache, shouting his war-cry and charging like Don Quixote at the windmills. We did laugh.

RAINA. You dared to laugh!

THE MAN. Yes; but when the sergeant ran up as white as a sheet, and told us theyd sent us the wrong ammunition, and that we couldnt fire a round for the next ten minutes, we laughed at the other side of our mouths. I never felt so sick in my life; though Ive been in one or two very tight places. And I hadnt even a revolver cartridge: only chocolate. We'd no bayonets: nothing. Of course, they just cut us to bits. And there was Don Quixote flourishing like a drum major, thinking he'd done the cleverest thing ever known, whereas he ought to be courtmartialled for it. Of all the fools ever let loose on a field of battle, that man must be the very maddest. He and his regiment simply committed suicide; only the pistol missed fire: thats all.

RAINA [*deeply wounded, but steadfastly loyal to her ideals*] Indeed! Would you know him again if you ever saw him?

THE MAN. Shall I ever forget him!

She again goes to the chest of drawers. He watches her with a vague hope that she may have something more

*for him to eat. She takes the portrait from its stand and
brings it to him.*

RAINA. That is a photograph of the gentleman—the
patriot and hero—to whom I am betrothed.

THE MAN [*recognizing it with a shock*] I'm really very
sorry. [*Looking at her*] Was it fair to lead me on?
[*He looks at the portrait again*] Yes: thats Don Quixote:
not a doubt of it. [*He stifles a laugh.*]

RAINA [*quickly*] Why do you laugh?

THE MAN [*apologetic, but still greatly tickled*] I didnt
laugh, I assure you. At least I didnt mean to. But
when I think of him charging the windmills and
imagining he was doing the finest thing—[*He chokes
with suppressed laughter*].

RAINA [*sternly*] Give me back the portrait, sir.

THE MAN [*with sincere remorse*] Of course. Certainly.
I'm really very sorry. [*He hands her the picture. She
deliberately kisses it and looks him straight in the face
before returning to the chest of drawers to replace it. He
follows her, apologizing*]. Perhaps I'm quite wrong,
you know: no doubt I am. Most likely he had got
wind of the cartridge business somehow, and knew it
was a safe job.

RAINA. That is to say, he was a pretender and a
coward! You did not dare say that before.

THE MAN [*with a comic gesture of despair*] It's no use,
dear lady: I cant make you see it from the professional
point of view. [*As he turns away to get back to the ottoman, a couple of distant shots threaten renewed trouble*].

RAINA [*sternly, as she sees him listening to the shots*] So
much the better for you!

THE MAN [*turning*] How?

RAINA. You are my enemy; and you are at my mercy.
What would I do if I were a professional soldier?

THE MAN. Ah, true, dear young lady: youre always

[405]

right. I know how good youve been to me: to my last hour I shall remember those three chocolate creams. It was unsoldierly; but it was angelic.

RAINA [*coldly*] Thank you. And now I will do a soldierly thing. You cannot stay here after what you have just said about my future husband; but I will go out on the balcony and see whether it is safe for you to climb down into the street. [*She turns to the window*].

THE MAN [*changing countenance*] Down that waterpipe! Stop! Wait! I cant! I darent! The very thought of it makes me giddy. I came up it fast enough with death behind me. But to face it now in cold blood—! [*He sinks on the ottoman*]. It's no use: I give up: I'm beaten. Give the alarm. [*He drops his head on his hands in the deepest dejection*].

RAINA [*disarmed by pity*] Come: dont be disheartened. [*She stoops over him almost maternally: he shakes his head*]. Oh, you are a very poor soldier: a chocolate cream soldier! Come, cheer up! it takes less courage to climb down than to face capture: remember that.

THE MAN [*dreamily, lulled by her voice*] No: capture only means death; and death is sleep: oh, sleep, sleep, sleep, undisturbed sleep! Climbing down the pipe means doing something—exerting myself—thinking! Death ten times over first.

RAINA [*softly and wonderingly, catching the rhythm of his weariness*] Are you as sleepy as that?

THE MAN. Ive not had two hours undisturbed sleep since I joined. I havnt closed my eyes for forty-eight hours.

RAINA [*at her wit's end*] But what am I to do with you?

THE MAN [*staggering up, roused by her desperation*] Of course. I must do something. [*He shakes himself; pulls himself together; and speaks with rallied vigor and courage*]. You see, sleep or no sleep, hunger or no hunger, tired or not tired, you can always do a thing when you know it must be done. Well, that pipe must be got down: [*he hits himself on the chest*] do you hear that, you chocolate cream soldier? [*He turns to the window*].

RAINA [*anxiously*] But if you fall?

THE MAN. I shall sleep as if the stones were a feather bed. Goodbye. [*He makes boldly for the window; and his hand is on the shutter when there is a terrible burst of firing in the street beneath*].

RAINA [*rushing to him*] Stop! [*She seizes him recklessly, and pulls him quite round*]. Theyll kill you.

THE MAN [*coolly, but attentively*] Never mind: this sort of thing is all in my day's work. I'm bound to take my chance. [*Decisively*] Now do what I tell you. Put out the candle; so that they shant see the light when I open the shutters. And keep away from the window, whatever you do. If they see me theyre sure to have a shot at me.

RAINA [*clinging to him*] Theyre sure to see you: it's bright moonlight. I'll save you. Oh, how can you be so indifferent! You want me to save you, dont you?

THE MAN. I really dont want to be troublesome. [*She shakes him in her impatience*]. I am not indifferent, dear young lady, I assure you. But how is it to be done?

RAINA. Come away from the window. [*She takes him firmly back to the middle of the room. The moment she releases him he turns mechanically towards the window again. She seizes him and turns him back, exclaiming*] Please! [*He becomes motionless, like a hypnotized rabbit, his fatigue gaining fast on him. She releases him, and addresses him patronizingly*]. Now listen. You must trust to our hospitality. You do not yet know in whose house you are. I am a Petkoff.

THE MAN. A pet what?

RAINA [*rather indignantly*] I mean that I belong to the family of the Petkoffs, the richest and best known in our country.

THE MAN. Oh yes, of course. I beg your pardon. The Petkoffs, to be sure. How stupid of me!

RAINA. You know you never heard of them until this moment. How can you stoop to pretend!

THE MAN. Forgive me: I'm too tired to think; and the change of subject was too much for me. Dont scold me.

RAINA. I forgot. It might make you cry. [*He nods, quite seriously. She pouts and then resumes her patronizing tone*]. I must tell you that my father holds the highest command of any Bulgarian in our army. He is [*proudly*] a Major.

THE MAN [*pretending to be deeply impressed*] A Major! Bless me! Think of that!

RAINA. You shewed great ignorance in thinking that it was necessary to climb up to the balcony because ours is the only private house that has two rows of windows. There is a flight of stairs inside to get up and down by.

THE MAN. Stairs! How grand! You live in great luxury indeed, dear young lady.

RAINA. Do you know what a library is?

THE MAN. A library? A roomful of books?

RAINA. Yes. We have one, the only one in Bulgaria.

THE MAN. Actually a real library! I should like to see that.

RAINA [*affectedly*] I tell you these things to shew you that you are not in the house of ignorant country folk who would kill you the moment they saw your Serbian uniform, but among civilized people. We go to Bucharest every year for the opera season; and I have spent a whole month in Vienna.

THE MAN. I saw that, dear young lady. I saw at once that you knew the world.

RAINA. Have you ever seen the opera of Ernani?

THE MAN. Is that the one with the devil in it in red velvet, and a soldiers' chorus?

RAINA [*contemptuously*] No!

THE MAN [*stifling a heavy sigh of weariness*] Then I dont know it.

RAINA. I thought you might have remembered the great scene where Ernani, flying from his foes just as you are tonight, takes refuge in the castle of his bitterest enemy, an old Castilian noble. The noble refuses to give him up. His guest is sacred to him.

THE MAN [*quickly, waking up a little*] Have your people got that notion?

RAINA [*with dignity*] My mother and I can understand that notion, as you call it. And if instead of threatening me with your pistol as you did you had simply thrown yourself as a fugitive on our hospitality, you would have been as safe as in your father's house.

THE MAN. Quite sure?

RAINA [*turning her back on him in disgust*] Oh, it is useless to try to make you understand.

THE MAN. Dont be angry: you see how awkward it would be for me if there was any mistake. My father is a very hospitable man: he keeps six hotels; but I couldnt trust him as far as that. What about your father?

RAINA. He is away at Slivnitza fighting for his country. I answer for your safety. There is my hand in pledge of it. Will that reassure you? [*She offers him her hand*].

THE MAN [*looking dubiously at his own hand*] Better not touch my hand, dear young lady. I must have a wash first.

RAINA [*touched*] That is very nice of you. I see that you are a gentleman.

THE MAN [*puzzled*] Eh?

RAINA. You must not think I am surprised. Bulgarians of really good standing—people in our position—wash their hands nearly every day. So you see I can appreciate your delicacy. You may take my hand. [*She offers it again*].

THE MAN [*kissing it with his hands behind his back*] Thanks, gracious young lady: I feel safe at last. And now would you mind breaking the news to your mother? I had better not stay here secretly longer than is necessary.

RAINA. If you will be so good as to keep perfectly still whilst I am away.

THE MAN. Certainly. [*He sits down on the ottoman*].

Raina goes to the bed and wraps herself in the fur cloak. His eyes close. She goes to the door. Turning for a last look at him, she sees that he is dropping off to sleep.

RAINA [*at the door*] You are not going asleep, are you? [*He murmurs inarticulately: she runs to him and shakes him*]. Do you hear? Wake up: you are falling asleep.

THE MAN. Eh? Falling aslee—? Oh no: not the least in the world: I was only thinking. It's all right: I'm wide awake.

RAINA [*severely*] Will you please stand up while I am away. [*He rises reluctantly*]. All the time, mind.

THE MAN [*standing unsteadily*] Certainly. Certainly: you may depend on me.

Raina looks doubtfully at him. He smiles weakly. She goes reluctantly, turning again at the door, and almost catching him in the act of yawning. She goes out.

THE MAN [*drowsily*] Sleep, sleep, sleep, sleep, slee— [*The words trail off into a murmur. He wakes again with a shock on the point of falling*]. Where am I ? Thats what I want to know: where am I ? Must keep awake. Nothing keeps me awake except danger: remember that: [*intently*] danger, danger, danger, dan—[*trailing off again: another shock*] Wheres danger ? Mus' find it. [*He starts off vaguely round the room in search of it*]. What am I looking for ? Sleep—danger—dont know. [*He stumbles against the bed*]. Ah yes: now I know. All right now. I'm to go to bed, but not to sleep. Be sure not to sleep, because of danger. Not to lie down either, only sit down. [*He sits on the bed. A blissful expression comes into his face*]. Ah! [*With a happy sigh he sinks back at full length; lifts his boots into the bed with a final effort; and falls fast asleep instantly*].

Catherine comes in, followed by Raina.

RAINA [*looking at the ottoman*] He's gone! I left him here.

CATHERINE. Here! Then he must have climbed down from the—

RAINA [*seeing him*] Oh! [*She points*].

CATHERINE [*scandalized*] Well! [*She strides to the bed, Raina following until she is opposite her on the other side*]. He's fast asleep. The brute!

RAINA [*anxiously*] Sh!

CATHERINE [*shaking him*] Sir! [*Shaking him again, harder*] Sir!! [*Vehemently, shaking very hard*] Sir!!!

RAINA [*catching her arm*] Dont, mamma: the poor darling is worn out. Let him sleep.

CATHERINE [*letting him go, and turning amazed to Raina*] The poor darling! Raina!!! [*She looks sternly at her daughter*].

The man sleeps profoundly.

[ACT II]

The sixth of March, 1886. In the garden of Major Petkoff's house. It is a fine spring morning: the garden looks fresh and pretty. Beyond the paling the tops of a couple of minarets can be seen, shewing that there is a valley there, with the little town in it. A few miles further the Balkan mountains rise and shut in the landscape. Looking towards them from within the garden, the side of the house is seen on the left, with a garden door reached by a little flight of steps. On the right the stable yard, with its gateway, encroaches on the garden. There are fruit bushes along the paling and house, covered with washing spread out to dry. A path runs by the house, and rises by two steps at the corner, where it turns out of sight. In the middle, a small table, with two bent wood chairs at it, is laid for breakfast with Turkish coffee pot, cups, rolls, etc.; but the cups have been used and the bread broken. There is a wooden garden seat against the wall on the right.

Louka, smoking a cigaret, is standing between the table and the house, turning her back with angry disdain on a man servant who is lecturing her. He is a middle-aged man of cool temperament and low but clear and keen intelligence, with the complacency of the servant who values himself on his rank in servitude, and the imperturbability of the accurate calculator who has no illusions. He wears a white Bulgarian costume: jacket with embroidered border, sash, wide knickerbockers, and decorated gaiters. His head is shaved up to the crown, giving him a high Japanese forehead. His name is Nicola.

NICOLA. Be warned in time, Louka: mend your manners. I know the mistress. She is so grand that she never dreams that any servant could dare be disrespectful to her; but if she once suspects that you are defying her, out you go.

LOUKA. I do defy her. I will defy her. What do I care for her?

NICOLA. If you quarrel with the family, I never can marry you. It's the same as if you quarrelled with me!

LOUKA. You take her part against me, do you?

NICOLA [*sedately*] I shall always be dependent on the good will of the family. When I leave their service and start a shop in Sofia, their custom will be half my capital: their bad word would ruin me.

LOUKA. You have no spirit. I should like to catch them saying a word against me!

NICOLA [*pityingly*] I should have expected more sense from you, Louka. But youre young: youre young!

LOUKA. Yes; and you like me the better for it, dont you? But I know some family secrets they wouldnt care to have told, young as I am. Let them quarrel with me if they dare!

NICOLA [*with compassionate superiority*] Do you know what they would do if they heard you talk like that?

LOUKA. What could they do?

NICOLA. Discharge you for untruthfulness. Who would believe any stories you told after that? Who would give you another situation? Who in this house would dare be seen speaking to you ever again? How long would your father be left on his little farm? [*She impatiently throws away the end of her cigaret, and stamps on it*]. Child: you dont know the power such high people have over the like of you and me when we try to rise out of our poverty against them. [*He goes close to her and lowers his voice*]. Look at me,

[413]

ten years in their service. Do you think I know no secrets? I know things about the mistress that she wouldnt have the master know for a thousand levas. I know things about him that she wouldnt let him hear the last of for six months if I blabbed them to her. I know things about Raina that would break off her match with Sergius if—

LOUKA [*turning on him quickly*] How do you know? I never told you!

NICOLA [*opening his eyes cunningly*] So thats your little secret, is it? I thought it might be something like that. Well, you take my advice and be respectful; and make the mistress feel that no matter what you know or dont know, she can depend on you to hold your tongue and serve the family faithfully. Thats what they like; and thats how youll make most out of them.

LOUKA [*with searching scorn*] You have the soul of a servant, Nicola.

NICOLA [*complacently*] Yes: thats the secret of success in service.

A loud knocking with a whip handle on a wooden door is heard from the stable yard.

MALE VOICE OUTSIDE. Hollo! Hollo there! Nicola!

LOUKA. Master! back from the war!

NICOLA [*quickly*] My word for it, Louka, the war's over. Off with you and get some fresh coffee. [*He runs out into the stable yard*].

LOUKA [*as she collects the coffee pot and cups on the tray, and carries it into the house*] Youll never put the soul of a servant into me.

Major Petkoff comes from the stable yard, followed by Nicola. He is a cheerful, excitable, insignificant, unpolished man of about 50, naturally unambitious except as to his income and his importance in local society, but just now greatly pleased with the military rank which the war has thrust on him as a man of consequence in his town. The fever of plucky patriotism which the Serbian attack roused in all the Bulgarians has pulled him through the war; but he is obviously glad to be home again.

PETKOFF [*pointing to the table with his whip*] Breakfast out here, eh?

NICOLA. Yes, sir. The mistress and Miss Raina have just gone in.

PETKOFF [*sitting down and taking a roll*] Go in and say Ive come; and get me some fresh coffee.

NICOLA. It's coming, sir. [*He goes to the house door. Louka, with fresh coffee, a clean cup, and a brandy bottle on her tray, meets him*]. Have you told the mistress?

LOUKA. Yes: she's coming.

Nicola goes into the house. Louka brings the coffee to the table.

PETKOFF. Well: the Serbs havnt run away with you, have they?

LOUKA. No, sir.

PETKOFF. Thats right. Have you brought me some cognac?

LOUKA [*putting the bottle on the table*] Here, sir.

PETKOFF. Thats right. [*He pours some into his coffee*].

Catherine, who, having at this early hour made only a very perfunctory toilet, wears a Bulgarian apron over a once brilliant but now half worn-out dressing gown, and a colored handkerchief tied over her thick black hair, comes from the house with Turkish slippers on her bare feet, looking astonishingly handsome and stately under all the circumstances. Louka goes into the house.

CATHERINE. My dear Paul: what a surprise for us! [*She stoops over the back of his chair to kiss him*]. Have they brought you fresh coffee?

PETKOFF. Yes: Louka's been looking after me. The war's over. The treaty was signed three days ago at Bucharest; and the decree for our army to demobilize was issued yesterday.

CATHERINE [*springing erect, with flashing eyes*] Paul: have you let the Austrians force you to make peace?

PETKOFF [*submissively*] My dear: they didnt consult me. What could *I* do? [*She sits down and turns away from him*]. But of course we saw to it that the treaty was an honorable one. It declares peace—

CATHERINE [*outraged*] Peace!

PETKOFF [*appeasing her*]—but not friendly relations: remember that. They wanted to put that in; but I insisted on its being struck out. What more could I do?

CATHERINE. You could have annexed Serbia and made Prince Alexander Emperor of the Balkans. Thats what I would have done.

PETKOFF. I dont doubt it in the least, my dear. But I should have had to subdue the whole Austrian Empire first; and that would have kept me too long away from you. I missed you greatly.

CATHERINE [*relenting*] Ah! [*She stretches her hand affectionately across the table to squeeze his*].

PETKOFF. And how have you been, my dear?

CATHERINE. Oh, my usual sore throats: thats all.

PETKOFF [*with conviction*] That comes from washing your neck every day. Ive often told you so.

CATHERINE. Nonsense, Paul!

PETKOFF [*over his coffee and cigaret*] I dont believe in going too far with these modern customs. All this washing cant be good for the health: it's not natural. There was an Englishman at Philippopolis who used to wet himself all over with cold water every morning when he got up. Disgusting! It all comes from the English: their climate makes them so dirty that they have to be perpetually washing themselves. Look at my father! he never had a bath in his life; and he lived to be ninety-eight, the healthiest man in Bulgaria. I dont mind a good wash once a week to keep up my position; but once a day is carrying the thing to a ridiculous extreme.

CATHERINE. You are a barbarian at heart still, Paul. I hope you behaved yourself before all those Russian officers.

PETKOFF. I did my best. I took care to let them know that we have a library.

CATHERINE. Ah; but you didnt tell them that we have an electric bell in it? I have had one put up.

PETKOFF. Whats an electric bell?

CATHERINE. You touch a button; something tinkles in the kitchen; and then Nicola comes up.

PETKOFF. Why not shout for him?

CATHERINE. Civilized people never shout for their servants. Ive learnt that while you were away.

PETKOFF. Well, I'll tell you something Ive learnt too. Civilized people dont hang out their washing to dry where visitors can see it; so youd better have all that [*indicating the clothes on the bushes*] put somewhere else.

CATHERINE. Oh, thats absurd, Paul: I dont believe really refined people notice such things.

SERGIUS [*knocking at the stable gates*] Gate, Nicola!

PETKOFF. Theres Sergius. [*Shouting*] Hollo, Nicola!

CATHERINE. Oh, dont shout, Paul: it really isnt nice.

PETKOFF. Bosh! [*He shouts louder than before*] Nicola!

NICOLA [*appearing at the house door*] Yes, sir.

PETKOFF. Are you deaf? Dont you hear Major

Saranoff knocking? Bring him round this way. [*He pronounces the name with the stress on the second syllable: Sarahnoff*].

NICOLA. Yes, major. [*He goes into the stable yard*].

PETKOFF. You must talk to him, my dear, until Raina takes him off our hands. He bores my life out about our not promoting him. Over my head, if you please.

CATHERINE. He certainly ought to be promoted when he marries Raina. Besides, the country should insist on having at least one native general.

PETKOFF. Yes; so that he could throw away whole brigades instead of regiments. It's no use, my dear: he hasnt the slightest chance of promotion until we're quite sure that the peace will be a lasting one.

NICOLA [*at the gate, announcing*] Major Sergius Saranoff! [*He goes into the house and returns presently with a third chair, which he places at the table. He then withdraws*].

Major Sergius Saranoff, the original of the portrait in Raina's room, is a tall romantically handsome man, with the physical hardihood, the high spirit, and the susceptible imagination of an untamed mountaineer chieftain. But his remarkable personal distinction is of a characteristically civilized type. The ridges of his eyebrows, curving with an interrogative twist round the projections at the outer corners; his jealously observant eye; his nose, thin, keen, and apprehensive in spite of the pugnacious high bridge and large nostril; his assertive chin, would not be out of place in a Parisian salon, shewing that the clever imaginative barbarian has an acute critical faculty which has been thrown into intense activity by the arrival of western civilization in the Balkans. The result is precisely what the advent of nineteenth century thought first produced in England:

[418]

to wit, Byronism. By his brooding on the perpetual failure, not only of others, but of himself, to live up to his ideals; by his consequent cynical scorn for humanity; by his jejune credulity as to the absolute validity of his concepts and the unworthiness of the world in disregarding them; by his wincings and mockeries under the sting of the petty disillusions which every hour spent among men brings to his sensitive observation, he has acquired the half tragic, half ironic air, the mysterious moodiness, the suggestion of a strange and terrible history that has left nothing but undying remorse, by which Childe Harold fascinated the grandmothers of his English contemporaries. It is clear that here or nowhere is Raina's ideal hero. Catherine is hardly less enthusiastic about him than her daughter, and much less reserved in shewing her enthusiasm. As he enters from the stable gate, she rises effusively to greet him. Petkoff is distinctly less disposed to make a fuss about him.

PETKOFF. Here already, Sergius! Glad to see you.

CATHERINE. My dear Sergius! [*She holds out both her hands*].

SERGIUS [*kissing them with a scrupulous gallantry*] My dear mother, if I may call you so.

PETKOFF [*drily*] Mother-in-law, Sergius: mother-in-law! Sit down; and have some coffee.

SERGIUS. Thank you: none for me. [*He gets away from the table with a certain distaste for Petkoff's enjoyment of it, and posts himself with conscious dignity against the rail of the steps leading to the house*].

CATHERINE. You look superb. The campaign has improved you, Sergius. Everybody here is mad about you. We were all wild with enthusiasm about that magnificent cavalry charge.

SERGIUS [*with grave irony*] Madam: it was the cradle and the grave of my military reputation.

CATHERINE. How so?

SERGIUS. I won the battle the wrong way when our worthy Russian generals were losing it the right way. In short, I upset their plans, and wounded their self-esteem. Two Cossack colonels had their regiments routed on the most correct principles of scientific warfare. Two major-generals got killed strictly according to military etiquette. The two colonels are now major-generals; and I am still a simple major.

CATHERINE. You shall not remain so, Sergius. The women are on your side; and they will see that justice is done you.

SERGIUS. It is too late. I have only waited for the peace to send in my resignation.

PETKOFF [*dropping his cup in his amazement*] Your resignation!

CATHERINE. Oh, you must withdraw it!

SERGIUS [*with resolute measured emphasis, folding his arms*] I never withdraw.

PETKOFF [*vexed*] Now who could have supposed you were going to do such a thing?

SERGIUS [*with fire*] Everyone that knew me. But enough of myself and my affairs. How is Raina; and where is Raina?

RAINA [*suddenly coming round the corner of the house and standing at the top of the steps in the path*] Raina is here.

She makes a charming picture as they turn to look at her. She wears an underdress of pale green silk, draped with an overdress of thin ecru canvas embroidered with gold. She is crowned with a dainty eastern cap of gold tinsel. Sergius goes impulsively to meet her. Posing regally, she presents her hand: he drops chivalrously on one knee and kisses it.

PETKOFF [*aside to Catherine, beaming with parental pride*] Pretty, isnt it? She always appears at the right moment.

CATHERINE [*impatiently*] Yes: she listens for it. It is an abominable habit.

Sergius leads Raina forward with splendid gallantry. When they arrive at the table, she turns to him with a bend of the head: he bows; and thus they separate, he coming to his place, and she going behind her father's chair.

RAINA [*stooping and kissing her father*] Dear father! Welcome home!

PETKOFF [*patting her cheek*] My little pet girl. [*He kisses her. She goes to the chair left by Nicola for Sergius, and sits down*].

CATHERINE. And so youre no longer a soldier, Sergius.

SERGIUS. I am no longer a soldier. Soldiering, my dear madam, is the coward's art of attacking mercilessly when you are strong, and keeping out of harm's way when you are weak. That is the whole secret of successful fighting. Get your enemy at a disadvantage; and never, on any account, fight him on equal terms.

PETKOFF. They wouldnt let us make a fair stand-up fight of it. However, I suppose soldiering has to be a trade like any other trade.

SERGIUS. Precisely. But I have no ambition to shine as a tradesman; so I have taken the advice of that bagman of a captain that settled the exchange of prisoners with us at Pirot, and given it up.

PETKOFF. What! that Swiss fellow? Sergius: Ive often thought of that exchange since. He over-reached us about those horses.

SERGIUS. Of course he over-reached us. His father was a hotel and livery stable keeper; and he owed his first step to his knowledge of horse-dealing. [*With mock enthusiasm*] Ah, he was a soldier: every inch a soldier! If only I had bought the horses for my regiment instead of foolishly leading it into danger, I should have been a field-marshal now!

CATHERINE. A Swiss? What was he doing in the Serbian army?

PETKOFF. A volunteer, of course: keen on picking up his profession. [*Chuckling*] We shouldnt have been able to begin fighting if these foreigners hadnt shewn us how to do it: we knew nothing about it; and neither did the Serbs. Egad, there'd have been no war without them!

RAINA. Are there many Swiss officers in the Serbian Army?

PETKOFF. No. All Austrians, just as our officers were all Russians. This was the only Swiss I came across. I'll never trust a Swiss again. He humbugged us into giving him fifty ablebodied men for two hundred worn out chargers. They werent even eatable!

SERGIUS. We were two children in the hands of that consummate soldier, Major: simply two innocent little children.

RAINA. What was he like?

CATHERINE. Oh, Raina, what a silly question!

SERGIUS. He was like a commercial traveller in uniform. Bourgeois to his boots!

PETKOFF [*grinning*] Sergius: tell Catherine that queer story his friend told us about how he escaped after Slivnitza. You remember. About his being hid by two women.

SERGIUS [*with bitter irony*] Oh yes: quite a romance! He was serving in the very battery I so unprofessionally charged. Being a thorough soldier, he ran away like the rest of them, with our cavalry at his heels. To escape their sabres he climbed a waterpipe and made his way into the bedroom of a young Bulgarian lady. The young lady was enchanted by his persuasive commercial traveller's manners. She very modestly entertained him for an hour or so, and then called in her mother lest her conduct should appear unmaidenly. The old lady was equally fascinated; and the fugitive was sent on his way in the morning, disguised in an old coat belonging to the master of the house, who was away at the war.

RAINA [*rising with marked stateliness*] Your life in the camp has made you coarse, Sergius. I did not think you would have repeated such a story before me. [*She turns away coldly*].

CATHERINE [*also rising*] She is right, Sergius. If such women exist, we should be spared the knowledge of them.

PETKOFF. Pooh! nonsense! what does it matter?

SERGIUS [*ashamed*] No, Petkoff: I was wrong. [*To Raina, with earnest humility*] I beg your pardon. I have behaved abominably. Forgive me, Raina. [*She bows reservedly*]. And you too, madam. [*Catherine bows graciously and sits down. He proceeds solemnly, again addressing Raina*] The glimpses I have had of the seamy side of life during the last few months have made me cynical; but I should not have brought my cynicism here: least of all into your presence, Raina. I—[*Here, turning to the others. he is evidently going to begin a long speech when the Major interrupts him*].

PETKOFF. Stuff and nonsense, Sergius! Thats quite enough fuss about nothing: a soldier's daughter should be able to stand up without flinching to a little strong conversation. [*He rises*]. Come: it's time for us to get to business. We have to make up our minds how those three regiments are to get back to Philippopolis: theres no forage for them on the Sofia route. [*He goes towards the house*]. Come along. [*Sergius is about to follow him when Catherine rises and intervenes*].

CATHERINE. Oh, Paul, cant you spare Sergius for a few moments? Raina has hardly seen him yet. Perhaps I can help you to settle about the regiments.

SERGIUS [*protesting*] My dear madam, impossible: you—

CATHERINE [*stopping him playfully*] You stay here, my dear Sergius: theres no hurry. I have a word or two to say to Paul. [*Sergius instantly bows and steps back*]. Now, dear [*taking Petkoff's arm*]: come and see the electric bell.

PETKOFF. Oh, very well, very well.

They go into the house together affectionately. Sergius, left alone with Raina, looks anxiously at her, fearing that she is still offended. She smiles, and stretches out her arms to him.

SERGIUS [*hastening to her*] Am I forgiven?

RAINA [*placing her hands on his shoulders as she looks up at him with admiration and worship*] My hero! My king!

SERGIUS. My queen! [*He kisses her on the forehead*].

RAINA. How I have envied you, Sergius! You have been out in the world, on the field of battle, able to prove yourself there worthy of any woman in the world; whilst I have had to sit at home inactive— dreaming—useless—doing nothing that could give me the right to call myself worthy of any man.

SERGIUS. Dearest: all my deeds have been yours. You inspired me. I have gone through the war like a knight in a tournament with his lady looking down at him!

RAINA. And you have never been absent from my

thoughts for a moment. [*Very solemnly*] Sergius: I think we two have found the higher love. When I think of you, I feel that I could never do a base deed, or think an ignoble thought.

SERGIUS. My lady and my saint! [*He clasps her reverently*].

RAINA [*returning his embrace*] My lord and my—

SERGIUS. Sh—sh! Let me be the worshipper, dear. You little know how unworthy even the best man is of a girl's pure passion!

RAINA. I trust you. I love you. You will never disappoint me, Sergius. [*Louka is heard singing within the house. They quickly release each other*]. I cant pretend to talk indifferently before her: my heart is too full. [*Louka comes from the house with her tray. She goes to the table, and begins to clear it, with her back turned to them*]. I will get my hat; and then we can go out until lunch time. Wouldnt you like that?

SERGIUS. Be quick. If you are away five minutes, it will seem five hours. [*Raina runs to the top of the steps, and turns there to exchange looks with him and wave him a kiss with both hands. He looks after her with emotion for a moment; then turns slowly away, his face radiant with the loftiest exaltation. The movement shifts his field of vision, into the corner of which there now comes the tail of Louka's double apron. His attention is arrested at once. He takes a stealthy look at her, and begins to twirl his moustache mischievously, with his left hand akimbo on his hip. Finally, striking the ground with his heels in something of a cavalry swagger, he strolls over to the other side of the table, opposite her, and says*] Louka: do you know what the higher love is?

LOUKA [*astonished*] No, sir.

SERGIUS. Very fatiguing thing to keep up for any

length of time, Louka. One feels the need of some relief after it.

LOUKA [*innocently*] Perhaps you would like some coffee, sir? [*She stretches her hand across the table for the coffee pot*].

SERGIUS [*taking her hand*] Thank you, Louka.

LOUKA [*pretending to pull*] Oh, sir, you know I didnt mean that. I'm surprised at you!

SERGIUS [*coming clear of the table and drawing her with him*] I am surprised at myself, Louka. What would Sergius, the hero of Slivnitza, say if he saw me now? What would Sergius, the apostle of the higher love, say if he saw me now? What would the half dozen Sergiuses who keep popping in and out of this handsome figure of mine say if they caught us here? [*Letting go her hand and slipping his arm dexterously round her waist*] Do you consider my figure handsome, Louka?

LOUKA. Let me go, sir. I shall be disgraced. [*She struggles: he holds her inexorably*]. Oh, will you let go?

SERGIUS [*looking straight into her eyes*] No.

LOUKA. Then stand back where we cant be seen. Have you no common sense?

SERGIUS. Ah! thats reasonable. [*He takes her into the stableyard gateway, where they are hidden from the house*].

LOUKA [*plaintively*] I may have been seen from the windows: Miss Raina is sure to be spying about after you.

SERGIUS [*stung: letting her go*] Take care, Louka. I may be worthless enough to betray the higher love; but do not you insult it.

LOUKA [*demurely*] Not for the world, sir, I'm sure. May I go on with my work, please, now?

SERGIUS [*again putting his arm round her*] You are a

provoking little witch, Louka. If you were in love
with me, would you spy out of windows on me?

LOUKA. Well, you see, sir, since you say you are half
a dozen different gentlemen all at once, I should have
a great deal to look after.

SERGIUS [*charmed*] Witty as well as pretty. [*He tries
to kiss her*].

LOUKA [*avoiding him*] No: I dont want your kisses.
Gentlefolk are all alike: you making love to me
behind Miss Raina's back; and she doing the same
behind yours.

SERGIUS [*recoiling a step*] Louka!

LOUKA. It shews how little you really care.

SERGIUS [*dropping his familiarity, and speaking with
freezing politeness*] If our conversation is to continue,
Louka, you will please remember that a gentleman
does not discuss the conduct of the lady he is engaged
to with her maid.

LOUKA. It's so hard to know what a gentleman considers right. I thought from your trying to kiss me
that you had given up being so particular.

SERGIUS [*turning from her and striking his forehead as
he comes back into the garden from the gateway*] Devil!
devil!

LOUKA. Ha! ha! I expect one of the six of you is very
like me, sir; though I am only Miss Raina's maid.
[*She goes back to her work at the table, taking no further
notice of him*].

SERGIUS [*speaking to himself*] Which of the six is the
real man? thats the question that torments me. One
of them is a hero, another a buffoon, another a humbug, another perhaps a bit of a blackguard. [*He pauses,
and looks furtively at Louka as he adds, with deep
bitterness*] And one, at least, is a coward: jealous, like
all cowards. [*He goes to the table*]. Louka.

LOUKA. Yes?

SERGIUS. Who is my rival?

LOUKA. You shall never get that out of me, for love or money.

SERGIUS. Why?

LOUKA. Never mind why. Besides, you would tell that I told you; and I should lose my place.

SERGIUS [*holding out his right hand in affirmation*] No! on the honor of a—[*He checks himself; and his hand drops, nerveless, as he concludes sardonically*]— of a man capable of behaving as I have been behaving for the last five minutes. Who is he?

LOUKA. I dont know. I never saw him. I only heard his voice through the door of her room.

SERGIUS. Damnation! How dare you?

LOUKA [*retreating*] Oh, I mean no harm: youve no right to take up my words like that. The mistress knows all about it. And I tell you that if that gentleman ever comes here again, Miss Raina will marry him, whether he likes it or not. I know the difference between the sort of manner you and she put on before one another and the real manner.

Sergius shivers as if she had stabbed him. Then, setting his face like iron, he strides grimly to her, and grips her above the elbows with both hands.

SERGIUS. Now listen you to me.

LOUKA [*wincing*] Not so tight: youre hurting me.

SERGIUS. That doesnt matter. You have stained my honor by making me a party to your eavesdropping. And you have betrayed your mistress.

LOUKA [*writhing*] Please—

SERGIUS. That shews that you are an abominable little clod of common clay, with the soul of a servant. [*He lets her go as if she were an unclean thing, and turns away, dusting his hands of her, to the bench by the wall, where he sits down with averted head, meditating gloomily*].

LOUKA [*whimpering angrily with her hands up her sleeves, feeling her bruised arms*] You know how to hurt with your tongue as well as with your hands. But I dont care, now Ive found out that whatever clay I'm made of, youre made of the same. As for her, she's a liar; and her fine airs are a cheat; and I'm worth six of her. [*She shakes the pain off hardily; tosses her head; and sets to work to put the things on the tray*].

He looks doubtfully at her. She finishes packing the tray, and laps the cloth over the edges, so as to carry all out together. As she stoops to lift it, he rises.

SERGIUS. Louka! [*She stops and looks defiantly at him*]. A gentleman has no right to hurt a woman under any circumstances. [*With profound humility, uncovering his head*] I beg your pardon.

LOUKA. That sort of apology may satisfy a lady. Of what use is it to a servant?

SERGIUS [*rudely crossed in his chivalry, throws it off with a bitter laugh, and says slightingly*] Oh! you wish to be paid for the hurt? [*He puts on his shako, and takes some money from his pocket*].

LOUKA [*her eyes filling with tears in spite of herself*] No: I want my hurt made well.

SERGIUS [*sobered by her tone*] How?

She rolls up her left sleeve; clasps her arm with the thumb and fingers of her right hand; and looks down at the bruise. Then she raises her head and looks straight at him. Finally, with a superb gesture, she presents her arm to be kissed. Amazed, he looks at her; at the arm; at her again; hesitates; and then, with shuddering intensity, exclaims Never! *and gets away as far as possible from her.*

Her arm drops. Without a word, and with unaffected dignity, she takes her tray, and is approaching the house

[429]

when Raina returns, wearing a hat and jacket in the height of the Vienna fashion of the previous year, 1885. Louka makes way proudly for her, and then goes into the house.

RAINA. I'm ready. Whats the matter? [*Gaily*] Have you been flirting with Louka?

SERGIUS [*hastily*] No, no. How can you think such a thing?

RAINA [*ashamed of herself*] Forgive me, dear: it was only a jest. I am so happy today.

He goes quickly to her, and kisses her hand remorsefully. Catherine comes out and calls to them from the top of the steps.

CATHERINE [*coming down to them*] I am sorry to disturb you, children; but Paul is distracted over those three regiments. He doesnt know how to send them to Philippopolis; and he objects to every suggestion of mine. You must go and help him, Sergius. He is in the library.

RAINA [*disappointed*] But we are just going out for a walk.

SERGIUS. I shall not be long. Wait for me just five minutes. [*He runs up the steps to the door*].

RAINA [*following him to the foot of the steps and looking up at him with timid coquetry*] I shall go round and wait in full view of the library windows. Be sure you draw father's attention to me. If you are a moment longer than five minutes, I shall go in and fetch you, regiments or no regiments.

SERGIUS [*laughing*] Very well. [*He goes in*].

Raina watches him until he is out of her sight. Then, with a perceptible relaxation of manner, she begins to pace up and down the garden in a brown study.

CATHERINE. Imagine their meeting that Swiss and hearing the whole story! The very first thing your

father asked for was the old coat we sent him off in.
A nice mess you have got us into!

RAINA [*gazing thoughtfully at the gravel as she walks*]
The little beast!

CATHERINE. Little beast! What little beast?

RAINA. To go and tell! Oh, if I had him here, I'd
cram him with chocolate creams til he couldnt ever
speak again!

CATHERINE. Dont talk such stuff. Tell me the truth,
Raina. How long was he in your room before you
came to me?

RAINA [*whisking round and recommencing her march
in the opposite direction*] Oh, I forget.

CATHERINE. You cannot forget! Did he really climb
up after the soldiers were gone; or was he there when
that officer searched the room?

RAINA. No. Yes: I think he must have been there
then.

CATHERINE. You think! Oh, Raina! Raina! Will
anything ever make you straightforward? If Sergius
finds out, it will be all over between you.

RAINA [*with cool impertinence*] Oh, I know Sergius is
your pet. I sometimes wish you could marry him
instead of me. You would just suit him. You would
pet him, and spoil him, and mother him to perfection.

CATHERINE [*opening her eyes very widely indeed*]
Well, upon my word!

RAINA [*capriciously: half to herself*] I always feel a
longing to do or say something dreadful to him—
to shock his propriety—to scandalize the five senses
out of him. [*To Catherine, perversely*] I dont care
whether he finds out about the chocolate cream soldier
or not. I half hope he may. [*She again turns and strolls
flippantly away up the path to the corner of the house*].

CATHERINE. And what should I be able to say to your father, pray?

RAINA [*over her shoulder, from the top of the two steps*] Oh, poor father! As if he could help himself! [*She turns the corner and passes out of sight*].

CATHERINE [*looking after her, her fingers itching*] Oh, if you were only ten years younger! [*Louka comes from the house with a salver, which she carries hanging down by her side*]. Well?

LOUKA. Theres a gentleman just called, madam. A Serbian officer.

CATHERINE [*flaming*] A Serb! And how dare he— [*checking herself bitterly*] Oh, I forgot. We are at peace now. I suppose we shall have them calling every day to pay their compliments. Well: if he is an officer why dont you tell your master? He is in the library with Major Saranoff. Why do you come to me?

LOUKA. But he asks for you, madam. And I dont think he knows who you are: he said the lady of the house. He gave me this little ticket for you. [*She takes a card out of her bosom; puts it on the salver; and offers it to Catherine*].

CATHERINE [*reading*] "Captain Bluntschli"? Thats a German name.

LOUKA. Swiss, madam, I think.

CATHERINE [*with a bound that makes Louka jump back*] Swiss! What is he like?

LOUKA [*timidly*] He has a big carpet bag, madam.

CATHERINE. Oh Heavens! he's come to return the coat. Send him away: say we're not at home: ask him to leave his address and I'll write to him. Oh stop: that will never do. Wait! [*She throws herself into a chair to think it out. Louka waits*]. The master and Major Saranoff are busy in the library, arnt they?

LOUKA. Yes, madam.

CATHERINE [*decisively*] Bring the gentleman out here at once. [*Peremptorily*] And be very polite to him. Dont delay. Here [*impatiently snatching the salver from her*]: leave that here; and go straight back to him.

LOUKA. Yes, madam [*going*].

CATHERINE. Louka!

LOUKA [*stopping*] Yes, madam.

CATHERINE. Is the library door shut?

LOUKA. I think so, madam.

CATHERINE. If not, shut it as you pass through.

LOUKA. Yes, madam [*going*].

CATHERINE. Stop! [*Louka stops*]. He will have to go that way [*indicating the gate of the stableyard*]. Tell Nicola to bring his bag here after him. Dont forget.

LOUKA [*surprised*] His bag?

CATHERINE. Yes: here: as soon as possible. [*Vehemently*] Be quick! [*Louka runs into the house. Catherine snatches her apron off and throws it behind a bush. She then takes up the salver and uses it as a mirror, with the result that the handkerchief tied round her head follows the apron. A touch to her hair and a shake to her dressing gown make her presentable*]. Oh, how? how? how can a man be such a fool! Such a moment to select! [*Louka appears at the door of the house, announcing* Captain Bluntschli. *She stands aside at the top of the steps to let him pass before she goes in again. He is the man of the midnight adventure in Raina's room, clean, well brushed, smartly uniformed, and out of trouble, but still unmistakably the same man. The moment Louka's back is turned, Catherine swoops on him with impetuous, urgent, coaxing appeal*]. Captain Bluntschli: I am very glad to see you; but you must leave this house at once. [*He raises his eyebrows*]. My husband has just returned with my future

[433]

son-in-law; and they know nothing. If they did, the consequences would be terrible. You are a foreigner: you do not feel our national animosities as we do. We still hate the Serbs: the effect of the peace on my husband has been to make him feel like a lion baulked of his prey. If he discovers our secret, he will never forgive me; and my daughter's life will hardly be safe. Will you, like the chivalrous gentleman and soldier you are, leave at once before he finds you here?

BLUNTSCHLI [*disappointed, but philosophical*] At once, gracious lady. I only came to thank you and return the coat you lent me. If you will allow me to take it out of my bag and leave it with your servant as I pass out, I need detain you no further. [*He turns to go into the house*].

CATHERINE [*catching him by the sleeve*] Oh, you must not think of going back that way. [*Coaxing him across to the stable gates*] This is the shortest way out. Many thanks. So glad to have been of service to you. Goodbye.

BLUNTSCHLI. But my bag?

CATHERINE. It shall be sent on. You will leave me your address.

BLUNTSCHLI. True. Allow me. [*He takes out his card-case, and stops to write his address, keeping Catherine in an agony of impatience. As he hands her the card, Petkoff, hatless, rushes from the house in a fluster of hospitality, followed by Sergius*].

PETKOFF [*as he hurries down the steps*] My dear Captain Bluntschli—

CATHERINE. Oh Heavens! [*She sinks on the seat against the wall*].

PETKOFF [*too preoccupied to notice her as he shakes Bluntschli's hand heartily*] Those stupid people of mine thought I was out here, instead of in the—haw!

—library [*he cannot mention the library without betraying how proud he is of it*]. I saw you through the window. I was wondering why you didnt come in. Saranoff is with me: you remember him, dont you?

SERGIUS [*saluting humorously, and then offering his hand with great charm of manner*] Welcome, our friend the enemy!

PETKOFF. No longer the enemy, happily. [*Rather anxiously*] I hope youve called as a friend, and not about horses or prisoners.

CATHERINE. Oh, quite as a friend, Paul. I was just asking Captain Bluntschli to stay to lunch; but he declares he must go at once.

SERGIUS [*sardonically*] Impossible, Bluntschli. We want you here badly. We have to send on three cavalry regiments to Philippopolis; and we dont in the least know how to do it.

BLUNTSCHLI [*suddenly attentive and businesslike*] Philippopolis? The forage is the trouble, I suppose.

PETKOFF [*eagerly*] Yes: thats it. [*To Sergius*] He sees the whole thing at once.

BLUNTSCHLI. I think I can shew you how to manage that.

SERGIUS. Invaluable man! Come along! [*Towering over Bluntschli, he puts his hand on his shoulder and takes him to the steps, Petkoff following*].

Raina comes from the house as Bluntschli puts his foot on the first step.

RAINA. Oh! The chocolate cream soldier!

Bluntschli stands rigid. Sergius, amazed, looks at Raina, then at Petkoff, who looks back at him and then at his wife.

CATHERINE [*with commanding presence of mind*] My dear Raina, dont you see that we have a guest here? Captain Bluntschli: one of our new Serbian friends.

Raina bows: Bluntschli bows.

RAINA. How silly of me! [*She comes down into the centre of the group, between Bluntschli and Petkoff*]. I made a beautiful ornament this morning for the ice pudding; and that stupid Nicola has just put down a pile of plates on it and spoilt it. [*To Bluntschli, winningly*] I hope you didnt think that you were the chocolate cream soldier, Captain Bluntschli.

BLUNTSCHLI [*laughing*] I assure you I did. [*Stealing a whimsical glance at her*] Your explanation was a relief.

PETKOFF [*suspiciously, to Raina*] And since when, pray, have you taken to cooking?

CATHERINE. Oh, whilst you were away. It is her latest fancy.

PETKOFF [*testily*] And has Nicola taken to drinking? He used to be careful enough. First he shews Captain Bluntschli out here when he knew quite well I was in the library; and then he goes downstairs and breaks Raina's chocolate soldier. He must—[*Nicola appears at the top of the steps with the bag. He descends; places it respectfully before Bluntschli; and waits for further orders. General amazement. Nicola, unconscious of the effect he is producing, looks perfectly satisfied with himself. When Petkoff recovers his power of speech, he breaks out at him with*] Are you mad, Nicola?

NICOLA [*taken aback*] Sir?

PETKOFF. What have you brought that for?

NICOLA. My lady's orders, major. Louka told me that—

CATHERINE [*interrupting him*] My orders! Why should I order you to bring Captain Bluntschli's luggage out here? What are you thinking of, Nicola?

NICOLA [*after a moment's bewilderment, picking up the bag as he addresses Bluntschli with the very perfection of servile discretion*] I beg your pardon, captain,

[436]

I am sure. [*To Catherine*] My fault, madam: I hope youll overlook it. [*He bows, and is going to the steps with the bag, when Petkoff addresses him angrily*].

PETKOFF. Youd better go and slam that bag, too, down on Miss Raina's ice pudding! [*This is too much for Nicola. The bag drops from his hand almost on his master's toes, eliciting a roar of*] Begone, you butter-fingered donkey.

NICOLA [*snatching up the bag, and escaping into the house*] Yes, major.

CATHERINE. Oh, never mind, Paul: dont be angry.

PETKOFF [*blustering*] Scoundrel! He's got out of hand while I was away. I'll teach him. Infernal blackguard! The sack next Saturday! I'll clear out the whole establishment— [*He is stifled by the caresses of his wife and daughter, who hang round his neck, petting him*].

CATHERINE
RAINA }[*together*]{ Now, now, now, it mustnt be angry. He meant no harm. Be good to please me, dear. Sh-sh-sh-sh!

Wow, wow, wow: not on your first day at home. I'll make another ice pudding. Tch-ch-ch!

PETKOFF [*yielding*] Oh well, never mind. Come, Bluntschli: lets have no more nonsense about going away. You know very well youre not going back to Switzerland yet. Until you do go back youll stay with us.

RAINA. Oh, do, Captain Bluntschli.

PETKOFF [*to Catherine*] Now, Catherine: it's of you he's afraid. Press him; and he'll stay.

CATHERINE. Of course I shall be only too delighted if [*appealingly*] Captain Bluntschli really wishes to stay. He knows my wishes.

BLUNTSCHLI [*in his driest military manner*] I am at madam's orders.

SERGIUS [*cordially*] That settles it!

PETKOFF [*heartily*] Of course!

RAINA. You see you must stay.

BLUNTSCHLI [*smiling*] Well, if I must, I must.

Gesture of despair from Catherine.

[ACT III]

In the library after lunch. It is not much of a library. Its literary equipment consists of a single fixed shelf stocked with old paper covered novels, broken backed, coffee stained, torn and thumbed; and a couple of little hanging shelves with a few gift books on them: the rest of the wall space being occupied by trophies of war and the chase. But it is a most comfortable sitting room. A row of three large windows shews a mountain panorama, just now seen in one of its friendliest aspects in the mellowing afternoon light. In the corner next the right hand window a square earthenware stove, a perfect tower of glistening pottery, rises nearly to the ceiling and guarantees plenty of warmth. The ottoman is like that in Raina's room, and similarly placed; and the window seats are luxurious with decorated cushions. There is one object, however, hopelessly out of keeping with its surroundings. This is a small kitchen table, much the worse for wear, fitted as a writing table with an old canister full of pens, an eggcup filled with ink, and a deplorable scrap of heavily used pink blotting paper.

At the side of this table, which stands to the left of anyone facing the window, Bluntschli is hard at work with a couple of maps before him, writing orders. At the head of it sits Sergius, who is supposed to be also at work, but is actually gnawing the feather of a pen, and contemplating Bluntschli's quick, sure, businesslike progress with a mixture of envious irritation at his own incapacity and awestruck wonder at an ability which seems to him almost miraculous, though its prosaic character forbids him to esteem it. The Major is comfortably established on the ottoman, with a newspaper in his hand and the tube of his hookah within easy reach. Catherine sits at the stove, with her back to them, embroidering. Raina, reclining on the divan, is gazing in a daydream out at the Balkan landscape, with a neglected novel in her lap.

The door is on the same side as the stove, farther from the window. The button of the electric bell is at the opposite side, behind Bluntschli.

PETKOFF [*looking up from his paper to watch how they are getting on at the table*] Are you sure I cant help you in any way, Bluntschli?

BLUNTSCHLI [*without interrupting his writing or looking up*] Quite sure, thank you. Saranoff and I will manage it.

SERGIUS [*grimly*] Yes: we'll manage it. He finds out what to do; draws up the orders; and I sign em. Division of labor! [*Bluntschli passes him a paper*]. Another one? Thank you. [*He plants the paper squarely before him; sets his chair carefully parallel to it; and signs with his cheek on his elbow and his protruded tongue following the movements of his pen*]. This hand is more accustomed to the sword than to the pen.

PETKOFF. It's very good of you, Bluntschli: it is indeed, to let yourself be put upon in this way. Now are you quite sure I can do nothing?

CATHERINE [*in a low warning tone*] You can stop interrupting, Paul.

PETKOFF [*starting and looking round at her*] Eh? Oh! Quite right, my love: quite right. [*He takes his newspaper up again, but presently lets it drop*]. Ah, you havnt been campaigning, Catherine: you dont know how pleasant it is for us to sit here, after a good lunch, with nothing to do but enjoy ourselves. Theres only one thing I want to make me thoroughly comfortable.

CATHERINE. What is that?

PETKOFF. My old coat. I'm not at home in this one: I feel as if I were on parade.

CATHERINE. My dear Paul, how absurd you are about that old coat! It must be hanging in the blue closet where you left it.

PETKOFF. My dear Catherine, I tell you Ive looked there. Am I to believe my own eyes or not? [*Catherine rises and crosses the room to press the button of the electric bell*]. What are you shewing off that bell for? [*She looks at him majestically, and silently resumes her chair and her needlework*]. My dear: if you think the obstinacy of your sex can make a coat out of two old dressing gowns of Raina's, your waterproof, and my mackintosh, youre mistaken. Thats exactly what the blue closet contains at present.

Nicola presents himself.

CATHERINE. Nicola: go to the blue closet and bring your master's old coat here: the braided one he wears in the house.

NICOLA. Yes, madam. [*He goes out*].

PETKOFF. Catherine.

CATHERINE. Yes, Paul.

PETKOFF. I bet you any piece of jewellery you like to order from Sofia against a week's housekeeping money that the coat isnt there.

CATHERINE. Done, Paul!

PETKOFF [*excited by the prospect of a gamble*] Come: heres an opportunity for some sport. Wholl bet on it? Bluntschli: I'll give you six to one.

BLUNTSCHLI [*imperturbably*] It would be robbing

you, major. Madam is sure to be right. [*Without looking up, he passes another batch of papers to Sergius*].

SERGIUS [*also excited*] Bravo, Switzerland! Major: I bet my best charger against an Arab mare for Raina that Nicola finds the coat in the blue closet.

PETKOFF [*eagerly*] Your best char—

CATHERINE [*hastily interrupting him*] Dont be foolish, Paul. An Arabian mare will cost you 50,000 levas.

RAINA [*suddenly coming out of her picturesque revery*] Really, mother, if you are going to take the jewellery, I dont see why you should grudge me my Arab.

Nicola comes back with the coat, and brings it to Petkoff, who can hardly believe his eyes.

CATHERINE. Where was it, Nicola?

NICOLA. Hanging in the blue closet, madam.

PETKOFF. Well, I am d—

CATHERINE [*stopping him*] Paul!

PETKOFF. I could have sworn it wasnt there. Age is beginning to tell on me. I'm getting hallucinations. [*To Nicola*] Here: help me to change. Excuse me, Bluntschli. [*He begins changing coats, Nicola acting as valet*]. Remember: I didnt take that bet of yours, Sergius. Youd better give Raina that Arab steed yourself, since youve roused her expectations. Eh, Raina? [*He looks round at her; but she is again rapt in the landscape. With a little gush of parental affection and pride, he points her out to them, and says*] She's dreaming, as usual.

SERGIUS. Assuredly she shall not be the loser.

PETKOFF. So much the better for her. *I* shant come off so cheaply, I expect. [*The change is now complete. Nicola goes out with the discarded coat*]. Ah, now I feel at home at last. [*He sits down and takes his newspaper with a grunt of relief*].

BLUNTSCHLI [*to Sergius, handing a paper*] Thats the last order.

PETKOFF [*jumping up*] What! Finished?

BLUNTSCHLI. Finished.

PETKOFF [*with childlike envy*] Havnt you anything for me to sign?

BLUNTSCHLI. Not necessary. His signature will do.

PETKOFF [*inflating his chest and thumping it*] Ah well, I think weve done a thundering good day's work. Can I do anything more?

BLUNTSCHLI. You had better both see the fellows that are to take these. [*Sergius rises*] Pack them off at once; and shew them that Ive marked on the orders the time they should hand them in by. Tell them that if they stop to drink or tell stories—if theyre five minutes late, theyll have the skin taken off their backs.

SERGIUS [*stiffening indignantly*] I'll say so. [*He strides to the door*]. And if one of them is man enough to spit in my face for insulting him, I'll buy his discharge and give him a pension. [*He goes out*].

BLUNTSCHLI [*confidentially*] Just see that he talks to them properly, major, will you?

PETKOFF [*officiously*] Quite right, Bluntschli, quite right. I'll see to it. [*He goes to the door importantly, but hesitates on the threshold*]. By the bye, Catherine, you may as well come too. Theyll be far more frightened of you than of me.

CATHERINE [*putting down her embroidery*] I daresay I had better. You would only splutter at them. [*She goes out, Petkoff holding the door for her and following her*].

BLUNTSCHLI. What an army! They make cannons out of cherry trees; and the officers send for their wives to keep discipline! [*He begins to fold and docket the papers*].

Raina, who has risen from the divan, marches slowly down the room with her hands clasped behind her, and looks mischievously at him.

RAINA. You look ever so much nicer than when we last met. [*He looks up, surprised*]. What have you done to yourself?

BLUNTSCHLI. Washed; brushed; good night's sleep and breakfast. Thats all.

RAINA. Did you get back safely that morning?

BLUNTSCHLI. Quite, thanks.

RAINA. Were they angry with you for running away from Sergius's charge?

BLUNTSCHLI [*grinning*] No: they were glad; because theyd all just run away themselves.

RAINA [*going to the table, and leaning over it towards him*] It must have made a lovely story for them: all that about me and my room.

BLUNTSCHLI. Capital story. But I only told it to one of them: a particular friend.

RAINA. On whose discretion you could absolutely rely?

BLUNTSCHLI. Absolutely.

RAINA. Hm! He told it all to my father and Sergius the day you exchanged the prisoners. [*She turns away and strolls carelessly across to the other side of the room*].

BLUNTSCHLI [*deeply concerned, and half incredulous*] No! You dont mean that, do you?

RAINA [*turning, with sudden earnestness*] I do indeed. But they dont know that it was in this house you took refuge. If Sergius knew, he would challenge you and kill you in a duel.

BLUNTSCHLI. Bless me! then dont tell him.

RAINA. Please be serious, Captain Bluntschli. Can you not realize what it is to me to deceive him? I want to be quite perfect with Sergius: no meanness, no smallness, no deceit. My relation to him is the one really beautiful and noble part of my life. I hope you can understand that.

BLUNTSCHLI [*sceptically*] You mean that you wouldnt like him to find out that the story about the ice pudding was a—a—a—You know.

RAINA [*wincing*] Ah, dont talk of it in that flippant way. I lied: I know it. But I did it to save your life. He would have killed you. That was the second time I ever uttered a falsehood. [*Bluntschli rises quickly and looks doubtfully and somewhat severely at her*]. Do you remember the first time?

BLUNTSCHLI. I! No. Was I present?

RAINA. Yes; and I told the officer who was searching for you that you were not present.

BLUNTSCHLI. True. I should have remembered it.

RAINA [*greatly encouraged*] Ah, it is natural that you should forget it first. It cost you nothing: it cost me a lie! A lie!

She sits down on the ottoman, looking straight before her with her hands clasped round her knee. Bluntschli, quite touched, goes to the ottoman with a particularly reassuring and considerate air, and sits down beside her.

BLUNTSCHLI. My dear young lady, dont let this worry you. Remember: I'm a soldier. Now what are the two things that happen to a soldier so often that he comes to think nothing of them? One is hearing people tell lies [*Raina recoils*]: the other is getting his life saved in all sorts of ways by all sorts of people.

RAINA [*rising in indignant protest*] And so he becomes a creature incapable of faith and of gratitude.

BLUNTSCHLI [*making a wry face*] Do you like gratitude? I dont. If pity is akin to love, gratitude is akin to the other thing.

RAINA. Gratitude! [*Turning on him*] If you are incapable of gratitude you are incapable of any noble sentiment. Even animals are grateful. Oh, I see now exactly what you think of me! You were not surprised to hear me lie. To you it was something I probably did every day! every hour!! That is how men think of women. [*She paces the room tragically*].

BLUNTSCHLI [*dubiously*] Theres reason in everything. You said youd told only two lies in your whole life. Dear young lady: isnt that rather a short allowance? I'm quite a straightforward man myself; but it wouldnt last me a whole morning.

RAINA [*staring haughtily at him*] Do you know, sir, that you are insulting me?

BLUNTSCHLI. I cant help it. When you strike that noble attitude and speak in that thrilling voice, I admire you; but I find it impossible to believe a single word you say.

RAINA [*superbly*] Captain Bluntschli!

BLUNTSCHLI [*unmoved*] Yes?

RAINA [*standing over him, as if she could not believe her senses*] Do you mean what you said just now? Do you know what you said just now?

BLUNTSCHLI. I do.

RAINA [*gasping*] I! I!!! [*She points to herself incredulously, meaning "I, Raina Petkoff tell lies!" He meets her gaze unflinchingly. She suddenly sits down beside him, and adds, with a complete change of manner from the heroic to a babyish familiarity*] How did you find me out?

BLUNTSCHLI [*promptly*] Instinct, dear young lady. Instinct, and experience of the world.

RAINA [*wonderingly*] Do you know, you are the first man I ever met who did not take me seriously?

BLUNTSCHLI. You mean, dont you, that I am the first man that has ever taken you quite seriously?

RAINA. Yes: I suppose I do mean that. [*Cosily, quite at her ease with him*] How strange it is to be talked to in such a way! You know, Ive always gone on like that.

BLUNTSCHLI. You mean the— ?

RAINA. I mean the noble attitude and the thrilling voice. [*They laugh together*]. I did it when I was a tiny child to my nurse. She believed in it. I do it before my parents. They believe in it. I do it before Sergius. He believes in it.

BLUNTSCHLI. Yes: he's a little in that line himself, isnt he?

RAINA [*startled*] Oh! Do you think so?

BLUNTSCHLI. You know him better than I do.

RAINA. I wonder—I wonder is he? If I thought that—! [*Discouraged*] Ah, well: what does it matter? I suppose now youve found me out, you despise me.

BLUNTSCHLI [*warmly, rising*] No, my dear young lady, no, no, no a thousand times. It's part of your youth: part of your charm. I'm like all the rest of them: the nurse, your parents, Sergius: I'm your infatuated admirer.

RAINA [*pleased*] Really?

BLUNTSCHLI [*slapping his breast smartly with his hand, German fashion*] Hand aufs Herz! Really and truly.

RAINA [*very happy*] But what did you think of me for giving you my portrait?

BLUNTSCHLI [*astonished*] Your portrait! You never gave me your portrait.

RAINA [*quickly*] Do you mean to say you never got it?

BLUNTSCHLI. No. [*He sits down beside her, with renewed interest, and says, with some complacency*] When did you send it to me?

RAINA [*indignantly*] I did not send it to you. [*She turns her head away, and adds, reluctantly*] It was in the pocket of that coat.

[447]

BLUNTSCHLI [*pursing his lips and rounding his eyes*] Oh-o-oh! I never found it. It must be there still.

RAINA [*springing up*] There still! for my father to find the first time he puts his hand in his pocket! Oh, how could you be so stupid?

BLUNTSCHLI [*rising also*] It doesnt matter: I suppose it's only a photograph: how can he tell who it was intended for? Tell him he put it there himself.

RAINA [*bitterly*] Yes: that is so clever! isnt it? [*Distractedly*] Oh! what shall I do?

BLUNTSCHLI. Ah, I see. You wrote something on it. That was rash.

RAINA [*vexed almost to tears*] Oh, to have done such a thing for you, who care no more—except to laugh at me—oh! Are you sure nobody has touched it?

BLUNTSCHLI. Well. I cant be quite sure. You see, I couldnt carry it about with me all the time: one cant take much luggage on active service.

RAINA. What did you do with it?

BLUNTSCHLI. When I got through to Pirot I had to put it in safe keeping somehow. I thought of the railway cloak room; but thats the surest place to get looted in modern warfare. So I pawned it.

RAINA. Pawned it!!!

BLUNTSCHLI. I know it doesnt sound nice; but it was much the safest plan. I redeemed it the day before yesterday. Heaven only knows whether the pawnbroker cleared out the pockets or not.

RAINA [*furious: throwing the words right into his face*] You have a low shopkeeping mind. You think of things that would never come into a gentleman's head.

BLUNTSCHLI [*phlegmatically*] Thats the Swiss national character, dear lady. [*He returns to the table*].

RAINA. Oh, I wish I had never met you. [*She flounces away, and sits at the window fuming.*]

Louka comes in with a heap of letters and telegrams on her salver, and crosses, with her bold free gait, to the table. Her left sleeve is looped up to the shoulder with a brooch, shewing her naked arm, with a broad gilt bracelet covering the bruise.

LOUKA [*to Bluntschli*] For you. [*She empties the salver with a fling on to the table*]. The messenger is waiting. [*She is determined not to be civil to an enemy, even if she must bring him his letters*].

BLUNTSCHLI [*to Raina*] Will you excuse me: the last postal delivery that reached me was three weeks ago. These are the subsequent accumulations. Four telegrams: a week old. [*He opens one*]. Oho! Bad news!

RAINA [*rising and advancing a little remorsefully*] Bad news?

BLUNTSCHLI. My father's dead. [*He looks at the telegram with his lips pursed, musing on the unexpected changes in his arrangements. Louka crosses herself hastily*].

RAINA. Oh, how very sad!

BLUNTSCHLI. Yes: I shall have to start for home in an hour. He has left a lot of big hotels behind him to be looked after. [*He takes up a fat letter in a long blue envelope*]. Here's a whacking letter from the family solicitor. [*He pulls out the enclosures and glances over them*]. Great Heavens! Seventy! Two hundred! [*In a crescendo of dismay*] Four hundred! Four thousand!! Nine thousand six hundred!!! What on earth am I to do with them all?

RAINA [*timidly*] Nine thousand hotels?

BLUNTSCHLI. Hotels! nonsense. If you only knew! Oh, it's too ridiculous! Excuse me: I must give my fellow orders about starting. [*He leaves the room hastily, with the documents in his hand*].

LOUKA [*knowing instinctively that she cannot annoy Raina by disparaging Bluntschli*] He has not much heart that Swiss. He has not a word of grief for his poor father.

RAINA [*bitterly*] Grief! A man who has been doing nothing but killing people for years! What does he care? What does any soldier care? [*She goes to the door, restraining her tears with difficulty*].

LOUKA. Major Saranoff has been fighting too; and he has plenty of heart left. [*Raina, at the door, draws herself up haughtily and goes out*]. Aha! I thought you wouldnt get much feeling out of your soldier. [*She is following Raina when Nicola enters with an armful of logs for the stove*].

NICOLA [*grinning amorously at her*] Ive been trying all the afternoon to get a minute alone with you, my girl. [*His countenance changes as he notices her arm*]. Why, what fashion is that of wearing your sleeve, child?

LOUKA [*proudly*] My own fashion.

NICOLA. Indeed! If the mistress catches you, she'll talk to you. [*He puts the logs down, and seats himself comfortably on the ottoman*].

LOUKA. Is that any reason why you should take it on yourself to talk to me?

NICOLA. Come! dont be so contrary with me. Ive some good news for you. [*She sits down beside him. He takes out some paper money. Louka, with an eager gleam in her eyes, tries to snatch it; but he shifts it quickly to his left hand, out of her reach*]. See! a twenty leva bill! Sergius gave me that, out of pure swagger. A fool and his money are soon parted. Theres ten levas more. The Swiss gave me that for backing up the mistress's and Raina's lies about him. He's no fool, he isnt. You should have heard old Catherine downstairs as polite as you please to me, telling me not to mind the Major being a little impatient; for they knew what a good servant I was—after making a fool and liar of me before them all! The twenty will go to our savings; and you shall have the ten to spend if youll only talk to me so as to remind me I'm a human being. I get tired of being a servant occasionally.

LOUKA. Yes: sell your manhood for 30 levas, and buy me for 10! [*Rising scornfully*] Keep your money. You were born to be a servant. I was not. When you set up your shop you will only be everybody's servant instead of somebody's servant. [*She goes moodily to the table and seats herself regally in Sergius's chair*].

NICOLA [*picking up his logs, and going to the stove*] Ah, wait til you see. We shall have our evenings to ourselves; and I shall be master in my own house, I promise you. [*He throws the logs down and kneels at the stove*].

LOUKA. You shall never be master in mine.

NICOLA [*turning, still on his knees, and squatting down rather forlornly on his calves, daunted by her implacable disdain*] You have a great ambition in you, Louka. Remember: if any luck comes to you, it was I that made a woman of you.

LOUKA. You!

NICOLA [*scrambling up and going at her*] Yes, me. Who was it made you give up wearing a couple of pounds of false black hair on your head and reddening your lips and cheeks like any other Bulgarian girl! I did. Who taught you to trim your nails, and keep your hands clean, and be dainty about yourself, like a fine Russian lady? Me: do you hear that? me! [*She tosses her head defiantly; and he turns away, adding, more coolly*] Ive often thought that if Raina were out of the way, and you just a little less of a fool and Sergius just a little more of one, you might come to be one of my grandest customers, instead of only being my wife and costing me money.

LOUKA. I believe you would rather be my servant than my husband. You would make more out of me. Oh, I know that soul of yours.

NICOLA [*going closer to her for greater emphasis*] Never you mind my soul; but just listen to my advice. If you want to be a lady, your present behavior to me wont do at all, unless when we're alone. It's too sharp and impudent; and impudence is a sort of familiarity: it shews affection for me. And dont you try being high and mighty with me, either. Youre like all country girls: you think it's genteel to treat a servant the way I treat a stableboy. Thats only your ignorance; and dont you forget it. And dont be so ready to defy everybody. Act as if you expected to have your own way, not as if you expected to be ordered about. The way to get on as a lady is the same as the way to get on as a servant: youve got to know your place: thats the secret of it. And you may depend on me to know my place if you get promoted. Think over it, my girl. I'll stand by you: one servant should always stand by another.

LOUKA [*rising impatiently*] Oh, I must behave in my own way. You take all the courage out of me with your cold-blooded wisdom. Go and put those logs on the fire: thats the sort of thing you understand.

Before Nicola can retort, Sergius comes in. He checks himself a moment on seeing Louka; then goes to the stove.

SERGIUS [*to Nicola*] I am not in the way of your work, I hope.

NICOLA [*in a smooth, elderly manner*] Oh no, sir:

[452]

thank you kindly. I was only speaking to this foolish girl about her habit of running up here to the library whenever she gets a chance, to look at the books. Thats the worst of her education, sir: it gives her habits above her station. [*To Louka*] Make that table tidy, Louka, for the Major. [*He goes out sedately*].

Louka, without looking at Sergius, pretends to arrange the papers on the table. He crosses slowly to her, and studies the arrangement of her sleeve reflectively.

SERGIUS. Let me see: is there a mark there? [*He turns up the bracelet and sees the bruise made by his grasp. She stands motionless, not looking at him: fascinated, but on her guard*]. Ffff! Does it hurt?

LOUKA. Yes.

SERGIUS. Shall I cure it?

LOUKA [*instantly withdrawing herself proudly, but still not looking at him*] No. You cannot cure it now.

SERGIUS [*masterfully*] Quite sure? [*He makes a movement as if to take her in his arms*].

LOUKA. Dont trifle with me, please. An officer should not trifle with a servant.

SERGIUS [*indicating the bruise with a merciless stroke of his forefinger*] That was no trifle, Louka.

LOUKA [*flinching; then looking at him for the first time*] Are you sorry?

SERGIUS [*with measured emphasis, folding his arms*] I am never sorry.

LOUKA [*wistfully*] I wish I could believe a man could be as unlike a woman as that. I wonder are you really a brave man?

SERGIUS [*unaffectedly, relaxing his attitude*] Yes: I am a brave man. My heart jumped like a woman's at the first shot; but in the charge I found that I was brave. Yes: that at least is real about me.

LOUKA. Did you find in the charge that the men whose

fathers are poor like mine were any less brave than the men who are rich like you.

SERGIUS [*with bitter levity*] Not a bit. They all slashed and cursed and yelled like heroes. Psha! the courage to rage and kill is cheap. I have an English bull terrier who has as much of that sort of courage as the whole Bulgarian nation, and the whole Russian nation at its back. But he lets my groom thrash him, all the same. Thats your soldier all over! No, Louka: your poor men can cut throats; but they are afraid of their officers; they put up with insults and blows; they stand by and see one another punished like children: aye, and help to do it when they are ordered. And the officers!!! Well [*with a short harsh laugh*] I am an officer. Oh, [*fervently*] give me the man who will defy to the death any power on earth or in heaven that sets itself up against his own will and conscience: he alone is the brave man.

LOUKA. How easy it is to talk! Men never seem to me to grow up: they all have schoolboy's ideas. You dont know what true courage is.

SERGIUS [*ironically*] Indeed! I am willing to be instructed. [*He sits on the ottoman, sprawling magnificently*].

LOUKA. Look at me! how much am I allowed to have my own will? I have to get your room ready for you: to sweep and dust, to fetch and carry. How could that degrade me if it did not degrade you to have it done for you? But [*with subdued passion*] if I were Empress of Russia, above everyone in the world, then!! Ah then, though according to you I could shew no courage at all, you should see, you should see.

SERGIUS. What would you do, most noble Empress?

LOUKA. I would marry the man I loved, which no

other queen in Europe has the courage to do. If I
loved you, though you would be as far beneath me as
I am beneath you, I would dare to be the equal of my
inferior. Would you dare as much if you loved me?
No: if you felt the beginnings of love for me you would
not let it grow. You would not dare: you would marry
a rich man's daughter because you would be afraid of
what other people would say of you.

SERGIUS [*bounding up*] You lie: it is not so, by all the
stars! If I loved you, and I were the Czar himself, I
would set you on the throne by my side. You know
that I love another woman, a woman as high above you
as heaven is above earth. And you are jealous of her.

LOUKA. I have no reason to be. She will never marry
you now. The man I told you of has come back. She
will marry the Swiss.

SERGIUS [*recoiling*] The Swiss!

LOUKA. A man worth ten of you. Then you can come
to me; and I will refuse you. You are not good
enough for me. [*She turns to the door*].

SERGIUS [*springing after her and catching her fiercely
in his arms*] I will kill the Swiss; and afterwards I
will do as I please with you.

LOUKA [*in his arms, passive and steadfast*] The Swiss
will kill you, perhaps. He has beaten you in love. He
may beat you in war.

SERGIUS [*tormentedly*] Do you think I believe that
she—she! whose worst thoughts are higher than your
best ones, is capable of trifling with another man
behind my back?

LOUKA. Do you think she would believe the Swiss if
he told her now that I am in your arms?

SERGIUS [*releasing her in despair*] Damnation! Oh,
damnation! Mockery! mockery everywhere! everything I think is mocked by everything I do. [*He strikes*

[455]

himself frantically on the breast]. Coward! liar! fool! Shall I kill myself like a man, or live and pretend to laugh at myself? [*She again turns to go*]. Louka! [*She stops near the door*]. Remember: you belong to me.

LOUKA [*turning*] What does that mean? An insult?

SERGIUS [*commandingly*] It means that you love me, and that I have had you here in my arms, and will perhaps have you there again. Whether that is an insult I neither know nor care: take it as you please. But [*vehemently*] I will not be a coward and a trifler. If I choose to love you, I dare marry you, in spite of all Bulgaria. If these hands ever touch you again, they shall touch my affianced bride.

LOUKA. We shall see whether you dare keep your word. And take care. I will not wait long.

SERGIUS [*again folding his arms and standing motionless in the middle of the room*] Yes: we shall see. And you shall wait my pleasure.

Bluntschli, much preoccupied, with his papers still in his hand, enters, leaving the door open for Louka to go out. He goes across to the table, glancing at her as he passes. Sergius, without altering his resolute attitude, watches him steadily. Louka goes out, leaving the door open.

BLUNTSCHLI [*absently, sitting at the table as before, and putting down his papers*] Thats a remarkable looking young woman.

SERGIUS [*gravely, without moving*] Captain Bluntschli.

BLUNTSCHLI. Eh?

SERGIUS. You have deceived me. You are my rival. I brook no rivals. At six oclock I shall be in the drilling-ground on the Klissoura road, alone, on horseback, with my sabre. Do you understand?

BLUNTSCHLI [*staring, but sitting quite at his ease*]

Oh, thank you: thats a cavalry man's proposal. I'm in the artillery; and I have the choice of weapons. If I go, I shall take a machine gun. And there shall be no mistake about the cartridges this time.

SERGIUS [*flushing, but with deadly coldness*] Take care, sir. It is not our custom in Bulgaria to allow invitations of that kind to be trifled with.

BLUNTSCHLI [*warmly*] Pooh! dont talk to me about Bulgaria. You dont know what fighting is. But have it your own way. Bring your sabre along. I'll meet you.

SERGIUS [*fiercely delighted to find his opponent a man of spirit*] Well said. Switzer. Shall I lend you my best horse?

BLUNTSCHLI. No: damn your horse! thank you all the same, my dear fellow. [*Raina comes in, and hears the next sentence*]. I shall fight you on foot. Horseback's too dangerous: I dont want to kill you if I can help it.

RAINA [*hurrying forward anxiously*] I have heard what Captain Bluntschli said, Sergius. You are going to fight. Why? [*Sergius turns away in silence, and goes to the stove, where he stands watching her as she continues, to Bluntschli*] What about?

BLUNTSCHLI. I dont know: he hasnt told me. Better not interfere, dear young lady. No harm will be done: Ive often acted as sword instructor. He wont be able to touch me; and I'll not hurt him. It will save explanations. In the morning I shall be off home; and youll never see me or hear of me again. You and he will then make it up and live happily ever after.

RAINA [*turning away deeply hurt, almost with a sob in her voice*] I never said I wanted to see you again.

SERGIUS [*striding forward*] Ha! That is a confession.

RAINA [*haughtily*] What do you mean?

SERGIUS. You love that man!

RAINA [*scandalized*] Sergius!

SERGIUS. You allow him to make love to you behind my back, just as you treat me as your affianced husband behind his. Bluntschli: you knew our relations; you deceived me. It is for that I call you to account, not for having received favors *I* never enjoyed.

BLUNTSCHLI [*jumping up indignantly*] Stuff! Rubbish! I have received no favors. Why, the young lady doesnt even know whether I'm married or not.

RAINA [*forgetting herself*] Oh! [*Collapsing on the ottoman*] Are you?

SERGIUS. You see the young lady's concern, Captain Bluntschli. Denial is useless. You have enjoyed the privilege of being received in her own room, late at night—

BLUNTSCHLI [*interrupting him pepperily*] Yes, you blockhead! she received me with a pistol at her head. Your cavalry were at my heels. I'd have blown out her brains if she'd uttered a cry.

SERGIUS [*taken aback*] Bluntschli! Raina: is this true?

RAINA [*rising in wrathful majesty*] Oh, how dare you, how dare you?

BLUNTSCHLI. Apologize, man: apologize. [*He resumes his seat at the table*].

SERGIUS [*with the old measured emphasis, folding his arms*] I never apologize!

RAINA [*passionately*] This is the doing of that friend of yours, Captain Bluntschli. It is he who is spreading this horrible story about me. [*She walks about excitedly*].

BLUNTSCHLI. No: he's dead. Burnt alive.

RAINA [*stopping, shocked*] Burnt alive!

BLUNTSCHLI. Shot in the hip in a woodyard. Couldnt drag himself out. Your fellows' shells set the timber on fire and burnt him, with half a dozen other poor devils in the same predicament.

RAINA. How horrible!

SERGIUS. And how ridiculous! Oh, war! war! the dream of patriots and heroes! A fraud, Bluntschli. A hollow sham, like love.

RAINA [*outraged*] Like love! You say that before me!

BLUNTSCHLI. Come, Saranoff: that matter is explained.

SERGIUS. A hollow sham, I say. Would you have come back here if nothing had passed between you except at the muzzle of your pistol? Raina is mistaken about your friend who was burnt. He was not my informant.

RAINA. Who then? [*Suddenly guessing the truth*] Ah, Louka! my maid! my servant! You were with her this morning all that time after—after—Oh, what sort of god is this I have been worshipping! [*He meets her gaze with sardonic enjoyment of her disenchantment. Angered all the more, she goes closer to him, and says, in a lower, intenser tone*] Do you know that I looked out of the window as I went upstairs, to have another sight of my hero; and I saw something I did not understand then. I know now that you were making love to her.

SERGIUS [*with grim humor*] You saw that?

RAINA. Only too well. [*She turns away, and throws herelf on the divan under the centre window, quite overcome*].

SERGIUS [*cynically*] Raina: our romance is shattered. Life's a farce.

BLUNTSCHLI [*to Raina, whimsically*] You see: he's found himself out now.

SERGIUS [*going to him*] Bluntschli: I have allowed you to call me a blockhead. You may now call me a coward as well. I refuse to fight you. Do you know why?

BLUNTSCHLI. No; but it doesnt matter. I didnt ask the reason when you cried on; and I dont ask the reason now that you cry off. I'm a professional soldier: I fight when I have to, and am very glad to get out of it when I havnt to. Youre only an amateur: you think fighting's an amusement.

SERGIUS [*sitting down at the table, nose to nose with him*] You shall hear the reason all the same, my professional. The reason is that it takes two men—real men—men of heart, blood and honor—to make a genuine combat. I could no more fight with you than I could make love to an ugly woman. Youve no magnetism: youre not a man: youre a machine.

BLUNTSCHLI [*apologetically*] Quite true, quite true. I always was that sort of chap. I'm very sorry.

SERGIUS. Psha!

BLUNTSCHLI. But now that youve found that life isnt a farce, but something quite sensible and serious, what further obstacle is there to your happiness?

RAINA [*rising*] You are very solicitous about my happiness and his. Do you forget his new love—Louka? It is not you that he must fight now, but his rival, Nicola.

SERGIUS. Rival!! [*bounding half across the room*].

RAINA. Dont you know that theyre engaged?

SERGIUS. Nicola! Are fresh abysses opening? Nicola!!

RAINA [*sarcastically*] A shocking sacrifice, isnt it? Such beauty! such intellect! such modesty! wasted on a middle-aged servant man. Really, Sergius, you cannot stand by and allow such a thing. It would be unworthy of your chivalry.

SERGIUS [*losing all self-control*] Viper! Viper! [*He rushes to and fro, raging*].

BLUNTSCHLI. Look here, Saranoff: youre getting the worst of this.

RAINA [*getting angrier*] Do you realize what he has done, Captain Bluntschli? He has set this girl as a spy on us; and her reward is that he makes love to her.

SERGIUS. False! Monstrous!

RAINA. Monstrous! [*Confronting him*] Do you deny that she told you about Captain Bluntschli being in my room?

SERGIUS. No; but—

RAINA [*interrupting*] Do you deny that you were making love to her when she told you?

SERGIUS. No; but I tell you—

RAINA [*cutting him short contemptuously*] It is unnecessary to tell us anything more. That is quite enough for us. [*She turns away from him and sweeps majestically back to the window*].

BLUNTSCHLI [*quietly, as Sergius, in an agony of mortification, sinks on the ottoman, clutching his averted head between his fists*] I told you you were getting the worst of it, Saranoff.

SERGIUS. Tiger cat!

RAINA [*running excitedly to Bluntschli*] You hear this man calling me names, Captain Bluntschli?

BLUNTSCHLI. What else can he do, dear lady? He must defend himself somehow. Come [*very persuasively*]: dont quarrel. What good does it do?

Raina, with a gasp, sits down on the ottoman, and after a vain effort to look vexedly at Bluntschli, falls a victim to her sense of humor, and actually leans back babyishly against the writhing shoulder of Sergius.

SERGIUS. Engaged to Nicola! Ha! ha! Ah well, Bluntschli, you are right to take this huge imposture of a world coolly.

RAINA [*quaintly to Bluntschli, with an intuitive guess at his state of mind*] I daresay you think us a couple of grown-up babies, dont you?

[461]

SERGIUS [*grinning savagely*] He does: he does. Swiss civilization nursetending Bulgarian barbarism, eh?

BLUNTSCHLI [*blushing*] Not at all, I assure you. I'm only very glad to get you two quieted. There! there! let's be pleasant and talk it over in a friendly way. Where is this other young lady?

RAINA. Listening at the door, probably.

SERGIUS [*shivering as if a bullet had struck him, and speaking with quiet but deep indignation*] I will prove that that, at least, is a calumny. [*He goes with dignity to the door and opens it. A yell of fury bursts from him as he looks out. He darts into the passage, and returns dragging in Louka, whom he flings violently against the table, exclaiming*] Judge her, Bluntschli. You, the cool impartial man: judge the eavesdropper.

Louka stands her ground, proud and silent.

BLUNTSCHLI [*shaking his head*] I mustnt judge her. I once listened myself outside a tent when there was a mutiny brewing. It's all a question of the degree of provocation. My life was at stake.

LOUKA. My love was at stake. I am not ashamed.

RAINA [*contemptuously*] Your love! Your curiosity, you mean.

LOUKA [*facing her and retorting her contempt with interest*] My love, stronger than anything you can feel, even for your chocolate cream soldier.

SERGIUS [*with quick suspicion, to Louka*] What does that mean?

LOUKA [*fiercely*] It means—

SERGIUS [*interrupting her slightingly*] Oh, I remember: the ice pudding. A paltry taunt, girl!

Major Petkoff enters, in his shirtsleeves.

PETKOFF. Excuse my shirtsleeves, gentlemen. Raina: somebody has been wearing that coat of mine: I'll swear it. Somebody with a differently shaped back.

It's all burst open at the sleeve. Your mother is mending it. I wish she'd make haste: I shall catch cold. [*He looks more attentively at them*]. Is anything the matter?

RAINA. No. [*She sits down at the stove, with a tranquil air*].

SERGIUS. Oh no. [*He sits down at the end of the table, as at first*].

BLUNTSCHLI [*who is already seated*] Nothing. Nothing.

PETKOFF [*sitting down on the ottoman in his old place*] Thats all right. [*He notices Louka*]. Anything the matter, Louka?

LOUKA. No, sir.

PETKOFF [*genially*] Thats all right. [*He sneezes*] Go and ask your mistress for my coat, like a good girl, will you?

Nicola enters with the coat. Louka makes a pretence of having business in the room by taking the little table with the hookah away to the wall near the windows.

RAINA [*rising quickly as she sees the coat on Nicola's arm*] Here it is, papa. Give it to me, Nicola; and do you put some more wood on the fire. [*She takes the coat, and brings it to the Major, who stands up to put it on. Nicola attends to the fire*].

PETKOFF [*to Raina, teasing her affectionately*] Aha! Going to be very good to poor old papa just for one day after his return from the wars, eh?

RAINA [*with solemn reproach*] Ah, how can you say that to me, father?

PETKOFF. Well, well, only a joke, little one. Come: give me a kiss. [*She kisses him*]. Now give me the coat.

RAINA. No: I am going to put it on for you. Turn your back. [*He turns his back and feels behind him with his*

[463]

arms for the sleeves. She dexterously takes the photograph from the pocket and throws it on the table before Bluntschli, who covers it with a sheet of paper under the very nose of Sergius, who looks on amazed, with his suspicions roused in the highest degree. She then helps Petkoff on with his coat]. There, dear! Now are you comfortable?

PETKOFF. Quite, little love. Thanks. [*He sits down; and Raina returns to her seat near the stove*]. Oh, by the bye, Ive found something funny. Whats the meaning of this? [*He puts his hand into the picked pocket*]. Eh? Hallo! [*He tries the other pocket*]. Well, I could have sworn—! [*Much puzzled, he tries the breast pocket*]. I wonder—[*trying the original pocket*]. Where can it—? [*He rises, exclaiming*] Your mother's taken it!.

RAINA [*very red*] Taken what?

PETKOFF. Your photograph, with the inscription: "Raina, to her Chocolate Cream Soldier: a Souvenir." Now you know theres something more in this than meets the eye; and I'm going to find it out. [*Shouting*] Nicola!

NICOLA [*coming to him*] Sir!

PETKOFF. Did you spoil any pastry of Miss Raina's this morning?

NICOLA. You heard Miss Raina say that I did, sir.

PETKOFF. I know that, you idiot. Was it true?

NICOLA. I am sure Miss Raina is incapable of saying anything that is not true, sir.

PETKOFF. Are you? Then I'm not. [*Turning to the others*] Come: do you think I dont see it all? [*He goes to Sergius, and slaps him on the shoulder*]. Sergius: youre the chocolate cream soldier, arnt you?

SERGIUS [*starting up*] I! A chocolate cream soldier! Certainly not.

PETKOFF. Not! [*He looks at them. They are all very serious and very conscious*]. Do you mean to tell me that Raina sends things like that to other men?

SERGIUS [*enigmatically*] The world is not such an innocent place as we used to think, Petkoff.

BLUNTSCHLI [*rising*] It's all right, Major. I'm the chocolate cream soldier. [*Petkoff and Sergius are equally astonished*]. The gracious young lady saved my life by giving me chocolate creams when I was starving: shall I ever forget their flavour! My late friend Stolz told you the story at Pirot. I was the fugitive.

PETKOFF. You! [*He gasps*]. Sergius: do you remember how those two women went on this morning when we mentioned it? [*Sergius smiles cynically. Petkoff confronts Raina severely*]. Youre a nice young woman, arnt you?

RAINA [*bitterly*] Major Saranoff has changed his mind. And when I wrote that on the photograph, I did not know that Captain Bluntschli was married.

BLUNTSCHLI [*startled into vehement protest*] I'm not married.

RAINA [*with deep reproach*] You said you were.

BLUNTSCHLI. I did not. I positively did not. I never was married in my life.

PETKOFF [*exasperated*] Raina: will you kindly inform me, if I am not asking too much, which of these gentlemen you are engaged to?

RAINA. To neither of them. This young lady [*introducing Louka, who faces them all proudly*] is the object of Major Saranoff's affections at present.

PETKOFF. Louka! Are you mad, Sergius? Why, this girl's engaged to Nicola.

NICOLA. I beg your pardon, sir. There is a mistake. Louka is not engaged to me.

PETKOFF. Not engaged to you, you scoundrel! Why, you had twenty-five levas from me on the day of your betrothal; and she had that gilt bracelet from Miss Raina.

NICOLA [*with cool unction*] We gave it out so, sir. But it was only to give Louka protection. She had a soul above her station; and I have been no more than her confidential servant. I intend, as you know, sir, to set up a shop later on in Sofia; and I look forward to her custom and recommendation should she marry into the nobility. [*He goes out with impressive discretion, leaving them all staring after him*].

PETKOFF [*breaking the silence*] Well, I am—hm!

SERGIUS. This is either the finest heroism or the most crawling baseness. Which is it, Bluntschli?

BLUNTSCHLI. Never mind whether it's heroism or baseness. Nicola's the ablest man Ive met in Bulgaria. I'll make him manager of a hotel if he can speak French and German.

LOUKA [*suddenly breaking out at Sergius*] I have been insulted by everyone here. You set them the example. You owe me an apology.

Sergius, like a repeating clock of which the spring has been touched, immediately begins to fold his arms.

BLUNTSCHLI [*before he can speak*] It's no use. He never apologizes.

LOUKA. Not to you, his equal and his enemy. To me, his poor servant, he will not refuse to apologize.

SERGIUS [*approvingly*] You are right. [*He bends his knee in his grandest manner*] Forgive me.

LOUKA. I forgive you. [*She timidly gives him her hand, which he kisses*]. That touch makes me your affianced wife.

SERGIUS [*springing up*] Ah! I forgot that.

LOUKA [*coldly*] You can withdraw if you like.

SERGIUS. Withdraw! Never! You belong to me. [*He puts his arm about her*].

Catherine comes in and finds Louka in Sergius's arms, with all the rest gazing at them in bewildered astonishment.

CATHERINE. What does this mean?

Sergius releases Louka.

PETKOFF. Well, my dear, it appears that Sergius is going to marry Louka instead of Raina. [*She is about to break out indignantly at him: he stops her by exclaiming testily*] Dont blame me: Ive nothing to do with it. [*He retreats to the stove*].

CATHERINE. Marry Louka! Sergius: you are bound by your word to us!

SERGIUS [*folding his arms*] Nothing binds me.

BLUNTSCHLI [*much pleased by this piece of common sense*] Saranoff: your hand. My congratulations. These heroics of yours have their practical side after all. [*To Louka*] Gracious young lady: the best wishes of a good Republican! [*He kisses her hand, to Raina's great disgust, and returns to his seat*].

CATHERINE. Louka: you have been telling stories.

LOUKA. I have done Raina no harm.

CATHERINE [*haughtily*] Raina!

Raina, equally indignant, almost snorts at the liberty.

LOUKA. I have a right to call her Raina: she calls me Louka. I told Major Saranoff she would never marry him if the Swiss gentleman came back.

BLUNTSCHLI [*rising, much surprised*] Hallo!

LOUKA [*turning to Raina*] I thought you were fonder of him than of Sergius. You know best whether I was right.

BLUNTSCHLI. What nonsense! I assure you, my dear Major, my dear Madam, the gracious young lady simply saved my life, nothing else. She never cared two straws for me. Why, bless my heart and soul, look at the young lady and look at me. She, rich, young, beautiful, with her imagination full of fairy princes and noble natures and cavalry charges and goodness knows what! And I, a commonplace Swiss soldier who hardly knows what a decent life is after fifteen years of barracks and battles: a vagabond, a man who has spoiled all his chances in life through an incurably romantic disposition, a man—

SERGIUS [*starting as if a needle had pricked him and interrupting Bluntschli in incredulous amazement*] Excuse me, Bluntschli: what did you say had spoiled your chances in life?

BLUNTSCHLI [*promptly*] An incurably romantic disposition. I ran away from home twice when I was a boy. I went into the army instead of into my father's business. I climbed the balcony of this house when a man of sense would have dived into the nearest cellar. I came sneaking back here to have another look at the young lady when any other man of my age would have sent the coat back—

PETKOFF. My coat!

BLUNTSCHLI. —yes: thats the coat I mean—would have sent it back and gone quietly home. Do you suppose I am the sort of fellow a young girl falls in love with? Why, look at our ages! I'm thirty-four: I dont suppose the young lady is much over seventeen. [*This estimate produces a marked sensation, all the rest turning and staring at one another. He proceeds innocently*] All that adventure which was life or death to me, was only a schoolgirl's game to her—chocolate creams and hide and seek. Heres the proof! [*He takes the photograph from the table*]. Now, I ask you, would a woman who took the affair seriously have sent me this and written on it "Raina, to her Chocolate Cream

Soldier: a Souvenir"? [*He exhibits the photograph triumphantly, as if it settled the matter beyond all possibility of refutation*].

PETKOFF. Thats what I was looking for. How the deuce did it get there? [*He comes from the stove to look at it, and sits down at the ottoman*].

BLUNTSCHLI [*to Raina, complacently*] I have put everything right, I hope, gracious young lady.

RAINA [*going to the table to face him*] I quite agree with your account of yourself. You are a romantic idiot. [*Bluntschli is unspeakably taken aback*]. Next time, I hope you will know the difference between a schoolgirl of seventeen and a woman of twenty-three.

BLUNTSCHLI [*stupefied*] Twenty-three!

Raina snaps the photograph contemptuously from his hand; tears it up; throws the pieces in his face; and sweeps back to her former place.

SERGIUS [*with grim enjoyment of his rival's discomfiture*] Bluntschli: my one last belief is gone. Your sagacity is a fraud, like everything else. You have less sense than even I!

BLUNTSCHLI [*overwhelmed*] Twenty-three! Twenty-three!! [*He considers*]. Hm! [*Swiftly making up his mind and coming to his host*] In that case, Major Petkoff, I beg to propose formally to become a suitor for your daughter's hand, in place of Major Saranoff retired.

RAINA. You dare!

BLUNTSCHLI. If you were twenty-three when you said those things to me this afternoon, I shall take them seriously.

CATHERINE [*loftily polite*] I doubt, sir, whether you quite realize either my daughter's position or that of Major Sergius Saranoff, whose place you propose to take. The Petkoffs and the Saranoffs are known as the richest and most important families in the country. Our position is almost historical: we can go back for twenty years.

PETKOFF. Oh never mind that, Catherine. [*To Bluntschli*] We should be most happy, Bluntschli, if it were only a question of your position; but hang it, you know, Raina is accustomed to a very comfortable establishment. Sergius keeps twenty horses.

BLUNTSCHLI. But who wants twenty horses? We're not going to keep a circus.

CATHERINE [*severely*] My daughter, sir, is accustomed to a first-rate stable.

RAINA. Hush, mother: youre making me ridiculous.

BLUNTSCHLI. Oh well, if it comes to a question of an establishment, here goes! [*He darts impetuously to the table; seizes the papers in the blue envelope; and turns to Sergius*]. How many horses did you say?

SERGIUS. Twenty, noble Switzer.

BLUNTSCHLI. I have two hundred horses. [*They are amazed*]. How many carriages?

SERGIUS. Three.

BLUNTSCHLI. I have seventy. Twenty-four of them will hold twelve inside, besides two on the box, without counting the driver and conductor. How many tablecloths have you?

SERGIUS. How the deuce do I know?

BLUNTSCHLI. Have you four thousand?

SERGIUS. No.

BLUNTSCHLI. I have. I have nine thousand six hundred pairs of sheets and blankets, with two thousand four hundred eider-down quilts. I have ten thousand knives and forks, and the same quantity of dessert spoons. I have three hundred servants. I have six palatial establishments, besides two livery stables, a tea gardens, and a private house. I have four medals for distinguished services; I have the rank of an officer and the standing of a gentleman; and I have three native languages. Shew me any man in Bulgaria that can offer as much!

PETKOFF [*with childish awe*] Are you Emperor of Switzerland?

BLUNTSCHLI. My rank is the highest known in Switzerland: I am a free citizen.

CATHERINE. Then, Captain Bluntschli, since you are my daughter's choice—

RAINA [*mutinously*] He's not.

CATHERINE [*ignoring her*]—I shall not stand in the way of her happiness. [*Petkoff is about to speak*] That is Major Petkoff's feeling also.

PETKOFF. Oh, I shall be only too glad. Two hundred horses! Whew!

SERGIUS. What says the lady?

RAINA [*pretending to sulk*] The lady says that he can keep his tablecloths and his omnibuses. I am not here to be sold to the highest bidder. [*She turns her back on him*].

BLUNTSCHLI. I wont take that answer. I appealed to you as a fugitive, a beggar, and a starving man. You accepted me. You gave me your hand to kiss, your bed to sleep in, and your roof to shelter me.

RAINA. I did not give them to the Emperor of Switzerland.

BLUNTSCHLI. Thats just what I say. [*He catches her by the shoulders and turns her face-to-face with him*]. Now tell us whom you did give them to.

RAINA [*succumbing with a shy smile*] To my chocolate cream soldier.

BLUNTSCHLI [*with a boyish laugh of delight*] Thatll do. Thank you. [*He looks at his watch and suddenly becomes businesslike*]. Time's up, Major. Youve managed those regiments so well that youre sure to be asked to get rid of some of the infantry of the Timok division. Send them home by way of Lom Palanka. Saranoff: dont get married until I come back: I shall be here punctually at five in the evening on Tuesday fortnight. Gracious ladies [*his heels click*] good evening. [*He makes them a military bow, and goes*].

SERGIUS. What a man! Is he a man!

Arms and the Man

(An interview drafted by Shaw for
The Star, *14 April 1894*)

The extra special *Star* man who is retained for the
sole purpose of interviewing Mr. Bernard Shaw on
great occasions presented himself at the Avenue
Theatre after rehearsal yesterday afternoon, and found
a very animated scene in progress. In the middle of the
stage was a table littered with drawings of gorgeous
uniforms, of scimitars, of kepis, Peninsular and Oriental costumes of all sorts, with sketches of delightful
little towns in the Bulgarian rose valleys, backgrounds
of the velvety Balkans, foregrounds of rugged mountain passes with field batteries struggling through,
and innumerable photographs of ladies and peasants,
Serbian, Roumanian, and Bulgarian, in every degree
of attractiveness, from hardy females in Wellington
boots and moustaches to adorable creatures (Cir-
cassians, the *Star* man guessed) in exquisitely embroidered blouses and aprons resembling some delicate and gorgeous Oriental variety of hearthrug. At
the table sat the author of the sketches, Mr. Schönberg, who acted as special artist for the *Illustrated
London News* during the Servo-Bulgarian war of
1885-6. In the little crowd round him the *Star* man
soon picked out Miss Alma Murray, Mr. Yorke
Stephens, Miss Farr, and Mrs. Charles Calvert.
Mr. Bernard Gould was discussing the drawings with
the double interest of draughtsman and actor with
Mr. Foss; and Mr. Welch stared, fascinated, at a
brilliantly colored sketch of himself as a ferocious
Bulgarian major. Mr. Schönberg was having a busy
time with the inquiries which rained on him. "How

do you pronounce Slivnitza?" "Is the sword worn upside down, like *that*?" "Must I wear these things in the bedroom scene?" "I suppose I shall look like this blue hero when I've got them all on?" &c., &c., &c. The *Star* man,

looked round wistfully for his prey. Presently somebody who had been stooping over the table rose, red-bearded, to the surface; and the *Star* man pounced promptly.

"Ten minutes, Mr. Shaw. Only ten minutes."

"Five," said the Fabian, sternly, leading the way to a private box. "What do you want to know?"

"First, the name of the new piece."

"'Arms and the Man.'"

"I beg your pardon?"

"'Arms and the Man,' I tell you."

"Oh, I see. Some lady's arms, I suppose?"

"A most unseemly jape!" exclaimed Mr. Shaw indignantly. "Why cannot *The Star* send an educated man to interview me? Don't you know your Virgil, or at least your Dryden?—

'Arms and the man I sing, who first by fate
And naughty Juno's unrelenting hate'"—

"'Arma virumque cano,' in fact," said the *Star* man. "The scene of the play is in Bulgaria, is it not?"

"Yes, in 1885 and 1886, during the triumphant repulse of the Serbian invasion. It will perhaps heighten your interest in the play if I give you some idea of the history of the two countries from the ninth century to the present time."

The *Star* man hung on the eloquence of the Fabian orator for exactly thirty-four minutes, at the end of which he unintentionally exasperated Mr. Shaw by asking—not unnaturally, he thinks—whether all that was to be in the play.

"May I ask, sir," was the reply, "whether you suppose that people go to the theatre to be bothered with the Eastern question? I am improving your mind, not

TALKING ABOUT MY OWN WORKS."

The *Star* man expressed his obligation, and ventured to inquire whether it is true, as has been stated, that "Arms and the Man" is a skit on Adelphi melodrama. The question proved a most unfortunate one. Mr. Shaw positively ground his teeth with rage. Then, controlling himself with a visible effort, he said, pointing to the stage:—

"Young man, do you see the artists on whose reputation and skill most of the expectations of the public with regard to this play are founded? Do you know the position they occupy in their profession, and the years of work it has cost them to attain that position? Do you suppose I am asking them to waste their talent on what you call a skit? If you cannot understand the value of an artist, you at least know that money is valuable. Well, do you know how much capital it will cost to put this play on the stage; and do you think it likely that I propose to waste that money in tomfoolery?"

The *Star* man tried vainly to sink into the earth as he pleaded that he was only repeating what the papers had said.

"The rumor is easily explained," Mr. Shaw condescended to add. "Bulgaria is like the Adelphi Theatre in one respect. Romantic dreams and Quixotic ideals flourish luxuriantly in the rose valleys of that country. They play their due part in 'Arms and the Man'; and I have not represented them as standing the test of reality any better or any worse than they do IN ACTUAL LIFE."

"At least, Mr. Shaw, I may assume that the play will be original and unconventional?"

This innocent and well-meant compliment drove the dramatist almost beside himself. "There is nothing whatever original or unconventional about it," he declared. "I made it up out of my own head, if that is what you mean. It is just like any other play written for a modern theatre."

"Then you are really aiming at a popular success?"

"Now deliver me from this foolish man!" cried Mr. Shaw in a heartrending voice. "Did you suppose I was aiming at a failure?"

The *Star* worm turned at last. "How is a man to know?" he said. "Miss Farr said she was going to produce plays that no ordinary management would care to take up."

"Precisely. And a certain able critic got a flash of satire out of the phrase at Miss Farr's expense. But for you to sit here and pretend that you do not understand that Miss Farr meant simply that her capital was entrusted to her for artistic and not for commercial purposes is not satirical criticism, but partly prevarication and partly congenital imbecility. I wish you would go away. You enrage me. I have kept my temper for eighteen years, and have never been uncivil to an interviewer in my life until to-day. But you would drive anybody mad with your chatter about unconventionality and originality and the rest of it. I am an author working at my trade; and what skill I have has been acquired in the ordinary way by practice and drudgery. I never offered a play to a manager in my life, so I cannot say whether an ordinary management would have anything to do with my plays or not. If my dramatic work turns out worth anything, my business in that department will increase without my having to

HAWK MY WARES

about. If not, I can make myself useful in other ways."

The *Star* man, who had crawled under a chair at an early stage of the above speech, emerged cautiously, and begged for a word or two about the cast.

"The names of the cast are a sufficient guarantee that if the play fails the fault will be mine."

"But who is to be the hero?"

"Everybody is a hero in Bulgaria. Mr. Gould will embody the chivalry of the Balkans;—you know what Mr. Gould can do with parts which have a touch of the fantastic. The audience can choose, for their pet hero, between him and Mr. Yorke Stephens, who will be the incarnation of the comparative coolness, good sense, efficiency, and social training of the higher civilisation of Western Europe. Then there is Mr. Welch; you remember him as Lickcheese in my 'Widowers' Houses'? How admirably he drove home the lessons in political economy in which that highly instructive play abounded! Well, in 'Arms and the Man' he has an equally serious part. On him will fall the duty of expounding the ethnology of Bulgaria, the peculiar customs and prejudices of the native races, and the eccentricities of their military system. He will thus supply a grave scientific background for the lighter scenes in which the other characters will participate."

"Not a comic part, then?"

"Certainly not. Some of his observations may raise a smile at first among the least thoughtful section of the audience; but that impression will be removed on a second or third visit to the play."

[477]

"And now the ladies, Mr. Shaw? I already know that your play will bring

MISS ALMA MURRAY

back to the stage after a long rest."

"It will have that honor, which I greatly appreciate. It will also give you an opportunity of renewing your acquaintance with the art of Mrs. Charles Calvert. Miss Murray will play the sympathetic heroine—as far as any heroine of mine can be claimed sympathetic."

"Why not Miss Farr?"

Mr. Shaw bounded from his chair; and the *Star* man again sought cover. "Have you any manners—have you any tact, any sense, any discretion, that you ask such a question? Do you know what has just happened at this very theatre? Miss Farr began by taking the advice of the critics, and getting a play from Mr. John Todhunter, whom they had all proclaimed, on the occasion of the production of his 'Black Cat' by the Independent Theatre Society, as the coming playwright. 'Give us some more of the clever conversation in the "Black Cat," without the tragic part,' they said. He took them at their word; and they promptly damned him most heartily. But why did they do it? The play was no worse than the 'Black Cat,' and it was much more expensively mounted and cast. Why, then, did it rouse the worse passions of everyone who heard it? Why was it received by the more impressionable critics not with mere disapproval, but with frantic detestation? I can tell you; for I was present and felt it all myself. The dramatist had tried the very dangerous experiment of trying to combine in one character the personality of a beautiful, winning, and sympathetic woman with the ideas of Hedda Gabler, whose morbid recoil from marriage and maternity as 'disgusting experiences,' as well as her swagger, her impulses to deliberate insolence, her heartlessly sensual coquetry, and her cowardice, are all reproduced in the heroine of a 'Comedy of Sighs' as material for sentimental comedy. What does

MISS FARR

do with the part, if you please? Seizes on all the odious points in the character, changes them from the intellectual affectations of an immature woman into the convictions of an experienced one, paints out her personal attractions, ages herself so as to owe nothing to the sort of admiration which Duse so pointedly does without, and pitches to the winds the sentimental charms which the other characters in the play keep attributing to her with exasperating iteration. The effect was so powerfully unpleasant that I positively hated Miss Farr for days after the performance; and it was sufficiently evident that some of the critics shared my feelings. Naturally Miss Farr laughed consumedly at me. But she did not propose that I should court Dr. Todhunter's doom by casting her for the sympathetic heroine when my play contained another important part far more congenial to her. Now your maladroit question is answered fully. Had you not better leave before you commit yourself again?"

"Am I taking up too much of your valuable time, Mr. Shaw?"

"YES."

The *Star* man had no alternative but to make for the door. On his way over the stage he resolved to say something to soften his irritable host. Turning with his most winning smile, he said, "I presume, Mr. Shaw, that when the eventful night comes, the most enjoyable part of it will be your speech after——"

But the sentence was never finished. The face of the Fabian suddenly turned a frightful greenish purple as he snatched up a length of iron gaspipe. The next moment he was struggling in the arms of the stage door keeper, a black-bearded veteran, who shouted to the *Star* man:—

"Get out of it, will you, before he gets loose and kills you. You ought to know better at your age than to come interviewing a man with rehearsals on his nerves. Steady, sir, steady; he isn't worth your no——."

The *Star* man, already flying for his life along the Embankment, heard no more. He signifies his intention of raising his terms for future interviews with the author of "Arms and the Man."

Ten Minutes
with Mr Bernard Shaw

(A questionnaire in *To-day*, 28 April 1894)

Since last Saturday Mr. Bernard Shaw, critic, Fabian, and speaker, and, last not least, dramatist, has become, in a special sense, the man of the hour. To a representative of To-Day he has kindly consented to describe something of his methods and ideas concerning stage-craft.

"You have laid the scene of your play in Bulgaria. Do you consider that an historical play is bound to be substantially accurate as to facts, etc?"

"Not more so than any other sort of play. Historical facts are not a bit more sacred than any other class of facts. In making a play out of them you must adapt them to the stage, and that alters them at once, more or less. Why, you cannot even write a history without adapting the facts to the conditions of literary narrative, which are in some respects much more distorting than the dramatic conditions of representation on the stage. Things do not happen in the form of stories or dramas; and since they must be told in some such form, all reports, even by eyewitnesses, all histories, all stories, all dramatic representations, are only attempts to arrange the facts in a thinkable, intelligible, interesting form—that is, when they are not more or less intentional efforts to hide the truth, as they very often are. But my play is not an historical play in your sense at all. It was written without the slightest reference to Bulgaria. In the original MS. the names of the places were blank, and the characters were called simply The Father, The Daughter, The Stranger, The Heroic Lover, and so on. The incident of the machine-gun bound me to a recent war; that was all. My own historical information being rather confused, I asked Mr. Sidney Webb to find out a good war for my purpose. He spent about two minutes in a rapid survey of every war that has ever been waged, and then told me that the Servo-Bulgarian was what I wanted. I then read the account of the war in the *Annual Register*, with a modern railway map of the Balkan Peninsula before me, and filled in my blanks, making all the action take place in Servia, in the house of a Servian family. I then read the play to Stepniak, and to the Admiral who commanded the Bulgarian Fleet during the war, who happens to reside in London just now. He made me change the scene from Servia to Bulgaria, and the characters from Servians to Bulgarians, and gave me descriptions of Bulgarian life and ideas, which enabled me to fit my play exactly with local colour and character. I followed the facts he gave me as closely as I could, because invented facts are the same stale stuff in all plays, one man's imagination being much the same as another's in such matters, whilst real facts are fresh and varied. So you can judge exactly how far my historical conscience goes. If I were to write a play about Julius Cæsar, it would not really be historical; but I should take care not let him appear with a revolver and a field-glass all the same."

"Do you assign an important part to the stage manager? Do you think that costumes, scenery, and general *mise-en-scène* have much to do nowadays with the success or failure of a new play?"

"The stage-manager is as important a functionary as the conductor of an orchestra, and good ones are almost as rare. An adequate *mise-en-scène* is necessary to the complete effect of a theatrical representation, whether it is *Box and Cox* or a grand opera. But if you ask what my choice would be between 'four boards and passion' and a sumptuous *mise-en-scène* without the passion, I am for the four boards. There is no rule that applies to all plays except the rule that no play should look shabby."

"Should a play simply aim at telling a story, or be used as a medium for embodying certain theories and ideas?"

"There is no such alternative presented to the playwright. You really cannot put the case exactly in that way. The greatest story-tellers are the most inveterate moralists; and no man who is not an idiot can tell a story without shaping it in such a way as to move the sympathy of the audience by appealing to their moral ideas. Molière's plays are full of preaching; whilst Joyce's Scientific Dialogues are confined mostly to statements of objective fact. Joyce should be the ideal dramatist of the people who complain of moral didactism in plays. For my part I prefer Molière, and so does the public."

"Are you an advocate of stage realism? Do the methods of the Théâtre Libre, for instance, appeal to you?"

"I am an advocate for stage illusion; stage realism is a contradiction in terms. I am only a realist in a Platonic sense. I am really a classicist, as far as my taste for other people's work goes. As to my own, I write what comes into my head, without reference to any theory of what is good or bad. I avoid what jars on me, either in sound or sense. I have never seen a performance at the Théâtre Libre. I should be satisfied with the Théâtre Français if I were allowed to make a clean sweep of the mass of superstitions which M. Antoine quite rightly protests against. Our own stage is in great need of reform, but it would take me too far to go into that. We require much greater force, vivacity, crispness, and alert intelligence in our actors. Our school is one of chronic sentimentality and solemn feebleness. A typical 'London leading man' is fit to be nothing else in the world than an undertaker's mute."

"Is it long since you first began writing plays? Are you engaged on a new one now?"

"In 1885 Mr. William Archer asked me to write a drama in collaboration with him, and under that external pressure I wrote the first two acts of *Widowers' Houses*. The breakdown of the collaboration, owing to the way in which I outraged all Mr. Archer's plans, was described by him in his *World* article on the performance of the play in 1892 by the Independent Theatre Society, for which occasion I finished the third act. You will find Mr. Archer's account in the preface to the published play. The Independent Theatre asked me for a second play, which I accordingly wrote; but when it was completed the actress upon whom I was relying for the principal character—a very difficult part—could not bring herself to face a certain scene in which she had to act a violent transport of grief for a dog which was erroneously supposed to have been vivisected. So I threw the play aside and wrote another, which, however, even if it escapes suppression by that intolerable social nuisance, the Censorship, will appeal to an audience rather more terribly in earnest in social questions than the ordinary playgoer. So that, too, was thrown aside to wait its opportunity. Finally I wrote *Arms and the Man* for Miss Farr, whose enterprise at the Avenue Theatre was just then in its initial stage. I am not at present engaged on a play, as nobody wants one from me. I have more than enough of other work, political and literary, to do; and my plays get scrawled in pocket-books in trains and on omnibuses, or when I am forced to seek some relief from the far harder work of musical and economic criticism. By the time I have made half a dozen more attempts I shall acquire a fair degree of skill in developing a dramatic theme. At present I am unable to do this to the utmost. My grip slips; and though I can cover up my shortcomings with sufficient address by a stroke of comedy or something of the sort, I am, I hope, too good a critic to be satisfied by myself yet."

To-Day, *London, April 28,* 1894

A Dramatic Realist to His Critics

(*The New Review*, London, July 1894, and, unauthorized, in *Eclectic Magazine*, New York, September 1894. Reprinted in *Shaw on Theatre*, ed. E. J. West, 1958)

I think very few people know how troublesome dramatic critics are. It is not that they are morally worse than other people; but they know nothing. Or, rather, it is a good deal worse than that: they know everything wrong. Put a thing on the stage for them as it is in real life, and instead of receiving it with the blank wonder of plain ignorance, they reject it with scorn as an imposture, on the ground that the real thing is known to the whole world to be quite different. Offer them Mr Crummles's real pump and tubs, and they will denounce both as spurious on the ground that tubs have no handles, and the pump no bung-hole.

I am, among other things, a dramatist; but I am not an original one, and so have to take all my dramatic material either from real life at first hand, or from authentic documents. The more usual course is to take it out of other dramas, in which case, on tracing it back from one drama to another, you finally come to its origin in the inventive imagination of some original dramatist. Now a fact as invented by a dramatist differs widely from the fact of the same name as it exists or occurs objectively in real life. Not only stage pumps and tubs, but (much more) stage morality and stage human nature differ from the realities of these things. Consequently to a man who derives all his knowledge of life from witnessing plays, nothing appears more unreal than objective life. A dramatic critic is generally such a man; and the more exactly

I reproduce objective life for him on the stage, the more certain he is to call my play an extravaganza.

It may be asked here whether it is possible for one who every day contemplates the real world for fourteen of his waking hours, and the stage for only two, to know more of the stage world than the real world. As well might it be argued that a farmer's wife, churning for only two hours a week, and contemplating nature almost constantly, must know more about geology, forestry, and botany than about butter. A man knows what he works at, not what he idly stares at. A dramatic critic works at the stage, writes about the stage, thinks about the stage, and understands nothing of the real life he idly stares at until he has translated it into stage terms. For the rest, seeing men daily building houses, driving engines, marching to the band, making political speeches, and what not, he is stimulated by these spectacles to *imagine* what it is to be a builder, an engine driver, a soldier, or a statesman. Of course, he imagines a stage builder, engine driver, soldier, and so on, not a real one. Simple as this is, few dramatic critics are intelligent enough to discover it for themselves. No class is more idiotically confident of the reality of its own unreal knowledge than the literary class in general and dramatic critics in particular.

We have, then, two sorts of life to deal with: one subjective or stagey, the other objective or real. What are the comparative advantages of the two for the purposes of the dramatist? Stage life is artificially simple and well understood by the masses; but it is very stale; its feeling is conventional; it is totally unsuggestive of thought because all its conclusions are foregone; and it is constantly in conflict with the real knowledge which the separate members of the audience derive from their own daily occupations.

For instance, a naval or military melodrama only goes down with civilians. Real life, on the other hand, is so ill understood, even by its clearest observers, that no sort of consistency is discoverable in it; there is no "natural justice" corresponding to that simple and pleasant concept, "poetic justice"; and, as a whole, it is unthinkable. But, on the other hand, it is credible, stimulating, suggestive, various, free from creeds and systems—in short, it is real.

This rough contrast will suffice to show that the two sorts of life, each presenting dramatic potentialities to the author, will, when reproduced on the stage, affect different men differently. The stage world is for the people who cannot bear to look facts in the face, because they dare not be pessimists, and yet cannot see real life otherwise than as the pessimist sees it. It might be supposed that those who conceive all the operations of our bodies as repulsive, and of our minds as sinful, would take refuge in the sects which abstain from playgoing on principle. But this is by no means what happens. If such a man has an artistic or romantic turn, he takes refuge, not in the conventicle, but in the theatre, where, in the contemplation of the idealised, or stage life, he finds some relief from his haunting conviction of omnipresent foulness and baseness. Confront him with anything like reality, and his chronic pain is aggravated instead of relieved: he raises a terrible outcry against the spectacle of cowardice, selfishness, faithlessness, sensuality—in short, everything that he went to the theatre to escape from. This is not the effect on those pessimists who dare face facts and profess their own faith. They are great admirers of the realist playwright, whom they embarrass greatly by their applause. Their cry is "Quite right: strip off the whitewash from the sepulchre; expose human nature in all its tragi-comic baseness; tear the mask of respectability from the smug bourgeois, and show the liar, the thief, the coward, the libertine beneath."

Now to me, as a realist playwright, the applause of the conscious, hardy pessimist is more exasperating than the abuse of the unconscious, fearful one. I am not a pessimist at all. It does not concern me that, according to certain ethical systems, all human beings fall into classes labelled liar, coward, thief, and so on. I am myself, according to these systems, a liar, a coward, a thief, and a sensualist; and it is my deliberate cheerful, and entirely self-respecting intention to continue to the end of my life deceiving people, avoiding danger, making my bargains with publishers and managers on principles of supply and demand instead of abstract justice, and indulging all my appetites, whenever circumstances commend such actions to my judgment. If any creed or system deduces from this that I am a rascal incapable on occasion of telling the truth, facing a risk, foregoing a commercial advantage, or resisting an intemperate impulse of any sort, then so much the worse for the creed or system, since I have done all these things, and will probably do them again. The saying "All have sinned," is, in the sense in which it was written, certainly true of all the people I have ever known. But the sinfulness of my friends is not unmixed with saintliness: some of their actions are sinful, others saintly. And here, again, if the ethical system to which the classifications of saint and sinner belong, involves the conclusion that a line of cleavage drawn between my friends' sinful actions and their saintly ones will coincide exactly with one drawn between their mistakes and their successes (I include the highest and widest sense of the two terms), then so much the worse for the system; for the facts contradict it. Persons obsessed by systems may retort: "No; so much the worse for your friends"—implying that I must move in a circle of rare blackguards; but I am quite prepared not only to publish a list of friends of mine whose names would put such a retort to open shame, but to take any human being, alive or dead, of whose actions a genuinely miscellaneous unselected dozen can be brought to light, to show that none of the ethical systems habitually applied by dramatic critics (not to mention other people) can verify their inferences. As a realist dramatist, therefore, it is my business to get outside these systems. For instance, in the play of mine which is most in evidence in London just now, the heroine has been classified by critics as a minx, a liar, and a *poseuse*. I have nothing to do with that: the only moral question for me is, does she do good or harm? If you admit that she does good, that she generously saves a man's life and wisely extricates herself from a false position with another man, then you may classify her as you please—brave, generous, and affectionate; or artful, dangerous, faithless—it is all one to me: you can no more prejudice me for or against her by such artificial categorising than you could have made Molière dislike Monsieur Jourdain by a lecture on the vanity and pretentiousness of that amiable "bourgeois gentilhomme." The fact is, though I am willing and anxious to see the human race improved, if possible, still I find that, with reasonably sound specimens, the more intimately I know people the better I like them; and when a man concludes from this that I am a cynic, and that he, who prefers stage monsters—walking catalogues of the systematised virtues—to his own species, is a person of wholesome philanthropic tastes,

[489]

why, how can I feel towards him except as an English-woman feels towards the Arab who, faithful to *his* system, denounces her indecency in appearing in public with her mouth uncovered.

The production of "Arms and the Man" at the Avenue Theatre, about nine weeks ago, brought the misunderstanding between my real world and the stage world of the critics to a climax, because the misunderstanding was itself, in a sense, the subject of the play. I need not describe the action of the piece in any detail: suffice it to say that the scene is laid in Bulgaria in 1885-6, at a moment when the need for repelling the onslaught of the Servians made the Bulgarians for six months a nation of heroes. But as they had only just been redeemed from centuries of miserable bondage to the Turks, and were, therefore, but beginning to work out their own redemption from barbarism—or, if you prefer it, beginning to contract the disease of civilisation—they were very ignorant heroes, with boundless courage and patriotic en-thusiasm, but with so little military skill that they had to place themselves under the command of Russian officers. And their attempts at Western civilisa-tion were much the same as their attempts at war—instructive, romantic, ignorant. They were a nation of plucky beginners in every department. Into their country comes, in the play, a professional officer from the high democratic civilisation of Switzerland—a man completely acquainted by long, practical ex-perience with the realities of war. The comedy arises, of course, from the collision of the knowledge of the Swiss with the illusions of the Bulgarians. In this dramatic scheme Bulgaria may be taken as symbolic of the stalls on the first night of a play. The Bulgarians are dramatic critics; the Swiss is the realist playwright invading their realm; and the comedy is the comedy of the collision of the realities represented by the realist playwright with the preconceptions of stageland. Let us follow this comedy a little into particulars.

War, as we all know, appeals very strongly to the romantic imagination. We owe the greatest realistic novel in the world, "Don Quixote," to the awakening lesson which a romantically imaginative man received from some practical experience of real soldiering. Nobody is now foolish enough to call Cervantes a cynic because he laughed at Amadis de Gaul, or Don Quixote a worthless creature because he charged windmills and flocks of sheep. But I have been plentifully denounced as a cynic, my Swiss soldier as a coward, and my Bulgarian Don Quixote as a humbug, because I have acted on the same impulse and pursued the same method as Cervantes. Not being myself a soldier like Cervantes, I had to take my facts at second hand; but the difficulties were not very great, as such wars as the Franco-Prussian and Russo-Turkish have left a considerable number of experienced soldiers who may occasionally be met and consulted even in England; whilst the publication of such long-delayed works as Marbot's Memoirs, and the success with which magazine editors have drawn some of our generals, both here and in America, on the enthralling subject of military courage, has placed a mass of documentary evidence at the disposal of the realist. Even realistic fiction has become valuable in this way: for instance, it is clear that Zola, in his "Débâcle," has gone into the evidence carefully enough to give high authority to his description of what a battle is really like.

The extent to which this method brought me into conflict with the martial imaginings of the critics is hardly to be conveyed by language. The notion that there could be any limit to a soldier's courage, or any preference on his part for life and a whole skin over a glorious death in the service of his country, was inexpressibly revolting to them. Their view was simple, manly, and straightforward, like most impracticable views. A man is either a coward or he is not. If a brave man, then he is afraid of nothing. If a coward, then he is no true soldier; and to represent him as such is to libel a noble profession.

The tone of men who know what they are talking about is remarkably different. Compare, for instance, this significant little passage from no less an authority than Lord Wolseley, who, far from being a cynic, writes about war with an almost schoolboyish enthusiasm, considering that he has seen so much of it:—

"One of the most trying things for the captain or subaltern is to make their men who have found some temporary haven of refuge from the enemy's fire, leave it and spring forward in a body to advance over the open upon a position to be attacked. It is even difficult to make a line of men who have lain down, perhaps to take breath after a long advance at a running pace, rise up together."—*Fortnightly Review*, Aug., 1888.

This, you will observe, is your British soldier, who is quite as brave as any soldier in the world. It may be objected, however, by believers in the gameness of blue blood, that it is the British officer who wins our battles, on the playing fields of Eton and elsewhere. Let me, therefore, quote another passage from our veteran commander:—

"I have seen a whole division literally crazy with terror when suddenly aroused in the dark by some

senseless alarm. I have known even officers to tackle
and wound their own comrades upon such occasions.
Reasoning men are for the time reduced to the
condition of unreasoning animals who, stricken
with terror, will charge walls or houses, unconscious
of what they do.... [Here Lord Wolseley describes
a scare which took place on a certain occasion.]
In that night's panic several lost their lives; and
many still bear the marks of wounds then received."
Ib., pp. 284-5.

Now let us hear General Horace Porter, a veteran
of the American War, which had the advantage of
being a civil war, the most respectable sort of war,
since there is generally a valuable idea of some kind at
stake in it. General Porter, a cooler writer than our
General, having evidently been trained in the world,
and not in the army, delivers himself as follows:—

"The question most frequently asked of soldiers
is 'How does a man feel in battle?' There is a belief,
among some who have never indulged in the pastime
of setting themselves up as targets to be shot at,
that there is a delicious sort of exhilaration experienced in battle, which arouses a romantic
enthusiasm; surfeits the mind with delightful
sensations; makes one yearn for a lifetime of
fighting, and feel that peace is a pusillanimous sort
of thing at best. Others suppose, on the contrary,
that one's knees rattle like a Spanish ballerina's
castanets, and that one's mind dwells on little else
than the most approved means of running away.

"A happy mean between these two extremes
would doubtless define the condition of the average
man when he finds that, as a soldier, he is compelled to devote himself to stopping bullets as well

as directing them. He stands his ground and faces
the dangers into which his profession leads him,
under a sense of duty and a regard for his self-
respect, but often feels that the sooner the firing
ceases, the better it would accord with his notion
of the general fitness of things, and that if the
enemy is going to fall back, the present moment
would be as good a time as any at which to begin
such a highly judicious and commendable movement. Braving danger, of course, has its compen-
sations. 'The blood more stirs to rouse a lion than
to start a hare.' In the excitement of a charge, or
in the enthusiasm of approaching victory there is a
sense of pleasure which no one should attempt to
underrate. It is the gratification which is always
born of success, and, coming to one at the supreme
moment of a favourable crisis in battle, rewards the
soldier for many severe trials and perilous tasks."—
(Article in *The Century*, June, 1888, p. 251.)

Probably nothing could convey a more sickening
sense of abandoned pusillanimity to the dramatic critic
than the ignoble spectacle of a soldier dodging a bullet.
[Alfred] Bunn's sublime conception of Don Cæsar de
Bazan, with his breast "expanding to the ball," has
fixed for ever the stage ideal of the soldier under fire.
General Porter falls far beneath Bunn in this pasage:—

"I can recall only two persons who, throughout
a rattling musketry fire, always sat in their saddles
without moving a muscle or even winking an eye.
One was a bugler in the regular cavalry, and the
other was General Grant."

It may be urged against me here that in my play I
have represented a soldier as shying like a nervous
horse, not at bullets, but at such trifles as a young

lady snatching a box of sweets from him and throwing
it away. But my soldier explains that he has been
three days under fire; and though that would, of
course, make no difference to the ideal soldier, it
makes a considerable difference to the real one,
according to General Porter.

"Courage, like everything else, wears out. Troops
used to go into action during our late war, displaying a coolness and steadiness the first day that
made them seem as if the screeching of shot and
shell was the music on which they had been brought
up. After fighting a couple of days their nerves
gradually lost their tension; their buoyancy of
spirits gave way; and dangers they would have
laughed at the first day, often sent them panic-
stricken to the rear on the third. It was always a
curious sight in camp after a three days' fight to
watch the effect of the sensitiveness of the nerves:
men would start at the slightest sound, and dodge
the flight of a bird or a pebble tossed at them. One
of the chief amusements on such occasions used to
be to throw stones and chips past one another's
heads to see the active dodging that would follow."

A simple dramatic paraphrase of that matter-of-
fact statement in the first act of "Arms and the Man"
has been received as a wild topsy-turvyist invention;
and when Captain Bluntschli said to the young
lady, "If I were in camp now they'd play all sorts of
tricks on me," he was supposed to be confessing
himself the champion coward of the Servian army.
But the truth is that he was rather showing off, in the
style characteristic of the old military hand. When an
officer gets over the youthful vanity of cutting a figure
as a hero, and comes to understand that courage is a

quality for use and not for display, and that the soldier who wins with the least risk is the best soldier, his vanity takes another turn; and, if he is a bit of a humorist, he begins to appreciate the comedy latent in the incongruity between himself and the stage soldier which civilians suppose him. General Porter puts this characteristic of the veteran before us with perfect clearness:—

"At the beginning of the war officers felt that, as untested men, they ought to do many things for the sake of appearance that were wholly unnecessary. This at times led to a great deal of posing for effect and useless exposure of life. Officers used to accompany assaulting columns over causeways on horseback, and occupy the most exposed positions that could be found. They were not playing the bravo: they were confirming their own belief in their courage, and acting under the impression that bravery ought not only to be undoubted, but conspicuous. They were simply putting their courage beyond suspicion.

"At a later period of the war, *when men began to plume themselves as veterans*, they could afford to be more conservative: they had won their spurs; their reputations were established; they were beyond reproach. Officers then dismounted to lead close assaults, dodged shots to their hearts' content, did not hesitate to avail themselves of the cover of earthworks when it was wise to seek such shelter, and resorted to many acts which conserved human life and in no wise detracted from their efficiency as soldiers. There was no longer anything done for buncombe: they had settled down to practical business."—*Ib.*, p. 249.

In Arms and the Man, this very simple and intelligible picture is dramatized by the contrast between the experienced Swiss officer, with a high record for distinguished services, and the Bulgarian hero who wins the battle by an insanely courageous charge for which the Swiss thinks he ought to be court-martialled. Result: the dramatic critics pronounce the Swiss "a poltroon." I again appeal to General Porter for a precedent both for the Swiss's opinion of the heroic Bulgarian, and the possibility of a novice, in "sheer ignorance of the art of war" (as the Swiss puts it), achieving just such a success as I have attributed to Sergius Saranoff:—

> "Recruits sometimes rush into dangers from which veterans would shrink. When Thomas was holding on to his position at Chickamauga on the afternoon of the second day, and resisting charge after charge of an enemy flushed with success, General Granger came up with a division of troops, many of whom had never before been under fire. As soon as they were deployed in front of the enemy, they set up a yell, sprang over the earthworks, charged into the ranks, and created such consternation that the Confederate veterans were paralysed by the very audacity of such conduct. Granger said, as he watched their movements, 'Just look at them: they don't know any better; they think that's the way it ought to be done. I'll bet they'll never do it again.'"

According to the critics, Granger was a cynic and a worldling, incapable of appreciating true courage.

I shall perhaps here be reminded by some of my critics that the charge in "Arms and the Man" was a cavalry charge; and that I am suppressing the damning sneer at military courage implied in Captain Bluntschli's reply to Raïna Petkoff's demand to have a cavalry charge described to her:—

"Bluntschli—You never saw a cavalry charge, did you?

"Raïna—No: how could I?

"Bluntschli—Of course not. Well, it's a funny sight. It's like slinging a handful of peas against a window-pane—first one comes, then two or three close behind them, and then all the rest in a lump.

"Raïna (*thinking of her lover, who has just covered himself with glory in a cavalry charge*)—Yes; first one, the bravest of the brave!

"Bluntschli—Hm! you should see the poor devil pulling at his horse.

"Raïna—Why should he pull at his horse?

"Bluntschli—It's running away with him, of course: do you suppose the fellow wants to get there before the others and be killed?"

Imagine the feelings of the critics—countrymen of the heroes of Balaclava, and trained in warfare by repeated contemplation of the reproduction of Miss Elizabeth Thompson's pictures in the Regent Street shop windows, not to mention the recitations of Tennyson's "Charge of the Light Brigade," which they have criticised—on hearing this speech from a mere Swiss! I ask them now to put aside these authorities for a moment and tell me whether they have ever seen a horse bolt in Piccadilly or the Row. If so, I would then ask them to consider whether it is not rather likely that in a battlefield, which is, on the whole, rather a startling place, it is not conceivable and even likely that at least one horse out a squadron may bolt in a charge. Having gently led them to this point, I further ask them how they think they would feel if they happened to be on the back of that horse, with the danger that has so often ended in death in Rotten Row complicated with the glory of charging a regiment practically single-handed. If we are to believe their criticisms, they would be delighted at the distinction. The Swiss captain in my play takes it for granted that they would pull the horse's head off. Leaving the difference of opinion unsettled, there can be no doubt as to what their duty would be if they were soldiers. A cavalry charge attains its maximum effect only when it strikes the enemy solid. This fact ought to be particularly well known to Balaclava amateurs; for Kinglake, the popular authority on the subject, gives us specimens of the orders that were heard during the frightful advance down "the valley of death." The dramatic-critical formula on that occasion would undoubtedly have been, "Charge, Chester, charge! on, Stanley, on!" Here is the reality:—

"The crash of dragoons overthrown by round shot, by grape and by rifle-ball, was alternate with dry technical precepts: 'Back, right flank!' 'Keep back, private This,' 'Keep back, private That!' 'Close in to your centre!' 'Do look to your dressing! 'Right squadron, right squadron, keep back!'"

There is no cynicism for you! Nothing but "keep back!" Then consider the conduct of Lord Cardigan, who rode at the head of the Light Brigade. Though he, too, said "Keep back," when Captain White tried to force the pace, he charged the centre gun of the battery just like a dramatic critic, and was the first man to sweep through the Russian gunners. In fact, he got clean out at the other side of the battery, happening to hit on a narrow opening by chance. The result was that he found himself presently riding down, quite alone, upon a mass of Russian cavalry. Here was a chance to cut them all down single-handed and plant the British flag on a mountain of Muscovite corpses. By refusing it, he flinched from the first-nighter's ideal. Realising the situation when he was twenty yards from the foe, he pulled up and converted that twenty yards into 200 as quickly as was consistent with his dignity as an officer. The stage hero finds in death the supreme consolation of being able to get up and go home when the curtain falls; but the real soldier, even when he leads Balaclava charges under conditions of appalling and prolonged danger, does not commit suicide for nothing. The fact is, Captain Bluntschli's description of the cavalry charge is taken almost verbatim from an account given privately to a friend of mine by an officer who served in the Franco-Prussian war. I am well aware that if I choose to be guided by men grossly ignorant of dramatic criticism, whose sole qualification is that they have seen cavalry charges on stricken fields, I must take the consequences. Happily, as between myself and the public, the consequences have not been unpleasant; and I recommend the experiment to my fellow dramatists with every confidence.

But great as has been the offence taken at my treating a soldier as a man with no stomach for unnecessary danger, I have given still greater by treating him as a man with a stomach for necessary food. Nature provides the defenders of our country with regular and efficient appetites. The taxpayer provides, at considerable cost to himself, rations for the soldier which are insufficient in time of peace and occasionally irregular in time of war. The result is that our young, growing soldiers sometimes go for months without once experiencing the sensation of having had enough to eat, and will often, under stress of famine, condescend to borrow florins and other trifles in silver from the young ladies who walk out with them, in order to eke out "the living wage." Let me quote a passage from Cobbett's description of his soldiering days in his "Advice to Young Men," which nobody who has read the book ever forgets:—

> "I remember, and well I may! that, upon occasion I, after all absolutely necessary expenses, had, on Friday, made shift to have a halfpenny in reserve, which I had destined for the purchase of a *red herring* in the morning; but, when I pulled off my clothes at night, so hungry then as to be hardly able to endure life, I found that I had *lost my halfpenny*. I buried my head under the miserable sheet and rug and cried like a child."

I am by no means convinced that the hidden tears still shed by young soldiers (who would rather die than confess to them) on similar provocation would not fill a larger cask than those shed over lost comrades or wounds to the national honour of England. In the field the matter is more serious. It is a mistake to suppose that in a battle the waiters come round regularly with soup, fish, an entrée, a snack of game, a cut from the joint, ice pudding, coffee and cigarettes, with drinks at discretion. When battles last for several days, as modern battles often do, the service of food and ammunition may get disorganised or cut off at any point; and the soldier may suffer exceedingly from hunger in consequence. To guard against this the veteran would add a picnic hamper to his equipment if it were portable enough and he could afford it, or if Fortnum and Mason would open a shop on the field. As it is, he falls back on the cheapest, most portable and most easily purchased sort of stomach-stayer, which, as every cyclist knows, is chocolate. This chocolate, which so shocks Raïna in the play—for she, poor innocent, classes it as "sweets"—and which seems to so many of my critics to be the climax of my audacious extravagances, is a commonplace of modern warfare. I know of a man who lived on it for two days in the Shipka Pass.

By the way I have been laughed at in this connection for making my officer carry an empty pistol, preferring chocolate to cartridges. But I might have gone further and represented him as going without any pistol at all. Lord Wolseley mentions two officers who seldom carried any weapons. One of them had to defend himself by shying stones when the Russians broke into his battery at Sebastopol. The other was Gordon.

The report that my military realism is a huge joke has once or twice led audiences at the Avenue Theatre to laugh at certain grim touches which form no part of the comedy of disillusionment elsewhere so constant between the young lady and the Swiss. Readers of General Marbot's Memoirs will remember his description of how, at the battle of Wagram, the standing corn was set on fire by the shells and many of the wounded were roasted alive. "This often happens," says Marbot, coolly, "in battles fought in summer." The Servo-Bulgarian war was fought in winter; but Marbot will be readily recognised as the source of the incident of Bluntschli's friend Stolz, who is shot in the hip in a wood-yard and burnt in the conflagration of the timber caused by the Servian shells. There is, no doubt, a certain barbarous humour in the situation —enough to explain why the Bulgarian, on hearing

Raïna exclaim, "How horrible!" adds bitterly, "And how ridiculous!" but I can assure those who are anxious to fully appreciate the fun of the travesty of war discovered in my work by the critics, and whose rule is, "When in doubt, laugh," that I should not laugh at that passage myself were I looking at my own play. Marbot's picture of the fire-eaters fire-eaten is one which I recommend to our music-hall tableauists when they are in need of a change. Who that has read that Wagram chapter does not remember Marbot forcing his wretched horse to gallop through the red-hot straw embers on his way to Massena; finding that general with no *aide-de-camp* left to send on a probably fatal errand except his only son; being sent in the son's place as soon as he had changed the roasted horse for a fresh one; being followed into the danger by the indignant son; and, finally—Nature seldom fails with her touch of farce—discovering that the son could not handle his sabre, and having to defend him against the pursuing cavalry of the enemy, who, as Bluntschli would have prophesied, no sooner found that they had to choose between two men who stood to fight and hundreds who were running away and allowing themselves to be slaughtered like sheep, [than they] devoted themselves entirely to the sheep, and left Marbot to come out of the battle of Wagram with a whole skin?

I might considerably multiply my citations of documents; but the above will, I hope, suffice to show that what struck my critics as topsy-turvy extravaganza, having no more relation to real soldiering than Mr. Gilbert's "Pinafore" has to real sailoring, is the plainest matter-of-fact. There is no burlesque: I have stuck to the routine of war, as described by real warriors, and avoided such farcical incidents as Sir William Gordon defending his battery by throwing stones, or General Porter's story of the two generals who, though brave and capable men, always got sick under fire, to their own great mortification. I claim that the dramatic effect produced by the shock which these realities give to the notions of romantic young ladies and fierce civilians is not burlesque, but legitimate comedy, none the less pungent because, on the first night at least, the romantic young lady was on the stage and the fierce civilians in the stalls. And since my authorities, who record many acts almost too brave to make pleasant reading, are beyond suspicion of that cynical disbelief in courage which has been freely attributed to me, I would ask whether it is not plain that the difference between my authenticated conception of real warfare and the stage conception lies in the fact that in real warfare there is real personal danger, the sense of which is constantly present to the mind of the soldier, whereas in stage warfare there is nothing but glory? Hence Captain Bluntschli, who thinks of a battlefield as a very busy and very dangerous place, is incredible to the critic who thinks of it only as a theatre in which to enjoy the luxurious excitements of patriotism, victory, and bloodshed without risk of retribution.

There are one or two general points in the play on which I may as well say a word whilst I have the opportunity. It is a common practice in England to speak of the courage of the common soldier as "bulldog pluck." I grant that it is an insulting practice—who would dream of comparing the spirit in which an ancient Greek went to battle with the ferocity of an animal?—though it is not so intended, as it generally comes from people who are thoughtless enough to suppose that they are paying the army a compliment.

A passage in the play which drove home the true significance of the comparison greatly startled these same thoughtless ones. Can we reasonably apply such a word as valour to the quality exhibited in the field by, for instance, the armies of Frederick the Great, consisting of kidnapped men, drilled, caned, and flogged to the verge of suicide, and sometimes over it? Flogging, sickeningly common in English barracks all through the most "glorious" periods of our military history, was not abolished here by any revolt of the English soldier against it: our warriors would be flogging one another to-day as abjectly as ever but for the interference of humanitarians who hated the whole conception of military glory. We still hear of soldiers severely punished for posting up in the barrack stables a newspaper paragraph on the subject of an army grievance. Such absurd tyranny would, in a dockyard or a factory full of matchgirls, produce a strike; but it cows a whole regiment of soldiers. The fact is, armies as we know them are made possible, not by valour in the rank and file, but by the lack of it; not by physical courage (we test the eyes and lungs of our recruits, never their courage), but by civic impotence and moral cowardice. I am afraid of a soldier, not because he is a brave man, but because he is so utterly unmanned by discipline that he will kill me if he is told, even when he knows that the order is given because I am trying to overthrow the oppression which he fears and hates. I respect a regiment for a mutiny more than for a hundred victories; and I confess to the heartiest contempt for the warlike civilian who pays poor men a pittance to induce them to submit to be used as pawns on a battlefield in time of war, he himself, meanwhile, sitting at home talking impudent nonsense about patriotism, heroism, devotion to duty, the inspiring sound of the British cheer, and so on. "Bulldog pluck" is much more sensible and candid. And so the idealist in my play continues to admit nightly that his bull terrier, which will fight as fiercely as a soldier, will let himself be thrashed as helplessly by the man in authority over him. One critic seems to think that it requires so much courage to say such things that he describes me as "protecting" myself by "ostensibly throwing the burden of my attack upon a couple of small and unimportant nationalities," since "there would have been a certain danger in bringing my malevolent mockery too near home." I can assure the gentleman that I meant no mockery at all. The observation is made in the play in a manner dramatically appropriate to the character of an idealist who is made a pessimist by the shattering of his illusions. His conclusion is that "life is a farce." My conclusion is that a soldier ought to be made a citizen and treated like any other citizen. And I am not conscious of running any risk in making that proposal, except the risk of being foolishly criticised.

I have been much lectured for my vulgarity in introducing certain references to soap and water in Bulgaria. I did so as the shortest and most effective way of bringing home to the audience the stage of civilisation in which the Bulgarians were in 1885, when, having clean air and clean clothes, which made them much cleaner than any frequency of ablution can make us in the dirty air of London, they were adopting the washing habits of big western cities as pure ceremonies of culture and civilisation, and not on hygienic grounds. I had not the slightest intention of suggesting that my Bulgarian major, who submits to a good wash for the sake of his social position, or his father, who never had a bath in his life, are uncleanly people, though a cockney, who by simple exposure to the atmosphere becomes more unpresentable in three hours than a Balkan mountaineer in three years, may feel bound to pretend to be shocked at them, and to shrink with disgust from even a single omission of the daily bath which, as he knows very well, the majority of English, Irish, and Scotch people do not take, and which the majority of the inhabitants of the world do not even tell lies about.

Major Petkoff is quite right in his intuitive perception that soap, instead of being the radical remedy for dirt, is really one of its worst consequences. And his remark that the cultus of soap comes from the English because their climate makes them exceptionally dirty, is one of the most grimly and literally accurate passages in the play, as we who dwell in smoky towns know to our cost. However, I am sorry that my piece of realism should have been construed as an insult to the Bulgarian nation; and perhaps I should have hesitated to introduce it had I known that a passionate belief in the scrupulous cleanliness of the inhabitants of the Balkan peninsula is a vital part of Liberal views on foreign policy. But what is done is done. I close the incident by quoting from the daily papers of the 5th May last the following item of Parliamentary intelligence, which gives a basis for a rough calculation of the value of English cleanliness as measured by the pecuniary sacrifices we are willing to make for it:—

"ARMY BEDDING

"The SECRETARY for WAR, replying to Mr. Hanbury's question as to the provision made in the Army for the washing of soldiers' bedding, stated that soldiers are now allowed to have their sheets washed once a month, and their blankets

once a year; and the right hon. gentleman stated
that the cost of allowing clean sheets fortnightly
instead of monthly would amount to something
like £10,000 a year, money which might be spent
more advantageously in other directions, he thought.
(Hear, hear.)"

I am afraid most of my critics will receive the above
explanations with an indignant sense of personal ingratitude on my part. The burden of their mostly very
kind notices has been that I am a monstrously clever
fellow, who has snatched a brilliant success by
amusingly whimsical perversions of patent facts and
piquantly cynical ridicule of human nature. I hardly
have the heart to turn upon such friendly help with a
cold-blooded confession that all my audacious ori-
ginalities are simple liftings from stores of evidence
which lie ready to everybody's hand. Even that triumph
of eccentric invention which nightly brings down the
house, Captain Bluntschli's proposal for the hand of
Raïna, is a paraphrase of an actual proposal made by
an Austrian hotel proprietor for the hand of a member
of my own family. To that gentleman, and to him
alone, is due the merit of the irresistible joke of the
four thousand tablecloths and the seventy equipages
of which twenty-four will hold twelve inside. I have
plundered him as I have plundered Lord Wolseley
and General Porter and everyone else who had anything that was good to steal. I created nothing; I
invented nothing; I imagined nothing; I perverted
nothing; I simply discovered drama in real life.

I now plead strongly for a theatre to supply the
want of this sort of drama. I declare that I am tired
to utter disgust of imaginary life, imaginary law,
imaginary ethics, science, peace, war, love, virtue,

villainy, and imaginary everything else, both on the stage and off it. I demand respect, interest, affection for human nature as it is, and life as we must still live it even when we have bettered it and ourselves to the utmost. If the critics really believe all their futile sermonising about "poor humanity" and the "seamy side of life" and meanness, cowardice, selfishness, and all the other names they give to qualities which are as much and as obviously a necessary part of themselves as their arms and legs, why do they not shoot themselves like men instead of coming whimpering to the dramatist to pretend that they are something else? I, being a man like to themselves, know what they are perfectly well; and as I do not find that I dislike them for what they persist in calling their vanity, and sensuality, and mendacity, and dishonesty, and hypocrisy, and venality, and so forth; as, furthermore, they would not interest me in the least if they were otherwise, I shall continue to put them on the stage as they are to the best of my ability, in the hope that some day it may strike them that if they were to try a little self-respect, and stop calling themselves offensive names, they would discover that the affection of their friends, wives, and sweethearts for them is not a reasoned tribute to their virtues, but a human impulse towards their very selves. When Raïna says in the play, "Now that you have found me out, I suppose you despise me," she discovers that that result does not follow in the least, Captain Bluntschli not being quite dramatic critic enough to feel bound to repudiate the woman who has saved his life as "a false and lying minx," because, at twenty-three, she has some generous illusions which lead her into a good deal of pretty nonsense.

I demand, moreover, that when I deal with facts

into which the critic has never inquired, and of which he has had no personal experience, he shall not make his vain imaginings the criterion of my accuracy. I really cannot undertake, every time I write a play, to follow it up by a text-book on mortgages, or soldiering, or whatever else it may be about, for the instruction of gentlemen who will neither accept the result of my study of the subject (lest it should destroy their cherished ideals), nor undertake any study on their own account. When I have written a play the whole novelty of which lies in the fact that it is void of malice to my fellow creatures, and laboriously exact as to all essential facts, I object to be complimented on my "brilliancy" as a fabricator of cynical extravaganzas. Nor do I consider it decent for critics to call their own ignorance "the British public," as they almost invariably do.

It must not be supposed that the whole Press has gone wrong over "Arms and the Man" to the same extent and in the same direction. Several of the London correspondents of the provincial papers, accustomed to deal with the objective world outside the theatre, came off with greater credit than the hopelessly specialised critics. Some of the latter saved themselves by a strong liking for the play, highly agreeable to me; but most of them hopelessly misunderstood me. I should have lain open to the retort that I had failed to make myself comprehensible had it not been for the masterly critical exploit achieved by Mr. A. B. Walkley, whose article in the *Speaker* was a completely successful analysis of my position. Mr. Walkley here saved the critics from the reproach of having failed where the actors had succeeded. Nobody who has seen Mr. Yorke Stephens's impersonation of the Swiss captain will suspect him for a moment of mistaking his man, as most of the critics did, for "a poltroon who prefers chocolate to fighting." It was Mr. Walkley who recognised that Bluntschli, "dogged, hopelessly unromantic, incurably frank, always *terre à terre*, yet a man every inch of him, is one of the most artistic things Mr. Yorke Stephens has done."

Here we have the actor making Bluntschli appear to a fine critic, as he undoubtedly did to the gallery, a brave sincere unaffected soldier; and yet some of the other critics, unable to rise to the actor's level, moralised in a positively dastardly way about a "cowardly and cynical mercenary." Imagine English dramatic critics, who, like myself, criticise for the paper that pays them best, without regard to its politics, and whose country's regular army is exclusively a paid professional one, waxing virtuous over a "mercenary" soldier! After that, one hardly noticed their paying tribute to the ideal woman (a sort of female George Washington) by calling Raïna a minx, and feebly remonstrating with Miss Alma Murray for charming them in such a character; whilst as to the heroic Sergius, obsessed with their own ideals, and desperately resolved to live up to them in spite of his real nature, which he is foolish enough to despise, I half expected them to stone him; and I leave Mr. Bernard Gould and Mr Walkley to divide the credit, as actor and critic, the one of having realised the man, and the other of having analysed him—the nicety of the second operation proving the success of the first.

Here I must break off, lest I should appear to talk too much about my own play. I should have broken off sooner but for the temptation of asserting the right of the authors to decide who is the best critic, since the critics take it upon themselves to decide who is the best author.

Candida

WITH

An Extraordinary Ordinary Play

Author's Note to 1937 Production

Shaw Reveals Who Was Candida

Composition begun 2 October 1894; completed 7 December 1894. Published in *Plays Pleasant and Unpleasant*, 1898. Revised text in Collected Edition, 1930. Copyright reading at the Theatre Royal, South Shields, on 30 March 1895. First presented by the Independent Theatre Company at Her Majesty's Theatre, Aberdeen, on 30 July 1897, at the start of a provincial tour. Presented by the Stage Society at the Strand Theatre, London, on 1 July 1900, with the same cast except for the substitution of H. Granville Barker as Eugene Marchbanks (originally called Marjoribanks).

The Reverend James Mavor Morell *Charles Charrington*

Eugene Marchbanks *Courtney Thorpe*

Mr Burgess *Lionel Belmore*

The Reverend Alexander Mill *Robert Farquharson*

Miss Proserpine Garnett *Edith Craig*

Candida Morell *Janet Achurch*

Scene: The Study and General Sitting-room, St Dominic's Vicarage, Victoria Park, London. Time: October 1894.

ACT I *Morning*

ACT II *Afternoon*

ACT III *Evening*

*A fine morning in October 1894 in the north east quarter
of London, a vast district miles away from the London
of Mayfair and St James's, and much less narrow,
squalid, fetid and airless in its slums. It is strong in
unfashionable middle class life: wide-streeted; myriad-
populated; well served with ugly iron urinals, Radical
clubs, and tram lines carrying a perpetual stream of
yellow cars; enjoying in its main thoroughfares the
luxury of grass-grown "front gardens" untrodden by
the foot of man save as to the path from the gate to the
hall doors; blighted by a callously endured monotony
of miles and miles of unlovely brick houses, black iron
railings, stony pavements, slated roofs, and respectably
ill dressed or disreputably worse dressed people, quite
accustomed to the place, and mostly plodding unin-
terestedly about somebody else's work. The little energy
and eagerness that crop up shew themselves in cockney
cupidity and business "push." Even the policemen and
the chapels are not infrequent enough to break the
monotony. The sun is shining cheerfully: there is no fog;
and though the smoke effectually prevents anything,
whether faces and hands or bricks and mortar, from
looking fresh and clean, it is not hanging heavily enough
to trouble a Londoner.*

*The desert of unattractiveness has its oasis. Near the
outer end of the Hackney Road is a park of 217 acres,
fenced in, not by railings, but by a wooden paling, and
containing plenty of greensward, trees, a lake for bathers,
flower beds which are triumphs of the admired cockney*

art of carpet gardening, and a sandpit, originally imported from the seaside for the delight of children, but speedily deserted on its becoming a natural vermin preserve for all the petty fauna of Kingsland, Hackney, and Hoxton. A bandstand, an unfurnished forum for religious, anti-religious, and political orators, cricket pitches, a gymnasium, and an old fashioned stone kiosk are among its attractions. Wherever the prospect is bounded by trees or rising green grounds, it is a pleasant place. Where the ground stretches flat to the grey palings, with bricks and mortar, sky signs, crowded chimneys and smoke beyond, the prospect makes it desolate and sordid.

The best view of Victoria Park is commanded by the front window of St Dominic's Parsonage, from which not a brick is visible. The parsonage is semi-detached, with a front garden and a porch. Visitors go up the flight of steps to the porch: tradespeople and members of the family go down by a door under the steps to the basement, with a breakfast room, used for all meals, in front, and the kitchen at the back. Upstairs, on the level of the hall door, is the drawingroom, with its large plate glass window looking out on the park. In this, the only sitting room that can be spared from the children and the family meals, the parson, the Reverend James Mavor Morell, does his work. He is sitting in a strong round backed revolving chair at the end of a long table, which stands across the window, so that he can cheer himself with a view of the park over his left shoulder. At the opposite end of the table, adjoining it, is a little table only half as wide as the other, with a typewriter on it. His typist is sitting at this machine, with her back to the window. The large table is littered with pamphlets, journals, letters, nests of drawers, an office diary, postage scales and the like. A spare chair for visitors having business with the parson is in the middle, turned to his end. Within reach of his hand is a stationery case, and a photograph in a frame. The wall behind him is fitted with bookshelves, on which an adept eye can measure the parson's casuistry and divinity by Maurice's Theological Essays and a complete set of Browning's poems, and the reformer's politics by a yellow backed Progress and Poverty, Fabian Essays, A Dream of John Ball, Marx's Capital, and half a dozen other literary landmarks in Socialism. Facing him on the other side of the room, near the typewriter, is the door. Further down opposite the fireplace, a bookcase stands on a cellaret, with a sofa near it. There is a generous fire burning; and the hearth, with a comfortable arm-chair and a black japanned flower-painted coal scuttle at one side, a miniature chair for children on the other, a varnished wooden mantelpiece, with neatly moulded shelves, tiny bits of mirror let into the panels, a travelling clock in a leather case (the inevitable wedding present), and on the wall above a large autotype of the chief figure in Titian's Assumption of the Virgin, is very inviting. Altogether the room is the room of a good housekeeper, vanquished, as far as the table is concerned, by an untidy man, but elsewhere mistress of the situation. The furniture, in its ornamental aspect, betrays the style of the advertized "drawingroom suite" of the pushing suburban furniture dealer; but there is nothing useless or pretentious in the room, money being too scarce in the house of an east end parson to be wasted on snobbish trimmings.

The Reverend James Mavor Morell is a Christian Socialist clergyman of the Church of England, and an active member of the Guild of St Matthew and the Christian Social Union. A vigorous, genial, popular man of forty, robust and goodlooking, full of energy, with pleasant, hearty, considerate manners, and a sound unaffected voice, which he uses with the clean athletic articulation of a practised orator, and with a wide range and perfect command of expression. He is a first rate clergyman, able to say what he likes to whom he likes, to lecture people without setting himself up against them, to impose his authority on them without humiliating them, and, on occasion, to interfere in their business without impertinence. His well-spring of enthusiasm and sympathetic emotion has never run dry for a moment: he still eats and sleeps heartily enough to win the daily battle between exhaustion and recuperation triumphantly. Withal, a great baby, pardonably vain of his powers and unconsciously pleased with himself. He has a healthy complexion: good forehead, with the brows somewhat blunt, and the eyes bright and eager, mouth resolute but not particularly well cut, and a substantial nose, with the mobile spreading nostrils of the dramatic orator, void, like all his features, of subtlety.

The typist, Miss Proserpine Garnett, is a brisk little woman of about 30, of the lower middle class, neatly but cheaply dressed in a black merino skirt and a blouse, notably pert and quick of speech, and not very civil in her manner, but sensitive and affectionate. She is clattering away busily at her machine whilst Morell opens the last of his morning's letters. He realizes its contents with a comic groan of despair.

PROSERPINE. Another lecture?

MORELL. Yes. The Hoxton Freedom Group want me to address them on Sunday morning [*he lays great emphasis on Sunday, this being the unreasonable part of the business*]. What are they?

PROSERPINE. Communist Anarchists, I think.

MORELL. Just like Anarchists not to know that they cant have a parson on Sunday! Tell them to come to church if they want to hear me: it will do them good. Say I can come on Mondays and Thursdays only. Have you the diary there?

PROSERPINE [*taking up the diary*] Yes.

MORELL. Have I any lecture on for next Monday?

PROSERPINE [*referring to the diary*] Tower Hamlets Radical Club.

MORELL. Well, Thursday then?

PROSERPINE. English Land Restoration League.

MORELL. What next?

PROSERPINE. Guild of St Matthew on Monday. Independent Labor Party, Greenwich Branch, on Thursday. Monday, Social-Democratic Federation, Mile End Branch. Thursday, first Confirmation class. [*Impatiently*] Oh, I'd better tell them you cant come. Theyre only half a dozen ignorant and conceited costermongers without five shillings between them.

MORELL [*amused*] Ah; but you see theyre near relatives of mine.

PROSERPINE [*staring at him*] Relatives of yours!

MORELL. Yes: we have the same father—in Heaven.

PROSERPINE [*relieved*] Oh, is that all?

MORELL [*with a sadness which is a luxury to a man whose voice expresses it so finely*] Ah, you dont believe it. Everybody says it: nobody believes it: nobody. [*Briskly, getting back to business*] Well, well! Come, Miss Proserpine: cant you find a date for the costers? what about the 25th? That was vacant the day before yesterday.

PROSERPINE [*referring to diary*] Engaged. The Fabian Society.

MORELL. Bother the Fabian Society! Is the 28th gone too?

PROSERPINE. City dinner. Youre invited to dine with the Founders' Company.

MORELL. Thatll do: I'll go to the Hoxton Group of Freedom instead. [*She enters the engagement in silence, with implacable disparagement of the Hoxton Anarchists in every line of her face. Morell bursts open the cover of a copy of The Church Reformer, which has come by post, and glances through Mr Stewart Headlam's leader and the Guild of St Matthew news. These proceedings are presently enlivened by the appearance of Morell's curate, the Reverend Alexander Mill, a young gentleman gathered by Morell from the nearest University settlement, whither he had come from Oxford to give the east end of London the benefit of his university training. He is a conceitedly well intentioned, enthusiastic, immature novice, with nothing positively unbearable about him except a habit of speaking with his lips carefully closed a full half inch from each corner for the sake of a finicking articulation and a set of university vowels, this being his chief means so far of bringing his Oxford refinement (as he calls his habits) to bear on Hackney vulgarity. Morell, whom he has won over by a doglike devotion, looks up indulgently from The Church Reformer, and remarks*] Well, Lexy? Late again, as usual!

LEXY. I'm afraid so. I wish I could get up in the morning.

MORELL [*exulting in his own energy*] Ha! ha! [*Whimsically*] Watch and pray, Lexy: watch and pray.

LEXY. I know. [*Rising wittily to the occasion*] But how can I watch and pray when I am asleep? Isnt that so, Miss Prossy? [*He makes for the warmth of the fire*].

PROSERPINE [*sharply*] Miss Garnett, if you please.

LEXY. I beg your pardon. Miss Garnett.

PROSERPINE. Youve got to do all the work today.

LEXY [*on the hearth*] Why?

PROSERPINE. Never mind why. It will do you good to earn your supper before you eat it, for once in a way, as I do. Come! dont dawdle. You should have been off on your rounds half an hour ago.

LEXY [*perplexed*] Is she in earnest, Morell?

MORELL [*in the highest spirits: his eyes dancing*] Yes. *I* am going to dawdle today.

LEXY. You! You dont know how.

MORELL [*rising*] Ha! ha! Dont I? I'm going to have this morning all to myself. My wife's coming back: she's due here at 11.45.

LEXY [*surprised*] Coming back already! with the children? I thought they were to stay to the end of the month.

MORELL. So they are: she's only coming up for two days, to get some flannel things for Jimmy, and to see how we're getting on without her.

LEXY [*anxiously*] But, my dear Morell, if what Jimmy and Fluffy had was scarlatina, do you think it wise—

MORELL. Scarlatina! Rubbish! it was German measles. I brought it into the house myself from the Pycroft Street school. A parson is like a doctor, my boy: he must face infection as a soldier must face bullets. [*He claps Lexy manfully on the shoulders*]. Catch the measles if you can, Lexy: she'll nurse you; and what a piece of luck that will be for you! Eh?

LEXY [*smiling uneasily*] It's so hard to understand you about Mrs Morell—

MORELL [*tenderly*] Ah, my boy, get married: get married to a good woman; and then youll understand. Thats a foretaste of what will be best in the Kingdom of Heaven we are trying to establish on earth. That will cure you of dawdling. An honest man feels that he must pay Heaven for every hour of happiness with a good spell of hard unselfish work to make others happy. We have no more right to consume happiness without producing it than to consume wealth without producing it. Get a wife like my Candida; and youll always be in arrear with your repayment. [*He pats Lexy affectionately and moves to leave the room*].

LEXY. Oh, wait a bit: I forgot. [*Morell halts and turns with the door knob in his hand*]. Your father-in-law is coming round to see you.

Morell, surprised and not pleased, shuts the door again, with a complete change of manner.

MORELL. Mr Burgess?

LEXY. Yes. I passed him in the park, arguing with somebody. He asked me to let you know that he was coming.

MORELL [*half incredulous*] But he hasnt called here for three years. Are you sure, Lexy? Youre not joking, are you?

LEXY [*earnestly*] No sir, really.

MORELL [*thoughtfully*] Hm! Time for him to take another look at Candida before she grows out of his knowledge. [*He resigns himself to the inevitable, and goes out*].

Lexy looks after him with beaming worship. Miss Garnett, not being able to shake Lexy, relieves her feelings by worrying the typewriter.

LEXY. What a good man! What a thorough loving soul he is! [*He takes Morell's place at the table, making himself very comfortable as he takes out a cigaret*].

PROSERPINE [*impatiently, pulling the letter she has been working at off the typewriter and folding it*] Oh, a man ought to be able to be fond of his wife without making a fool of himself about her.

LEXY [*shocked*] Oh, Miss Prossy!

PROSERPINE [*snatching at the stationery case for an envelope, in which she encloses the letter as she speaks*] Candida here, and Candida there, and Candida everywhere! [*She licks the envelope*]. It's enough to drive anyone out of their s e n s e s [*thumping the envelope to make it stick*] to hear a woman raved about in that absurd manner merely because she's got good hair and a tolerable figure.

LEXY [*with reproachful gravity*] I think her extremely beautiful, Miss Garnett. [*He takes the photograph up; looks at it; and adds, with even greater impressiveness*] extremely beautiful. How fine her eyes are!

PROSERPINE. Her eyes are not a bit better than mine: now! [*He puts down the photograph and stares austerely at her*]. And you know very well you think me dowdy and second rate enough.

LEXY [*rising majestically*] Heaven forbid that I should think of any of God's creatures in such a way! [*He moves stiffly away from her across the room to the neighborhood of the bookcase*].

PROSERPINE [*sarcastically*] Thank you. Thats very nice and comforting.

LEXY [*saddened by her depravity*] I had no idea you had any feeling against Mrs Morell.

PROSERPINE [*indignantly*] I have no feeling against her. She's very nice, very good-hearted: I'm very fond of her, and can appreciate her real qualities far better than any man can. [*He shakes his head sadly. She rises and comes at him with intense pepperiness*]. You dont believe me? You think I'm jealous? Oh, what a knowledge of the human heart you have, Mr Lexy Mill! How well you know the weaknesses of Woman, dont you? It must be so nice to be a man and have a fine penetrating intellect instead of mere emotions like us, and to know that the reason we dont share

[523]

your amorous delusions is that we're all jealous of one another! [*She abandons him with a toss of her shoulders, and crosses to the fire to warm her hands*].

LEXY. Ah, if you women only had the same clue to Man's strength that you have to his weakness, Miss Prossy, there would be no Woman Question.

PROSERPINE [*over her shoulder, as she stoops, holding her hands to the blaze*] Where did you hear Morell say that? You didnt invent it yourself: youre not clever enough.

LEXY. Thats quite true. I am not ashamed of owing him that, as I owe him so many other spiritual truths. He said it at the annual conference of the Women's Liberal Federation. Allow me to add that though they didnt appreciate it, I, a mere man, did. [*He turns to the bookcase again, hoping that this may leave her crushed*].

PROSERPINE [*putting her hair straight at a panel of mirror in the mantelpiece*] Well, when you talk to me, give me your own ideas, such as they are, and not his. You never cut a poorer figure than when you are trying to imitate him.

LEXY [*stung*] I try to follow his example, not to imitate him.

PROSERPINE [*coming at him again on her way back to her work*] Yes, you do: you imitate him. Why do you tuck your umbrella under your left arm instead of carrying it in your hand like anyone else? Why do you walk with your chin stuck out before you, hurrying along with that eager look in your eyes? you! who never get up before half past nine in the morning. Why do you say "knoaledge" in church, though you always say "knolledge" in private conversation! Bah! do you think I dont know? [*She goes back to the typewriter*]. Here! come and set about your work: weve wasted enough time for one morning. Here's a copy of the diary for today. [*She hands him a memorandum*].

LEXY [*deeply offended*] Thank you. [*He takes it and stands at the table with his back to her, reading it. She begins to transcribe her shorthand notes on the typewriter without troubling herself about his feelings*].

The door opens; and Mr Burgess enters unannounced. He is a man of sixty, made coarse and sordid by the compulsory selfishness of petty commerce, and later on softened into sluggish bumptiousness by overfeeding and commercial success. A vulgar ignorant guzzling man, offensive and contemptuous to people whose labor is cheap, respectful to wealth and rank, and quite sincere and without rancor or envy in both attitudes. The world has offered him no decently paid work except that of a sweater; and he has become, in consequence, somewhat hoggish. But he has no suspicion of this himself, and honestly regards his commercial prosperity as the inevitable and socially wholesome triumph of the ability, industry, shrewdness, and experience in business of a man who in private is easygoing, affectionate, and humorously convivial to a fault. Corporeally he is podgy, with a snoutish nose in the centre of a flat square face, a dust colored beard with a patch of grey in the centre under his chin, and small watery blue eyes with a plaintively sentimental expression, which he transfers easily to his voice by his habit of pompously intoning his sentences.

BURGESS [*stopping on the threshold, and looking round*] They told me Mr Morell was here.

PROSERPINE [*rising*] I'll fetch him for you.

BURGESS [*staring disappointedly at her*] Youre not the same young lady as hused to typewrite for him?

PROSERPINE. No.

BURGESS [*grumbling on his way to the hearthrug*] No:

she was young-er. [*Miss Garnett stares at him; then goes out, slamming the door*]. Startin on your rounds, Mr Mill?

LEXY [*folding his memorandum and pocketing it*] Yes: I must be off presently.

BURGESS [*momentously*] Dont let me detain you, Mr Mill. What I come about is private between me and Mr Morell.

LEXY [*huffily*] I have no intention of intruding, I am sure, Mr Burgess. Good morning.

BURGESS [*patronizingly*] Oh, good morning to you.

Morell returns as Lexy is making for the door.

MORELL [*to Lexy*] Off to work?

LEXY. Yes, sir.

MORELL. Take my silk handkerchief and wrap your throat up. Theres a cold wind. Away with you.

Lexy, more than consoled for Burgess's rudeness, brightens up and goes out.

BURGESS. Spoilin your korates as usu'l, James. Good mornin. When I pay a man, an' 'is livin depens on me, I keep him in 'is place.

MORELL [*rather shortly*] I always keep my curates in their places as my helpers and comrades. If you get as much work out of your clerks and warehousemen as I do out of my curates you must be getting rich pretty fast. Will you take your old chair.

He points with curt authority to the armchair beside the fireplace; then takes the spare chair from the table and sits down at an unfamiliar distance from his visitor.

BURGESS [*without moving*] Just the same as hever, James!

MORELL. When you last called—it was about three years ago, I think—you said the same thing a little more frankly. Your exact words then were "Just as big a fool as ever, James!"

BURGESS [*soothingly*] Well, praps I did; but [*with
conciliatory cheerfulness*] I meant no hoffence by it.
A clorgyman is privileged to be a bit of a fool, you
know: it's ony becomin in 'is profession that he should.
Anyhow, I come here, not to rake up hold differences,
but to let bygones be bygones. [*Suddenly becoming
very solemn, and approaching Morell*] James: three
years ago, you done me a hil turn. You done me hout
of a contrac; an when I gev you arsh words in my
natral disappointment, you turned my daughrter
again me. Well, Ive come to hact the part of a Kerischin. [*Offering his hand*] I forgive you, James.

MORELL [*starting up*] Confound your impudence!

BURGESS [*retreating, with almost lachrymose de-
precation of this treatment*] Is that becomin language
for a clorgyman, James? And you so particlar, too!

MORELL [*hotly*] No, sir: it is not becoming language
for a clergyman. I used the wrong word. I should have
said damn your impudence: thats what St Paul or
any honest priest would have said to you. Do you
think I have forgotten that tender of yours for the
contract to supply clothing to the workhouse?

BURGESS [*in a paroxysm of public spirit*] I hacted in
the hinterest of the ratepayers, James. It was the
lowest tender: you carnt deny that.

MORELL. Yes, the lowest, because you paid worse
wages than any other employer—starvation wages—
aye, worse than starvation wages—to the women
who made the clothing. Your wages would have
driven them to the streets to keep body and soul
together. [*Getting angrier and angrier*] Those women
were my parishioners. I shamed the Guardians out of
accepting your tender: I shamed the ratepayers out of
letting them do it: I shamed everybody but you.
[*Boiling over*] How dare you, sir, come here and

CANDIDA

offer to forgive me, and talk about your daughter, and—

BURGESS. Heasy, James! heasy! heasy! Dont git hinto a fluster about nothink. Ive howned I was wrong.

MORELL. Have you? I didnt hear you.

BURGESS. Of course I did. I hown it now. Come: I harsk your pardon for the letter I wrote you. Is that enough?

MORELL [snapping his fingers] Thats nothing. Have you raised the wages?

BURGESS [triumphantly] Yes.

MORELL. What!

BURGESS [unctuously] Ive turned a moddle hemployer. I dont hemploy no women now: theyre all sacked; and the work is done by machinery. Not a man 'as less than sixpence a *hour*; and the skilled ands gits the Trade Union rate. [Proudly] What ave you to say to me now?

MORELL [overwhelmed] Is it possible! Well, theres more joy in heaven over one sinner that repenteth!— [Going to Burgess with an explosion of apologetic cordiality] My dear Burgess: how splendid of you! I most heartily beg your pardon for my hard thoughts. [Grasping his hand] And now, dont you feel the better for the change? Come! confess! youre happier. You look happier.

BURGESS [ruefully] Well, praps I do. I spose I must, since you notice it. At all events, I git my contrax assepted by the County Council. [Savagely] They dussent ave nothink to do with me unless I paid fair wages: curse em for a parcel o meddlin fools!

MORELL [dropping his hand, utterly discouraged] So that was why you raised the wages! [He sits down moodily].

BURGESS [*severely, in spreading, mounting tones*] Woy helse should I do it? What does it lead to but drink and huppishness in workin men? [*He seats himself magisterially in the easy chair*]. It's hall very well for you, James: it gits you hinto the papers and makes a great man of you; but you never think of the arm you do, puttin money into the pockets of workin men that they dunno ow to spend, and takin it from people that might be makin a good huse on it.

MORELL [*with a heavy sigh, speaking with cold politeness*] What is your business with me this morning? I shall not pretend to believe that you are here merely out of family sentiment.

BURGESS [*obstinately*] Yes I ham: just family sentiment and nothink helse.

MORELL [*with weary calm*] I dont believe you.

BURGESS [*rising threateningly*] Dont say that to me again, James Mavor Morell.

MORELL [*unmoved*] I'll say it just as often as may be necessary to convince you that it's true. I dont believe you.

BURGESS [*collapsing into an abyss of wounded feeling*] Oh, well, if youre detormined to be hunfriendly, I spose I'd better go. [*He moves reluctantly towards the door. Morell makes no sign. He lingers*]. I didnt hexpect to find a hunforgin spirit in you, James. [*Morell still not responding, he takes a few more reluctant steps doorwards. Then he comes back, whining*]. We huseter git on well enough, spite of our different hopinions. Woy are you so changed to me? I give you my word I come here in peeorr [pure] frenliness, not wishin to be hon bad terms with my hown daughrter's usban. Come, James: be a Kerischin, and shake ands. [*He puts his hand sentimentally on Morell's shoulder*].

MORELL [*looking up at him thoughtfully*] Look here, Burgess. Do you want to be as welcome here as you were before you lost that contract?

BURGESS. I do, James. I do—*h*onest.

MORELL. Then why dont you behave as you did then?

BURGESS [*cautiously removing his hand*] Ow d'y'mean?

MORELL. I'll tell you. You thought me a young fool then.

BURGESS [*coaxingly*] No I didnt, James. I—

MORELL [*cutting him short*] Yes, you did. And I thought you an old scoundrel.

BURGESS [*most vehemently deprecating this gross self-accusation on Morell's part*] No you didnt, James. Now you do yourself a hinjustice.

MORELL. Yes I did. Well, that did not prevent our getting on very well together. God made you what I call a scoundrel as He made me what you call a fool. [*The effect of this observation on Burgess is to remove the keystone of his moral arch. He becomes bodily weak, and, with his eyes fixed on Morell in a helpless stare, puts out his hand apprehensively to balance himself, as if the floor had suddenly sloped under him. Morell proceeds, in the same tone of quiet conviction*] It was not for me to quarrel with His handiwork in the one case more than in the other. So long as you come here honestly as a self-respecting, thorough, convinced scoundrel, justifying your scoundrelism and proud of it, you are welcome. But [*and now Morell's tone becomes formidable; and he rises and strikes the back of the chair for greater emphasis*] I wont have you here snivelling about being a model employer and a converted man when youre only an apostate with your coat turned for the sake of a County Council contract. [*He nods at him to enforce the point; then goes to the hearth-rug,*

[530]

*where he takes up a comfortably commanding position
with his back to the fire, and continues*] No: I like a man
to be true to himself, even in wickedness. Come now:
either take your hat and go; or else sit down and
give me a good scoundrelly reason for wanting to be
friends with me. [*Burgess, whose emotions have subsided sufficiently to be expressed by a dazed grin, is
relieved by this concrete proposition. He ponders it for
a moment, and then, slowly and very modestly, sits down
in the chair Morell has just left*]. Thats right. Now out
with it.

BURGESS [*chuckling in spite of himself*] Well, you orr
a queer bird, James, and no mistake. But [*almost
enthusiastically*] one carnt elp likin you: besides, as I
said afore, of course one dont take hall a clorgyman
says seriously, or the world couldnt go on. Could it
now? [*He composes himself for graver discourse, and,
turning his eyes on Morell, proceeds with dull seriousness*]
Well, I dont mind tellin you, since it's your wish we
should be free with one another, that I did think you
a bit of a fool once; but I'm beginnin to think that
praps I was be'ind the times a bit.

MORELL [*exultant*] Aha! Youre finding that out at
last, are you?

BURGESS [*portentously*] Yes: times 'as changed mor'n
I could a believed. Five yorr [year] ago, no sensible
man would a thought o takin hup with your hidears.
I hused to wonder you was let preach at all. Why, I
know a clorgyman what 'as bin kep hout of his job
for yorrs by the Bishop o London, although the pore
feller's not a bit more religious than you are. But
today, if hennyone was to horffer to bet me a thousan
poun that youll hend by bein a bishop yourself, I
dussent take the bet. [*Very impressively*] You and
your crew are gittin hinfluential: I can see that.

Theyll ave to give you somethink someday, if it's honly to stop your mouth. You ad the right instinc arter all, James: the line you took is the payin line in the long run for a man o your sort.

MORELL [*offering his hand with thorough decision*] Shake hands, Burgess. Now youre talking honestly. I dont think theyll make me a bishop; but if they do, I'll introduce you to the biggest jobbers I can get to come to my dinner parties.

BURGESS [*who has risen with a sheepish grin and accepted the hand of friendship*] You will ave your joke, James. Our quarrel's made up now, aint it?

A WOMAN'S VOICE. Say yes, James.

Startled, they turn quickly and find that Candida has just come in, and is looking at them with an amused maternal indulgence which is her characteristic expression. She is a woman of 33, well built, well nourished, likely, one guesses, to become matronly later on, but now quite at her best, with the double charm of youth and motherhood. Her ways are those of a woman who has found that she can always manage people by engaging their affection, and who does so frankly and instinctively without the smallest scruple. So far, she is like any other pretty woman who is just clever enough to make the most of her sexual attractions for trivially selfish ends; but Candida's serene brow, courageous eyes, and well set mouth and chin signify largeness of mind and dignity of character to ennoble her cunning in the affections. A wise-hearted observer, looking at her, would at once guess that whoever had placed the Virgin of the Assumption over her hearth did so because he fancied some spiritual resemblance between them, and yet would not suspect either her husband or herself of any such idea, or indeed of any concern with the art of Titian.

Just now she is in bonnet and mantle, carrying a

strapped rug with her umbrella stuck through it, a handbag, and a supply of illustrated papers.

MORELL [*shocked at his remissness*] Candida! Why— [*he looks at his watch, and is horrified to find it so late*]. My darling! [*Hurrying to her and seizing the rug strap, pouring forth his remorseful regrets all the time*] I intended to meet you at the train. I let the time slip. [*Flinging the rug on the sofa*] I was so engrossed by— [*returning to her*] —I forgot—oh! [*He embraces her with penitent emotion*].

BURGESS [*a little shamefaced and doubtful of his reception*] How orr you, Candy? [*She, still in Morell's arms, offers him her cheek, which he kisses*]. James and me is come to a nunnerstannin. A *h*onorable unnerstannin. Ain we, James?

MORELL [*impetuously*] Oh bother your understanding! youve kept me late for Candida. [*With compassionate fervor*] My poor love: how did you manage about the luggage? How—

CANDIDA [*stopping him and disengaging herself*] There! there! there! I wasnt alone. Eugene has been down with us; and we travelled together.

MORELL [*pleased*] Eugene!

CANDIDA. Yes: he's struggling with my luggage, poor boy. Go out, dear, at once; or he'll pay for the cab; and I dont want that. [*Morell hurries out. Candida puts down her handbag; then takes off her mantle and bonnet and puts them on the sofa with the rug, chatting meanwhile*]. Well, papa: how are you getting on at home?

BURGESS. The ouse aint worth livin in since you left it, Candy. I wish youd come round and give the gurl a talkin to. Who's this Eugene thats come with you?

CANDIDA. Oh, Eugene's one of James's discoveries. He found him sleeping on the Embankment last

June. Havnt you noticed our new picture [*pointing to the Virgin*]? He gave us that.

BURGESS [*incredulously*] Garn! D'you mean to tell me—your hown father!—that cab touts or such like, orf the Embankment, buys pictures like that? [*Severely*] Dont deceive me, Candy: it's a 'Igh Church picture; and James chose it hisself.

CANDIDA. Guess again. Eugene isnt a cab tout.

BURGESS. Then what is he? [*Sarcastically*] A nobleman, I spose.

CANDIDA [*nodding delightedly*] Yes. His uncle's a peer! A real live earl.

BURGESS [*not daring to believe such good news*] No!

CANDIDA. Yes. He had a seven day bill for £55 in his pocket when James found him on the Embankment. He thought he couldnt get any money for it until the seven days were up; and he was too shy to ask for credit. Oh, he's a dear boy! We are very fond of him.

BURGESS [*pretending to belittle the aristocracy, but with his eyes gleaming*] Hm! I thort you wouldnt git a hearl's nevvy visitin in Victawriar Pawrk unless he were a bit of a flat. [*Looking again at the picture*] Of course I dont old with that picture, Candy; but still it's a 'igh class fust rate work of ort: I can see that. Be sure you hintrodooce me to im, Candy. [*He looks at his watch anxiously*]. I can ony stay about two minutes.

Morell comes back with Eugene, whom Burgess contemplates moist-eyed with enthusiasm. He is a strange, shy youth of eighteen, slight, effeminate, with a delicate childish voice, and a hunted tormented expression and shrinking manner that shew the painful sensitiveness of very swift and acute apprehensiveness in youth, before the character has grown to its full strength.

Miserably irresolute, he does not know where to stand or what to do. He is afraid of Burgess, and would run away into solitude if he dared; but the very intensity with which he feels a perfectly commonplace position comes from excessive nervous force; and his nostrils, mouth, and eyes betray a fiercely petulant wilfulness, as to the bent of which his brow, already lined with pity, is reassuring. He is so uncommon as to be almost unearthly; and to prosaic people there is something noxious in this unearthliness, just as to poetic people there is something angelic in it. His dress is anarchic. He wears an old blue serge jacket, unbuttoned, over a woollen lawn tennis shirt, with a silk handkerchief for a cravat, trousers matching the jacket, and brown canvas shoes. In these garments he has apparently lain in the heather and waded through the waters; and there is no evidence of his having ever brushed them.

As he catches sight of a stranger on entering, he stops, and edges along the wall on the opposite side of the room.

MORELL [*as he enters*] Come along: you can spare us quarter of an hour at all events. This is my father-in-law. Mr Burgess— Mr Marchbanks.

MARCHBANKS [*nervously backing against the bookcase*] Glad to meet you, sir.

BURGESS [*crossing to him with great heartiness, whilst Morell joins Candida at the fire*] Glad to meet you, I'm shore. Mr Morchbanks [*Forcing him to shake hands*] Ow do you find yoreself this weather? Ope you aint lettin James put no foolish ideas into your ed?

MARCHBANKS. Foolish ideas? Oh, you mean Socialism? No.

BURGESS. Thats right. [*Again looking at his watch*] Well, I must go now: theres no elp for it. Yore not comin my way, orr you, Mr Morchbanks?

MARCHBANKS. Which way is that?

BURGESS. Victawriar Pawrk Station. Theres a city train at 12.25.

MORELL. Nonsense. Eugene will stay to lunch with us, I expect.

MARCHBANKS [*anxiously excusing himself*] No—I—I

BURGESS. Well, well, I shornt press you: I bet youd rather lunch with Candy. Some night, I ope, youll come and dine with me at my club, the Freeman Founders in Nortn Folgit. Come: say you will!

MARCHBANKS. Thank you, Mr Burgess. Where is Norton Folgate? Down in Surrey, isnt it?

Burgess, inexpressibly tickled, begins to splutter with laughter.

CANDIDA [*coming to the rescue*] Youll lose your train, papa, if you dont go at once. Come back in the afternoon and tell Mr Marchbanks where to find the club.

BURGESS [*roaring with glee*] Down in Surrey! Har, har! thats not a bad one. Well, I never met a man as didnt know Nortn Folgit afore. [*Abashed at his own noisiness*] Goodbye, Mr Morchbanks: I know yore too ighbred to take my pleasantry in bad part. [*He again offers his hand*].

MARCHBANKS [*taking it with a nervous jerk*] Not at all.

BURGESS. Bye, bye, Candy. I'll look in again later on. So long, James.

MORELL. Must you go?

BURGESS. Dont stir. [*He goes out with unabated heartiness*].

MORELL. Oh, I'll see you off. [*He follows him*].

Eugene stares after them apprehensively, holding his breath until Burgess disappears.

CANDIDA [*laughing*] Well, Eugene? [*He turns with a start, and comes eagerly towards her, but stops ir-*

resolutely as he meets her amused look]. What do you think of my father?

MARCHBANKS. I—I hardly know him yet. He seems to be a very nice old gentleman.

CANDIDA [*with gentle irony*] And youll go to the Freeman Founders to dine with him, wont you?

MARCHBANKS [*miserably, taking it quite seriously*] Yes, if it will please you.

CANDIDA [*touched*] Do you know, you are a very nice boy, Eugene, with all your queerness. If you had laughed at my father I shouldnt have minded; but I like you ever so much better for being nice to him.

MARCHBANKS. Ought I to have laughed? I noticed that he said something funny; but I am so ill at ease with strangers; and I never can see a joke. I'm very sorry. [*He sits down on the sofa, his elbows on his knees and his temples between his fists, with an expression of hopeless suffering*].

CANDIDA [*bustling him goodnaturedly*] Oh come! You great baby, you! You are worse than usual this morning. Why were you so melancholy as we came along in the cab?

MARCHBANKS. Oh, that was nothing. I was wondering how much I ought to give the cabman. I know it's utterly silly; but you dont know how dreadful such things are to me—how I shrink from having to deal with strange people. [*Quickly and reassuringly*] But it's all right. He beamed all over and touched his hat when Morell gave him two shillings. I was on the point of offering him ten.

Morell comes back with a few letters and newspapers which have come by the midday post.

CANDIDA. Oh, James dear, he was going to give the cabman ten shillings! ten shillings for a three minutes drive! Oh dear!

MORELL [*at the table, glancing through the letters*] Never mind her, Marchbanks. The overpaying instinct is a generous one: better than the underpaying instinct, and not so common.

MARCHBANKS [*relapsing into dejection*] No: cowardice, incompetence. Mrs Morell's quite right.

CANDIDA. Of course she is. [*She takes up her handbag*]. And now I must leave you to James for the present. I suppose you are too much of a poet to know the state a woman finds her house in when she's been away for three weeks. Give me my rug. [*Eugene takes the strapped rug from the couch, and gives it to her. She takes it in her left hand, having the bag in her right*]. Now hang my cloak across my arm. [*He obeys*]. Now my hat. [*He puts it into the hand which has the bag*]. Now open the door for me. [*He hurries before her and opens the door*]. Thanks. [*She goes out; and Marchbanks shuts the door*].

MORELL [*still busy at the table*] Youll stay to lunch, Marchbanks, of course.

MARCHBANKS [*scared*] I mustnt. [*He glances quickly at Morell, but at once avoids his frank look, and adds, with obvious disingenuousness*] I mean I cant.

MORELL. You mean you wont.

MARCHBANKS [*earnestly*] No: I should like to, indeed. Thank you very much. But—but—

MORELL. But—but—but—but—Bosh! If youd like to stay, stay. If youre shy, go and take a turn in the park and write poetry until half past one; and then come in and have a good feed.

MARCHBANKS. Thank you, I should like that very much. But I really mustnt. The truth is, Mrs Morell told me not to. She said she didnt think youd ask me to stay to lunch, but that I was to remember, if you did, that you didnt really want me to. [*Plain-*

tively] She said I'd understand; but I dont. Please dont tell her I told you.

MORELL [*drolly*] Oh, is that all? Wont my suggestion that you should take a turn in the park meet the difficulty?

MARCHBANKS. How?

MORELL [*exploding good-humoredly*] Why, you duffer —[*But this boisterousness jars himself as well as Eugene. He checks himself*]. No: I wont put it in that way. [*He comes to Eugene with affectionate seriousness*]. My dear lad: in a happy marriage like ours, there is something very sacred in the return of the wife to her home. [*Marchbanks looks quickly at him, half anticipating his meaning*]. An old friend or a truly noble and sympathetic soul is not in the way on such occasions; but a chance visitor is. [*The hunted horrorstricken expression comes out with sudden vividness in Eugene's face as he understands. Morell, occupied with his own thoughts, goes on without noticing this*]. Candida thought I would rather not have you here; but she was wrong. I'm very fond of you, my boy; and I should like you to see for yourself what a happy thing it is to be married as I am.

MARCHBANKS. Happy! Your marriage! You think that! You believe that!

MORELL [*buoyantly*] I know it, my lad. Larochefoucauld said that there are convenient marriages but no delightful ones. You dont know the comfort of seeing through and through a thundering liar and rotten cynic like that fellow. Ha! ha! Now, off with you to the park, and write your poem. Half past one, sharp, mind: we never wait for anybody.

MARCHBANKS [*wildly*] No: stop: you shant. I'll force it into the light.

MORELL [*puzzled*] Eh? Force what?

MARCHBANKS. I must speak to you. There is something that must be settled between us.

MORELL [*with a whimsical glance at his watch*] Now?

MARCHBANKS [*passionately*] Now. Before you leave this room. [*He retreats a few steps, and stands as if to bar Morell's way to the door*].

MORELL [*without moving, and gravely, perceiving now that there is something serious the matter*] I'm not going to leave it, my dear boy: I thought you were. [*Eugene, baffled by his firm tone, turns his back on him, writhing with anger. Morell goes to him and puts his hand on his shoulder strongly and kindly, disregarding his attempt to shake it off*]. Come: sit down quietly; and tell me what it is. And remember: we are friends, and need not fear that either of us will be anything but patient and kind to the other, whatever we may have to say.

MARCHBANKS [*twisting himself round on him*] Oh, I am not forgetting myself: I am only [*covering his face desperately with his hands*] full of horror. [*Then, dropping his hands, and thrusting his face forward fiercely at Morell, he goes on threateningly*] You shall see whether this is a time for patience and kindness. [*Morell, firm as a rock, looks indulgently at him*]. Dont look at me in that self-complacent way. You think yourself stronger than I am; but I shall stagger you if you have a heart in your breast.

MORELL [*powerfully confident*] Stagger me, my boy. Out with it.

MARCHBANKS. First—

MORELL. First?

MARCHBANKS. I love your wife.

Morell recoils, and, after staring at him for a moment in utter amazement, bursts into uncontrollable laughter. Eugene is taken aback, but not disconcerted; and he soon becomes indignant and contemptuous.

MORELL [*sitting down to have his laugh out*] Why, my dear child, of course you do. Everybody loves her: they cant help it. I like it. But [*looking up jocosely at him*] I say, Eugene: do you think yours is a case to be talked about? Youre under twenty: she's over thirty. Doesnt it look rather too like a case of calf love?

MARCHBANKS [*vehemently*] You dare say that of her! You think that way of the love she inspires! It is an insult to her!

MORELL [*rising quickly, in an altered tone*] To her! Eugene: take care. I have been patient. I hope to remain patient. But there are some things I wont allow. Dont force me to shew you the indulgence I should shew to a child. Be a man.

MARCHBANKS [*with a gesture as if sweeping something behind him*] Oh, let us put aside all that cant. It horrifies me when I think of the doses of it she has had to endure in all the weary years during which you have selfishly and blindly sacrificed her to minister to your self-sufficiency: you! [*turning on him*] who have not one thought—one sense—in common with her.

MORELL [*philosophically*] She seems to bear it pretty well. [*Looking him straight in the face*] Eugene, my boy: you are making a fool of yourself: a very great fool of yourself. Theres a piece of wholesome plain speaking for you. [*He knocks in the lesson with a nod in his old way, and posts himself on the hearthrug, holding his hands behind him to warm them*].

MARCHBANKS. Oh, do you think I dont know all that? Do you think that the things people make fools of themselves about are any less real and true than the things they behave sensibly about? [*Morell's gaze wavers for the first time. He forgets to warm his hands, and stands listening, startled and thoughtful*]. They are more true: they are the only things that are true. You are very calm and sensible and moderate with me because you can see that I am a fool about your wife; just as no doubt that old man who was here just now is very wise over your Socialism, because he sees that you are a fool about it. [*Morell's perplexity deepens markedly. Eugene follows up his advantage, plying him fiercely with questions*]. Does that prove you wrong? Does your complacent superiority to me prove that *I* am wrong?

MORELL. Marchbanks: some devil is putting these words into your mouth. It is easy—terribly easy—to shake a man's faith in himself. To take advantage of that to break a man's spirit is devil's work. Take care of what you are doing. Take care.

MARCHBANKS [*ruthlessly*] I know. I'm doing it on purpose. I told you I should stagger you.

They confront one another threateningly for a moment. Then Morell recovers his dignity.

MORELL [*with noble tenderness*] Eugene: listen to me. Some day, I hope and trust, you will be a happy man like me. [*Eugene chafes intolerantly, repudiating the worth of his happiness. Morell, deeply insulted, controls himself with fine forbearance, and continues steadily with great artistic beauty of delivery*] You will be married; and you will be working with all your might and valor to make every spot on earth as happy as your own home. You will be one of the makers of the Kingdom of Heaven on earth; and—who knows?—you may be a master builder where I am only a humble journeyman; for dont think, my boy, that I cannot see in you, young as you are, promise of higher powers than I can ever pretend to. I well know that it is in the poet that the holy spirit of man—the god within him—is most godlike. It should make you tremble to think

[542]

of that—to think that the heavy burthen and great gift of a poet may be laid upon you.

MARCHBANKS [*unimpressed and remorseless, his boyish crudity of assertion telling sharply against Morell's oratory*] It does not make me tremble. It is the want of it in others that makes me tremble.

MORELL [*redoubling his force of style under the stimulus of his genuine feeling and Eugene's obduracy*] Then help to kindle it in them—in me—not to extinguish it. In the future, when you are as happy as I am, I will be your true brother in the faith. I will help you to believe that God has given us a world that nothing but our own folly keeps from being a paradise. I will help you to believe that every stroke of your work is sowing happiness for the great harvest that all—even the humblest—shall one day reap. And last, but trust me, not least, I will help you to believe that your wife loves you and is happy in her home. We need such help, Marchbanks: we need it greatly and always. There are so many things to make us doubt, if once we let our understanding be troubled. Even at home, we sit as if in camp, encompassed by a hostile army of doubts. Will you play the traitor and let them in on me?

MARCHBANKS [*looking round wildly*] Is it like this for her here always? A woman, with a great soul, craving for reality, truth, freedom; and being fed on metaphors, sermons, stale perorations, mere rhetoric. Do you think a woman's soul can live on your talent for preaching?

MORELL [*stung*] Marchbanks: you make it hard for me to control myself. My talent is like yours insofar as it has any real worth at all. It is the gift of finding words for divine truth.

MARCHBANKS [*impetuously*] It's the gift of the gab,

nothing more and nothing less. What has your knack of fine talking to do with the truth, any more than playing the organ has? Ive never been in your church; but Ive been to your political meetings; and Ive seen you do whats called rousing the meeting to enthusiasm: that is, you excited them until they behaved exactly as if they were drunk. And their wives looked on and saw what fools they were. Oh, it's an old story: youll find it in the Bible. I imagine King David, in his fits of enthusiasm, was very like you. [*Stabbing him with the words*] "But his wife despised him in her heart."

MORELL [*wrathfully*] Leave my house. Do you hear? [*He advances on him threateningly*].

MARCHBANKS [*shrinking back against the couch*] Let me alone. Dont touch me. [*Morell grasps him powerfully by the lappell of his coat: he cowers down on the sofa and screams passionately*] Stop, Morell: if you strike me, I'll kill myself: I wont bear it. [*Almost in hysterics*] Let me go. Take your hand away.

MORELL [*with slow emphatic scorn*] You little snivelling cowardly whelp. [*He releases him*]. Go, before you frighten yourself into a fit.

MARCHBANKS [*on the sofa, gasping, but relieved by the withdrawal of Morell's hand*] I'm not afraid of you: it's you who are afraid of me.

MORELL [*quietly, as he stands over him*] It looks like it, doesnt it?

MARCHBANKS [*with petulant vehemence*] Yes, it does. [*Morell turns away contemptuously. Eugene scrambles to his feet and follows him*]. You think because I shrink from being brutally handled—because [*with tears in his voice*] I can do nothing but cry with rage when I am met with violence—because I cant lift a heavy trunk down from the top of a cab like you—because I cant fight you for your wife as a drunken navvy would:

all that makes you think I'm afraid of you. But youre wrong. If I havnt got what you call British pluck, I havnt British cowardice either: I'm not afraid of a clergyman's ideas. I'll fight your ideas. I'll rescue her from her slavery to them. I'll pit my own ideas against them. You are driving me out of the house because you darent let her choose between your ideas and mine. You are afraid to let me see her again. [*Morell, angered, turns suddenly on him. He flies to the door in involuntary dread*]. Let me alone, I say. I'm going.

MORELL [*with cold scorn*] Wait a moment: I am not going to touch you: dont be afraid. When my wife comes back she will want to know why you have gone. And when she finds that you are never going to cross our threshold again, she will want to have that explained too. Now I dont wish to distress her by telling her that you have behaved like a blackguard.

MARCHBANKS [*coming back with renewed vehemence*] You shall. You must. If you give any explanation but the true one, you are a liar and a coward. Tell her what I said; and how you were strong and manly, and shook me as a terrier shakes a rat; and how I shrank and was terrified; and how you called me a snivelling little whelp and put me out of the house. If you dont tell her, I will: I'll write it to her.

MORELL [*puzzled*] Why do you want her to know this?

MARCHBANKS [*with lyric rapture*] Because she will understand me, and know that I understand her. If you keep back one word of it from her—if you are not ready to lay the truth at her feet as I am—then you will know to the end of your days that she really belongs to me and not to you. Goodbye. [*Going*].

MORELL [*terribly disquieted*] Stop: I will not tell her.

MARCHBANKS [*turning near the door*] Either the truth or a lie you must tell her, if I go.

MORELL [*temporizing*] Marchbanks: it is sometimes justifiable—

MARCHBANKS [*cutting him short*] I know: to lie. It will be useless. Goodbye, Mr Clergyman.

As he turns to the door, it opens and Candida enters in her housekeeping dress.

CANDIDA. Are you going, Eugene? [*Looking more observantly at him*] Well, dear me, just look at you, going out into the street in that state! You are a poet, certainly. Look at him, James! [*She takes him by the coat, and brings him forward, shewing him to Morell*]. Look at his collar! look at his tie! look at his hair! One would think somebody had been throttling you. [*Eugene instinctively tries to look round at Morell; but she pulls him back*]. Here! Stand still. [*She buttons his collar; ties his neckerchief in a bow; and arranges his hair*]. There! Now you look so nice that I think youd better stay to lunch after all, though I told you you musnt. It will be ready in half an hour. [*She puts a final touch to the bow. He kisses her hand*]. Dont be silly.

MARCHBANKS. I want to stay, of course; unless the reverend gentleman your husband has anything to advance to the contrary.

CANDIDA. Shall he stay, James, if he promises to be a good boy and help me to lay the table?

MORELL [*shortly*] Oh yes, certainly: he had better. [*He goes to the table and pretends to busy himself with his papers there*].

MARCHBANKS [*offering his arm to Candida*] Come and lay the table [*She takes it. They go to the door together. As they pass out he adds*] I am the happiest of mortals.

MORELL. So was I—an hour ago.

[ACT II]

*The same day later in the afternoon. The same room.
The chair for visitors has been replaced at the table.
Marchbanks, alone and idle, is trying to find out how
the typewriter works. Hearing someone at the door,
he steals guiltily away to the window and pretends to be
absorbed in the view. Miss Garnett, carrying the note-
book in which she takes down Morell's letters in shorthand from his dictation, sits down at the typewriter and
sets to work transcribing them, much too busy to notice
Eugene. When she begins the second line she stops and
stares at the machine. Something wrong evidently.*

PROSERPINE. Bother! Youve been meddling with my
typewriter, Mr Marchbanks; and theres not the least
use in your trying to look as if you hadnt.

MARCHBANKS [*timidly*] I'm very sorry, Miss Garnett.
I only tried to make it write. [*Plaintively*] But it
wouldnt.

PROSERPINE. Well, youve altered the spacing.

MARCHBANKS [*earnestly*] I assure you I didnt. I
didnt indeed. I only turned a little wheel. It gave a
sort of click.

PROSERPINE. Oh, now I understand. [*She restores
the spacing, talking volubly all the time*]. I suppose you
thought it was a sort of barrel-organ. Nothing to do
but turn the handle, and it would write a beautiful
love letter for you straight off, eh?

MARCHBANKS [*seriously*] I suppose a machine

[547]

could be made to write love letters. Theyre all the same, arnt they?

PROSERPINE [*somewhat indignantly: any such discussion, except by way of pleasantry, being outside her code of manners*] How do I know? Why do you ask me?

MARCHBANKS. I beg your pardon. I thought clever people—people who can do business and write letters and that sort of thing—always had to have love affairs to keep them from going mad.

PROSERPINE [*rising, outraged*] Mr Marchbanks! [*She looks severely at him, and marches majestically to the bookcase*].

MARCHBANKS [*approaching her humbly*] I hope I havnt offended you. Perhaps I shouldnt have alluded to your love affairs.

PROSERPINE [*plucking a blue book from the shelf and turning sharply on him*] I havnt any love affairs. How dare you say such a thing? The idea! [*She tucks the book under her arm, and is flouncing back to her machine when he addresses her with awakened interest and sympathy*].

MARCHBANKS. Really! Oh, then you are shy, like me.

PROSERPINE. Certainly I am not shy. What do you mean?

MARCHBANKS [*secretly*] You must be: that is the reason there are so few love affairs in the world. We all go about longing for love: it is the first need of our natures, the first prayer of our hearts; but we dare not utter our longing: we are too shy. [*Very earnestly*] Oh, Miss Garnett, what would you not give to be without fear, without shame—

PROSERPINE [*scandalized*] Well, upon my word!

MARCHBANKS [*with petulant impatience*] Ah, dont say those stupid things to me: they dont deceive me:

[548]

what use are they? Why are you afraid to be your real self with me? I am just like you.

PROSERPINE. Like me! Pray are you flattering me or flattering yourself? I dont feel quite sure which. [*She again tries to get back to her work*].

MARCHBANKS [*stopping her mysteriously*] Hush! I go about in search of love; and I find it in unmeasured stores in the bosoms of others. But when I try to ask for it, this horrible shyness strangles me; and I stand dumb, or worse than dumb, saying meaningless things: foolish lies. And I see the affection I am longing for given to dogs and cats and pet birds, because they come and ask for it. [*Almost whispering*] It must be asked for: it is like a ghost: it cannot speak unless it is first spoken to. [*At his usual pitch, but with deep melancholy*] All the love in the world is longing to speak; only it dare not, because it is shy! shy! shy! That is the world's tragedy. [*With a deep sigh he sits in the visitors' chair and buries his face in his hands*].

PROSERPINE [*amazed, but keeping her wits about her: her point of honor in encounters with strange young men*] Wicked people get over that shyness occasionally, dont they?

MARCHBANKS [*scrambling up almost fiercely*] Wicked people means people who have no love: therefore they have no shame. They have the power to ask love because they dont need it: they have the power to offer it because they have none to give. [*He collapses into his seat, and adds, mournfully*] But we, who have love, and long to mingle it with the love of others: we cannot utter a word. [*Timidly*] You find that, dont you?

PROSERPINE. Look here: if you dont stop talking like this, I'll leave the room, Mr Marchbanks: I really will. It's not proper.

[549]

She resumes her seat at the typewriter, opening the blue book and preparing to copy a passage from it.

MARCHBANKS [*hopelessly*] Nothing thats worth saying is proper. [*He rises, and wanders about the room in his lost way*]. I cant understand you, Miss Garnett. What am I to talk about?

PROSERPINE [*snubbing him*] Talk about indifferent things. Talk about the weather.

MARCHBANKS. Would you talk about indifferent things if a child were by, crying bitterly with hunger?

PROSERPINE. I suppose not.

MARCHBANKS. Well: *I* cant talk about indifferent things with my heart crying out bitterly in its hunger.

PROSERPINE. Then hold your tongue.

MARCHBANKS. Yes: that is what it always comes to. We hold our tongues. Does that stop the cry of your heart? for it does cry: doesnt it? It must, if you have a heart.

PROSERPINE [*suddenly rising with her hand pressed on her heart*] Oh, it's no use trying to work while you talk like that. [*She leaves her little table and sits on the sofa. Her feelings are keenly stirred*]. It's no business of yours whether my heart cried or not; but I have a mind to tell you, for all that.

MARCHBANKS. You neednt. I know already that it must.

PROSERPINE. But mind! if you ever say I said so, I'll deny it.

MARCHBANKS [*compassionately*] Yes, I know. And so you havnt the courage to tell him?

PROSERPINE [*bouncing up*] Him! Who?

MARCHBANKS. Whoever he is. The man you love. It might be anybody. The curate, Mr. Mill, perhaps.

PROSERPINE [*with disdain*] Mr Mill!!! A fine man to break my heart about, indeed! I'd rather have you than Mr Mill.

MARCHBANKS [*recoiling*] No, really: I'm very sorry; but you mustnt think of that. I—

PROSERPINE [*testily, going to the fire-place and standing at it with her back to him*] Oh, dont be frightened: it's not you. It's not any one particular person.

MARCHBANKS. I know. You feel that you could love anybody that offered—

PROSERPINE [*turning, exasperated*] Anybody that offered! No, I do not. What do you take me for?

MARCHBANKS [*discouraged*] No use. You wont make me real answers: only those things that everybody says. [*He strays to the sofa and sits down disconsolately*].

PROSERPINE [*nettled at what she takes to be a disparagement of her manners by an aristocrat*] Oh well, if you want original conversation, youd better go and talk to yourself.

MARCHBANKS. That is what all poets do: they talk to themselves out loud; and the world overhears them. But it's horribly lonely not to hear someone else talk sometimes.

PROSERPINE. Wait until Mr Morell comes. He'll talk to you. [*Marchbanks shudders*]. Oh, you neednt make wry faces over him: he can talk better than you. [*With temper*] He'd talk your little head off. [*She is going back angrily to her place, when he, suddenly, enlightened, springs up and stops her*].

MARCHBANKS. Ah! I understand now.

PROSERPINE [*reddening*] What do you understand?

MARCHBANKS. Your secret. Tell me: is it really and truly possible for a woman to love him?

PROSERPINE [*as if this were beyond all bounds*] Well!!

MARCHBANKS [*passionately*] No: answer me. I want

to know: I must know. *I* cant understand it. I can see nothing in him but words, pious resolutions, what people call goodness. You cant love that.

PROSERPINE [*attempting to snub him by an air of cool propriety*] I simply dont know what youre talking about. I dont understand you.

MARCHBANKS [*vehemently*] You do. You lie.

PROSERPINE. Oh!

MARCHBANKS. You do understand; and you know. [*Determined to have an answer*] Is it possible for a woman to love him?

PROSERPINE [*looking him straight in the face*] Yes. [*He covers his face with his hands*]. Whatever is the matter with you! [*He takes down his hands. Frightened at the tragic mask presented to her, she hurries past him at the utmost possible distance, keeping her eyes on his face until he turns from her and goes to the child's chair beside the hearth, where he sits in the deepest dejection. As she approaches the door, it opens and Burgess enters. Seeing him, she ejaculates*] Praise heaven! here's somebody [*and feels safe enough to resume her place at the table. She puts a fresh sheet of paper into the typewriter as Burgess crosses to Eugene*].

BURGESS [*bent on taking care of the distinguished visitor*] Well: so this is the way they leave you to yoreself, Mr Morchbanks. Ive come to keep you company. [*Marchbanks looks up at him in consternation, which is quite lost on him*]. James is receivin a deppitation in the dinin room; and Candy is hupstairs heducating of a young stitcher gurl she's hinterested in. [*Condolingly*] You must find it lonesome here with no one but the typist to talk to. [*He pulls round the easy chair, and sits down*].

PROSERPINE [*highly incensed*] He'll be all right now that he has the advantage of your polished conversation: thats one comfort, anyhow. [*She begins to typewrite with clattering asperity*].

BURGESS [*amazed at her audacity*] Hi was not addressin myself to you, young woman, that I'm awerr of.

PROSERPINE. Did you ever see worse manners, Mr Marchbanks?

BURGESS [*with pompous severity*] Mr Morchbanks is a gentleman, and knows his place, which is more than some people do.

PROSERPINE [*fretfully*] It's well you and I are not ladies and gentlemen: I'd talk to you pretty straight if Mr Marchbanks wasnt here. [*She pulls the letter out of the machine so crossly that it tears*]. There! now I've spoiled this letter! have to be done all over again! Oh, I cant contain myself: silly old fathead!

BURGESS [*rising, breathless with indignation*] Ho! I'm a silly ole fat'ead, am I? Ho, indeed [*gasping*]! Hall right, my gurl! Hall right. You just wait till I tell that to yore hemployer. Youll see. I'll teach you: see if I dont.

PROSERPINE [*conscious of having gone too far*] I—

BURGESS [*cutting her short*] No: youve done it now. No huse a-talkin to me. I'll let you know who I am. [*Proserpine shifts her paper carriage with a defiant bang, and disdainfully goes on with her work*]. Dont you take no notice of her, Mr Morchbanks. She's beneath it. [*He loftily sits down again*].

MARCHBANKS [*miserably nervous and disconcerted*] Hadnt we better change the subject? I—I dont think Miss Garnett meant anything.

PROSERPINE [*with intense conviction*] Oh, didnt I though, just!

BURGESS. I wouldnt demean myself to take notice on her.

An electric bell rings twice.

PROSERPINE [*gathering up her note-book and papers*] Thats for me. [*She hurries out*].

BURGESS [*calling after her*] Oh, we can spare you. [*Somewhat relieved by the triumph of having the last word, and yet half inclined to try to improve on it, he looks after her for a moment; then subsides into his seat by Eugene, and addresses him very confidentially*]. Now we're alone, Mr Morchbanks, let me give you a friendly int that I wouldnt give to heverybody. Ow long ave you known my son-in-law James ere?

MARCHBANKS. I dont know. I never can remember dates. A few months, perhaps.

BURGESS. Ever notice hennythink queer about him?

MARCHBANKS. I dont think so.

BURGESS [*impressively*] No more you wouldnt. Thats the danger on it. Well, he's mad.

MARCHBANKS. Mad!

BURGESS. Mad as a Morch 'are. You take notice on him and youll see.

MARCHBANKS [*uneasily*] But surely that is only because his opinions—

BURGESS [*touching him on the knee with his forefinger, and pressing it to hold his attention*] Thats the same what I hused to think, Mr Morchbanks. Hi thought long enough that it was ony his opinions; though, mind you, hopinions becomes vurry serious things when people takes to hactin on em as e does. But thats not what I go on. [*He looks round to make sure that they are alone, and bends over to Eugene's ear*]. What do you think he sez to me this morning in this very room?

MARCHBANKS. What?

BURGESS. He sez to me—this is as sure as we're settin here now—he sez "I'm a fool," he sez; "and

[554]

yore a scounderl." Me a scounderl, mind you! And then shook ands with me on it, as if it was to my credit! Do you mean to tell me as that man's sane?

MORELL [*outside, calling to Proserpine as he opens the door*] Get all their names and addresses, Miss Garnett.

PROSERPINE [*in the distance*] Yes, Mr Morell.

Morell comes in, with the deputation's documents in his hands.

BURGESS [*aside to Marchbanks*] Yorr he is. Just you keep your heye on im and see. [*Rising momentously*] I'm sorry, James, to ave to make a complaint to you. I dont want to do it; but I feel I oughter, as a matter o right and dooty.

MORELL. Whats the matter?

BURGESS. Mr Morchbanks will bear me hout: he was a witness. [*Very solemnly*] Yore young woman so far forgot herself as to call me a silly ole fat'ead.

MORELL [*with tremendous heartiness*] Oh, now, isnt that exactly like Prossy? She's so frank: she cant contain herself! Poor Prossy! Ha! ha!

BURGESS [*trembling with rage*] And do you hexpec me to put up with it from the like of er?

MORELL. Pooh, nonsense! you cant take any notice of it. Never mind. [*He goes to the cellaret and puts the papers into one of the drawers*].

BURGESS. Oh, Hi dont mind. Hi'm above it. But is it right? thats what I want to know. Is it right?

MORELL. Thats a question for the Church, not for the laity. Has it done you any harm? thats the question for you, eh? Of course it hasnt. Think no more of it. [*He dismisses the subject by going to his place at the table and setting to work at his correspondence*].

BURGESS [*aside to Marchbanks*] What did I tell you? Mad as a atter. [*He goes to the table and asks, with the sickly civility of a hungry man*] When's dinner, James?

MORELL. Not for a couple of hours yet.

BURGESS [*with plaintive resignation*] Gimme a nice book to read over the fire, will you, James: thur's a good chap.

MORELL. What sort of book? A good one?

BURGESS [*with almost a yell of remonstrance*] Nah-oo! Summat pleasant, just to pass the time. [*Morell takes an illustrated paper from the table and offers it. He accepts it humbly*]. Thank yer, James. [*He goes back to the big chair at the fire, and sits there at his ease, reading*].

MORELL [*as he writes*] Candida will come to entertain you presently. She has got rid of her pupil. She is filling the lamps.

MARCHBANKS [*starting up in the wildest consternation*] But that will soil her hands. I cant bear that, Morell: it's a shame. I'll go and fill them. [*He makes for the door*].

MORELL. Youd better not. [*Marchbanks stops irresolutely*]. She'd only set you to clean my boots, to save me the trouble of doing it myself in the morning.

BURGESS [*with grave disapproval*] Dont you keep a servant now, James?

MORELL. Yes; but she isnt a slave; and the house looks as if I kept three. That means that everyone has to lend a hand. It's not a bad plan: Prossy and I can talk business after breakfast while we're washing up. Washing up's no trouble when there are two people to do it.

MARCHBANKS [*tormentedly*] Do you think every woman is as coarse-grained as Miss Garnett?

BURGESS [*emphatically*] Thats quite right, Mr Morchbanks: thats quite right. She is corse-grained.

MORELL [*quietly and significantly*] Marchbanks!

MARCHBANKS. Yes?

MORELL. How many servants does your father keep?

MARCHBANKS [*pettishly*] Oh, I dont know. [*He moves to the sofa, as if to get as far as possible from Morell's questioning, and sits down in great agony of spirit, thinking of the paraffin*].

MORELL [*very gravely*] So many that you dont know! [*More aggressively*] When theres anything coarse-grained to be done, you just ring the bell and throw it on to somebody else, eh?

MARCHBANKS. Oh, dont torture me. You dont even ring the bell. But your wife's beautiful fingers are dabbling in paraffin oil while you sit here comfortably preaching about it: everlasting preaching! preaching! words! words! words!

BURGESS [*intensely appreciating this retort*] Har, har! Devil a better! [*Radiantly*] Ad you there, James, straight.

Candida comes in, well aproned, with a reading lamp trimmed, filled, and ready for lighting. She places it on the table near Morell, ready for use.

CANDIDA [*brushing her finger tips together with a slight twitch of her nose*] If you stay with us, Eugene, I think I will hand over the lamps to you.

MARCHBANKS. I will stay on condition that you hand over all the rough work to me.

CANDIDA. Thats very gallant; but I think I should like to see how you do it first. [*Turning to Morell*] James: youve not been looking after the house properly.

MORELL. What have I done—or not done—my love?

CANDIDA [*with serious vexation*] My own particular pet scrubbing brush has been used for blackleading. [*A heart-breaking wail bursts from Marchbanks. Burgess looks round, amazed. Candida hurries to the sofa.*] Whats the matter? Are you ill, Eugene?

MARCHBANKS. No: not ill. Only horror! horror! horror! [*He bows his head on his hands*].

BURGESS [*shocked*] What! Got the orrors, Mr Morchbanks! Oh, thats bad, at your age, You must leave it off grajally.

CANDIDA [*reassured*] Nonsense, papa! It's only poetic horror, isnt it, Eugene [*petting him*]?

BURGESS [*abashed*] Oh, poetic orror, is it? I beg your pordon, I'm shore. [*He turns to the fire again, deprecating his hasty conclusion*].

CANDIDA. What is it, Eugene? the scrubbing brush? [*He shudders*] Well, there! never mind. [*She sits down beside him*]. Wouldnt you like to present me with a nice new one, with an ivory back inlaid with mother-of-pearl?

MARCHBANKS [*softly and musically, but sadly and longingly*] No, not a scrubbing brush, but a boat: a tiny shallop to sail away in, far from the world, where the marble floors are washed by the rain and dried by the sun; where the south wind dusts the beautiful green and purple carpets. Or a chariot! to carry us up into the sky, where the lamps are stars, and dont need to be filled with paraffin oil every day.

MORELL [*harshly*] And where there is nothing to do but to be idle, selfish and useless.

CANDIDA [*jarred*] Oh, James! how could you spoil it all?

MARCHBANKS [*firing up*] Yes, to be idle, selfish, and useless: that is, to be beautiful and free and happy: hasnt every man desired that with all his soul for the woman he loves? Thats my ideal: whats yours, and that of all the dreadful people who live in these hideous rows of houses? Sermons and scrubbing brushes! With you to preach the sermon and your wife to scrub.

CANDIDA [*quaintly*] He cleans the boots, Eugene. You will have to clean them to-morrow for saying that about him.

MARCHBANKS. Oh, dont talk about boots! Your feet should be beautiful on the mountains.

CANDIDA. My feet would not be beautiful on the Hackney Road without boots.

BURGESS [*scandalized*] Come, Candy! dont be vulgar. Mr Morchbanks aint accustomed to it. Youre givin him the orrors again. I mean the poetic ones.

Morell is silent. Apparently he is busy with his letters: really he is puzzling with misgiving over his new and alarming experience that the surer he is of his moral thrusts, the more swiftly and effectively Eugene parries them. To find himself beginning to fear a man whom he does not respect afflicts him bitterly.

Miss Garnett comes in with a telegram.

PROSERPINE [*handing the telegram to Morell*] Reply paid. The boy's waiting. [*To Candida, coming back to her machine and sitting down*] Maria is ready for you now in the kitchen, Mrs Morell [*Candida rises*]. The onions have come.

MARCHBANKS [*conclusively*] Onions!

CANDIDA. Yes, onions. Not even Spanish ones: nasty little red onions. You shall help me to slice them. Come along.

She catches him by the wrist and runs out, pulling him after her. Burgess rises in consternation, and stands aghast on the hearth-rug, staring after them.

BURGESS. Candy didnt oughter andle a hearl's nevvy like that. It's goin too fur with it. Lookee ere, James: do e often git taken queer like that?

MORELL [*shortly, writing a telegram*] I dont know.

BURGESS [*sentimentally*] He talks very pretty. I awlus had a turn for a bit of poetry. Candy takes arter me that-a-way. Huseter make me tell er fairy stories when she was ony a little kiddy not that igh [*indicating a stature of two feet or thereabouts*].

MORELL [*preoccupied*] Ah, indeed. [*He blots the telegram and goes out*].

PROSERPINE. Used you to make the fairy stories up out of your own head?

Burgess, not deigning to reply, strikes an attitude of the haughtiest disdain on the hearth-rug.

PROSERPINE [*calmly*] I should never have supposed you had it in you. By the way, I'd better warn you, since youve taken such a fancy to Mr Marchbanks. He's mad.

BURGESS. Mad! What! Im too!!

PROSERPINE. Mad as a March hare. He did frighten me, I can tell you, just before you came in that time. Havent you noticed the queer things he says?

BURGESS. So thats what the poetic orrors means. Blame me if it didnt come into my ed once or twyst that he was a bit horff is chump! [*He crosses the room to the door, lifting up his voice as he goes*]. Well, this is a pretty sort of asylum for a man to be in, with no one but you to take care of him!

PROSERPINE [*as he passes her*] Yes, what a dreadful thing it would be if anything happened to you!

BURGESS [*loftily*] Dont you haddress no remarks to me. Tell your hemployer that Ive gone into the gorden for a smoke.

PROSERPINE [*mocking*] Oh!

Before Burgess can retort, Morell comes back.

BURGESS [*sentimentally*] Goin for a turn in the gording to smoke, James.

MORELL [*brusquely*] Oh, all right, all right. [*Burgess goes out pathetically in the character of a weary old man. Morell stands at the table, turning over his papers, and adding, across to Proserpine, half humorously, half absently*] Well, Miss Prossy, why have you been calling my father-in-law names?

PROSERPINE [*blushing fiery red, and looking quickly up at him, half scared, half reproachful*] I—[*She bursts into tears*].

MORELL [*with tender gaiety, leaning across the table towards her, and consoling her*] Oh, come! come! come! Never mind, Pross: he is a silly old fathead, isnt he?

With an explosive sob, she makes a dash at the door, and vanishes, banging it. Morell, shaking his head resignedly, sighs, and goes wearily to his chair, where he sits down and sets to work, looking old and careworn.

Candida comes in. She has finished her household work and taken off the apron. She at once notices his dejected appearance, and posts herself quietly at the visitors' chair, looking down at him attentively. She says nothing.

MORELL [*looking up, but with his pen raised ready to resume his work*] Well? Where is Eugene?

CANDIDA. Washing his hands in the scullery under the tap. He will make an excellent cook if he can only get over his dread of Maria.

MORELL [*shortly*] Ha! No doubt. [*He begins writing again*]

CANDIDA [*going nearer, and putting her hand down softly on his to stop him as she says*] Come here, dear. Let me look at you. [*He drops his pen and yields himself to her disposal. She makes him rise, and brings him a little away from the table, looking at him critically all the time*]. Turn your face to the light. [*She places him facing the window*]. My boy is not looking well. Has he been overworking?

MORELL. Nothing more than usual.

CANDIDA. He looks very pale, and grey, and wrinkled, and old. [*His melancholy deepens; and she attacks it with wilful gaiety*] Here: [*pulling him towards the easy chair*] youve done enough writing for today. Leave Prossy to finish it. Come and talk to me.

MORELL. But—

CANDIDA [*insisting*] Yes, I must be talked to. [*She makes him sit down, and seats herself on the carpet beside his knee*]. Now [*patting his hand*] youre beginning to look better already. Why must you go out every night lecturing and talking? I hardly have one evening a week with you. Of course what you say is all very true; but it does no good: they dont mind what you say to them one little bit. They think they agree with you; but whats the use of their agreeing with you if they go and do just the opposite of what you tell them the moment your back is turned? Look at our congregation at St Dominic's! Why do they come to hear you talking about Christianity every Sunday? Why, just because theyve been so full of business and money-making for six days that they want to forget all about it and have a rest on the seventh; so that they can go back fresh and make money harder than ever! You positively help them at it instead of hindering them.

MORELL [*with energetic seriousness*] You know very well, Candida, that I often blow them up soundly for that. And if there is nothing in their churchgoing but rest and diversion, why dont they try something more amusing? more self-indulgent? There must be some good in the fact that they prefer St Dominic's to worse places on Sundays.

CANDIDA. Oh, the worse places arnt open; and even if they were, they darent be seen going to them. Besides, James dear, you preach so splendidly that it's as good as a play for them. Why do you think the women are so enthusiastic?

MORELL [*shocked*] Candida!

[562]

CANDIDA. Oh, *I* know. You silly boy: you think it's your Socialism and your religion; but if it were that, theyd do what you tell them instead of only coming to look at you. They all have Prossy's complaint.

MORELL. Prossy's complaint! What do you mean, Candida?

CANDIDA. Yes, Prossy, and all the other secretaries you ever had. Why does Prossy condescend to wash up the things, and to peel potatoes and abase herself in all manner of ways for six shillings a week less than she used to get in a city office? She's in love with you, James: thats the reason. Theyre all in love with you. And you are in love with preaching because you do it so beautifully. And you think it's all enthusiasm for the kingdom of Heaven on earth; and so do they. You dear silly!

MORELL. Candida: what dreadful! what soul-destroying cynicism! Are you jesting? Or—can it be?—are you jealous?

CANDIDA [*with curious thoughtfulness*] Yes, I feel a little jealous sometimes.

MORELL [*incredulously*] Of Prossy?

CANDIDA [*laughing*] No, no, no, no. Not jealous of anybody. Jealous for somebody else, who is not loved as he ought to be.

MORELL. Me?

CANDIDA. You! Why, youre spoiled with love and worship: you get far more than is good for you. No: I mean Eugene.

MORELL [*startled*] Eugene!

CANDIDA. It seems unfair that all the love should go to you, and none to him; although he needs it so much more than you do. [*A convulsive movement shakes him in spite of himself*]. Whats the matter? Am I worrying you?

MORELL [*hastily*] Not at all. [*Looking at her with troubled intensity*] You know that I have perfect confidence in you, Candida.

CANDIDA. You vain thing! Are you so sure of your irresistible attractions?

MORELL. Candida: you are shocking me. I never thought of my attractions. I thought of your goodness, of your purity. That is what I confide in.

CANDIDA. What a nasty uncomfortable thing to say to me! Oh, you are a clergyman, James: a thorough clergyman!

MORELL [*turning away from her, heart-stricken*] So Eugene says.

CANDIDA [*with lively interest, leaning over to him with her arms on his knee*] Eugene's always right. He's a wonderful boy: I have grown fonder and fonder of him all the time I was away. Do you know, James, that though he has not the least suspicion of it himself, he is ready to fall madly in love with me?

MORELL [*grimly*] Oh, he has no suspicion of it himself, hasnt he?

CANDIDA. Not a bit. [*She takes her arms from his knee, and turns thoughtfully, sinking into a more restful attitude with her hands in her lap*]. Some day he will know: when he is grown up and experienced, like you. And he will know that I must have known. I wonder what he will think of me then.

MORELL. No evil, Candida. I hope and trust, no evil.

CANDIDA [*dubiously*] That will depend.

MORELL [*bewildered*] Depend!

CANDIDA [*looking at him*] Yes: it will depend on what happens to him. [*He looks vacantly at her*]. Dont you see? It will depend on how he comes to learn what love really is. I mean on the sort of woman who will teach it to him.

MORELL [*quite at a loss*] Yes. No. I dont know what you mean.

CANDIDA [*explaining*] If he learns it from a good woman, then it will be all right: he will forgive me.

MORELL. Forgive?

CANDIDA. But suppose he learns it from a bad woman, as so many men do, especially poetic men, who imagine all women are angels! Suppose he only discovers the value of love when he has thrown it away and degraded himself in his ignorance! Will he forgive me then, do you think?

MORELL. Forgive you for what?

CANDIDA [*realizing how stupid he is, and a little disappointed, though quite tenderly so*] Dont you understand? [*He shakes his head. She turns to him again, so as to explain with the fondest intimacy*]. I mean, will he forgive me for not teaching him myself? For abandoning him to the bad women for the sake of my goodness, of my purity, as you call it? Ah, James, how little you understand me, to talk of your confidence in my goodness and purity! I would give them both to poor Eugene as willingly as I would give my shawl to a beggar dying of cold, if there were nothing else to restrain me. Put your trust in my love for you, James: for if that went, I should care very little for your sermons: mere phrases that you cheat yourself and others with every day. [*She is about to rise*].

MORELL. His words!

CANDIDA [*checking herself quickly in the act of getting up*] Whose words?

MORELL. Eugene's.

CANDIDA [*delighted*] He is always right. He understands you; he understands me; he understands Prossy; and you, darling, you understand nothing.

[*She laughs, and kisses him to console him. He recoils as if stabbed, and springs up*].

MORELL. How can you bear to do that when—Oh, Candida [*with anguish in his voice*] I had rather you had plunged a grappling iron into my heart than given me that kiss.

CANDIDA [*amazed*] My dear: whats the matter?

MORELL [*frantically waving her off*] Dont touch me.

CANDIDA. James!!!

They are interrupted by the entrance of Marchbanks with Burgess, who stop near the door, staring.

MARCHBANKS. Is anything the matter?

MORELL [*deadly white, putting an iron constraint on himself*] Nothing but this: that either you were right this morning, or Candida is mad.

BURGESS [*in loudest protest*] What! Candy mad too! Oh, come! come! come! [*He crosses the room to the fireplace, protesting as he goes, and knocks the ashes out of his pipe on the bars*].

Morell sits down at his table desperately, leaning forward to hide his face, and interlacing his fingers rigidly to keep them steady.

CANDIDA [*to Morell, relieved and laughing*] Oh, youre only shocked! Is that all? How conventional all you unconventional people are! [*She sits gaily on the arm of the chair*].

BURGESS. Come: be'ave yourself, Candy. Whatll Mr Morchbanks think of you?

CANDIDA. This comes of James teaching me to think for myself, and never to hold back out of fear of what other people may think of me. It works beautifully as long as I think the same things as he does. But now! because I have just thought something different! look at him! Just look! [*She points to Morell, greatly amused*].

Eugene looks, and instantly presses his hand on his heart, as if some pain had shot through it. He sits down on the sofa like a man witnessing a tragedy.

BURGESS [*on the hearthrug*] Well, James, you certnly haint as himpressive lookin as usu'l.

MORELL [*with a laugh which is half a sob*] I suppose not. I beg all your pardons: I was not conscious of making a fuss. [*Pulling himself together*] Well, well, well, well, well! [*He sets to work at his papers again with resolute cheerfulness*].

CANDIDA [*going to the sofa and sitting beside Marchbanks, still in a bantering humor*] Well, Eugene: why are you so sad? Did the onions make you cry?

MARCHBANKS [*aside to her*] It is your cruelty. I hate cruelty. It is a horrible thing to see one person make another suffer.

CANDIDA [*petting him ironically*] Poor boy! have I been cruel? Did I make it slice nasty little red onions?

MARCHBANKS [*earnestly*] Oh, stop, stop: I dont mean myself. You have made him suffer frightfully. I feel his pain in my own heart. I know that it is not your fault: it is something that must happen; but dont make light of it. I shudder when you torture him and laugh.

CANDIDA [*incredulously*] *I* torture James! Nonsense, Eugene: how you exaggerate! Silly! [*She rises and goes to the table, a little troubled*]. Dont work any more, dear. Come and talk to us.

MORELL [*affectionately but bitterly*] Ah no: *I* cant talk. I can only preach.

CANDIDA [*caressing his hand*] Well, come and preach.

BURGESS [*strongly remonstrating*] Aw no, Candy. Ang it all!

Lexy Mill comes in, anxious and important.

LEXY [*hastening to shake hands with Candida*] How

do you do, Mrs Morell? So glad to see you back again.

CANDIDA. Thank you, Lexy. You know Eugene, dont you?

LEXY. Oh yes. How do you do, Marchbanks?

MARCHBANKS. Quite well, thanks.

LEXY [to Morell] Ive just come from the Guild of St Matthew. They are in the greatest consternation about your telegram.

CANDIDA. What did you telegraph about, James?

LEXY [to Candida] He was to have spoken for them tonight. Theyve taken the large hall in Mare Street and spent a lot of money on posters. Morell's telegram was to say he couldnt come. It came on them like a thunderbolt.

CANDIDA [surprised, and beginning to suspect something wrong] Given up an engagement to speak!

BURGESS. Fust time in his life, I'll bet. Ain it, Candy?

LEXY [to Morell] They decided to send an urgent telegram to you asking whether you could not change your mind. Have you received it?

MORELL [with restrained impatience] Yes, yes: I got it.

LEXY. It was reply paid.

MORELL. Yes, I know. I answered it. I cant go.

CANDIDA. But why, James?

MORELL [almost fiercely] Because I dont choose. These people forget that I am a man: they think I am a talking machine to be turned on for their pleasure every evening of my life. May I not have one night at home, with my wife, and my friends?

They are all amazed at this outburst, except Eugene. His expression remains unchanged.

CANDIDA. Oh, James, you musnt mind what I said about that. And if you dont go youll have an attack of bad conscience tomorrow.

LEXY [*intimidated, but urgent*] I know, of course, that they make the most unreasonable demands on you. But they have been telegraphing all over the place for another speaker; and they can get nobody but the President of the Agnostic League.

MORELL [*promptly*] Well, an excellent man. What better do they want?

LEXY. But he always insists so powerfully on the divorce of Socialism from Christianity. He will undo all the good we have been doing. Of course you know best; but—[*he shrugs his shoulders and wanders to the hearth beside Burgess*].

CANDIDA [*coaxingly*] Oh, do go, James. We'll all go.

BURGESS [*grumblingly*] Look ere, Candy! I say! Lets stay at home by the fire, comfortable. He wont need to be more'n a couple-o-hour away.

CANDIDA. Youll be just as comfortable at the meeting. We'll all sit on the platform and be great people.

EUGENE [*terrified*] Oh please dont let us go on the platform. No: everyone will stare at us: I couldnt. I'll sit at the back of the room.

CANDIDA. Dont be afraid. Theyll be too busy looking at James to notice you.

MORELL. Prossy's complaint, Candida! Eh?

CANDIDA [*gaily*] Yes: Prossy's complaint.

BURGESS [*mystified*] Prossy's complaint! What are you talkin about, James?

MORELL [*not heeding him, rises; goes to the door; and holds it open, calling in a commanding tone*] Miss Garnett.

PROSERPINE [*in the distance*] Yes, Mr Morell. Coming.

They all wait, except Burgess, who turns stealthily to Lexy.

BURGESS. Listen ere, Mr Mill. Whats Prossy's complaint? Whats wrong with er?

LEXY [*confidentially*] Well, I dont exactly know; but she spoke very strangely to me this morning. I'm afraid she's a little out of her mind sometimes.

BURGESS [*overwhelmed*] Why, it must be catchin! Four in the same ouse!

PROSERPINE [*appearing on the threshold*] What is it, Mr Morell?

MORELL. Telegraph to the Guild of St Matthew that I am coming.

PROSERPINE [*surprised*] Dont they expect you?

MORELL [*peremptorily*] Do as I tell you.

Proserpine, frightened, sits down at her typewriter, and obeys. Morell, now unaccountably resolute and forceful, goes across to Burgess. Candida watches his movements with growing wonder and misgiving.

MORELL. Burgess: you dont want to come.

BURGESS. Oh, dont put it like that, James. It's ony that it aint Sunday, you know.

MORELL. I'm sorry. I thought you might like to be introduced to the chairman. He's on the Works Committee of the County Council, and has some influence in the matter of contracts. [*Burgess wakes up at once*]. Youll come?

BURGESS [*with enthusiasm*] Cawrse I'll come, James. Aint it awlus a pleasure to ear you!

MORELL [*turning to Prossy*] I shall want you to take some notes at the meeting, Miss Garnett, if you have no other engagement. [*She nods, afraid to speak*]. You are coming, Lexy, I suppose?

LEXY. Certainly.

CANDIDA. We're all coming, James.

MORELL. No: you are not coming; and Eugene is not coming. You will stay here and entertain him—to

celebrate your return home. [*Eugene rises, breathless*].
CANDIDA. But, James—
MORELL [*authoritatively*] I insist. You do not want
to come; and he does not want to come. [*Candida is
about to protest*]. Oh, dont concern yourselves: I shall
have plenty of people without you: your chairs will be
wanted by unconverted people who have never heard
me before.
CANDIDA [*troubled*] Eugene: wouldnt you like to
come?
MORELL. I should be afraid to let myself go before
Eugene: he is so critical of sermons. [*Looking at him*]
He knows I am afraid of him: he told me as much this
morning. Well, I shall shew him how much afraid I
am by leaving him here in your custody, Candida.
MARCHBANKS [*to himself, with vivid feeling*] Thats
brave. Thats beautiful.
CANDIDA [*with anxious misgiving*] But—but—Is anything the matter, James? [*Greatly troubled*] I cant
understand—
MORELL [*taking her tenderly in his arms and kissing her
on the forehead*] Ah, I thought it was *I* who couldnt
understand, dear.

[ACT III]

Past ten in the evening. The curtains are drawn, and the lamps lighted. The typewriter is in its case: the large table has been cleared and tidied: everything indicates that the day's work is over.

Candida and Marchbanks are sitting by the fire. The reading lamp is on the mantelshelf above Marchbanks, who is in the small chair, reading aloud. A little pile of manuscripts and a couple of volumes of poetry are on the carpet beside him. Candida is in the easy chair. The poker, a light brass one, is upright in her hand. Leaning back and looking intently at the point of it, with her feet stretched towards the blaze, she is in a waking dream, miles away from the surroundings and completely oblivious of Eugene.

MARCHBANKS [*breaking off in his recitation*] Every poet that ever lived has put that thought into a sonnet. He must: he cant help it. [*He looks to her for assent, and notices her absorption in the poker*]. Havnt you been listening? [*No response*]. Mrs Morell!

CANDIDA [*starting*] Eh?

MARCHBANKS. Havnt you been listening?

CANDIDA [*with a guilty excess of politeness*] Oh yes. It's very nice. Go on, Eugene. I'm longing to hear what happens to the angel.

MARCHBANKS [*letting the manuscript drop from his hand to the floor*] I beg your pardon for boring you.

CANDIDA. But you are not boring me, I assure you. Please go on. Do, Eugene.

MARCHBANKS. I finished the poem about the angel quarter of an hour ago. Ive read you several things since.

CANDIDA [*remorsefully*] I'm so sorry, Eugene. I think the poker must have hypnotized me. [*She puts it down*].

MARCHBANKS. It made me horribly uneasy.

CANDIDA. Why didnt you tell me? I'd have put it down at once.

MARCHBANKS. I was afraid of making you uneasy too. It looked as if it were a weapon. If I were a hero of old I should have laid my drawn sword between us. If Morell had come in he would have thought you had taken up the poker because there was no sword between us.

CANDIDA [*wondering*] What? [*With a puzzled glance at him*] I cant quite follow that. Those sonnets of yours have perfectly addled me. Why should there be a sword between us?

MARCHBANKS [*evasively*] Oh, never mind. [*He stoops to pick up the manuscript*].

CANDIDA. Put that down again, Eugene. There are limits to my appetite for poetry: even your poetry. Youve been reading to me for more than two hours, ever since James went out. I want to talk.

MARCHBANKS [*rising, scared*] No: I musnt talk. [*He looks round him in his lost way, and adds, suddenly*] I think I'll go out and take a walk in the park. [*He makes for the door*].

CANDIDA. Nonsense: it's closed long ago. Come and sit down on the hearth-rug, and talk moonshine as you usually do. I want to be amused. Dont you want to?

MARCHBANKS [*half in terror, half enraptured*] Yes.

CANDIDA. Then come along. [*She moves her chair back a little to make room*].

He hesitates; then timidly stretches himself on the hearth-rug, face upwards, and throws back his head across her knees, looking up at her.

MARCHBANKS. Oh, Ive been so miserable all the evening, because I was doing right. Now I'm doing wrong; and I'm happy.

CANDIDA [*tenderly amused at him*] Yes: I'm sure you feel a great grown-up wicked deceiver. Quite proud of yourself, arnt you?

MARCHBANKS [*raising his head quickly and turning a little to look round at her*] Take care. I'm ever so much older than you, if you only knew. [*He turns quite over on his knees, with his hands clasped and his arms on her lap, and speaks with growing impulse, his blood beginning to stir*]. May I say some wicked things to you?

CANDIDA [*without the least fear or coldness, and with perfect respect for his passion, but with a touch of her wise-hearted maternal humor*] No. But you may say anything you really and truly feel. Anything at all, no matter what it is. I am not afraid, so long as it is your real self that speaks, and not a mere attitude: a gallant attitude, or a wicked attitude, or even a poetic attitude. I put you on your honor and truth. Now say whatever you want to.

MARCHBANKS [*the eager expression vanishing utterly from his lips and nostrils as his eyes light up with pathetic spirituality*] Oh, now I cant say anything: all the words I know belong to some attitude or other—all except one.

CANDIDA. What one is that?

MARCHBANKS [*softly, losing himself in the music of the name*] Candida, Candida, Candida, Candida, Candida.

I must say that now, because you have put me on my honor and truth; and I never think or feel Mrs Morell: it is always Candida.

CANDIDA. Of course. And what have you to say to Candida?

MARCHBANKS. Nothing but to repeat your name a thousand times. Dont you feel that every time is a prayer to you?

CANDIDA. Doesnt it make you happy to be able to pray?

MARCHBANKS. Yes, very happy.

CANDIDA. Well, that happiness is the answer to your prayer. Do you want anything more?

MARCHBANKS. No: I have come into heaven, where want is unknown.

Morell comes in. He halts on the threshold, and takes in the scene at a glance.

MORELL [*grave and self-contained*] I hope I dont disturb you.

Candida starts up violently, but without the smallest embarrassment, laughing at herself. Eugene, capsized by her sudden movement, recovers himself without rising, and sits on the rug hugging his ankles, also quite unembarrassed.

CANDIDA. Oh, James, how you startled me! I was so taken up with Eugene that I didnt hear your latchkey. How did the meeting go off? Did you speak well?

MORELL. I have never spoken better in my life.

CANDIDA. That was first rate! How much was the collection?

MORELL. I forgot to ask.

CANDIDA [*to Eugene*] He must have spoken splendidly, or he would never have forgotten that. [*To Morell*] Where are all the others?

MORELL. They left long before I could get away: I thought I should never escape. I believe they are having supper somewhere.

CANDIDA [*in her domestic business tone*] Oh, in that case, Maria may go to bed. I'll tell her. [*She goes out to the kitchen*].

MORELL [*looking sternly down at Marchbanks*] Well?

MARCHBANKS [*squatting grotesquely on the hearth-rug, and actually at ease with Morell: even impishly humorous*] Well?

MORELL. Have you anything to tell me?

MARCHBANKS. Only that I have been making a fool of myself here in private whilst you have been making a fool of yourself in public.

MORELL. Hardly in the same way, I think.

MARCHBANKS [*eagerly, scrambling up*] The very, very very same way. I have been playing the Good Man. Just like you. When you began your heroics about leaving me here with Candida—

MORELL [*involuntarily*] Candida!

MARCHBANKS. Oh yes: Ive got that far. But dont be afraid. Heroics are infectious: I caught the disease from you. I swore not to say a word in your absence that I would not have said a month ago in your presence.

MORELL. Did you keep your oath?

MARCHBANKS [*suddenly perching himself on the back of the easy chair*] It kept itself somehow until about ten minutes ago. Up to that moment I went on desperately reading to her—reading my own poems—anybody's poems—to stave off a conversation. I was standing outside the gate of Heaven, and refusing to go in. Oh, you cant think how heroic it was, and how uncomfortable! Then—

MORELL [*steadily controlling his suspense*] Then?

MARCHBANKS [*prosaically slipping down into a quite ordinary attitude on the seat of the chair*] Then she couldnt bear being read to any longer.

MORELL. And you approached the gate of Heaven at last?

MARCHBANKS. Yes.

MORELL. Well? [*Fiercely*] Speak, man: have you no feeling for me?

MARCHBANKS [*softly and musically*] Then she became an angel; and there was a flaming sword that turned every way, so that I couldnt go in; for I saw that that gate was really the gate of Hell.

MORELL [*triumphantly*] She repulsed you!

MARCHBANKS [*rising in wild scorn*] No, you fool: if she had done that I should never have seen that I was in Heaven already. Repulsed me! You think that would have saved us! virtuous indignation! Oh, you are not worthy to live in the same world with her. [*He turns away contemptuously to the other side of the room*].

MORELL [*who has watched him quietly without changing his place*] Do you think you make yourself more worthy by reviling me, Eugene?

MARCHBANKS. Here endeth the thousand and first lesson. Morell: I dont think much of your preaching after all: I believe I could do it better myself. The man I want to meet is the man that Candida married.

MORELL. The man that—? Do you mean me?

MARCHBANKS. I dont mean the Reverend James Mavor Morell, moralist and windbag. I mean the real man that the Reverend James must have hidden somewhere inside his black coat: the man that Candida loved. You cant make a woman like Candida love you by merely buttoning your collar at the back instead of in front.

MORELL [*boldly and steadily*] When Candida promised to marry me, I was the same moralist and windbag you now see. I wore my black coat; and my collar was buttoned behind instead of in front. Do you think she would have loved me any the better for being insincere in my profession?

MARCHBANKS [*on the sofa, hugging his ankles*] Oh, she forgave you, just as she forgives me for being a coward, and a weakling, and what you call a snivelling little whelp and all the rest of it. [*Dreamily*] A woman like that has divine insight: she loves our souls, and not our follies and vanities and illusions, nor our collars and coats, nor any other of the rags and tatters we are rolled up in. [*He reflects on this for an instant; then turns intently to question Morell*]. What I want to know is how you got past the flaming sword that stopped me.

MORELL. Perhaps because I was not interrupted at the end of ten minutes.

MARCHBANKS [*taken aback*] What!

MORELL. Man can climb to the highest summits; but he cannot dwell there long.

MARCHBANKS [*springing up*] It's false: there can he dwell for ever, and there only. It's in the other moments that he can find no rest, no sense of the silent glory of life. Where would you have me spend my moments, if not on the summits?

MORELL. In the scullery, slicing onions and filling lamps.

MARCHBANKS. Or in the pulpit, scrubbing cheap earthenware souls?

MORELL. Yes, that too. It was there that I earned my golden moment, and the right, in that moment, to ask her to love me. *I* did not take the moment on credit; nor did I use it to steal another man's happiness.

MARCHBANKS [*rather disgustedly, trotting back to-wards the fireplace*] I have no doubt you conducted the transaction as honestly as if you were buying a pound of cheese. [*He stops on the brink of the hearth-rug, and adds, thoughtfully, to himself, with his back turned to Morell*] I could only go to her as a beggar.

MORELL [*starting*] A beggar dying of cold! asking for her shawl!

MARCHBANKS [*turning, surprised*] Thank you for touching up my poetry. Yes, if you like: a beggar dying of cold, asking for her shawl.

MORELL [*excitedly*] And she refused. Shall I tell you why she refused? I can tell you, on her own authority. It was because of—

MARCHBANKS. She didnt refuse.

MORELL. Not!

MARCHBANKS. She offered me all I chose to ask for: her shawl, her wings, the wreath of stars on her head, the lilies in her hand, the crescent moon beneath her feet—

MORELL [*seizing him*] Out with the truth, man: my wife is my wife: I want no more of your poetic frip-peries. I know well that if I have lost her love and you have gained it, no law will bind her.

MARCHBANKS [*quaintly, without fear or resistance*] Catch me by the shirt collar, Morell: she will arrange it for me afterwards as she did this morning. [*With quiet rapture*] I shall feel her hands touch me.

MORELL. You young imp, do you know how danger-ous it is to say that to me? Or [*with a sudden misgiving*] has something made you brave?

MARCHBANKS. I'm not afraid now. I disliked you before: that was why I shrank from your touch. But I saw today—when she tortured you—that you love her. Since then I have been your friend: you may strangle me if you like.

MORELL [*releasing him*] Eugene: if that is not a heartless lie—if you have a spark of human feeling left in
you—will you tell me what has happened during my
absence?

MARCHBANKS. What happened! Why, the flaming
sword [*Morell stamps with impatience*]—Well, in plain
prose, I loved her so exquisitely that I wanted nothing
more than the happiness of being in such love. And
before I had time to come down from the highest
summits, you came in.

MORELL [*suffering deeply*] So it is still unsettled. Still
the misery of doubt.

MARCHBANKS. Misery! I am the happiest of men. I
desire nothing now but her happiness. [*In a passion of
sentiment*] Oh, Morell, let us both give her up. Why
should she have to choose between a wretched little
nervous disease like me, and a pig-headed parson like
you? Let us go on a pilgrimage, you to the east and I
to the west, in search of a worthy lover for her: some
beautiful archangel with purple wings—

MORELL. Some fiddlestick! Oh, if she is mad enough
to leave me for you, who will protect her? who will
help her? who will work for her? who will be a father
to her children? [*He sits down distractedly on the sofa,
with his elbows on his knees and his head propped on his
clenched fists*].

MARCHBANKS [*snapping his fingers wildly*] She does
not ask those silly questions. It is she who wants
somebody to protect, to help, to work for: somebody
to give her children to protect, to help and to work
for. Some grown up man who has become as a little
child again. Oh, you fool, you fool, you triple fool! I
am the man, Morell: I am the man. [*He dances about
excitedly, crying*] You dont understand what a woman
is. Send for her, Morell: send for her and let her

[580]

choose between—[*The door opens and Candida enters. He stops as if petrified*].

CANDIDA [*amazed, on the threshold*] What on earth are you at, Eugene?

MARCHBANKS [*oddly*] James and I are having a preaching match; and he is getting the worst of it.

Candida looks quickly round at Morell. Seeing that he is distressed, she hurries down to him, greatly vexed.

CANDIDA. You have been annoying him. Now I wont have it, Eugene: do you hear? [*She puts her hand on Morell's shoulder, and quite forgets her wifely tact in her anger*]. My boy shall not be worried: I will protect him.

MORELL [*rising proudly*] Protect!

CANDIDA [*not heeding him: to Eugene*] What have you been saying?

MARCHBANKS [*appalled*] Nothing. I—

CANDIDA. Eugene! Nothing?

MARCHBANKS [*piteously*] I mean—I—I'm very sorry. I wont do it again: indeed I wont. I'll let him alone.

MORELL [*indignantly, with an agressive movement towards Eugene*] Let me alone! You young—

CANDIDA [*stopping him*] Sh!—no: let me deal with him, James.

MARCHBANKS. Oh, youre not angry with me, are you?

CANDIDA [*severely*] Yes I am: very angry. I have a good mind to pack you out of the house.

MORELL [*taken aback by Candida's vigour, and by no means relishing the position of being rescued by her from another man*] Gently, Candida, gently. I am able to take care of myself.

CANDIDA [*petting him*] Yes, dear: of course you are. But you musnt be annoyed and made miserable.

MARCHBANKS [*almost in tears, turning to the door*] I'll go.

CANDIDA. Oh, you neednt go: I cant turn you out at this time of night. [*Vehemently*] Shame on you! For shame!

MARCHBANKS [*desperately*] But what have I done?

CANDIDA. I know what you have done: as well as if I had been here all the time. Oh, it was unworthy! You are like a child: you cannot hold your tongue.

MARCHBANKS. I would die ten times over sooner than give you a moment's pain.

CANDIDA [*with infinite contempt for this puerility*] Much good your dying would do me!

MORELL. Candida, my dear: this altercation is hardly quite seemly. It is a matter between two men; and I am the right person to settle it.

CANDIDA. Two men! Do you call that a man? [*To Eugene*] You bad boy!

MARCHBANKS [*gathering a whimsically affectionate courage from the scolding*] If I am to be scolded like a boy, I must make a boy's excuse. He began it. And he's bigger than I am.

CANDIDA [*losing confidence a little as her concern for Morell's dignity takes the alarm*] That cant be true. [*To Morell*] You didnt begin it, James, did you?

MORELL [*contemptuously*] No.

MARCHBANKS [*indignant*] Oh!

MORELL [*to Eugene*] You began it: this morning. [*Candida, instantly connecting this with his mysterious allusion in the afternoon to something told him by Eugene in the morning, looks at him with quick suspicion. Morell proceeds, with the emphasis of offended superiority*] But your other point is true. I am certainly the bigger of the two, and, I hope, the stronger,

[582]

Candida. So you had better leave the matter in my hands.

CANDIDA [*again soothing him*] Yes, dear; but— [*troubled*] I dont understand about this morning.

MORELL [*gently snubbing her*] You need not understand, my dear.

CANDIDA. But James, I [*the street bell rings*]—Oh bother! Here they all come. [*She goes out to let them in*].

MARCHBANKS [*running to Morell*] Oh, Morell, isnt it dreadful? She's angry with us: she hates me. What shall I do?

MORELL [*with quaint desperation, walking up and down the middle of the room*] Eugene: my head is spinning round. I shall begin to laugh presently.

MARCHBANKS [*following him anxiously*] No, no: she'll think Ive thrown you into hysterics. Dont laugh.

Boisterous voices and laughter are heard approaching. Lexy Mill, his eyes sparkling, and his bearing denoting unwonted elevation of spirit, enters with Burgess, who is greasy and self-complacent, but has all his wits about him. Miss Garnett, with her smartest hat and jacket on, follows them; but though her eyes are brighter than before, she is evidently a prey to misgiving. She places herself with her back to her typewriting table, with one hand on it to steady herself, passing the other across her forehead as if she were a little tired and giddy. Marchbanks relapses into shyness and edges away into the corner near the window, where Morell's books are.

LEXY [*exhilarated*] Morell: I must congratulate you. [*Grasping his hand*] What a noble, splendid, inspired address you gave us! You surpassed yourself.

BURGESS. So you did, James. It fair kep me awake to the lars' word. Didnt it, Miss Gornett?

PROSERPINE [*worriedly*] Oh, I wasnt minding you: I

was trying to make notes. [*She takes out her note-book, and looks at her stenography, which nearly makes her cry*].

MORELL. Did I go too fast, Pross?

PROSERPINE. Much too fast. You know I cant do more than ninety words a minute. [*She relieves her feelings by throwing her note-book angrily beside her machine, ready for use next morning*].

MORELL [*soothingly*] Oh well, well, never mind, never mind, never mind. Have you all had supper?

LEXY. Mr Burgess has been kind enough to give us a really splendid supper at the Belgrave.

BURGESS [*with effusive magnanimity*] Dont mention it, Mr Mill. [*Modestly*] Youre arty welcome to my little treat.

PROSERPINE. We had champagne. I never tasted it before. I feel quite giddy.

MORELL [*surprised*] A champagne supper! That was very handsome. Was it my eloquence that produced all this extravagance?

LEXY [*rhetorically*] Your eloquence, and Mr Burgess's goodness of heart. [*With a fresh burst of exhilaration*] And what a very fine fellow the chairman is, Morell! He came to supper with us.

MORELL [*with long drawn significance, looking at Burgess*] O-o-o-h! the chairman. Now I understand.

Burgess covers with a deprecatory cough a lively satisfaction with his own diplomatic cunning. Lexy folds his arms and leans against the head of the sofa in a high-spirited attitude after nearly losing his balance. Candida comes in with glasses, lemons, and a jug of hot water on a tray.

CANDIDA. Who will have some lemonade? You know our rules: total abstinence. [*She puts the tray on the*

*table, and takes up the lemon squeezer, looking enquir-
ingly round at them].*

MORELL. No use, dear. Theyve all had champagne.
Pross has broken her pledge.

CANDIDA [*to Proserpine*] You dont mean to say youve
been drinking champagne!

PROSERPINE [*stubbornly*] Yes I do. I'm only a beer
teetotaller, not a champagne teetotaller. I dont like
beer. Are there any letters for me to answer, Mr
Morell?

MORELL. No more to-night.

PROSERPINE. Very well. Goodnight, everybody.

LEXY [*gallantly*] Had I not better see you home, Miss
Garnett?

PROSERPINE. No thank you. I shant trust myself
with anybody tonight. I wish I hadnt taken any of that
stuff. [*She takes uncertain aim at the door; dashes at it;
and barely escapes without disaster*].

BURGESS [*indignantly*] Stuff indeed! That gurl dunno
what champagne is! Pommery and Greeno at twelve
and six a bottle. She took two glasses amost straight
horff.

MORELL [*anxious about her*] Go and look after her,
Lexy.

LEXY [*alarmed*] But if she should really be— Suppose
she began to sing in the street, or anything of that
sort.

MORELL. Just so: she may. Thats why youd better see
her safely home.

CANDIDA. Do, Lexy: theres a good fellow. [*She shakes
his hand and pushes him gently to the door*].

LEXY. It's evidently my duty to go. I hope it may not
be necessary. Goodnight, Mrs Morell. [*To the rest*]
Goodnight. [*He goes. Candida shuts the door*].

BURGESS. He was gushin with hextra piety hisself

arter two sips. People carnt drink like they huseter.
[*Bustling across to the hearth*] Well, James: it's time to
lock up. Mr Morchbanks: shall I ave the pleasure of
your company for a bit o the way ome?

MARCHBANKS [*affrightedly*] Yes: I'd better go. [*He
hurries towards the door; but Candida places herself
before it, barring his way*].

CANDIDA [*with quiet authority*] You sit down. Youre
not going yet.

MARCHBANKS [*quailing*] No: I—I didnt mean to.
[*He sits down abjectly on the sofa*].

CANDIDA. Mr Marchbanks will stay the night with
us, papa.

BURGESS. Oh well, I'll say goodnight. So long, James.
[*He shakes hands with Morell, and goes over to Eugene*].
Make em give you a nightlight by your bed, Mr
Morchbanks: itll comfort you if you wake up in the
night with a touch of that complaint of yores. Good-
night.

MARCHBANKS. Thank you: I will. Goodnight, Mr
Burgess. [*They shake hands. Burgess goes to the door*].

CANDIDA [*intercepting Morell, who is following
Burgess*] Stay here, dear: I'll put on papa's coat for
him. [*She goes out with Burgess*].

MARCHBANKS [*rising and stealing over to Morell*]
Morell: theres going to be a terrible scene. Arnt you
afraid?

MORELL. Not in the least.

MARCHBANKS. I never envied you your courage
before. [*He puts his hand appealingly on Morell's fore-
arm*]. Stand by me, wont you?

MORELL [*casting him off resolutely*] Each for himself,
Eugene. She must choose between us now.

*Candida returns. Eugene creeps back to the sofa like
a guilty schoolboy.*

CANDIDA [*between them, addressing Eugene*] Are you sorry?

MARCHBANKS [*earnestly*] Yes. Heartbroken.

CANDIDA. Well then, you are forgiven. Now go off to bed like a good little boy: I want to talk to James about you.

MARCHBANKS [*rising in great consternation*] Oh, I cant do that, Morell. I must be here. I'll not go away. Tell her.

CANDIDA [*her suspicions confirmed*] Tell me what? [*His eyes avoid hers furtively. She turns and mutely transfers the question to Morell*].

MORELL [*bracing himself for the catastrophe*] I have nothing to tell her, except [*here his voice deepens to a measured and mournful tenderness*] that she is my greatest treasure on earth—if she is really mine.

CANDIDA [*coldly, offended by his yielding to his orator's instinct and treating her as if she were the audience at the Guild of St Matthew*] I am sure Eugene can say no less, if that is all.

MARCHBANKS [*discouraged*] Morell: she's laughing at us.

MORELL [*with a quick touch of temper*] There is nothing to laugh at. Are you laughing at us, Candida?

CANDIDA [*with quiet anger*] Eugene is very quick-witted, James. I hope I am going to laugh; but I am not sure that I am not going to be very angry. [*She goes to the fireplace, and stands there leaning with her arm on the mantelpiece, and her foot on the fender, whilst Eugene steals to Morell and plucks him by the sleeve*].

MARCHBANKS [*whispering*] Stop, Morell. Dont let us say anything.

MORELL [*pushing Eugene away without deigning to look at him*] I hope you dont mean that as a threat, Candida.

CANDIDA [*with emphatic warning*] Take care, James. Eugene: I asked you to go. Are you going?

MORELL [*putting his foot down*] He shall not go. I wish him to remain.

MARCHBANKS. I'll go. I'll do whatever you want. [*He turns to the door*].

CANDIDA. Stop! [*He obeys*]. Didnt you hear James say he wished you to stay? James is master here. Dont you know that?

MARCHBANKS [*flushing with a young poet's rage against tyranny*] By what right is he master?

CANDIDA [*quietly*] Tell him, James.

MORELL [*taken aback*] My dear: I dont know of any right that makes me master. I assert no such right.

CANDIDA [*with infinite reproach*] You dont know! Oh, James! James! [*To Eugene, musingly*] I wonder do you understand, Eugene! [*He shakes his head helplessly, not daring to look at her*]. No: youre too young. Well, I give you leave to stay: to stay and learn. [*She comes away from the hearth and places herself between them*]. Now, James! whats the matter? Come: tell me.

MARCHBANKS [*whispering tremulously across to him*] Dont.

CANDIDA. Come. Out with it!

MORELL [*slowly*] I meant to prepare your mind carefully, Candida, so as to prevent misunderstanding.

CANDIDA. Yes, dear: I am sure you did. But never mind: I shant misunderstand.

MORELL. Well—er— [*he hesitates, unable to find the long explanation which he supposed to be available*].

CANDIDA. Well?

MORELL [*blurting it out baldy*] Eugene declares that you are in love with him.

MARCHBANKS [*frantically*] No, no, no, no, never. I did not, Mrs Morell: it's not true. I said I loved you.

[588]

I said I understood you, and that he couldnt. And it was not after what passed there before the fire that I spoke: it was not, on my word. It was this morning.

CANDIDA [*enlightened*] This morning!

MARCHBANKS. Yes. [*He looks at her, pleading for credence, and then adds simply*] That was what was the matter with my collar.

CANDIDA. Your collar? [*Suddenly taking in his meaning she turns to Morell, shocked*]. Oh, James: did you— [*she stops*]?

MORELL [*ashamed*] You know, Candida, that I have a temper to struggle with. And he said [*shuddering*] that you despised me in your heart.

CANDIDA [*turning quickly on Eugene*] Did you say that?

MARCHBANKS [*terrified*] No.

CANDIDA [*almost fiercely*] Then James has just told me a falsehood. Is that what you mean?

MARCHBANKS. No, no: I—I— [*desperately*] it was David's wife. And it wasnt at home: it was when she saw him dancing before all the people.

MORELL [*taking the cue with a debater's adroitness*] Dancing before all the people, Candida; and thinking he was moving their hearts by his mission when they were only suffering from—Prossy's complaint. [*She is about to protest: he raises his hand to silence her*]. Dont try to look indignant, Candida—

CANDIDA. Try!

MORELL [*continuing*] Eugene was right. As you told me a few hours after, he is always right. He said nothing that you did not say far better yourself. He is the poet, who sees everything; and I am the poor parson, who understands nothing.

CANDIDA [*remorsefully*] Do you mind what is said by a foolish boy, because I said something like it in jest?

MORELL. That foolish boy can speak with the inspiration of a child and the cunning of a serpent. He has claimed that you belong to him and not to me; and, rightly or wrongly, I have come to fear that it may be true. I will not go about tortured with doubts and suspicions. I will not live with you and keep a secret from you. I will not suffer the intolerable degradation of jealousy. We have agreed—he and I—that you shall choose between us now. I await your decision.

CANDIDA [*slowly recoiling a step, her heart hardened by his rhetoric in spite of the sincere feeling behind it*] Oh! I am to choose am I? I suppose it is quite settled that I must belong to one or the other.

MORELL [*firmly*] Quite. You must choose definitely.

MARCHBANKS [*anxiously*] Morell: you dont understand. She means that she belongs to herself.

CANDIDA [*turning on him*] I mean that, and a good deal more, Master Eugene, as you will both find out presently. And pray, my lords and masters, what have you to offer for my choice? I am up for auction, it seems. What do you bid, James?

MORELL [*reproachfully*] Cand— [*He breaks down: his eyes and throat fill with tears: the orator becomes a wounded animal*]. I cant speak—

CANDIDA [*impulsively going to him*] Ah, dearest—

MARCHBANKS [*in wild alarm*] Stop: it's not fair. You musnt shew her that you suffer, Morell. I am on the rack too; but I am not crying.

MORELL [*rallying all his forces*] Yes: you are right. It is not for pity that I am bidding. [*He disengages himself from Candida*].

CANDIDA [*retreating, chilled*] I beg your pardon, James: I did not mean to touch you. I am waiting to hear your bid.

MORELL [*with proud humility*] I have nothing to offer

you but my strength for your defence, my honesty for your surety, my ability and industry for your livelihood, and my authority and position for your dignity. That is all it becomes a man to offer to a woman.

CANDIDA [*quite quietly*] And you, Eugene? What do you offer?

MARCHBANKS. My weakness. My desolation. My heart's need.

CANDIDA [*impressed*] Thats a good bid, Eugene. Now I know how to make my choice.

She pauses and looks curiously from one to the other, as if weighing them. Morell, whose lofty confidence has changed into heartbreaking dread at Eugene's bid, loses all power of concealing his anxiety. Eugene, strung to the highest tension, does not move a muscle.

MORELL [*in a suffocated voice: the appeal bursting from the depths of his anguish*] Candida!

MARCHBANKS [*aside, in a flash of contempt*] Coward!

CANDIDA [*significantly*] I give myself to the weaker of the two.

Eugene divines her meaning at once: his face whitens like steel in a furnace.

MORELL [*bowing his head with the calm of collapse*] I accept your sentence, Candida.

CANDIDA. Do you understand, Eugene?

MARCHBANKS. Oh, I feel I'm lost. He cannot bear the burden.

MORELL [*incredulously, raising his head and voice with comic abruptness*] Do you mean me, Candida?

CANDIDA [*smiling a little*] Let us sit and talk comfortably over it like three friends. [*To Morell*] Sit down, dear. [*Morell, quite lost, takes the chair from the fireside: the children's chair*]. Bring me that chair, Eugene. [*She indicates the easy chair. He fetches it silently, even with something like cold strength, and places it next Morell, a little behind him. She sits down. He takes the visitors' chair himself, and sits, inscrutable. When they are all settled she begins, throwing a spell of quietness on them by her calm, sane, tender tone].* You remember what you told me about yourself, Eugene: how nobody has cared for you since your old nurse died: how those clever fashionable sisters and successful brothers of yours were your mother's and father's pets: how miserable you were at Eton: how your father is trying to starve you into returning to Oxford: how you have had to live without comfort or welcome or refuge: always lonely, and nearly always disliked and misunderstood, poor boy!

MARCHBANKS [*faithful to the nobility of his lot*] I had my books. I had Nature. And at last I met you.

CANDIDA. Never mind that just at present. Now I want you to look at this other boy here: my boy! spoiled from his cradle. We go once a fortnight to see his parents. You should come with us, Eugene, to see the pictures of the hero of that household. James as a baby! the most wonderful of all babies. James holding his first school prize, won at the ripe age of eight! James as the captain of his eleven! James in his first frock coat! James under all sorts of glorious circumstances! You know how strong he is (I hope he didnt hurt you): how clever he is: how happy. [*With deepening gravity*] Ask James's mother and his three sisters what it cost to save James the trouble of doing anything but be strong and clever and happy. Ask me what it costs to be James's mother and three sisters and wife and mother to his children all in one. Ask Prossy and Maria how troublesome the house is even when we have no visitors to help us to slice the onions. Ask the tradesmen who want to worry James and spoil his beautiful sermons who it is that puts them off. When there is money to give, he gives it: when there is money to refuse, I refuse it. I build a castle of comfort and indulgence and love for him, and stand sentinel always to keep little vulgar cares out. I make him master here, though he does not know it, and could not tell you a moment ago how it came to be so. [*With sweet irony*] And when he thought I might go away with you, his only anxiety was—what should become of me! And to tempt me to stay he offered me [*leaning forward to stroke his hair caressingly at each phrase*] his strength for my defence! his industry for my livelihood! his dignity for my position! his— [*relenting*] ah, I am mixing up your beautiful cadences and spoiling them, am I not, darling? [*She lays her cheek fondly against his*].

MORELL [*quite overcome, kneeling beside her chair and embracing her with boyish ingenuousness*] It's all true, every word. What I am you have made me with the labor of your hands and the love of your heart. You are my wife, my mother, my sisters: you are the sum of all loving care to me.

CANDIDA [*in his arms, smiling, to Eugene*] Am I your mother and sisters to you, Eugene?

MARCHBANKS [*rising with a fierce gesture of disgust*] Ah, never. Out, then, into the night with me!

CANDIDA [*rising quickly*] You are not going like that, Eugene?

MARCHBANKS [*with the ring of a man's voice—no longer a boy's—in the words*] I know the hour when it strikes. I am impatient to do what must be done.

MORELL [*who has also risen*] Candida: dont let him do anything rash.

CANDIDA [*confident, smiling at Eugene*] Oh, there is no fear. He has learnt to live without happiness.

MARCHBANKS. I no longer desire happiness: life is nobler than that. Parson James: I give you my happiness with both hands: I love you because you have filled the heart of the woman I loved. Goodbye. [*He goes towards the door*].

CANDIDA. One last word. [*He stops, but without turning to her. She goes to him*]. How old are you, Eugene?

MARCHBANKS. As old as the world now. This morning I was eighteen.

CANDIDA. Eighteen! Will you, for my sake, make a little poem out of the two sentences I am going to say to you? And will you promise to repeat it to yourself whenever you think of me?

MARCHBANKS [*without moving*] Say the sentences.

CANDIDA. When I am thirty, she will be forty-five. When I am sixty, she will be seventy-five.

MARCHBANKS [*turning to her*] In a hundred years, we shall be the same age. But I have a better secret than that in my heart. Let me go now. The night outside grows impatient.

CANDIDA. Goodbye. [*She takes his face in her hands; and as he divines her intention and falls on his knees, she kisses his forehead. Then he flies out into the night. She turns to Morell, holding out her arms to him*]. Ah, James!

They embrace. But they do not know the secret in the poet's heart.

An Extraordinary Ordinary Play

(An interview drafted by Shaw for
The New Budget, *4 April 1895*)

It is one of the most difficult things in London to
catch Mr Bernard Shaw in an idle hour, pin him down
in an easy-chair, and bleed his intellect. For when Mr
Shaw is not writing plays of his own, he is criticizing
those of other people; and when he is doing neither he
is shewing the democracy the way to the Promised
Land, where every man has a fowl in his pot and no
man sweats his fellow. When I found Mr Shaw the
other day he had just delivered two lectures and
polished off a batch of copy. He sank into a chair and
said:

"I am the laziest man in London, really."

"You have told me that before," I said. "Now
please tell me about Candida. From the reports in the
morning papers, I gather that the whole play pivots
on the question whether a man who is an altruist and
a Socialist should hand over his wife to another man,
who says he wants her, always supposing no active
opposition on the part of the wife. Is that so?"

Mr Shaw had not seen the report. I handed him a
paper.

"It is as correct as most newspaper descriptions of
a play," replied Mr Shaw, after a few moments. "That
is, ingeniously the reverse of the actual position. It
runs on a false scent entirely."

"Perhaps you can put me on the right one. What is
the purpose of the play?"

"It has no purpose."

"Well—what is the plot?"

"It has no plot."

"Then it has characters?" I persisted, by the method of exhaustion.

"That is the point. It has characterization, and dialogue—pregnant dialogue."

"The heroine is the wife of an East-end clergyman, is she not? What particular type of cleric?"

"I have chosen a type which, so far as I know, has not yet been taken seriously on the stage. I mean the Christian Socialist, the member of the Guild of St Matthew, the regenerator of the Church of England. In short, the man who would be found working with Canon Shuttleworth [then Rector of St Nicholas Cole-Abbey] and the Rev. Stewart Headlam, and the advance guard of the Christian Social Union."

"And for the rest?"

"The third main character—there are only six in all—is that of Eugene Marjoribanks, a young poet. He is in love with Candida, the wife of the clergyman, and tells him so quite early in the play. The plot—what there is of it—consists mainly in the persistent efforts of Eugene to attain his object, and the growing fear of Morell—the clergyman—that he may succeed, together, of course, with the attitude of Candida, who inadvertently, by her conduct, increases her husband's uneasiness."

"This is quite commonplace," I said, disappointedly.

"Quite," said Mr Shaw, cheerfully. "That is the point of it. But come to New York and see it, and you wont find it dull."

"Well, how does it end?"

"You see, there is a strong contrast throughout between Morell—a burly, well-fed fellow, and a trifle ordinary—and Eugene, the poet, who is a real genius. I make him say things which prove he is a genius."

"I see."

"And the contrast is accentuated by the fact that Morell, though apparently strong, is really weak, and that Eugene, with all his fragility and poeticism, is really strong."

"And how does the contrast work out?"

"It would take too long to explain that; besides, it would be giving the play away. But I may tell you that Morell finally decides to ask his wife to decide between them—in the presence of Eugene. He does so. And the wife replies that she will 'choose the weaker.' For a moment the husband supposes she means Eugene. But Eugene knows better. He knows that he is the stronger—and goes."

"So the wife remains with her husband?"

"Precisely."

"How absurdly commonplace!"

"Ah," said Mr Shaw, rather wearily, "you miss the point; I thought you would."

"But, seriously, tell me why the real production is to take place in America, while we are put off with a 'copyright' performance."

"Because Mr Mansfield was the first to secure the play. Besides, the principal part, you will have seen, presents a certain difficulty. It is that of a boy in his 'teens, and rather fragile and effeminate at that. The difficulty was to find in London an actor-manager whose impersonative skill was equal to the rejuvenation. Mr Esmond was suggested on all hands. And I have no doubt he would have played it excellently. Unluckily, Mr Esmond is not an actor-manager. Mr Mansfield's powers of transforming himself are almost miraculous. Besides, he has been remarkably successful in *Arms and the Man*. So it happened that, before *Candida* got beyond the discussion stage here, it was accepted and announced by Mr Mansfield at New York."

"But that does not preclude its independent production here?"

"You forget Candida herself—a character of the utmost importance to the play. I have made it an absolute condition that Miss Janet Achurch shall be cast for the part. Obviously she cannot play on both sides of the Atlantic at the same time. And therefore, if the play is successful in New York, it will be given in London by Miss Janet Achurch and Mr Mansfield, under the management of the latter."

"And a company otherwise American?"

"No. The other four parts will in that case be played by well-known London artists."

"You will excuse the question—but had you any difficulty with the Censor?"

"None whatever. Mr Redford actually wrote a letter to the manager at South Shields, warning him that one of the most delicate situations in the piece would be coarsened and spoiled if my directions were not faithfully carried out. I am infinitely obliged to him for that. It is, I admit, almost enough to disarm me in my crusade against his office. But really, you know, my play is absolutely innocuous. The Rev. Hugh Price Hughes would license it without blinking. Wait till I send up my other play—*Mrs Warren's Profession*. That will put them to the test. It will also make the public sit up."

"What was her profession?"

"The oldest."

"Ah! And are you going to apply for a licence?"

"Yes, and if it is refused I shall make it the text of another tremendous sermon against the Censorship.

"But tell me," said Mr Shaw, "what do you think of *Candida*—so far?"

"It seems to me," I replied, "a very ordinary play."

"That's just it," said Mr Shaw, as he rose to go. "It's extraordinary ordinariness makes it the most extraordinary play ever produced."

Wherewith he departed. And it was not till he had turned the corner of the stairs that the significance of the date struck me. It was Monday, the First of April. It might have been a mere coincidence. But still—

However, I had nothing which I could afford to throw at him.

So I wrote this.

Author's Note

[From the programme of the production at the Globe Theatre, London, 10 February 1937]

As Candida's age is now over 40, the circumstances of her birth are quite forgotten. Let me recall some of them. In the nineties of last century, the theatre was staggering under the shock given to it by the great Norwegian playwright, Henrik Ibsen, who crashed into it when it was in a condition of barren staleness and detachment from the cultural life of the country incredible nowadays. The particular play which acted as the spearhead of his attack was the famous Doll's House, inhabited by a gentleman with all the ideas and attributes of a perfect hero of the theatrical romance of that day, and his charming young wife with her tiny tots of children. Thus A Doll's House began with the happy ending of all the drawing-room comedies in vogue at that time. And the development of the play shewed ruthlessly that the hero was a moral coxcomb, conceited, selfish, and pitifully small in emergencies. And it left the charming wife so completely convinced that she was only the man's pretty doll and that she was quite unfit to have charge of her children, or indeed of anything, that she finished the play by walking out of the house and slamming the door behind her to find out what the world was really like.

This startled Europe and scandalized its silly old theatres so much that they did not notice that it had obliged the playwright to introduce a new constructional feature. The old rule for the playwright was to put the "situation" which was the climax of his story at the end of the last act but one, and then bundle the audience out of the house as best he could by registering a happy ending for the last act. Not thus Ibsen. He made what was then an astounding innovation by first finishing his story completely, and then, instead of bringing down the curtain as quickly as possible, making his characters sit down to discuss the play and draw the moral.

Now this is what happens in Candida; and it was still so novel in 1895 that even so openminded a great actress as Ellen Terry told me that it was utterly impossible for a stage heroine to say calmly, just when the audience was feeling for its hats and caps, "Let us sit and talk comfortably over it like three friends."

When the first shock of this innovation was over, and playgoers discovered that the discussion could be the most interesting part of the play, it soon ceased to appear as a separate and formally announced feature just before the final curtain and spread itself over the entire play, thus bringing the drama back to the classic practice of Shakespeare and the ancient Greek playwrights.

However, audiences do not trouble themselves about technical points; and the surprise in Candida 40 years ago was its turning the tables on A Doll's House. For though the cards are not packed against the husband as they were in Ibsen's play, and he is unquestionably a genuine good fellow of high character and unselfish spirit, yet it is shewn irresistibly that domestically he is the pet and the doll, and that it is his wife who runs the establishment and makes all his public triumphs possible.

That is why Candida made me many women friends and a few male enemies (among the less generous of their sex) 40 years ago. I have no fear of its proving out of date, though some of its first audiences were certainly in that condition. A play that will not last 40 years and be all the better for it is not worth writing.

G. B. S.

11.12.36.

Shaw Reveals Who Was Candida

Evening Standard, November 28, 1944

I count Mr. Beverley Baxter among the friendliest of my up-to-date (my date) critics; for was he not the only one who rose enthusiastically to Heartbreak House when that masterpiece was exploded on an unprepared London twenty years ago?

But in his notice of Candida, at the Lyric Theatre, he has given me a shock that would have killed any other man of my age. He really should be more careful.

Describing the origin of Candida, Mr. Baxter wrote: "It was an open secret at the time that Shaw drew the preacher from Sir Henry Irving and took Candida from Ellen Terry. We need not ask who the poet was. The boy has no beard, but he was Shaw."

This is quite the worst shot ever made by a twentieth century critic at the nineteenth century.

Irving did not know that the Christian Socialist world or such men as the Reverend James Mavor Morell existed. If I had read the play to him he would not have known what I was talking about. He could make-up as the Vicar of Wakefield in Wills's version, with Goldsmith's political economy left out, or as Becket in twelfth century costume; but as an ultramodern parson living in Victoria Park, no.

Irving's world was the Strand, and revolution to him meant the flight of its theatres to the new Shaftesbury-avenue through Seven Dials. He was offered (not by me) two plays in which, with Ellen Terry, he could have made a success and caught up with the times which were leaving him behind; but, unlike Mr. Beverley Baxter, he could not rise to the occasion.

Ellen Terry was a wise and good woman considering the intense segregation in her time of the profession into which she was born; but having tried five husbands and discarded them all without losing their friendship she was hardly a model for Candida.

I knew practically all the leading Christian Socialist clergymen. The nearest to Morell was Stopford Brooke, with touches of Canon Shuttleworth and Fleming Williams.

I had no models for Candida. I borrowed her name from an Italian lady I never met: Candida Bartolucci, afterwards a British marchioness. Candida Morell is entirely imagined: and the play is a counterblast to Ibsen's Doll's House, showing that in the real typical doll's house it is the man who is the doll.

When I began writing the part of the young poet, I had in mind De Quincey's account of his adolescence in his Confessions. I certainly never thought of myself as a model.

Heaven forgive you, Beverley Baxter!

The Man of Destiny

WITH

An interview drafted by Shaw for
The Daily Mail, *15 May 1897*

Composition begun 10 May 1895; completed 24 August 1895. Published in *Plays Pleasant and Unpleasant*, 1898. Revised text in Collected Edition, 1930.

First presented by Murray Carson at the Grand Theatre, Croydon, on 1 July 1897 (3 performances).

Napoleon   *Murray Carson*
A Lieutenant   *E. H. Kelly*
Giuseppe   *Horace Hodges*
A Strange Lady   *Florence West*

Scene: Tavazzano, Italy. An Inn on the road from Lodi to Milan. Period: May 12, 1796. Time: 7.30 in the Evening.

$\begin{bmatrix} \text{ACT I} \end{bmatrix}$

The twelfth of May, 1796, in north Italy, at Tavaz-
zano, on the road from Lodi to Milan. The afternoon
sun is blazing serenely over the plains of Lombardy,
treating the Alps with respect and the ant-hills with in-
dulgence, neither disgusted by the basking of the swine in
the villages nor hurt by its cool reception in the churches,
but ruthlessly disdainful of two hordes of mischievous
insects which are the French and Austrian armies. Two
days before, at Lodi, the Austrians tried to prevent the
French from crossing the river by the narrow bridge
there; but the French, commanded by a general aged 27,
Napoleon Bonaparte, who does not respect the rules of
war, rushed the fireswept bridge, supported by a tremen-
dous cannonade in which the young general assisted with
his own hands. Cannonading is his technical speciality:
he has been trained in the artillery under the old régime,
and made perfect in the military arts of shirking his
duties, swindling the paymaster over travelling expenses,
and dignifying war with the noise and smoke of cannon,
as depicted in all military portraits. He is, however, an
original observer, and has perceived, for the first time
since the invention of gunpowder, that a cannon ball, if
it strikes a man, will kill him. To a thorough grasp of
this remarkable discovery he adds a highly evolved
faculty for physical geography and for the calculation of
times and distances. He has prodigious powers of work,
and a clear realistic knowledge of human nature in
public affairs, having seen it exhaustively tested in
that department during the French Revolution. He is

imaginative without illusions, and creative without religion, loyalty, patriotism or any of the common ideals. Not that he is incapable of these ideals: on the contrary, he has swallowed them all in his boyhood, and now, having a keen dramatic faculty, is extremely clever at playing upon them by the arts of the actor and stage manager. Withal, he is no spoiled child. Poverty, ill-luck, the shifts of impecunious shabby-gentility, repeated failure as a would-be author, humiliation as a rebuffed time server, reproof and punishment as an incompetent and dishonest officer, an escape from dismissal from the service so narrow that if the emigration of the nobles had not raised the value of even the most rascally lieutenant to the famine price of a general he would have been swept contemptuously from the army: these trials have ground his conceit out of him, and forced him to be self-sufficient and to understand that to such men as he is the world will give nothing that he cannot take from it by force. In this the world is not free from cowardice and folly; for Napoleon, as a merciless cannonader of political rubbish, is making himself useful: indeed, it is even now impossible to live in England without sometimes feeling how much that country lost in not being conquered by him as well as by Julius Caesar.

However, on this May afternoon in 1796, it is early days with him. He has but recently been promoted general, partly by using his wife to seduce the Directory (then governing France); partly by the scarcity of officers caused by the emigration as aforesaid; partly by his faculty of knowing a country, with all its roads, rivers, hills and valleys, as he knows the palm of his hand; and largely by that new faith of his in the efficacy of firing cannons at people. His army is, as to discipline, in a state which has so greatly shocked some modern writers before whom the following story has been en-

*acted, that they, impressed with the later glory of
"L'Empereur," have altogether refused to credit it. But
Napoleon is not L'Empereur yet: his men call him Le
Petit Caporal, as he is still in the stage of gaining influence over them by displays of pluck. He is not in a
position to force his will on them in orthodox military
fashion by the cat o' nine tails. The French Revolution,
which has escaped suppression solely through the mon-
archy's habit of being at least four years in arrear with its
soldiers in the matter of pay, has substituted for that
habit, as far as possible, the habit of not paying at all,
except in promises and patriotic flatteries which are not
compatible with martial law of the Prussian type.
Napoleon has therefore approached the Alps in command of men without money, in rags, and consequently
indisposed to stand much discipline, especially from upstart generals. This circumstance, which would have
embarrassed an idealist soldier, has been worth a
thousand cannon to Napoleon. He has said to his army
" You have patriotism and courage; but you have no
money, no clothes, and hardly anything to eat. In Italy
there are all these things, and glory as well, to be gained
by a devoted army led by a general who regards loot as
the natural right of the soldier. I am such a general. En
avant, mes enfants!" The result has entirely justified
him. The army conquers Italy as the locusts conquered
Cyprus. They fight all day and march all night, covering
impossible distances and appearing in incredible places,
not because every soldier carries a field marshal's baton
in his knapsack, but because he hopes to carry at least
half a dozen silver forks there next day.*

*It must be understood, by the way, that the French
army does not make war on the Italians. It is there to
rescue them from the tyranny of their Austrian con-
querors, and confer republican institutions on them; so*

that in incidentally looting them it merely makes free with the property of its friends, who ought to be grateful to it, and perhaps would be if ingratitude were not the proverbial failing of their country. The Austrians, whom it fights, are a thoroughly respectable regular army, well disciplined, commanded by gentlemen versed in orthodox campaigning: at the head of them Beaulieu, practising the classic art of war under orders from Vienna, and getting horribly beaten by Napoleon, who acts on his own responsibility in defiance of professional precedents or orders from Paris. Even when the Austrians win a battle, all that is necessary is to wait until their routine obliges them to return to their quarters for afternoon tea, so to speak, and win it back again from them: a course pursued later on with brilliant success at Marengo. On the whole, with his foe handicapped by Austrian statesmanship, classic generalship, and the exigencies of the aristocratic social structure of Viennese society, Napoleon finds it possible to be irresistible without working heroic miracles. The world, however, likes miracles and heroes, and is quite incapable of conceiving the action of such forces as academic militarism or Viennese drawing-roomism. Hence it has already begun to manufacture "L'Empereur," and thus to make it difficult for the romanticists of a hundred years later to credit the hitherto unrecorded little scene now in question at Tavazzano.

The best quarters in Tavazzano are at a little inn, the first house reached by travellers passing through the place from Milan to Lodi. It stands in a vineyard; and its principal room, a pleasant refuge from the summer heat, is open so widely at the back to this vineyard that it is almost a large veranda. The bolder children, much excited by the alarums and excursions of the past few days, and by an irruption of French troops at six o'clock,

*know that the French commander has quartered himself
in this room, and are divided between a craving to peep
in at the front windows, and a mortal dread of the sentinel, a young gentleman-soldier who, having no natural
moustache, has had a most ferocious one painted on his
face with boot blacking by his sergeant. As his heavy
uniform, like all the uniforms of that day, is designed for
parade without the least reference to his health or comfort, he perspires profusely in the sun; and his painted
moustache has run in little streaks down his chin and
round his neck, except where it has dried in stiff japanned
flakes and had its sweeping outline chipped off in grotesque little bays and headlands, making him unspeakably
ridiculous in the eye of History a hundred years later,
but monstrous and horrible to the contemporary north
Italian infant, to whom nothing would seem more
natural than that he should relieve the monotony of his
guard by pitchforking a stray child up on his bayonet,
and eating it uncooked. Nevertheless one girl of bad
character, in whom an instinct of privilege with soldiers
is already stirring, does peep in at the safest window for
a moment before a glance and a clink from the sentinel
sends her flying. Most of what she sees she has seen before:
the vineyard at the back, with the old winepress and a
cart among the vines; the door close on her right leading
to the street entry; the landlord's best sideboard, now in
full action for dinner, further back on the same side; the
fireplace on the other side with a couch near it; another
door, leading to the inner rooms, between it and the vineyard; and the table in the middle set out with a repast
of Milanese risotto, cheese, grapes, bread, olives, and a
big wickered flask of red wine.*

*The landlord, Giuseppe Grandi, she knows well. He
is a swarthy vivacious shrewdly cheerful black-curled
bullet headed grinning little innkeeper of 40. Naturally*

*an excellent host, he is in the highest spirits this evening
at his good fortune in having as his guest the French
commander to protect him against the license of the
troops. He actually sports a pair of gold earrings which
would otherwise have been hidden carefully under the
winepress with his little equipment of silver plate.*

*Napoleon, sitting facing her on the further side of the
table, she sees for the first time. He is working hard,
partly at his meal, which he has discovered how to dis-
patch in ten minutes by attacking all the courses simultaneously (this practice is the beginning of his downfall),
and partly at a military map on which he from time to
time marks the position of the forces by taking a grape-
skin from his mouth and planting it on the map with his
thumb like a wafer. There is no revolutionary untidiness
about his dress or person; but his elbow has displaced
most of the dishes and glasses; and his long hair trails
into the risotto when he forgets it and leans more
intently over the map.*

GIUSEPPE. Will your excellency—
NAPOLEON [*intent on his map, but cramming himself
mechanically with his left hand*] Dont talk. I'm busy.
GIUSEPPE [*with perfect goodhumor*] Excellency: I
obey.
NAPOLEON. Some red ink.
GIUSEPPE. Alas! excellency, there is none.
NAPOLEON [*with Corsican facetiousness*] Kill some-
thing and bring me its blood.
GIUSEPPE [*grinning*] There is nothing but your
excellency's horse, the sentinel, the lady upstairs, and
my wife.
NAPOLEON. Kill your wife.

GIUSEPPE. Willingly, your excellency; but unhappily
I am not strong enough. She would kill me.

NAPOLEON. That will do equally well.

GIUSEPPE. Your excellency does me too much honor.
[*Stretching his hand towards the flask*] Perhaps some
wine will answer your excellency's purpose.

NAPOLEON [*hastily protecting the flask, and becoming
quite serious*] Wine! No: that would be waste. You are
all the same: waste! waste! waste! *He marks the map
with gravy, using his fork as a pen*]. Clear away. [*He
finishes his wine; pushes back his chair; and uses his
napkin, stretching his legs and leaning back, but still
frowning and thinking*].

GIUSEPPE [*clearing the table and removing the things
to a tray on the sideboard*] Every man to his trade,
excellency. We innkeepers have plenty of cheap wine:
we think nothing of spilling it. You great generals
have plenty of cheap blood: you think nothing of
spilling it. Is it not so, excellency?

NAPOLEON. Blood costs nothing: wine costs money.
[*He rises and goes to the fireplace*].

GIUSEPPE. They say you are careful of everything
except human life, excellency.

NAPOLEON. Human life, my friend, is the only thing
that takes care of itself. [*He throws himself at his ease
on the couch*].

GIUSEPPE [*admiring him*] Ah, excellency, what fools
we all are beside you! If I could only find out the
secret of your success!

NAPOLEON. You would make yourself Emperor of
Italy, eh?

GIUSEPPE. Too troublesome, excellency: I leave all
that to you. Besides, what would become of my inn if
I were Emperor? See how you enjoy looking on at
me whilst I keep the inn for you and wait on you!

Well, I shall enjoy looking on at you whilst you become Emperor of Europe, and govern the country for me. [*As he chatters, he takes the cloth off deftly without removing the map, and finally takes the corners in his hands and the middle in his mouth, to fold it up*].

NAPOLEON. Emperor of Europe, eh? Why only Europe?

GIUSEPPE. Why, indeed? Emperor of the world, excellency! Why not? [*He folds and rolls up the cloth, emphasizing his phrases by the steps of the process*]. One man is like another [*fold*]: one country is like another [*fold*]: one battle is like another. [*At the last fold, he slaps the cloth on the table and deftly rolls it up, adding, by way of peroration*] Conquer one: conquer all. [*He takes the cloth to the sideboard, and puts it in a drawer*].

NAPOLEON. And govern for all; fight for all; be everybody's servant under cover of being everybody's master. Guiseppe.

GIUSEPPE [*at the sideboard*] Excellency?

NAPOLEON. I forbid you to talk to me about myself.

GIUSEPPE [*coming to the foot of the couch*] Pardon. Your excellency is so unlike other great men. It is the subject they like best.

NAPOLEON. Well, talk to me about the subject they like next best, whatever that may be.

GIUSEPPE [*unabashed*] Willingly, your excellency. Has your excellency by any chance caught a glimpse of the lady upstairs?

NAPOLEON [*sitting up promptly*] How old is she?

GIUSEPPE. The right age, excellency.

NAPOLEON. Do you mean seventeen or thirty?

GIUSEPPE. Thirty, excellency.

NAPOLEON. Goodlooking?

GIUSEPPE. I cannot see with your excellency's eyes: every man must judge that for himself. In my opinion,

[614]

excellency, a fine figure of a lady. [*Slyly*] Shall I lay the table for her collation here?

NAPOLEON. [*brusquely, rising*] No: lay nothing here until the officer for whom I am waiting comes back. [*He looks at his watch, and takes to walking to and fro between the fireplace and the vineyard*].

GIUSEPPE [*with conviction*] Excellency: believe me, he has been captured by the accursed Austrians. He dare not keep you waiting if he were at liberty.

NAPOLEON [*turning at the edge of the shadow of the veranda*] Giuseppe: if that turns out to be true, it will put me into such a temper that nothing short of hanging you and your whole household, including the lady upstairs, will satisfy me.

GIUSEPPE. We are all cheerfully at your excellency's disposal, except the lady. I cannot answer for her; but no lady could resist you, General.

NAPOLEON [*sourly, resuming his march*] Hm! You will never be hanged. There is no satisfaction in hanging a man who does not object to it.

GIUSEPPE [*sympathetically*] Not the least in the world, excellency: is there? [*Napoleon again looks at his watch, evidently growing anxious*]. Ah, one can see that you are a great man, General: you know how to wait. If it were a corporal now, or a sub-lieutenant, at the end of three minutes he would be swearing, fuming, threatening, pulling the house about our ears.

NAPOLEON. Giuseppe: your flatteries are insufferable. Go and talk outside. [*He sits down again at the table, with his jaws in his hands, and his elbows propped on the map, poring over it with a troubled expression*].

GIUSEPPE. Willingly, your excellency. You shall not be disturbed. [*He takes up the tray and prepares to withdraw*].

[615]

NAPOLEON. The moment he comes back, send him to me.

GIUSEPPE. Instantaneously, your excellency.

A LADY'S VOICE [*calling from some distant part of the inn*] Giusep-pe! [*The voice is very musical, and the two final notes make an ascending interval*].

NAPOLEON. [*startled*] Who's that?

GIUSEPPE. The lady, excellency.

NAPOLEON. The lady upstairs?

GIUSEPPE. Yes, excellency. The strange lady.

NAPOLEON. Strange? Where does she come from?

GIUSEPPE [*with a shrug*] Who knows? She arrived here just before your excellency in a hired carriage belonging to the Golden Eagle at Borghetto. By herself, excellency. No servants. A dressing bag and a trunk: that is all. The postillion says she left a horse at the Golden Eagle. A charger, with military trappings.

NAPOLEON. A woman with a charger! French or Austrian?

GIUSEPPE. French, excellency.

NAPOLEON. Her husband's charger, no doubt. Killed at Lodi, poor fellow.

THE LADY'S VOICE [*the two final notes now making a peremptory descending interval*] Giuseppe!

NAPOLEON [*rising to listen*] Thats not the voice of a woman whose husband was killed yesterday.

GIUSEPPE. Husbands are not always regretted, excellency. [*Calling*] Coming, lady, coming. [*He makes for the inner door*].

NAPOLEON [*arresting him with a strong hand on his shoulder*] Stop. Let her come.

VOICE. Giuseppe!! [*impatiently*].

GIUSEPPE. Let me go, excellency. It is my point of honor as an innkeeper to come when I am called. I appeal to you as a soldier.

A MAN'S VOICE [*outside, at the inn door, shouting*] Here, someone. Hollo! Landlord! Where are you? [*Somebody raps vigorously with a whip handle on a bench in the passage*].

NAPOLEON [*suddenly becoming the commanding officer again and throwing Giuseppe off*] My man at last. [*Pointing to the inner door*] Go. Attend to your business: the lady is calling you. [*He goes to the fireplace and stands with his back to it with a determined military air*].

GIUSEPPE [*with bated breath, snatching up his tray*] Certainly, excellency. [*He hurries out by the inner door*].

THE MAN'S VOICE [*impatiently*] Are you all asleep here?

The other door is kicked rudely open. A dusty sublieutenant bursts into the room. He is a tall chuckleheaded young man of 24, with the complexion and style of a man of rank, and a self-assurance on that ground which the French Revolution has failed to shake in the smallest degree. He has a thick silly lip, an eager credulous eye, an obstinate nose, and a loud confident voice. A young man without fear, without reverence, without imagination, without sense, hopelessly insusceptible to the Napoleonic or any other idea, stupendously egotistical, eminently qualified to rush in where angels fear to tread, yet of a vigorous babbling vitality which bustles him into the thick of things. He is just now boiling with vexation, attributable by a superficial observer to his impatience at not being promptly attended to by the staff of the inn, but in which a more discerning eye can perceive a certain moral depth, indicating a more permanent and momentous grievance. On seeing Napoleon, he is sufficiently taken aback to check himself and salute; but he does not betray by his manner any of that prophetic consciousness of Marengo and Austerlitz, Water-

*loo and St Helena, or the Napoleonic pictures of
Delaroche and Meissonier, which later ages expect from
him.*

NAPOLEON [*watch in hand*] Well, sir, you have come
at last. Your instructions were that I should arrive
here at six, and find you waiting for me with my mail
from Paris and with despatches. It is now twenty
minutes to eight. You were sent on this service as a
hard rider with the fastest horse in the camp. You
arrive a hundred minutes late, on foot. Where is your
horse?

THE LIEUTENANT [*moodily pulling off his gloves and
dashing them with his cap and whip on the table*] Ah!
where indeed? Thats just what I should like to know,
General. [*With emotion*] You dont know how fond I
was of that horse.

NAPOLEON [*angrily sarcastic*] Indeed! [*With sudden
misgiving*] Where are the letters and despatches?

THE LIEUTENANT [*importantly, rather pleased than
otherwise at having some remarkable news*] I dont know.

NAPOLEON [*unable to believe his ears*] You dont
know!

LIEUTENANT. No more than you do, General. Now
I suppose I shall be court-martialled. Well, I dont
mind being court-martialled; but [*with solemn determination*] I tell you, General, if ever I catch that
innocent looking youth, I'll spoil his beauty, the slimy
little liar! I'll make a picture of him. I'll—

NAPOLEON. [*advancing from the hearth to the table*]
What innocent looking youth? Pull yourself together,
sir, will you; and give an account of yourself.

LIEUTENANT [*facing him at the opposite side of the
table, leaning on it with his fists*] Oh, I'm all right,
General: I'm perfectly ready to give an account of
myself. I shall make the court-martial thoroughly

understand that the fault was not mine. Advantage has been taken of the better side of my nature; and I'm not ashamed of it. But with all respect to you as my commanding officer, General, I say again that if ever I set eyes on that son of Satan, Ill—

NAPOLEON [*angrily*] So you said before.

LIEUTENANT [*drawing himself upright*] I say it again. Just wait until I catch him. Just wait: thats all. [*He folds his arms resolutely, and breathes hard, with compressed lips*].

NAPOLEON. I am waiting, sir. For your explanation.

LIEUTENANT [*confidently*] Youll change your tone, General, when you hear what has happened to me.

NAPOLEON. Nothing has happened to you, sir: you are alive and not disabled. Where are the papers entrusted to you?

LIEUTENANT. Nothing happened to me! Nothing!! He swore eternal brotherhood with me. Was that nothing? He said my eyes reminded him of his sister's eyes. Was that nothing? He cried—actually cried— over the story of my separation from Angelica. Was that nothing? He paid for both bottles of wine, though he only ate bread and grapes himself. Perhaps you call that nothing. He gave me his pistols and his horse and his despatches—most important despatches—and let me go away with them. [*Triumphantly, seeing that he has reduced Napoleon to blank stupefaction*] Was that nothing?

NAPOLEON [*enfeebled by astonishment*] What did he do that for?

LIEUTENANT [*as if the reason were obvious*] To shew his confidence in me, of course. [*Napoleon's jaw does not exactly drop; but its hinges becomes nerveless*]. And I was worthy of his confidence: I brought them all back honorably. But would you believe it? when I trusted him with my pistols, and my horse, and my despatches—

NAPOLEON. What the devil did you do that for?

LIEUTENANT. I'm telling you: to shew my confidence in him. And he betrayed it! abused it! never came back again! The thief! the swindler! the heartless treacherous little blackguard! You call that nothing, I suppose. But look here, General: [*again resorting to the table with his fists for greater emphasis*] you may put up with this outrage from the Austrians if you like; but speaking for myself personally, I tell you that if ever I catch—

NAPOLEON [*turning on his heel in disgust and irritably resuming his march to and fro*] Yes: you have said that more than once already.

LIEUTENANT [*excitedly*] More than once! I'll say it fifty times; and whats more, I'll do it. Youll see, General. I'll shew my confidence in him, so I will. I'll—

NAPOLEON. Yes, yes, sir: no doubt you will. What kind of man was he?

LIEUTENANT. Well, I should think you ought to be able to tell from his conduct the kind of man he was.

NAPOLEON. Psha! What was he like?

LIEUTENANT. Like! He was like—well, you ought to have just seen the fellow: that will give you a notion of what he was like. He wont be like it five minutes after I catch him; for I tell you that if ever—

NAPOLEON [*shouting furiously for the innkeeper*] Giuseppe! [*To the Lieutenant, out of all patience*] Hold your tongue, sir, if you can.

LIEUTENANT [*plaintively*] I warn you it's no use trying to put the blame on me. How was I to know the sort of fellow he was? [*He takes a chair from between the sideboard and the outer door; places it near the table; and sits down*]. If you only knew how hungry and tired I am, youd have more consideration.

GIUSEPPE [*returning*] What is it, excellency?

NAPOLEON [*struggling with his temper*] Take this— this officer. Feed him; and put him to bed, if necessary. When he is in his right mind again, find out what has happened to him and bring me word. [*To the Lieutenant*] Consider yourself under arrest, sir.

LIEUTENANT [*with sulky stiffness*] I was prepared for that. It takes a gentleman to understand a gentleman. [*He throws his sword on the table*].

GIUSEPPE [*with sympathetic concern*] Have you been attacked by the Austrians, lieutenant? Dear! dear! dear!

LIEUTENANT [*contemptuously*] Attacked! I could have broken his back between my finger and thumb. I wish I had, now. No: it was by appealing to the better side of my nature: thats what I cant get over. He said he'd never met a man he liked so much as me. He put his handkerchief round my neck because a gnat bit me, and my stock was chafing it. Look! [*He pulls a handkerchief from his stock. Giuseppe takes it and examines it*].

GIUSEPPE [*to Napoleon*] A lady's handkerchief, excellency. [*He smells it*]. Perfumed.

NAPOLEON. Eh? [*He takes it and looks at it attentively*]. Hm! [*He smells it*]. Ha! [*He walks thoughtfully across the room, looking at the handkerchief, which he finally sticks in the breast of his coat*].

LIEUTENANT. Good enough for him, anyhow. I noticed that he had a woman's hands when he touched my neck, with his coaxing fawning ways, the mean effeminate little hound. [*Lowering his voice with thrilling intensity*] But mark my words, General. If ever—

THE LADY'S VOICE [*outside as before*] Giuseppe!

LIEUTENANT [*petrified*] What was that?

GIUSEPPE. Only a lady upstairs, lieutenant, calling me.

LIEUTENANT. Lady!

VOICE. Giuseppe, Giuseppe: where are you?

LIEUTENANT [*murderously*] Give me that sword. [*He snatches up the sword and draws it*].

GIUSEPPE [*rushing forward and seizing his right arm*] What are you thinking of, lieutenant? It's a lady: dont you hear? It's a woman's voice.

LIEUTENANT. It's his voice, I tell you. Let me go. [*He breaks away, and rushes to the edge of the veranda, where he posts himself, sword in hand, watching the door like a cat watching a mousehole*].

It opens; and the Strange Lady steps in. She is tall and extraordinarily graceful, with a delicately intelligent, apprehensive, questioning face: perception in the brow, sensitiveness in the nostrils, character in the chin: all keen, refined, and original. She is very feminine, but by no means weak: the lithe tender figure is hung on a strong frame: the hands and feet, neck and shoulders, are useful vigorous members, of full size in proportion to her stature, which perceptibly exceeds that of Napoleon and the innkeeper, and leaves her at no disadvantage with the lieutenant. Only, her elegance and radiant charm keep the secret of her size and strength. She is not, judging by her dress, an admirer of the latest fashions of the Directory; or perhaps she uses up her old dresses for travelling. At all events she wears no jacket with extravagant lappels, no Greco-Tallien sham chiton, nothing, indeed, that the Princesse de Lamballe might not have worn. Her dress of flowered silk is long waisted, with a Watteau pleat behind, but with the paniers reduced to mere rudiments, as she is too tall for them. It is cut low

*in the neck, where it is eked out by a creamy fichu. She
is fair, with golden brown hair and grey eyes.*

*She enters with the self-possession of a woman accus-
tomed to the privileges of rank and beauty. The innkeeper, who has excellent natural manners, is highly
appreciative of her. Napoleon is smitten self-conscious.
His color deepens: he becomes stiffer and less at ease than
before. She is advancing in an infinitely well bred manner to pay her respects to him when the lieutenant
pounces on her and seizes her right wrist. As she recognizes him, she becomes deadly pale. There is no mistaking
her expression: a revelation of some fatal error, utterly
unexpected, has suddenly appalled her in the midst of
tranquillity, security, and victory. The next moment a
wave of angry color rushes up from beneath the creamy
fichu and drowns her whole face. One can see that she is
blushing all over her body. Even the lieutenant, ordinarily
incapable of observation, can see a thing when it is painted
red for him. Interpreting the blush as the involuntary
confession of black deceit confronted with its victim, he
addresses her in a loud crow of retributive triumph.*

LIEUTENANT. So Ive got you, my lad. So youve disguised yourself, have you? [*In a voice of thunder,
releasing her wrist*] Take off that skirt.

GIUSEPPE [*remonstrating*] Oh, lieutenant!

LADY [*affrighted, but highly indignant at his having
dared to touch her*] Gentlemen: I appeal to you. [*To
Napoleon*] You, sir, are an officer: a general. You will
protect me, will you not?

LIEUTENANT. Never you mind him, General. Leave
me to deal with him.

NAPOLEON. With him! With whom, sir? Why do
you treat this lady in such a fashion?

LIEUTENANT. Lady! He's a man! the man I shewed
my confidence in. [*Raising his sword*] Here, you—

LADY [*running behind Napoleon and in her agitation clasping to her breast the arm which he extends before her as a fortification*] Oh, thank you, General. Keep him away.

NAPOLEON. Nonsense, sir. This is certainly a lady [*she suddenly drops his arm and blushes again*]; and you are under arrest. Put down your sword, sir, instantly.

LIEUTENANT. General: I tell you he's an Austrian spy. He passed himself off on me as one of General Masséna's staff this afternoon; and now he's passing himself off on you as a woman. Am I to believe my own eyes or not?

LADY. General: it must be my brother. He is on General Masséna's staff. He is very like me.

LIEUTENANT [*his mind giving way*] Do you mean to say that youre not your brother, but your sister? the sister who was so like me? who had my beautiful blue eyes? It's a lie: your eyes are not like mine: theyre exactly like your own.

NAPOLEON [*with contained exasperation*] Lieutenant: will you obey my orders and leave the room, since you are convinced at last that this is no gentleman?

LIEUTENANT. Gentleman! I should think not. No gentleman would have abused my confid—

NAPOLEON [*out of all patience*] That will do, sir: do you hear? Will you leave the room? I order you to leave the room.

LADY. Oh pray let me go instead.

NAPOLEON [*drily*] Excuse me, madam. With all possible respect for your brother, I do not yet understand what an officer on General Masséna's staff wants with my letters. I have some questions to put to you.

GIUSEPPE [*discreetly*] Come, lieutenant. [*He opens the door*].

LIEUTENANT. I'm off. General: take warning by me:

be on your guard against the better side of your nature. [*To the lady*] Madam: my apologies. I thought you were the same person, only of the opposite sex; and that naturally misled me.

LADY [*recovering her good humor*] It was not your fault, was it? I'm so glad youre not angry with me any longer, lieutenant. [*She offers her hand*].

LIEUTENANT [*bending gallantly to kiss it*] Oh, madam, not the lea—[*Checking himself and looking at it*] You have your brother's hand. And the same sort of ring!

LADY [*sweetly*] We are twins.

LIEUTENANT. That accounts for it. [*He kisses her hand*]. A thousand pardons. I didnt mind about the despatches at all: thats more the General's affair than mine: it was the abuse of my confidence through the better side of my nature. [*Taking his cap, gloves and whip from the table and going*] Youll excuse my leaving you, General, I hope. Very sorry, I'm sure. [*He talks himself out of the room. Giuseppe follows him and shuts the door*].

NAPOLEON [*looking after them with concentrated irritation*] Idiot!

The Strange Lady smiles sympathetically. He comes frowning down the room between the table and the fireplace, all his awkwardness gone now that he is alone with her.

LADY. How can I thank you, General, for your protection?

NAPOLEON [*turning on her suddenly*] My despatches: come! [*He puts out his hand for them*].

LADY. General! [*She involuntarily puts her hands on her fichu as if to protect something there*].

NAPOLEON. You tricked that blockhead out of them. You disguised yourself as a man. I want my des-

patches. They are there in the bosom of your dress,
under your hands.

LADY [*quickly removing her hands*] Oh, how unkindly
you are speaking to me! [*She takes her handkerchief
from her fichu*] You frighten me. [*She touches her eyes
as if to wipe away a tear*].

NAPOLEON. I see you dont know me, madam, or you
would save yourself the trouble of pretending to cry.

LADY [*producing an effect of smiling through her tears*]
Yes, I do know you. You are the famous General
Buonaparte. [*She gives the name a marked Italian pro-
nunciation: Bwawna-parr-te*].

NAPOLEON [*angrily, with the French pronunciation*]
Bonaparte, Madam, Bonaparte. The papers, if you
please.

LADY. But I assure you— [*He snatches the handkerchief rudely*]. General! [*indignantly*].

NAPOLEON [*taking the other handkerchief from his
breast*] You lent one of your handkerchiefs to my
lieutenant when you robbed him. [*He looks at the two
handkerchiefs*]. They match one another. [*He smells
them*]. The same scent. [*He flings them down on the
table*]. I am waiting for my despatches. I shall take
them, if necessary, with as little ceremony as I took
the handkerchief.

LADY [*in dignified reproof*] General: do you threaten
women?

NAPOLEON [*bluntly*] Yes.

LADY [*disconcerted, trying to gain time*] But I dont
understand. I—

NAPOLEON. You understand perfectly. You came
here because your Austrian employers calculated that
I was six leagues away. I am always to be found where
my enemies dont expect me. You have walked into
the lion's den. Come! you are a brave woman. Be a

sensible one: I have no time to waste. The papers.
[*He advances a step ominously*].

LADY [*breaking down in the childish rage of impotence,
and throwing herself in tears on the chair left beside the
table by the lieutenant*] I brave! How little you know!
I have spent the day in an agony of fear. I have a pain
here from the tightening of my heart at every sus-
picious look, every threatening movement. Do you
think everyone is as brave as you? Oh, why will not you
brave people do the brave things? Why do you leave
them to us, who have no courage at all? I'm not
brave: I shrink from violence: danger makes me
miserable.

NAPOLEON [*interested*] Then why have you thrust
yourself into danger?

LADY. Because there is no other way: I can trust
nobody else. And now it is all useless: all because of
you, who have no fear because you have no heart, no
feeling, no—[*She breaks off, and throws herself on her
knees*]. Ah, General, let me go: let me go without
asking any questions. You shall have your despatches
and letters: I swear it.

NAPOLEON [*holding out his hand*] Yes: I am waiting
for them.

*She gasps, daunted by his ruthless promptitude into
despair of moving him by cajolery. She looks up perplexedly at him, racking her brains for some device to
outwit him. He meets her regard inflexibly.*

LADY [*rising at last with a quiet little sigh*] I will get
them for you. They are in my room. [*She turns to the
door*].

NAPOLEON. I shall accompany you, madam.

LADY [*drawing herself up with a noble air of offended
delicacy*] I cannot permit you, General to enter my
chamber.

NAPOLEON. Then you shall stay here, madam, whilst I have your chamber searched for my papers.

LADY [*spitefully, openly giving up her plan*] You may save yourself the trouble. They are not there.

NAPOLEON. No: I have already told you where they are [*pointing to her breast*].

LADY [*with pretty piteousness*] General: I only want to keep one little private letter. Only one. Let me have it.

NAPOLEON [*cold and stern*] Is that a reasonable demand, madam?

LADY [*encouraged by his not refusing point-blank*] No; but that is why you must grant it. Are your own demands reasonable? thousands of lives for the sake of your victories, your ambitions, your destiny! And what I ask is such a little thing. And I am only a weak woman, and you a brave man. [*She looks at him with her eyes full of tender pleading, and is about to kneel to him again*].

NAPOLEON [*brusquely*] Get up, get up. [*He turns moodily away and takes a turn across the room, pausing for a moment to say, over his shoulder*] Youre talking nonsense; and you know it. [*She sits down submissively on the couch. When he turns and sees her despair, he feels that his victory is complete, and that he may now indulge in a little play with his victim. He comes back and sits beside her. She looks alarmed and moves a little away from him; but a ray of rallying hope beams from her eye. He begins like a man enjoying some secret joke*]. How do you know I am a brave man?

LADY [*amazed*] You! General Buonaparte [*Italian pronounciation*].

NAPOLEON. Yes, I, General Bonaparte [*emphasizing the French pronunciation*].

LADY. Oh, how can you ask such a question? you!

[628]

who stood only two days ago at the bridge at Lodi, with the air full of death, fighting a duel with cannons across the river! [*Shuddering*]. Oh, you do brave things.

NAPOLEON. So do you.

LADY. I! [*With a sudden odd thought*] Oh! Are you a coward?

NAPOLEON [*laughing grimly and slapping his knees*] That is the one question you must never ask a soldier. The sergeant asks after the recruit's height, his age, his wind, his limb, but never after his courage.

LADY [*as if she had found it no laughing matter*] Ah, you can laugh at fear. Then you dont know what fear is.

NAPOLEON. Tell me this. Suppose you could have got that letter by coming to me over the bridge at Lodi the day before yesterday! Suppose there had been no other way, and that this was a sure way—if only you escaped the cannon! [*She shudders and covers her eyes for a moment with her hands*]. Would you have been afraid?

LADY. Oh, horribly afraid, agonizingly afraid. [*She presses her hands on her heart*]. It hurts only to imagine it.

NAPOLEON [*inflexibly*] Would you have come for the despatches?

LADY [*overcome by the imagined horror*] Dont ask me. I must have come.

NAPOLEON. Why?

LADY. Because I must. Because there would have been no other way.

NAPOLEON [*with conviction*] Because you would have wanted my letter enough to bear your fear. [*He rises suddenly, and deliberately poses for an oration*]. There is only one universal passion: fear. Of all the thousand qualities a man may have, the only one you will find as certainly in the youngest drummer boy in my army as in me, is fear. It is fear that makes men fight: it is indifference that makes them run away: fear is the mainspring of war. Fear! I know fear well, better than you, better than any woman. I once saw a regiment of good Swiss soldiers massacred by a mob in Paris because I was afraid to interfere: I felt myself a coward to the tips of my toes as I looked on at it. Seven months ago I revenged my shame by pounding that mob to death with cannon balls. Well, what of that? Has fear ever held a man back from anything he really wanted—or a woman either? Never. Come with me; and I will shew you twenty thousand cowards who will risk death every day for the price of a glass of brandy. And do you think there are no women in the army, braver than the men, though their lives are worth more? Psha! I think nothing of your fear or your bravery. If you had had to come across to me at Lodi, you would not have been afraid: once on the bridge, every other feeling would have gone down before the necessity—the necessity—for making your way to my side and getting what you wanted.

And now, suppose you had done all this! suppose you had come safely out with that letter in your hand, knowing that when the hour came, your fear had tightened, not your heart, but your grip of your own purpose! that it had ceased to be fear, and had become strength, penetration, vigilance, iron resolution! how would you answer then if you were asked whether you were a coward?

LADY [*rising*] Ah, you are a hero, a real hero.

NAPOLEON. Pooh! theres no such thing as a real hero. [*He strolls about the room, making light of her enthusi-*

asm, but by no means displeased with himself for having evoked it].

LADY. Ah yes, there is. There is a difference between what you call my bravery and yours. You wanted to win the battle of Lodi for yourself and not for anyone else, didnt you?

NAPOLEON. Of course. [*Suddenly recollecting himself*] Stop: no [*He pulls himself piously together, and says, like a man conducting a religious service*] I am only the servant of the French republic, following humbly in the footsteps of the heroes of classical antiquity. I win battles for humanity: for my country, not for myself.

LADY [*disappointed*] Oh, then you are only a womanish hero after all. [*She sits down again, all her enthusiasm gone*].

NAPOLEON [*greatly astonished*] Womanish!

LADY [*listlessly*] Yes, like me. [*With deep melancholy*] Do you think that if I wanted those despatches only for myself, I dare venture into a battle for them? No: if that were all, I should not have the courage to ask to see you at your hotel, even. My courage is mere slavishness: it is of no use to me for my own purposes. It is only through love, through pity, through the instinct to save and protect someone else, that I can do the things that terrify me.

NAPOLEON [*contemptuously*] Pshaw! [*He turns slightingly away from her*].

LADY. Aha! now you see that I'm not really brave. [*Relapsing into petulant listlessness*] But what right have you to despise me if you only win your battles for others? for your country! through patriotism! That is what I call womanish: it is so like a Frenchman!

NAPOLEON [*furiously*] I am no Frenchman.

LADY [*innocently*] I thought you said you won the battle of Lodi for your country, General Bu— shall I pronounce it in Italian or French?

NAPOLEON. You are presuming on my patience, madam. I was born a French subject, but not in France.

LADY [*affecting a marked access of interest in him*] You were not born a subject at all, I think.

NAPOLEON. [*greatly pleased*] Eh? Eh? You think not.

LADY. I am sure of it.

NAPOLEON. Well, well, perhaps not. [*The self-complacency of his assent catches his own ear. He stops short, reddening. Then composing himself into a solemn attitude, modelled on the heroes of classical antiquity, he takes a high moral tone*]. But we must not live for ourselves alone, little one. Never forget that we should always think of others, and work for others, and lead and govern them for their own good. Self-sacrifice is the foundation of all true nobility of character.

LADY [*again relaxing her attitude with a sigh*] Ah, it is easy to see that you have never tried it, General.

NAPOLEON [*indignantly, forgetting all about Brutus and Scipio*] What do you mean by that speech, madam?

LADY. Havnt you noticed that people always exaggerate the value of the things they havnt got? The poor think they need nothing but riches to be quite happy and good. Everybody worships truth, purity, unselfishness, for the same reason: because they have no experience of them. Oh, if they only knew!

NAPOLEON [*with angry derision*] If they only knew! Pray do you know?

LADY. Yes. I had the misfortune to be born good. [*Glancing up at him for a moment*] And it is a mis-

[632]

fortune, I can tell you, General. I really am truthful and unselfish and all the rest of it; and it's nothing but cowardice; want of character; want of being really, strongly, positively oneself.

NAPOLEON. Ha? [*turning to her quickly with a flash of strong interest*].

LADY [*earnestly, with rising enthusiasm*] What is the secret of your power? Only that you believe in yourself. You can fight and conquer for yourself and for nobody else. You are not afraid of your own destiny. You teach us what we all might be if we had the will and courage; and that [*suddenly sinking on her knees before him*] is why we all begin to worship you. [*She kisses his hand*].

NAPOLEON [*embarrassed*] Tut! tut! Pray rise, madam.

LADY. Do not refuse my homage: it is your right. You will be Emperor of France—

NAPOLEON [*hurriedly*] Take care. Treason!

LADY [*insisting*] Yes, Emperor of France; then of Europe; perhaps of the world. I am only the first subject to swear allegiance. [*Again kissing his hand*] My Emperor!

NAPOLEON [*overcome, raising her*] Pray! pray! No, no: this is folly. Come: be calm, be calm. [*Petting her*] There! there! my girl.

LADY [*struggling with happy tears*] Yes, I know it is an impertinence in me to tell you what you must know far better than I do. But you are not angry with me, are you?

NAPOLEON. Angry! No, no: not a bit, not a bit. Come: you are a very clever and sensible and interesting woman. [*He pats her on the cheek*]. Shall we be friends?

LADY [*enraptured*] Your friend! You will let me be your friend! Oh! [*She offers him both her hands with a radiant smile*]. You see: I shew my confidence in you.

This incautious echo of the lieutenant undoes her. Napoleon starts: his eyes flash: he utters a yell of rage.

NAPOLEON. What!!!

LADY. Whats the matter?

NAPOLEON. Shew your confidence in me! So that I may shew my confidence in you in return by letting you give me the slip with the despatches, eh? Ah, Dalila, Dalila, you have been trying your tricks on me; and I have been as gross a gull as my jackass of a lieutenant. [*Menacingly*] Come: the despatches, Quick: I am not to be trifled with now.

LADY [*flying round the couch*] General—

NAPOLEON. Quick, I tell you. [*He passes swiftly up the middle of the room and intercepts her as she makes for the vineyard*].

LADY [*at bay, confronting him and giving way to her temper*] You dare address me in that tone.

NAPOLEON. Dare!

LADY. Yes, dare. Who are you that you should presume to speak to me in that coarse way. Oh, the vile, vulgar Corsican adventurer comes out in you very easily.

NAPOLEON [*beside himself*] You she devil! [*Savagely*] Once more, and only once, will you give me those papers or shall I tear them from you?—by force!

LADY. Tear them from me: by force!

As he glares at her like a tiger about to spring, she crosses her arms on her breasts in the attitude of a martyr. The gesture and pose instantly awaken his theatrical instinct: he forgets his rage in the desire to shew her that in acting, too, she has met her match. He keeps her a moment in suspense; then suddenly clears up his countenance; puts his hands behind him with pro-

voking coolness; looks at her up and down a couple of times; takes a pinch of snuff; wipes his fingers carefully and puts up his handkerchief, her heroic pose becoming more and more ridiculous all the time.

NAPOLEON [*at last*] Well?

LADY [*disconcerted, but with her arms still crossed devotedly*] Well: what are you going to do?

NAPOLEON. Spoil your attitude.

LADY. You brute! [*Abandoning the attitude, she comes to the end of the couch, where she turns with her back to it, leaning against it and facing him with her hands behind her*].

NAPOLEON. Ah, thats better. Now listen to me. I like you. Whats more, I value your respect.

LADY. You value what you have not got, then.

NAPOLEON. I shall have it presently. Now attend to me. Suppose I were to allow myself to be abashed by the respect due to your sex, your beauty, your heroism and all the rest of it! Suppose I, with nothing but such sentimental stuff to stand between these muscles of mine and those papers which you have about you, and which I want and mean to have! suppose I, with the prize within my grasp, were to falter and sneak away with my hands empty; or, what would be worse, cover up my weakness by playing the magnanimous hero, and sparing you the violence I dared not use! would you not despise me from the depths of your woman's soul? Would any woman be such a fool? Well, Bonaparte can rise to the situation and act like a woman when it is necessary. Do you understand?

The lady, without speaking, stands upright, and takes a packet of papers from her bosom. For a moment she has an intense impulse to dash them in his face. But her good breeding cuts her off from any vulgar method of relief. She hands them to him politely, only averting her head.

The moment he takes them, she hurries across to the other side of the room; sits down; and covers her face with her hands.

NAPOLEON [*gloating over the papers*] Aha! Thats right. Thats right. [*Before he opens them, he looks at her and says*] Excuse me. [*He sees that she is hiding her face*]. Very angry with me, eh? [*He unties the packet, the seal of which is already broken, and puts it on the table to examine its contents*].

LADY [*quietly, taking down her hands and shewing that she is not crying, but only thinking*] No. You were right. But I am sorry for you.

NAPOLEON [*pausing in the act of taking the uppermost paper from the packet*] Sorry for me! Why?

LADY. I am going to see you lose your honor.

NAPOLEON. Hm! Nothing worse than that? [*He takes up the paper*].

LADY. And your happiness.

NAPOLEON. Happiness! Happiness is the most tedious thing in the world to me. Should I be what I am if I cared for happiness? Anything else?

LADY. Nothing.

NAPOLEON. Good.

LADY. Except that you will cut a very foolish figure in the eyes of France.

NAPOLEON [*quickly*] What? [*The hand unfolding the paper involuntarily stops. The lady looks at him enigmatically, in tranquil silence. He throws the letter down and breaks out in a torrent of scolding*]. What do you mean? Eh? Are you at your tricks again? Do you think I dont know what these papers contain? I'll tell you. First, my information as to Beaulieu's retreat. There are only two things he can do—leather-brained idiot that he is!—shut himself up in Mantua or violate the neutrality of Venice by taking Peschiera. You are

[636]

one of old Leatherbrain's spies: he has discovered that he has been betrayed, and has sent you to intercept the information at all hazards. As if that could save him from me, the old fool! The other papers are only my private letters from Paris, of which you know nothing.

LADY [*prompt and businesslike*] General: let us make a fair division. Take the information your spies have sent you about the Austrian army; and give me the Paris correspondence. That will content me.

NAPOLEON [*his breath taken away by the coolness of the proposal*] A fair di— [*he gasps*]. It seems to me, madam, that you have come to regard my letters as your own property, of which I am trying to rob you.

LADY [*earnestly*] No: on my honour I ask for no letter of yours: not a word that has been written by you or to you. That packet contains a stolen letter: a letter written by a woman to a man: a man not her husband: a letter that means disgrace, infamy—

NAPOLEON. A love letter?

LADY [*bitter-sweetly*] What else but a love letter could stir up so much hate?

NAPOLEON. Why is it sent to me? To put the husband in my power, eh?

LADY. No, no: it can be of no use to you: I swear that it will cost you nothing to give it to me. It has been sent to you out of sheer malice: solely to injure the woman who wrote it.

NAPOLEON. Then why not send it to her husband instead of to me?

LADY [*completely taken aback*] Oh! [*Sinking back into the chair*] I—I dont know. [*She breaks down*].

NAPOLEON. Aha! I thought so: a little romance to get the papers back. Per Bacco, I cant help admiring you. I wish I could lie like that. It would save me a great deal of trouble.

LADY [*wringing her hands*] Oh, how *I* wish I really had told you some lie! You would have believed me then. The truth is the one thing nobody will believe.

NAPOLEON [*with coarse familiarity, treating her as if she were a vivandière*] Capital! Capital! [*He puts his hands behind him on the table, and lifts himself on to it, sitting with his arms akimbo and his legs wide apart*] Come: I am a true Corsican in my love for stories. But I could tell them better than you if I set my mind to it. Next time you are asked why a letter compromising a wife should not be sent to her husband, answer simply that the husband wouldnt read it. Do you suppose, you goose, that a man wants to be compelled by public opinion to make a scene, to fight a duel, to break up his household, to injure his career by a scandal, when he can avoid it all by taking care not to know?

LADY [*revolted*] Suppose that packet contained a letter about your own wife?

NAPOLEON [*offended, coming off the table*] You are impertinent, madam.

LADY [*humbly*] I beg your pardon. Caesar's wife is above suspicion.

NAPOLEON [*with a deliberate assumption of superiority*] You have committed an indiscretion. I pardon you. In future, do not permit yourself to introduce real persons in your romances.

LADY [*politely ignoring a speech which is to her only a breach of good manners*] General: there really is a woman's letter there. [*Pointing to the packet*] Give it to me.

NAPOLEON [*with brute conciseness*] Why?

LADY. She is an old friend: we were at school together. She has written to me imploring me to prevent the letter falling into your hands.

NAPOLEON. Why has it been sent to me?

LADY. Because it compromises the director Barras.

NAPOLEON [*frowning, evidently startled*] Barras! [*Haughtily*] Take care, madam. The director Barras is my attached personal friend.

LADY [*nodding placidly*] Yes. You became friends through your wife.

NAPOLEON. Again! Have I not forbidden you to speak of my wife? [*She keeps looking curiously at him, taking no account of the rebuke. More and more irritated, he drops his haughty manner, of which he is himself somewhat impatient, and says suspiciously, lowering his voice*] Who is this woman with whom you sympathize so deeply?

LADY. Oh, General! How could I tell you that?

NAPOLEON [*ill humoredly, beginning to walk about again in angry perplexity*] Ay, ay: stand by one another. You are all the same, you women.

LADY [*indignantly*] We are not all the same, any more than you are. Do you think that if *I* loved another man, I should pretend to go on loving my husband, or be afraid to tell him or all the world? But this woman is not made that way. She governs men by cheating them; and they like it, and let her govern them. [*She turns her back to him in disdain*].

NAPOLEON [*not attending to her*] Barras? Barras? [*Very threateningly, his face darkening*] Take care. Take care: do you hear? You may go too far.

LADY [*innocently turning her face to him*] Whats the matter?

NAPOLEON. What are you hinting at? Who is this woman?

LADY [*meeting his angry searching gaze with tranquil*

indifference as she sits looking up at him] A vain, silly, extravagant creature, with a very able and ambitious husband who knows her through and through: knows that she has lied to him about her age, her income, her social position, about everything that silly women lie about: knows that she is incapable of fidelity to any principle or any person; and yet cannot help loving her—cannot help his man's instinct to make use of her for his own advancement with Barras.

NAPOLEON [*in a stealthy coldly furious whisper*] This is your revenge, you she cat, for having had to give me the letters.

LADY. Nonsense! Or do you mean that you are that sort of man?

NAPOLEON [*exasperated, clasps his hands behind him, his fingers twitching, and says, as he walks irritably away from her to the fireplace*] This woman will drive me out of my senses. [*To her*] Begone.

LADY [*seated immovably*] Not without that letter.

NAPOLEON. Begone, I tell you. [*Walking from the fireplace to the vineyard and back to the table*] You shall have no letter. I dont like you. Youre a detestable woman, and as ugly as Satan. I dont choose to be pestered by strange women. Be off. [*He turns his back on her. In quiet amusement, she leans her cheek on her hand and laughs at him. He turns again, angrily mocking her*]. Ha! ha! ha! What are you laughing at?

LADY. At you, General. I have often seen persons of your sex getting into a pet and behaving like children; but I never saw a really great man do it before.

NAPOLEON [*brutally, flinging the words in her face*] Psha! Flattery! Flattery! Coarse, impudent flattery!

LADY [*springing up with a bright flush in her cheeks*] Oh, you are too bad. Keep your letters. Read the story of your own dishonor in them; and much good may they do you. Goodbye. [*She goes indignantly to-wards the inner door*].

NAPOLEON. My own—! Stop. Come back. Come back, I order you. [*She proudly disregards his savagely peremptory tone and continues on her way to the door. He rushes at her; seizes her by the arm; and drags her back*]. Now, what do you mean? Explain. Explain. I tell you, or— [*threatening her. She looks at him with unflinching defiance*]. Rrrr! you obstinate devil, you. [*Throwing her arm away*] Why cant you answer a civil question?

LADY [*deeply offended by his violence*] Why do you ask me? You have the explanation.

NAPOLEON. Where?

LADY [*pointing to the letters on the table*] There. You have only to read it.

He snatches the packet up; hesitates; looks at her suspiciously; and throws it down again.

NAPOLEON. You seem to have forgotten your solici-tude for the honor of your old friend.

LADY. I do not think she runs any risk now. She does not quite understand her husband.

NAPOLEON. I am to read the letter, then? [*He stretches out his hand as if to take up the packet again, with his eye on her*].

LADY. I do not see how you can very well avoid doing so now. [*He instantly withdraws his hand*]. Oh, dont be afraid. You will find many interesting things in it.

NAPOLEON. For instance?

LADY. For instance, a duel with Barras, a domestic scene, a broken household, a public scandal, a checked career, all sorts of things.

NAPOLEON. Hm! [*He looks at her; takes up the packet and looks at it, pursing his lips and balancing it in his hand; looks at her again; passes the packet into his left*

*hand and puts it behind his back, raising his right to
scratch the back of his head as he turns and goes up to
the edge of the vineyard, where he stands for a moment
looking out into the vines, deep in thought. The lady
watches him in silence, somewhat slightingly. Suddenly
he turns and comes back again, full of force and de-
cision].* I grant your request, madam. Your courage
and resolution deserve to succeed. Take the letters for
which you have fought so well; and remember hence-
forth that you found the vile vulgar Corsican adventurer as generous to the vanquished after the battle as
he was resolute in the face of the enemy before it.
[He offers her the packet].

LADY *[without taking it, looking hard at him]* What are
you at now, I wonder? *[He dashes the packet furiously
to the floor].* Aha! Ive spoilt that attitude, I think.
[She makes him a pretty mocking curtsey].

NAPOLEON *[snatching it up again]* Will you take the
letters and begone *[advancing and thrusting them upon
her]*?

LADY *[escaping round the table]* No: I dont want your
letters.

NAPOLEON. Ten minutes ago, nothing else would
satisfy you.

LADY *[keeping the table carefully between them]* Ten
minutes ago you had not insulted me beyond all
bearing.

NAPOLEON. I— *[swallowing his spleen]* I apologize.

LADY *[coolly]* Thanks. *[With forced politeness he offers
her the packet across the table. She retreats a step out of
its reach and says]* But dont you want to know whether
the Austrians are at Mantua or Peschiera?

NAPOLEON. I have already told you that I can conquer my enemies without the aid of spies, madam.

LADY. And the letter? dont you want to read that?

NAPOLEON. You have said that it is not addressed to me. I am not in the habit of reading other people's letters. [*He again offers the packet*].

LADY. In that case there can be no objection to your keeping it. All I wanted was to prevent your reading it. [*Cheerfully*] Good afternoon, General. [*She turns coolly towards the inner door*].

NAPOLEON [*angrily flinging the packet on the couch*] Heaven grant me patience! [*He goes determinedly to the door, and places himself before it*]. Have you any sense of personal danger? Or are you one of those women who like to be beaten black and blue?

LADY. Thank you, General: I have no doubt the sensation is very voluptuous; but I had rather not. I simply want to go home: thats all. I was wicked enough to steal your despatches; but you have got them back; and you have forgiven me, because [*delicately reproducing his rhetorical cadence*] you are as generous to the vanquished after the battle as you are resolute in the face of the enemy before it. Wont you say goodbye to me? [*She offers her hand sweetly*].

NAPOLEON [*repulsing the advance with a gesture of concentrated rage, and opening the door to call fiercely*] Giuseppe! [*Louder*] Giuseppe! [*He bangs the door to, and comes to the middle of the room. The lady goes a little way into the vineyard to avoid him*].

GIUSEPPE [*appearing at the door*] Excellency?

NAPOLEON. Where is that fool?

GIUSEPPE. He has had a good dinner, according to your instructions, excellency, and is now doing me the honor to gamble with me to pass the time.

NAPOLEON. Send him here. Bring him here. Come with him. [*Giuseppe, with unruffled readiness, hurries off. Napoleon turns curtly to the lady, saying*] I must trouble you to remain some moments longer, madam. [*He comes to the couch*].

She comes from the vineyard along the opposite side of the room to the sideboard, and posts herself there, leaning against it, watching him. He takes the packet from the couch and deliberately buttons it carefully into his breast pocket, looking at her meanwhile with an expression which suggests that she will soon find out the meaning of his proceedings, and will not like it. Nothing more is said until the Lieutenant arrives followed by Giuseppe, who stands modestly in attendance at the table. The Lieutenant, without cap, sword or gloves, and much improved in temper and spirits by his meal, chooses the lady's side of the room, and waits, much at his ease, for Napoleon to begin.

NAPOLEON. Lieutenant.

LIEUTENANT [*encouragingly*] General.

NAPOLEON. I cannot persuade this lady to give me much information; but there can be no doubt that the man who tricked you out of your charge was, as she admitted to you, her brother.

LIEUTENANT [*triumphantly*] What did I tell you, General! What did I tell you!

NAPOLEON. You must find that man. Your honor is at stake; and the fate of the campaign, the destiny of France, of Europe, of humanity, perhaps, may depend on the information those despatches contain.

LIEUTENANT. Yes, I suppose they really are rather serious [*as if this had hardly occurred to him before*].

NAPOLEON [*energetically*] They are so serious, sir, that if you do not recover them, you will be degraded in the presence of your regiment.

LIEUTENANT. Whew! The regiment wont like that, I can tell you.

NAPOLEON. Personally I am sorry for you. I would

willingly hush up the affair if it were possible. But I shall be called to account for not acting on the despatches. I shall have to prove to all the world that I never received them, no matter what the consequences may be to you. I am sorry; but you see that I cannot help myself.

LIEUTENANT [*goodnaturedly*] Oh, dont take it to heart, General: it's really very good of you. Never mind what happens to me: I shall scrape through somehow; and we'll beat the Austrians for you, despatches or no despatches. I hope you wont insist on my starting off on a wild goose chase after the fellow now. I havnt a notion where to look for him.

GIUSEPPE [*deferentially*] You forget, Lieutenant: he has your horse.

LIEUTENANT [*starting*] I forgot that. [*Resolutely*] I'll go after him, General: I'll find that horse if it's alive anywhere in Italy. And I shant forget the despatches: never fear. Giuseppe: go and saddle one of those mangy old post-horses of yours while I get my cap and sword and things. Quick march. Off with you [*bustling him*].

GIUSEPPE. Instantly, Lieutenant, instantly [*He disappears in the vineyard, where the light is now reddening with the sunset*].

LIEUTENANT [*looking about him on his way to the inner door*] By the way, General, did I give you my sword or did I not? Oh, I remember now. [*Fretfully*] It's all that nonsense about putting a man under arrest: one never knows where to find— [*he talks himself out of the room*].

LADY [*still at the sideboard*] What does all this mean, General?

NAPOLEON. He will not find your brother.

LADY. Of course not. Theres no such person.

NAPOLEON. The despatches will be irrecoverably lost.

LADY. Nonsense! They are inside your coat.

NAPOLEON. You will find it hard, I think, to prove that wild statement. [*The lady starts. He adds, with clinching emphasis*] Those papers are lost.

LADY [*anxiously, advancing to the corner of the table*] And that unfortunate young man's career will be sacrificed?

NAPOLEON. His career! The fellow is not worth the gunpowder it would cost to have him shot. [*He turns contemptuously and goes to the hearth, where he stands with his back to her*].

LADY [*wistfully*] You are very hard. Men and women are nothing to you but things to be used, even if they are broken in the use.

NAPOLEON [*turning on her*] Which of us has broken this fellow? I or you? Who tricked him out of the despatches? Did you think of his career then?

LADY [*conscience-stricken*] Oh, I never thought of that. It was wicked of me; but I couldnt help it, could I? How else could I have got the papers? [*Supplicating*] General: you will save him from disgrace.

NAPOLEON [*laughing sourly*] Save him yourself, since you are so clever: it was you who ruined him. [*With savage intensity*] I hate a bad soldier.

He goes out determinedly through the vineyard. She follows him a few steps with an appealing gesture, but is interrupted by the return of the Lieutenant, gloved and capped, with his sword on, ready for the road. He is crossing to the outer door when she intercepts him.

LADY. Lieutenant.

LIEUTENANT [*importantly*] You musnt delay me, you know. Duty, madam, duty.

LADY [*imploringly*] Oh, sir, what are you going to do to my poor brother?

LIEUTENANT. Are you very fond of him?

LADY. I should die if anything happened to him. You must spare him. [*The Lieutenant shakes his head gloomily*]. Yes, yes: you must: you shall: he is not fit to die. Listen to me. If I tell you where to find him— if I undertake to place him in your hands a prisoner, to be delivered up by you to General Bonaparte—will you promise me on your honor as an officer and a gentleman not to fight with him or treat him unkindly in any way?

LIEUTENANT. But suppose he attacks me. He has my pistols.

LADY. He is too great a coward.

LIEUTENANT. I dont feel so sure about that. He's capable of anything.

LADY. If he attacks you, or resists you in any way, I release you from your promise.

LIEUTENANT. My promise! I didnt mean to promise. Look here: youre as bad as he is: youve taken an advantage of me through the better side of my nature. What about my horse?

LADY. It is part of the bargain that you are to have your horse and pistols back.

LIEUTENANT. Honor bright?

LADY. Honor bright. [*She offers her hand*].

LIEUTENANT [*taking it and holding it*] All right: I'll be as gentle as a lamb with him. His sister's a very pretty woman. [*He attempts to kiss her*].

LADY [*slipping away from him*] Oh, Lieutenant! You forget: your career is at stake—the destiny of Europe —of humanity.

LIEUTENANT. Oh, bother the destiny of humanity! [*Making for her*] Only a kiss.

LADY [*retreating round the table*] Not until you have regained your honor as an officer. Remember: you have not captured my brother yet.

LIEUTENANT [*seductively*] Youll tell me where he is, wont you?

LADY. I have only to send him a certain signal; and he will be here in quarter of an hour.

LIEUTENANT. He's not far off, then.

LADY. No: quite close. Wait here for him: when he gets my message he will come here at once and surrender himself to you. You understand?

LIEUTENANT [*intellectually overtaxed*] Well, it's a little complicated; but I daresay it will be all right.

LADY. And now, whilst youre waiting, dont you think you had better make terms with the General?

LIEUTENANT. Oh, look here: this is getting frightfully complicated. What terms?

LADY. Make him promise that if you catch my brother he will consider that you have cleared your character as a soldier. He will promise anything you ask on that condition.

LIEUTENANT. Thats not a bad idea. Thank you: I think I'll try it.

LADY. Do. And mind, above all things, dont let him see how clever you are.

LIEUTENANT. I understand. He'd be jealous.

LADY. Dont tell him anything except that you are resolved to capture my brother or perish in the attempt. He wont believe you. Then you will produce my brother—

LIEUTENANT [*interrupting as he masters the plot*] And have the laugh at him! I say: what a jolly clever woman you are! [*Shouting*] Giuseppe!

LADY. Sh! Not a word to Giuseppe about me. [*She puts her finger on her lips. He does the same. They look at one another warningly. Then, with a ravishing smile, she changes the gesture into wafting him a kiss, and runs out through the inner door. Electrified, he bursts into a volley of chuckles].*

Giuseppe comes back by the outer door.

GIUSEPPE. The horse is ready, Lieutenant.

LIEUTENANT. I'm not going just yet. Go and find the General and tell him I want to speak to him.

GIUSEPPE [*shaking his head*] That will never do, Lieutenant.

LIEUTENANT. Why not?

GIUSEPPE. In this wicked world a general may send for a lieutenant; but a lieutenant must not send for a general.

LIEUTENANT. Oh, you think he wouldnt like it. Well, perhaps youre right: one has to be awfully particular about that sort of thing now we're a republic.

Napoleon reappears, advancing from the vineyard, buttoning the breast of his coat, pale and full of gnawing thoughts.

GIUSEPPE [*unconscious of Napoleon's approach*] Quite true, Lieutenant, quite true. You are all like innkeepers now in France: you have to be polite to everybody.

NAPOLEON [*putting his hand on Giuseppe's shoulder*] And that destroys the whole value of politeness, eh?

LIEUTENANT. The very man I wanted! See here, General: suppose I catch that fellow for you!

NAPOLEON [*with ironical gravity*] You will not catch him, my friend.

LIEUTENANT. Aha! you think so; but youll see. Just wait. Only, if I do catch him and hand him over to you, will you cry quits? Will you drop all this about degrading me in the presence of my regiment? Not that *I* mind, you know; but still no regiment likes to have all the other regiments laughing at it.

NAPOLEON [*a cold ray of humor striking pallidly across his gloom*] What shall we do with this officer, Giuseppe? Everything he says is wrong.

GIUSEPPE [*promptly*] Make him a general, excellency; and then everything he says will be right.

LIEUTENANT [*crowing*] Haw-aw! [*He throws himself ecstatically on the couch to enjoy the joke*].

NAPOLEON [*laughing and pinching Giuseppe's ear*] You are thrown away in this inn, Giuseppe. [*He sits down and places Giuseppe before him like a schoolmaster with a pupil*]. Shall I take you away with me and make a man of you?

GIUSEPPE [*shaking his head rapidly and repeatedly*] No no no no no no no. All my life long people have wanted to make a man of me. When I was a boy, our good priest wanted to make a man of me by teaching me to read and write. Then the organist at Melegnano wanted to make a man of me by teaching me to read music. The recruiting sergeant would have made a man of me if I had been a few inches taller. But it always meant making me work; and I am too lazy for that, thank Heaven! So I taught myself to cook and became an innkeeper; and now I keep servants to do the work, and have nothing to do myself except talk, which suits me perfectly.

NAPOLEON [*looking at him thoughtfully*] You are satisfied?

GIUSEPPE [*with cheerful conviction*] Quite, excellency.

NAPOLEON. And you have no devouring devil inside you who must be fed with action and victory: gorged with them night and day: who makes you pay, with the sweat of your brain and body, weeks of Herculean toil for ten minutes of enjoyment: who is at once your

slave and your tyrant, your genius and your doom:
who brings you a crown in one hand and the oar of a
galley slave in the other: who shews you all the kingdoms of the earth and offers to make you their master
on condition that you become their servant! have you
nothing of that in you?

GIUSEPPE. Nothing of it! Oh, I assure you, excellency, my devouring devil is far worse than that. He
offers me no crowns and kingdoms: he expects to get
everything for nothing: sausages! omelettes! grapes!
cheese! polenta! wine! three times a day, excellency:
nothing less will content him.

LIEUTENANT. Come: drop it, Giuseppe: youre
making me feel hungry again.

*Giuseppe, with an apologetic shrug, retires from the
conversation.*

NAPOLEON [*turning to the Lieutenant with sardonic
politeness*] I hope *I* have not been making you feel
ambitious.

LIEUTENANT. Not at all: I dont fly so high. Besides,
I'm better as I am: men like me are wanted in the
army just now. The fact is, the Revolution was all
very well for civilians; but it wont work in the army.
You know what soldiers are, General: they will have
men of family for their officers. A subaltern must be
a gentleman, because he's so much in contact with the
men. But a general, or even a colonel, may be any sort
of riff-raff if he understands his job well enough. A
lieutenant is a gentleman: all the rest is chance. Why,
who do you suppose won the battle of Lodi? I'll tell
you. My horse did.

NAPOLEON [*rising*] Your folly is carrying you too far,
sir. Take care.

LIEUTENANT. Not a bit of it. You remember all that
red-hot cannonade across the river: the Austrians

blazing away at you to keep you from crossing, and you blazing away at them to keep them from setting the bridge on fire? Did you notice where I was then?

NAPOLEON. I am sorry. I am afraid I was rather occupied at the moment.

GIUSEPPE [*with eager admiration*] They say you jumped off your horse and worked the big guns with your own hands, General.

LIEUTENANT. That was a mistake: an officer should never let himself down to the level of his men. [*Napoleon looks at him dangerously, and begins to walk tigerishly to and fro*]. But you might have been firing away at the Austrians still if we cavalry fellows hadnt found the ford and got across and turned old Beaulieu's flank for you. You know you didnt dare give the order to charge the bridge until you saw us on the other side. Consequently, I say that whoever found that ford won the battle of Lodi. Well, who found it? I was the first man to cross; and I know. It was my horse that found it. [*With conviction, as he rises from the couch*] That horse is the true conqueror of the Austrians.

NAPOLEON [*passionately*] You idiot: I'll have you shot for losing those despatches: I'll have you blown from the mouth of a cannon: nothing less could make any impression on you. [*Baying at him*] Do you hear? Do you understand?

A French officer enters unobserved, carrying his sheathed sabre in his hand.

LIEUTENANT [*unabashed*] If I dont capture him, General. Remember the if.

NAPOLEON. If!! Ass: there is no such man.

THE OFFICER [*suddenly stepping between them and speaking in the unmistakeable voice of the Strange Lady*]

Lieutenant: I am your prisoner. [*She offers him her sabre*].

Napoleon gazes at her for a moment thunderstruck; then seizes her by the wrist and drags her roughly to him, looking closely and fiercely at her to satisfy himself as to her identity; for it now begins to darken rapidly into night, the red glow over the vineyard giving way to clear starlight.

NAPOLEON. Pah! [*He flings her hand away with an exclamation of disgust, and turns his back on them with his hand in his breast, his brow lowering, and his toes twitching*].

LIEUTENANT [*triumphantly, taking the sabre*] No such man! eh, General? [*To the Lady*] I say: wheres my horse?

LADY. Safe at Borghetto, waiting for you, Lieutenant.

NAPOLEON [*turning on them*] Where are the despatches?

LADY. You would never guess. They are in the most unlikely place in the world. Did you meet my sister here, any of you?

LIEUTENANT. Yes. Very nice woman. She's wonderfully like you; but of course she's better-looking.

LADY [*mysteriously*] Well, do you know that she is a witch?

GIUSEPPE [*in terror, crossing himself*] Oh, no, no, no. It is not safe to jest about such things. I cannot have it in my house, excellency.

LIEUTENANT. Yes, drop it. Youre my prisoner, you know. Of course I dont believe in any such rubbish; but still it's not a proper subject for joking.

LADY. But this is very serious. My sister has bewitched the General. [*Giuseppe and the lieutenant recoil from Napoleon*]. General: open your coat: you will find the despatches in the breast of it. [*She puts her hand quickly on his breast*]. Yes: there they are: I can feel them. Eh? [*She looks up into his face half coaxingly, half mockingly*]. Will you allow me, General? [*She takes a button as if to unbutton his coat, and pauses for permission*].

NAPOLEON [*inscrutably*] If you dare.

LADY. Thank you. [*She opens his coat and takes out the despatches*]. There! [*To Giuseppe, shewing him the despatches*] See!

GIUSEPPE [*flying to the outer door*] No, in heaven's name! Theyre bewitched.

LADY [*turning to the lieutenant*] Here, Lieutenant: you are not afraid of them.

LIEUTENANT [*retreating*] Keep off. [*Seizing the hilt of the sabre*] Keep off, I tell you.

LADY [*to Napoleon*] They belong to you, General. Take them.

GIUSEPPE. Dont touch them, excellency. Have nothing to do with them.

LIEUTENANT. Be careful, General: be careful.

GIUSEPPE. Burn them. And burn the witch too.

LADY [*to Napoleon*] Shall I burn them?

NAPOLEON [*thoughtfully*] Yes, burn them. Giuseppe: go and fetch a light.

GIUSEPPE [*trembling and stammering*] Do you mean go alone? in the dark? with a witch in the house?

NAPOLEON. Psha! Youre a poltroon. [*To the lieutenant*] Oblige me by going, Lieutenant.

LIEUTENANT [*remonstrating*] Oh, I say, General! No, look here, you know: nobody can say I'm a coward after Lodi. But to ask me to go into the dark by myself without a candle after such an awful conversation is a little too much. How would you like to do it yourself?

NAPOLEON [*irritably*] You refuse to obey my order?

LIEUTENANT [*resolutely*] Yes I do. It's not reasonable. But I'll tell you what I'll do. If Guiseppe goes, I'll go with him and protect him.

NAPOLEON [*to Giuseppe*] There! will that satisfy you? Be off, both of you.

GIUSEPPE [*humbly, his lips trembling*] W-willingly, your excellency. [*He goes reluctantly towards the inner door*]. Heaven protect me! [*To the lieutenant*] After you, Lieutenant.

LIEUTENANT. Youd better go first: I dont know the way.

GIUSEPPE. You cant miss it. Besides [*imploringly, laying his hand on his sleeve*] I am only a poor inn keeper: you are a man of family.

LIEUTENANT. Theres something in that. Here: you neednt be in such a fright. Take my arm. [*Giuseppe does so*]. Thats the way. [*They go out, arm in arm*].

It is now starry night. The lady throws the packet on the table and seats herself at her ease on the couch, enjoying the sensation of freedom from petticoats.

LADY. Well, General: Ive beaten you.

NAPOLEON [*walking about*] You are guilty of indelicacy: of unwomanliness. Is that costume proper?

LADY. It seems to me much the same as yours.

NAPOLEON. Psha! I blush for you.

LADY [*naïvely*] Yes: soldiers blush so easily. [*He growls and turns away. She looks mischievously at him, balancing the despatches in her hand*]. Wouldnt you like to read these before theyre burnt, General? You must be dying with curiosity. Take a peep. [*She throws the packet on the table, and turns her face away from it*]. I wont look.

NAPOLEON. I have no curiosity whatever, madam. But since you are evidently burning to read them, I give you leave to do so.

LADY. Oh, Ive read them already.

NAPOLEON [*starting*] What!

LADY. I read them the first thing after I rode away on that poor lieutenant's horse. So you see I know whats in them; and you dont.

NAPOLEON. Excuse me: I read them when I was out there in the vineyard ten minutes ago.

LADY. Oh! [*Jumping up*] Oh, General: Ive not beaten you after all. I do admire you so. [*He laughs and pats her cheek*]. This time, really and truly without shamming, I do you homage [*kissing his hand*].

NAPOLEON [*quickly withdrawing it*] Brr! Dont do that. No more witchcraft.

LADY. I want to say something to you; only you would misunderstand it.

NAPOLEON. Need that stop you?

LADY. Well, it is this. I adore a man who is not afraid to be mean and selfish.

NAPOLEON [*indignantly*] I am neither mean nor selfish.

LADY. Oh, you dont appreciate yourself. Besides, I dont really mean meanness and selfishness.

NAPOLEON. Thank you. I thought perhaps you did.

LADY. Well, of course I do. But what I mean is a certain strong simplicity about you.

NAPOLEON. Thats better.

LADY. You didnt want to read the letters; but you were curious about what was in them. So you went into the garden and read them when no one was looking, and then came back and pretended you hadnt. Thats the meanest thing I ever knew any man do; but it exactly fulfilled your purpose; and so you wernt a bit afraid or ashamed to do it.

NAPOLEON [*abruptly*] Where did you pick up all these vulgar scruples? this [*with contemptuous emphasis*] conscience of yours? I took you for a lady: an aristocrat. Was your grandfather a shopkeeper, pray?

LADY. No: he was an Englishman.

NAPOLEON. That accounts for it. The English are a nation of shopkeepers. Now I understand why youve beaten me.

LADY. Oh, I havnt beaten you. And I'm not English.

NAPOLEON. Yes you are: English to the backbone. Listen to me: I will explain the English to you.

LADY [*eagerly*] Do. [*With a lively air of anticipating an intellectual treat, she sits down on the couch and composes herself to listen to him. Secure of his audience, he at once nerves himself for a performance. He considers a little before he begins; so as to fix her attention by a moment of suspense. His style is at first modelled on Talma's in Corneille's Cinna; but it is somewhat lost in the darkness, and Talma presently gives way to Napoleon, the voice coming through the gloom with startling intensity*].

NAPOLEON. There are three sorts of people in the world: the low people, the middle people, and the high people. The low people and the high people are alike in one thing: they have no scruples, no morality. The low are beneath morality, the high above it. I am not afraid of either of them; for the low are unscrupulous without knowledge, so that they make an idol of me; whilst the high are unscrupulous without purpose, so that they go down before my will. Look you: I shall go over all the mobs and all the courts of Europe as a plough goes over a field. It is the middle people who are dangerous: they have both knowledge and purpose. But they, too, have their weak point. They are full of scruples: chained hand and foot by their morality and respectability.

LADY. Then you will beat the English; for all shopkeepers are middle people.

NAPOLEON. No, because the English are a race apart. No Englishman is too low to have scruples: no Englishman is high enough to be free from their tyranny. But every Englishman is born with a certain miraculous power that makes him master of the world. When he wants a thing, he never tells himself that he wants it. He waits patiently until there comes into his mind, no one knows how, a burning conviction that it is his moral and religious duty to conquer those who possess the thing he wants. Then he becomes irresistible. Like the aristocrat, he does what pleases him and grabs what he covets: like the shopkeeper, he pursues his purpose with the industry and steadfastness that come from strong religious conviction and deep sense of moral responsibility. He is never at a loss for an effective moral attitude. As the great champion of freedom and national independence, he conquers and annexes half the world, and calls it Colonization. When he wants a new market for his adulterated Manchester goods, he sends a missionary to teach the natives the Gospel of Peace. The natives kill the missionary: he flies to arms in defence of Christianity; fights for it; conquers for it; and takes the market as a reward from heaven. In defence of his island shores, he puts a chaplain on board his ship; nails a flag with a cross on it to his top-gallant mast; and sails to the ends of the earth, sinking, burning, and destroying all who dispute the empire of the seas with him. He boasts that a slave is free the moment his foot touches British soil; and he sells the children of his poor at six years of age to work under the lash in his factories for sixteen hours a day. He makes two revolutions, and then declares war on our one in the name of law and order. There is nothing so bad or so good that you will not find Englishmen doing it; but

you will never find an Englishman in the wrong. He
does everything on principle. He fights you on patriotic principles; he robs you on business principles;
he enslaves you on imperial principles; he bullies you
on manly principles; he supports his king on loyal
principles and cuts off his king's head on republican
principles. His watchword is always Duty; and he
never forgets that the nation which lets its duty get on
the opposite side to its interest is lost. He—

LADY. W-w-w-w-w-wh! Do stop a moment. I want
to know how you make me out to be English at this
rate.

NAPOLEON [*dropping his rhetorical style*] It's plain
enough. You wanted some letters that belonged to me.
You have spent the morning in stealing them: yes,
stealing them, by highway robbery. And you have
spent the afternoon in putting me in the wrong about
them: in assuming that it was *I* who wanted to steal
your letters: in explaining that it all came about
through my meanness and selfishness, and your goodness, your devotion, your self-sacrifice. Thats English.

LADY. Nonsense! I am sure I am not a bit English.
The English are a very stupid people.

NAPOLEON. Yes, too stupid sometimes to know when
theyre beaten. But I grant that your brains are not
English. You see, though your grandfather was an
Englishman, your grandmother was—what? A
Frenchwoman?

LADY. Oh no. An Irishwoman.

NAPOLEON [*quickly*] Irish! [*Thoughtfully*] Yes: I
forgot the Irish. An English army led by an Irish
general: that might be a match for a French army led
by an Italian general. [*He pauses, and adds, half jest-
ingly, half moodily*] At all events, you have beaten me;
and what beats a man first will beat him last. [*He*

goes meditatively into the moonlit vineyard and looks up].

She steals out after him. She ventures to rest her hand on his shoulder, overcome by the beauty of the night and emboldened by its obscurity.

LADY [*softly*] What are you looking at?

NAPOLEON [*pointing up*] My star.

LADY. You believe in that?

NAPOLEON. I do.

They look at it for a moment, she leaning a little on his shoulder.

LADY. Do you know that the English say that a man's star is not complete without a woman's garter?

NAPOLEON [*scandalized: abruptly shaking her off and coming back into the room*] Pah! The hypocrites! If the French said that, how they would hold up their hands in pious horror! [*He goes to the inner door and holds it open, shouting*] Hallo! Giuseppe! Wheres that light, man? [*He comes between the table and the sideboard, and moves the second chair to the table, beside his own*]. We have still to burn the letter. [*He takes up the packet*].

Giuseppe comes back, pale and still trembling, carrying in one hand a branched candlestick with a couple of candles alight, and a broad snuffers tray in the other.

GIUSEPPE [*piteously, as he places the light on the table*] Excellency: what were you looking up at just now? Out there! [*He points across his shoulder to the vineyard, but is afraid to look round*].

NAPOLEON [*unfolding the packet*] What is that to you?

GIUSEPPE. Because the witch is gone: vanished; and no one saw her go out.

LADY [*coming behind him from the vineyard*] We were watching her riding up to the moon on your broomstick, Giuseppe. You will never see her again.

GIUSEPPE. Gesu Maria! [*He crosses himself and hurries out*].

NAPOLEON [*throwing down the letters in a heap on the table*] Now! [*He sits down at the table in the chair which he has just placed*].

LADY. Yes; but you know you have THE letter in your pocket. [*He smiles; takes a letter from his pocket; and tosses it on top of the heap. She holds it up and looks at him, saying*] About Caesar's wife.

NAPOLEON. Caesar's wife is above suspicion. Burn it.

LADY [*taking up the snuffers and holding the letter to the candle flame with it*] I wonder would Caesar's wife be above suspicion if she saw us here together!

NAPOLEON [*echoing her, with his elbows on the table and his cheeks on his hands, looking at the letter*] I wonder!

The Strange Lady puts the letter down alight on the snuffers tray, and sits down beside Napoleon, in the same attitude, elbows on table, cheeks on hands, watching it burn. When it is burnt, they simultaneously turn their eyes and look at one another. The curtain steals down and hides them.

The Man of Destiny

(An interview, drafted by Shaw,
Daily Mail, 15 May 1897)

During the last fortnight or so, no man has been so liberally be-paragraphed in the Dramatic World as Mr. Bernard Shaw, none more consistently abused on the one side, more assiduously lauded on the other—and according as the taste of the writer ran anti-Ibsen-wards or the reverse. Just as the announcement, some eighteen months ago, that Sir Henry Irving had accepted a one-act play entitled "The Man of Destiny" from "The Saturday Review" set the town by the ears in amazement that this most modern of the moderns, high priest to Ibsen and contemner of Shakespeare, had gained admission to the shrine of the Lyceum, sacred to the memory of "W. S."; so the statement, which has been current within the past few weeks to the effect that the play is now once again in the author's hands, has been the signal for many a tongue to start clattering. Wherever two or three were gathered together, there the subject of "G. B. S." and "A Man of Destiny" cropped up and, so surely, one of the party would assume an air of mystery—wholly foreign to his nature—and with some doubtful phrase as "I could an I would" or "were I not in honour bound," assert that he individually had some inner knowledge of the affair denied to the meaner herd. This state of things was obviously destined to end and, judging from the absolutely opposed statements scattered broadcast, that the psychological moment for an official pronouncement had arrived, a representative of this paper set out in search of the same. As the portals of the Lyceum however, bear the

Dante legend "all hope abandon, ye who enter here" —to journalists and seekers after "copy"—his feet led him past Wellington Street in a westerly direction to Fitzroy Square.

Having climbed innumerable stairs, knocked at a door and been cordially welcomed on the doormat, he subsided into the nearest available chair and after a brief rest for recovery of breath et cetera, plunged in medias res with the query:—

"Can you be persuaded to say anything about the reports which have been circulating as to your Lyceum play?"

"By all means. Do you want the history from the beginning?" was the courteous reply.

"If you please, Mr. Shaw."

"Well, the matter is very simple. About eighteen months ago, when Sir Henry Irving was touring in America, one of my admirers shewed him a trumpery little one-act play of mine called "The Man of Destiny." Sir Henry, whose literary judgment is his weak point, enormously overrated the play, and made me an offer for it. I, of course, held the play at his disposal and made no further attempt to deal with it; but I put the business off until he should have time to think twice about it. Nothing more passed until the night when he announced from the stage his intention of producing "Madame Sans-Gène." I then represented to him that he could not very well play the two Napoleons—Sardou's and mine, and proposed that we should cry off. But I found him still obstinately under the spell of my genius. He saw no reason why he should not play the two—he had always wanted to play the young Napoleon—he had a medallion of him—he had looked like him in the last act of Claude Melnotte—the part gave him what was missing in the

[663]

older, coarser Napoleon of forty in "Sans-Gène", in fact he gave me a thousand and one reasons for keeping to his resolution. I told him he overrated the play, and offered to write him a better one. He provoked me extremely by assuring me, with unmistakeable sincerity, that he was sure I should never write a better one: in fact, I think he was surprised that I had written anything so good. It was on this point that our main difficulty arose. Sir Henry Irving wanted to be free to produce the play when he could really do it justice by arranging for a run: I, on the other hand, declared that I had rather destroy the piece than have it produced as my latest achievement at some remote date when I had long outgrown it. In the end, he very reluctantly agreed to produce it before the end of the present year (this passed, you must understand, in July 1896 or thereabouts). A contract was drawn up: here it is!"—and with this the portentous-looking document, full of legal technicalities, duly signed and witnessed by Miss Edith Wardell (Miss Edith Craig) was placed in my hands. "If you look through the clauses you will see that it is not an ordinary commercial affair. Sir Henry desired that we should deal with one another as men of honour; and I accepted that basis gladly. You see!—there is no question of money, no advances, no penalties, a very modest fee (as such things go) for actual performances, payable out of the money paid by the public, and ample reservations to Sir Henry Irving of performing rights both here and in America, without any of the usual pecuniary considerations which attend such reservations. But, please, let it be clear that this is not due to any illiberality on Sir Henry Irving's part. He gave me practically carte blanche as to money terms; but my position as a dramatic critic ties my hands in respect

of advances and penalties, and prevents managers
from objecting to special arrangements, which have a
great air of being nobly disinterested on my part, but
which are—as a matter of fact—inconvenient and
exasperating in the highest degree to the unfortunate
managers. You see then, that the agreement, though
it effectually locked up my play, only bound Sir
Henry Irving to produce before the end of 1897; and,
by providing no penalty for non-compliance, left even
that on the footing of an understanding (in Sir
Henry's own phrase) between men of honour. You
may take the agreement away and study it if you like;
for I think it effectually disposes of the inventions
which have been circulating recently as to the spirit
in which Sir Henry Irving and I dealt with one
another."

"But is the play to be produced, then, after all?"

"No! That is the second chapter of the story. The
lapse of a year brings many disillusions with it; and I
suspect that when "Madame Sans-Gène" brought
Sir Henry Irving face to face with his rash engagement to play Napoleon twice, he began to realise what
a piffling little affair this play of mine is, and how
extremely difficult it would be to fit it into the
Lyceum bill. Naturally, he has not recanted his former opinion of the play to me, whatever his private
sentiments may be; but after the accident which
interrupted the career of "Richard III" and upset his
arrangements for the season, we had a correspondence
from which I gathered that, if I insisted on my pound
of flesh in the shape of a production of the play this
year, I should put him in a very disagreeable situation. His desire was that I should leave him free to
produce it a little later, with a view to combining it
with a certain play by one of our leading dramatists,

which will create a good deal of interest when it is produced at the Lyceum. But I held to my old position, and preferred to settle the difficulty by cancelling the agreement, getting the play back, and crying off the whole bargain.

"Unfortunately, secrets in London are never more than half kept; and before the conclusion of the matter left me at liberty to speak, a paragraph appeared stating that a play of mine had been rejected at the Lyceum. Immediately the cry was taken up on all hands and garnished with all sorts of ridiculous inventions. Our good old anti-Ibsenite grandmother, "The Era," solemnly scolded the wicked people who had stated that plays by wicked people like myself were accepted at the Lyceum Theatre. A London correspondent, with a clever air of inside knowledge, described how my play had been returned "with a handsome present." One stupendous ass explained that Sir Henry returned "The Man of Destiny" to rebuke me for writing excessively adulatory articles about him in the "Saturday Review." All this nonsense seems to have created an appetite for a few authoritative words on the real state of the case. Well, you have them. Are you satisfied?"

"Somewhat disappointed that we are not to see your play, Mr. Shaw."

"You need not be. My reputation as a dramatist grows with every play of mine that is *not* performed. Besides, Irving should go to the real Man of Destiny— Ibsen. 'A Doll's House,' 'Borkman,' eh?"

The rest of Mr. Shaw's conversation was not directed to the Lyceum affair.

You Never Can Tell

WITH

GBS and His Play

Chapter XVI of Cyril Maude's
The Haymarket Theatre, *1903,*
written by Shaw

Composition begun December 1895 (after an
abortive effort in July 1895); completed 18
May 1896. Published in *Plays Pleasant and
Unpleasant*, 1898. Revised text in Collected
Edition, 1930.

Copyright reading at the Victoria Hall (Bijou
Theatre), London, on 23 March 1898. First
presented by the Stage Society at the Royalty
Theatre, London, on 26 November 1899.

Mr Valentine   *Yorke Stephens*
Dolly Clandon   *Winifred Fraser*
Philip Clandon   *Roland Bottomley*
Gloria Clandon   *Margaret Halstan*
Mrs Lanfrey Clandon   *Elsie Chester*
Fergus Crampton   *Hermann Vezin*
Waiter   *James Welch*
Finch M'Comas   *Sydney Warden*
Walter Bohun   *Charles Charrington*
Parlormaid   *Mabel Hardinge*
Jo   *Edward Knoblauch*
The Cook   *Leopold Profeit*

Scene: At the Seaside. Time: August 1896.
ACT I *A Dentist's Operating-room. Morning.*
ACT II *The Marine Hotel. Luncheon.*
ACT III *Sitting-room at the Hotel. Afternoon
Tea.*
ACT IV *Sitting-room in the Hotel. After Din-
ner.*

$\begin{bmatrix}\text{ACT I}\end{bmatrix}$

In a dentist's operating room on a fine August morning in 1896. It is the best sitting room of a furnished lodging in a terrace on the sea front at a watering place on the coast of Torbay in Devon. The operating chair, with a gas pump and cylinder beside it, is half way between the centre of the room and one of the corners. If you could look into the room through the window facing the chair, you would see the fireplace in the middle of the wall opposite you, with the door beside it to your left, a dental surgeon's diploma in a frame above the mantel-shelf, an easy chair on the hearth, and a neat stool and bench, with vice, tools, and a mortar and pestle, in the corner to the right. In the wall on your left is a broad window looking on the sea. Beneath it a writing table with a blotter and a diary on it, and a chair. Also a sofa, farther along. A cabinet of instruments is handy to the operating chair. The furniture, carpet, and wall-paper are those of a mid-Victorian drawing room, formally bright and festive, not for everyday use.

Two persons just now occupy the room. One of them, a very pretty woman in miniature, her tiny figure dressed with the daintiest gaiety, is hardly eighteen yet. This darling little creature clearly does not belong to the room, or even to the country; for her complexion, though very delicate, has been burnt biscuit color by some warmer sun than England's. She has a glass of water in her hand, and a rapidly clearing cloud of Spartan endurance on her small firm set mouth and quaintly squared eyebrows.

The dentist, contemplating her with the self-satisfaction of a successful operator, is a young man of thirty or thereabouts. He does not give the impression of being much of a workman: the professional manner of the newly set-up dentist in search of patients is underlain by a thoughtless pleasantry which betrays the young gentleman, still unsettled and in search of amusing adventures. He is not without gravity of demeanor; but the strained nostrils stamp it as the gravity of the humorist. His eyes are clear, alert, of sceptically moderate size, and yet a little rash; his forehead is an excellent one, with plenty of room behind it; his nose and chin are cavalierly handsome. On the whole, an attractive noticeable beginner, of whose prospects a man of business might form a tolerably favorable estimate.

THE YOUNG LADY [*handing him the glass*] Thank you. [*In spite of the biscuit complexion she has not the slightest foreign accent*].

THE DENTIST [*putting it down on the ledge of his cabinet of instruments*] That was my first tooth.

THE YOUNG LADY [*aghast*] Your first! Do you mean to say that you began practising on me?

THE DENTIST. Every dentist has to begin with somebody.

THE YOUNG LADY. Yes: somebody in a hospital, not people who pay.

THE DENTIST [*laughing*] Oh, the hospital doesnt count. I only meant my first tooth in private practice. Why didnt you let me give you gas?

THE YOUNG LADY. Because you said it would be five shillings extra.

THE DENTIST [*shocked*] Oh, dont say that. It makes

[670]

me feel as if I had hurt you for the sake of five shillings.

THE YOUNG LADY [*with cool insolence*] Well, so you have. [*She gets up*] Why shouldnt you? it's your business to hurt people. [*It amuses him to be treated in this fashion: he chuckles secretly as he proceeds to clean and replace his instruments. She shakes her dress into order: looks inquisitively about her; and goes to the broad window*]. You have a good view of the sea from your rooms! Are they expensive?

THE DENTIST. Yes.

THE YOUNG LADY. You dont own the whole house, do you?

THE DENTIST. No.

THE YOUNG LADY. I thought not. [*Tilting the chair which stands at the writing-table and looking critically at it as she spins it round on one leg*] Your furniture isnt quite the latest thing, is it?

THE DENTIST. It's my landlord's.

THE YOUNG LADY. Does he own that toothache chair? [*pointing to the operating chair*].

THE DENTIST. No: I have that on the hire-purchase system.

THE YOUNG LADY [*disparagingly*] I thought so. [*Looking about in search of further conclusions*] I suppose you havnt been here long?

THE DENTIST. Six weeks. Is there anything else you would like to know?

THE YOUNG LADY [*the hint quite lost on her*] Any family?

THE DENTIST. I am not married.

THE YOUNG LADY. Of course not: anybody can see that. I meant sisters and mother and that sort of thing.

THE DENTIST. Not on the premises.

THE YOUNG LADY. Hm! If youve been here six weeks, and mine was your first tooth, the practice cant be very large, can it?

THE DENTIST. Not as yet. [*He shuts the cabinet, having tidied up everything*].

THE YOUNG LADY. Well, good luck! [*She takes out her purse*]. Five shillings, you said it would be?

THE DENTIST. Five shillings.

THE YOUNG LADY [*producing a crown piece*] Do you charge five shillings for everything?

THE DENTIST. Yes.

THE YOUNG LADY. Why?

THE DENTIST. It's my system. I'm whats called a five shilling dentist.

THE YOUNG LADY. How nice! Well, here! [*holding up the crown piece*] a nice new five-shilling piece! your first fee! Make a hole in it with the thing you drill people's teeth with; and wear it on your watch-chain.

THE DENTIST. Thank you.

THE PARLORMAID [*appearing at the door*] The young lady's brother, sir.

A handsome man in miniature, obviously the young lady's twin, comes in eagerly. He wears a suit of terra cotta cashmere, the elegantly cut frock coat lined in brown silk, and carries in his hand a brown tall hat and tan gloves to match. He has his sister's delicate biscuit complexion, and is built on the same small scale; but he is elastic and strong in muscle, decisive in movement, unexpectedly deeptoned and trenchant in speech, and with perfect manners and a finished personal style which might be envied by a man twice his age. Suavity and self-possession are points of honor with him; and though this, rightly considered, is only a mode of boyish self-consciousness, its effect is none the less staggering to his elders, and would be quite insufferable in a less pre-

possessing youth. He is promptitude itself, and has a question ready the moment he enters.

THE YOUNG GENTLEMAN. Am I in time?

THE YOUNG LADY. No: it's all over.

THE YOUNG GENTLEMAN. Did you howl?

THE YOUNG LADY. Oh, something awful. Mr Valentine: this is my brother Phil. Phil: this is Mr Valentine, our new dentist. [*Valentine and Phil bow to one another. She proceeds, all in one breath*] He's only been here six weeks and he's a bachelor the house isnt his and the furniture is the landlord's but the professional plant is hired he got my tooth out beautifully at the first go and he and I are great friends.

PHILIP. Been asking a lot of questions?

THE YOUNG LADY [*as if incapable of doing such a thing*] Oh no.

PHILIP. Glad to hear it. [*To Valentine*] So good of you not to mind us, Mr Valentine. The fact is, weve never been in England before; and our mother tells us that the people here simply wont stand us. Come and lunch with us.

Valentine, bewildered by the leaps and bounds with which their acquaintanceship is proceeding, gasps, but has no time to reply, as the conversation of the twins is swift and continuous.

THE YOUNG LADY. Oh, do, Mr Valentine.

PHILIP. At the Marine Hotel: half past one.

THE YOUNG LADY. We shall be able to tell mamma that a respectable Englishman has promised to lunch with us.

PHILIP. Say no more, Mr Valentine: youll come.

VALENTINE. Say no more! I havnt said anything. May I ask whom I have the pleasure of entertaining? It's really quite impossible for me to lunch at the Marine Hotel with two perfect strangers.

[673]

THE YOUNG LADY [*flippantly*] Ooooh! what bosh! One patient in six weeks! What difference does it make to you?

PHILIP [*maturely*] No, Dolly: my knowledge of human nature confirms Mr Valentine's judgment. He is right. Let me introduce Miss Dorothy Clandon, commonly called Dolly. [*Valentine bows to Dolly. She nods to him*]. I'm Philip Clandon. We're from Madeira, but perfectly respectable, so far.

VALENTINE. Clandon! Are you related to—

DOLLY [*unexpectedly crying out in despair*] Yes we are.

VALENTINE [*astonished*] I beg your pardon?

DOLLY. Oh, we are, we are. It's all over, Phil: they know all about us in England. [*To Valentine*] Oh, you cant think how maddening it is to be related to a celebrated person, and never be valued anywhere for o r own sakes.

VALENTINE. But excuse me: the gentleman I was thinking of is not celebrated.

DOLLY AND PHILIP [*staring at him*] Gentleman!

VALENTINE. Yes. I was going to ask whether you were by any chance a daughter of Mr Densmore Clandon of Newbury Hall.

DOLLY [*vacantly*] No.

PHILIP. Well, come, Dolly: how do you know youre not?

DOLLY [*cheered*] Oh, I forgot. Of course. Perhaps I am.

VALENTINE. Dont you know?

PHILIP. Not in the least.

DOLLY. It's a wise child—

PHILIP [*cutting her short*] Sh! [*Valentine starts nervously; for the sound made by Phil, though but momentary, is like cutting a sheet of silk in two with a flash of lightning. It is the result of long practice in checking*

[674]

Dolly's indiscretions]. The fact is, Mr Valentine, we are the children of the celebrated Mrs Lanfrey Clandon, an authoress of great repute—in Madeira. No household is complete without her works. We came to England to get away from them. They are called the Twentieth Century Treatises.

DOLLY. Twentieth Century Cooking.

PHILIP. Twentieth Century Creeds.

DOLLY. Twentieth Century Clothing.

PHILIP. Twentieth Century Conduct.

DOLLY. Twentieth Century Children.

PHILIP. Twentieth Century Parents.

DOLLY. Cloth limp, half a dollar.

PHILIP. Or mounted on linen for hard family use, two dollars. No family should be without them. Read them, Mr Valentine: theyll improve your mind.

DOLLY. But not till weve gone, please.

PHILIP. Quite so: we prefer people with unimproved minds. Our own minds have successfully resisted all our mother's efforts to improve them.

VALENTINE [*dubiously*] Hm!

DOLLY [*echoing him inquiringly*] Hm? Phil: he prefers people whose minds are improved.

PHILIP. In that case we shall have to introduce him to the other member of the family: the Woman of the Twentieth Century: our sister Gloria!

DOLLY [*dithyrambically*] Nature's masterpiece!

PHILIP. Learning's daughter!

DOLLY. Madeira's pride!

PHILIP. Beauty's paragon!

DOLLY [*suddenly descending to prose*] Bosh! No complexion.

VALENTINE [*desperately*] May I have a word?

PHILIP [*politely*] Excuse us. Go ahead.

DOLLY [*very nicely*] So sorry.

VALENTINE [*attempting to take them paternally*] I really must give a hint to you young people—

DOLLY [*breaking out again*] Oh come! I like that. How old are you?

PHILIP. Over thirty.

DOLLY. He's not.

PHILIP [*confidently*] He is.

DOLLY [*emphatically*] Twenty-seven.

PHILIP [*imperturbably*] Thirty-three.

DOLLY. Stuff.

PHILIP [*to Valentine*] I appeal to you, Mr Valentine.

VALENTINE [*remonstrating*] Well, really—[*resigning himself*] Thirty-one.

PHILIP [*to Dolly*] You were wrong.

DOLLY. So were you.

PHILIP [*suddenly conscientious*] We're forgetting our manners, Dolly.

DOLLY. [*remorseful*] Yes, so we are.

PHILIP [*apologetic*] We interrupted you, Mr Valentine.

DOLLY. You were going to improve our minds, I think.

VALENTINE. The fact is, your—

PHILIP [*anticipating him*] Our manners?

DOLLY. Our appearance?

VALENTINE [*ad misericordiam*] Oh do let me speak.

DOLLY. The old story. We talk too much.

PHILIP. We do. Shut up, both. [*He seats himself on the arm of the operating chair*].

DOLLY. Mum! [*She sits down in the writing-table chair, and closes her lips with the tips of her fingers*].

VALENTINE. Thank you. [*He brings the stool from the bench in the corner; places it between them; and sits down with a judicial air. They attend to him with extreme gravity. He addresses himself first to Dolly*].

Now may I ask, to begin with, have you ever been in an English seaside resort before? [*She shakes her head slowly and solemnly. He turns to Phil, who shakes his head quickly and expressively*]. I thought so. Well, Mr Clandon, our acquaintance has been short; but it has been voluble; and I have gathered enough to convince me that you are neither of you capable of conceiving what life in an English seaside resort is. Believe me, it's not a question of manner and appearance. In those respects we enjoy a freedom unknown in Madeira. [*Dolly shakes her head vehemently*]. Oh yes, I assure you. Lord de Cresci's sister bicycles in knickerbockers; and the rector's wife advocates dress reform and wears hygienic boots. [*Dolly furtively looks at her own shoe: Valentine catches her in the act, and deftly adds*] No, thats not the sort of boot I mean. [*Dolly's shoe vanishes*]. We dont bother much about dress and manners in England, because, as a nation, we dont dress well and weve no manners. But—and now will you excuse my frankness? [*They nod*]. Thank you. Well, in a seaside resort theres one thing you must have before anybody can afford to be seen going about with you; and thats a father, alive or dead. Am I to infer that you have omitted that indispensable part of your social equipment? [*They confirm him by melancholy nods*]. Then I'm sorry to say that if you are going to stay here for any length of time, it will be impossible for me to accept your kind invitation to lunch. [*He rises with an air of finality, and replaces the stool by the bench*].

PHILIP [*rising with grave politeness*] Come, Dolly. [*He gives her his arm*].

DOLLY. Good morning. [*They go together to the door with perfect dignity*].

VALENTINE [*overwhelmed with remorse*] Oh stop!

stop! [*They halt and turn, arm in arm*]. You make me feel a perfect beast.

DOLLY. Thats your conscience: not us.

VALENTINE [*energetically, throwing off all pretence of a professional manner*] My conscience! My conscience has been my ruin. Listen to me. Twice before I have set up as a respectable medical practitioner in various parts of England. On both occasions I acted conscientiously, and told my patients the brute truth instead of what they wanted to be told. Result, ruin. Now Ive set up as a dentist, a five shilling dentist; and Ive done with conscience for ever. This is my last chance. I spent my last sovereign on moving in; and I havnt paid a shilling of rent yet. I'm eating and drinking on credit; my landlord is as rich as a Jew and as hard as nails; and Ive made five shillings in six weeks. If I swerve by a hair's breadth from the straight line of the most rigid respectability, I'm done for. Under such circumstances is it fair to ask me to lunch with you when you dont know your own father?

DOLLY. After all, our grandfather is a canon of Lincoln Cathedral.

VALENTINE [*like a castaway mariner who sees a sail on the horizon*] What! Have you a grandfather?

DOLLY. Only one.

VALENTINE. My dear good young friends, why on earth didnt you tell me that before? A canon of Lincoln! That makes it all right, of course. Just excuse me while I change my coat. [*He reaches the door in a bound and vanishes*].

Dolly and Phil stare after him, and then at one another. Missing their audience, they discard their style at once.

PHILIP [*throwing away Dolly's arm and coming ill-humoredly towards the operating chair*] That wretched bankrupt ivory snatcher makes a compliment of allowing us to stand him a lunch: probably the first square meal he has had for months. [*He gives the chair a kick, as if it were Valentine*].

DOLLY. It's too beastly. I wont stand it any longer, Phil. Here in England everybody asks whether you have a father the very first thing.

PHILIP. I wont stand it either. Mamma must tell us who he was.

DOLLY. Or who he is. He may be alive.

PHILIP. I hope not. No man alive shall father me.

DOLLY. He might have a lot of money, though.

PHILIP. I doubt it. My knowledge of human nature leads me to believe that if he had a lot of money he wouldnt have got rid of his affectionate family so easily. Anyhow, let's look at the bright side of things. Depend on it, he's dead.

He goes to the hearth and stands with his back to the fireplace. The parlormaid appears.

THE PARLORMAID. Two ladies for you, miss. Your mother and sister, miss, I think.

Mrs Clandon and Gloria come in. Mrs Clandon is a veteran of the Old Guard of the Women's Rights movement which had for its Bible John Stuart Mill's treatise on The Subjection of Women. She has never made herself ugly or ridiculous by affecting masculine waistcoats, collars, and watchchains, like some of her old comrades who had more aggressiveness than taste; and she is too militant an Agnostic to care to be mistaken for a Quaker. She therefore dresses in as businesslike a way as she can without making a guy of herself, ruling out all attempt at sex attraction and imposing respect on frivolous mankind and fashionable womankind. She belongs to the forefront of her own period (say 1860-80) in a jealously assertive attitude of character and intellect, and in being a woman of cultivated interests rather than passionately developed personal affections. Her voice and ways are entirely kindly and humane; and she lends herself conscientiously to the occasional demonstrations of fondness by which her children mark their esteem for her; but displays of personal sentiment secretly embarrass her: passion in her is humanitarian rather than human: she feels strongly about social questions and principles, not about persons. Only, one observes that this reasonableness and intense personal privacy, which leaves her relations with Gloria and Phil much as they might be between her and the children of any other woman, breaks down in the case of Dolly. Though almost every word she addresses to her is necessarily in the nature of a remonstrance for some breach of decorum, the tenderness in her voice is unmistakeable; and it is not surprising that years of such remonstrance have left Dolly hopelessly spoiled.

Gloria, who is hardly past twenty, is a much more formidable person than her mother. She is the incarnation of haughty high-mindedness, raging with the impatience of a mettlesome dominative character paralyzed by the inexperience of her youth, and unwillingly disciplined by the constant danger of ridicule from her irreverent juniors. Unlike her mother, she is all passion; and the conflict of her passion with her obstinate pride and intense fastidiousness results in a freezing coldness of manner. In an ugly woman all this would be repulsive; but Gloria is attractive. A dangerous girl, one would say, if the moral passions were not also marked, and even nobly marked, in a fine brow. Her tailormade skirt-and-jacket dress, of saffron brown cloth, seems conventional when her back is turned; but it displays in front a blouse of sea-green silk which scatters its conventionality with one stroke, and sets her apart as effectually as the twins from the ordinary run of fashionable seaside humanity.

Mrs Clandon comes a little way into the room looking round to see who is present. Gloria, who studiously avoids encouraging the twins by betraying any interest in them, wanders to the window and looks out to sea with her thoughts far away. The parlormaid, instead of withdrawing, shuts the door and waits at it.

MRS CLANDON. Well, children? How is the tooth-ache, Dolly?

DOLLY. Cured, thank Heaven. Ive had it out. [*She sits down on the step of the operating chair*].

Mrs Clandon takes the writing-table chair.

PHILIP [*striking in gravely from the hearth*] And the dentist, a first rate professional man of the highest standing, is coming to lunch with us.

MRS CLANDON [*looking round apprehensively at the servant*] Phil!

THE PARLORMAID. Beg pardon, maam. I'm waiting for Mr Valentine. I have a message for him.

DOLLY. Who from?

MRS CLANDON [*shocked*] Dolly!

Dolly catches her lips suppressively with her finger tips.

THE PARLORMAID. Only the landlord, maam.

Valentine, in a blue serge suit, with a straw hat in his hand, comes back in high spirits, out of breath with the haste he has made. Gloria turns from the window and studies him with chilling attention.

PHILIP. Let me introduce you, Mr Valentine. My mother, Mrs Lanfrey Clandon. [*Mrs Clandon bows. Valentine bows, self-possessed and quite equal to the occasion*]. My sister Gloria. [*Gloria bows with cold dignity and sits down on the sofa*].

Valentine falls abjectly in love at first sight. He

fingers his hat nervously, and makes her a sneaking bow.

MRS CLANDON. I understand that we are to have the pleasure of seeing you at luncheon today, Mr Valentine.

VALENTINE. Thank you—er—if you dont mind—I mean if you will be so kind—[*to the parlormaid, testily*] What is it?

THE PARLORMAID. The landlord, sir, wishes to speak to you before you go out.

VALENTINE. Oh, tell him I have four patients here. [*The Clandons look surprised, except Phil, who is imperturbable*]. If he wouldnt mind waiting just two minutes, I—I'll slip down and see him for a moment. [*Throwing himself confidentially on her sense of the position*] Say I'm busy, but that I want to see him.

THE PARLORMAID [*reassuringly*] Yes, sir. [*She goes*].

MRS CLANDON [*on the point of rising*] We are detaining you, I am afraid.

VALENTINE. Not at all, not at all. Your presence here will be the greatest help to me. The fact is, I owe six weeks rent; and Ive had no patients until today. My interview with my landlord will be considerably smoothed by the apparent boom in my business.

DOLLY [*vexed*] Oh, how tiresome of you to let it all out! And weve just been pretending that you were a respectable professional man in a first rate position.

MRS CLANDON [*horrified*] Oh Dolly! Dolly! My dearest: how can you be so rude? [*To Valentine*] Will you excuse these barbarian children of mine, Mr Valentine?

VALENTINE. Dont mention it: I'm used to them. Would it be too much to ask you to wait five minutes while I get rid of my landlord downstairs?

DOLLY. Dont be long. We're hungry.

MRS CLANDON [*again remonstrating*] Dolly, dear!

VALENTINE [*to Dolly*] All right. [*To Mrs Clandon*] Thank you: I shant be long. [*He steals a look at Gloria as he turns to go. She is looking gravely at him. He falls into confusion*]. I—er—er—yes—thank you [*he succeeds at last in blundering himself out of the room; but the exhibition is a pitiful one*].

PHILIP. Did you observe? [*Pointing to Gloria*] Love at first sight. Another scalp for your collection, Gloria. Number fifteen.

MRS CLANDON. Sh—sh pray, Phil. He may have heard you.

PHILIP. Not he. [*Bracing himself for a scene*] And now look here, mamma. [*He takes the stool from the bench; and seats himself majestically in the middle of the room, copying Valentine's recent demonstration. Dolly, feeling that her position on the step of the operating chair is unworthy the dignity of the occasion, rises, looking important and uncompromising. She crosses to the window, and stands with her back to the end of the writing-table, her hands behind her and on the table. Mrs Clandon looks at them, wondering what is coming. Gloria becomes attentive. Phil straightens his back; places his knuckles symmetrically on his knees; and opens his case*]. Dolly and I have been talking over things a good deal lately; and I dont think, judging from my knowledge of human nature—we dont think that you [*speaking very pointedly, with the words detached*] quite. Appreciate. The fact—

DOLLY [*seating herself on the end of the table with a spring*] That weve grown up.

MRS CLANDON. Indeed? In what way have I given you any reason to complain?

PHILIP. Well, there are certain matters upon which we are beginning to feel that you might take us a little more into your confidence.

MRS CLANDON [*rising, with all the placidity of her age suddenly breaking up into a curious hard excitement, dignified but dogged, ladylike but implacable: the manner of the Old Guard*] Phil: take care. What have I always taught you? There are two sorts of family life, Phil; and your experience of human nature only extends, so far, to one of them. [*Rhetorically*] The sort you know is based on mutual respect, on recognition of the right of every member of the household to independence and privacy [*her emphasis on "privacy" is intense*] in their personal concerns. And because you have always enjoyed that, it seems such a matter of course to you that you dont value it. But [*with biting acrimony*] there is another sort of family life: a life in which husbands open their wives' letters, and call on them to account for every farthing of their expenditure and every moment of their time; in which women do the same to their children; in which no room is private and no hour sacred; in which duty, obedience, affection, home, morality and religion are detestable tyrannies, and life is a vulgar round of punishments and lies, coercion and rebellion, jealousy, suspicion, recrimination— Oh! I cannot describe it to you: fortunately for you, you know nothing about it. [*She sits down, panting*].

DOLLY [*inaccessible to rhetoric*] See Twentieth Century Parents, chapter on Liberty, passim.

MRS CLANDON [*touching her shoulder affectionately, softened even by a gibe from her*] My dear Dolly: if you only knew how glad I am that it is nothing but a joke to you, though it is such bitter earnest to me. [*More resolutely, turning to Phil*] Phil: I never ask you questions about your private concerns. You are not going to question me, are you?

PHILIP. I think it due to ourselves to say that the

question we wanted to ask is as much our business as yours.

DOLLY. Besides, it cant be good to keep a lot of questions bottled up inside you. You did it, mamma; but see how awfully it's broken out again in me.

MRS CLANDON. I see you want to ask your question. Ask it.

DOLLY AND PHILIP [*beginning   simultaneously*] Who—[*They stop*].

PHILIP. Now look here, Dolly: am I going to conduct this business or are you?

DOLLY. You.

PHILIP. Then hold your mouth. [*Dolly does so, literally*]. The question is a simple one. When the ivory snatcher—

MRS CLANDON [*remonstrating*] Phil!

PHILIP. Dentist is an ugly word. The man of ivory and gold asked us whether we were the children of Mr Densmore Clandon of Newbury Hall. In pursuance of the precepts in your treatise on Twentieth Century Conduct, and your repeated personal exhortations to us to curtail the number of unnecessary lies we tell, we replied truthfully that we didnt know.

DOLLY. Neither did we.

PHILIP. Sh! The result was that the gum architect made considerable difficulties about accepting our invitation to lunch, although I doubt if he has had anything but tea and bread and butter for a fortnight past. Now my knowledge of human nature leads me to believe that we had a father, and that you probably know who he was.

MRS CLANDON [*her agitation returning*] Stop, Phil. Your father is nothing to you, nor to me. [*Vehemently*] That is enough.

The twins are silenced, but not satisfied. Their faces

[685]

fall. But Gloria, who has been following the altercation attentively, suddenly intervenes.

GLORIA [*advancing*] Mother: we have a right to know.

MRS CLANDON [*rising and facing her*] Gloria! "We"! Who is "we"?

GLORIA [*steadfastly*] We three. [*Her tone is unmistakeable: she is pitting her strength against her mother's for the first time. The twins instantly go over to the enemy*].

MRS CLANDON [*wounded*] In your mouth "we" used to mean you and I, Gloria.

PHILIP [*rising decisively and putting away the stool*] We're hurting you: let's drop it. We didnt think youd mind. *I* dont want to know.

DOLLY [*coming off the table*] I'm sure *I* dont. Oh, dont look like that, mamma. [*She looks angrily at Gloria and flings her arms round her mother's neck*].

MRS CLANDON. Thank you, my dear. Thanks, Phil. [*She detaches Dolly gently and sits down again*].

GLORIA [*inexorably*] We have a right to know, mother.

MRS CLANDON [*indignantly*] Ah! You insist.

GLORIA. Do you intend that we shall never know?

DOLLY. Oh Gloria, dont. It's barbarous.

GLORIA [*with quiet scorn*] What is the use of being weak? You see what has happened with this gentleman here, mother. The same thing has happened to me.

MRS CLANDON
DOLLY
PHILIP
[*all together*] {What do you mean? / Oh, tell us! / What happened to you?}

GLORIA. Oh, nothing of any consequence. [*She turns away from them and strolls up to the easy chair at the fireplace, where she sits down, almost with her back to them. As they wait expectantly, she adds, over her shoulder, with studied indifference*] On board the

steamer, the first officer did me the honor to propose
to me.

DOLLY. No: it was to me.

MRS CLANDON. The first officer! Are you serious,
Gloria? What did you say to him? [*Correcting herself*] Excuse me: I have no right to ask that.

GLORIA. The answer is pretty obvious. A woman who
does not know who her father was cannot accept such
an offer.

MRS CLANDON. Surely you did not want to accept
it!

GLORIA [*turning a little and raising her voice*] No; but
suppose I had wanted to!

PHILIP. Did that difficulty strike you, Dolly?

DOLLY. No. I accepted him.

GLORIA ⎫ [*all crying* ⎧ Accepted him!
MRS CLANDON ⎬ *out together*] ⎨ Dolly!
PHILIP ⎭ ⎩ Oh, I say!

DOLLY [*naïvely*] He did look such a fool!

MRS CLANDON. But why did you do such a thing,
Dolly?

DOLLY. For fun, I suppose. He had to measure my
finger for a ring. Youd have done the same thing
yourself.

MRS CLANDON. No, Dolly, I would not. As a matter
of fact the first officer did propose to me; and I told
him to keep that sort of thing for women who were
young enough to be amused by it. He appears to have
acted on my advice. [*She rises and goes to the hearth*].
Gloria: I am sorry you think me weak; but I cannot
tell you what you want. You are all too young.

PHILIP. This is rather a startling departure from
Twentieth Century principles.

DOLLY [*quoting*] "Answer all your children's questions, and answer them truthfully, as soon as they are

old enough to ask them." See Twentieth Century Motherhood—

PHILIP. Page one.

DOLLY. Chapter one.

PHILIP. Sentence one.

MRS CLANDON. My dears: I do not mean that you are too young to know. I mean that you are too young to be taken into my confidence. You are very bright children, all of you; but you are still very inexperienced and consequently sometimes very unsympathetic. There are experiences of mine that I cannot bear to speak of except to those who have gone through what I have gone through. I hope you will never be qualified for such confidences.

PHILIP. Another grievance, Dolly!

DOLLY. We're not sympathetic.

GLORIA [*leaning forward in her chair and looking earnestly up at her mother*] Mother: I did not mean to be unsympathetic.

MRS CLANDON [*affectionately*] Of course not, dear. I quite understand!

GLORIA [*rising*] But, mother—

MRS CLANDON [*drawing back a little*] Yes?

GLORIA [*obstinately*] It is nonsense to tell us that our father is nothing to us.

MRS CLANDON [*provoked to sudden resolution*] Do you remember your father?

GLORIA [*meditatively, as if the recollection were a tender one*] I am not quite sure. I think so.

MRS CLANDON [*grimly*] You are not sure?

GLORIA. No.

MRS CLANDON [*with quiet force*] Gloria: if I had ever struck you [*Gloria recoils: Phil and Dolly are disagreeably shocked: all three stare at her, revolted, as she continues mercilessly*]—struck you purposely, de-

[688]

liberately, with the intention of hurting you, with a whip bought for the purpose! would you remember that, do you think? [*Gloria utters an exclamation of indignant repulsion*]. That would have been your last recollection of your father, Gloria, if I had not taken you away from him. I have kept him out of your life: keep him now out of mine by never mentioning him to me again.

Gloria, with a shudder, covers her face with her hands until, hearing someone at the door, she recomposes herself. Mrs Clandon sits down on the sofa. Valentine returns.

VALENTINE. I hope Ive not kept you waiting. That landlord of mine is really an extraordinary old character.

DOLLY [*eagerly*] Oh, tell us. How long has he given you to pay?

MRS CLANDON [*distracted by her child's manners*] Dolly, Dolly, Dolly dear! You must not ask questions.

DOLLY [*demurely*] So sorry. Youll tell us, wont you, Mr Valentine?

VALENTINE. He doesnt want his rent at all. He's broken his tooth on a Brazil nut; and he wants me to look at it and to lunch with him afterwards.

DOLLY. Then have him up and pull his tooth out at once; and we'll bring him to lunch too. Tell the maid to fetch him along. [*She runs to the bell and rings it vigorously. Then, with a sudden doubt, she turns to Valentine and adds*] I suppose he's respectable? really respectable?

VALENTINE. Perfectly. Not like me.

DOLLY. Honest Injun?

Mrs Clandon gasps faintly; but her powers of remonstrance are exhausted.

VALENTINE. Honest Injun!

[689]

DOLLY. Then off with you and bring him up.

VALENTINE [*looking dubiously at Mrs Clandon*] I dare say he'd be delighted if—er— ?

MRS CLANDON [*rising and looking at her watch*] I shall be happy to see your friend at lunch if you can persuade him to come; but I cant wait to see him now: I have an appointment at the hotel at a quarter to one with an old friend whom I have not seen since I left England eighteen years ago. Will you excuse me?

VALENTINE. Certainly, Mrs Clandon.

GLORIA. Shall I come?

MRS CLANDON. No, dear. I want to be alone. [*She goes out, evidently still a good deal troubled*].

Valentine opens the door for her and follows her.

PHILIP [*significantly to Dolly*] Hmhm!

DOLLY [*significantly to Phil*] Ahah!

The parlormaid answers the bell.

DOLLY. Shew the old gentleman up.

THE PARLORMAID [*puzzled*] Madam?

DOLLY. The old gentleman with the toothache.

PHILIP. The landlord.

THE PARLORMAID. Mr Crampton, sir?

PHILIP. Is his name Crampton?

DOLLY [*to Phil*] Sounds rheumaticky, doesnt it?

PHILIP. Chalkstones, probably.

DOLLY. Shew Mr Crampstones up.

THE PARLORMAID [*going out*] Mr Crampton, miss.

DOLLY [*repeating it to herself like a lesson*] Crampton, Crampton, Crampton, Crampton, Crampton. [*She sits down studiously at the writing-table*] I must get that name right, or Heaven knows what I shall call him.

GLORIA. Phil: can you believe such a horrible thing as that about our father? what mother said just now.

PHILIP. Oh, there are lots of people of that kind. Old Chamico used to thrash his wife and daughters with a cart whip.

DOLLY [*contemptuously*] Yes, a Portuguese!

PHILIP. When you come to men who are brutes, there is much in common between the Portuguese and the English variety, Doll. Trust my knowledge of human nature. [*He resumes his position on the hearth-rug with an elderly and responsible air*].

GLORIA [*with angered remorse*] I dont think we shall ever play again at our old game of guessing what our father was to be like. Dolly: are you sorry for your father? the father with lots of money!

DOLLY. Oh come! What about your father? the lonely old man with the tender aching heart! He's pretty well burst up, I think.

PHILIP. There can be no doubt that the governor is an exploded superstition. [*Valentine is heard talking to somebody outside the door*]. But hark! he comes.

GLORIA [*nervously*] Who?

DOLLY. Chalkstones.

PHILIP. Sh! Attention! [*They put on their best manners. Phil adds in a lower voice to Gloria*] If he's good enough for the lunch, I'll nod to Dolly; and if she nods to you, invite him straight away.

Valentine comes back with his landlord. Mr Fergus Crampton is a man of about sixty, with an atrociously obstinate ill tempered grasping mouth, and a dogmatic voice. There is no sign of strained means or commercial diffidence about him: he is well dressed, and would be classed at a guess as a prosperous master-manufacturer in a business inherited from an old family in the aristocracy of trade. His navy blue coat is not of the usual fashionable pattern. It is not exactly a pilot's coat; but it is cut that way, double breasted, and with stout buttons and broad lappels: a coat for a shipyard rather than a counting house. He has taken a fancy to Valentine, who cares nothing for his crossness of grain, and treats him with a disrespectful humanity for which he is secretly grateful.

VALENTINE. May I introduce? This is Mr Crampton: Miss Dorothy Clandon, Mr Philip Clandon, Miss Clandon. [*Crampton stands nervously bowing. They all bow*]. Sit down, Mr Crampton.

DOLLY [*pointing to the operating chair*] That is the most comfortable chair, Mr Ch-crampton.

CRAMPTON. Thank you; but wont this young lady—[*indicating Gloria, who is close to the chair*]?

GLORIA. Thank you, Mr Crampton: we are just going.

VALENTINE [*bustling him across to the chair with good-humored peremptoriness*] Sit down, sit down. Youre tired.

CRAMPTON. Well, perhaps as I am considerably the oldest person present, I—[*he finishes the sentence by sitting down a little rheumatically in the operating chair. Meanwhile Phil, having studied him critically during his passage across the room, nods to Dolly; and Dolly nods to Gloria*].

GLORIA. Mr Crampton: we understand that we are preventing Mr Valentine from lunching with you by taking him away ourselves. My mother would be very glad indeed if you would come too.

CRAMPTON [*gratefully, after looking at her earnestly for a moment*] Thank you. I will come with pleasure.

GLORIA		Thank you very much—er—
DOLLY	[*politely murmuring*]	So glad—er—
PHILIP		Delighted, I'm sure—er—

The conversation drops. Gloria and Dolly look at one another; then at Valentine and Phil. Valentine and

Phil, unequal to the occasion, look away from them at one another, and are instantly so disconcerted by catching one another's eye, that they look back again and catch the eyes of Gloria and Dolly. Thus, catching one another all round, they all look at nothing and are quite at a loss. Crampton looks at them, waiting for them to begin. The silence becomes unbearable.

DOLLY [*suddenly, to keep things going*] How old are you, Mr Crampton?

GLORIA [*hastily*] I am afraid we must be going, Mr Valentine. It is understood, then, that we meet at half past one. [*She makes for the door. Phil goes with her. Valentine retreats to the bell*].

VALENTINE. Half past one. [*He rings the bell*]. Many thanks. [*He follows Gloria and Phil to the door, and goes out with them*].

DOLLY [*who has meanwhile stolen across to Crampton*] Make him give you gas. It's five shillings extra; but it's worth it.

CRAMPTON [*amused*] Very well. [*Looking more earnestly at her*] So you want to know my age, do you? I'm fifty seven.

DOLLY [*with conviction*] You look it.

CRAMPTON [*grimly*] I dare say I do.

DOLLY. What are you looking at me so hard for? Anything wrong? [*She feels whether her hat is right*].

CRAMPTON. Youre like somebody.

DOLLY. Who?

CRAMPTON. Well, you have a curious look of my mother.

DOLLY [*incredulously*] Your mother!!! Quite sure you dont mean your daughter?

CRAMPTON [*suddenly blackening with hate*] Yes: I'm quite sure I dont mean my daughter.

DOLLY [*sympathetically*] Tooth bad?

CRAMPTON. No, no: nothing. A twinge of memory, Miss Clandon, not of toothache.

DOLLY. Have it out. "Pluck from the memory a rooted sorrow." With gas, five shillings extra.

CRAMPTON [*vindictively*] No, not a sorrow. An injury that was done me once: thats all. I dont forget injuries: and I dont want to forget them. [*His features settle into an implacable frown*].

DOLLY [*looking critically at him*] I dont think we shall like you when you are brooding over your injuries.

PHILIP [*who has entered the room unobserved, and stolen behind her*] My sister means well, Mr Crampton; but she is indiscreet. Now Dolly: outside! [*He takes her towards the door*].

DOLLY [*in a perfectly audible undertone*] He says he's only fifty seven and he thinks me the image of his mother and he hates his daughter and— [*She is interrupted by the return of Valentine*].

VALENTINE. Miss Clandon has gone on.

PHILIP. Dont forget half past one.

DOLLY. Mind you leave Mr Crampton enough teeth to eat with. [*They go out*].

Valentine comes to his cabinet, and opens it.

CRAMPTON. Thats a spoiled child, Mr Valentine. Thats one of your modern products. When I was her age, I had many a good hiding fresh in my memory to teach me manners.

VALENTINE [*taking up his dental mirror and probe*] What did you think of her sister?

CRAMPTON. You liked her better, eh?

VALENTINE [*rhapsodically*] She struck me as being— [*He checks himself, and adds, prosaically*] However, thats not business. [*He assumes his professional tone*]. Open, please. [*Crampton opens his mouth. Valentine puts the mirror in, and examines his teeth*]. Hm! Youve smashed that one. What a pity to spoil such a splendid set of teeth! Why do you crack nuts with them? [*He withdraws the mirror, and comes forward to converse with his patient*].

CRAMPTON. Ive always cracked nuts with them: what else are they for? [*Dogmatically*] The proper way to keep teeth good is to give them plenty of use on bones and nuts, and wash them every day with soap: plain yellow soap.

VALENTINE. Soap! Why soap?

CRAMPTON. I began using it as a boy because I was made to; and Ive used it ever since. And Ive never had toothache in my life.

VALENTINE. Dont you find it rather nasty?

CRAMPTON. I found that most things that were good for me were nasty. But I was taught to put up with them, and made to put up with them. I'm used to it now: in fact I like the taste when the soap is really good.

VALENTINE [*making a wry face in spite of himself*] You seem to have been very carefully educated, Mr Crampton.

CRAMPTON [*grimly*] I wasnt spoiled, at all events.

VALENTINE [*smiling a little to himself*] Are you quite sure?

CRAMPTON [*crustily*] What d'y' mean?

VALENTINE. Well, your teeth are good, I admit. But Ive seen just as good in very self-indulgent mouths. [*He goes to the cabinet and changes the probe for another one*].

CRAMPTON. It's not the effect on the teeth: it's the effect on the character.

VALENTINE [*placably*] Oh, the character! I see. [*He recommences operations*]. A little wider, please. Hm! Why do you bite so hard? youve broken the tooth worse than you broke the Brazil nut. It will have to come out: it's past saving. [*He withdraws the probe and again comes to the side of the chair to converse*]. Dont be alarmed: you shant feel anything. I'll give you gas.

CRAMPTON. Rubbish, man: I want none of your gas. Out with it! People were taught to bear necessary pain in my day.

VALENTINE. Oh, if you like being hurt, all right. I'll hurt you as much as you like, without any extra charge for the beneficial effect on your character.

CRAMPTON [*rising and glaring at him*] Young man: you owe me six weeks rent.

VALENTINE. I do.

CRAMPTON. Can you pay me?

VALENTINE. No.

CRAMPTON [*satisfied with his advantage*] I thought not. [*He sits down again*]. How soon d'y' think youll be able to pay me if you have no better manners than to make game of your patients?

VALENTINE. My good sir: my patients havnt all formed their characters on kitchen soap.

CRAMPTON [*suddenly gripping him by the arm as he turns away again to the cabinet*] So much the worse for them! I tell you you dont understand my character. If I could spare all my teeth, I'd make you pull them out one after another to shew you what a properly hardened man can go through with when he's made up his mind to it. [*He nods at Valentine to emphasize this declaration, and releases him*].

VALENTINE [*his careless pleasantry quite unruffled*] And you want to be more hardened, do you?

CRAMPTON. Yes.

VALENTINE [*strolling away to the bell*] Well, youre quite hard enough for me already—as a landlord.

[*Crampton receives this with a growl of grim humor. Valentine rings the bell, and remarks in a cheerful casual way, whilst waiting for it to be answered*] Why did you never get married, Mr Crampton ? A wife and children would have taken some of the hardness out of you.

CRAMPTON [*with unexpected ferocity*] What the devil is that to you ?

The parlormaid appears at the door.

VALENTINE [*politely*] Some warm water, please. [*She retires; and Valentine comes back to the cabinet, not at all put out by Crampton's rudeness, and carries on the conversation whilst he selects a forceps and places it ready to his hand with a gag and a tumbler*] You were asking me what the devil that was to me. Well, I have an idea of getting married myself.

CRAMPTON [*with grumbling irony*] Naturally, sir, naturally. When a young man has come to his last farthing, and is within twenty four hours of having his furniture distrained upon by his landlord, he marries. Ive noticed that before. Well, marry; and be miserable.

VALENTINE. Oh come! what do you know about it ?

CRAMPTON. I'm not a bachelor.

VALENTINE. Then there is a Mrs Crampton ?

CRAMPTON [*wincing with a pang of resentment*] Yes: damn her!

VALENTINE [*unperturbed*] Hm! A father, too, perhaps, as well as a husband, Mr Crampton ?

CRAMPTON. Three children.

VALENTINE [*politely*] Damn them ? eh ?

CRAMPTON [*jealously*] No, sir: the children are as much mine as hers.

The parlormaid brings in a jug of hot water.

VALENTINE. Thank you. [*She gives him the jug and goes out. He brings it to the cabinet, continuing in the same idle strain*] I really should like to know your family, Mr Crampton. [*He pours some hot water into the tumbler*].

CRAMPTON. Sorry I cant introduce you, sir. I'm happy to say that I dont know where they are, and dont care, so long as they keep out of my way. [*Valentine, with a hitch of his eyebrows and shoulders, drops the forceps with a clink into the hot water*]. You neednt warm that thing to use on me. I'm not afraid of the cold steel. [*Valentine stoops to arrange the gas pump and cylinder beside the chair*]. Whats that heavy thing?

VALENTINE. Oh, never mind. Something to put my foot on, to get the necessary purchase for a good pull. [*Crampton looks alarmed in spite of himself. Valentine stands upright and places the glass with the forceps ready to his hand, chatting on with provoking indifference*]. And so you advise me not to get married, Mr Crampton? [*He puts his foot on the lever by which the chair is raised and lowered*].

CRAMPTON [*irritably*] I advise you to get my tooth out and have done reminding me of my wife. Come along, man. [*He grips the arms of the chair and braces himself*].

VALENTINE. What do you bet that I dont get that tooth out without your feeling it?

CRAMPTON. Your six weeks rent, young man. Dont you gammon me.

VALENTINE [*jumping at the bet and sending him aloft vigorously*] Done! Are you ready?

Crampton, who has lost his grip of the chair in his alarm at its sudden ascent, folds his arms; sits stiffly upright; and prepares for the worst. Valentine suddenly lets down the back of the chair to an obtuse angle.

CRAMPTON [*clutching at the arms of the chair as he*

falls back] P! take care, man! I'm quite helpless in this
po—

VALENTINE [*deftly stopping him with the gag, and
snatching up the mouthpiece of the gas machine*] Youll
be more helpless presently.

*He presses the mouthpiece over Crampton's mouth and
nose, leaning over his chest so as to hold his head and
shoulders well down on the chair. Crampton makes an
inarticulate sound in the mouthpiece and tries to lay
hands on Valentine, whom he supposes to be in front of
him. After a moment his arms wave aimlessly, then subside and drop. He is quite insensible. Valentine throws
aside the mouthpiece quickly; picks the forceps adroitly
from the glass; and—.*

[ACT II]

---

*On the terrace at the Marine Hotel. It is a square
flagged platform, glaring in the sun, and fenced on the
seaward edge by a parapet. The head waiter, busy
laying napkins on a luncheon table with his back to the
sea, has the hotel on his right, and on his left, in the
corner nearest the sea, a flight of steps leading down to
the beach. When he looks down the terrace in front of
him he sees, a little to his left, a middle aged gentleman
sitting on a chair of iron laths at a little iron table with
a bowl of lump sugar on it, reading an ultra-Conserva-
tive newspaper, with his umbrella up to defend him from
the sun, which, in August and at less than an hour after
noon, is toasting his protended insteps. At the hotel side
of the terrace, there is a garden seat of the ordinary
esplanade pattern. Access to the hotel for visitors is by an
entrance in the middle of its façade. Nearer the parapet
there lurks a way to the kitchen, masked by a little
trellis porch. The table at which the waiter is occupied is
a long one, set across the terrace with covers and chairs
for five, two at each side and one at the end next the
hotel. Against the parapet another table is prepared as
a buffet to serve from.*

*The waiter is a remarkable person in his way. A silky
old man, white haired and delicate looking, but so cheerful and contented that in his encouraging presence
ambition stands rebuked as vulgarity, and imagination
as treason to the abounding sufficiency and interest of
the actual. He has a certain expression peculiar to
men who are pre-eminent in their callings, and who,*

whilst aware of the vanity of success, are untouched by envy.

The gentleman at the iron table is not dressed for the seaside. He wears his London frock coat and gloves; and his tall silk hat is on the table beside the sugarbowl. The excellent condition and quality of these garments and the gold-rimmed folding spectacles through which he is reading, testify to his respectability. He is about fifty, clean-shaven and close-cropped, with the corners of his mouth turned down purposely, as if he suspected them of wanting to turn up, and was determined not to let them have their way. He keeps his brow resolutely wide open, as if, again, he had resolved in his youth to be truthful, magnanimous, and incorruptible, but had never suc-ceeded in making that habit of mind automatic and unconscious. Still, he is by no means to be laughed at. There is no sign of stupidity or infirmity of will about him: on the contrary, he would pass anywhere at sight as a man of more than average professional capacity and responsibility. Just at present he is enjoying the weather and the sea too much to be out of patience; but he has exhausted all the news in his paper, and is at present reduced to the advertisements, which are not sufficiently succulent to induce him to persevere with them.

THE GENTLEMAN [*yawning and giving up the paper as a bad job*] Waiter!

WAITER. Sir? [*coming to him*].

THE GENTLEMAN. Are you quite sure Mrs Clandon is coming back before lunch?

WAITER. Quite sure, sir. She expects you at a quarter to one, sir. [*The gentleman, soothed at once by the waiter's voice, looks at him with a lazy smile. It is a quiet voice, with a gentle melody in it that gives sympathetic*

*interest to his most commonplace remark; and he speaks
with the sweetest propriety, neither dropping his aitches
nor misplacing them, nor committing any other vulgarism.
He looks at his watch as he continues*] Not that yet,
sir, is it? 12.43, sir. Only two minutes more to wait,
sir. Nice morning, sir!

THE GENTLEMAN. Yes: very fresh after London.

WAITER. Yes, sir: so all our visitors say, sir. Very
nice family, Mrs Clandon's, sir.

THE GENTLEMAN. You like them, do you?

WAITER. Yes, sir. They have a free way with them
that is very taking, sir, very taking indeed: especially
the young lady and gentleman.

THE GENTLEMAN. Miss Dorothea and Mr Philip, I
suppose.

WAITER. Yes, sir. The young lady, in giving an order,
or the like of that, will say, "Remember, William: we
came to this hotel on your account, having heard what
a perfect waiter you are." The young gentleman will
tell me that I remind him strongly of his father [*the
gentleman starts at this*] and that he expects me to act
by him as such. [*With a soothing sunny cadence*] Oh,
very pleasant, sir, very affable and pleasant indeed!

THE GENTLEMAN. You like his father! [*He laughs
at the notion*].

WAITER. Oh sir, we must not take what they say too
seriously. Of course, sir, if it were true, the young
lady would have seen the resemblance too, sir.

THE GENTLEMAN. Did she?

WAITER. No, sir. She thought me like the bust of
Shakespear in Stratford Church, sir. That is why she
calls me William, sir. My real name is Walter, sir. [*He
turns to go back to the table, and sees Mrs Clandon
coming up to the terrace from the beach by the steps*].
Here is Mrs Clandon, sir. [*To Mrs Clandon in an un-*

obtrusively confidential tone] Gentleman for you, maam.

MRS CLANDON. We shall have two more gentlemen at lunch, William.

WAITER. Right, maam. Thank you, maam. [*He withdraws into the hotel*].

Mrs Clandon comes forward looking for her visitor, but passes over the gentleman without any sign of recognition.

THE GENTLEMAN [*peering at her quaintly from under the umbrella*] Dont you know me?

MRS CLANDON [*incredulously, looking hard at him*] Are you Finch M'Comas?

M'COMAS. Cant you guess? [*He shuts the umbrella; puts it aside; and jocularly plants himself with his hands on his hips to be inspected*].

MRS CLANDON. I believe you are. [*She gives him her hand. The shake that ensues is that of old friends after a long separation*]. Wheres your beard?

M'COMAS [*humorously solemn*] Would you employ a solicitor with a beard?

MRS CLANDON [*pointing to the silk hat on the table*] Is that your hat?

M'COMAS. Would you employ a solicitor with a sombrero?

MRS CLANDON. I have thought of you all these eighteen years with the beard and the sombrero. [*She sits down on the garden seat. M'Comas takes his chair again*]. Do you go to the meetings of the Dialectical Society still?

M'COMAS [*gravely*] I do not frequent meetings now.

MRS CLANDON. Finch: I see what has happened. You have become respectable.

M'COMAS. Havnt you?

MRS CLANDON. Not a bit.

[703]

M'COMAS. You hold to our old opinions still?

MRS CLANDON. As firmly as ever.

M'COMAS. Bless me! And you are still ready to make speeches in public, in spite of your sex [*Mrs Clandon nods*]; to insist on a married woman's right to her own separate property [*she nods again*]; to champion Darwin's view of the origin of species and John Stuart Mill's Essay on Liberty [*nod*]; to read Huxley, Tyndall, and George Eliot [*three nods*]; and to demand University degrees, the opening of the professions, and the parliamentary franchise for women as well as men?

MRS CLANDON [*resolutely*] Yes: I have not gone back one inch; and I have educated Gloria to take up my work when I must leave it. That is what has brought me back to England. I felt I had no right to bury her alive in Madeira: my St Helena, Finch. I suppose she will be howled at as I was; but she is prepared for that.

M'COMAS. Howled at! My dear good lady: there is nothing in any of those views nowadays to prevent her marrying an archbishop. You reproached me just now for having become respectable. You were wrong: I hold to our old opinions as strongly as ever. I dont go to church; and I dont pretend I do. I call myself what I am: a Philosophic Radical standing for liberty and the rights of the individual, as I learnt to do from my master Herbert Spencer. Am I howled at? No: I'm indulged as an old fogey. I'm out of everything, because Ive refused to bow the knee to Socialism.

MRS CLANDON [*shocked*] Socialism!

M'COMAS. Yes: Socialism. Thats what Miss Gloria will be up to her ears in before the end of the month if you let her loose here.

MRS CLANDON [*emphatically*] But I can prove to her that Socialism is a fallacy.

M'COMAS [*touchingly*] It is by proving that, Mrs Clandon, that I have lost all my young disciples. Be careful what you do: let her go her own way. [*With some bitterness*] We're old fashioned: the world thinks it has left us behind. There is only one place in all England where your opinions would still pass as advanced.

MRS CLANDON [*scornfully unconvinced*] The Church, perhaps?

M'COMAS. No: the theatre. And now to business! Why have you made me come down here?

MRS CLANDON. Well, partly because I wanted to see you—

M'COMAS [*with good-humored irony*] Thanks.

MRS CLANDON. —and partly because I want you to explain everything to the children. They know nothing; and now that we have come back to England it is impossible to leave them in ignorance any longer. [*Agitated*] Finch: I cannot bring myself to tell them. I—

She is interrupted by the twins and Gloria. Dolly comes tearing up the steps, racing Phil, who combines terrific speed with an unhurried propriety of bearing which, however, costs him the race, as Dolly reaches her mother first and almost upsets the garden seat by the precipitancy of her embrace.

DOLLY [*breathless*] It's all right, mamma. The dentist is coming; and he's bringing his old man.

MRS CLANDON. Dolly, dear: dont you see Mr M'Comas? [*M'Comas rises, smiling*].

DOLLY [*her face falling with the most disparagingly obvious disappointment*] This! Where are the flowing locks?

PHILIP [*seconding her warmly*] Where the beard? the cloak? the poetic exterior?

DOLLY. Oh, Mr M'Comas, youve gone and spoiled yourself. Why didnt you wait til we'd seen you?

M'COMAS [*taken aback, but rallying his humor to meet the emergency*] Because eighteen years is too long for a solicitor to go without having his hair cut.

GLORIA [*at the other side of M'Comas*] How do you do, Mr M'Comas? [*He turns; and she takes his hand and presses it, with a frank straight look into his eyes*]. We are glad to meet you at last.

M'COMAS. Miss Gloria, I presume? [*Gloria smiles assent; releases his hand after a final pressure; and retires behind the garden seat, leaning over the back beside Mrs Clandon*]. And this young gentleman?

PHILIP. I was christened in a comparatively prosaic mood. My name is—

DOLLY [*completing his sentence for him declamatorily*] "Norval. On the Grampian hills"—

PHILIP [*declaiming gravely*] "My father feeds his flock, a frugal swain"—

MRS CLANDON [*remonstrating*] Dear, dear children: dont be silly. Everything is so new to them here, Finch, that they are in the wildest spirits. They think every Englishman they meet is a joke.

DOLLY. Well, so he is: it's not our fault.

PHILIP. My knowledge of human nature is fairly extensive, Mr M'Comas; but I find it impossible to take the inhabitants of this island seriously.

M'COMAS. I presume, sir, you are Master Philip [*offering his hand*].

PHILIP [*taking M'Comas's hand and looking solemnly at him*] I was Master Philip: was so for many years; just as you were once Master Finch. [*He gives the hand a single shake and drops it; then turns away, exclaiming meditatively*] How strange it is to look back on our boyhood!

[706]

DOLLY [*to Mrs Clandon*] Has Finch had a drink?

MRS CLANDON [*remonstrating*] Dearest: Mr M'Comas will lunch with us.

DOLLY. Have you ordered for seven? Dont forget the old gentleman.

MRS CLANDON. I have not forgotten him, dear. What is his name?

DOLLY. Chalkstones. He'll be here at half past one. [*To M'Comas*] Are we like what you expected?

MRS CLANDON [*earnestly, even a little peremptorily*] Dolly: Mr M'Comas has something more serious than that to tell you. Children: I have asked my old friend to answer the question you asked this morning. He is your father's friend as well as mine; and he will tell you the story of my married life more fairly than I could. Gloria: are you satisfied?

GLORIA [*gravely attentive*] Mr M'Comas is very kind.

M'COMAS [*nervously*] Not at all, my dear young lady: not at all. At the same time, this is rather sudden. I was hardly prepared—er—

DOLLY [*suspiciously*] Oh, we dont want anything prepared.

PHILIP [*exhorting him*] Tell us the truth.

DOLLY [*emphatically*] Bald headed.

M'COMAS [*nettled*] I hope you intend to take what I have to say seriously.

PHILIP [*with profound gravity*] I hope it will deserve it, Mr M'Comas. My knowledge of human nature teaches me not to expect too much.

MRS CLANDON [*remonstrating*] Phil—

PHILIP. Yes, mother: all right. I beg your pardon, Mr M'Comas: dont mind us.

DOLLY [*in conciliation*] We mean well.

PHILIP. Shut up, both.

Dolly holds her lips. M'Comas takes a chair from the luncheon table; places it between the little table and the garden seat, with Dolly on his right and Phil on his left; and settles himself in it with the air of a man about to begin a long communication. The Clandons watch him expectantly.

M'COMAS. Ahem! Your father—

DOLLY. How old is he?

PHILIP. Sh!

MRS CLANDON [*softly*] Dear Dolly: dont let us interrupt Mr M'Comas.

M'COMAS [*emphatically*] Thank you, Mrs Clandon. Thank you. [*To Dolly*] Your father is fifty-seven.

DOLLY [*with a bound, startled and excited*] Fifty-seven!! Where does he live?

MRS CLANDON [*remonstrating*] Dolly! Dolly!

M'COMAS [*stopping her*] Let me answer that, Mrs Clandon. The answer will surprise you considerably. He lives in this town.

Mrs Clandon rises, intensely angry, but sits down again, speechless: Gloria watching her perplexedly.

DOLLY [*with conviction*] I knew it. Phil: Chalkstones is our father!

M'COMAS. Chalkstones!

DOLLY. Oh, Crampstones, or whatever it is. He said I was like his mother. I knew he must mean his daughter.

PHILIP [*very seriously*] Mr M'Comas: I desire to consider your feelings in every possible way; but I warn you that if you stretch the long arm of coincidence to the length of telling me that Mr Crampton of this town is my father, I shall decline to entertain the information for a moment.

M'COMAS. And pray why?

PHILIP. Because I have seen the gentleman; and he

[708]

is entirely unfit to be my father, or Dolly's father, or Gloria's father, or my mother's husband.

M'COMAS. Oh, indeed! Well, sir, let me tell you that whether you like it or not, he is your father, and your sisters' father, and Mrs Clandon's husband. Now! What have you to say to that?

DOLLY [*whimpering*] You neednt be so cross. Crampton isnt your father.

PHILIP. Mr M'Comas: your conduct is heartless. Here you find a family enjoying the unspeakable peace and freedom of being orphans. We have never seen the face of a relative: never known a claim except the claim of freely chosen friendship. And now you wish to thrust into the most intimate relationship with us a man whom we dont know—

DOLLY [*vehemently*] An awful old man [*Reproachfully*] And you began as if you had quite a nice father for us!

M'COMAS [*angrily*] How do you know that he is not nice? And what right have you to choose your own father? [*Raising his voice*] Let me tell you, Miss Clandon, that you are too young to—

DOLLY [*interrupting him suddenly and eagerly*] Stop: I forgot! Has he any money?

M'COMAS. He has a great deal of money.

DOLLY [*delighted*] Oh, what did I always say, Phil?

PHILIP. Dolly: we have perhaps been condemning the old man too hastily. Proceed, Mr M'Comas.

M'COMAS. I shall not proceed, sir. I am too hurt, too shocked, to proceed.

MRS CLANDON [*struggling with her temper*] Finch: do you realize what is happening? Do you understand that my children have invited that man to lunch, and that he will be here in a few moments?

M'COMAS [*completely upset*] What! Do you mean? am I to understand? is it—

PHILIP [*impressively*] Steady, Finch. Think it out slowly and carefully. He's coming: coming to lunch.

GLORIA. Which of us is to tell him the truth? Have you thought of that?

MRS CLANDON. Finch: you must tell him.

DOLLY. Oh, Finch is no good at telling things. Look at the mess he has made of telling us.

M'COMAS. I have not been allowed to speak. I protest against this.

DOLLY [*taking his arm coaxingly*] Dear Finch: dont be cross.

MRS CLANDON. Gloria: let us go in. He may arrive at any moment.

GLORIA [*proudly*] Do not stir, mother. *I* shall not stir. We must not run away.

MRS CLANDON. My dear: we cannot sit down to lunch just as we are. We shall come back again. We must have no bravado. [*Gloria winces, and goes into the hotel without a word*]. Come, Dolly. [*As she goes to the hotel door, the waiter comes out with a tray of plates, etc. for two additional covers*].

WAITER. Gentlemen come yet, maam?

MRS CLANDON. Two more to come still, thank you. They will be here immediately. [*She goes into the hotel*].

The waiter takes his tray to the service table.

PHILIP. I have an idea. Mr M'Comas: this communication should be made, should it not, by a man of infinite tact?

M'COMAS. It will require tact, certainly.

PHILIP. Good! Dolly: whose tact were you noticing only this morning?

DOLLY [*seizing the idea with rapture*] Oh yes, I declare!

PHILIP. The very man! [*Calling*] William!

WAITER. Coming, sir.

M'COMAS [*horrified*] The waiter! Stop! stop! I will not permit this. I—

WAITER [*presenting himself between Phil and M'Comas*] Yes, sir.

M'Comas's complexion fades into stone grey: all movement and expression desert his eyes. He sits down stupefied.

PHILIP. William: you remember my request to you to regard me as your son?

WAITER [*with respectful indulgence*] Yes, sir. Anything you please, sir.

PHILIP. William: at the very outset of your career as my father, a rival has appeared on the scene.

WAITER. Your real father, sir? Well, that was to be expected, sooner or later, sir, wasnt it? [*Turning with a happy smile to M'Comas*] Is it you, sir?

M'COMAS [*renerved by indignation*] Certainly not. My children know how to behave themselves.

PHILIP. No, William: this gentleman was very nearly my father: he wooed my mother, but wooed her in vain.

M'COMAS [*outraged*] Well, of all the—

PHILIP. Sh! Consequently, he is only our solicitor. Do you know one Crampton, of this town?

WAITER. Cock-eyed Crampton, sir, of the Crooked Billet, is it?

PHILIP. I dont know. Finch: does he keep a public house?

M'COMAS [*rising, scandalized*] No, no, no. Your father, sir, is a well known yacht builder, an eminent man here.

WAITER [*impressed*] Oh! Beg pardon, sir, I'm sure. A son of Mr Crampton's! Dear me!

PHILIP. Mr Crampton is coming to lunch with us.

WAITER [*puzzled*] Yes, sir. [*Diplomatically*] Dont usually lunch with his family, perhaps, sir?

PHILIP [*impressively*] William: he does not know that we are his family. He has not seen us for eighteen years. He wont know us. [*To emphasize the communication, Phil seats himself on the iron table with a spring, and looks at the waiter with his lips compressed and his legs swinging*].

DOLLY. We want you to break the news to him, William.

WAITER. But I should think he'd guess when he sees your mother, miss.

Phil's legs become motionless. He contemplates the waiter raptly

DOLLY [*dazzled*] I never thought of that.

PHILIP. Nor I. [*Coming off the table and turning reproachfully on M'Comas*] Nor you!

DOLLY. And you a solicitor!

PHILIP. Finch: your professional incompetence is appalling. William: your sagacity puts us all to shame.

DOLLY. You really are like Shakespear, William.

WAITER. Not at all, sir. Dont mention it, miss. Most happy, I'm sure, sir. [*He goes back modestly to the luncheon table and lays the two additional covers, one at the end next the steps, and the other so as to make a third on the side furthest from the balustrade*].

PHILIP [*abruptly seizing M'Comas's arm and leading him towards the hotel*] Finch: come and wash your hands.

M'COMAS. I am thoroughly vexed and hurt, Mr Clandon—

PHILIP [*interrupting him*] You will get used to us. Come, Dolly. [*M'Comas shakes him off and marches into the hotel. Phil follows with unruffled composure*].

DOLLY [*turning for a moment on the steps as she follows them*] Keep your wits about you, William. There will be fireworks.

WAITER. Right, miss. You may depend on me, miss. [*She goes into the hotel*].

Valentine comes lightly up the steps from the beach, followed doggedly by Crampton. Valentine carries a walking stick. Crampton, either because he is old and chilly, or with some idea of extenuating the unfashionableness of his reefer jacket, wears a light overcoat. He stops at the chair left by M'Comas in the middle of the terrace, and steadies himself for a moment by placing his hand on the back of it.

CRAMPTON. Those steps make me giddy. [*He passes his hand over his forehead*]. I have not got over that infernal gas yet.

He goes to the iron chair, so that he can lean his elbows on the little table to prop his head as he sits. He soon recovers, and begins to unbutton his overcoat. Meanwhile Valentine interviews the waiter.

VALENTINE. Waiter!

WAITER [*coming forward between them*] Yes, sir.

VALENTINE. Mrs Lanfrey Clandon.

WAITER [*with a sweet smile of welcome*] Yes, sir. We're expecting you, sir. That is your table, sir. Mrs Clandon will be down presently, sir. The young lady and gentleman were just talking about your friend, sir.

VALENTINE. Indeed!

WAITER [*smoothly melodious*] Yes, sir. Great flow of spirits, sir. A vein of pleasantry, as you might say, sir. [*Quickly, to Crampton, who has risen to get the overcoat off*] Beg pardon, sir; but if youll allow me [*helping him to get the overcoat off, and taking it from him*]. Thank you, sir. [*Crampton sits down again; and the waiter resumes the broken melody*]. The young gentleman's latest is that youre his father, sir.

CRAMPTON. What!

WAITER. Only his joke, sir, his favorite joke. Yesterday, *I* was to be his father. Today, as soon as he knew you were coming, sir, he tried to put it up on me that you were his father: his long lost father! Not seen you for eighteen years, he said.

CRAMPTON [*startled*] Eighteen years!

WAITER. Yes, sir. [*With gentle archness*] But I was up to his tricks, sir. I saw the idea coming into his head as he stood there, thinking what new joke he'd have with me. Yes, sir: thats the sort he is: very pleasant, ve—ry offhand and affable indeed, sir. [*Again changing his tempo to say to Valentine, who is putting his stick down against the corner of the garden seat*] If youll allow me, sir? [*He takes Valentine's stick*]. Thank you, sir. [*Valentine strolls up to the luncheon table and looks at the menu. The waiter turns to Crampton and continues his lay*]. Even the solicitor took up the joke, although he was in a manner of speaking in my confidence about the young gentleman, sir. Yes, sir, I assure you, sir. You would never imagine what respectable professional gentlemen from London will do on an outing, when the sea air takes them, sir.

CRAMPTON. Oh, theres a solicitor with them, is there?

WAITER. The family solicitor, sir: yes, sir. Name of M'Comas, sir. [*He goes towards the hotel entrance with the coat and stick, happily unconscious of the bomblike effect the name has produced on Crampton*].

CRAMPTON [*rising in angry alarm*] M'Comas! [*Calling to Valentine*] Valentine! [*Again, fiercely*] Valentine!!

[714]

[*Valentine turns*]. This is a plant, a conspiracy. This is my family! my children! my infernal wife.

VALENTINE [*coolly*] Oh indeed! Interesting meeting! [*He resumes his study of the menu*].

CRAMPTON. Meeting! Not for me. Let me out of this. [*Calling across to the waiter*] Give me that coat.

WAITER. Yes, sir. [*He comes back; puts Valentine's stick carefully down against the luncheon table; and delicately shakes the coat out and holds it for Crampton to put on*]. I seem to have done the young gentleman an injustice, sir, havnt I, sir?

CRAMPTON. Rrrh! [*He stops on the point of putting his arms into the sleeves, and turns on Valentine with sudden suspicion*]. Valentine: you are in this. You made this plot. You—

VALENTINE [*decisively*] Bosh! [*He throws the menu down and goes round the table to look out unconcernedly over the parapet*].

CRAMPTON [*angrily*] What d'ye—

M'Comas, followed by Phil and Dolly, comes out, but recoils on seeing Crampton.

WAITER [*softly interrupting Crampton*] Steady, sir. Here they come, sir. [*He takes up Valentine's stick and makes for the hotel, throwing the coat across his arm.*]

M'Comas turns the corners of his mouth resolutely down and crosses to Crampton, who draws back and glares, with his hands behind him. M'Comas, with his brow opener than ever, confronts him in the majesty of a spotless conscience.

WAITER [*aside, as he passes Phil on his way out*] Ive broke it to him, sir.

PHILIP. Invaluable William! [*He passes on to the table*].

DOLLY [*aside to the waiter*] How did he take it?

WAITER [*aside to her*] Startled at first, miss: but

[715]

resigned: very resigned indeed, miss. [*He takes the stick and coat into the hotel*].

M'COMAS [*having stared Crampton out of countenance*] So here you are, Mr Crampton.

CRAMPTON. Yes, here: caught in a trap: a mean trap. Are those my children?

PHILIP [*with deadly politeness*] Is this our father, Mr M'Comas?

M'COMAS [*stoutly*] He is.

DOLLY [*conventionally*] Pleased to meet you again. [*She wanders idly round the table, exchanging a grimace with Valentine on the way*].

PHILIP. Allow me to discharge my first duty as host by ordering your wine. [*He takes the wine list from the table. His polite attention, and Dolly's unconcerned indifference, leave Crampton on the footing of a casual acquaintance picked up that morning at the dentist's. The consciousness of it goes through the father with so keen a pang that he trembles all over; his brow becomes wet; and he stares dumbly at his son, who, just sensible enough of his own callousness to intensely enjoy the humor and adroitness of it, proceeds pleasantly*] Finch: some crusted old port for you, as a respectable family solicitor, eh?

M'COMAS [*firmly*] Apollinaris only. Nothing heating. [*He walks away to the side of the terrace, like a man putting temptation behind him*].

PHILIP. Valentine—?

VALENTINE. Would Lager be considered vulgar?

PHILIP. Probably. We'll order some. [*Turning to Crampton with cheerful politeness*] And now, Mr Crampton, what can we do for you?

CRAMPTON. What d'ye mean, boy?

PHILIP. Boy! [*Very solemnly*] Whose fault is it that I am a boy?

[716]

Crampton snatches the wine list rudely from him and irresolutely pretends to read it. Philip abandons it to him with perfect politeness.

DOLLY [*looking over Crampton's right shoulder*] The whisky's on the last page but one.

CRAMPTON. Let me alone, child.

DOLLY. Child! No, no: you may call me Dolly if you like; but you musnt call me child. [*She slips her arm through Phil's; and the two stand looking at Crampton as if he were some eccentric stranger*].

CRAMPTON [*mopping his brow in rage and agony, and yet relieved even by their playing with him*] M'Comas: we are—ha!—going to have a pleasant meal.

M'COMAS [*resolutely cheerful*] There is no reason why it should not be pleasant.

PHILIP. Finch's face is a feast in itself.

Mrs Clandon and Gloria come from the hotel. Mrs Clandon advances with courageous self-possession and marked dignity of manner. She stops at the foot of the steps to address Valentine, who is in her path. Gloria also stops, looking at Crampton with a certain repulsion.

MRS CLANDON. Glad to see you again, Mr Valentine. [*He smiles. She passes on and confronts Crampton, intending to address him with complete composure; but his aspect shakes her. She stops suddenly and says anxiously, with a touch of remorse*] Fergus: you are greatly changed.

CRAMPTON [*grimly*] I daresay. A man does change in eighteen years.

MRS CLANDON [*troubled*] I—I did not mean that. I hope your health is good.

CRAMPTON. Thank you. No: it's not my health. It's my happiness: thats the change you meant, I think. [*Breaking out suddenly*] Look at her, M'Comas! Look at her; and [*with a half laugh, half sob*] look at me!

[717]

PHILIP. Sh! [*Pointing to the hotel entrance, where the waiter has just appeared*] Order before William!

DOLLY [*touching Crampton's arm warningly*] Ahem!

The waiter goes to the service table and beckons to the kitchen entrance, whence issue a young waiter with soup plates, and a cook, in white apron and cap, with the soup tureen. The young waiter remains and serves: the cook goes out, and reappears from time to time bringing in the courses. He carves, but does not serve. The waiter comes to the end of the luncheon table next the steps.

MRS CLANDON [*as they assemble at the table*] I think you have all met one another already today. Oh no: excuse me. [*Introducing*] Mr Valentine: Mr M'Comas. [*She goes to the end of the table nearest the hotel*]. Fergus: will you take the head of the table, please.

CRAMPTON. Ha! [*Bitterly*] The head of the table!

WAITER [*holding the chair for him with inoffensive encouragement*] This end, sir. [*Crampton submits, and takes his seat*]. Thank you, sir.

MRS CLANDON. Mr Valentine: will you take that side [*indicating the side next the parapet*] with Gloria? [*Valentine and Gloria take their places, Gloria next Crampton and Valentine next Mrs Clandon*]. Finch: I must put you on this side, between Dolly and Phil. You must protect yourself as best you can.

The three take the remaining side of the table, Dolly next her mother, Phil next his father. Soup is served.

WAITER [*to Crampton*] Thick or clear, sir?

CRAMPTON [*to Mrs Clandon*] Does nobody ask a blessing in this household?

PHILIP [*interposing smartly*] Let us first settle what we are about to receive. William!

WAITER. Yes, sir. [*He glides swiftly round the table to Phil's left elbow. On his way he whispers to the younger waiter*] Thick.

PHILIP. Two small Lagers for the children as usual, William; and one large for this gentleman [*indicating Valentine*]. Large Apollinaris for Mr M'Comas.

WAITER. Yes, sir.

DOLLY. Have a six of Irish in it, Finch?

M'COMAS [*scandalized*] No. No, thank you.

PHILIP. Number 413 for my mother and Miss Gloria as before; and—[*turning inquiringly to Crampton*] Eh?

CRAMPTON [*scowling and about to reply offensively*] I—

WAITER [*striking in mellifluously*] All right, sir. We know what Mr Crampton likes here, sir. [*He goes into the hotel*].

PHILIP [*looking gravely at his father*] You frequent bars. Bad habit!

The cook, followed by a waiter with hot plates, brings in the fish from the kitchen to the service table, and begins slicing it.

CRAMPTON. You have learnt your lesson from your mother, I see.

MRS CLANDON. Phil: will you please remember that your jokes are apt to irritate people who are not accustomed to us, and that your father is our guest today.

CRAMPTON [*bitterly*] Yes: a guest at the head of my own table. [*The soup plates are removed*].

DOLLY [*sympathetically*] It's embarrassing, isnt it? It's just as bad for us, you know.

PHILIP. Sh! Dolly: we are both wanting in tact. [*To Crampton*] We mean well, Mr Crampton; but we are not yet strong in the filial line. [*The waiter returns from the hotel with the drinks*]. William: come and restore good feeling.

WAITER [*cheerfully*] Yes, sir. Certainly, sir. Small Lager for you, sir. [*To Crampton*] Seltzer and Irish,

sir. [*To M'Comas*] Appollinaris, sir. [*To Dolly*] Small
Lager, miss. [*To Mrs Clandon, pouring out wine*] 413,
madam. [*To Valentine*] Large Lager for you, sir. [*To
Gloria*] 413, miss.

DOLLY [*drinking*] To the family!

PHILIP [*drinking*] Hearth and Home!

Fish is served.

M'COMAS. We are getting on very nicely after all.

DOLLY [*critically*] After all! After all what, Finch!

CRAMPTON [*sarcastically*] He means that you are
getting on very nicely in spite of the presence of your
father. Do I take your point rightly, Mr M'Comas?

M'COMAS [*disconcerted*] No, no. I only said "after
all" to round off the sentence. I—er—er—er—

WAITER [*tactfully*] Turbot, sir?

M'COMAS [*intensely grateful for the interruption*]
Thank you, waiter: thank you.

WAITER [*sotto voce*] Dont mention it, sir. [*He returns
to the service table*].

CRAMPTON [*to Phil*] Have you thought of choosing
a profession yet?

PHILIP. I am keeping my mind open on that subject.
William!

WAITER. Yes, sir.

PHILIP. How long do you think it would take me to
learn to be a really smart waiter?

WAITER. Cant be learnt, sir. It's in the character, sir.
[*Confidentially to Valentine, who is looking about for
something*] Bread for the lady, sir? yes, sir. [*He serves
bread to Gloria, and resumes, at his former pitch*] Very
few are born to it, sir.

PHILIP. You dont happen to have such a thing as a
son, yourself, have you?

WAITER. Yes, sir: oh yes, sir. [*To Gloria, again drop-*

ping his voice] A little more fish, miss? you wont care for the joint in the middle of the day.

GLORIA. No, thank you.

The fish plates are removed, and the next course served.

DOLLY. Is your son a waiter too, William?

WAITER [*serving Gloria with fowl*] Oh no, miss: he's too impetuous. He's at the Bar.

M'COMAS [*patronizingly*] A potman, eh?

WAITER [*with a touch of melancholy, as if recalling a disappointment softened by time*] No, sir: the other bar. Your profession, sir. A Q.C., sir.

M'COMAS [*embarrassed*] I'm sure I beg your pardon.

WAITER. Not at all, sir. Very natural mistake, I'm sure, sir. Ive often wished he was a potman, sir. Would have been off my hands ever so much sooner, sir. [*Aside to Valentine, who is again in difficulties*] Salt at your elbow, sir. [*Resuming*] Yes, sir: had to support him until he was thirty-seven, sir. But doing well now, sir: very satisfactory indeed, sir: Nothing less than fifty guineas, sir.

M'COMAS. Democracy, Crampton! Modern democracy!

WAITER [*calmly*] No, sir, not democracy: only education, sir. Scholarships, sir. Cambridge Local, sir. Sidney Sussex College, sir. [*Dolly plucks his sleeve and whispers as he bends down*]. Stone ginger, miss? Right, miss. [*To M'Comas*] Very good thing for him, sir: he never had any turn for real work, sir. [*He goes into the hotel, leaving the company somewhat overwhelmed by his son's eminence*].

VALENTINE. Which of us dare give that man an order again!

DOLLY. I hope he wont mind my sending him for ginger-beer.

CRAMPTON [*doggedly*] While he's a waiter it's his business to wait. If you had treated him as a waiter ought to be treated, he'd have held his tongue.

DOLLY. What a loss that would have been! Perhaps he'll give us an introduction to his son and get us into London society.

The waiter reappears with the ginger-beer.

CRAMPTON [*growling contemptuously*] London society! London society! Youre not fit for any society, child.

DOLLY [*losing her temper*] Now look here, Mr Crampton. If you think—

WAITER [*softly, at her elbow*] Stone ginger, miss.

DOLLY [*taken aback, recovers her good humor after a long breath, and says sweetly*] Thank you, dear William. You were just in time [*She drinks*].

M'COMAS. If I may be allowed to change the subject, Miss Clandon, what is the established religion in Madeira?

GLORIA. I suppose the Portuguese religion. I never inquired.

DOLLY. The servants come in Lent and kneel down before you and confess all the things theyve done; and you have to pretend to forgive them. Do they do that in England, William?

WAITER. Not usually, miss. They may in some parts; but it has not come under my notice, miss. [*Catching Mrs Clandon's eye as the young waiter offers her the salad bowl*] You like it without dressing, maam: yes, maam, I have some for you. [*To his young colleague, motioning him to serve Gloria*] This side, Jo. [*He takes a special portion of salad from the service table and puts it beside Mrs Clandon's plate. In doing so he observes that Dolly is making a wry face*]. Only a bit of water-cress, miss, got in by mistake [*he takes her salad away*].

Thank you, miss. [*To the young waiter, admonishing him to serve Dolly afresh*] Jo. [*Resuming*] Mostly members of the Church of England, miss.

DOLLY. Members of the Church of England? Whats the subscription?

CRAMPTON [*rising violently amid general consternation*] You see how my children have been brought up, M'Comas. You see it: you hear it. I call all of you to witness— [*He becomes inarticulate, and is about to strike his fist recklessly on the table when the waiter considerately takes away his plate*].

MRS CLANDON [*firmly*] Sit down, Fergus. There is no occasion at all for this outburst. You must remember that Dolly is just like a foreigner here. Pray sit down.

CRAMPTON [*subsiding unwillingly*] I doubt whether I ought to sit here and countenance all this. I doubt it.

WAITER. Cheese, sir? or would you like a cold sweet?

CRAMPTON [*taken aback*] What? Oh! Cheese, cheese.

DOLLY. Bring a box of cigarets, William.

WAITER. All ready, miss. [*He takes a box of cigarets from the service table and places them before Dolly, who selects one and prepares to smoke. He then returns to his table for the matches*].

CRAMPTON [*staring aghast at Dolly*] Does she smoke?

DOLLY [*out of patience*] Really, Mr Crampton, I'm afraid I'm spoiling your lunch. I'll go and have my cigaret on the beach. [*She leaves the table with petulant suddenness and goes to the steps. The waiter strikes a match and adroitly lights her cigaret*]. Thank you, dear William. [*She vanishes down the steps*].

CRAMPTON [*furiously*] Margaret: call that girl back. Call her back, I say.

M'COMAS [*trying to make peace*] Come, Crampton: never mind. She's her father's daughter: thats all.

MRS CLANDON [*with deep resentment*] I hope not,

Finch. [*She rises: they all rise a little*]. Mr Valentine:
will you excuse me? I am afraid Dolly is hurt and put
out by what has passed. I must go to her.

CRAMPTON. To take her part against me, you mean.

MRS ·CLANDON [*ignoring him*] Gloria: will you take
my place whilst I am away, dear. [*She crosses to the
steps and goes down to the beach*].

*Crampton's expression is one of bitter hatred. The
rest watch her in embarrassed silence, feeling the incident
to be a very painful one. The waiter discreetly shepherds
his assistant along with him into the hotel by the kitchen
entrance, leaving the luncheon party to themselves.*

CRAMPTON [*throwing himself back in his chair*] Theres
a mother for you, M'Comas! Theres a mother for you!

GLORIA [*steadfastly*] Yes: a good mother.

CRAMPTON. And a bad father? Thats what you mean,
eh?

VALENTINE [*rising indignantly and addressing Gloria*]
Miss Clandon: I—

CRAMPTON [*turning on him*] That girl's name is
Crampton, Mr Valentine, not Clandon. Do you wish
to join them in insulting me?

VALENTINE [*ignoring him*] I'm overwhelmed, Miss
Clandon. It's all my fault: I brought him here: I'm
responsible for him. And I'm ashamed of him.

CRAMPTON. What d'y' mean?

GLORIA [*rising coldly*] No harm has been done, Mr
Valentine. We have all been a little childish, I am
afraid. Our party has been a failure: let us break it up
and have done with it. [*She puts her chair aside and
turns to the steps, adding, with slighting composure, as
she passes Crampton*] Goodbye, father.

*She descends the steps with cold disgusted indifference.
They all look after her, and so do not notice the return
of the waiter from the hotel, laden with Crampton's*

coat, Valentine's stick, a couple of shawls and parasols, and some camp stools, which he deposits on the bench.

CRAMPTON [*to himself, staring after Gloria with a ghastly expression*] Father! Father!! [*He strikes his fist violently on the table*]. Now—

WAITER [*offering the coat*] This is yours, sir, I think, sir. [*Crampton glares at him, then snatches it rudely and comes down the terrace towards the garden seat, struggling with the coat in his angry efforts to put it on. M'Comas rises and goes to his assistance: then takes his hat and umbrella from the little iron table, and turns towards the steps. Meanwhile the waiter, after thanking Crampton with unruffled sweetness for taking the coat, picks up the other articles and offers the parasols to Phil*]. The ladies' sunshades, sir. Nasty glare off the sea today, sir: very trying to the complexion, sir. I shall carry down the camp stools myself, sir.

PHILIP. You are old, Father William; but you are the most thoughtful of men. No: keep the sunshades and give me the camp stools [*taking them*].

WAITER [*with flattering gratitude*] Thank you, sir.

PHILIP. Finch: share with me [*giving him a couple*]. Come along. [*They go down the steps together*].

VALENTINE [*to the waiter*] Leave me something to bring down. One of these [*offering to take a sunshade*].

WAITER [*discreetly*] Thats the younger lady's, sir. [*Valentine lets it go*]. Thank you, sir. If youll allow me, sir, I think you had better take this. [*He puts down his burden on Crampton's chair, and produces from the tail pocket of his dress coat a book with a lady's handkerchief between the leaves to mark the page*]. The elder young lady is reading it at present. [*Valentine takes it eagerly*]. Thank you, sir. The Subjection of Women, sir, you see. [*He takes up the burden again*]. Heavier reading than you and I would care for at the seaside, sir. [*He goes down the steps*].

VALENTINE [*coming rather excitedly to Crampton*] Now look here, Crampton: are you at all ashamed of yourself?

CRAMPTON [*pugnaciously*] Ashamed of myself! What for?

VALENTINE. For behaving like a bear. What will your daughter think of me for having brought you here?

CRAMPTON. I was not thinking of what my daughter was thinking of you.

VALENTINE. No, you were thinking of yourself. Youre a perfect egomaniac.

CRAMPTON [*heartrent*] She told you what I am: a father: a father robbed of his children. What are the hearts of this generation like? Am I to come here after all these years? to see what my children are for the first time! to hear their voices! and carry it all off like a fashionable visitor; drop in to lunch; be Mr Crampton? Mister Crampton! What right have they to talk to me like that? I'm their father: do they deny that? I'm a man, with the feelings of our common humanity: have I no rights, no claims? In all these years who have I had round me? Servants, clerks, business acquaintances. Ive had respect from them: aye, kindness. Would one of them have spoken to me as that girl spoke? Would one of them have laughed at me as that boy was laughing at me all the time? [*Frantically*] My own children! Mister Crampton! My—

VALENTINE. Come, come! theyre only children. She called you father.

CRAMPTON. Yes: "goodbye, father." Goodbye! Oh yes: she got at my feelings: with a stab!

VALENTINE [*taking this in very bad part*] Now look

here, Crampton: you just let her alone: she's treated you very well. I had a much worse time of it at lunch than you.

CRAMPTON. You!

VALENTINE [*with growing impetuosity*] Yes: I. I sat next her; and I never said a single thing to her the whole time: couldnt think of a blessed word. And not a word did she say to me.

CRAMPTON. Well?

VALENTINE. Well? Well??? [*Tackling him very seriously, and talking faster and faster*] Crampton: do you know whats been the matter with me today? You dont suppose, do you, that I'm in the habit of playing such tricks on my patients as I played on you?

CRAMPTON. I hope not.

VALENTINE. The explanation is that I'm stark mad, or rather that Ive never been in my real senses before. I'm capable of anything: Ive grown up at last: I'm a Man; and it's your daughter thats made a man of me.

CRAMPTON [*incredulously*] Are you in love with my daughter?

VALENTINE [*his words now coming in a perfect torrent*] Love! Nonsense: it's something far above and beyond that. It's life, it's faith, it's strength, certainty, paradise—

CRAMPTON [*interrupting him with acrid contempt*] Rubbish, man! What have you to keep a wife on? You cant marry her.

VALENTINE. Who wants to marry her? I'll kiss her hands; I'll kneel at her feet; I'll live for her; I'll die for her; and thatll be enough for me. Look at her book! See! [*He kisses the handkerchief*]. If you offered me all your money for this excuse for going down to the beach and speaking to her again, I'd only laugh at you. [*He rushes buoyantly off to the steps, where he bounces right into the arms of the waiter, who is coming up from the beach. The two save themselves from falling by clutching one another tightly round the waist and whirling one another round*].

WAITER [*delicately*] Steady, sir, steady!

VALENTINE [*shocked at his own violence*] I beg your pardon.

WAITER. Not at all, sir, not at all. Very natural, sir, I'm sure, sir, at your age. The lady has sent me for her book, sir. Might I take the liberty of asking you to let her have it at once, sir.

VALENTINE. With pleasure. And if you will allow me to present you with a professional man's earnings for six weeks—[*offering him Dolly's crown piece*]?

WAITER [*as if the sum were beyond his utmost expectations*] Thank you, sir: much obliged. [*Valentine dashes down the steps*]. Very high-spirited young gentleman, sir: very manly and straight set up.

CRAMPTON [*in grumbling disparagement*] And making his fortune in a hurry, no doubt. *I* know what his six weeks' earnings come to. [*He crosses the terrace to the iron table, and sits down*].

WAITER [*philosophically*] Well, sir, you never can tell. Thats a principle in life with me, sir, if youll excuse my having such a thing, sir. [*Delicately sinking the philosopher in the waiter for a moment*] Perhaps you havnt noticed that you hadnt touched that seltzer and Irish, sir, when the party broke up. [*He takes the tumbler from the luncheon table and sets it before Crampton*]. Yes, sir, you never can tell. There was my son, sir! who ever thought that he would rise to wear a silk gown, sir? And yet, today, sir, nothing less than fifty guineas. What a lesson, sir!

CRAMPTON. Well, I hope he is grateful to you, and recognizes what he owes you, as a son should.

WAITER. We get on together very well, very well indeed, sir, considering the difference in our stations. [*Crampton is about to take a drink*]. A small lump of sugar, sir, will take the flatness out of the seltzer without noticeably sweetening the drink, sir. Allow me, sir. [*He drops a lump of sugar into the tumbler*]. But as I say to him, wheres the difference after all? If I must put on a dress coat to shew what I am, sir, he must put on a wig and gown to shew what he is. If my income is mostly tips, and theres a pretence that I dont get them, why, his income is mostly fees, sir; and I understand theres a pretence that he dont get them! If he likes society, and his profession brings him into contact with all ranks, so does mine too, sir. If it's a little against a barrister to have a waiter for his father, sir, it's a little against a waiter to have a barrister for a son: many people consider it a great liberty, sir, I assure you, sir. Can I get you anything else, sir?

CRAMPTON. No, thank you. [*With bitter humility*] I suppose theres no objection to my sitting here for a while: I cant disturb the party on the beach here.

WAITER [*with emotion*] Very kind of you, sir, to put it as if it was not a compliment and an honor to us, Mr Crampton, very kind indeed. The more you are at home here, sir, the better for us.

CRAMPTON [*in poignant irony*] Home!

WAITER [*reflectively*] Well, yes, sir: thats a way of looking at it too, sir. I have always said that the great advantage of a hotel is that it's a refuge from home life, sir.

CRAMPTON. I missed that advantage today, I think.

WAITER. You did, sir: you did. Dear me! It's the unexpected that always happens, isnt it? [*Shaking his head*] You never can tell, sir: you never can tell. [*He goes into the hotel*].

CRAMPTON [*his eyes shining hardly as he props his drawn miserable face on his hands*] Home! Home!! [*Hearing someone approaching he hastily sits bolt upright. It is Gloria, who has come up the steps alone, with her sunshade and her book in her hands. He looks defiantly at her, with the brutal obstinacy of his mouth and the wistfulness of his eyes contradicting each other pathetically. She comes to the corner of the garden seat and stands with her back to it, leaning against the end of it, and looking down at him as if wondering at his weakness: too curious about him to be cold, but supremely indifferent to their kinship. He greets her with a growl*]. Well?

GLORIA. I want to speak to you for a moment.

CRAMPTON [*looking steadily at her*] Indeed? Thats surprising. You meet your father after eighteen years; and you actually want to speak to him for a moment! Thats touching: isnt it?

GLORIA. All that is what seems to me so nonsensical, so uncalled for. What do you expect us to feel for you? to do for you? What is it you want? Why are you less civil to us than other people are? You are evidently not very fond of us: why should you be? But surely we can meet without quarrelling.

CRAMPTON [*a dreadful grey shade passing over his face*] Do you realize that I am your father?

GLORIA. Perfectly.

CRAMPTON. Do you know what is due to me as your father?

GLORIA. For instance—?

CRAMPTON [*rising as if to combat a monster*] For instance! For instance!! For instance, duty, affection, respect, obedience—

GLORIA [*quitting her careless leaning attitude and confronting him promptly and proudly*] I obey nothing but my sense of what is right. I respect nothing that is not noble. That is my duty. [*She adds, less firmly*] As to affection, it is not within my control. I am not sure that I quite know what affection means. [*She turns away with an evident distaste for that part of the subject, and goes to the luncheon table for a comfortable chair, putting down her book and sunshade*].

CRAMPTON [*following her with his eyes*] Do you really mean what you are saying?

GLORIA [*turning on him quickly and severely*] Excuse me: that is an uncivil question. I am speaking seriously to you; and I expect you to take me seriously. [*She takes one of the luncheon chairs; turns it away from the table; and sits down a little wearily, saying*] Can you not discuss this matter coolly and rationally?

CRAMPTON. Coolly and rationally! No I cant. Do you understand that? I cant.

GLORIA [*emphatically*] No. That I cannot understand. I have no sympathy with—

CRAMPTON [*shrinking nervously*] Stop! Dont say anything more yet: you dont know what youre doing. Do you want to drive me mad? [*She frowns, finding such petulance intolerable. He adds hastily*] No: I'm not angry: indeed I'm not. Wait, wait: give me a little time to think. [*He stands for a moment, screwing and clinching his brows and hands in his perplexity; then takes the end chair from the luncheon table and sits down beside her, saying, with a touching effort to be gentle and patient*] Now I think I have it. At least I'll try.

GLORIA [*firmly*] You see! Everything comes right if we only think it resolutely out.

CRAMPTON [*in sudden dread*] No: dont think. I want you to feel: thats the only thing that can help us. Listen! Do you—but first—I forgot. Whats your name? I mean your pet name. They cant very well call you Sophronia.

GLORIA [*with astonished disgust*] Sophronia! My name is Gloria. I am always called by it.

CRAMPTON [*his temper rising again*] Your name is Sophronia, girl: you were called after your aunt Sophronia, my sister: she gave you your first Bible with your name written in it.

GLORIA. Then my mother gave me a new name.

CRAMPTON [*angrily*] She had no right to do it. I will not allow this.

GLORIA. You had no right to give me your sister's name. I dont know her.

CRAMPTON. Youre talking nonsense. There are bounds to what I will put up with. I will not have it. Do you hear that?

GLORIA [*rising warningly*] Are you resolved to quarrel?

CRAMPTON [*terrified, pleading*] No, no: sit down. Sit down, wont you? [*She looks at him, keeping him in suspense. He forces himself to utter the obnoxious name*]. Gloria. [*She marks her satisfaction with a slight tightening of the lips, and sits down*]. There! You see I only want to shew you that I am your father, my—my dear child. [*The endearment is so plaintively inept that she smiles in spite of herself, and resigns herself to indulge him a little*]. Listen now. What I want to ask you is this. Dont you remember me at all? You were only a tiny child when you were taken away from me; but you took plenty of notice of things. Cant you remember someone whom you loved, or [*shyly*] at least liked in a childish way? Come! someone who let you stay in his study and look at his toy boats, as you thought them? [*He looks anxiously into her face for some response, and continues less hopefully and more urgently*] Someone who let you do as you liked there, and never said a word to you except to tell you that you must sit still and not speak? Someone who was something that no one else was to you—who was your father?

GLORIA [*unmoved*] If you describe things to me, no doubt I shall presently imagine that I remember them. But I really remember nothing.

CRAMPTON [*wistfully*] Has your mother never told you anything about me?

GLORIA. She has never mentioned your name to me. [*He groans involuntarily. She looks at him rather contemptuously, and continues*] Except once; and then she did remind me of something I had forgotten.

CRAMPTON [*looking up hopefully*] What was that?

GLORIA [*mercilessly*] The whip you bought to beat me with.

CRAMPTON [*gnashing his teeth*] Oh! To bring that up against me! To turn you from me! When you need never have known. [*Under a grinding, agonized breath*] Curse her!

GLORIA [*springing up*] You wretch! [*With intense emphasis*] You wretch! You dare curse my mother!

CRAMPTON. Stop; or youll be sorry afterwards. I'm your father.

GLORIA. How I hate the name! How I love the name of Mother! You had better go.

CRAMPTON. I—I'm choking. You want to kill me. Some—I— [*His voice stifles: he is almost in a fit*].

GLORIA [*going up to the balustrade with cool quick resourcefulness, and calling over it to the beach*] Mr Valentine!

VALENTINE [*answering from below*] Yes.

GLORIA. Come here for a moment, please. Mr

Crampton wants you. [*She returns to the table and pours out a glass of water*].

CRAMPTON [*recovering his speech*] No: let me alone. I dont want him. I'm all right, I tell you. I need neither his help nor yours. [*He rises and pulls himself together*]. As you say, I had better go. [*He puts on his hat*]. Is that your last word?

GLORIA. I hope so.

He looks stubbornly at her for a moment; nods grimly, as if he agreed to that; and goes into the hotel. She looks at him with equal steadiness until he disappears, when, with a gesture of relief, she turns to Valentine, who comes running up the steps.

VALENTINE [*panting*] Whats the matter? [*Looking round*] Wheres Crampton?

GLORIA. Gone. [*Valentine's face lights up with sudden joy, dread, and mischief as he realizes that he is alone with Gloria. She continues indifferently*] I thought he was ill; but he recovered himself. He wouldnt wait for you. I am sorry. [*She goes for her book and parasol*].

VALENTINE. So much the better. He gets on my nerves after a while. [*Pretending to forget himself*] How could that man have so beautiful a daughter!

GLORIA [*taken aback for a moment; then answering him with polite but intentional contempt*] That seems to be an attempt at what is called a pretty speech. Let me say at once, Mr Valentine, that pretty speeches make very sickly conversation. Pray let us be friends, if we are to be friends, in a sensible and wholesome way. I have no intention of getting married; and unless you are content to accept that state of things, we had much better not cultivate each other's acquaintance.

VALENTINE [*cautiously*] I see. May I ask just this one question? Is your objection an objection to marriage as an institution, or merely an objection to marrying me personally?

GLORIA. I do not know you well enough, Mr Valentine, to have any opinion on the subject of your personal merits. [*She turns away from him with infinite indifference, and sits down with her book on the garden seat*]. I do not think the conditions of marriage at present are such as any self-respecting woman can accept.

VALENTINE [*instantly changing his tone for one of cordial sincerity, as if he frankly accepted her terms and was delighted and reassured by her principles*] Oh, then thats a point of sympathy between us already. I quite agree with you: the conditions are most unfair. [*He takes off his hat and throws it gaily on the iron table*]. No: what I want is to get rid of all that nonsense. [*He sits down beside her, so naturally that she does not think of objecting, and proceeds, with enthusiasm*] Dont you think it a horrible thing that a man and a woman can hardly know one another without being supposed to have designs of that kind? As if there were no other interests! no other subjects of conversation! As if women were capable of nothing better!

GLORIA [*interested*] Ah, now you are beginning to talk humanly and sensibly, Mr Valentine.

VALENTINE [*with a gleam in his eye at the success of his hunter's guile*] Of course! two intelligent people like us! Isnt it pleasant, in this stupid convention-ridden world, to meet with someone on the same plane? someone with an unprejudiced enlightened mind?

GLORIA [*earnestly*] I hope to meet many such people in England.

VALENTINE [*dubiously*] Hm! there are a good many people here: nearly forty millions. Theyre not all consumptive members of the highly educated classes like the people in Madeira.

GLORIA [*now full of her subject*] Oh, everybody is stupid and prejudiced in Madeira: weak sentimental creatures. I hate weakness; and I hate sentiment.

VALENTINE. Thats what makes you so inspiring.

GLORIA [*with a slight laugh*] Am I inspiring?

VALENTINE. Yes. Strength's infectious.

GLORIA. Weakness is, I know.

VALENTINE [*with conviction*] Youre strong. Do you know that you changed the world for me this morning? I was in the dumps, thinking of my unpaid rent, frightened about the future. When you came in, I was dazzled. [*Her brow clouds a little. He goes on quickly*] That was silly, of course; but really and truly something happened to me. Explain it how you will, my blood got—[*he hesitates, trying to think of a sufficiently unimpassioned word*]—oxygenated: my muscles braced; my mind cleared; my courage rose. Thats odd, isnt it? considering that I am not at all a sentimental man.

GLORIA [*uneasily, rising*] Let us go back to the beach.

VALENTINE [*darkly: looking up at her*] What! you feel it too?

GLORIA. Feel what?

VALENTINE. Dread.

GLORIA. Dread!

VALENTINE. As if something were going to happen. It came over me suddenly just before you proposed that we should run away to the others.

GLORIA [*amazed*] Thats strange: very strange! I had the same presentiment.

VALENTINE [*solemnly*] How extraordinary! [*Rising*] Well: shall we run away?

GLORIA. Run away! Oh no: that would be childish.

[*She sits down again. He resumes his seat beside her, and watches her with a gravely sympathetic air. She is thoughtful and a little troubled as she adds*] I wonder what is the scientific explanation of those fancies that cross us occasionally!

VALENTINE. Ah, I wonder! It's a curiously helpless sensation: isnt it?

GLORIA [*rebelling against the word*] Helpless?

VALENTINE. Yes, helpless. As if Nature, after letting us belong to ourselves and do what we judged right and reasonable for all these years, were suddenly lifting her great hand to take us—her two little children —by the scruffs of our little necks, and use us, in spite of ourselves, for her own purposes, in her own way.

GLORIA. Isnt that rather fanciful?

VALENTINE [*with a new and startling transition to a tone of utter recklessness*] I dont know. I dont care. [*Bursting out reproachfully*] Oh, Miss Clandon, Miss Clandon: how could you?

GLORIA. What have I done?

VALENTINE. Thrown this enchantment on me. I'm honestly trying to be sensible and scientific and everything that you wish me to be. But—but—oh, dont you see what you have set to work in my imagination?

GLORIA. I hope you are not going to be so foolish— so vulgar—as to say love.

VALENTINE. No, no, no, no, no. Not love: we know better than that. Let's call it chemistry. You cant deny that there is such a thing as chemical action, chemical affinity, chemical combination: the most irresistible of all natural forces. Well, youre attracting me irresistibly. Chemically.

GLORIA [*contemptuously*] Nonsense!

VALENTINE. Of course it's nonsense, you stupid girl. [*Gloria recoils in outraged surprise*]. Yes, stupid girl:

thats a scientific fact, anyhow. Youre a prig: a feminine prig: thats what you are. [*Rising*] Now I suppose youve done with me for ever. [*He goes to the iron table and takes up his hat*].

GLORIA [*with elaborate calm, sitting up like a High-school-mistress posing to be photographed*]. That shews how very little you understand my real character. I am not in the least offended. [*He pauses and puts his hat down again*]. I am always willing to be told my own defects, Mr Valentine, by my friends, even when they are as absurdly mistaken about me as you are. I have many faults—very serious faults—of character and temper; but if there is one thing that I am not, it is what you call a prig. [*She closes her lips trimly and looks steadily and challengingly at him as she sits more collectedly than ever*].

VALENTINE [*returning to the end of the garden seat to confront her more emphatically*] Oh yes, you are. My reason tells me so: my knowledge tells me so: my experience tells me so.

GLORIA. Excuse my reminding you that your reason and your knowledge and your experience are not infallible. At least I hope not.

VALENTINE. I must believe them. Unless you wish me to believe my eyes, my heart, my instincts, my imagination, which are all telling me the most monstrous lies about you.

GLORIA [*the collectedness beginning to relax*] Lies!

VALENTINE [*obstinately*] Yes, lies. [*He sits down again beside her*] Do you expect me to believe that you are the most beautiful woman in the world?

GLORIA. That is ridiculous, and rather personal.

VALENTINE. Of course it's ridiculous. Well, thats what my eyes tell me. [*Gloria makes a movement of contemptuous protest*]. No: I'm not flattering. I tell you

I dont believe it. [*She is ashamed to find that this does not quite please her either*]. Do you think that if you were to turn away in disgust from my weakness, I should sit down here and cry like a child?

GLORIA [*beginning to find that she must speak shortly and pointedly to keep her voice steady*] Why should you, pray?

VALENTINE. Of course not: I'm not such an idiot. And yet my heart tells me I should: my fool of a heart. But I'll argue with my heart and bring it to reason. If I loved you a thousand times, I'll force myself to look the truth steadily in the face. After all, it's easy to be sensible: the facts are the facts. Whats this place? it's not heaven: it's the Marine Hotel. Whats the time? it's not eternity: it's about half past one in the afternoon. What am I? a dentist: a five shilling dentist!

GLORIA. And I am a feminine prig.

VALENTINE [*passionately*] No, no: I cant face that: I must have one illusion left: the illusion about you. I love you. [*He turns towards her as if the impulse to touch her were ungovernable: she rises and stands on her guard wrathfully. He springs up impatiently and retreats a step*]. Oh, what a fool I am! an idiot! You dont understand: I might as well talk to the stones on the beach. [*He turns away, discouraged*].

GLORIA [*reassured by his withdrawal, and a little remorseful*] I am sorry. I do not mean to be unsympathetic, Mr Valentine; but what can I say?

VALENTINE [*returning to her with all his recklessness of manner replaced by an engaging and chivalrous respect*] You can say nothing, Miss Clandon. I beg your pardon: it was my own fault, or rather my own bad luck. You see, it all depended on your naturally liking me. [*She is about to speak: he stops her depre-*

catingly] Oh, I know you musnt tell me whether you like me or not; but—

GLORIA [*her principles up in arms at once*] Must not! Why not? I am a free woman: why should I not tell you?

VALENTINE [*pleading in terror, and retreating*] Dont. I'm afraid to hear.

GLORIA [*no longer scornful*] You need not be afraid. I think you are sentimental, and a little foolish; but I like you.

VALENTINE [*dropping into the nearest chair as if crushed*] Then it's all over. [*He becomes the picture of despair*].

GLORIA [*puzzled, approaching him*] But why?

VALENTINE. Because liking is not enough. Now that I think down into it seriously, I dont know whether I like you or not.

GLORIA [*looking down at him with wondering concern*] I'm sorry.

VALENTINE [*in an agony of restrained passion*] Oh, dont pity me. Your voice is tearing my heart to pieces. Let me alone, Gloria. You go down into the very depths of me, troubling and stirring me. I cant struggle with it. I cant tell you—

GLORIA [*breaking down suddenly*] Oh, stop telling me what you feel: I cant bear it.

VALENTINE [*springing up triumphantly, the agonized voice now solid, ringing, and jubilant*] Ah, it's come at last: my moment of courage. [*He seizes her hands: she looks at him in terror*]. Our moment of courage! [*He draws her to him; kisses her with impetuous strength; and laughs boyishly*]. Now youve done it, Gloria. It's all over: we're in love with one another. [*She can only gasp at him*]. But what a dragon you were! And how hideously afraid I was!

PHILIP'S VOICE [*calling from the beach*] Valentine!

DOLLY'S VOICE. Mr Valentine!

VALENTINE. Goodbye. Forgive me. [*He rapidly kisses her hands and runs away to the steps, where he meets Mrs Clandon ascending*].

Gloria, quite lost, can only stare after him.

MRS CLANDON. The children want you, Mr Valentine. [*She looks anxiously round*]. Is he gone?

VALENTINE [*puzzled*] He? [*Recollecting*] Oh, Crampton. Gone this long time, Mrs Clandon. [*He runs off buoyantly down the steps*].

GLORIA [*sinking upon the bench*] Mother!

MRS CLANDON [*hurrying to her in alarm*] What is it, dear?

GLORIA [*with heartfelt appealing reproach*] Why didnt you educate me properly?

MRS CLANDON [*amazed*] My child: I did my best.

GLORIA. Oh, you taught me nothing: nothing.

MRS CLANDON. What is the matter with you?

GLORIA [*with the most intense expression*] Only shame! shame!! shame!!! [*Blushing unendurably, she covers her face with her hands and turns away from her mother*].

[ACT III]

The Clandons' sitting room in the hotel. An expensive apartment on the ground floor, with a French window leading to the gardens. In the centre of the room is a substantial table, surrounded by chairs, and draped with a maroon cloth on which opulently bound hotel and railway guides are displayed. A visitor entering through the window and coming down to this central table would have the fireplace on his left, and a writing table against the wall on his right, next the door, which is further down. He would, if his taste lay that way, admire the wall decoration of Lincrusta Walton in plum color and bronze lacquer, with dado and cornice; the ormolu consoles in the corners; the vases on pillar pedestals of veined marble with bases of polished black wood, one on each side of the window; the ornamental cabinet next the vase on the side nearest the fireplace, its centre compartment closed by an inlaid door, and its corners rounded off with curved panes of glass protecting shelves of cheap blue and white pottery; the bamboo tea table, with folding shelves, in the corresponding space on the other side of the window; the photogravures after Burton and Stacy Marks; the saddlebag ottoman in line with the door but on the other side of the room; the two comfortable seats of the same pattern on the hearth-rug; and finally, on turning round and looking up, the massive brass pole above the window, sustaining a pair of maroon rep curtains with decorated borders of staid green. Altogether, a room well arranged to flatter the middle-class occupant's sense of gentility, and reconcile him to a charge of a pound a day for its use.

Mrs Clandon sits at the writing table, correcting proofs. Gloria is standing at the window, looking out in tormented revery.

The clock on the mantelpiece strikes five with a sickly clink, the bell being unable to bear up against the black marble cenotaph in which it is immured.

MRS CLANDON. Five! I dont think we need wait any longer for the children. They are sure to get tea somewhere.

GLORIA [*wearily*] Shall I ring?

MRS CLANDON. Do, my dear. [*Gloria goes to the hearth and rings*]. I have finished these proofs at last, thank goodness!

GLORIA [*strolling listlessly across the room and coming behind her mother's chair*] What proofs?

MRS CLANDON. The new edition of Twentieth Century Women.

GLORIA [*with a bitter smile*] Theres a chapter missing.

MRS CLANDON [*beginning to hunt among her proofs*] Is there? Surely not.

GLORIA. I mean an unwritten one. Perhaps I shall write it for you—when I know the end of it. [*She goes back to the window*].

MRS CLANDON. Gloria! More enigmas!

GLORIA. Oh no. The same enigma.

MRS CLANDON [*puzzled and rather troubled; after watching her for a moment*] My dear?

GLORIA [*returning*] Yes.

MRS CLANDON. You know I never ask questions.

GLORIA [*kneeling beside her chair*] I know, I know. [*She suddenly throws her arm about her mother and embraces her almost passionately*].

[743]

MRS CLANDON [*gently, smiling but embarrassed*] My dear: you are getting quite sentimental.

GLORIA [*recoiling*] Ah no, no. Oh, dont say that. Oh! [*She rises and turns away with a gesture as if tearing herself*].

MRS CLANDON [*mildly*] My dear: what is the matter? What—

The waiter enters with the tea-tray.

WAITER [*balmily*] Was this what you rang for, maam?

MRS CLANDON. Thank you, yes. [*She turns her chair away from the writing table, and sits down again. Gloria crosses to the hearth and sits crouching there with her face averted*].

WAITER [*placing the tray temporarily on the centre table*] I thought so, maam. Curious how the nerves seem to give out in the afternoon without a cup of tea. [*He fetches the tea table and places it in front of Mrs Clandon, conversing meanwhile*]. The young lady and gentleman have just come back, maam: they have been out in a boat, maam. Very pleasant on a fine afternoon like this: very pleasant and invigorating indeed. [*He takes the tray from the centre table and puts it on the tea table*]. Mr M'Comas will not come to tea, maam: he has gone to call upon Mr Crampton. [*He takes a couple of chairs and sets one at each end of the tea table*].

GLORIA [*looking round with an impulse of terror*] And the other gentleman?

WAITER [*reassuringly, as he unconsciously drops for a moment into the measure of "Ive been roaming," which he sang when a boy*] Oh, he's coming, miss: he's coming. He has been rowing the boat, miss, and has just run down the road to the chemist's for something to put on the blisters. But he will be here directly, miss: directly. [*Gloria, in ungovernable apprehension, rises and hurries towards the door*].

MRS CLANDON [*half rising*] Glo—

Gloria goes out. Mrs Clandon looks perplexedly at the waiter, whose composure is unruffled.

WAITER [*cheerfully*] Anything more, maam?

MRS CLANDON. Nothing, thank you.

WAITER. Thank you, maam. [*As he withdraws, Phil and Dolly, in the highest spirits, come tearing in. He holds the door open for them: then goes out and closes it*].

DOLLY [*ravenously*] Oh, give me some tea. [*Mrs Clandon pours out a cup for her*]. Weve been out in a boat. Valentine will be here presently.

PHILIP. He is unaccustomed to navigation. Wheres Gloria?

MRS CLANDON [*anxiously, as she pours out his tea*] Phil: there is something the matter with Gloria. Has anything happened? [*Phil and Dolly look at one another and stifle a laugh*]. What is it?

PHILIP [*sitting down on her left*] Romeo—

DOLLY [*sitting down on her right*]—and Juliet.

PHILIP [*taking his cup of tea from Mrs Clandon*] Yes, my dear mother: the old, old story. Dolly: dont take all the milk [*he deftly takes the jug from her*]. Yes: in the spring—

DOLLY.—a young man's fancy—

PHILIP.—lightly turns to— thank you [*to Mrs Clandon, who has passed the biscuits*] —thoughts of love. It also occurs in the autumn. The young man in this case is—

DOLLY. Valentine.

PHILIP. And his fancy has turned to Gloria to the extent of—

DOLLY. —kissing her—

PHILIP. —on the terrace—

DOLLY [*correcting him*] —on the lips, before everybody.

MRS CLANDON [*incredulously*] Phil! Dolly! Are you joking? [*They shake their heads*]. Did she allow it?

PHILIP. We waited to see him struck to earth by the lightning of her scorn; but—

DOLLY. —but he wasnt.

PHILIP. She appeared to like it.

DOLLY. As far as we could judge. [*Stopping Phil, who is about to pour out another cup*] No: youve sworn off two cups.

MRS CLANDON [*much troubled*] Children: you must not be here when Mr Valentine comes. I must speak very seriously to him about this.

PHILIP. To ask him his intentions? What a violation of Twentieth Century principles!

DOLLY. Quite right, mamma: bring him to book. Make the most of the nineteenth century while it lasts.

PHILIP. Sh! Here he is.

VALENTINE [*entering*] Very sorry to be late, Mrs Clandon. [*She takes up the tea-pot*]. No, thank you: I never take any. No doubt Miss Dolly and Phil have explained what happened to me.

PHILIP [*momentously, rising*] Yes, Valentine: we have explained.

DOLLY [*significantly, also rising*] We have explained very thoroughly.

PHILIP. It was our duty. [*Very seriously*] Come, Dolly. [*He offers Dolly his arm, which she takes. They look sadly at him, and go out gravely arm in arm, leaving Valentine staring*].

MRS CLANDON [*rising and leaving the tea table*] Will you sit down, Mr Valentine. I want to speak to you a little, if you will allow me. [*Valentine goes slowly to the ottoman, his conscience presaging a bad quarter of an hour. Mrs Clandon takes Phil's chair, and seats herself with gentle dignity. Valentine sits down*]. I must begin by throwing myself somewhat on your consideration. I am going to speak of a subject of which I know very little: perhaps nothing. I mean love.

VALENTINE. Love!

MRS CLANDON. Yes, love. Oh, you need not look so alarmed as that, Mr Valentine: I am not in love with you.

VALENTINE [*overwhelmed*] Oh, really, Mrs— [*Recovering himself*] I should be only too proud if you were.

MRS CLANDON. Thank you, Mr Valentine. But I am too old to begin.

VALENTINE. Begin! Have you never—?

MRS CLANDON. Never. My case is a very common one, Mr Valentine. I married before I was old enough to know what I was doing. As you have seen for yourself, the result was a bitter disappointment for both my husband and myself. So you see, though I am a married woman, I have never been in love; I have never had a love affair; and, to be quite frank with you Mr Valentine, what I have seen of the love affairs of other people has not led me to regret that deficiency in my experience. [*Valentine, looking very glum, glances sceptically at her, and says nothing. Her color rises a little; and she adds, with restrained anger*] You do not believe me?

VALENTINE [*confused at having his thought read*] Oh, why not? Why not?

MRS CLANDON. Let me tell you, Mr Valentine, that a life devoted to the Cause of Humanity has enthusiasms and passions to offer which far transcend the selfish personal infatuations and sentimentalities of romance. Those are not your enthusiasms and passions, I take it? [*Valentine, quite aware that she despises him for it, answers in the negative with a melancholy shake of his head*]. I thought not. Well, I am equally at a disadvantage in discussing those so-called affairs of the heart in which you appear to be an expert.

VALENTINE [*restlessly*] What are you driving at, Mrs Clandon?

MRS CLANDON. I think you know.

VALENTINE. Gloria?

MRS CLANDON. Yes. Gloria.

VALENTINE [*surrendering*] Well, yes: I'm in love with Gloria. [*Interposing as she is about to speak*] I know what youre going to say: Ive no money.

MRS CLANDON. I care very little about money, Mr Valentine.

VALENTINE. Then youre very different to all the other mothers who have interviewed me.

MRS CLANDON. Ah, now we are coming to it, Mr Valentine. You are an old hand at this. [*He opens his mouth to protest: she cuts him short with some indignation*]. Oh, do you think, little as I understand these matters, that I have not common sense enough to know that a man who could make as much way in one interview with such a woman as my daughter, can hardly be a novice?

VALENTINE. I assure you——

MRS CLANDON [*stopping him*] I am not blaming you, Mr Valentine. It is Gloria's business to take care of herself, and you have a right to amuse yourself as you please. But—

VALENTINE [*protesting*] Amuse myself! Oh, Mrs Clandon!

MRS CLANDON [*relentlessly*] On your honor, Mr Valentine, are you in earnest?

VALENTINE [*desperately*] On my honor I am in earnest. [*She looks searchingly at him. His sense of humor gets the better of him; and he adds quaintly*] Only, I always have been in earnest; and yet—! Well, here I am, you see.

MRS CLANDON. This is just what I suspected. [*Severely*] Mr Valentine: you are one of those men who play with women's affections.

VALENTINE. Well, why not, if the Cause of Humanity is the only thing worth being serious about? However, I understand. [*Rising and taking his hat with formal politeness*] You wish me to discontinue my visits.

MRS CLANDON. No: I am sensible enough to be well aware that Gloria's best chance of escape from you now is to become better acquainted with you.

VALENTINE [*unaffectedly alarmed*] Oh, dont say that, Mrs Clandon. You dont think that, do you?

MRS CLANDON. I have great faith, Mr Valentine, in the sound training Gloria's mind has had since she was a child.

VALENTINE [*amazingly relieved*] O-oh! Oh, thats all right. [*He sits down again and throws his hat flippantly aside with the air of a man who has no longer anything to fear*].

MRS CLANDON [*indignant at his assurance*] What do you mean?

VALENTINE [*turning confidentially to her*] Come! shall I teach you something, Mrs Clandon?

MRS CLANDON [*stiffly*] I am always willing to learn.

VALENTINE. Have you ever studied the subject of gunnery? artillery? cannons and war-ships and so on?

MRS CLANDON. Has gunnery anything to do with Gloria?

VALENTINE. A great deal. By way of illustration.

During this whole century, my dear Mrs Clandon, the progress of artillery has been a duel between the maker of cannons and the maker of armor plates to keep the cannon balls out. You build a ship proof against the best gun known: somebody makes a better gun and sinks your ship. You build a heavier ship, proof against that gun: somebody makes a heavier gun and sinks you again. And so on. Well, the duel of sex is just like that.

MRS CLANDON. The duel of sex!

VALENTINE. Yes: youve heard of the duel of sex, havnt you? Oh, I forgot: youve been in Madeira: the expression has come up since your time. Need I explain it?

MRS CLANDON [*contemptuously*] No.

VALENTINE. Of course not. Now what happens in the duel of sex? The old fashioned daughter received an old fashioned education to protect her against the wiles of man. Well, you know the result: the old fashioned man got round her. The old fashioned mother resolved to protect her daughter more effectually—to find some armor too strong for the old fashioned man. So she gave her daughter a scientific education: your plan. That was a corker for the old fashioned man: he thought it unfair, and tried to howl it down as unwomanly and all the rest of it. But that didnt do him any good. So he had to give up his old fashioned plan of attack: you know: going down on his knees and swearing to love, honor, and obey and so on.

MRS CLANDON. Excuse me: that was what the woman swore.

VALENTINE. Was it? Ah, perhaps youre right. Yes: of course it was. Well, what did the man do? Just what the artillery man does: went one better than the woman: educated himself scientifically and beat her at that game just as he had beaten her at the old game. I learnt how to circumvent the Women's Rights woman before I was twenty-three: it's all been found out long ago. You see, my methods are thoroughly modern.

MRS CLANDON [*with quiet disgust*] No doubt.

VALENTINE. But for that very reason theres one sort of girl against whom they are of no use.

MRS CLANDON. Pray which sort?

VALENTINE. The thoroughly old fashioned girl. If you had brought up Gloria in the old way, it would have taken me eighteen months to get to the point I got to this afternoon in eighteen minutes. Yes, Mrs Clandon: the Higher Education of Women delivered Gloria into my hands; and it was you who taught her to believe in the Higher Education of Women.

MRS CLANDON [*rising*] Mr Valentine: you are very clever.

VALENTINE [*rising also*] Oh, Mrs Clandon!

MRS CLANDON. And you have taught me—nothing. Goodbye.

VALENTINE [*horrified*] Goodbye! Oh, maynt I see her before I go?

MRS CLANDON. I am afraid she will not return until you have gone, Mr Valentine. She left the room expressly to avoid you.

VALENTINE [*thoughtfully*] Thats a good sign. Goodbye. [*He bows and makes for the door, apparently well satisfied*].

MRS CLANDON [*alarmed*] Why do you think it a good sign?

VALENTINE [*turning near the door*] Because I am mortally afraid of her; and it looks as if she were mortally afraid of me.

He turns to go and finds himself face to face with

Gloria, who has just entered. She looks steadfastly at him. He stares helplessly at her; then round at Mrs Clandon; then at Gloria again, completely at a loss.

GLORIA [*white, and controlling herself with difficulty*] Mother: is what Dolly told me true?

MRS CLANDON. What did she tell you, dear?

GLORIA. That you have been speaking about me to this gentleman?

VALENTINE [*murmuring*] This gentleman! Oh!

MRS CLANDON [*sharply*] Mr Valentine: can you hold your tongue for a moment?

He looks piteously at them; then, with a despairing shrug, goes back to the ottoman and throws his hat on it.

GLORIA [*confronting her mother, with deep reproach*] Mother: what right had you to do it?

MRS CLANDON. I dont think I have said anything I have no right to say, Gloria.

VALENTINE [*confirming her officiously*] Nothing. Nothing whatever. [*The two women look at him crushingly*]. I beg your pardon. [*He sits down ignominiously on the ottoman*].

GLORIA. I cannot believe that anyone has any right even to think about things that concern me only. [*She turns away from them to conceal a painful struggle with her emotion*].

MRS CLANDON. My dear: if I have wounded your pride—

GLORIA [*turning on them for a moment*] My pride! My pride! Oh, it's gone: I have learnt now that I have no strength to be proud of. [*Turning away again*] But if a woman cannot protect herself, no one can protect her. No one has any right to try: not even her mother. I know I have lost your confidence, just as I have lost this man's respect;—[*She stops to regain command of her voice*].

VALENTINE. This man! Oh!

MRS CLANDON. Pray be silent, sir.

GLORIA [*continuing*] —but I have at least the right to be left alone in my disgrace. I am one of those weak creatures born to be mastered by the first man whose eye is caught by them; and I must fulfil my destiny, I suppose. At least spare me the humiliation of trying to save me. [*She sits down, with her handkerchief to her eyes, at the further end of the table*].

VALENTINE [*jumping up*] Look here—

MRS CLANDON [*severely*] Mr Va—

VALENTINE [*recklessly*] No: I will speak: Ive been silent for nearly thirty seconds. [*He goes resolutely to Gloria*]. Miss Clandon—

GLORIA [*bitterly*] Oh, not Miss Clandon: you have found it quite safe to call me Gloria.

VALENTINE. No I wont: youll throw it in my teeth afterwards and accuse me of disrespect. I say it's a heartbreaking falsehood that I dont respect you. It's true that I didnt respect your old pride: why should I? it was nothing but cowardice. I didnt respect your intellect: Ive a better one myself: it's a masculine speciality. But when the depths stirred! when my moment came! when you made me brave! ah, then! then!! then!!!

GLORIA. Then you respected me, I suppose.

VALENTINE. No I didnt: I adored you. [*She rises quickly and turns her back on him*]. And you can never take that moment away from me. So now I dont care what happens. [*He comes back to the ottoman, addressing a cheerful explanation to nobody in particular*] I'm perfectly aware that I'm talking nonsense. I cant help it. [*To Mrs Clandon*] I love Gloria; and theres an end of it.

MRS CLANDON [*emphatically*] Mr Valentine: you

are a most dangerous man. Gloria: come here. [*Gloria wondering a little at the command, obeys, and stands, with drooping head, on her mother's right hand, Valentine being on the opposite side. Mrs Clandon then begins, with intense scorn*] Ask this man whom you have inspired and made brave, how many women have inspired him before [*Gloria looks up suddenly with a flash of jealous anger and amazement*]; how many times he has laid the trap in which he has caught you; how often he has baited it with the same speeches; how much practice it has taken to make him perfect in his chosen part in life as the Duellist of Sex.

VALENTINE. This isnt fair. Youre abusing my confidence, Mrs Clandon.

MRS CLANDON. Ask him, Gloria.

GLORIA [*in a flush of rage, going over to him with her fists clenched*] Is that true?

VALENTINE. Dont be angry—

GLORIA [*interrupting him implacably*] Is it true? Did you ever say that before? Did you ever feel that before? for another woman?

VALENTINE [*bluntly*] Yes.

Gloria raises her clenched hands.

MRS CLANDON [*horrified, catching her uplifted arm*] Gloria!! My dear! Youre forgetting yourself.

Gloria, with a deep expiration, slowly relaxes her threatening attitude.

VALENTINE. Remember: a man's power of love and admiration is like any other of his powers: he has to throw it away many times before he learns what is really worthy of it.

MRS CLANDON. Another of the old speeches, Gloria. Take care.

VALENTINE [*remonstrating*] Oh!

GLORIA [*to Mrs Clandon, with contemptuous self-*

possession] Do you think I need to be warned now? [*To Valentine*] You have tried to make me love you.

VALENTINE. I have.

GLORIA. Well, you have succeeded in making me hate you: passionately.

VALENTINE [*philosophically*] It's surprising how little difference there is between the two. [*Gloria turns indignantly away from him. He continues, to Mrs Clandon*] I know men whose wives love them; and they go on exactly like that.

MRS CLANDON. Excuse me, Mr Valentine; but had you not better go?

GLORIA. You need not send him away on my account, mother. He is nothing to me now; and he will amuse Dolly and Phil. [*She sits down with slighting indifference, at the end of the table nearest the window*].

VALENTINE [*gaily*] Of course: thats the sensible way of looking at it. Come, Mrs Clandon! you cant quarrel with a mere butterfly like me!

MRS CLANDON. I very greatly mistrust you, Mr Valentine. But I do not like to think that your unfortunate levity of disposition is mere shamelessness and worthlessness;—

GLORIA [*to herself, but aloud*] It is shameless; and it is worthless.

MRS CLANDON [*continuing*] so perhaps we had better send for Phil and Dolly, and allow you to end your visit in the ordinary way.

VALENTINE [*as if she had paid him the highest compliment*] You overwhelm me, Mrs Clandon. Thank you.

The waiter returns.

WAITER. Mr M'Comas, maam.

MRS CLANDON. Oh, certainly. Bring him in.

WAITER. He wishes to see you in the reception-room, maam.

MRS CLANDON. Why not here?

WAITER. Well, if you will excuse my mentioning it, maam, I think Mr M'Comas feels that he would get fairer play if he could speak to you away from the younger members of your family, maam.

MRS CLANDON. Tell him they are not here.

WAITER. They are within sight of the door, maam; and very watchful, for some reason or other.

MRS CLANDON [*going*] Oh, very well: I'll go to him.

WAITER [*holding the door open for her*] Thank you, maam. [*She goes out. He comes back into the room, and meets the eye of Valentine who wants him to go*]. All right, sir. Only the tea-things, sir. [*Taking the tray*] Excuse me, sir. Thank you, sir. [*He goes out*].

VALENTINE [*to Gloria*] Look here. Youll forgive me, sooner or later. Forgive me now.

GLORIA [*rising to level the declaration more intensely at him*] Never! While grass grows or water runs, never! never!! never!!!

VALENTINE [*unabashed*] Well, I dont care. I cant be unhappy about anything. I shall never be unhappy again, never, never, never, while grass grows or water runs. The thought of you will always make me wild with joy. [*Some quick taunt is on her lips: he interposes swiftly*] No: I never said that before: thats new.

GLORIA. It will not be new when you say it to the next woman.

VALENTINE. Oh dont, Gloria, dont. [*He kneels at her feet*].

GLORIA. Get up! Get up! How dare you?

Phil and Dolly, racing, as usual, for first place, burst into the room. They check themselves on seeing what is passing. Valentine springs up.

PHILIP [*discreetly*] I beg your pardon. Come, Dolly. [*He offers her his arm and turns to go*].

GLORIA [*annoyed*] Mother will be back in a moment, Phil. [*Severely*] Please wait here for her. [*She turns away to the window, where she stands looking out with her back to them*].

PHILIP [*significantly*] Oh, indeed. Hmhm!

DOLLY. Ahah!

PHILIP. You seem in excellent spirits, Valentine.

VALENTINE. I am. [*He comes between them*]. Now look here. You both know whats going on: dont you?

Gloria turns quickly, as if anticipating some fresh outrage.

DOLLY. Perfectly.

VALENTINE. Well, it's all over. Ive been refused. Scorned. I'm here on sufferance only. You understand? it's all over. Your sister is in no sense entertaining my addresses, or condescending to interest herself in me in any way. [*Gloria, satisfied, turns back contemptuously to the window*]. Is that clear?

DOLLY. Serve you right. You were in too great a hurry.

PHILIP [*patting him on the shoulder*] Never mind: youd never have been able to call your soul your own if she'd married you. You can now begin a new chapter in your life.

DOLLY. Chapter seventeen or thereabouts, I should imagine.

VALENTINE [*much put out by this pleasantry*] No: dont say things like that. Thats just the sort of thoughtless remark that makes a lot of mischief.

DOLLY. Oh, indeed? Hmhm!

PHILIP. Ahah! [*He goes to the hearth and plants himself there in his best head-of-the-family attitude*].

M'Comas, looking very serious, comes in quickly with Mrs Clandon, whose first anxiety is about Gloria. She looks round to see where she is, and is going to join her

*at the window when Gloria comes down to meet her with
a marked air of trust and affection. Finally Mrs
Clandon takes her former seat, and Gloria posts herself
behind it. M'Comas, on his way to the ottoman, is
hailed by Dolly.*

DOLLY. What cheer, Finch?

M'COMAS [*sternly*] Very serious news from your
father, Miss Clandon. Very serious news indeed. [*He
passes impressively to the ottoman, and sits down*].

*Dolly, duly impressed, follows and sits beside him on
his right.*

VALENTINE. Perhaps I had better go.

M'COMAS. By no means, Mr Valentine. You are
deeply concerned in this. [*Valentine takes a chair from
the table and sits astride of it, leaning over the back, near
the ottoman*]. Mrs Clandon: your husband demands
the custody of his two younger children, who are not
of age.

MRS CLANDON [*in quick alarm*] To take Dolly from
me?

DOLLY [*touched*] But how nice of him! He likes us,
mamma.

M'COMAS. I am sorry to have to disabuse you of any
such illusion, Miss Dorothea.

DOLLY [*cooing ecstatically*] Dorothee-ee-ee-a! [*Nest-
ling against his shoulder, quite overcome*]. Oh, Finch!

M'COMAS [*nervously, shrinking away*] No, no, no, no!

MRS CLANDON. The deed of separation gives me the
custody of the children.

M'COMAS. It also contains a covenant that you are not
to approach or molest him in any way.

MRS CLANDON. Well: have I done so?

M'COMAS. Whether the behavior of your younger
children amounts to legal molestation is a question on
which it may be necessary to take counsel's opinion.

At all events, Mr Crampton not only claims to have been molested; but he believes that he was brought here by a plot in which Mr Valentine acted as your agent.

VALENTINE. Whats that? Eh?

M'COMAS. He alleges that you drugged him, Mr Valentine.

VALENTINE. So I did.

M'COMAS. But what did you do that for?

DOLLY. Five shillings extra.

M'COMAS [*to Dolly, short-temperedly*] I must really ask you, Miss Clandon, not to interrupt this very serious conversation with irrelevant interjections. [*Vehemently*] I insist on having earnest matters earnestly and reverently discussed. [*This outburst produces an apologetic silence, and puts M'Comas himself out of countenance. He coughs, and starts afresh, addressing himself to Gloria*]. Miss Clandon: it is my duty to tell you that your father has also persuaded himself that Mr Valentine wishes to marry you—

VALENTINE [*interposing adroitly*] I do.

M'COMAS [*huffily*] In that case, sir, you must not be surprised to find yourself regarded by the young lady's father as a fortune hunter.

VALENTINE. So I am. Do you expect my wife to live on what I earn? tenpence a week!

M'COMAS [*revolted*] I have nothing more to say, sir. I shall return and tell Mr Crampton that this family is no place for a father. [*He makes for the door*].

MRS CLANDON [*With quiet authority*] Finch! [*He halts*]. If Mr Valentine cannot be serious, you can. Sit down. [*M'Comas, after a brief struggle between his dignity and his friendship succumbs, seating himself this time midway between Dolly and Mrs Clandon*]. You know that all this is a made up case—that Fergus does not believe in it any more than you do. Now give me your real advice: your sincere, friendly advice. You know I have always trusted your judgment. I promise you the children will be quiet.

M'COMAS [*resigning himself*] Well, well! What I want to say is this. In the old arrangement with your husband, Mrs Clandon, you had him at a terrible disadvantage.

MRS CLANDON. How so, pray?

M'COMAS. Well, you were an advanced woman, accustomed to defy public opinion, and with no regard for what the world might say of you.

MRS CLANDON [*proud of it*] Yes: that is true.

Gloria, behind the chair, stoops and kisses her mother's hair, a demonstration which disconcerts her extremely.

M'COMAS. On the other hand, Mrs Clandon, your husband had a great horror of anything getting into the papers. There was his business to be considered, as well as the prejudices of an old fashioned family.

MRS CLANDON. Not to mention his own prejudices.

M'COMAS. Now no doubt he behaved badly, Mrs Clandon.

MRS CLANDON [*scornfully*] No doubt.

M'COMAS. But was it altogether his fault?

MRS CLANDON. Was it mine?

M'COMAS [*hastily*] No. Of course not.

GLORIA [*observing him attentively*] You do not mean that, Mr M'Comas.

M'COMAS. My dear young lady, you pick me up very sharply. But let me just put this to you. When a man makes an unsuitable marriage (nobody's fault, you know, but purely accidental incompatibility of tastes); when he is deprived by that misfortune of the domestic sympathy which, I take it, is what a man marries for; when, in short, his wife is rather worse than no wife at all (through no fault of her own, of course), is it to be wondered at if he makes matters worse at first by blaming her, and even, in his desperation, by occasionally drinking himself into a violent condition or seeking sympathy elsewhere?

MRS CLANDON. I did not blame him: I simply rescued myself and the children from him.

M'COMAS. Yes; but you made hard terms, Mrs Clandon. You had him at your mercy: you brought him to his knees when you threatened to make the matter public by applying to the Courts for a judicial separation. Suppose he had had that power over you, and used it to take your children away from you and bring them up in ignorance of your very name, how would you feel? what would you do? Well, wont you make some allowance for his feelings? in common humanity.

MRS CLANDON. I never discovered his feelings. I discovered his temper, and his— [*she shivers*] the rest of his common humanity.

M'COMAS [*wistfully*] Women can be very hard, Mrs Clandon.

VALENTINE. Thats true.

GLORIA [*angrily*] Be silent. [*He subsides*].

M'COMAS [*rallying all his forces*] Let me make one last appeal. Mrs Clandon: believe me, there are men who have a good deal of feeling, and kind feeling too, which they are not able to express. What you miss in Crampton is that mere veneer of civilization, the art of shewing worthless attentions and paying insincere compliments in a kindly charming way. If you lived in London, where the whole system is one of false good-fellowship, and you may know a man for twenty years without finding out that he hates you like poison, you would soon have your eyes opened. There we do unkind things in a kind way: we say bitter things in a sweet voice: we always give our friends chloroform when we tear them to pieces. But think of the other side of it! Think of the people who do kind things in an unkind way! people whose touch hurts, whose voices jar, whose tempers play them false, who wound and worry the people they love in the very act of trying to conciliate them, and who yet need affection as much as the rest of us. Crampton has an abominable temper, I admit. He has no manners, no tact, no grace. He'll never be able to gain anyone's affection unless they will take his desire for it on trust. Is he to have none? not even pity? from his own flesh and blood?

DOLLY [*quite melted*] Oh how beautiful, Finch! How nice of you!

PHILIP [*with conviction*] Finch: this is eloquence: positive eloquence.

DOLLY. Oh mamma, let us give him another chance. Let us have him to dinner.

MRS CLANDON [*unmoved*] No, Dolly: I hardly got any lunch. My dear Finch: there is not the least use in talking to me about Fergus. You have never been married to him: I have.

M'COMAS [*to Gloria*] Miss Clandon: I have hitherto refrained from appealing to you, because, if what Mr Crampton told me be true, you have been more merciless even than your mother.

GLORIA [*defiantly*] You appeal from her strength to my weakness!

M'COMAS. Not your weakness, Miss Clandon. I appeal from her intellect to your heart.

GLORIA. I have learnt to mistrust my heart. [*With an angry glance at Valentine*] I would tear my heart out

[762]

and throw it away if I could. My answer to you is my mother's answer.

M'COMAS [*defeated*] Well, I am sorry. Very sorry. I have done my best. [*He rises and prepares to go, deeply dissatisfied*].

MRS CLANDON. But what did you expect, Finch? What do you want us to do?

M'COMAS. The first step for both you and Crampton is to obtain counsel's opinion as to whether he is bound by the deed of separation or not. Now why not obtain this opinion at once, and have a friendly meeting [*her face hardens*] or shall we say a neutral meeting? to settle the difficulty? Here? In this hotel? Tonight? What do you say?

MRS CLANDON. But where is the counsel's opinion to come from?

M'COMAS. It has dropped down on us out of the clouds. On my way back here from Crampton's I met a most eminent Q.C.: a man whom I briefed in the case that made his name for him. He has come down here from Saturday to Monday for the sea air, and to visit a relative of his who lives here. He has been good enough to say that if I can arrange a meeting of the parties he will come and help us with his opinion. Now do let us seize this chance of a quiet friendly family adjustment. Let me bring my friend here and try to persuade Crampton to come too. Come: consent.

MRS CLANDON [*rather ominously, after a moment's consideration*] Finch: I dont want counsel's opinion, because I intend to be guided by my own opinion. I dont want to meet Fergus again, because I dont like him, and dont believe the meeting will do any good. However [*rising*], you have persuaded the children that he is not quite hopeless. Do as you please.

M'COMAS [*taking her hand and shaking it*] Thank you, Mrs Clandon. Will nine o'clock suit you?

MRS CLANDON. Perfectly. Phil: will you ring, please. [*Phil rings the bell*]. But if I am to be accused of conspiring with Mr Valentine, I think he had better be present.

VALENTINE [*rising*] I quite agree with you. I think it's most important.

M'COMAS. There can be no objection to that, I think. I have the greatest hopes of a happy settlement. Goodbye for the present. [*He goes out, meeting the waiter, who holds the door open for him*].

MRS CLANDON. We expect some visitors at nine, William. Can we have dinner at seven instead of half past?

WAITER [*at the door*] Seven, maam? Certainly, maam. It will be a convenience to us this busy evening, maam. There will be the band and the arranging of the fairy lights and one thing or another maam.

DOLLY. Fairy lights!

PHILIP. A band! William: what mean you?

WAITER. The fancy ball, miss.

DOLLY AND PHILIP [*simultaneously rushing to him*] Fancy ball!!!

WAITER. Oh yes, sir. Given by the regatta committee for the benefit of the Life-boat, sir. [*To Mrs Clandon*] We often have them, maam: Chinese lanterns in the garden, maam: very bright and pleasant, very gay and innocent indeed. [*To Phil*] Tickets downstairs at the office, sir, five shillings: ladies half price if accompanied by a gentleman.

PHILIP [*seizing his arm to drag him off*] To the office, William!

DOLLY [*breathlessly, seizing his other arm*] Quick,

before theyre all sold. [*They rush him out of the room between them*].

MRS CLANDON [*following them*] But they musnt go off dancing this evening. They must be here to meet— [*She disappears*].

    Gloria stares coolly at Valentine, and then deliberately looks at her watch.

VALENTINE. I understand. Ive stayed too long. I'm going.

GLORIA [*with disdainful punctiliousness*] I owe you some apology, Mr Valentine. I am conscious of having spoken to you somewhat sharply. Perhaps rudely.

VALENTINE. Not at all.

GLORIA. My only excuse is that it is very difficult to give consideration and respect when there is no dignity of character on the other side to command it.

VALENTINE. How is a man to look dignified when he's infatuated?

GLORIA [*angrily*] Dont say those things to me. I forbid you. They are insults.

VALENTINE. No: theyre only follies. I cant help them.

GLORIA. If you were really in love, it would not make you foolish: it would give you dignity! earnestness! even beauty.

VALENTINE. Do you really think it would make me beautiful? [*She turns her back on him with the coldest contempt*]. Ah, you see youre not in earnest. Love cant give any man new gifts. It can only heighten the gifts he was born with.

GLORIA [*sweeping round at him again*] What gifts were you born with, pray?

VALENTINE. Lightness of heart.

GLORIA. And lightness of head, and lightness of faith, and lightness of everything that makes a man.

VALENTINE. Yes, the whole world is like a feather

dancing in the light now; and Gloria is the sun. [*She rears her head haughtily*]. Beg pardon: I'm off. Back at nine. Goodbye. [*He runs off gaily, leaving her standing in the middle of the room staring after him*].

GLORIA [*at the top of her voice; suddenly furious with him for leaving her*] Idiot!

[ACT IV]

The same room. Nine o'clock. Nobody present. The lamps are lighted; but the curtains are not drawn. The window stands wide open; and strings of Chinese lanterns are glowing among the trees outside, with the starry sky beyond. The band is playing dance-music in the garden, drowning the sound of the sea.

The waiter enters, shewing in Crampton and M'Comas. Crampton looks cowed and anxious. He sits down wearily and timidly on the ottoman.

WAITER. The ladies have gone for a turn through the grounds to see the fancy dresses, sir. If you will be so good as to take seats, gentlemen, I shall tell them. [*He is about to go into the garden through the window when M'Comas stops him*].

M'COMAS. Stop a bit. If another gentleman comes, shew him in without any delay: we are expecting him.

WAITER. Right, sir. What name, sir?

M'COMAS. Boon. Mr Boon. He is a stranger to Mrs Clandon; so he may give you a card. If so, the name is spelt B.O.H.U.N. You will not forget.

WAITER [*smiling*] You may depend on me for that, sir. My own name is Boon, sir, though I am best known down here as Balmy Walters, sir. By rights I should spell it with the aitch you, sir; but I think it best not to take that liberty, sir. There is Norman blood in it, sir; and Norman blood is not a recommendation to a waiter.

M'COMAS. Well, well: "True hearts are more than coronets, and simple faith than Norman blood."

WAITER. That depends a good deal on one's station in life, sir. If you were a waiter, sir, youd find that simple faith would leave you just as short as Norman blood. I find it best to spell myself B. double-O.N., and to keep my wits pretty sharp about me. But I'm taking up your time, sir. Youll excuse me, sir: your own fault for being so affable, sir. I'll tell the ladies youre here, sir. [*He goes out into the garden through the window*].

M'COMAS. Crampton: I can depend on you, cant I?

CRAMPTON. Yes, yes. I'll be quiet. I'll be patient. I'll do my best.

M'COMAS. Remember: Ive not given you away. Ive told them it was all their fault.

CRAMPTON. You told me that it was all my fault.

M'COMAS. I told you the truth.

CRAMPTON [*plaintively*] If they will only be fair to me!

M'COMAS. My dear Crampton, they wont be fair to you: it's not to be expected from them at their age. If youre going to make impossible conditions of this kind, we may as well go back home at once.

CRAMPTON. But surely I have a right—

M'COMAS [*intolerantly*] You wont get your rights. Now, once for all, Crampton, did your promise of good behavior only mean that you wont complain if theres nothing to complain of? Because, if so— [*He moves as if to go*].

CRAMPTON [*miserably*] No, no: let me alone, cant you? Ive been bullied enough: Ive been tormented enough. I tell you I'll do my best. But if that girl begins to talk to me like that and to look at me like— [*He breaks off and buries his head in his hands*].

M'COMAS [*relenting*] There, there: itll be all right, if
you will only bear and forbear. Come: pull yourself
together: theres someone coming. [*Crampton, too
dejected to care much, hardly changes his attitude.
Gloria enters from the garden. M'Comas goes to meet
her at the window; so that he can speak to her without
being heard by Crampton*]. There he is, Miss Clandon.
Be kind to him. I'll leave you with him for a moment.
[*He goes into the garden*].

    *Gloria comes in and strolls coolly down the middle of
the room.*

CRAMPTON [*looking round in alarm*] Wheres
M'Comas?

GLORIA [*listlessly, but not unsympathetically*] Gone
out. To leave us together. Delicacy on his part, I
suppose. [*She stops beside him and looks quaintly down
at him*]. Well, father?

CRAMPTON [*submissively*] Well, daughter?

    *They look at one another with a melancholy sense of
humor, though humor is not their strong point.*

GLORIA. Shake hands. [*They shake hands*].

CRAMPTON [*holding her hand*] My dear: I'm afraid I
spoke very improperly of your mother this afternoon.

GLORIA. Oh, dont apologize. I was very high and
mighty myself; but Ive come down since: oh, yes:
Ive been brought down. [*She sits down on the floor
beside his chair*].

CRAMPTON. What has happened to you, my child?

GLORIA. Oh, never mind. I was playing the part of
my mother's daughter then; but I'm not: I'm my
father's daughter. [*Looking at him forlornly*] Thats a
come down, isnt it?

CRAMPTON [*angry*] What! [*Her expression does not
alter. He surrenders*]. Well, yes, my dear: I suppose it
is, I suppose it is. I'm afraid I'm sometimes a little

irritable; but I know whats right and reasonable all the time, even when I dont act on it. Can you believe that?

GLORIA. Believe it! Why, thats myself: myself all over. *I* know whats right and dignified and strong and noble, just as well as she does; but oh, the things I do! the things I do! the things I let other people do!!

CRAMPTON [*a little grudgingly in spite of himself*] As well as she does? You mean your mother?

GLORIA [*quickly*] Yes, mother. [*She turns to him on her knees and seizes his hands*]. Now listen. No treason to her: no word, no thought against her. She is our superior: yours and mine: high heavens above us. Is that agreed?

CRAMPTON. Yes, yes. Just as you please, my dear.

GLORIA [*not satisfied, letting go his hands and drawing back from him*] You dont like her?

CRAMPTON. My child: you havnt been married to her. I have. [*She raises herself slowly to her feet, looking at him with growing coldness*]. She did me a great wrong in marrying me without really caring for me. But after that, the wrong was all on my side, I dare say. [*He offers her his hand again*].

GLORIA [*taking it firmly and warningly*] Take care. Thats my dangerous subject. My feelings—my miserable cowardly womanly feelings—may be on your side; but my conscience is on hers.

CRAMPTON. I'm very well content with that division, my dear. Thank you.

Valentine arrives. Gloria immediately becomes deliberately haughty.

VALENTINE. Excuse me; but it's impossible to find a servant to announce one: even the never failing William seems to be at the ball. I should have gone myself; only I havnt five shillings to buy a ticket. How are you getting on, Crampton? Better, eh?

CRAMPTON. I am myself again, Mr Valentine, no thanks to you.

VALENTINE. Look at this ungrateful parent of yours, Miss Clandon! I saved him from an excruciating pang; and he reviles me!

GLORIA [*coldly*] I am sorry my mother is not here to receive you, Mr Valentine. It is not quite nine o'clock; and the gentleman of whom Mr M'Comas spoke, the lawyer, has not yet come.

VALENTINE. Oh yes he has. Ive met him and talked to him. [*With gay malice*] Youll like him, Miss Clandon: he's the very incarnation of intellect. You can hear his mind working.

GLORIA [*ignoring the jibe*] Where is he?

VALENTINE. Bought a false nose and gone to the fancy ball.

CRAMPTON [*crustily, looking at his watch*] It seems that everybody has gone to this fancy ball instead of keeping to our appointment here.

VALENTINE. Oh, he'll come all right enough: that was half an hour ago. I didnt like to borrow five shillings from him and go in with him; so I joined the mob and looked through the railings until Miss Clandon disappeared into the hotel through the window.

GLORIA. So it has come to this, that you follow me about in public to stare at me.

VALENTINE. Yes: somebody ought to chain me up.

Gloria turns her back on him and goes to the fireplace. He takes the snub very philosophically, and goes to the opposite side of the room. The waiter appears at the window, ushering in Mrs Clandon and M'Comas.

MRS CLANDON. I am so sorry to have kept you all waiting.

A grotesquely majestic stranger, in a domino and false nose with goggles, appears at the window.

WAITER [*to the stranger*] Beg pardon, sir; but this is a private apartment, sir. If you will allow me, sir, I will shew you the American bar and supper rooms, sir. This way, sir.

He goes into the garden, leading the way under the impression that the stranger is following him. The majestic one, however, comes straight into the room to the end of the table, where, with impressive deliberation, he takes off the false nose and then the domino, rolling up the nose in the domino and throwing the bundle on the table like a champion throwing down his glove. He is now seen to be a tall stout man between forty and fifty, clean shaven, with a midnight oil pallor emphasized by stiff black hair, cropped short and oiled, and eyebrows like early Victorian horsehair upholstery. Physically and spiritually a coarsened man: in cunning and logic a ruthlessly sharpened one. His bearing as he enters is sufficiently imposing and disquieting; but when he speaks, his powerful menacing voice, impressively articulated speech, strong inexorable manner, and a terrifying power of intensely critical listening, raise the impression produced by him to absolute tremendousness.

THE STRANGER. My name is Bohun. [*General awe*]. Have I the honor of addressing Mrs Clandon? [*Mrs Clandon bows. Bohun bows*]. Miss Clandon? [*Gloria bows. Bohun bows*]. Mr Clandon?

CRAMPTON [*insisting on his rightful name as angrily as he dares*] My name is Crampton, sir.

BOHUN. Oh, indeed. [*Passing him over without further notice and turning to Valentine*] Are you Mr Clandon?

VALENTINE [*making it a point of honor not to be im-*

pressed by him] Do I look like it? My name is Valentine. I did the drugging.

BOHUN. Ah, quite so. Then Mr Clandon has not yet arrived?

WAITER [*entering anxiously through the window*] Beg pardon, maam; but can you tell me what became of that— [*He recognizes Bohun, and loses all his self-possession. Bohun waits rigidly for him to pull himself together*]. Beg pardon, sir, I'm sure, sir. [*Brokenly*] Was—was it you, sir?

BOHUN [*remorselessly*] It was I.

WAITER [*Unable to restrain his tears*] You in a false nose, Walter! [*He clings to a chair to support himself*]. I beg your pardon, maam. A little giddiness—

BOHUN [*commandingly*] You will excuse him, Mrs Clandon, when I inform you that he is my father.

WAITER [*heartbroken*] Oh no, no, Walter. A waiter for your father on top of a false nose! What will they think of you?

MRS CLANDON. I am delighted to hear it, Mr Bohun. Your father has been an excellent friend to us since we came here.

Bohun bows gravely.

WAITER [*shaking his head*] Oh no, maam. It's very kind of you: very ladylike and affable indeed, maam; but I should feel at a great disadvantage off my own proper footing. Never mind my being the gentleman's father, maam: it is only the accident of birth after all, maam. Youll excuse me, I'm sure, having interrupted your business. [*He begins to make his way along the table, supporting himself from chair to chair, with his eye on the door*].

BOHUN. One moment. [*The waiter stops, with a sinking heart*]. My father was a witness of what passed today, was he not, Mrs Clandon?

MRS CLANDON. Yes, most of it, I think.

BOHUN. In that case we shall want him.

WAITER [*pleading*] I hope it may not be necessary, sir. Busy evening for me, sir, with that ball: very busy evening indeed, sir.

BOHUN [*inexorably*] We shall want you.

MRS CLANDON [*politely*] Sit down, wont you?

WAITER [*earnestly*] Oh, if you please, maam, I really must draw the line at sitting down. I couldnt let myself be seen doing such a thing, maam: thank you, I am sure, all the same. [*He looks round from face to face wretchedly, with an expression that would melt a heart of stone*].

GLORIA. Dont let us waste time. William only wants to go on taking care of us. I should like a cup of coffee.

WAITER [*brightening perceptibly*] Coffee, miss? [*He gives a little gasp of hope*]. Certainly, miss. Thank you, miss: very timely, miss, very thoughtful and considerate indeed. [*To Mrs Clandon, timidly but expectantly*] Anything for you, maam?

MRS CLANDON. Er—oh yes: it's so hot, I think we might have a jug of claret cup.

WAITER [*beaming*] Claret cup, maam! Certainly, maam.

GLORIA. Oh well, I'll have claret cup instead of coffee. Put some cucumber in it.

WAITER [*delighted*] Cucumber, miss! yes miss. [*To Bohun*] Anything special for you, sir? You dont like cucumber, sir.

BOHUN. If Mrs Clandon will allow me: syphon: Scotch.

WAITER. Right, sir. [*To Crampton*] Irish for you, sir, I think, sir? [*Crampton assents with a grunt. The waiter looks inquiringly at Valentine*].

VALENTINE. I like cucumber.

WAITER. Right, sir. [*Summing up*] Claret cup, syphon, one Scotch and one Irish?

MRS CLANDON. I think thats right.

WAITER [*himself again*] Right, maam. Directly, maam. Thank you. [*He ambles off through the window, having sounded the whole gamut of human happiness, from despair to ecstasy, in fifty seconds*].

M'COMAS. We can begin now, I suppose.

BOHUN. We had better wait until Mrs Clandon's husband arrives.

CRAMPTON. What d'y' mean? I'm her husband.

BOHUN [*instantly pouncing on the inconsistency between this and his previous statement*] You said just now that your name was Crampton.

CRAMPTON. So it is.

MRS CLANDON			I—
GLORIA	[*all four speaking simultaneously*]		My—
M'COMAS			Mrs—
VALENTINE			You—

BOHUN [*drowning them in two thunderous words*] One moment. [*Dead silence*]. Pray allow me. Sit down, everybody. [*They obey humbly. Gloria takes the saddle-bag chair on the hearth. Valentine slips round to her side of the room and sits on the ottoman facing the window, so that he can look at her. Crampton sits on the ottoman with his back to Valentine's. Mrs Clandon, who has all along kept at the opposite side of the room in order to avoid Crampton as much as possible, sits near the door, with M'Comas beside her on the left. Bohun places himself magisterially in the centre of the group, near the corner of the table on Mrs Clandon's side. When they are settled, he fixes Crampton with his eye, and begins*] In this family, it appears the husband's name is Crampton: the wife's, Clandon. Thus we have on the very threshold of the case an element of confusion.

VALENTINE [*getting up and speaking across to him with one knee on the ottoman*] But it's perfectly simple—

BOHUN [*annihilating him with a vocal thunderbolt*] It is. Mrs Clandon has adopted another name. That is the obvious explanation which you feared I could not find out for myself. You mistrust my intelligence, Mr Valentine—[*stopping him as he is about to protest*] no: I dont want you to answer that: I want you to think over it when you feel your next impulse to interrupt me.

VALENTINE [*dazed*] This is simply breaking a butterfly on a wheel. What does it matter? [*He sits down again*].

BOHUN. I will tell you what it matters, sir. It matters that if this family difference is to be smoothed over as we all hope it may be, Mrs Clandon, as a matter of social convenience and decency, will have to resume her husband's name [*Mrs Clandon assumes an expression of the most determined obstinacy*] or else Mr Crampton will have to call himself Mr Clandon. [*Crampton looks indomitably resolved to do nothing of the sort*]. No doubt you think that an easy matter, Mr Valentine. [*He looks pointedly at Mrs Clandon, then at Crampton*]. I differ from you. [*He throws himself back in his chair, frowning heavily*].

M'COMAS [*timidly*] I think, Bohun, we had perhaps better dispose of the important questions first.

BOHUN. M'Comas: there will be no difficulty about the important questions. There never is. It is the trifles that will wreck you at the harbor mouth. [*M'Comas looks as if he considered this a paradox*]. You dont agree with me, eh?

M'COMAS [*flatteringly*] If I did—

BOHUN [*interrupting him*] If you did, you would be me, instead of being what you are.

M'COMAS [*fawning on him*] Of course, Bohun, your speciality—

BOHUN [*again interrupting him*] My speciality is being right when other people are wrong. If you agreed with me I should be no use here. [*He nods at him to drive the point home; then turns suddenly and forcibly on Crampton*]. Now you, Mr Crampton: what point in this business have you most at heart?

CRAMPTON [*beginning slowly*] I wish to put all considerations of self aside in this matter—

BOHUN [*cutting him short*] So do we all, Mr Crampton. [*To Mrs Clandon*] You wish to put self aside, Mrs Clandon?

MRS CLANDON. Yes: I am not consulting my own feelings in being here.

BOHUN. So do you, Miss Clandon?

GLORIA. Yes.

BOHUN. I thought so. We all do.

VALENTINE. Except me. My aims are selfish.

BOHUN. Thats because you think an affectation of sincerity will produce a better effect on Miss Clandon than an affectation of disinterestedness. [*Valentine, utterly dismantled and destroyed by this just remark, takes refuge in a feeble speechless smile. Bohun, satisfied at having now effectually crushed all rebellion, again throws himself back in his chair, with an air of being prepared to listen tolerantly to their grievances*]. Now, Mr Crampton, go on. It's understood that self is put aside. Human nature always begins by saying that.

CRAMPTON. But I mean it, sir.

BOHUN. Quite so. Now for your point.

CRAMPTON. Every reasonable person will admit that it's an unselfish one. It's about the children.

BOHUN. Well? What about the children?

CRAMPTON [*with emotion*] They have—

BOHUN [*pouncing forward again*] Stop. Youre going to tell me about your feelings, Mr Crampton. Dont. I sympathize with them; but theyre not my business. Tell us exactly what you want: thats what we have to get at.

CRAMPTON [*uneasily*] It's a very difficult question to answer, Mr Bohun.

BOHUN. Come: I'll help you out. What do you object to in the present circumstances of the children?

CRAMPTON. I object to the way they have been brought up.

Mrs Clandon's brow contracts ominously.

BOHUN. How do you propose to alter that now?

CRAMPTON. I think they ought to dress more quietly.

VALENTINE. Nonsense.

BOHUN [*instantly flinging himself back in his chair, outraged by the interruption*] When you are done, Mr Valentine: when you are quite done.

VALENTINE. Whats wrong with Miss Clandon's dress?

CRAMPTON [*hotly to Valentine*] My opinion is as good as yours.

GLORIA [*warningly*] Father!

CRAMPTON [*subsiding piteously*] I didnt mean you, my dear. [*Pleading earnestly to Bohun*] But the two younger ones! you have not seen them, Mr Bohun; and indeed I think you would agree with me that there is something very noticeable, something almost gay and frivolous in their style of dressing.

MRS CLANDON [*impatiently*] Do you suppose I choose their clothes for them? Really, this is childish.

CRAMPTON [*furious, rising*] Childish!

Mrs Clandon rises indignantly.

M'COMAS	[*all	Crampton, you promised—
VALENTINE	*rising*	Ridiculous. They dress
	and	charmingly.
GLORIA	*speaking*	Pray let us behave reason-
	together]	ably.

Tumult. Suddenly they hear a warning chime of glasses in the room behind them. They turn guiltily and find that the waiter has just come back from the bar in the garden, and is jingling his tray as he comes softly to the table with it. Dead silence.

WAITER [*to Crampton, setting a tumbler apart on the table*] Irish for you, sir. [*Crampton sits down a little shamefacedly. The waiter sets another tumbler and a syphon apart, saying to Bohun*] Scotch and syphon for you, sir. [*Bohun waves his hand impatiently. The waiter places a large glass jug and three tumblers in the middle*]. And claret cup. [*All subside into their seats. Peace reigns*].

MRS CLANDON. I am afraid we interrupted you, Mr Bohun.

BOHUN [*calmly*] You did. [*To the waiter, who is going out*] Just wait a bit.

WAITER. Yes, sir. Certainly, sir. [*He takes his stand behind Bohun's chair*].

MRS CLANDON [*to the waiter*] You dont mind our detaining you, I hope. Mr Bohun wishes it.

WAITER [*now quite at his ease*] Oh no, maam, not at all, maam. It is a pleasure to me to watch the working of his trained and powerful mind: very stimulating, very entertaining and instructive indeed, maam.

BOHUN [*resuming command of the proceedings*] Now, Mr Crampton: we are waiting for you. Do you give up your objection to the dressing or do you stick to it?

CRAMPTON [*pleading*] Mr Bohun: consider my position for a moment. I havnt got myself alone to consider: theres my sister Sophronia and my brother-in-law and all their circle. They have a great horror of anything that is at all—at all—well—

BOHUN. Out with it. Fast? Loud? Gay?

CRAMPTON. Not in any unprincipled sense, of course; but—but—[*blurting it out desperately*] those two children would shock them. Theyre not fit to mix with their own people. Thats what I complain of.

MRS CLANDON [*with suppressed anger*] Mr Valentine: do you think there is anything fast or loud about Phil and Dolly?

VALENTINE. Certainly not. It's utter bosh. Nothing can be in better taste.

CRAMPTON. Oh yes: of course you say so.

MRS CLANDON. William: you see a great deal of good English society. Are my children overdressed?

WAITER [*reassuringly*] Oh dear no, maam. [*Persuasively*] Oh no, sir, not at all. A little pretty and tasty no doubt, but very choice and classy, very genteel and high toned indeed. Might be the son and daughter of a Dean, sir, I assure you, sir. You have only to look at them, sir, to—

At this moment a harlequin and columbine, waltzing to the band in the garden, whirl one another into the room. The harlequin's dress is made of lozenges, an inch square, of turquoise blue silk and gold alternately. His bat is gilt and his mask turned up. The columbine's petticoats are the epitome of a harvest field, golden orange and poppy crimson, with a tiny velvet jacket for the poppy stamens. They pass, an exquisite and dazzling apparition, between M'Comas and Bohun, and then back in a circle to the end of the table, where, as the final chord of the waltz is struck, they make a tableau in the middle of the company, the harlequin down on his left knee, and the columbine standing on his right knee, with her arms curved over her head. Unlike their dancing, which is charmingly graceful, their attitudinizing is hardly a success, and threatens to end in a catastrophe.

THE COLUMBINE [*screaming*] Lift me down, somebody: I'm going to fall. Papa: lift me down.

CRAMPTON [*anxiously running to her and taking her hands*] My child!

DOLLY [*jumping down, with his help*] Thanks: so nice of you. [*Phil sits on the edge of the table and pours out some claret cup. Crampton returns to the ottoman in great perplexity*]. Oh, what fun! Oh dear! [*She seats herself with a vault on the front edge of the table, panting*]. Oh, claret cup! [*She drinks*].

BOHUN [*in powerful tones*] This is the younger lady, is it?

DOLLY [*slipping down off the table in alarm at his formidable voice and manner*] Yes, sir. Please, who are you?

MRS CLANDON. This is Mr Bohun, Dolly, who has very kindly come to help us this evening.

DOLLY. Oh, then he comes as a boon and a blessing—

PHILIP. Sh!

CRAMPTON. Mr Bohun—M'Comas: I appeal to you. Is this right? Would you blame my sister's family for objecting to it?

DOLLY [*flushing ominously*] Have you begun again?

CRAMPTON [*propitiating her*] No, no. It's perhaps natural at your age.

DOLLY [*obstinately*] Never mind my age. Is it pretty?

CRAMPTON. Yes, dear, yes. [*He sits down in token of submission*].

DOLLY [*insistently*] Do you like it?

CRAMPTON. My child: how can you expect me to like it or to approve of it?

DOLLY [*determined not to let him off*] How can you think it pretty and not like it?

M'COMAS [*rising, scandalized*] Really I must say—

Bohun, who has listened to Dolly with the highest approval, is down on him instantly.

BOHUN. No: dont interrupt, M'Comas. The young lady's method is right. [*To Dolly, with tremendous emphasis*] Press your questions, Miss Clandon: press your questions.

DOLLY [*turning to Bohun*] Oh dear, you are a regular overwhelmer! Do you always go on like this?

BOHUN [*rising*] Yes. Dont you try to put me out of countenance young lady: youre too young to do it. [*He takes M'Comas's chair from beside Mrs Clandon's and sets it beside his own*]. Sit down. [*Dolly, fascinated, obeys; and Bohun sits down again. M'Comas, robbed of his seat, takes a chair on the other side, between the table and the ottoman*]. Now, Mr Crampton, the facts are before you: both of them. You think youd like to have your two youngest children to live with you. Well, you wouldnt— [*Crampton tries to protest; but Bohun will not have it on any terms*] no you wouldnt: you think you would; but I know better than you. Youd want this young lady here to give up dressing like a stage columbine in the evening and like a fashionable columbine in the morning. Well, she wont: never. She thinks she will; but—

DOLLY [*interrupting him*] No I dont. [*Resolutely*] I'll never give up dressing prettily. Never. As Gloria said to that man in Madeira, never, never, never! while grass grows or water runs.

VALENTINE [*rising in the wildest agitation*] What!

What! [*Beginning to speak very fast*] When did she say that? Who did she say that to?

BOHUN [*throwing himself back with massive pitying remonstrance*] Mr Valentine—

VALENTINE [*pepperily*] Dont you interrupt me, sir: this is something really serious. I insist on knowing who Miss Clandon said that to.

DOLLY. Perhaps Phil remembers. Which was it, Phil? number three or number five?

VALENTINE. Number five!!!

PHILIP. Courage, Valentine! It wasnt number five: it was only a tame naval lieutenant who was always on hand: the most patient and harmless of mortals.

GLORIA [*coldly*] What are we discussing now, pray?

VALENTINE [*very red*] Excuse me: I am sorry I interrupted. I shall intrude no further, Mrs Clandon. [*He bows to Mrs Clandon and marches away into the garden, boiling with suppressed rage*].

DOLLY. Hmhm!

PHILIP. Ahah!

GLORIA. Please go on, Mr Bohun.

DOLLY [*striking in as Bohun, frowning formidably, collects himself for a fresh grapple with the case*] Youre going to bully us, Mr Bohun.

BOHUN. I—

DOLLY [*interrupting him*] Oh yes you are: you think youre not; but you are. I know by your eyebrows.

BOHUN [*capitulating*] Mrs Clandon: these are clever children: clear headed well brought up children. I make that admission deliberately. Can you, in return, point out to me any way of inducing them to hold their tongues?

MRS CLANDON. Dolly, dearest—!

PHILIP. Our old failing, Dolly. Silence!

Dolly holds her mouth.

MRS CLANDON. Now, Mr Bohun, before they begin again—

WAITER [*softly*] Be quick, sir: be quick.

DOLLY [*beaming at him*] Dear William!

PHILIP. Sh!

BOHUN [*unexpectedly beginning by hurling a question straight at Dolly*] Have you any intention of getting married?

DOLLY. I! Well, Finch calls me by my Christian name.

M'COMAS [*starting violently*] I will not have this. Mr Bohun: I use the young lady's Christian name naturally as an old friend of her mother's.

DOLLY. Yes, you call me Dolly as an old friend of my mother's. But what about Dorothee-ee-a?

M'Comas rises indignantly.

CRAMPTON [*anxiously, rising to restrain him*] Keep your temper, M'Comas. Dont let us quarrel. Be patient.

M'COMAS. I will not be patient. You are shewing the most wretched weakness of character, Crampton. I say this is monstrous.

DOLLY. Mr Bohun: please bully Finch for us.

BOHUN. I will. M'Comas: youre making yourself ridiculous. Sit down.

M'COMAS. I—

BOHUN [*waving him down imperiously*] No: sit down, sit down.

M'Comas sits down sulkily; and Crampton, much relieved, follows his example.

DOLLY [*to Bohun, meekly*] Thank you.

BOHUN. Now listen to me, all of you. I give no opinion, M'Comas, as to how far you may or may not have committed yourself in the direction indicated by this young lady. [*M'Comas is about to protest*]. No:

dont interrupt me: if she doesnt marry you she will marry somebody else. That is the solution of the difficulty as to her not bearing her father's name. The other lady intends to get married.

GLORIA [*flushing*] Mr Bohun!

BOHUN. Oh yes you do: you dont know it; but you do.

GLORIA [*rising*] Stop. I warn you, Mr Bohun, not to answer for my intentions.

BOHUN [*rising*] It's no use, Miss Clandon: you cant put me down. I tell you your name will soon be neither Clandon nor Crampton; and I could tell you what it will be if I chose. [*He goes to the table and takes up his domino. They all rise; and Phil goes to the window. Bohun, with a gesture, summons the waiter to help him to robe*]. Mr Crampton: your notion of going to law is all nonsense: your children will be of age before you can get the point decided. [*Allowing the waiter to put the domino on his shoulders*] You can do nothing but make a friendly arrangement. If you want your family more than they want you, youll get the worst of the arrangement: if they want you more than you want them youll get the better of it. [*He shakes the domino into becoming folds and takes up the false nose. Dolly gazes admiringly at him*]. The strength of their position lies in their being very agreeable people personally. The strength of your position lies in your income. [*He claps on the false nose, and is again grotesquely transfigured*].

DOLLY [*running to him*] Oh, now you look quite like a human being. Maynt I have just one dance with you? Can you dance?

Phil, resuming his part of harlequin, waves his bat as if casting a spell on them.

BOHUN [*thunderously*] Yes: you think I cant: but I can. Allow me. [*He seizes her and dances off with her*

[785]

through the window in a most powerful manner, but with studied propriety and grace].

PHILIP. "On with the dance: let joy be unconfined." William.

WAITER. Yes, sir.

PHILIP. Can you procure a couple of dominos and false noses for my father and Mr M'Comas?

M'COMAS. Most certainly not. I protest—

CRAMPTON. Yes, yes. What harm will it do, just for once, M'Comas? Dont let us be spoil-sports.

M'COMAS. Crampton: you are not the man I took you for. [*Pointedly*] Bullies are always cowards. [*He goes disgustedly towards the window*].

CRAMPTON [*following him*] Well, never mind. We must indulge them a little. Can you get us something to wear, waiter?

WAITER. Certainly, sir. [*He precedes them to the window, and stands aside there to let them pass out before him*]. This way, sir, Dominos and noses, sir?

M'COMAS [*angrily, on his way out*] I shall wear my own nose.

WAITER [*suavely*] Oh dear yes, sir: the false one will fit over it quite easily, sir: plenty of room, sir, plenty of room. [*He goes out after M'Comas*].

CRAMPTON [*turning at the window to Phil with an attempt at genial fatherliness*] Come along, my boy. Come along. [*He goes*].

PHILIP [*cheerily, following him*] Coming, dad, coming. [*On the window threshold he stops; looks after Crampton; then turns fantastically with his bat bent into a halo round his head, and says with lowered voice to Mrs Clandon and Gloria*] Did you feel the pathos of that? [*He vanishes*].

MRS CLANDON [*left alone with Gloria*] Why did Mr Valentine go away so suddenly, I wonder?

GLORIA [*petulantly*] I dont know. Yes, I do know. Let us go and see the dancing.

They go towards the window, and are met by Valentine, who comes in from the garden walking quickly, with his face set and sulky.

VALENTINE [*stiffly*] Excuse me. I thought the party had quite broken up.

GLORIA [*nagging*] Then why did you come back?

VALENTINE. I came back because I am penniless. I cant get out that way without a five-shilling ticket.

MRS CLANDON. Has anything annoyed you, Mr Valentine?

GLORIA. Never mind him, mother. This is a fresh insult to me: that is all.

MRS CLANDON [*hardly able to realize that Gloria is deliberately provoking an altercation*] Gloria!

VALENTINE. Mrs Clandon: have I said anything insulting? Have I done anything insulting?

GLORIA. You have implied that my past has been like yours. That is the worst of insults.

VALENTINE. I imply nothing of the sort. I declare that my past has been blameless in comparison with yours.

MRS CLANDON [*most indignantly*] Mr Valentine!

VALENTINE. Well, what am I to think when I learn that Miss Clandon has made exactly the same speeches to other men that she has made to me? Five former lovers, with a tame naval lieutenant thrown in! Oh, it's too bad.

MRS CLANDON. But you surely do not believe that these affairs—mere jokes of the children's—were serious, Mr Valentine?

VALENTINE. Not to you. Not to her, perhaps. But I know what the men felt. [*With ludicrously genuine earnestness*] Have you ever thought of the wrecked

lives, the unhappy marriages contracted in the recklessness of despair, the suicides, the—the—the—

GLORIA [*interrupting him contemptuously*] Mother:
this man is a sentimental idiot. [*She sweeps away to the
fireplace*].

MRS CLANDON [*shocked*] Oh, my dearest Gloria, Mr
Valentine will think that rude.

VALENTINE. I am not a sentimental idiot. I am cured
of sentiment for ever. [*He turns away in dudgeon*].

MRS CLANDON. Mr Valentine: you must excuse us
all. Women have to unlearn the false good manners of
their slavery before they acquire the genuine good
manners of their freedom. Dont think Gloria vulgar
[*Gloria turns, astonished*]: she is not really so.

GLORIA. Mother! You apologize for me to him!

MRS CLANDON. My dear: you have some of the
faults of youth as well as its qualities; and Mr
Valentine seems rather too old fashioned in his ideas
about his own sex to like being called an idiot. And
now had we not better go and see what Dolly is doing?
[*She goes towards the window*].

GLORIA. Do you go, mother. I wish to speak to Mr
Valentine alone.

MRS CLANDON [*startled into a remonstrance*] My
dear! [*Recollecting herself*] I beg your pardon, Gloria.
Certainly, if you wish. [*She goes out*].

VALENTINE. Oh, if your mother were only a widow!
She's worth six of you.

GLORIA. That is the first thing I have heard you say
that does you honor.

VALENTINE. Stuff! Come: say what you want to say
and let me go.

GLORIA. I have only this to say. You dragged me
down to your level for a moment this afternoon. Do
you think, if that had ever happened before, that I

should not have been on my guard? that I should not have known what was coming, and known my own miserable weakness?

VALENTINE [*scolding at her passionately*] Dont talk of it in that way. What do I care for anything in you but your weakness, as you call it? You thought yourself very safe, didnt you, behind your advanced ideas? I amused myself by upsetting them pretty easily.

GLORIA [*insolently, feeling that now she can do as she likes with him*] Indeed!

VALENTINE. But why did I do it? Because I was being tempted to awaken your heart: to stir the depths in you. Why was I tempted? Because Nature was in deadly earnest with me when I was in jest with her. When the great moment came, who was awakened? who was stirred? in whom did the depths break up? In myself—myself. *I* was transported: you were only offended—shocked. You are just an ordinary lady, too ordinary to allow tame lieutenants to go as far as I went. Thats all. I shall not trouble you with conventional apologies. Goodbye. [*He makes resolutely for the door*].

GLORIA. Stop. [*He hesitates*]. Oh, will you understand, if I tell you the truth, that I am not making advances to you?

VALENTINE. Pooh! I know what youre going to say. You think youre not ordinary: that I was right: that you really have those depths in your nature. It flatters you to believe it. [*She recoils*]. Well, I grant that you are not ordinary in some ways: you are a clever girl [*Gloria stifles an exclamation of rage, and takes a threatening step towards him*]; but youve not been awakened yet. You didnt care: you dont care. It was my tragedy, not yours. Goodbye. [*He turns to the door. She watches him, appalled to see him slipping from*

*her grasp. As he turns the handle, he pauses; then turns
again to her, offering his hand*]. Let us part kindly.

GLORIA [*enormously relieved, and immediately turning
her back on him deliberately*] Goodbye. I trust you will
soon recover from the wound.

VALENTINE [*brightening up as it flashes on him that he
is master of the situation after all*] I shall recover: such
wounds heal more than they harm. After all, I still
have my own Gloria.

GLORIA [*facing him quickly*] What do you mean?

VALENTINE. The Gloria of my imagination.

GLORIA [*proudly*] Keep your own Gloria: the Gloria
of your imagination. [*Her emotion begins to break
through her pride*]. The real Gloria: the Gloria who
was shocked, offended, horrified—oh yes, quite truly
—who was driven almost mad with shame by the
feeling that all her power over herself had broken
down at her first real encounter with—with— [*The
color rushes over her face again. She covers it with her
left hand, and puts her right on his left arm to support
herself*].

VALENTINE. Take care. I'm losing my senses again.
[*Summoning all her courage, she takes away her hand
from her face and puts it on his right shoulder, turning
him towards her and looking him straight in the eyes. He
begins to protest agitatedly*]. Gloria: be sensible: it's no
use: I havnt a penny in the world.

GLORIA. Cant you earn one? Other people do.

VALENTINE [*half delighted, half frightened*] I never
could: youd be unhappy. My dearest love: I should
be the merest fortune-hunting adventurer if— [*Her
grip of his arms tightens; and she kisses him*]. Oh Lord!
[*Breathless*] Oh, I—[*he gasps*] I dont know anything
about women: twelve years experience is not enough.
[*In a gust of jealously she throws him away from her; and*

[790]

he reels back into a chair like a leaf before the wind].

Dolly dances in, waltzing with the waiter, followed by Mrs Clandon and Finch, also waltzing, and Phil pirouetting by himself.

DOLLY [*sinking on the chair at the writing-table*] Oh, I'm out of breath. How beautifully you waltz, William!

MRS CLANDON [*sinking on the saddle-bag seat on the hearth*] Oh, how could you make me do such a silly thing, Finch! I havnt danced since the soirée at South Place twenty years ago.

GLORIA [*peremptorily to Valentine*] Get up. [*Valentine gets up abjectly*]. Now let us have no false delicacy. Tell my mother that we have agreed to marry one another.

A silence of stupefaction ensues. Valentine, dumb with panic, looks at them with an obvious impulse to run away.

DOLLY [*breaking the silence*] Number Six!

PHILIP. Sh!

DOLLY [*tumultuously*] Oh, my feelings! I want to kiss somebody; and we bar it in the family. Wheres Finch?

M'COMAS. No, positively.

Crampton appears at the window.

DOLLY [*running to Crampton*] Oh, youre just in time. [*She kisses him*]. Now [*leading him forward*] bless them.

GLORIA. No. I will have no such thing, even in jest. When I need a blessing, I shall ask my mother's.

CRAMPTON [*to Gloria, with deep disappointment*] Am I to understand that you have engaged yourself to this young gentleman?

GLORIA [*resolutely*] Yes. Do you intend to be our friend or—

DOLLY. —or our father?

CRAMPTON. I should like to be both, my child. But

surely—! Mr Valentine: I appeal to your sense of honor.

VALENTINE. Youre quite right. It's perfect madness. If we go out to dance together I shall have to borrow five shillings from her for a ticket. Gloria: dont be rash: youre throwing yourself away. I'd much better clear straight out of this, and never see any of you again. I shant commit suicide: I shant even be unhappy. Itll be a relief to me: I—I'm frightened, I'm positively frightened; and that's the plain truth.

GLORIA [determinedly] You shall not go.

VALENTINE [quailing] No, dearest: of course not. But—oh, will somebody only talk sense for a moment and bring us all to reason! *I* cant. Where's Bohun? Bohun's the man. Phil: go and summon Bohun.

PHILIP. From the vasty deep. I go. [*He makes his bat quiver in the air and darts away through the window*].

WAITER [harmoniously to Valentine] If you will excuse my putting in a word, sir, do not let a matter of five shillings stand between you and your happiness, sir. We shall be only too pleased to put the ticket down to you; and you can settle at your convenience. Very glad to meet you in any way, very happy and pleased indeed, sir.

PHILIP [reappearing] He comes. [*He waves his bat over the window*].

Bohun comes in, taking off his false nose and throwing it on the table in passing as he comes between Gloria and Valentine.

VALENTINE. The point is, Mr Bohun—

M'COMAS [interrupting from the hearthrug] Excuse me, sir: the point must be put to him by a solicitor. The question is one of an engagement between these two young people. The lady has some property, and [look-

ing at Crampton] will probably have a good deal more.

CRAMPTON. Possibly. I hope so.

VALENTINE. And the gentleman hasnt a rap.

BOHUN [*nailing Valentine to the point instantly*] Then insist on a settlement. That shocks your delicacy: most sensible precautions do. But you ask my advice; and I give it to you. Have a settlement.

GLORIA [*proudly*] He shall have a settlement.

VALENTINE. My good sir, I dont want advice for myself. Give her some advice.

BOHUN. She wont take it. When youre married, she wont take yours either— [*turning suddenly on Gloria*] oh no you wont: you think you will; but you wont. He'll set to work and earn his living— [*turning suddenly on Valentine*] oh yes you will: you think you wont; but you will. She'll make you.

CRAMPTON [*only half persuaded*] Then, Mr Bohun, you dont think this match an unwise one?

BOHUN. Yes I do: all matches are unwise. It's unwise to be born; it's unwise to be married; it's unwise to live; and it's wise to die.

WAITER [*insinuating himself between Crampton and Valentine*] Then, if I may respectfully put a word in, sir, so much the worse for wisdom!

PHILIP. Allow me to remark that if Gloria has made up her mind—

DOLLY. The matter's settled; and Valentine's done for. And we're missing all the dances.

VALENTINE [*to Gloria, gallantly making the best of it*] May I have a dance—

BOHUN [*interposing in his grandest diapason*] Excuse me: I claim that privilege as counsel's fee. May I have the honor? thank you. [*He dances away with Gloria, and disappears among the lanterns, leaving Valentine gasping*].

VALENTINE [*recovering his breath*] Dolly: may I— [*offering himself as her partner*]?

DOLLY. Nonsense! [*eluding him and running round the table to the fireplace*]. Finch: my Finch! [*She pounces on M'Comas and makes him dance*].

M'COMAS [*protesting*] Pray restrain—really— [*He is borne off dancing through the window*].

VALENTINE [*making a last effort*] Mrs Clandon: may I—

PHILIP [*forestalling him*] Come, mother. [*He seizes his mother and whirls her away*].

MRS CLANDON [*remonstrating*] Phil, Phil—[*She shares M'Comas's fate*].

CRAMPTON [*following them with senile glee*] Ho! ho! He! he! he! [*He goes into the garden chuckling*].

VALENTINE [*collapsing on the ottoman and staring at the waiter*] I might as well be a married man already.

WAITER [*contemplating the defeated Duellist of Sex with ineffable benignity*] Cheer up, sir, cheer up. Every man is frightened of marriage when it comes to the point; but it often turns out very comfortable, very enjoyable and happy indeed, sir—from time to time. *I* never was master in my own house, sir: my wife was like your young lady: she was of a commanding and masterful disposition, which my son has inherited. But if I had my life to live twice over, I'd do it again: I'd do it again, I assure you. You never can tell, sir: you never can tell.

"G. B. S." and His Play

(*Daily Mail*, 4 May 1900)

"Yes, it is a beautiful situation," said Mr. Bernard Shaw yesterday, as he rose from the writing-table in his study in Adelphi-terrace, and moved towards the open window.

Outside, in the sudden sunshine of a changing May afternoon, the fresh green of the Embankment lay beneath, while the broad Thames rolled sluggishly through the white stone bridges beyond.

"But I do not find inspiration here," he continued to a "Daily Mail" representative. "When I want to work I have to go in the country, in the fresh air, early in the morning. That is what makes my work different from that of other writers. They write in town, at night. First they poison themselves with alcohol and tobacco, drinking and smoking at their dinner, then they go in their studies, draw the blinds, turn on the light, and work. The consequence is that almost all of modern literature is drunken. The taint of tobacco, of wine, of meat-eating runs right through it.

"You want to know my opinion of my new play? What is the use of coming to me. I was busy yesterday with the important public duty of attending a meeting of my vestry, and could not neglect that merely to attend the first performance of a play, even though I wrote that play myself.

"And I will admit that I do not care to attend my own plays. After the last rehearsal is over, I can do no more to alter them, and my presence only makes the performers nervous. I am of no use there. Why should I go?

"I do not in the least know why public performances of my play should be given. The public, I feel sure, do not wish for it. It was written for acting before a private society, and Mr. Yorke Stephens saw it there and wanted it. I have done my best to dissuade him from staging it, but in vain.

ON THE CRITICS' EFFORTS

"The mere fact that a few people go to see it does not prove that I am wrong. London is so vast a city that some folks can be found for almost anything. There are, I believe, eighteen thousand policemen in London keeping in control a great army of criminals. One might write something that tickled the fancy of the thieves and burglars, so that they rushed to see it. Think how they would fill a theatre. But that would not make the play really popular. So with mine.

"The painful efforts the dramatic critics make to say kind things about any play I write are very amusing. They do not in the least understand what I am driving at, and they are continually trying to read into my work some conventional stage meaning. They say to themselves, 'Shaw is a very clever fellow; his work is really brilliant; so we will ignore the bad sides of his work, and say the best we can for him?'

"They look at man from quite a different point of view to what I do. They go on the old conventions of right and wrong, crime and punishment, vengeance for the offender, reward for the good. They ask for what they call clearly-marked characters. They want an innocent heroine, not realising that when they put such a character on the stage she has to be wholly uninteresting, saying little, and acting like a stock figure.

"They want a wholly bad villain. I ignore all their conventions. I regard man as a specimen to be studied, the same as one would study any other member of the animal kingdom. He interests me, and so I study him. My plays represent my studies. But reward and punishment—!"

You Never Can Tell

(Chapter XVI of Cyril Maude's
The Haymarket Theatre,
1903, written by Shaw)

I now come to an episode in the history of the theatre which might have wrecked our enterprise had not Providence, which has never yet disappointed our humble trust in it, caused the danger into which we had stumbled to withdraw itself at the eleventh hour.

I think it must have been in the year 1895 that the devil put it into the mind of a friend of mine to tempt me with news of a play called "Candida" by a writer named Bernard Shaw, of whom until then I had never heard. I wrote to him suggesting that he should let me see the play. He instantly undertook the management of our theatre to the extent of informing me that "Candida" would not suit us, but that he would write a new play for us—which I protest I never asked him to do. As I learnt subsequently, he then took a chair in Regent's Park for the whole season, and sat there in the public eye writing the threatened play.

In the winter of 1897 this play, which was called "You Never Can Tell," came to hand. Some of our friends thought well of the author, and Harrison (who, as my readers have doubtless already gathered, is a perfect ignoramus in all matters connected with plays and acting) liked the play. In short, I allowed myself to be overpersuaded, and we actually put the play into rehearsal.

From the first the author showed the perversity of his disposition and his utter want of practical knowledge of the stage. He proposed impossible casts. He forced us into incomprehensible agreements by torturing us with endless talk until we were ready to sign anything rather than argue for another hour. Had I been properly supported by my colleagues I should not have tolerated his proceedings for a moment. I do not wish to complain of anybody, but as a matter of fact I was not so supported. I expected nothing better from Harrison, because with all his excellent qualities he is too vain—I say it though he is my best friend—to be trusted in so delicate an undertaking as the management of a theatre. The truth is, Shaw flattered him, and thus detached him from me by playing on his one fatal weakness.

The world knows, I think, that whatever my faults may be, I am an affectionate and devoted husband. But I have never pretended that my wife is perfect. No woman is, and but few men. Still, I do think she might have supported me better than she did through our greatest trial. This man from the first exercised a malign influence over her. With my full consent and approval she selected for herself a certain part in his play. He had privately resolved—out of mere love of contradiction—that she should play another. When he read the play he contrived to balance the parts in such a way that my unfortunate and misguided wife actually there and then gave up her part and accepted the one he had determined to throw upon her. I then recognised for the first time that I had to deal with a veritable Svengali.

Our mistake in admitting an author of this type to our theatre soon became apparent. At the reading, that excellent actor, Jack Barnes, whose very name calls up the idea of sound judgment, withdrew, overpowered by fatigue and disgust, at the end of the first act, and presently threw up the part with which we proposed to insult him—and I now publicly apologise to him for that outrage. Miss Coleman soon followed his example, with a very natural protest against a part in which, as she rightly said, there were "no laughs and no exits." Any author with the slightest decency of feeling would have withdrawn in the face of rebuffs so pointed as these, But Mr. Shaw—encouraged, I must say, by Harrison—persisted in what had now become an intolerable intrusion.

I can hardly describe the rehearsals that followed. It may well be that my recollection of them is confused; for my nerves soon gave way; sleep became a stranger to me; and there were moments at which I was hardly in possession of my faculties. I had to stage-manage as well as act—to stage-manage with that demon sitting beside me casting an evil spell on all our efforts!

On one occasion Mr. Shaw insulted the entire profession by wanting a large table on the stage, on the ground that the company would fall over it unless they behaved as if they were coming into a real room instead of, as he coarsely observed, rushing to the float to pick up the band at the beginning of a comic song. This was a personal attack on me, as my vivacity of character and *diable au corps* make me specially impatient of obstacles.

Mr. Shaw was one of those persons who use a

certain superficial reasonableness and dexterity of manner to cover an invincible obstinacy in their own opinion. We had engaged for the leading part (I myself having accepted an insignificant part as a mere waiter) no less an artist than Mr. Allan Aynesworth, whose reputation and subsequent achievements make it unnecessary for me to justify our choice. Mr. Shaw had from the first contended that one of the scenes lay outside Mr. Aynesworth's peculiar province. There can be no doubt now that Mr. Shaw deliberately used his hypnotic power at rehearsal to compel Mr. Aynsworth to fulfil his prediction. In every other scene Mr. Aynesworth surpassed himself. In this he became conscious and confused; his high spirits were suddenly extinguished; even his good-humour left him. He was like a man under a spell—as no doubt he actually was—and his embarrassment communicated itself most painfully to my dear wife, who had to sit on the stage whilst Svengali deliberately tortured his victim.

At the same time I must say that Mrs. Maude's conduct was not all I could have desired. I greatly dreaded an open rupture between her and the author; and the fiend somehow divined this, and used it as a means of annoying me. Sometimes, when he had cynically watched one of her scenes without any symptom of pleasure, I would venture to ask him his opinion of it. On such occasions he invariably rose with every appearance of angry disapproval, informed me that he would give his opinion to Miss Emery herself, and stalked up the stage to her in a threatening manner, leaving me in a state of apprehension that my overstrained nerves were ill able to bear. Not until afterwards did I learn that on these occasions he flattered my wife disgracefully, and actually made her a party to his systematic attempt to drive me out of my senses. I have never reproached her with this, and I never shall. I mention it here only because it is the truth; and truth has always been with me the first consideration.

At last Aynesworth broke down under the torture. Mr. Shaw, with that perfidious air of making the best of everything which never deserted him, hypnotised him into complaining of the number of speeches he had to deliver, whereupon Mr. Shaw cut out no less than seventeen of them. This naturally disabled the artist totally. On the question of cutting, Mr. Shaw's attitude was nothing less than Satanic. When I suggested cutting he handed me the play, begged me to cut it freely, and then hypnotised me so that I could not collect my thoughts sufficiently to cut a single line. On the other hand, if I showed the least pleasure in a scene at rehearsal he at once cut it out on the ground that the play was too long. What I suffered from that man at that time will never be fully known. The heart alone knoweth its own bitterness.

The end came suddenly and unexpectedly. We had made a special effort to fulfil our unfortunate contract, of which even Harrison was now beginning to have his doubts. We had brought back Miss Kate Bishop from Australia to replace Miss Coleman. Mr. Valentine had taken the part repudiated by Mr. Barnes. The scenery had been modelled, and a real dentist's chair obtained for the first act. Harrison, whose folly was responsible for the whole wretched business, came down to the rehearsal. We were honestly anxious to retrieve the situation by a great effort, and save our dear little theatre from the disgrace of a failure.

Suddenly the author entered, *in a new suit of clothes ! !*

I have little more to say. Nobody who had not seen Mr. Shaw sitting there day after day in a costume which the least self-respecting carpenter would have discarded months before, could possibly have understood the devastating effect of the new suit on our minds. That this was a calculated *coup de théâtre* I have not the slightest doubt. That it fulfilled its purpose I cannot deny. With distracted attentions, demented imaginations, and enfeebled reasons we made a bewildered effort to go through the first two acts. I saw with inexpressible aggravation that Harrison's face grew longer and longer as he contemplated our company blundering through a rehearsal like disconcerted amateurs (as if it were anybody's fault but his own). Talma himself would have broken down before the famous pit of kings if that new suit had been in the house.

I neither know nor care how it all ended. I remember Svengali privately informing Harrison and myself that he felt that our ruin and disgrace could only be averted by a heroic sacrifice on his part. If Harrison had had a spark of manhood he would have kicked him then and there into the Haymarket. But Harrison's deplorable weakness of character again allowed our enemy to pose as our benevolent rescuer. As for me, the man was in some sort my guest; besides, I was too unspeakably relieved by the prospect of being rid of him and his absurd play to make any difficulties.

In concluding this sickening record of a disastrous experience I desire to say that I have the greatest admiration for Mr. Shaw's talents and the sincerest esteem for his personal character. In any other walk of life than that of a dramatic author I should expect him to achieve a high measure of success. I understand that he has made considerable mark as a vestryman, collecting dust with punctuality and supervising drainage with public-spirited keenness. I do not blame him for imposing on Harrison, for Harrison's credulity simply invites imposture. I wish him well in every way, and I am glad to hear from time to time that he is prospering. I met him in Garrick Street not long ago, and noticed that he still wore the suit which he purchased in 1897 in anticipation of the royalties on "You Never Can Tell."

His name is never mentioned in my household.